JEWISH MYSTICISM

Jewish Mysticism

From Ancient Times through Today

Marvin A. Sweeney

William B. Eerdmans Publishing Company
Grand Rapids, Michigan

Wm. B. Eerdmans Publishing Co.
4035 Park East Court SE, Grand Rapids, Michigan 49546
www.eerdmans.com

26 25 24 23 22 21 20   1 2 3 4 5 6 7

ISBN 978-0-8028-6403-1

Library of Congress Cataloging-in-Publication Data

Names: Sweeney, Marvin A. (Marvin Alan), 1953– author.
Title: Jewish mysticism : from ancient times through today / Marvin A. Sweeney.
Description: Grand Rapids : Wm. B. Eerdmans Publishing Co., 2020. |
    Includes bibliographical references and index.
Identifiers: LCCN 2019040616 | ISBN 9780802864031 (cloth)
Subjects: LCSH: Mysticism—Judaism—History.
Classification: LCC BM723 .S93 2020 | DDC 296.7/1209—dc23
LC record available at https://lccn.loc.gov/2019040616

Dedicated to the blessed memory of my teacher
Rabbi Dr. J. Jerome Pine, z"l
Temple B'nai Abraham
Decatur, Illinois

CONTENTS

Preface

My interest in Jewish mysticism goes back to my adolescence in 1965, when Rabbi J. Jerome Pine, z"l, first came to Temple B'nai Abraham, Decatur, Illinois. Rabbi Pine guided me in preparation for my Bar Mitzvah, which took place on Shabbat evening, August 5, 1966, in keeping with Temple B'nai Abraham's classical Reform practice at the time. Rabbi Pine had a keen interest in kabbalism and Hasidism, and frequently spoke about both in his Shabbat sermons throughout my teen years and beyond; indeed, it was R. Pine who first introduced me to the Lurianic concept of Tzimtzum and to teachings based on the Hasidic tales. I doubt that I fully understood his teachings at the time, but the seeds were planted for what would become a major interest in my religious life and professional career.

My engagement with Jewish mysticism began to develop more fully when I arrived at the University of Miami in 1983 as a newly minted Assistant Professor in the Religious Studies Department and Jewish Studies Program with a PhD in Hebrew Bible from Claremont Graduate School. My responsibilities included teaching introductory courses in Hebrew Bible, the History of Judaism and Jewish Thought, and, ironically, Asian Religions (because I had the most interest and expertise in the department at the time!). I noticed that the University had already listed a course in Jewish mysticism in its catalog, and I realized that this presented an important opportunity for me to think and teach seriously about a subject that had piqued my interest years before. I first taught the course in the Spring 1985 semester, and I have been teaching it ever since in various iterations at the University of Miami, Claremont School of Theology, Claremont Graduate University, and the Academy for Jewish Religion California.

But one of my problems with the course was the need for good text-books. I had first read Gershom Scholem's *Major Trends in Jewish Mysticism* as one of the textbooks assigned in my "Introduction to Judaism" course at the University of Illinois in 1973. Scholem was the major figure in Jewish mysticism at the time, but his volume demands much from its readers, especially from those studying Judaism at the undergraduate level. Although I used *Major Trends* as one of my textbooks, I realized the need for something to complement it. I chose *Journeys: An Introductory Guide to Jewish Mysticism* by William E. Kaufman, which offers a very clear discussion, well suited to introductory undergraduate students.

Both volumes served well for many years, together with other volumes that presented source texts in English translation; but when I moved to the Claremont School of Theology in 1994, I encountered two major problems. One was that both volumes were becoming very dated, and no new edition of either was likely to appear. The other was that both volumes focus on Jewish mysticism beginning in the rabbinic period and spend little time dealing with biblical antecedents other than Ezekiel. But as a Jewish professor in a Methodist School of Theology with a specialization in Prophetic Literature—and a special focus in visionary texts at that—I found that the origins and development of Jewish mysticism needed more complete explanation. The prophets of ancient Israel and Judah had laid the groundwork for the development of Jewish mysticism in the rabbinic period and beyond with their own visionary experiences of the presence of G-d and their attempts to convey that experience. Ancient Near Eastern visionary and dream texts, texts from Qumran and elsewhere in the Judean Desert, and Jewish Apocalyptic texts also demanded attention, especially since so many Christian scholars read such texts in relation to the New Testament but knew little of subsequent Jewish developments following the Zealot Revolt of 66–74 CE and the Bar Kokhba revolt of 132–135 CE.

I never found a suitable textbook to cover the field as I understood it. When I was invited to write a book about Jewish apocalyptic by Allen Myers of Eerdmans, I explained that Jewish apocalyptic needed to be understood within the larger context of Jewish visionary and mystical experience. Allen agreed, and so the present book was born.

I owe a great debt of gratitude to many, including my teachers in Jewish studies, biblical studies, and ancient Near Eastern studies; my colleagues at the University of Miami, Claremont School of Theology,

Claremont Graduate University, and the Academy for Jewish Religion California; and my students who have taken up the study of visionary and mystical experience in their dissertations and beyond. I would also like to thank my research assistant, Dr. Pamela Nourse, who will start her own dissertation soon. She has saved me from many errors, but any that remain are my own.

Hanukkah
San Dimas, CA
25 Kislev, 5778
December 13, 2017

Abbreviations

	van der Toorn, Bob Becking, and Pieter W. van der Horst. 2nd rev. edition. Grand Rapids: Eerdmans, 1999
EncJud	*Encyclopedia Judaica*. Edited by Cecil Roth. 16 volumes; Jerusalem: Keter, n.d. (1972)
FAT	Forschungen zum Alten Testament
FOTL	Forms of the Old Testament Literature
HThKAT	Herders Theologischer Kommentar zum Alten Testament
IBT	Interpreting Biblical Texts
IEJ	*Israel Exploration Journal*
JAOS	*Journal of the American Oriental Society*
JBL	*Journal of Biblical Literature*
JCS	*Journal of Cuneiform Studies*
JPS	Jewish Publication Society
JR	*Journal of Religion*
JSJ	*Journal for the Study of Judaism*
JSOTSup	Journal for the Study of the Old Testament Supplements
LHBOTS	The Library of Hebrew Bible/Old Testament Studies
NEAEHL	*The New Encyclopedia of Archaeological Excavations of the Holy Land*. Edited by Ephraim Stern. 4 vols. Jerusalem: Israel Exploration Society and Carta, New York: Simon & Schuster, 1993
NIBCOT	New International Bible Commentary on the Old Testament
OTL	Old Testament Library
ROT	Reading the Old Testament
SBL	Society of Biblical Literature
SBLMS	Society of Biblical Literature Monograph Series
SBLSym	Society of Biblical Literature Symposium Series
SHBC	Smyth & Helwys Bible Commentary
SJSJ	Supplements to the Journal for the Study of Judaism
TSAJ	Texte und Studien zum antiken Judentum
VT	*Vetus Testamentum*
VTSup	Supplements to Vetus Testamentum
WBC	Word Biblical Commentary
YAB	Yale Anchor Bible

INTRODUCTION

Jewish mysticism has emerged over the course of the last century as a unique and growing subject of inquiry within the larger fields of Jewish studies and religious studies. Jewish mysticism is fundamentally concerned with understanding the presence of the divine in relation to the world of creation, including the cosmos and natural world of creation at large, the human self and psyche, and the Jewish textual tradition which gives expression to Jewish thought and practice. Although scholarship during the first centuries of the Enlightenment vilified Jewish mysticism as an expression of superstition and magic that was not worthy of the rationalist tradition of Jewish philosophy and theology, the twentieth century saw the emergence of Jewish mysticism as a serious field of academic inquiry, largely through the work of Gershom Scholem, his own disciples, and the many other scholars who were influenced by his work.[1] Scholem's work suffered from a number of problems and limitations related to his own unique perspectives on the field, but he nevertheless identified Jewish mysticism in its variety of forms as an important means by which Jews throughout history have come to understand both G-d and themselves in relation to the larger world of creation, and human—especially Jewish—life within that creation.

In the early twenty-first century, Jewish mysticism is one of the most dynamic fields of Jewish studies, insofar as it is increasingly recognized as a dimension of Jewish thought that dares to inquire concerning the essential nature of G-d and divine presence in the world, particularly in the aftermath of the Shoah and the emergence of a modern secular worldview. Is G-d all powerful? All present? All knowing? All just? And all active in the world of

---

1. See esp. Gershom Scholem, *Major Trends in Jewish Mysticism* (New York: Schocken, 1961).

creation and human affairs? Or is G-d simply a construct developed by Jews in their attempts to make sense out of a world that is increasingly recognized as amoral and profane? Jewish mysticism posits that G-d is present, powerful, just, and active, but it is also willing to examine questions of divine weakness and limitation in its attempts to explain the reverses suffered by the Jewish people during well over three thousand years of Jewish history and thought. Today, Jewish mysticism permeates Jewish thought and practice, and it enables Judaism to posit increasingly insightful and productive perspectives on the Jewish experience of history in relation to the divine.

Modern critical scholars during the first centuries of the Enlightenment viewed Jewish mysticism from the rationalist and empirical viewpoints of the Age of Reason. To them Jewish mysticism was an embarrassing expression of superstition and irrationality that marred attempts to present Judaism as a model form of rationalist thought and experience, one deserving of a place alongside rationalist Protestant Christianity among the true religions of the world. Heinrich Graetz, in his celebrated *History of the Jews*, first published in German in 1853–1875 and later in English in 1891–1898, charged that "the Kabbala is a daughter of embarrassment; its system was a way of escape from the dilemma between the simple, anthropomorphic interpretation of the Bible and the shallowness of Maimunist philosophy."[2] Graetz obviously had little regard for kabbalah and for Jewish mysticism in general, and his *History* reflects his view that Judaism must be a rational tradition, philosophically and historically based, in keeping with Enlightenment ideals. The reason that he also took issue with Maimonides lay in his view that Maimonides's philosophy ran contrary to Jewish tradition, insofar as Graetz charged that Maimonides did not hold to the notion of a personal G-d who was involved in human history, but instead upheld the Aristotelian principle of G-d as first mover who remained in cold isolation from the human realm once creation was put into motion.[3]

Indeed, Graetz's charges that Jewish mysticism was superstitious and irrational were typical of the scholarly and religious views at the time that valued reason and empirical observation as the arbiters of truth in human and religious experience. William James in his famed 1902 volume, *Varieties of Religious Experience*, argues that mysticism entails a psychological and emotional experience of religion or divine presence rather than a rational

2. Heinrich Graetz, *History of the Jews* (Philadelphia: Jewish Publication Society, 1894), 3:549.

3. Graetz, *History*, 3:486–87.

understanding.[4] He maintains that mysticism has four dimensions: (1) ineffability, as mystical experience of the divine cannot be described adequately to another; (2) noetic quality, as the mystical experience does not impart discursive knowledge, but instead imparts intuitive knowledge; (3) transiency, as mystical experience lasts only for a short period, half an hour to an hour or two, and fades when the experience concludes; and (4) passivity, as the mystic's will lapses as a superior power takes control. Altogether, James's description appears to presuppose ecstatic experience, which is non-rational, but which also hardly encapsulates the entirety of mysticism. It is important to note that experience of the divine, which cannot be defined in empirical terms, necessarily constitutes a form of non-rational experience. Consequently, we must also note Scholem's citation of Rufus Jones's 1909 comment that mysticism is "the type of religion which puts the emphasis on immediate awareness of relation with G-d, on direct and intimate consciousness of the divine presence. It is religion in its most acute, intense, and living stage."[5]

But we must consider that Jewish mysticism—and indeed mysticism in general—does not exclusively constitute trance possession or the notion of *unio mystica* as James's understanding of mystical experience suggests. Although mysticism comes to expression in the forms of metaphorical visions and sensations of divine presence both within and around the mystic, such visions and sensations of divine presence often convey fully rational considerations. Examples might include Isaiah's vision of G-d in Isa 6 in which G-d tells him that the people of Jerusalem and Judah will suffer until only one-tenth of them are left, which arguably took place in Isaiah's time, or G-d's statement to R. Nehunyah ben Haqanah in the Heikhalot Rabbati 29 that G-d's destruction of the temple and of Bar Kokhba's warriors at the hands of the Romans may well have been wrong, which is arguably the case. Other teachings are also known to be true, such as the kabbalistic view that intangible qualities attributed to the divine—including thought, morality, and the ever-changing nature of material reality—appear in human beings. Likewise, the Lurianic teaching that G-d might be limited and imperfect, as expressed through the notion of Tzimtzum, also point to a rational conclusion in the light of historical experience, i.e., that G-d might not be all powerful, all present, all engaged, or even all good, as experience such as

4. William James, *The Varieties of Religious Experience* (New York: The New American Library, 1958), 292–328.
5. Rufus M. Jones, *Studies in Mystical Religion* (London: Macmillan, 1909), xv.

the Spanish expulsion, the Chmielnitzki massacres, and later even the Shoah might suggest. Mysticism cannot be reduced to irrational or emotional experience, insofar as it addresses some very serious and rational problems concerning the nature of G-d, human beings, and the world in which we live.

Indeed, although Jewish mysticism employs some rather bizarre imagery to give expression to its understanding of the presence, character, and actions of the divine, it does not employ imagery that is otherwise unknown in Jewish tradition. Ezekiel's vision of G-d in Ezek 1–3 actually draws on the imagery of the ark of the covenant in the Jerusalem Temple, including the bronze-overlaid cherubim that are mounted atop and beside the ark in the holy of holies, the imagery of the menorot with their seventy burning lamps that appear in the heikhal of the temple before the holy of holies where the ark resides, and the wheels or rings associated with the ark that allow it to be transported in biblical narrative. Stephen Katz correctly argues that in all forms of mysticism, mystics employ the imagery that they know from their respective traditions; thus Buddhists employ Buddhist motifs, Hindus employ Hindu motifs, Christians employ Christian motifs, and Muslims employ Muslim motifs.[6] It stands to reason then that Jewish mystics employ Jewish motifs, such as the imagery of the ark of the covenant, the Jerusalem Temple, and aspects of the Torah narrative as well as other biblical, talmudic, midrashic, liturgical, and halakic literature to convey their concepts and ideas. Indeed, Elliot Wolfson demonstrates that the heikhalot and the kabbalistic literature build upon the visionary experience presented in the Bible.[7] There is a continuity in Jewish mysticism as the various stages of Jewish mystical movements progressively build on the imagery and understanding of past traditions as they attempt to solve or at least address the unresolved questions of the past.

The fields of Jewish studies and religious studies are indebted to Gershom Scholem for placing the study of Jewish mysticism on the table. Scholem essentially legitimized the study of Jewish mysticism with his groundbreaking 1938 lectures at the Jewish Theological Seminary published in 1941 under the title *Major Trends in Jewish Mysticism*. Scholem argued that Jewish mysticism came to expression especially through mythological imagery that was inspired largely by Judaism's interaction with ancient and

6. Steven T. Katz, "The Conservative Character of Mysticism," in *Mysticism and Religious Traditions* (Oxford: Oxford University Press, 1983), 3–60.

7. Elliot R. Wolfson, *Through a Speculum That Shines: Vision and Imagination in Medieval Jewish Mysticism* (Princeton: Princeton University Press, 1994).

medieval gnosticism. He employed a combination of historical, philosophical, and philological tools to elucidate a sequence of major individuals and movements from the rabbinic period through modern Hasidism, including the heikhalot or merkavah literature, the Hasidei Ashkenaz movement, the work of Abraham Abulafia, the Zohar written by Moses ben Shem Tov de León, Isaac Luria and Lurianic kabbalah, the failed messianic movement of Shabbetai Zevi, and the emergence of modern Hasidism. Overall, he argued that Jewish mysticism was a marginal and esoteric movement in Judaism that only came to major public attention with the emergence of Lurianic kabbalah, which was addressed to all Jews and became known especially through the messianic claims of Shabbetai Zevi. The Shabbetean movements that emerged in the aftermath of Shabbetai Zevi's failure played a key role in stimulating the emergence of the Hasidic movement under the leadership of the Baal Shem Tov.

Although Scholem deserves major credit for initiating the modern study of Jewish mysticism, his work is not without its faults. For one, his decision to bypass biblical literature and to begin with the merkavah/heikhalot literature is very questionable. He apparently viewed biblical literature as *sui generis* and therefore as fundamentally different from the mystical literature in part due to the understanding that biblical literature was inherently true and credible as revelatory literature, whereas later Jewish mystical texts were somehow suspect. But as the following analyses of biblical texts show, many of the fundamental concepts and terminology of Jewish mysticism originate in biblical texts, and it is therefore a mistake to overlook them when attempting to trace the development of Jewish mysticism. Furthermore, it is clear that ancient Israel and Judah developed as Canaanite cultures that drew heavily on their pre-Israelite Canaanite contexts and other ancient Near Eastern influences from Egypt, Phoenicia, Aram, Mesopotamia, and other cultures in formulating their visionary imagery and concepts. Consequently, the present volume gives considerable attention to the relevant biblical texts and to their ancient Near Eastern antecedents from Egypt, Canaan, and Mesopotamia in attempting to trace the development of Jewish visionary and mystical texts.

Much the same may be said of the Jewish apocalyptic literature, e.g., 1 Enoch, 4 Ezra, 2 Baruch, the War Scroll from Qumran, and the Songs of the Sabbath Sacrifice, which not only share concepts and terminology but indicate a much closer generic relationship with the heikhalot texts. Indeed, it has become customary for biblical scholars in general, such as John Collins, to read Jewish apocalyptic texts in relative isolation from the broader context of Jewish mysticism and instead to read them in relation to the apocalyptic concerns of the book of Revelation and other literature of the New Testament and early church.[8] Although they are certainly relevant for early Christianity, they are even more relevant for the development of Jewish visionary experience and mysticism in addressing the questions posed by events concerned with the Second Temple throughout the Persian and Hellenistic periods, the destruction of the Second Temple in 70 CE, and the failure of the Bar Kokhba revolt in 132–135 CE. Consequently, the present volume attempts to place the Jewish apocalyptic literature into the larger development of ancient Jewish visionary and mystical experience in an effort to fill some of the gaps left by the work of Scholem, Collins, and others who have been so important to the field.

We must also question Scholem's contention that the authors of Jewish mystical literature, including the heikhalot, kabbalistic, and Hasidic texts, were marginalized figures within the larger Jewish tradition. Although it is clear that the authors were not central figures such as R. Akiva, R. Ishmael, R. Shimon bar Yohai, and other luminaries, it is also clear that the authors of these texts were generally well grounded in rabbinic, talmudic, halakic, and other forms of the classical Jewish tradition. Indeed, m. Hag. 2:1 states that those who would study and expound on the topics and texts of Jewish mysticism must be figures who understand their own knowledge; and texts in the Tosefta and Gemara associated with this mishnah, such as the narrative concerning the four who attempted to enter Pardes, hold up a standard that one who would engage in such study must be well versed in the rabbinic tradition. Indeed, analysis of the heikhalot literature indicates that these texts are not concerned only with articulating gnostic ideas concerning the human capacity to journey to heaven to engage the divine. They articulate classical Jewish values; e.g., the Heikhalot Rabbati calls for knowledge of Torah as a key criterion for gaining access to the divine, and the Shiur Qomah, often vilified as a heretical text concerned with divine dimensions, actually focuses on reminding readers of the power and majesty of G-d before whom they stand in worship. Even the Baal Shem Tov, often brought forward as a figure who eschewed talmudic study, was competent in this literature. The authors of these texts were not marginalized figures; they were figures who were generally well-trained in Jewish literature and thought who opposed those with different understandings of the tradition, such as those who were

---

8. John J. Collins, *The Apocalyptic Imagination: An Introduction to Jewish Apocalyptic Literature*, 3rd ed. (Grand Rapids: Eerdmans, 2016).

grounded in philosophy or those who were grounded in the values and perspectives of the Haskalah, Jewish Enlightenment.

Scholem's own adherence to historical scholarship, philosophy, and philology as the bases for his understanding of Jewish mysticism apparently influenced his focus on the historical, philosophical, and textual dimensions of Jewish mysticism. But it is clear throughout the tradition that spiritual, theurgical, and magical practice also played key roles in the various movements. To be sure, Scholem does include a chapter on R. Abraham Abulafia, who especially employed gematria in his early kabbalistic interpretation of Torah; but scholars such as Moshe Idel have sought to reset the study of Jewish mysticism by focusing on mystical practice as the foundation of the movement.[9] Idel not only produced a major study of Abulafia, but he also wrote a monograph on Hasidism that focused on the key roles played by spiritual and magical practices such as faith healing that constituted the bases of much Hasidic practice and thought.[10] Likewise, Lawrence Fine produced a full study of such practice in the life, work, and thought of R. Isaac Luria and the subsequent movement of Lurianic kabbalah that so influenced the Hasidic movement and turned Jewish mysticism into a movement that influenced the masses of Jews rather than only a handful of scholars.[11] Judaism and Jewish life are based on a combination of study and worship, and the increasing focus on the spiritual and liturgical practices of the Jewish mystical movements provides an important complement to Scholem's philosophical, historical, and textual perspectives. Consequently, this volume gives greater attention to the roles played by Jewish liturgical and theurgical practice as well as textual interpretation in its presentation of the development of Jewish visionary and mystical experience. Indeed, the presentation emphasizes how each movement builds upon earlier movements and works to address questions raised and to resolve ongoing problems left open by earlier movements and texts.

One of the major problems in Scholem's analysis was his focus on the false messiah, Shabbetai Zevi, who was the subject of a massive study by Scholem. Scholem argued that Shabbetai Zevi suffered from manic-depressive syndrome; that he represented an embarrassment for Judaism,

---

9. Moshe Idel, *Kabbalah: New Perspectives* (New Haven: Yale University Press, 1988).

10. Moshe Idel, *The Mystical Experience in Abraham Abulafia* (Albany: SUNY Press, 1987), and *Hasidism: Between Ecstasy and Magic* (Albany: SUNY Press, 1995).

11. Lawrence Fine, *Physician of the Soul, Healer of the Cosmos: Isaac Luria and His Kabbalistic Fellowship* (Stanford, CA: Stanford University Press, 2003).

having falsely claimed to be the messiah and ultimately converted to Islam; and that the Shabbetean movements that arose in the aftermath of his lifetime played a major role in influencing the Baal Shem Tov and the origins of Hasidism. But Scholem was mistaken in his assessment of Shabbetai Zevi. Shabbetai Zevi was likely a manic depressive, and he was certainly an embarrassment for Judaism, but he did not influence the emergence of Hasidism as Scholem claims. Scholem's claims are based on the Hasidic traditions that Israel ben Eliezer, the founder of Hasidism, was a hidden messiah who eschewed talmudic study. Scholem claimed that the Baal Shem Tov was heavily influenced by a certain R. Adam, identified by Scholem as a Shabbetean figure known as R. Hershel Tzoref, and kept a manuscript of his work throughout his life from which he drew inspiration concerning the foundations of Hasidism. But no evidence for such a manuscript exists except in Hasidic legend. Furthermore, analysis of the early Hasidic movement shows a number of factors that countermand Scholem's claims. One is that the Baal Shem Tov did know the classical Jewish tradition; and certainly his disciples, such as R. Dov Ber and R. Shneur Zalman, had full competence in rabbinic tradition. In addition, the early Hasidim spent considerable time and energy combatting the heresies of early Shabbetean movements. Although the Hasidim were often vilified and excommunicated by the rabbinic authorities of Vilna, they eventually demonstrated that they had much in common with the so-called Vilna Mitnagdim (Opponents) with regard to talmudic knowledge and even allied with them in resisting the modern Jewish Haskalah (Enlightenment) movement that threatened traditional Jewish life and values. The early Hasidic movement was not inspired by the Shabbetean movements; instead, it was inspired by Lurianic kabbalah in relation to both Lurianic thought and practice.

In view of the above considerations, this volume presents an account of the development of visionary and mystical experience in Jewish tradition from antiquity to the present. It begins with accounts of ancient Near Eastern visionary and dream experience, which profoundly influenced ancient Israelite and Judean understandings and expressions of visionary experience concerning the presence of the divine within the world of creation and human experience. It turns to three chapters on biblical texts in the Pentateuch, the Former Prophets and Psalms, and the Latter Prophets in an effort to examine how visionary experience concerning the presence of G-d in the worlds of creation and human events was understood and expressed in ancient Israel and Judah. A chapter on Jewish apocalyptic texts then follows, in order to establish the interrelationship between biblical visionary texts and later rabbinic texts; this apocalyptic literature fundamentally concerns itself with the divine presence and purpose in relation to the Second Temple throughout the Persian, Hellenistic, and Roman periods in ancient Jerusalem and Judah. The chapter on the heikhalot or merkavah literature clarifies the literary intent of the individual works and their depictions of the journey through the seven levels of heaven to appear before the heavenly throne of G-d and address G-d with the issues posed by the destruction of the temple and the failure of the Bar Kokhba revolts. Three chapters then follow on the various dimensions of the emergence of the kabbalistic tradition. These include the early development of kabbalistic works such as the Sefer Habahir; the Zohar, which represents the premier text of kabbalistic tradition; and the emergence of Lurianic kabbalah, which played such an important role in ensuring that kabbalistic thought and practice influenced Judaism at large. A final chapter examines the emergence of the Hasidic movement in Eastern Europe, with special attention to Habad Hasidism, which constitutes the primary form of contemporary Jewish mysticism. In all cases, the presentation of visionary and mystical texts and traditions serves a primary goal of understanding how they addressed the particular challenges, problems, needs, and perspectives of Judaism and the Jewish people throughout their historical experience.

Chapter 1

VISIONARY EXPERIENCE
IN THE ANCIENT NEAR EAST

Origins and Development of Israel and Its Portrayals of G-d

Ancient Israel emerged as a discrete nation in Canaan during the latter portions of the Bronze Age in the fourteenth through the tenth centuries BCE.[1] The first known historical reference to Israel appears in the so-called victory stele of Pharaoh Merneptah (1224–1216 BCE) in which he claimed victory over a Canaanite coalition known as the Nine Bows.[2] Many familiar place names appear in Merneptah's stele, e.g., Ashkelon, Ashdod, Gaza, and others, but all of these place names indicated settled cities and the like, which is consistent with the socio-political structure of Canaan during this period as a collection of independent city-states lacking central authority. Israel appears among the list of Merneptah's enemies, but it is unique in that the name Israel is identified not as a settled, landed nation or city, but as a semi-nomadic tribal group residing in Canaan. Such a view is consistent with the portrayal of Israel's ancestors in Genesis, i.e., Abraham and Sarah; Isaac and Rebekah; Jacob, Rachel, and Leah; and the twelve sons of Jacob whose descendants would later constitute the tribes of Israel, even if there is no evidence to confirm the historicity of the ancestral narratives.

Egypt had dominated Canaan for much of the fifteenth through the thirteenth centuries BCE, which helped to ensure that Canaan did not unite; but by the time of Merneptah's reign, Canaan was slipping from Egyptian control.[3]

---

1. For an overview of ancient Near Eastern history, see esp. Amélie Kuhrt, *The Ancient Near East, c. 3000–330 BC* (London: Routledge, 1998).

2. *ANET*, 376–78.

3. Kuhrt, *The Ancient Near East*, 185–224; Donald B. Redford, *Egypt, Canaan, and Israel in Ancient Times* (Princeton: Princeton University Press, 1992), 125–237.

Merneptah's father, Pharaoh Rameses II (1290–1224 BCE), had been defeated by the Hittites at the Battle of Kadesh in 1274 BCE and consequently retreated with his army to Egypt. Merneptah's claim to victory rings rather hollow as archeological evidence confirms the decline of Egyptian influence in Canaan following his reign. Indeed, Egypt's decline following the reign of Merneptah in the late thirteenth century BCE left a power vacuum in Canaan. Canaan was the trading crossroads of the Eastern Mediterranean and West Asian world; it sat astride the sea and land routes that connected the major superpowers of the day, i.e., Egypt, Hatti, and Mesopotamia. But none of the other powers were able to capitalize on Egypt's decline. The Hittites collapsed as a result of invasion by the Sea Peoples, who originated in the Greek islands and traveled by sea and land along the eastern Mediterranean coast. The Sea Peoples destroyed the Hittite Empire, the port city of Ugarit, and other coastal cities before launching a failed invasion of Egypt during the reign of Pharaoh Rameses III (1186–1155 BCE) that forced them to settle along the coastal plain of southern Canaan where they would meld with the local Canaanite population to form the five-city coalition known in the Bible as the Philistines. The Mesopotamian empires of Assyria and Babylonia lacked the organization and power to move southward through Aram and into Canaan until the ninth and eighth centuries BCE. Thus, Canaan was largely left to develop on its own without major interference from the superpowers of the day from the late thirteenth through the late ninth centuries BCE.

The historical origins of Israel may be traced back even before this period. The Amarna letters, a cache of cuneiform tablets discovered at the site of Amarna in Egypt in the nineteenth century, provide evidence of the origins of Israel.[4] Most of the letters were written in Akkadian by many of the city-state rulers of ancient Canaan to their Egyptian overlords during the mid-fourteenth-century BCE reign of Pharaoh Amenhotep IV (1353–1336 BCE), otherwise known as Akhenaten, to request troops to defend against incursions by a semi-nomadic people identified as the Habiru. The Akkadian term, *habiru* (Egyptian rendering, *apiru*), is a term that means simply "barbarian," and refers to the semi-nomadic, Semitic-speaking tribal groups from the Arabian Desert that would enter the settled agricultural areas known as the Fertile Crescent, ranging from Assyria and Babylonia to the north and east and Aram and Canaan to the west. Although the issue is disputed, many scholars maintain that the Hebrew word, *ivri*, "Hebrew," is derived from the Akkadian word, *habiru*. In any case, the portrayal of the Habiru in the

---

4. *ANET*, 623–26.

Amarna Letters points to their concentration around the city of Shechem, ruled by King Labayu and his sons during the mid-fourteenth century BCE. Many of Shechem's neighbors, such as Megiddo and Jerusalem, complained to the Egyptian Pharaoh that Shechem had allied with the Habiru to threaten their own borders and requested archers to help defend against Habiru/Shechemite incursions. Amenhotep IV/Akhenaten was preoccupied with his own internal issues in Egypt, and it remains unclear whether he ever sent the requested support.

Shechem, situated on the border between the tribal territories of Ephraim and Manasseh in the Israelite hill country, served as a central political and religious focal point for early Israel. Deuteronomy 27 portrays Moses directing the tribes to gather the tribes at the site of Shechem between Mt. Ebal and Mt. Gerizim to affirm the covenant with YHWH; Joshua 8 and 24 portray Joshua's assembly of the Israelite tribes at Shechem for similar reasons; Judges 9 portrays Shechem as the focal point for the failed campaign by Abimelech ben Gideon to assert his rule over Israel; and 1 Kings 12 portrays Shechem as the gathering point for the northern Israelite tribes to choose their leadership following the death of King Solomon ben David. These biblical examples of Israelites coalescing at Shechem appear consistent with the claim that the Habiru are the forerunners of ancient Israel.

Ancient Israel emerged as a nation—or better, a monarchy—from ancient Canaan.[5] Although biblical sources, such as the wilderness narratives of Exodus, Numbers, and Deuteronomy and the conquest narratives of Joshua, portray Israel as foreign conquerors of Canaan, other biblical sources, such as Judges 1, and archeological sources point to Israel's cultural and linguistic ties to ancient Canaan. Indeed, the very name Israel (Hebrew, *yisra'el*) does not mean, "you have struggled with G-d and with humans," as claimed in Gen 32:28. Instead, the theophoric name *yisra'el* means "G-d rules"; it employs the name of the Canaanite creator god, El, known already from Ugaritic texts of the fifteenth–fourteenth century BCE and later from the late ninth–early eighth century BCE in the Aramaic inscription of the vision of Balaam bar Beor from Transjordanian Deir Alla. Israel emerged as a Canaanite monarchy, and over the course of its history attributed characteristics of Canaanite gods, such as El, Baal, and others, to the distinctive Israelite and Judean G-d, YHWH. Indeed, the divine name, YHWH, appears to have originated among semi-nomadic tribal groups in Edom from where it became known as the name of the G-d of Judah and Israel from their formation

5. Kuhrt, *The Ancient Near East*, 417–72.

during the premonarchic period (twelfth–tenth century BCE) through the monarchic period of Israelite and Judean kings (tenth–sixth century BCE) until the onset of the Babylonian Exile in 587 BCE.

Although Judah and Israel were self-standing monarchies throughout the tenth–sixth centuries BCE, they were heavily influenced by the Canaanite culture from which they emerged and by major powers, such as Egypt, Hatti, Aram, and the Mesopotamian empires of Assyria and Babylonia, which sought to control them and the trade routes on which they were situated. The structure of Solomon's administration shows clear Egyptian influence; biblical sources, such as the narrative of Abraham's purchase of the Machpelah Cave in Genesis 23, indicate Hittite influence; northern Israel's abandonment of its treaty with Assyria indicates Aramean influence; and the conceptualization of the covenant between YHWH and Israel/Judah indicates heavy dependence on Mesopotamian models.

Examination of ancient Near Eastern conceptualizations of the gods and of texts concerning interrelations with the gods, including visionary texts, dream reports, and omen interpretation, indicates that ancient Israel and Judah owed much to these cultures in their own understandings of the characterization of YHWH and their understandings of interaction with YHWH through visionary and dream experience. It is therefore imperative that interpreters understand such ancient Near Eastern conceptualization and experience as a means to understand the unique forms of Israelite and Judean conceptualization and experience that develop from them. A major issue in understanding this development is the recognition that ancient Near Eastern cultures understood their gods to be embodied, i.e., that they could be perceived and experienced in tangible form, particularly through the widespread portrayals of the embodiment of their gods in literature and art forms.[6] Ancient Near Eastern cultures were well-known for vivid portrayals of the physical forms of their gods in literature and pictorial art, particularly the construction of idols of their gods from wood, stone, precious metals and stones, and fabrics. Although recent scholarly discussion points to the understanding in Israel and Judah of the embodied nature of G-d or YHWH, Israel and Judah tended to avoid detailed portrayal of a tangible form of YHWH and chose instead to employ metaphorical imagery, such as that of

6. Esther J. Hamori, *"When Gods Were Men": The Embodied God in Biblical and Ancient Near Eastern Literature*, BZAW 384 (Berlin: Walter de Gruyter, 2008); Benjamin D. Sommer, *The Bodies of G-d and the World of Ancient Israel* (Cambridge: Cambridge University Press, 2009); Mark S. Smith, *Where the Gods Are: Spatial Dimensions of Anthropomorphism in the Biblical World* (New Haven: Yale University Press, 2016).

smoke or cloud, fire, and water, to portray the presence of YHWH. There is ongoing concern with the unwarranted construction of idols, whether of YHWH or of foreign gods, but Israel and Judah eschewed tangible description of the body of YHWH and attempts to construct tangible images of YHWH's divine presence.

Discussion now turns to the conceptualization of the gods and the visionary and dream experience of the gods in Egypt, Canaan, Hatti, Aram, and Mesopotamia as background for the understanding of such issues in ancient Israel and Judah.

Seeing and Hearing the Gods of Egypt

Egyptian religion includes a large variety of gods and goddesses from the origins of Egyptian society in the Archaic Period (Dynasties 1–2, 3000–2650 BCE) through the end of the Roman period in 324 CE.[7] The origins of the various gods and goddesses apparently lie in the local cultural areas that were ultimately incorporated into the larger Egyptian civilization through the course of unification that produced Upper and Lower Egypt, i.e., the highlands of Southern Egypt and the Nile River Plain and Delta of Northern Egypt ca. 3000 BCE. Egyptian religion includes multiple creator gods that form their own respective hierarchies that differ and change depending upon the shifting fortunes of Egyptian political centers. Thus, Ptah, the early Egyptian creator deity, is worshiped in Memphis during the Old Kingdom period (Dynasties 3–8; ca. 2650–2135 BCE) when Memphis served as the principal city and capital of ancient Egypt. During the New Kingdom period (Dynasties 18–20; ca. 1550–1080 BCE), the sun deity, Amun-Re, a synthesis of the gods Amun and Re, emerges as the chief creator deity of Thebes at a time when it served as the dominant city of Egypt. Khnum, the Egyptian creator god of southern Egypt, is often viewed as an aspect of Amun-Re, which likely reflects Memphite domination over Esna and Elephantine, locations where Khnum was worshiped.

The Egyptian gods are generally portrayed in a combination of human and animal forms, depending upon the specific qualities and characters of each deity. Ptah, the patron god of craftsmen, woodworkers, metalworkers,

---

7. See esp. Sigfried Morenz, *Egyptian Religion* (Ithaca: Cornell University Press, 1973); Denise M. Doxey, "Egyptian Religion," in *The Cambridge History of Religions in the Ancient World*, vol. 1: *From the Bronze Age to the Hellenistic Age*, ed. Michele Renee Salzman and Marvin A. Sweeney (Cambridge: Cambridge University Press, 2013), 177–204.

etc., is often portrayed in human form as a man with green skin and the divine beard, wrapped in a shroud, and holding a scepter that combines *was* ("power"), *ankh* ("life"), and *djed* ("stability") to symbolize the interplay of change and stability in the world of creation. Following his merger with Osiris, the god of the underworld, he can appear as half-human and half-hawk or as a falcon as he accompanies the dead on their journey to the west. When identified as the sun god, Re or Aten, Ptah appears as two birds with human heads, each of which supports a sun disk, to portray the two souls of Re, i.e., Shu and Tefnut.

Although Ptah appears in tangible forms, it is clear that Ptah's underlying character is intangible, insofar as he infuses creation with his divine presence. The multiplicity of his forms is telling; his character shifts in relation to the shifting relationships of geographical regions and cities in Egypt and the deities that represent them. Fundamentally, Ptah's shifting forms must be understood as metaphorical portrayals that enable his human worshipers to understand his underlying, intangible character and powers. The Memphite Theology of Creation portrays Ptah's underlying intangible qualities.[8] The Memphite Theology of Creation is a text that was originally written early in the Old Kingdom period on leather, but it was copied on stone ca. 710 BCE by Pharaoh Shabaka (Twenty-Fifth Dynasty) due to the deteriorated state of the original text. It describes Ptah as the early deity who employed his heart (mind) and tongue (spoken word) to create the *ka*s or life forces of other deities, such as Atun, the early form of the above-mentioned sun deity. The initial focus on heart and tongue points to an indigenous Egyptian form of philosophical idealism akin to later Platonic philosophy that sees creation initially dependent upon the conceptualization of creation in the mind, and the naming of such conceptualization by the tongue or spoken word. Having conceptualized and named the deity in question, Ptah's act of creation then turns to the tangible forms. Ptah vocalizes creation as an act of masturbation in which the semen and hand combine to create the physical form of Ptah's Ennead, i.e., the nine initial deities from whom creation proceeds, in tangible form. Through conceptualization, vocalization, and tangible formation, the Ennead then brings all of creation into being.

Such an understanding of Ptah and his role as creator points to an important aspect of the Egyptian deities and world of creation that they produce, viz., the deities and all creation are a combination of intangible

---

8. Miriam Lichtheim, *Ancient Egyptian Literature*, vol. 1: *The Old and Middle Kingdoms* (Berkeley: University of California Press, 1975), 51–57; *ANET*, 4–6.

conceptualization and vocalization on the one hand and tangible form on the other. In such an understanding, Egyptian deities and all creation are ultimately intangible and unseen principles which become embodied in a changing physical and tangible form. Such tangible portrayal of Ptah—as human, as half-human and half-hawk, as falcon, as two birds with sun disks, etc.—must be understood as metaphorical devices intended to personalize and concretize the abstract qualities contained within, so as to make the intangible qualities of the deities and creation at large comprehensible to human observers and readers.

Similar considerations apply to Amun-Re. Amun emerged as the king of the gods in the city of Thebes during the course of the Eighteenth Dynasty (1550–1305 BCE) when Thebes became the capital of Egypt. He merged with the sun god Re to become the sun deity Amun-Re, who in turn became the chief deity of Egypt and the new creator god. Amun-Re is typically portrayed in human form, much like a Pharaoh, wearing a double crown that symbolized the unification of Upper and Lower Egypt. Because of Thebes's political power, Amun-Re tended to absorb other deities as Egypt moved toward an early form of monotheism. As the sun god, Amun-Re was understood to be self-created as a hidden presence or principle in the world of creation at large that enabled creation to grow and thrive.

During the reign of Pharaoh Amenhotep IV (1365–1349 BCE), also known as Akhenaten, the Pharaoh turned to the worship of Aten in a bid to challenge the power of the priests of Amun-Re. Aten was the sun disk, which means he was the pupil in the eye of Amun-Re and thereby represented the true intangible character, power, and essence of Amun-Re on which Akhenaten wanted to focus. Past scholars have posited that Akhenaten's religious reforms represented a form of nascent monotheism, but interpreters must recognize that Akhenaten's reforms never denied the reality or power of other gods; they forbade the worship of such gods to focus instead on Aten in a bid to marginalize the others and thereby strengthen Akhenaten's political hand.[9] Both the religious and political dimensions of Akhenaten's reforms failed, and after his death his reforms were abolished.

Nevertheless, the characterization of Amun-Re as a sun deity and Aten as the sun disk point to the importance of the intangible character of both deities and the role of the sun and light, both very real but very intangible

9. See Donald B. Redford, *Akhenaten: The Heretic King* (Princeton: Princeton University Press, 1984).

phenomena, as the metaphorical means to portray that character to human observers and readers.

A hymn to Amun from the Eighteenth Dynasty makes clear the interplay between his unseen but very real power in creation and his physical form portrayed as a sun chariot coursing across the heavens.[10] He is lauded for rising at dawn and shining his rays on the faces of those who toil on earth. Such a description of course invokes the the sun itself. The hymn portrays Amun as self-made: he formed his own body; but the imagery of light and sun rays indicates a less tangible, although very real, presence in the world. The hymn turns to the imagery of a race—whether by foot, horse, or chariot, the hymn does not say—but it nevertheless depicts Amun in terms of the sun making its daily course across the sky as it moves from rising in the east to setting in the west. The hymn closes by noting that, by Amun's daily presence, all eyes on earth can see; and without Amun's presence at night, they cannot. A second hymn portrays Amun as both creator and craftsman. He is once again portrayed as self-created; but the hymn goes on to assert that Amun is the creator of all crops in the world, the shepherd of all flocks, the protector of all, illuminator of the land, creator of the seasons, and creator of all heat and cold. In short, Amun's intangible power as the sun god creates order in the world, the capacity to produce food, and therefore the capacity to create and sustain life.

The Great Hymn to Aten likewise focuses on Aten's portrayal as the sun disk and his capacity to create life and bring about order in the world. The hymn begins with a portrayal of the rising sun which all animals and human beings turn out to see. Aten is lauded as the one who causes seed to grow into human beings, who feeds the son in his mother's womb, and who enables the chick to break out of its shell and walk on its own feet. Aten sets humans into their places, differentiates their languages, provides food, and counts their time on earth. His rays likewise nurse the fields, create the seasons, and create the various forms of life on earth. All eyes are on Aten's beauty until he sets, and all labor ceases when he goes down in the west. Once again, the abstraction of light and the daily presence of the sun become the unseen and self-created power that ensures life, food, growth, and order in the world of creation.

The interplay between tangible, physical form and intangible character and power is not limited to the sun deities. A key example appears in the

---

10. Miriam Lichtheim, *Ancient Egyptian Literature*, vol. 2: *The New Kingdom* (Berkeley: University of California Press, 1976), 86–100; *ANET*, 365–72.

mythologies associated with Osiris, Isis, Seth, and Horus and their conflicts concerning rule over Egypt.[11] Osiris is often considered to be a god of the underworld, but he is perhaps best known as a god of transition, resurrection, and regeneration in creation. Osiris is an early divine king of Egypt, and he is typically portrayed in human form with green skin, a pharaoh's beard, partially mummy-wrapped legs, a crook and flail, and a large crown with ostrich feathers on either side. He is often credited with safeguarding life in the Nile by ensuring the life of the animals and fish in the river together with the growth of plant life along its banks. He is therefore especially associated with the Nile River and the Nile Delta region as the god who ensures its life. His brother Seth is a god of the desert, which stands in conflict with the Nile and the Delta as a region associated with the absence of water and with death. He is a warrior associated with violence, storms, chaos, and foreigners, although he is often useful as a defender of Re's solar boat. He appears as the Seth-animal, a beast of unknown origin, perhaps a composite of a jackal, a giraffe, a fox, an aardvark, a donkey, and others. He has a long, curved snout, rectangular ears, a long, forked tail, and a body that may be depicted as either human or canine. He is in conflict with his brother Osiris and ultimately kills him and cuts his body into pieces in an attempt to seize the power of the Egyptian throne. According to the Old Kingdom myth of Osiris, his wife Isis is portrayed as the ideal wife and mother with a throne-crown on her head. Indeed, her name means "throne," and she is the power behind the throne of Egypt. She gathers all the pieces of her husband—except the penis, which had been eaten by a fish—reassembles them, and brings him back to life. She then uses her powers to fashion a golden penis for her resurrected husband, which she then uses to impregnate herself with their son Horus, thereby ensuring the continuity of the dynasty and Egypt itself. Horus, backed by his mother Isis, comes to symbolize the power and stability of the Egyptian monarchy.

The later New Kingdom myth of the conflict between Seth and Horus, written during the reign of Pharaoh Rameses V (1149–1145 BCE), returns to the efforts of Seth to gain the throne of Egypt.[12] Following his murder of Osiris, Seth attempts to claim the throne of Egypt as the brother of the dead king. Isis opposes Seth's claims on behalf of her son, Horus, whose status as the son of Osiris becomes the basis for his own claim. The Ennead, i.e., the nine gods who serve as a divine council in Egypt, are conflicted concerning

11. See, e.g., Lichtheim, *Ancient Egyptian Literature*, 2:81–86.
12. Lichtheim, *Ancient Egyptian Literature*, 2:214–23.

their course of action. Atum, the leading member of the Ennead, attempts to appoint both Seth and Horus but encounters resistance at every move. Finally, Seth proposes to Horus that they change themselves into hippopotamuses and plunge into the Nile where they will fight for control of the throne. The thrashing in the water as a result of their conflict then explains the annual rise of the Nile River in the spring, spreading silt over the land and ensuring its fertility. Isis is distressed at the thought that Seth might kill her son, so she fashions a harpoon that she casts into the water in an attempt to spear Seth; but she misses and instead spears Horus, who becomes angry with his mother as a result. She tries again and spears Seth, who also becomes angry with her and demands to know why she would spear her own brother. Isis's spearing of both Horus and Seth explains the reddish cast of the Nile River water during the spring season when the waters rise and flood the land. This coloring of the waters is the result of reddish silt that the Nile carries from its headwaters in the hill country and carries into the Nile River Valley below. The issue is finally settled when Seth attempts to rape Horus. Horus catches the semen of Seth in his hand and shows it to his mother, Isis, who casts it on the waters of the Nile. She then takes semen from Horus and casts it upon the lettuce that Seth habitually eats. When Seth and Horus return to the Ennead to press their claims, Seth goes first to claim dominance over Horus. But when the Ennead call his semen forth to testify to his dominance, it answers from the river and invalidates his claim. When Horus then presses his claim, the Ennead call his semen forth and it answers from inside Seth, thereby validating Horus's claim to dominance over Seth. Horus is recognized as king of Egypt, especially the Nile River and Nile Delta region, and continues his father's role in ensuring the life and vitality of the Nile River and Egypt as a whole. Seth continues as Horus's opponent, but he is never able to overthrow him.

Horus's role as the mythological king of Egypt manifests itself in a vision experienced by Thutmose IV as he slept by the Great Sphinx of Egypt.[13] The Sphinx was originally built in the Old Kingdom period to represent a pharaoh of the Fourth Dynasty (2600–2450 BCE), Kephra son of Khufu. By the New Kingdom period, however, the Sphinx had become associated with Horus and known as Hor-em-akhet, "Horus of the Horizon." Thutmose IV (1401–1391) was the son of Amenhotep II (1427–1401 BCE), but he was apparently never named as Crown Prince nor slated to succeed his father. Scholars therefore surmise that there must have been a conflict over

---

13. *ANET*, 449.

the throne in which Thutmose deposed an older brother. Upon attaining the throne, Thutmose IV erected his famous Dream Stele in which he reports a vision that he experienced while he slept by the Sphinx. According to his stele, Hor-em-akhet Kephri Re Atum appeared to him in a dream and spoke to him with his own mouth to declare that Thutmose would become the next king of Egypt. It is important to note that there is no description of the appearance of the god, other than that he speaks with his own mouth. It is only the word that Hor-em-akhet speaks that is important in this visionary experience. Following the divine quote, Thutmose IV merely states that he was like one who was ill, and that he would then devote himself to maintaining the Sphinx so that the Hor-em-akhet could accomplish what he proposed to do.

An analogous dream vision is reported by Pharaoh Djoser of the Third Dynasty (2650–2600 BCE). According to the so-called Hunger Stele, the creator god Khnum appeared to him in a dream.[14] Khnum is one of the earliest gods of Egypt. He is associated with the headwaters of the Nile and credited with the birth of children, whom he creates on a potter's wheel before placing them in their mothers' wombs. He is typically depicted with a human body and the head of a ram. But in Djoser's stele, Khnum's physical description plays only a minimal role. After identifying himself to Djoser in the dream, Khnum announces that his arms are around Djoser to compose his body and heal his limbs. Khnum also states that he will grant to Djoser precious stones and hard stones that have not been worked, so that the Pharaoh can carry out necessary repairs and building projects, such as temples and shrines. Khnum promises to ensure the proper flow of the Nile River and its floods to ensure fertility and food in the land. Primarily, Khnum manifests to Djoser in spoken promises of divine support, prosperity, and food during his reign.

But the interpretation of imagery in a dream also plays a role. A dream by Pharaoh Tanutamun (664–656 BCE), of the Twenty-Fifth Dynasty, presents two serpents, one on the right and one on the left, that require interpretation.[15] When the Pharaoh awakes and reports the dream, his advisors tell him that Upper Egypt already belongs to him, but the dream indicates that he should take control of Lower Egypt as well. They claim that the two

---

14. A. Leo Oppenheim, *The Interpretation of Dreams in the Ancient Near East* (Philadelphia: The American Philosophical Society, 1956), 251–52; Miriam Lichtheim, *Ancient Egyptian Literature*, vol. 3: *The Late Period* (Berkeley: University of California Press, 1980), 94–103.

15. Oppenheim, *The Interpretation of Dreams*, 252.

serpents represent two goddesses who have granted him the entire land, its length and breadth.

The Bentresh Stele reports a dream by the Prince of Bekhtin (Bactria in the Hittite Empire) whose daughter, Bentresh, became the sister-in-law of Pharaoh Rameses II (1290–1224 BCE).[16] Scholars have concluded that the stele was actually written in a much later period, either during the periods of Persian domination (525–330 BCE) or even during the Ptolemaic period (332–330 BCE), in an attempt to assert the earlier glory of Egypt and perhaps to prompt action to restore that glory. The narrative relates how the Prince of Bekhtin became concerned about the welfare of his daughter, Bentresh, who appeared to be possessed by a demon. He therefore sent to Egypt for assistance; Egypt responded by sending a god, Khons the Provider, known for expelling demons. The god apparently arrived in the form of a statue and remained for several years as Bentresh was relieved of her affliction. But after several years of the god's residence in Bekhtin, the Prince had a dream: a vision of a falcon god, apparently an image of Khons the Provider, who flew up into the sky to Egypt. When the Prince awoke, a Priest of Khons the Provider explained it to him as a message that the god presently resided in Bekhtin but wished to return to his home sanctuary in Thebes. The Prince complied and sent the statue of the god to Egypt. Once again, the image of the god is less important than the verbal message portrayed in the text. Khons wielded divine power that would be useful in healing the problems of the Princess, here described as demon possession. When the god wearied of residing in Bekhtin, it appeared in a dream vision to convey its desires to the Prince.

The Egyptian emphasis on verbal communication from the gods comes to the forefront in the Journey of Wen Amun.[17] This text was written during the latter third of the reign of Pharaoh Rameses XI (1110–1078 BCE) of the Twentieth Dynasty; it was a time of Egyptian weakness when the Pharaoh yielded power to two other figures, Herihor in the South and Smendes in the North. Egypt had lost effective control of Canaan and Phoenicia at this time as well. The text recounts the efforts of an Egyptian official, Wen Amun, who was sent to Phoenician ports, here identified as ports of the Tjeker, to purchase timber for Egypt. After waiting in Tanis for authorization to sail, Wen Amun puts to sea bound for the port of Dor along the Canaanite coast south of Akko. When Wen Amun docks in Dor, Beder, the Prince of Dor,

---

16. Lichtheim, *Ancient Egyptian Literature*, 3:90–94.
17. Lichtheim, *Ancient Egyptian Literature*, 2:224–30; *ANET*, 25–29.

sends supplies of food and drink; but Wen Amun suffers a reversal when a member of his crew steals a quantity of gold and silver and flees from the ship into the city of Dor. Wen Amun demands that Beder, as the prince who has jurisdiction in the city, find the thief and return the stolen goods. But Beder informs Wen Amun that he is not responsible for resolving the situation, as the thief was in fact a member of Wen Amun's crew. There is a gap in the text at this point; but Wen Amun, apparently on the advice of Beder, waits in the harbor for nine days until he finally gives up and sails north. After passing Tyre, he seizes a Tjeker vessel and commandeers silver from the ship to replace his loss. Wen Amun's action infuriates the Phoenicians (Tjeker), especially after he enters the harbor at Byblos and sets up a tent to celebrate his "victory" and to wait for the Tjeker to catch the thief and restore his original silver and gold. Every day, the Prince of Byblos sends a messenger to Wen Amun to tell him to "Get out of my harbor!" and Wen Amun responds each time, "Where shall I go?" After twenty-nine days of standoff, a young man from the Prince's court has an ecstatic experience and speaks on behalf of an unnamed Phoenician god during the daily offerings of the Prince to the gods of Byblos. The text describes the young man as shaking when he enters a trance and speaks on behalf of the deity who commandeers his body. The Phoenician god speaking through the possessed young man states that Amun-Re, the god of Egypt, has sent Wen Amun, and he demands that Wen Amun and the envoy carrying him be brought before the Prince of Byblos to resolve the matter. No description of Amun-Re or the Phoenician god is given; only the verbal message is conveyed as the body of the young man becomes the vessel through which the amorphous and anonymous deity communicates. But even this message does not resolve the matter. The papyrus is incomplete, but it continues at length describing the Prince's suspicions of Wen Amun throughout extended negotiations, the confirmation and receipt of payment, and the eventual departure of Wen Amun with the lumber cut for him by the Prince of Byblos—who then sends after Wen Amun's ship to arrest him. The Prince's suspicions of Wen Amun overshadow and outlast the divine message.

The Prophecy of Neferti also points to the Egyptian interest in verbal communication, although there are problems with this text.[18] The present manuscript dates to the Eighteenth Dynasty (1550–1305 BCE), but it depicts an event that allegedly occurred during the reign of Pharaoh Snefru of the Fourth Dynasty (2600–2450 BCE). A reference to a new Pharaoh named

18. Lichtheim, *Ancient Egyptian Literature*, 1:139–45; *ANET*, 444–46.

Ameni, apparently a reference to the Twelfth Dynasty (1990–1785 BCE) Pharaoh, Amenemhet I, betrays the true setting of the composition of this text as a pseudepigraph designed to authorize the ascension of Amenemhet I, apparently an usurper, to the throne. Nevertheless, the text presents an Egyptian understanding of how prophecy and visionary experience work.

The narrative portrays Pharaoh Snefru sitting in court, apparently bored; he demands that a figure be brought forward to announce a prophecy before him as a form of entertainment. A lector priest named Neferti of Bastet, apparently an educated holy man, well-versed in the poetic arts of prophecy as a form of speech from the gods, is brought before Pharaoh to provide a well-polished vision before the bored Pharaoh. The description of the setting of the prophecy indicates that the Egyptians expect a prophetic statement to be a poetic and well-polished literary form that would represent the speech of the gods. Such an understanding is apparently consistent with the formulation of Israelite and Judean prophecy, which generally appears as erudite and well-crafted poetry that can easily be put to music despite its generally challenging message. When Neferti appears before the Pharaoh, he asks if the prophecy should be about something that has already happened, or something that will happen. When Snefru asks for a prophecy of the future, Neferti takes writing implements, ink, and papyrus in hand and begins to write his prophecy as he speaks before the monarch. There is no reference to any god as the source for what Neferti has to say. Neferti surprises everyone in court by speaking of hard times to come for Egypt rather than an expectation of well-being, wealth, and peace. He speaks of a time of evil in which the great are overthrown, the Nile River has gone dry, the fish have disappeared, the winds will stand in conflict, all happiness has disappeared from Egypt, and Asiatics (apparently a reference to West Semitic peoples from Canaan and beyond) have come down to Egypt to take control of the country. But Neferti turns to a prediction of a new king named Ameni, apparently a reference to Amenemhet I, who will arise in the south, take the red and white crown of Upper and Lower Egypt, and restore order to the land by defeating the Asiatics, the Libyans, and any rebels who support them.

In addition to demonstrating the political concerns of the text to justify Amenemhet's own seizure of the Egyptian throne, the text illustrates the Egyptian interest in the high literary and poetic quality of prophecy as speech that comes ultimately from the gods. Interpreters agree that the text does not describe a historical prediction of the reign of Amenemhet I; rather, it was written during his reign to justify his seizure of the Egyptian throne. The prophecy functions much like the prediction of the reign of Cyrus the Great of Persia that is prophesied in Isa 44:28 and 45:1—apparently the work of the anonymous prophet of the Babylonian Exile known to scholars as Deutero-Isaiah, but attributed like the rest of the book of Isaiah to the prophet of the eighth century BCE, Isaiah ben Amoz, who looked forward to a righteous monarch chosen by YHWH.

The Admonitions of Ipuwer are very similar in character to the Prophecy of Neferti, although no setting in the royal court—or any other setting for that matter—is mentioned in the heavily damaged text.[19] The papyrus on which the text is written dates to the Nineteenth Dynasty (1305–1195 BCE). Most scholars follow Gardiner who argues that the text was written in the Twelfth Dynasty (1990–1785 BCE) concerning the chaos that brought the Tenth Dynasty to an end ca. 2040 BCE. But Lichtheim points to the ahistorical character of the portrayal of chaos in the text and argues that it cannot be placed in any particular historical setting. The only hint of a historical setting to the text appears at the end, which is heavily damaged and describes Ipuwer as giving his speech at the request of a pharaoh whose name has been lost to the deterioration of the papyrus.

The surviving text begins in the midst of damage to the papyrus with a portrayal of the land of Egypt in chaos, in which the doorkeepers, who are responsible for security, say "let us go plunder!" Washermen do not carry their loads; the birds are lined up for battle; and the people of the Delta, one of the most secure places in Egypt, carry shields. He describes a land full of gangs; a plowman works with his shield by his side; faces are pale, apparently with anxiety; and crime appears everywhere. Every town states that it will expel its leaders, robbers have great riches, and nobles have become thieves. But the imagery is not limited to the human realm. Egyptian mythology—like most mythologies in the ancient Near East—sees an inherent connection between the stability or lack thereof in the human and natural worlds. Ipuwer goes on to describe the Nile as a river of blood.

This should not be unusual for Bible readers who are familiar with YHWH's first plague against Egypt. Although the Nile is known to look red as it surges in the spring to bring brownish-red silt from its headwaters into the Nile Valley below, our text suggests that the imagery of the Nile as blood is a common representation of chaos in ancient Egyptian thought. As noted above, the surging of the Nile, and its red, blood-like color, is viewed mythologically as the result of the combat between Seth and Horus. Even

19. Lichtheim, *Ancient Egyptian Literature*, 1:149–63; *ANET*, 441–44.

though the Nile brings the necessary silt to make the Nile Valley fertile, the flooding of the Nile nevertheless metaphorically depicts chaos in the land as the waters also threaten both human and animal life in Egypt. Crocodiles inhabit the water ready to catch what they will. Nets do the same as people living in the Nile Valley can fall victim to predators, both natural and human; people bury their brothers continually.

The text returns to imagery of social disruption in which women slaves wear the expensive jewelry and precious stones of their mistresses. Everyone's hair has fallen out, and both the paupers and the rich state that they wish they were dead. Ultimately, Ipuwer states that the land is deprived of kingship, but he gives no hint that a king will arise to restore order to the land. All he can say is that it is good to enjoy one's food as he calls upon his readers or listeners to consume their food in gladness, for god ordains such fortune for whomever god chooses. By the end of the document, Ipuwer appears to be accusing Pharaoh, stating, "If we had been fed, I would not have found you; one would not have summoned me." He continues by stating, "Authority, Knowledge, and Truth are with you—turmoil is what you let happen in the land, and the noise of strife." He admonishes his anonymous addressee, "If only you would taste a little of these miseries, then you would say . . . ," and he continues with statements that indicate the Pharaoh's role to decree and act upon the establishment of order in the land. Altogether, no god is apparent once again, although the text is heavily damaged, and no historical referent is mentioned. But the Admonitions of Ipuwer point once again to the power of speech in Egyptian culture. Insofar as the Pharaoh is divine, his critique also represents divine speech directed against a figure who is entirely inadequate to the task.

Although Egyptian literature and mythology are replete with examples of the embodied representation of gods and goddesses, often in multiple and shifting forms, the true significance of the gods is through their abstract and intangible qualities, whether it is Amun-Re's capacity as the sun to bring life and fertility to the world, or Isis's role to ensure the stability of the Egyptian royal throne by intervening to prepare for the survival and enthronement of her son Horus over against the challenges of her brother Seth. The gods appear to humans in dreams, sometimes in human and/or animal form, but the key element of divine interaction with human beings is through divine speech, conceived as well-crafted prophecy that represents the speech of the gods. Altogether, the tangible portrayal of the Egyptian gods and goddesses must be understood as a form of metaphor that enables the conveyance of the intangible speech and qualities of the divine.

Seeing and Hearing the Gods of Canaan

Ancient Israel and Judah grew out of Canaanite culture. The Pentateuchal narratives portray Abraham and Sarah, the ancestors of Israel, as foreigners who moved into Canaan from Ur of the Chaldeans and later Haran by divine direction and promise of land. But the archeological and historical records point to the origins of Israel as a movement of semi-nomadic Semitic-speaking tribes who moved into southern Canaan from the Arabian Desert across the Jordan River and ultimately assimilated into the resident Canaanite population in the hill country of northern Israel and southern Judah. Indeed, Israelite and Judean religious practice presupposes Canaanite models, including patterns for temples, conceptualizations of YHWH based on earlier traits of Canaanite deities such as El or Baal, and biblical texts that repeatedly assert that Canaanites remained in the land of Israel where they would have formed part of the Israelite and Judean populations.

Unfortunately, there is little written evidence of Canaanite culture in the area of south Canaan where Israel took root and grew. Rather, interpreters are compelled to rely especially on the body of cuneiform literature discovered at the site of ancient Ugarit, a fifteenth- through thirteenth-century BCE port city located in what is now northern Syria near the northeastern Mediterranean coast.[20] As a port city, Ugarit had extensive trade relations with the Hittites, the Phoenicians, the Egyptians, the Arameans, and the Mesopotamians throughout their history. They left a number of alphabetic cuneiform tablets, written in a Semitic language akin to Aramaic and Phoenician; these included economic records, ritual texts, and mythological texts among others. Ugarit was apparently destroyed by the Sea Peoples ca. 1200 BCE as they made their way down the Mediterranean toward Egypt.

The Ugaritic texts present a great deal of material concerning their gods: the creator god, El; El's consort, Athirat (a variation of Ishtar); the storm god, Baal; Baal's consort, Anath; the Chaos god of the Sea, Yamm; the god of the underworld, Mot; and others. They describe very few details of the gods' physical characteristics, and there is little artwork that helps us to understand their tangible forms. In their depiction the gods appear to have very human interests in combat, banqueting, drinking, sex, etc.; and they

---

20. See esp. N. Wyatt, *Religious Texts from Ugarit: The Words of Ilimilku and His Colleagues*, BibSem 56 (Sheffield: Sheffield Academic Press, 1998); David P. Wright, "Syro-Canaanite Religions," in Salzman and Sweeney, *The Cambridge History of Religions in the Ancient World*, 1:129–50.

interact with human beings, usually through a dream in which the deity in question provides instruction and insight to the human subject.

The chief god of the Ugaritic pantheon is El, whose name serves both as a proper name and as a term for a deity in general. El also appears in other West Semitic cultures, including Israel where he is often identified with YHWH. El is the creator god who fathered many of the other gods and goddesses and set creation in order. He dwells in a tent on Mt. Lel (Night) at the fountains of the two rivers that water the world of creation. This depiction points to El's role perhaps as a desert deity dwelling at an oasis that waters the world. He appears to symbolize the transition from semi-nomadic life in the wilderness to settled agricultural life in urban areas. He is often portrayed as a bull, which is a typical symbol of virility and strength; and he often appears wearing a horned crown, which is based on the bull imagery.

Texts that portray his role in setting creation in order are scarce, but one text—known as Shahar and Shalem (Dawn and Dusk) or the Gracious Gods—apparently provides an account of El's role as the Creator God.[21] The text portrays a sacred marriage between El and his two wives: Athirat, also known as Asherah, the Lady of the Sea, and Rahmay, who is associated with the womb. El approaches the sea from the steppe and sees the two women. Athirat and Rahmay dress themselves in garments and jewels, and El has sexual relations with both of them. In depicting the sexual encounter, the text focuses especially on El's erect penis, which is described as being as long as the sea. During the encounter, a bird roasting on a fire provides them with a meal. After repeated encounters, both Athirat and Rahmay give birth to children, Shahar and Shalem, who suck at their breasts. Shahar means "Dawn" and Shalem is taken to mean "Dusk," so the text appears to depict basic aspects of creation: the differentiation between the land and the sea as well as the definition of the day defined by Dawn and Dusk. Other gods and goddesses who will presumably be identified with various elements of creation are subsequently born. This encounter clearly portrays El in very human terms; but the concern with ordering basic aspects of creation, particularly the definition of the day, indicates his role as an element in instigating order and stability in the world.

But El is also capable of fault. He spends most of his time engaged in sex, banqueting, and drinking, generally to excess. One text, called the Myth of El's Banquet, portrays his excessive eating and drinking with the other

21. Wyatt, *Religious Texts*, 324–35.

gods.[22] During the feast, a god named Yarih, who looks and acts like a dog, hides under the table as pieces of meat are thrown to him. El drinks so much at this banquet that he must be helped back to his house by two gods, as he stumbles and falls into his own feces and urine before he is able to make it inside. His wife Athirat and his daughter Anat nurse him back to health, and the myth does include a recipe for a potion that might be used to relieve the symptoms of a hangover. The drinking bout may be related to a *mrzkh* ritual, in which copious drinking and vomiting apparently play a key role (cf. Isa 28). The full significance of this ritual is not yet understood, although it might be linked to a celebration of a fall agricultural festival (cf. Sukkot) that might focus on eating and imbibing the produce of the annual harvest. Elsewhere, Athirat and Anath are known for their hunting skills. Anath can be an impetuous young daughter—with hunting and military skills, no less!—who threatens to make blood run down her Father's gray beard if she does not get her way. El usually gives in when Anath threatens him in this manner. El appears as a very human husband and father with his own set of faults and weaknesses. He needs the support of his wife and his daughter, which points to the role that goddesses frequently play in ensuring stability in creation or kingship throughout ancient Near Eastern societies. Kings are always dependent on others to ensure the success of their rule, and El—though divine—is no exception.

El is forced to make way for the younger god, Baal, "Lord," "Master," or "Husband," who appears to be identified with the Aramean storm god, Hadad. Baal is a god of the storm and fertility, who brings rains to the earth and thereby ensures the growth of new crops to support life in the world of creation. It seems likely that the rise of Baal is linked to the continued arrival of new people in Canaan, perhaps Arameans or semi-nomadic desert dwellers who continue to settle the agricultural and urban areas of the Fertile Crescent through the history of ancient Near Eastern civilization. Baal does not create the natural world as El does; rather, he plays a role in protecting creation from threats and thereby ensures its stability as well as its fertility. The famous Baal cycle includes his combat with Yamm, "Sea," also known as Nahar, "River," apparently a son of El, who threatens the stability of earth by inundating it with flood.[23] In this respect, Baal's combat with Yamm is

---

22. Wyatt, *Religious Texts*, 404–13.

23. Wyatt, *Religious Texts*, 39–114; *ANET*, 129–42; cf. Mark S. Smith, *The Ugaritic Baal Cycle*, vol. 1: *Introduction with Text, Commentary and Translation of KTU 1.1–1.2*, VTSup 55 (Leiden: Brill, 1994).

an example of the typical combat myth in which the hero deity defeats a sea deity of chaos and is therefore granted kingship for protecting the created world. Baal is summoned by El to defend against the threats posed by Yamm, apparently emanating from Cyprus. The myth may have some basis in the threats posed by Sea Peoples who ultimately did destroy Ugarit. Yamm sends messengers to Baal to demand his submission, and Baal's consort Anat, the daughter of El, must restrain him from killing Yamm's messengers on the spot. At the instigation of El, Kothar-wa-Khasis, the craftsman god, goes to the foundry to manufacture two weapons, Crusher and Driver, which Baal then uses to fight and defeat Yamm. Although Yamm scores some hits on Baal, Baal uses Crusher and Driver to strike down Yamm. As a result of Baal's victory, the gods, again at the instigation of El, build a house for him. The house would then serve as the temple for Baal in the city of Ugarit and represent his newly acquired role as the chief deity of the city as his father-in-law El enters old age and potential retirement. The great banquet at Baal's house apparently symbolizes the liturgical celebration of the New Year in Ugarit as a recognition of Baal's kingship.

But Baal, like El, also requires support. When he is challenged by Mot, the god of the underworld and another son of El, Baal is killed in the combat.[24] Although Baal is able to defeat Lotan, apparently an Ugaritic version of Leviathan (cf. Isa 11:15–16; 27:1), he is unable to defeat Mot who opens his mouth and swallows him (cf. Hab 2:4–5). Baal descends into the underworld of the dead where he sits like a piece of dead meat. El and other deities go down to see him and attempt to bring him back to life, but they are unsuccessful and must return to the world of the living without their hero. In an attempt to bring Baal back to life, mourning rituals are devised; worshipers would shave the sides of their heads and gash themselves to draw blood, symbolizing the reversal of creation realized by the death of the god of fertility and life. Two goddesses, Shapsh and Anath, Baal's consort, then descend into the underworld to recover the dead Baal. Shapsh lifts him up and Anath carries him on her back to take him back to the world of the living where he is restored to life. This myth is a typical example of the dying-rising god motif in which the god of fertility dies, descends to the underworld, and is rescued by one or more goddesses who bring him back to life. The myth represents the end of the dry season, which lasts through the summer in the Middle East and concludes with the onset of rain in the fall. During the time of the dry season, Baal is dead in the underworld and the rains do not fall.

---

24. Wyatt, *Religious Texts*, 114–46.

But when the land goes into mourning, the goddesses take action to restore the stability and order of creation by retrieving and reviving the dead god, thereby bringing rain—and crops—back to the world of the living to support a revived creation. Baal is mortal to a certain extent, but his mortality, embedded in the seasonal patterns of the Near East, provides the basis for celebrating the fall festival when the summer drought ends, the rains come, and life is restored to the world of creation.

The Aqhat text is one of the Ugaritic mythological compositions that presents a visionary and dream experience of the gods by a human.[25] The narrative portrays the efforts of Dan-el, a sage who is cited in Ezek 14:14 together with Noah and Job as a figure who was able to save the lives of others because of his own righteousness. He may also stand in the background of the sage Daniel, the protagonist of the book of Daniel, though Daniel does not save anyone's life but his own. The beginning of the Aqhat tablet is damaged, but it portrays Dan-el, the ruler of Rapha and devotee of a god named Hrnm, robed and presenting offerings to the gods before he retires to bed for sleep. Upon completing the offerings, Dan-el removes his robe and goes to bed to wait for a dream vision from the gods. He repeats this procedure for six days without success, but finally on the seventh day Baal appears to him. There is no description of Baal's physical appearance, but the vision depicts Baal drawing near to El to intercede on behalf of the pious and righteous Dan-el. The problem is that Dan-el lacks a son like those of his brothers. Baal asks El, here named in customary manner as Bull El, to bless Dan-el with a son who will remove any cause for slander, support him when he is drunk, repair his roof when necessary, set up an ancestral stele, and fulfill any other tasks normally undertaken by a son on behalf of his presumably aging father. El grants Baal's request and blesses Dan-el with instructions to lie on his bed and have relations with his wife so that the son might be born. Upon the birth of his son, Dan-el presents offering to the Daughters of Ellil, the Bright Ones, who apparently have something to do with the conception of his son.

Following a break in the tablet, the next scene pictures Dan-el seated with his feet on a footstool as a king would sit deciding justice for the orphan and the widow in typical ancient Near Eastern form. From a distance, he sees the craftsman god, Kothar-wa-Khasis, approaching with a bow in his hand to give as a gift to Dan-el's son Aqhat. Dan-el once again demonstrates his piety

---

25. Wyatt, *Religious Texts*, 246–312; *ANET*, 149–55; cf. David P. Wright, *Ritual in Narrative: The Dynamics of Feasting, Mourning, and Retaliation Rites in the Ugaritic Tale of Aqhat* (Winona Lake, IN: Eisenbrauns, 2001).

by asking his wife to prepare food and drink to honor the god. Upon seeing the bow, the goddess Anath covets it and makes a series of offers, ranging from silver and gold to eternal life like that of Baal, if Aqhat will give her the bow. He rejects all of Anath's offers and suggests that she ask Kother-wa-Khasis to construct a similar bow for her, but she rejects Aqhat's suggestions and continues to demand his bow for herself. When Aqhat continues to refuse and suggests that bows are for warriors and not for women, Anath is incensed and appears before her father's throne to demand satisfaction. She tells El about Aqhat's insolence and threatens to make her father's blood run down his grey beard if he does not allow her to take revenge. El, of course, gives in, and Anath proceeds to take action. She invites Aqhat to join her on a hunt, and in the midst of a heavily damaged tablet, Aqhat's bow is apparently damaged. Anath approaches Yatipan, a mercenary god who controls falcons, and devises a plot to kill Aqhat. Anath hides herself among a group of falcons as Aqhat sits down to eat and strikes him on the head, killing him. Ironically, Anath mourns for the dead Aqhat as she hacks his body apart, apparently to feed him to the falcons. Upon Aqhat's death, fertility disappears from the land, and the text portrays Paqhat, the daughter of Dan-el and sister of Aqhat, sending her father to see the dried-up fields that have resulted from Aqhat's murder. Paqhat takes matters into her own hands, puts on armor, and takes up arms, for a westward journey to find Yatipan and recover the remains of her dead brother. After killing a number of falcons and splitting them open, she finally finds Aqhat's remains in a falcon named Sunul and approaches Yatipan to undertake a journey to restore Aqhat to life. Unfortunately, the tablet breaks off here, but it should be clear that this narrative is a variation on the dying and rising god motif in which Paqhat will descend into the netherworld to recover her dead brother, bring him back to life, and thereby restore fertility and life to the land. The protagonists Dan-el, Aqhat, and Paqhat are all human; yet, by worship, they have the capacities to influence the gods to carry out tasks that will either damage or ensure the fertility of the world and life on it. The narrative portrays communication between humans and gods, and the activities of each, but supplies few details of the visual appearance of the gods. Throughout the narrative, the gods act very much like human beings, but they do have the power to create marvelous weapons, shift their own shapes, and restore the dead to life.

Another Ugaritic myth with somewhat analogous concerns, including visionary experience of El, is the legend of King Keret.[26] Keret is the king of

---

26. Wyatt, *Religious Texts*, 176–243.

Khabur on the Khabur River, and the text is concerned with his need to produce a male heir to ensure the continuity of his dynasty. Some have speculated that the legend has a historical background connecting Keret somehow to the dynasty of King Niqmad II of Ugarit, the patron of the scribe Ilimilku who wrote the copies of many of the mythological texts in the Ugaritic corpus; but no secure evidence for such a claim has been forthcoming. Interpreters must remain contented for the present with seeing Keret as a text that is concerned with folkloric motifs of royal ideology, the continuity of a dynastic house, and human or royal interaction with the gods. The narrative begins with an account of the destruction of Keret's house (family). His wife "went away," which some interpret as rebelled, and his seven sons were all killed by one means or another. But El appears to Keret in a dream vision to ask what ails him. There is little attempt to describe El in tangible form, but he does describe himself as the Bull, his (Keret's) Father, and the Father of Humankind. El offers Keret gold, silver, slaves, charioteers, and horsemen to alleviate his sorrow, but Keret declines El's offer and insists that only descendants will satisfy his grief. At this point, El instructs Keret to cease his grieving, wash himself, and prepare to make an offering to both himself and Baal. Keret will then distribute food from the offering to the people of the city, assemble an army, and march against Udum, apparently a foreign land or city state, in order to convince its ruler, Pabil, to grant him the right to marry his daughter, Hurriy.

Following an elaborate description of Hurriy's beauty like those of the Song of Songs, Keret awakes from his dream vision and begins to prepare himself according to El's instructions. Keret assembles his army and after a three-day march arrives at the Sanctuary of Athirat of Tyre and Sidon. Keret offers sacrifices to Athirat and vows to give Athirat twice her weight in silver and three times her weight in gold if the goddess grants him success in his quest to marry Hurriy. Keret and his army arrive at Udum after four more days of marching and proceed to defeat Pabil's forces. When Pabil offers Keret silver, gold, and the production of slaves, Keret demands Hurriy, whose beauty is like that of Anath and Athirat, so that she might bear him children. Although the tablet is broken, Pabil apparently grants Keret's demand, and he returns with Hurriy to Khabur where he holds a great wedding feast. Even the gods, such as Baal and El, come, as Keret will accept no excuses. El himself blesses the marriage with promises of the birth of children. After the wedding feast, Hurriy does indeed bear many children to Keret, and Athirat then remembers Keret's vow.

Due to damage to the text, the reason for Keret's impending death is not clear, but a banquet is declared as Keret prepares to die and his son and successor, Yasib, prepares to ascend the throne. Ilhu, another son of Keret, takes his spear in hand and summons his sister, who has apparently been unaware of Keret's illness and impending death. The sister begins to lament for her father and strips herself naked as part of her efforts. She summons other gods, such as Ilsh and Kothar, to heal her father. Ultimately, El fashions a healing goddess named Shatiqat from clay, who succeeds in healing Keret. Unaware of Keret's recovery, Yasib goes to curse Keret as he prepares to ascend Keret's throne, but Keret curses Yasib instead. At this point, the text ends with the signature of Ilimilku the scribe.

Ultimately, the Keret narrative points to the success of Keret's efforts to restore his family and to protect himself with the help of the gods. Although several gods and goddesses take part in the narrative (El, Baal, Athirat, Anath, Kothar, and others), none of the gods or goddesses is ever described in detail. Their roles are to speak to Keret during a dream vision, in the case of El, or to interact with him as he seeks to secure his bride or searches for a cure from the maladies he suffers. Altogether, Keret proves to be a pious king who secures what he needs by properly approaching the gods. Although the gods featured in the narratives all represent some aspect of the world of creation, they conduct themselves as human protagonists might in playing their roles. Nevertheless, deities such as El and Athirat act to ensure the future of Keret's dynasty, including the births of his new children following his marriage with Hurriy; and in this way they do play some part in the role of the gods in sustaining the order of the world. Although the distinction between the human and the divine is somewhat pale, the text portrays a distinction insofar as the gods and goddesses influence creation and the course of human events.

In addition to the Ugaritic literary corpus discussed so far, other texts from the Transjordanian region of ancient Canaan and Israel bear upon this discussion. One is the Moabite Stone in which King Mesha of Moab celebrates his victory over Israel in the ninth century BCE. The other is the Deir Alla Inscription, from the late ninth or early eighth century, which portrays the vision of the Aramean seer, Balaam bar Beor, concerning the defeat of Israel in the Transjordanian region.

The background for both of these inscriptions is the war between Aram and Israel that saw Israel defeated by Aram, the overthrow of Israelite control in the Transjordan, and ultimately the overthrow of the royal House of Omri by Jehu, an Israelite army commander in the Transjordan.[27] The

27. For discussion of the northern kingdom of Israel and the texts from the book of

Omride dynasty, founded by an Israelite army officer named Omri (876–869 BCE), was one of the major power dynasties of ancient Israel. Following the revolt of northern Israel against the House of David after the death of Solomon, northern Israel saw a string of short-lived dynasties founded by Jeroboam ben Nebat and his son Nadab (922–900 BCE), Baasha and his son Elah (900–876 BCE), and Zimri (876 BCE). Omri overthrew Zimri in 876 BCE and consolidated his own power by founding a new city named Samaria to serve as the capital for northern Israel. Following his death in 869 BCE, Omri's son Ahab ruled northern Israel until he was killed in battle with the Arameans at Ramoth-gilead in the Transjordan in 850 BCE (1 Kgs 22). Ahab was succeeded in 850 BCE by his son Ahaziah, who died as a result of a fall through a second story window in his palace in 849 BCE. Ahaziah's brother, Joram, then served as king of northern Israel until he was assassinated and overthrown by Jehu in 842 BCE.

Interpreters have struggled to understand the Omride dynasty. The Assyrians considered it to be a very powerful dynasty, referring to Israel as the House of Omri even after Joram ben Ahab's assassination. The Assyrian monarch Shalmaneser III named Ahab as the leader of a powerful force of two thousand chariots and ten thousand men who joined the Aramean monarch Hadadezer (Ben Hadad) in battle against him at Qarqar in 853 BCE. Shalmaneser III was defeated by the coalition despite his claims to the contrary. Ahab and Hadadezer were clearly allies at this point, but the biblical narrative in 1 Kgs 20 and 22 indicates that Ahab and Ben Hadad were enemies. A likely explanation for the change of fortune is that Ahab withdrew from his alliance with Ben Hadad following the battle with Shalmaneser III due to the high cost of losing well-trained chariot soldiers and equipment. Ben Hadad would then have attacked Ahab to force him back into the coalition. Ultimately, Ahab was killed, and Jehu overthrew the Omride dynasty as Israel's position against the Arameans continued to deteriorate. The Tel Dan Inscription relates the claim by an Aramean figure, apparently identified with Jehu himself, that he had killed the kings of Israel and Judah, just as Jehu is reported to have done in 2 Kgs 9–10.[28] The biblical narrative indicates Jehu's submission to Aram early in his reign (842–815 BCE), but the Black Obelisk of Shalmaneser III indicates that Jehu submitted to Shalmaneser III in 841

Kings pertaining to that history, see Marvin A. Sweeney, *1 and 2 Kings: A Commentary*, OTL (Louisville: Westminster John Knox, 2007).

28. Avraham Biran and Joseph Naveh, "An Aramaic Stele Fragment from Tel Dan," *IEJ* 43 (1993): 81–98; Biran and Naveh, "The Tel Dan Inscription: A New Fragment," *IEJ* 45 (1995): 1–18.

BCE, apparently to gain an ally who would help him resist the Arameans.[29] Later, the Assyrian monarch Adad-Nirari III claims Jehu's grandson Joash as one of his tributaries.[30]

The Jehu dynasty of five monarchs (842–746 BCE) proved to be the strongest and longest-lasting dynasty of the northern kingdom of Israel. Nevertheless, it was very weak in its early years as Israel lost control of the Transjordan, apparently beginning in the late reign of Ahab, extending through the reign of Jehu (842–815 BCE), and continuing through the reigns of Jehoahaz (815–801 BCE) and Jehoash/Joash (801–786 BCE). Joash restored Israel's position, apparently through his alliance with Assyria, and paved the way for the peaceful, powerful, and prosperous reign of his son, Jeroboam II (786–746 BCE), who ruled a kingdom like that of Solomon from Lebo-Hamath to the Sea of the Arabah (2 Kgs 14:23–29). Jeroboam's son, Zechariah, was assassinated in 746 BCE by Shallum, thereby bringing the House of Jehu to an end.

Israel's loss of the Transjordan is confirmed by the above-mentioned Tel Dan Inscription as well as by the Mesha Inscription on the Moabite Stone and the Deir Alla Inscription; like Tel Dan, these other inscriptions also refer to communication from gods to humans.

The Mesha Inscription was written in the mid-ninth century BCE by a king of Moab, located to the east of the Dead Sea, named Mesha, known in the Bible in 2 Kgs 3.[31] The inscription celebrates Mesha's overthrow of Israelite power in the Transjordan. He specifically mentions the dominance of the Omride Dynasty over Moab under the rule of Omri's son Ahab. He speaks about his capture of the city of Atarot, where the men of the Israelite tribe of Gad lived, as well as about his capture of other Transjordanian cities and his consolidation of power in the aftermath of the Israelite defeat. Such a defeat would have correlated with the Arameans' defeat of Israel beginning with the death of Ahab in battle at Ramoth-gilead and continuing with the reverses suffered by Israel under Ahab's sons Ahaziah and Joram until the dynasty was overthrown by Jehu.

In the inscription, Mesha mentions communication from the Moabite god, Chemosh. Chemosh is known for his appetite for human blood. Mesha states that "Chemosh said to me, 'Go, take Nebo from Israel,'" and that he

---

29. *ANEP*, 351–55.

30. Stephanie Page, "A Stela of Adad Nirari III and Nergal-ereš from Tell al Rimah," *Iraq* 30 (1968): 139–53.

31. See *ANET*, 320–21.

complied with Chemosh's instructions, killing thousands of Israelite men, women, and children whom he considered as offerings for Chemosh. The means by which Chemosh communicated with Mesha are not made clear in the inscription, but the form of Chemosh's statement suggests a divinatory experience in which a question is posed to Chemosh, and Chemosh then replies. An analogy appears in David's inquiry to YHWH in 2 Samuel 2 in which David apparently employs divinatory means to ask YHWH if he should go up to Hebron, and YHWH replies, "Go up." Such an action indicates that divination is a form of visionary experience; in its most basic form a deity responds simply to a question in either visual or audial form. The vision might have occurred by reading smoke, oil, or water patterns in a divinatory inquiry, or by reading animal entrails or perhaps other physical signs that would be understood as a response to the question posed to the god.

The other inscription, the Deir Alla Inscription, was discovered during excavations at a site often identified as biblical Sukkoth along the Wadi Jabbok, now known as the Zerka River in Jordan.[32] It was written on a now-collapsed plaster wall inside of a destroyed building believed to have functioned as a temple or cultic center. Although the text, which presents the vision of the seer Balaam bar Beor, was originally identified as an Aramaic text, the mixture of Aramaic, Hebrew, and other elements has prompted scholars to suggest that it is an indigenous Canaanite or Ammonite text dated to the early or mid-eighth century BCE. Reconstruction of the inscription has been difficult due to the deteriorated condition of the plaster and the loss of many of its fragments. It begins with a superscription that identifies the text as "the admonitions of the Book of Balaam the son of Beor, who is a visionary of the gods." In that the name Balaam bar Beor is an Aramaic form of the Hebrew name Balaam ben Beor, the text appears to present an Aramaic, Canaanite, or Ammonite vision experienced by the Aramean seer hired by King Balak of Moab to curse Israel in Num 22–24.

The first portion of the Deir Alla Inscription describes Balaam's dream vision concerning the gods who came to him to present a pronouncement from El, generally identified as the Canaanite creator god. The text describes Balaam's efforts to prepare for the vision by summoning the heads of the assembly, perhaps a reference to Transjordanian leadership, fasting, and

---

32. Meindert Dijkstra, "Is Balaam Also among the Prophets?," *JBL* 114 (1995): 43–64; Baruch A. Levine, *Numbers 21–36*, AB 4A (New York: Doubleday, 2000), 241–75; Marvin A. Sweeney, "Balaam in Intertextual Perspective," in *Tell It in Gath: Studies in the History and Archaeology of Israel: Essays in Honor of Aren Maeir on the Occasion of His Sixtieth Birthday*, ed. Itzhaq Shai et al., ÄAT 90 (Münster: Zaphon, 2018), 534–47.

weeping for two days. When the people ask him what he has seen, he states that the gods, here identified as the Shadayin, established a council. The council directs the goddess Shagar-and-Ishtar to sew up the heavens with cloud, so that darkness, cloud, and obscurity will cover the land, plunging the birds and animals of creation into chaos. The chaos then prompts the augurers and armies to panic and flee the land. The second portion of the Inscription is very fragmentary and difficult to reconstruct and interpret, but it portrays El finishing with lovemaking and building an eternal house or temple; it also describes the dead lying decomposed in Sheol, the underworld where all the dead go.

What the first part of Balaam's Deir Alla vision appears to describe is the defeat and expulsion of the augurers and armies of an unidentified kingdom in the Transjordan. Although the second part of the Inscription is fragmentary, it appears to celebrate the building of a temple for El, perhaps the Deir Alla structure itself, and the enemies who now lie dead in Sheol. Such a scenario appears to presuppose the Aramean and Moabite defeats of Israel in the late ninth and early eighth centuries BCE, noted above, as the Omride and early Jehu dynasties were expelled from the Transjordan. Ironically, the oracles of Balaam ben Beor in Num 22–24 portray Balaam's blessings of Israel. Now since Num 22–24 celebrates Israel, it appears to belong to the mid-eighth century BCE as part of the foundational E or Ephraimite stratum of the Pentateuch. The portrayal of Balaam's blessing of Israel when he was hired by King Balak of Moab to curse Israel suggests that Num 22–24 was written as a response to the Deir Alla Inscription and its portrayal of the role of Balaam, announcing the curses of the Canaanite or Transjordanian gods that prompted Israel's defeat and withdrawal from the region.

The role of the gods in bringing darkness and chaos to the land indicates their close interrelationship with and control of the forces of creation that they employ to influence human events. Balaam, identified as an exemplar of the Mesopotamian *baru*-priest, or oracle diviner, reports his dream vision in typical fashion with both a report of the dream and its interpretation. Shagar-and-Ishtar's role emphasizes her activity, on behalf of the larger divine council, as that of a god exercising control of the world; in this respect Balaam's vision is consistent with the foregoing examples in which humans see the gods act, hear their messages, or receive visual answers to their questions much as on the report of their actions and/or their answers to human inquiry (divination), by which they direct the world.

Gods and Mortals of Ancient Mesopotamia

Ancient Mesopotamian civilization dates to as early as the mid-sixth millennium BCE, but the first three millennia remain largely undocumented
because cuneiform writing did not appear until the mid-third millennium.[33]
Cuneiform texts written in Sumerian indicate that Sumerian civilization
dominated southern Mesopotamia through approximately 1940 BCE when
the Elamites sacked ancient Uruk. But Semitic-speaking Amorite peoples
migrated into the Fertile Crescent from the Arabian Desert to form the Akkadian Empire, beginning with the reign of King Sargon the Great (2334–
2279 BCE) in the late twenty-fourth century BCE. The later First Babylonian Dynasty, of which King Hammurabi of Babylon (1728–1686 BCE) is
the best-known monarch, solidified Semitic control of Mesopotamia in the
nineteenth century BCE, which led to the origins of ancient Assyria and
Babylonia.

The Mesopotamian civilizations, Sumer, Babylonia, and Assyria, portrayed their gods and goddesses in a variety of forms based on a combination
of human and animal imagery, but it was always clear that the Mesopotamian
gods and goddesses were considered as luminous beings whose intangible
forms distinguished them from tangible human beings.[34] Such a portrayal is
evident in the mid-third millennium BCE cylinder seal of Adda, which portrays a number of deities at sunrise.[35] The Sumerian sun-god, Utu, appears in
the center rising from behind the mountain in the form of a human equipped
with sun rays emanating from his shoulders. To his left, Inanna, the goddess
of the Morning Star (Venus), hovers over the mountains as the first light to
be seen in the morning prior to dawn. She, too, emanates rays of light, and
she represents stability in creation. Further to the left is Ninurta, the god
of thunderstorms, holding his bow and followed by his lion, whose roar
represents the sound of thunder in the heavens. To the right of Utu stands
Enki, the god of sweet waters, holding a thunderbird in his left hand and

33. Kuhrt, *The Ancient Near East*, 19–117; A. Leo Oppenheim, *Ancient Mesopotamia:
Portrait of a Dead Civilization* (Chicago: University of Chicago Press, 1964).

34. Jean Bottéro, *Religion in Ancient Mesopotamia* (Chicago: University of Chicago
Press, 2004); Graham Cunningham, "Sumerian Religion," in Salzman and Sweeney, *The
Cambridge History of Religions in the Ancient World*, 1:31–53; Tammi J. Schneider, "Assyrian
and Babylonian Religions," in Salzman and Sweeney, *The Cambridge History of Religions in
the Ancient World*, 1:54–83.

35. Thorkild Jacobsen, *The Treasures of Darkness: A History of Mesopotamian Religion*
(New Haven: Yale University Press, 1976), 94.

pouring the waters of the Tigris and Euphrates Rivers from his shoulders. Behind Enki is his vizier, Isimud. Although all the figures are depicted in human or quasi-human form, most have characteristics that identify them with the natural features of creation that they represent, and each wears the horned cap signifying his or her divine status. Although the images portray tangible, physical forms, they appear to be designed as metaphors to facilitate comprehension of divine presence.

Mesopotamian religion presupposes that the gods are identified with the various features of creation and with the political structures of human civilization. Thus, Enlil, one of the chief gods of Sumerian civilization, is the god of the winds who uses his powers to defeat Tiamatu, the goddess of salt water chaos, who threatens to destroy the order of creation and the gods who inhabit it in the Sumerian version of the Mesopotamian creation epic. As god of the city of Nippur in southern Mesopotamia, Enlil's victory over chaos signaled the preeminent position of Nippur ca. 3000 BCE. When Babylon became the chief city of Mesopotamia in the nineteenth century BCE, Marduk, the city god of Babylon, supplanted Enlil as chief of the gods, but he continued to use the winds as his primary weapons to defeat Tiamatu in the Babylonian version of the creation epic, Enuma Elish.

Because the gods and goddesses were so closely identified with features of creation in Mesopotamian thought, *baru*-priests, specialists in reading omens from the world of creation, evolved over time as the experts who could discern the will of the gods.[36] The *baru* were highly trained in reading and writing cuneiform so they could record omens over the course of centuries in order to study them and discern their significance for interpreting the will of the gods. The *baru* read a large variety of omens, such as the stars and the planets. Each star or planet was identified with a particular god or goddess, and their movements through the heavens signaled the intentions of the gods that the *baru* would read, interpret, and declare to their patrons. Other omens might include smoke or oil patterns on water. The smoke would rise from incense or sacred fires and the *baru* would observe the patterns of the rising smoke to determine the will of the gods. Oil patterns were formed when oil was poured into water during the divinatory process where they could be read and interpreted. Other omens might include the movements of animals, unusual phenomena in creation such as a two-headed snake, or other anomalies that would signal to the trained *baru* a message from a god.

---

36. Frederick H. Cryer, *Divination in Ancient Israel and Its Near Eastern Environment*, JSOTSup 142 (Sheffield: Sheffield Academic Press, 1994), 124–228.

The reading of animal entrails, especially livers, was a well-known specialty of the *baru*. A question might be whispered into the ear of the sacrificial animal and the animal would be slaughtered and filleted to recover its entrails so that they could be read. The position of a lobe or "finger" on the liver was frequently an important means to determine the divine will. Dreams were another source for interpretation of the divine will, and the *baru* were experts in the interpretation of the symbolism represented in dreams that were taken to represent communication from the gods.

The correlation of the Mesopotamian gods and goddesses with the world of creation and human beings is evident in the first instance in the Mesopotamian creation epic.[37] Although it was known already in Sumerian civilization, in which the wind god Enlil was the deity who set the world in order, the creation epic is best known in its Babylonian form and by its first words in Akkadian, Enuma Elish, "when on high." The Enuma Elish features Marduk, the city god of Babylon, as the creator god who sets in order the natural world and thereby ensures that Babylon will be recognized as the leading city in all creation.

The Enuma Elish begins with a depiction of the two parental deities, Apsu, the male god of sweet waters, and Tiamatu, the female deity of saltwater and chaos, who often appears as a sea monster. Apsu and Tiamatu mix their waters together and thereby bring about the birth of all the various gods and goddesses of the Mesopotamian pantheon. But problems ensue when the multitude of gods and goddesses make so much noise that Apsu is unable to sleep. Apsu thereupon decides to kill all his offspring so that he might eliminate the noise and get some rest. Word of Apsu's plan becomes known to the god of the earth, Enki in Sumerian or Ea in Akkadian, who takes action to save his siblings by killing Apsu. Tiamatu, enraged by the murder of her husband, gathers an army from all the monsters of the deep to carry out her husband's plan and kill the gods and goddesses of the Mesopotamian pantheon. Enki brings word back to the gods and goddesses of Tiamatu's plan, and the gods assemble to consider what they should do. The divine assembly is the model for human assemblies that exercised power and frequently played a role in the selection of monarchs in the ancient Mesopotamian world. The gods debate the issue and ultimately choose Marduk, the city god of Babylon, as their hero to lead them in battle to face Tiamatu and her hordes.

---

37. Stephanie Dalley, *Myths from Mesopotamia: Creation, the Flood, Gilgamesh and Others* (Oxford: Oxford University Press, 1991), 228–77; *ANET*, 60–72, 501–3.

Marduk prepares for battle by rouging his lips and gathering his weapons: the wind, a net, a sword, bow and arrow, etc. The two armies face each other and begin with taunts as the two heroes, Tiamatu and Marduk, come to the forefront for individual combat. As Tiamatu approaches Marduk, she opens her mouth to swallow him, but Marduk blows the winds down her open throat, forcing it to remain open, as he aims an arrow and shoots it down her throat, killing her. He takes his sword and cuts Tiamatu's carcass in half, setting one half up as heaven and the other half down as earth. Marduk places the gods and goddesses in the heavens so that each becomes identified with an individual planet or star as his or her symbol in the Mesopotamian pantheon. When it is pointed out that there is no one to do the work of building houses or temples for the gods and goddesses or feeding them by offering sacrifices at the temples, Marduk takes action. He holds the defeated army of Tiamatu in his net and selects the god Kingu, who had been designated as Tiamatu's military commander, to be killed. He kills Kingu, takes his blood, and mixes it with earth to create the first human beings who will be tasked with doing the work of the gods and goddesses, i.e., building their houses or temples and seeing to their feeding by the offering of sacrifices. The gods and goddesses then celebrate the victory by having the Etemenanki temple built for Marduk in the city of Babylon, Bab-ilu in Akkadian, which means "gateway of the gods," to signify its status where human beings and the gods may meet. Marduk is given fifty names to signify his status as the ruler of the gods. Every year, the anniversary of creation is celebrated at the New Year or Akitu festival in which the Enuma Elish is read, and statues of the gods who represent the cities and nations of the Babylonian Empire are carried in procession through the streets of Babylon to the Etemenanki. The Babylonian king, who rules as Marduk's regent, is brought to the temple at the top of the Etemenanki, where he is met by a priestess who represents Marduk. In Sumerian practice, the king would have sexual intercourse with the priestess, but in Babylonian practice she would simply slap his face to remind him that he serves Marduk. The king would then receive the tablets of destiny, which would authorize him to rule on Marduk's behalf for another year, thereby ensuring the continuity of creation and the Babylonian Empire. The Enuma Elish ties the political order of the Babylonian Empire to the establishment of the natural world of creation itself, as it identifies the gods and goddesses with both the natural world of creation and the political order of Babylonia.

Another myth whose concerns overlap those of the Enuma Elish is the Babylonian Flood Narrative, named the Atrahasis Epic after the human

Babylonian flood hero.[38] The overlap with the Enuma Elish appears in the creation of human beings to do the work of the gods in the Atrahasis. The Atrahasis Epic is one of the major forms in which the Mesopotamian flood narrative appears. Atrahasis, whose name means "exceedingly wise," was the King of Shuruppak in south central Mesopotamia. He is mentioned in the Sumerian King List under his Sumerian name, Ziusudra, which also means "exceedingly wise" in Sumerian. A Sumerian form of the narrative features Ziusudra as the flood hero, but the Akkadian form of the narrative, written by the scribe Nur-Aya during the reign of King Ammi-Tzaduka of Babylon (1702–1682 BCE), represents the fullest known form of the text. A variant in which Utnapishtim, "he found life," an attribute of Atrahasis, serves as the flood hero, appears in the Gilgamesh epic to be treated below.

The Atrahasis Epic begins with a depiction of Igigi, a lower class of gods, who are working under the supervision of the Anunnaki, the upper class of the gods who were born to the sky god, Anu, and the earth goddess, Ki, to dig the canals of Mesopotamia. The Igigi are suffering greatly under their forced labor, and they propose sending the god Ellil, a variant of the name Enlil, the lord of the wind, to demand from Anu the sky god that the Igigi be given relief from their burdens. The attempt is successful, and Enki suggests that human beings be created to do the work of digging the canals so that the Igigi might find some relief. The mother goddess, Mami, makes clay figurines mixed with the flesh and blood of the slain god, Geshtu-E, to carry out the work of the gods. Human beings then flourish and become extremely numerous throughout the world.

With the proliferation of humans on earth, a problem emerges when they make so much noise that Enlil cannot get any sleep. Enlil decides to destroy all humankind, first by famine and then by flood; but Enki, typically the ally of human beings in Mesopotamian mythology, conveys to Atrahasis instructions for building a water-going vessel by which to save his family and other life on earth. Enki speaks to Atrahasis through a reed wall; this suggests a form of oracular communication. No description of Enki is given in the text, but the use of a reed wall indicates either some form of a barrier between Enki and Atrahasis, perhaps analogous to the veil worn by Moses when YHWH speaks to him, or the transcription and interpretation of the oracular message on papyrus by a *baru*-priest who is trained to interpret the omens that might be employed in oracular communication. In some versions

---

38. Dalley, *Myths*, 1–38; W. G. Lambert and A. R. Millard, *Atra-Ḥasīs: The Babylonian Story of the Flood* (Oxford: Clarendon, 1969).

of the text, Enki speaks to Atrahasis in dreams, which are also explained to Atrahasis through the wall of a reed hut. When Enlil decrees famine in the land to decrease the human population, Enki tells Atrahasis to cease giving offerings to the gods, except for the storm gods, such as the Aramean Hadad (Adad) who also appears in Mesopotamian texts. When Hadad delivers the rains to allow food to grow, Enlil then decides to send a flood to diminish humankind. Enki then tells Atrahasis to dismantle his house and use the timber to build a water-going vessel so that he and his family will survive the flood. The vessel shall be built like the roof of Apsu, the underground fresh-water stores that Enki controls, with bitumen like that of a ship (or the roof of Solomon's Temple; see 1 Kgs 7), to ensure that the vessel is watertight. Atrahasis builds the vessel and loads his family and animals in it to survive the flood. During the course of the flood, problems arise for the gods. No one is making offerings, and so the gods are starving for lack of food. When the seven-day flood comes to an end, Atrahasis offers sacrifices, and the famished gods crowd around like flies to get to the offered food. Enlil is angry that his decree of death was undermined, but Enki reminds him that he preserved life in the world that would otherwise have been wiped out. In order to control the growth of the human population, Enlil decrees that humankind will suffer plague, drought, stillbirth, and childlessness. The Atrahasis Epic therefore explains human mortality decreed by the gods as a means to limit human growth.

A similar concern appears in the Adapa myth.[39] The myth is known from Akkadian tablets of the fifteenth–fourteenth centuries BCE, discovered at Amarna in Egypt, and tablets from the mid-second millennium, discovered at Assur, the religious capital of Assyria. Adapa was the first of seven antediluvian sages sent by Enki/Ea to humankind to teach them the arts of civilization. Described as the son of Eridu, one of the earliest of the Sumerian cities located near what was then the Persian Gulf, Adapa acts as both a sage and a priest in teaching humans how to bake bread and offer it to the gods. Adapa is also a fisherman, and while he is out on the Gulf fishing, the South Wind blows, threatening to sink his boat. He curses the South Wind, here portrayed metaphorically as a bird, and breaks its wing so it cannot fly (blow) any longer. When Anu, the god of heaven, notes the absence of the South Wind, he makes inquiries and learns that Adapa is responsible. He therefore invites Adapa to ascend through the seven levels of heaven to appear before his throne to eat and drink. Enki/Ea, however, is suspicious

39. Dalley, *Myths*, 182–88; *ANET*, 101–3.

of Anu's invitation and advises Adapa to refuse any food and drink offered by Anu as it might prove to be poisonous. Adapa ascends through the levels of heaven to the gate of Anu and correctly identifies the various gods who guard the gates for each level so that he will pass in safety. When Adapa is brought before Anu, Anu offers him the bread of eternal life and the water of eternal life. But thinking that he is about to be poisoned, Adapa refuses the bread and water, and thereby refuses eternal life for humankind; and thus the myth explains how human beings are mortal. Adapa and the other sages are ultimately expelled to the Apsu controlled by Enki/Ea. The Adapa myth not only explains mortality as a characteristic of humankind; but it also points to the differentiation between humans who live on earth and gods who dwell above in the heavens, or below in the Apsu, and therefore require specialized means to facilitate communication between the human and the divine worlds.

The differentiation between the heavenly realm of the gods and the earthly existence of human beings is apparent in the Sumerian King List.[40] The Sumerian King List presents a chronicle of the various Mesopotamian dynasties, beginning with the antediluvian dynasties associated with the city of Eridu, the first major Mesopotamian city whose monarchs are credited with fantastic reigns as long as thirty-six thousand years, and culminating in the Dynasty of Isin (1953–1730 BCE) whose kings reigned for more reasonable periods of time. The antediluvian dynasties cannot be confirmed historically, but beginning with them points to the principle of dynastic movements among the cities of Mesopotamia as a means of demonstrating the legitimacy of the Dynasty of Isin in the Middle Bronze Age (ca. 2100–1550 BCE). The document begins, "When kingship was lowered from heaven, the kingship was in Eridu," to introduce the accounts of the various kings of Eridu and the other dynasties that follow.[41] It is noteworthy that the kings lowered from heaven are typically portrayed as metaphorical trees growing upside down from heaven. Their branches embody various qualities of the king—wisdom, righteousness, power, sweet scent, etc.—as metaphors that portray the ideal characteristics of the Mesopotamian kings (cf. Isa 11:1–10).

The differentiation between the realm of the gods and the realm of humans is also apparent in the myth of Ishtar's descent to the underworld,

40. Thorkild Jacobsen, *The Sumerian King List* (Chicago: University of Chicago Press, 1939).

41. Jacobsen, *The Sumerian King List*, 71.

which dates to the Late Bronze Age, ca. 1550–1200 BCE.[42] An earlier Sumerian form of the myth, the Descent of Inanna to the Underworld, presents a much fuller form of this text.[43] The Sumerian Inanna and the Akkadian Ishtar are names for the same goddess. She is often portrayed as a nude young woman or as a warrior armed with her own weapons. She is often declared to be the goddess of sexuality, love, and passion, because she displays these traits in the mythological texts written about her. But she is much more than this. Inanna/Ishtar is identified with planet Venus, and she appears in both the morning and the evening as the Morning Star and the Evening Star, which is the first and last of the heavenly bodies seen in the morning and at night. She must therefore be recognized as a goddess who embodies stability in the world of creation, and the Descent of Inanna/Ishtar illustrates this role. Her sister is Ereshkigal, the goddess who rules the underworld of the dead. For reasons unknown, Inanna journeys to the underworld, perhaps to seize the throne of her sister, much as Ereshkigal's consort, Nergal, does. As Inanna/Ishtar passes through each of the seven levels of the underworld, she must remove an article of clothing or jewelry, which signifies her giving up the ornaments and beauty of life as she progressively devolves into a corpse. By the time she appears before the throne of Ereshkigal, she is completely naked. She compels Ereshkigal to rise from her throne, and then sits upon it herself. This angers the Anna, the seven divine judges, who condemn her to death. Her corpse is hung on a hook and left to rot. After three days and nights, Inanna's servant Ninshubar follows his instructions and appeals to the major gods to rescue Inanna. Enki responds and creates two asexual beings, Galatura and Kurjula, from the dirt under the fingernails of the gods and goddesses. They descend to the underworld, where Ereshkigal demands that they bring Inanna back. They agree to do so, but in fact do not. They do follow instructions and bring back the corpse of Inanna to the world of the living and restore her life. An angry Ereshkigal sends demons to pursue them and to capture Inanna's servants, but initially they fail to do so. They ultimately settle on Inanna's consort, Dumuzi, known in Akkadian as Tammuz, a male god of fertility. Inanna had seen him lavishly clothed and surrounded by maidens during her absence; she decrees that he can be taken to the underworld to take her place. Dumuzi's sister offers to go instead, and ultimately the decision is made that Dumuzi will dwell in the underworld for six months of the year and in the world of the living for the other six months.

---

42. Dalley, *Myths*, 154–63; *ANET*, 106–9.
43. *ANET*, 50–57.

While he is in the underworld, there is no rain or fertility in the world of the living. When he is among the living, the rains come and the land bears fruit. This narrative explains climatological patterns in western Asia, which experiences a dry summer for half of the year and a wet winter that begins with the fall rains.

A related body of mythological literature is the Sumerian love songs.[44] The Sumerian love songs are a collection of twenty-seven poems written in Sumerian on cuneiform tablets; the highly erotic poetry speaks of the love between Inanna and Dumuzi. An example of the poems' language, in which Inanna speaks longingly of her desire for love, illustrates their metaphorical character: "My uncultivated land, that which is left fallow in the steppe; my field of ducks, where the ducks teem; my high field, that which is well-watered; my own nakedness, a well-watered, a rising mound—I, the maiden—who will plow it? My nakedness, the wet and well-watered ground—I the young lady—who will station there an ox?"[45]

The Sumerian love songs appear to be generically similar to the Song of Songs of the Hebrew Bible, which likewise speaks of the longing of a woman for her male lover and ultimately of the consummation of their relationship. The tablets were composed during the Third Dynasty of Ur and the early Old Babylonian period (ca. 2100–1800 BCE). They appear to play a role in the sacred marriage rites in the Sumerian cities of Ur, Uruk, and Isin, in which the king engages in sexual intercourse with a priestess as part of the Sumerian New Year festival, when the king is authorized by the gods, in this case Enlil, to rule on their behalf for another year. The king and the priestess assume their roles as Dumuzi and Inanna consummating their union in the fall New Year celebration.

Such a conceptualization points to the role of Inanna and Dumuzi—and in later Babylonian and Assyrian times, Ishtar and Tammuz—in ensuring the renewal of creation. The Sumerian love songs are hardly limited to the New Year festival, known in Babylonia as the Akitu festival. They also correlate with the mythological narrative of the Descent of Inanna to the Underworld in which Dumuzi was condemned to death in the underworld to take the place of Inanna, who had descended thither, perhaps to claim the throne of her sister, Ereshkigal. But the compromise, allowing Dumuzi to come back to earth for six months of the year, points to the concern with creation in

---

44. Yitschak Sefati, *Love Songs in Sumerian Literature: Critical Edition of the Dumuzi-Inanna Songs* (Ramat Gan, Israel: Bar Ilan University Press, 1998).

45. Sefati, *Love Songs in Sumerian Literature*, 224–25.

the Sumerian—and later, Babylonian and Assyrian—celebration of the fall New Year festival. Dumuzi's sojourn in the underworld lasts during the dry months of the year when no rain falls and no crops grow. His return to earth marks the onset of the fall rains that will water the earth and ensure the growth of crops in the land for the other six months of the year.

The reunion of Inanna and Dumuzi marks not only the authorization of kingship for another year; it also marks the renewal of creation for another year. The political structure of human civilization and the natural structure of creation are two aspects of the same reality in ancient Mesopotamian thought, and both are expressed mythically by the union of Inanna and Dumuzi—and in less explicit form by the union of Ishtar and Tammuz in Babylonian and Assyrian culture. Indeed, Inanna and Dumuzi symbolize not only the union of the gods, the union of the king and the priestess, and the renewal of creation; they also symbolize the union of every married couple in the land, indicating that one of the ways to experience the presence of the gods and goddesses in ancient Mesopotamia was through marriage and sexual union in which the bride and groom embodied the relationship between Inanna and Dumuzi.

The notion that the gods and goddesses are embodied in human sexuality, both at the level of kingship and at the level of common human marriages, does not represent the only means by which the divine is manifested in human life in ancient Mesopotamia. There are also the matters of the deep bonds of friendship and the role of mortality in human life. Although this chapter has already examined the issue of human and divine mortality in the Atrahasis, the Adapa myth, and the Descent of Inanna to the Underworld, the Gilgamesh Epic of ancient Mesopotamia provides an extended examination.

The Gilgamesh Epic was already known in fragmentary Sumerian tablets from Uruk, ca. 2150 BCE.[46] It includes a number of independently composed episodes that appear in the extensive later Akkadian version of the Epic, but it is clear that the text has gone through an extensive process of writing, expansion, and editing during the course of its compositional history. The standard Akkadian text employed for study is a twelve-tablet Akkadian version, ascribed to a master scribe and incantation priest named Sin-leqe-unnini of the Kassite period (ca. twelfth century BCE).[47] Some of the best copies of this version were discovered in the seventh-century BCE ruins of King Assurbanipal's library in Nineveh.

---

46. *ANET*, 42–52.
47. Dalley, *Myths*, 39–153; *ANET*, 72–99, 503–7.

Gilgamesh is described as the part-god, part-human ruler of Uruk. The Sumerian King List includes Gilgamesh among its antediluvian monarchs, and so it is possible that he is based upon a historical figure. He is a rambunctious monarch who disturbs his people with his constant battles, noise, and demands. The people appeal to the gods for a hero to challenge Gilgamesh and put an end to their suffering. The gods then create Enkidu, a human wild man, to meet the challenge. Gilgamesh is warned by the gods in a dream in which he sees a *kitzrum* from Anu fall from the heavens.[48] Gilgamesh's mother interprets it as a sign that someone as strong as Gilgamesh has been born in the wild, and that he and Gilgamesh will become fast friends when they meet. Enkidu lives in the wild with the wolves, but he is civilized when he comes upon a woman who was deliberately placed to tame him. After seven days of intercourse and training in the practices of the civilized world, Enkidu cannot return to his wild life and comes to Uruk to live and to challenge Gilgamesh. Enkidu and Gilgamesh fight, but neither is able to overcome and defeat the other. Each finally recognizes his equal in the other, and they become fast friends, roaming the land looking for adventure and defeating many monsters and divine beings along the way.

Gilgamesh has three dreams sent by the gods that signal divine approval for their quest.[49] Gilgamesh prepares the dreams by digging a canal to the west and scattering incense offerings, which were typically employed to welcome dream demons. He finally invokes a mountain, on which he and Enkidu ascend. The mountain responds by sending a dream in the form of a wind that puts Gilgamesh into a deep sleep, during which he sleeps while squatting on the ground with his chin touching his knees (cf. Elijah, 1 Kgs 18), apparently in a trance. Gilgamesh awakes and exclaims that he is wide awake; Enkidu did not call him, no god has passed by, and yet he feels paralyzed. He reports the three dreams, but the first is lost to damage in the text. The second portrays the collapse of the mountain, which traps Gilgamesh by his feet, but a man comes to rescue him. The third dream portrays the mountain burning to ashes, day turned to night, and death-dealing rain (cf. Elijah, 1 Kgs 18). The dreams warn Gilgamesh to leave the area, but Enkidu persuades him to stay. The narrative portends coming disaster, but it also shows something of the means by which dream omens were prepared and experienced.

Enkidu ultimately meets his end when Gilgamesh offends the goddess Ishtar by rejecting her sexual advances. Ishtar decrees death for Enkidu and

<hr>

48. Oppenheim, *The Interpretation of Dreams*, 246–47.
49. Oppenheim, *The Interpretation of Dreams*, 247–48.

sends a monster to kill him. Again, a dream plays a role in the narrative when Enkidu dreams of his coming demise.[50] He sees a griffin sent to convey him to the underworld. He is stripped of his garments and clothed in feathers as he is led on a path, by which one may never return, to a dark underworld of death. There he is met by Ereshkigal, the ruler of the underworld, who asks, "Who has sent this man hither?" Gilgamesh mourns for his friend and attempts to revive him, but finally gives up the effort when he sees a worm emerge from Enkidu's nose. He thereupon embarks upon a quest to find the flood hero Utnapishtim, who gained immortality by surviving the flood. Gilgamesh ultimately finds Utnapishtim, who relates the story of the flood to him in a form that is apparently derived from the Atrahasis Epic. When Utnapishtim completes his narrative, he gives Gilgamesh the secret to eternal life in the form of an olive branch which Gilgamesh must return to the world of the living. But traveling on the river back to the world of the living, Gilgamesh stops for the night, and a snake emerges from the waters to snatch the tree of life from Gilgamesh and then dives back into the water. The episode thereby explains why snakes, who shed their skins, are considered by the ancient Mesopotamians to live forever, whereas human beings remain mortal because Gilgamesh lost the secret of life.

Ancient Near East cultures display a variety of means by which human beings experience and relate to their gods and goddesses through dreams, visionary experience, and direct interaction. Altogether, ancient Near Eastern deities are very powerful, but undependable, self-interested, and frequently amoral. Human beings therefore must find ways to understand the deities so that they may better survive and flourish in the world.

50. Oppenheim, *The Interpretation of Dreams*, 248–49.

Chapter 2

VISIONARY AND DREAM EXPERIENCE IN THE PENTATEUCH

The Pentateuch presents numerous texts that illustrate how visionary and dream experience functioned in ancient Israelite and Judean thought. In most cases, they point to temple settings as the locus for such activity, and reasonably so, for temples generally serve as the settings for visionary experience in the ancient Near Eastern and Greco-Roman worlds.[1] Visions are typically experienced through either ecstatic or dream events. In all cases they employ imagery that would have been well known in ancient Israel and Judah. Visionary and dream account texts in the Pentateuch include Gen 15; Gen 28; Gen 35; Gen 37; Gen 40–41; Exod 3; Exod 19; Exod 24; Exod 33; Lev 16; Num 22–24.

Abram's Vision and YHWH's Covenant Obligation (Gen 15)

Genesis 15 presents an account of Abram's vision of YHWH in which YHWH concludes a covenant with the patriarch.[2] YHWH promises Abram numerous descendants who will possess the entire land of Canaan/Israel from the River of Egypt in the south to the Euphrates River in the north. This text is often misinterpreted as a statement of justification by faith, due to the New Testament readings of Gen 15:6 in Gal 3:6–9 and Heb 11:8–12 according to which YHWH reckons Abram as righteous due to his faith in YHWH.

---

1. Frances Flannery-Dailey, *Dreamers, Scribes, and Priests: Jewish Dreams in the Hellenistic and Roman Eras*, SJSJ 90 (Leiden: Brill, 2004).

2. For a detailed study of Gen 15, see Marvin A. Sweeney, "Form Criticism," in *To Each Its Own Meaning: An Introduction to Biblical Criticisms and Their Application*, ed. Steven L. McKenzie and Stephen R. Haynes (Louisville: Westminster John Knox, 1999), 58–89.

Genesis 15:6 reads, "and he believed in YHWH, and he reckoned it to him as righteous." Analysis of the syntax of Gen 15:6 and the function of its pronouns, however, indicates that it refers to Abram's reckoning of YHWH as righteous, i.e., that the childless Abram accepts YHWH's promise in v. 5 to make his offspring as numerous as the stars of the heavens. Indeed, the dialog between Abram and YHWH concerns YHWH's promises that Abram's reward will be great and Abram's assertion that any reward would be meaningless so long as he remains childless and a servant in his house will inherit his legacy. YHWH's covenant with Abram then confirms YHWH's promise to Abram and his wife Sarai as the ancestors of Israel.

Genesis 15 is formulated as a vision account of YHWH's word to Abram. Genesis 15:1 makes this context clear at the outset, "After these things, the word of YHWH came to Abram in a vision." The formal structure of the passage includes four major segments, including an account of YHWH's initial promise of a reward to Abram and Abram's response that he has no offspring in Gen 15:1–3; an account of YHWH's promise to Abram of many descendants like the stars of the heavens in Gen 15:4–5; a lengthy account of Abram's response to YHWH's promise and YHWH's visionary response to Abram in a deep sleep that ratifies the covenant and the promise of many descendants in Gen 15:6–17; and a summation of YHWH's covenant with Abram in Gen 15:18–21 which grants the land of Canaan/Israel from the River of Egypt to the Euphrates River to Abram and his descendants.

Genesis 15:6–17 is key to understanding the visionary material in this passage. It begins with Abram's above-mentioned affirmation of YHWH's righteousness in v. 6; it proceeds with YHWH's promise of land to Abram in v. 7, Abram's request for confirmation in v. 8, YHWH's instruction to prepare for a covenant ratification ritual by bringing sacrificial animals and cutting their carcasses in half in v. 9, Abram's compliance in vv. 10–11; and it culminates with the account of the covenant ritual by means of a dream vision in vv. 12–17.

The dream vision begins in v. 12 with the notice that a deep sleep fell upon Abram. The "deep sleep" is described by the Hebrew term, *tardema*, which is the same term employed in Gen 2:21 to describe the deep sleep that YHWH imposed on Adam before creating Eve from one of his "ribs" or "sides" (Hebrew, *tzal'otayw*). The first element of the vision is the account of YHWH's statements to Abram in vv. 13–14 that his many descendants will be foreigners who will be enslaved in Egypt for a period of four hundred years and that YHWH will redeem them from Egyptian bondage so that they will go free with great wealth. The second element in vv. 15–16 promises that

Abram will die in his old age in peace and be buried in the land promised to him. His descendants will return to the land in the fourth generation which will ensure that they will live in the land promised to Abram and his descendants. Following the account of YHWH's promises, v. 17 recounts a scene after sunset in which a smoking oven and flaming torch pass between the pieces of the sacrificial animals prepared by Abram in v. 9 to confirm the covenant with Abram promised by YHWH.

The imagery of the smoking oven (Hebrew, *tannur 'ashan*) and the flaming torch (Hebrew, *lappid 'esh*) is quite enigmatic. Ephraim A. Speiser explains this imagery in relation to Akkadian magical texts that portray smoking pots and flaming torches that were used together with incantations to expel witches.[3] Although this is an attractive explanation, it does not go far enough in explaining the symbolism and function of the two devices. They clearly symbolize the divine, as in fact the Mesopotamian incantations would call upon deities to aid in expelling witches or other malevolent beings. Yet the present context in Gen 15 does not require the expulsion of witches or the like, while it does presuppose the presence of the divine. In this case, the smoking oven and flaming torch symbolize features of ancient Israelite temples where YHWH would be manifested. Two features of Israelite temples immediately suggest themselves, viz., the incense altar and candelabra or menorahs that are placed in the heikhal or main hall of Israelite temples to evoke the presence of YHWH. The incense altar would emit smoke, a tangible and yet undefinable substance that suggests the smoke and cloud with which theophanic texts portray divine presence. The menorahs were seven-branched lamps with wicks fed by olive oil to supply light in the heikhal of Israelite temples, analogous to the lightning that together with the imagery of smoke and cloud portrays the divine presence. Both items appear in the instructions concerning the building of Solomon's Temple in 1 Kgs 7 where the incense altar appears in 1 Kgs 7:48, and the menorahs appear in 1 Kgs 7:49.[4]

Identification of the smoking oven and the flaming torch of Abram's vision with the temple incense burners and menorahs does not fully explain the vision. Also requiring explanation is that both of these items pass between the pieces of the sacrificial animals. Such explanation comes from ancient Near Eastern ceremonies for signing or ratifying treaties. Aramean

3. Ephraim A. Speiser, *Genesis*, AB 1 (Garden City, NY: Doubleday, 1965), 113–14.

4. See Marvin A. Sweeney, *1 and 2 Kings: A Commentary*, OTL (Louisville: Westminster John Knox, 2007), 121, 124.

and Assyrian practice called for the signatories of a treaty to pass between the pieces of severed sacrificial animals, declaring that the same must happen to them if they should violate the terms of the treaty that they have just sworn to observe before their own gods (cf. Jer 34:18).[5] Thus, the Aramean King Matti'el of Arpad declares in the eighth-century Sefire IA treaty with King Bargayah of KTK, "As this calf is cut up, thus Matti'el and his nobles shall be cut up (if Matti'el is false)."[6] In other words, if Matti'el violates the terms of the treaty with Bargayah, he is to be cut up just as the sacrificial calf is cut up.

Because YHWH is the primary signatory to this covenant, represented by the smoking oven and the flaming torch, the vision of these two symbols passing between the severed pieces of the sacrificial animals signifies YHWH's ratification and signing of the covenant with Abram. Abram does not sign the covenant in any appreciable manner in this chapter; after all, Gen 15 portrays YHWH's commitment to the covenant promised to Abram. Within the larger context of the Abram/Abraham and Sarai/Sarah narratives of Genesis, Abram's ratification of the covenant with YHWH comes in Gen 17 when Abram undergoes circumcision to signify his affirmation to observe the covenant made with YHWH. Although Gen 15 has been analyzed as a J narrative supplemented by E,[7] more recent recognition of the late composition of the J or Judean stratum of the Pentateuch during the late monarchic or exilic periods indicates that Gen 15 is fundamentally an E or Ephraimite narrative from eighth-century BCE northern Israel that has been edited by J or Judean editors during the late seventh or sixth centuries BCE.[8] YHWH's (or perhaps even G-d's) ratification of the covenant thus originates in northern Israel; the narrative was brought south and updated to suit Judean interests following the destruction of northern Israel in 722–721 BCE. The introduction, in the mid-fifth century, of the P or Priestly narrative in Gen 17 then completes the scenario by portraying Abram's ratification of the covenant.

---

5. Nahum Sarna, *Genesis*, JPS Torah Commentary (Philadelphia: Jewish Publication Society, 1989), 114–15; Moshe Weinfeld, "The Covenant of Grant in the Old Testament and the Ancient Near East," *JAOS* 90 (1970): 184–203.

6. See *ANET*, 660.

7. Antony F. Campbell and Mark A. O'Brien, *Sources of the Pentateuch: Texts, Introductions, Annotations* (Minneapolis: Fortress, 1993), 100–101, 166–67.

8. Marvin A. Sweeney, *The Pentateuch: Foundations of Identity in Israel and Judah*, CBS (Nashville: Abingdon, 2017), 9–14.

Jacob's First Vision at Beth El (Gen 28)

Genesis 28:10–22 presents the account of Jacob's initial vision of G-d at Beth El. The episode follows Gen 27:1–28:9 in which Jacob, at the instigation of his mother Rebekah, deceives Isaac into granting him the blessing of the father that was to have gone to his firstborn son, Esau. Consequently, Esau vows to kill Jacob. Rebekah recognizes the threat to Jacob and expresses her frustration with Esau's marriages to foreign women. She thereby convinces Isaac to send Jacob to Paddan-aram where he may take refuge with her brother Laban and find a suitable wife.

Jacob's first stop on his journey from Beer Sheba to Haran (in Paddan-aram) is at a place called Luz where he takes a stone to use as a pillow and spends the night. While sleeping, Jacob has a dream in which he sees a stairway to heaven with angels of G-d going up and down upon it. YHWH stands beside him and promises him the ground on which he is lying, many descendants who will spread out in all directions, the blessing of all the families of the land by him and his descendants; YHWH promises to be with him wherever he goes and to return him to the land. When Jacob awakes, he recognizes that he has had a vision of the divine and that the place where he had slept is sacred ground. He therefore erects the stone as a *matzevah* dedicated to G-d, renames the place Beth El, i.e., "house of G-d" in Hebrew, and vows that YHWH will be his god if YHWH protects him on this journey and brings him safely home.

Genesis 28:10–22 is clearly an etiological narrative concerning the foundation of the northern Israelite sanctuary at Beth El.[9] Beth El was founded as one of two royal sanctuaries of the northern kingdom of Israel by its first monarch, King Jeroboam ben Nebat. According to 1 Kgs 12:25–33, Jeroboam feared that his people would continue to go to the Jerusalem Temple following their revolt against the house of David, and so he established Beth El and Dan as the royal sanctuaries that would ensure their allegiance to the northern kingdom and the retention of their offerings. But 1 Kgs 12:25–33 also alleges that Jeroboam set up Beth El and Dan as idolatrous sanctuaries by erecting images of a golden calf for the people to worship. This charge must be qualified, however, by the observation that the golden calves were not gods per se, but only represented mounts for the normally invisible YHWH, much as the ark of the covenant served as the

9. George W. Coats, *Genesis, with an Introduction to Narrative Literature*, FOTL 1 (Grand Rapids: Eerdmans, 1983), 206–9.

throne where YHWH would be invisibly seated in the Jerusalem Temple.[10] The historical Jeroboam likely had no intention of setting up idolatrous gods, but he was charged with idolatry by the Judean authors from the late monarchic period whose writing of the Jeroboam narrative sought to defend YHWH from any charges of having failed to protect northern Israel by blaming the king and people for their own destruction at the hands of Assyria in 722–721 BCE. The purpose of their polemic against the northern kingdom was to prompt the people of Judah to adhere to YHWH by adhering to the Jerusalem Temple and the House of David—and thereby, presumably, to avoid the same fate.

Beth El was in fact a sanctuary dedicated to YHWH in the northern kingdom of Israel, and therefore it was the locus of visionary activity that was typical at Israelite and Judean sanctuaries in antiquity. Indeed, our narrative portrays the patriarch Jacob as the true founder of the sanctuary and attributes the first instance of visionary experience of YHWH at the site to him. There is no hint of any critique of Beth El, and so it appears that the narrative originated as part of the E or Ephraimite stratum of the Pentateuch.[11] Following the destruction of the northern kingdom of Israel in 722–721, the foundational E narrative of the Pentateuch would have come south with northern Israelite survivors seeking refuge in Judah, where J or Judean authors during the late monarchic period would have edited and expanded the E narrative that D or Deuteronomic material would also supplement. Following the Babylonian Exile, the EJD strata of the Pentateuch would have been edited by P or Priestly writers during the fifth or fourth centuries BCE to produce the present form of the Pentateuch.

Setting aside possible reasons to polemicize against a northern sanctuary in later strata, E's narrative of Jacob's vision of YHWH and his founding of Beth El presents several features relating to Israelite dream visions at shrines devoted to YHWH that demand attention.

First, Jacob's vision of YHWH appears in the form of a dream, like that of Abram in Gen 15. Dreams are one of the common means to convey visionary experience in Israel/Judah and throughout the ancient Near East.

Second, the dream vision takes place at the site of the future Israelite royal sanctuary. As Frances Flannery-Dailey demonstrates, temple sites

---

10. Marvin A. Sweeney, *Reading the Hebrew Bible after the Shoah: Engaging Holocaust Theology* (Minneapolis: Fortress, 2008), 52–57, 67–72; cf. Sweeney, *1 and 2 Kings*, 175–78.

11. Marvin A. Sweeney, "The Jacob Narratives: An Ephraimitic Text?" *CBQ* 78 (2016): 236–55; Sweeney, *The Pentateuch*, 17.

are typically the sites of visionary experience in the ancient Near East and Greco-Roman world.[12]

Third, although YHWH appears in the dream vision experience, YHWH's form is never described. Although YHWH is presumed to have a body or physical form that can be observed in some visionary experience,[13] other passages such as the Ten Commandments can be read as prohibiting the description of YHWH's form, or even as excluding the possibility of viewing it. Nevertheless, those texts that do attempt to describe the presence of YHWH often employ metaphorical imagery of light, smoke or cloud, and water to portray YHWH. Although YHWH is presumably seen by Jacob in the present vision, YHWH's presence is manifested in the narrative by speech to Jacob. Speech likewise lacks physical form, but it nevertheless is a very powerful force in the tangible world that prompts human beings to action in transforming the world in which they live.

Fourth, Jacob sets up the stone which he used as a pillow to function as a *matzevah*. A matzevah is an uninscribed stone pillar that is used to represent the presence of a deity in Canaanite and some Israelite/Judean sanctuaries during the Bronze and Iron Ages. The pillar may well have represented El or Baal prior to the emergence of Israel, but it could also be employed to represent YHWH. Indeed, the south Judean sanctuary for YHWH at Arad had a matzevah set up in its holy of holies.[14] The fact that it was uninscribed lends itself nicely to Israelite and Judean practice insofar as it very pointedly does not ascribe any physical form to YHWH.

Fifth, the angels going up and down the ladder to heaven are likewise mentioned without reference to their physical form. They play important roles in ancient Near Eastern texts, such as the Adapa myth, that portray the various gods who guard the ascent to heaven, as well as in later heikhalot literature that portrays angels as the figures who guard the ascent through the various levels of heaven.[15]

Sixth, the appearance of the ladder, Hebrew, *sullam*, indicates a characteristic feature of Mesopotamian temples or ziggurats that are built as stepped pyramids and employ a lengthy staircase that enables temple officials and others to climb to the top of the ziggurat. Some scholars argue that

12. Flannery-Dailey, *Dreamers, Scribes, and Priests.*

13. See Benjamin D. Sommer, *The Bodies of G-d and the World of Ancient Israel* (Cambridge: Cambridge University Press, 2011).

14. Miriam Aharoni, "Arad," *NEAEHL*, 1:75–87; see esp. the photograph on p. 84.

15. For the Adapa myth, see *ANET*, 101–3; for the heikhalot literature, see chapter 6 below.

such a feature points to the Babylonian Etemenanki, which was built in the form of a stepped ziggurat with such ramps facilitating ascent to the top. This feature then becomes the basis for arguing that the Beth El narrative was written during the Babylonian Exile when Babylon would have ruled Judah following the destruction of the Jerusalem Temple.[16] But such an argument misses an important connection to northern Israel when it was subject to Assyria from the late-ninth-century reign of King Jehu (842–815 BCE), founder of the Jehu dynasty. The Black Obelisk of King Shalmaneser III depicts Jehu bowing in submission at his feet.[17] By submitting to Assyria, King Jehu found the means to pressure Aram from the northeast and thereby to relieve Aramean pressure on northern Israel. Indeed, his grandson, King Jehoash ben Jehoahaz is also listed as a tributary of King Adad-nirari III of Assyria. Like the Babylonian ziggurat, Assyrian ziggurats were also built according to the pattern of a stepped pyramid with ramps along each side to enable ascent to the temple at the top of the ziggurat. Northern Israel was ultimately destroyed by the Assyrian Empire in 722–721 BCE for breaking its treaty during the reign of King Hoshea in 724 BCE (see 2 Kgs 17). Such an action would have triggered penalty clauses in a typical Assyrian treaty that called for the destruction of a rebellious ally. The portrayal of YHWH associated with such a structure in Jacob's vision at Beth El demonstrates that YHWH is the true ruler of Israel who surpasses the Assyrians in guaranteeing Israel's security in the world. Ironically, Israelite law prohibits the building of such a ramp on an Israelite altar (Exod 20:26), apparently to preserve the modesty of the priests; but Jacob's vision instead depicts Beth El as the site of the heavenly temple of YHWH.

Altogether, the imagery of the vision correlates well to Israelite sensibilities concerning the refusal to depict YHWH in physical form, both by employing an unmarked matzevah to depict the presence of YHWH at a holy temple in Israel and by employing YHWH's words to Jacob as the key representation of divine presence and power. At the same time, the use of Mesopotamian ziggurat and ramp imagery lends itself to the portrayal of YHWH—and not the Assyrian god, Assur—as the true deity of the world. YHWH is therefore capable of promising Jacob that Jacob will return to the

---

16. E.g., Victor Avigdor Hurowitz, "Babylon in Bethel—New Light on Jacob's Dream," in *Orientalism, Assyriology, and the Bible*, ed. Steven W. Holloway (Sheffield: Sheffield Phoenix Press, 2007), 436–48.

17. For the Black Obelisk of Shalmaneser III, see *ANEP*, 351–55; for the vassal list of Adad Nirari III, see Stephanie Page, "A Stela of Adad Nirari III and Nergal-ereš from Tell al Rimlah," *Iraq* 30 (1968): 139–53.

land, that he will have many descendants, and that he and his descendants will indeed possess the land of Israel. YHWH's promise is thereby well integrated into the Jacob narratives which depict YHWH's relationship with Jacob as the eponymous ancestor of Israel, who is about to go into exile where he will find his wives and father his children, the ancestors of the twelve tribes of Israel, and who ultimately will return with them to the land, where he will be able to settle issues with his fraternal twin brother Esau, so that he and his descendants will live peacefully in the land promised to him by YHWH.

Jacob's Second Vision at Beth El (Gen 35)

Genesis 35 presents a second instance of Jacob's visions of YHWH—or G-d as the case may be—at Beth El. The present form of the narrative is clearly designed to complement the earlier account in Gen 28:10–22, making repeated reference to the earlier episode. Most interpreters maintain that Gen 35 is largely a combination of E and P elements due to the consistent reference to YHWH as G-d or El Shaddai, with E elements in Gen 35:1–5, 7, 8, 14, and 16–20, and P elements in Gen 35:6, 9–13a, and 22b–29.[18] The E narrative appears to focus on Jacob's building of an altar at Beth El as well as other cultic installations and actions. It seems designed to complete the earlier narrative in Gen 28:10–22 by ensuring that Beth El be recognized as a holy site for the worship of G-d, including the presentation of sacred offerings. The E account in Gen 35:1–5 emphasizes G-d's requirement that Jacob's family give up their foreign gods and purify themselves before traveling to Beth El to build an altar and thereby to dedicate the site as holy to G-d.

The P narrative in Gen 35 resembles E at this point, insofar as both strata employ the term "G-d" for YHWH, but P appears to be designed to serve its own agenda. The P elements in Gen 35:9–13a present a vision account in which the portrayal of G-d makes several important points. The first is the blessing that G-d gives to Jacob in which Jacob's name is changed to Israel. This account builds upon the earlier J narrative in Gen 32:23–33 in which Jacob wrestled with a man apparently representing YHWH and had his name changed to Israel. Although the account in Gen 32:22–32 explains the name Israel as a statement that Jacob "had striven with G-d" and prevailed, the name actually signifies, "may El (G-d) rule," taking the verb root, *srh*, "to

18. Campbell and O'Brien, *Sources*, 33, 119, 174–75, 197.

rule," as the basis of a theophoric name in which El is the subject. El is well recognized as the name of the Canaanite creator god who was also venerated in Israel following the establishment of the Israelite nation. Although El was Canaanite in origin, El was absorbed into Israelites' conceptualization of YHWH. In P's thought, YHWH originally appeared as El Shaddai, "G-d Almighty," as indicated by YHWH's explanation to Moses in the P account of the revelation of the divine name in Exod 6. Indeed, G-d self-identifies as El Shaddai in Gen 35:11 following the statements concerning the change of Jacob's name. Altogether, the change of Jacob's name serves P's interest in portraying Jacob as the ancestor of the nation, Israel, an agenda previously served by E and J.

Second is the interest in portraying YHWH in continuity with the earlier Canaanite deity, El Shaddai, as well as any variations, such as El Elyon (Gen 14). The P and E narratives both recognize that Israel had worshiped foreign gods prior to the revelation of YHWH to the ancestors and later at Sinai, as the present form of the P vision account makes clear with the above-mentioned identification of YHWH as El Shaddai. Beth El likewise had some earlier function from Canaanite times as indicated by its earlier name of Luz. The present narrative thereby presents YHWH's revelation to the ancestors, and Israel at large, as a necessary evolutionary process by which Israel would dispense with earlier forms of idolatry or foreign worship to recognize YHWH as the true G-d of all creation and humanity.

Third is the issue of the sanctuary at Beth El per se. As noted in the discussion of Jacob's first vision at Beth El, the later history of Israel portrays Beth El as a very problematic site associated with idolatry. The golden calves that, according to the later Judean writers of 1 Kgs 12:25–13:34, King Jeroboam ben Nebat established at Beth El and Dan as gods for the northern kingdom of Israel to worship were apparently, in the view of northern Israelites themselves, nothing more than mounts for YHWH, seated invisibly upon them, just as ancient Near Eastern gods were typically mounted on animals. The northern Israelite E had no need to critique Beth El, especially if Jacob's vision there signified YHWH's kingship in contrast to Assyria's; the polemical narratives about Jeroboam in Kings, then, serve to blame Israel, not YHWH, for the Assyrian destruction and serve to instruct Judeans in how they might avoid a similar fate by observing YHWH's expectations. However, after the Judean exile to Babylonia, how to make sense of Beth El presented a problem for P in Gen 35.

P's problem in Gen 35, then, is how to explain that YHWH appeared to Jacob at Beth El and promised him a nation and a land when Beth El has such a sordid reputation in the Hebrew Bible. Much of the Bible is indeed written by Judeans, including both the Kings narratives of the late monarchic period and the Persian period P narratives from the time of Ezra and Nehemiah, who would view Beth El as an idolatrous sanctuary. The earlier EJ narrative in Gen 28 offers no hint that Beth El is a problematic site, other than the appearance of a matzevah; but even that can be dedicated to YHWH. The present P narrative within Gen 35 is likewise quite positive. It changes Jacob's name to Israel, thereby declaring that Jacob is the founding figure of the Israelite nation and that El rules that nation. But it also presents the iconic priestly blessing, "be fruitful and multiply," as a sign of YHWH's favor, and it continues by promising that Jacob/Israel will become a great nation, that kings will descend from him, and that his descendants will also possess the land that YHWH promised to Abraham and Isaac.

P does not suggest any critique of Beth El in its vision account. After all, the vision represents YHWH's promise to the eponymous patriarch and through him to the entire nation of Israel. But it takes up the critique of Beth El in the episodes that follow the vision account in Gen 35:16–21, 22. In the first instance, the blessing that kings would descend from Jacob comes into play when Rachel dies while giving birth to Benjamin. Rachel is Jacob's beloved wife, and her death in childbirth accentuates both the tragic dimension of their relationship and its impact on the nation at large. Jacob had earlier declared in Gen 31:32 that anyone possessing Laban's teraphim or household gods would die, not knowing that his beloved Rachel had them in her possession. Rachel is the mother of both Joseph and Benjamin, the two ancestors of the chief tribes of northern Israel. Joseph is the father of Ephraim and Manasseh, the two most powerful tribes of northern Israel located in the Israelite hill country; and Benjamin is the first royal tribe of Israel, from which King Saul ben Kish would come. Although Rachel is the ancestral mother of the most important tribes in northern Israel, her early death marks not only tragedy for her husband Jacob, but tragedy for the nation as well. Jacob is frequently portrayed in the Pentateuchal narratives as a flawed character, and one of his faults is the favoritism he displays, first to his beloved Rachel over his other wife, her sister Leah, as well as to her sons Joseph and Benjamin. Jacob's favorable treatment of Joseph will ultimately provoke the jealousy of his brothers who will sell him into slavery in Egypt, causing untold suffering to Jacob. Although Joseph's sojourn in Egypt will ultimately save the lives of his father and the rest of his family, it will result in Jacob's death in Egyptian exile. As for Benjamin, the youngest of Jacob's sons and the most spoiled after Joseph, he ultimately produces King Saul, Israel's first king, who proves to be a completely tragic and incompetent monarch; he suffers from manic-depressive syndrome, constantly oversteps his boundaries, fails to observe the instructions of YHWH, leads his country to defeat at the hands of the Philistines, and finally commits suicide as portrayed in 1 Samuel 31. As portrayed in the aftermath of G-d's blessing to Jacob at Beth El in Gen 35, that tragedy begins with the death of Rachel while giving birth to Benjamin—immediately after the family's sojourn at Beth El. The association of the death of Rachel with the family's sojourn at Beth El apparently functions as a form of value judgment on Beth El. Beth El is later known for its association with idolatry and tragedy in biblical literature. Rachel's death while on the journey from Beth El to Beth Lehem, the future birthplace of King David ben Jesse of Judah, highlights the contrast between the royal house of Saul and the royal house of David. Whereas Saul's house is defunct after two generations, the house of David rules for some four hundred years.

The brief notice of Reuben's affair with Bilhah, the concubine of his father, further accentuates the problematic association with Beth El. Beth El seems to bring out the worst in people. The fact that Reuben is the culprit also proves to be instructive. Reuben is the oldest son of Jacob and thereby destined to inherit the greatest share of his father's house, but he now loses that role because of his abominable actions. Simeon and Levi, Jacob's second and third sons, had also disgraced themselves by killing the men of Shechem in Gen 34. Although Shechem had despicably raped their sister, Dinah, Jacob had made a treaty with the Shechemites. The actions of Simeon and Levi meant that Jacob had violated his own treaty. With the displacement of Reuben, Simeon, and Levi, Judah remains as the fourth son destined to inherit the majority share of his father's house and serve as the leader of the family.

Jacob's second vision at Beth El (Gen 35) occurs in the midst of events of great moment, upheaval, and tragedy for the ancestors of Israel's tribes. Judah's eventual leadership, reflecting the interests of the Jerusalem Temple and the House of David, comes at the expense of Shechem, the name of another northern Israelite center of worship, in addition to the priestly ancestor Levi and Simeon, ancestor of a tribe that seems to have been absorbed into Judah. The changing fortunes of the tribes also parallels the journey— literally and metaphorically on the way from Beth El to Beth Lehem—in which they suffer the loss of Rachel, mother of the once-dominant Josephite tribes and Benjaminite king. Her death recalls the oath Jacob makes to Laban concerning his stolen gods, and thereby echoes Jacob's words to his family, urging them to put away their gods, just before they arrive at Beth El. Thus

Jacob's second vision is preceded by a reminder of the oath about the stolen gods that unwittingly dooms Rachel and is followed by her death upon
leaving the sanctuary of Jacob's G-d. Perhaps these associations between her
death and the other gods recalls not only the critique of Beth El from the
Judean point of view but also the covenant between Jacob and Laban that
follows the search for the stolen gods; they invoke YHWH's watching-over
in what turns out to be, for Rachel, an ominous echo of the divine promise
of divine supervision of Jacob's sojourn in the first vision at Beth El. The
weight of Jacob's vow about Laban's gods and their covenant that invokes
Jacob's G-d as witness does not fall upon Rachel until YHWH's kept promise
is affirmed and Jacob has made his vow in recognition of his G-d at Beth El
in the second visit and vision. In placing Jacob's second vision at Beth El in
the midst of narratives redolent of the varying fates of the northern tribes
especially, the second vision serves to extend the promise of the first vision
and amplifies the ambivalence about Beth El as a sanctuary associated with
the G-d who not only appears to Jacob there but also watches over Jacob/
Israel in every place for both good and ill.

Joseph's Dreams (Gen 37)

Genesis 37 introduces the Joseph narratives with a portrayal of a seventeen-
year-old Joseph who helps his father's wives, Bilhah and Zilpah, in tending
sheep. He is portrayed as a very arrogant young man who believes that he
is destined to rule Israel. The basis for his arrogance appears to lie in his
father's treatment. Jacob gives his son a special garment, described in Hebrew as *ketonet passim*, translated as "a coat of many colors" or as "a coat of
sleeves," which appears to be the same type of garment worn by the unmar-
ried daughters of King David (2 Sam 13:18).[19] Although the full meaning of
the garment's description is uncertain, it is a mark of special privileged status
that reflects Jacob's favored treatment of the son of his favorite, but now
dead, wife Rachel. Jacob's poor parenting skills appear to have been learned
from his parents, as Isaac favored Esau and Rebekah favored Jacob. Just as
Isaac's and Rebekah's favoritism provokes conflict between their sons, so
Jacob's special treatment of Joseph (and Benjamin) will have consequences
for his family and ultimately for himself. The narrative signals this issue at

19. Sarna, *Genesis*, 255–56.

the outset when it states that Joseph's brothers hated him as a result of his special treatment by Jacob.

Dreams play a key role in signaling both Joseph's arrogance and his destiny as father of the leading tribes of Israel. Genesis 37:5–8 presents an account of Joseph's first dream in which Joseph and his brothers were binding sheaves of grain in the field. Joseph relates how his sheaf rose and stood upright, prompting the sheaves of his brothers to gather around his sheaf and bow down to it. When his brothers hear of this dream, they recognize its message and ask if Joseph means to rule over them. A second dream account then follows, in which Joseph recounts how the sun, the moon, and eleven stars were bowing down to Joseph. When he reports the dream to his father and brothers, Jacob understands immediately and asked if he, Joseph's mother, and Joseph's eleven brothers are meant to bow down to him. Within the larger narrative of Genesis, Joseph's mother Rachel has already died, but the dream makes the point that she will bow to him together with his father and brothers. Joseph's brothers are again incensed, but Jacob characteristically does not discipline or rebuke Joseph.

There is no overt connection between Joseph's dreams and any Israelite sanctuary, as there were in the cases of Abram's vision in Gen 15 or Jacob's visions in Gen 28 and 35. The sheaves of grain likely would have been taken to a sanctuary as an offering of the first fruits of grain, but such an outcome is not even mentioned in the narrative. Rather, the dreams could be read as communications by YHWH to Joseph, much as YHWH informed Abimelech in a dream that Sarah was Abraham's wife in Gen 20:6–7, although YHWH is not identified as the source of the dream in Gen 37.

Indeed, the accounts of Joseph's dreams in Gen 37 appear to have a dual function that points to the potentially twofold sources of Joseph's dreams from YHWH and Joseph's own characterization.

In the first instance, the dreams appear to portend Joseph's leading role in Israel. Joseph will ultimately become the father of Manasseh and Ephraim in Gen 37–50. The order of the boys will be reversed to Ephraim and Manasseh when Jacob adopts them in Gen 48. The adoption was necessary in part because Joseph's wife who gave birth to his sons was not Israelite. She was Asenath, daughter of the Egyptian priest Potiphera according to Gen 41:41–46. Just as Esau's marriage to foreign women was a problem for Isaac and Rebekah, so was Joseph's marriage to a foreign woman an issue for Jacob. By adopting them as his own sons, Jacob attempted to alleviate the stigma of their foreign birth, but their Egyptian association is of course remembered.

Ephraim and Manasseh are the two key tribes of the northern kingdom of Israel; Ephraim is the more powerful tribe, positioned in the southern hill country of the northern kingdom of Israel, although Manasseh, positioned both in the Transjordan and in the northern Israelite hill country, may well have been the older tribe. Indeed, Ephraim's rise to power is noted in the book of Judges, when Ephraim threatens the judge, Gideon of Manasseh, because he fails to include them in the order of battle against Israel's enemies in Judg 8. Likewise, Ephraim goes to war against the Transjordanian (perhaps Gadite?) judge, Jephthah, in Judg 10–12 when he fails to include them in his plans for the defense of Israel. Ephraim forces its way into the role of the leading tribe of northern Israel, thereby creating great resentment, just as Joseph created great resentment by claiming status as the leading son of Jacob among his brothers. Although Joseph is resented for his dreams, they point to the future roles of his sons as the ancestors of the two most powerful tribes in the northern kingdom of Israel. Such a destiny suggests that YHWH is the source of the dreams, just as YHWH disclosed Abram's destiny to him in the dream vision of Gen 15.

In the second instance, Joseph's dreams give expression to his own arrogance and sense of entitlement. Joseph believes that he is superior to his brothers and, by communicating his dream to them, he asserts that he is. But the Joseph narrative is not simply a tale about how the young Joseph rose to power to become the leader of both Egypt and his people; it is also the story of a very spoiled and arrogant young man who by suffering and discipline grew up to become a worthy leader of his people. Joseph's arrogance in relating his dreams and aspirations to his father and his brothers incites the jealousy of his brothers and prompts them to attempt to murder him and sell him into slavery in Egypt. Joseph suffers for his arrogance, and he continues to do so in Egypt when he is falsely accused of attempting to seduce the wife of his master and imprisoned for his alleged crime. Joseph must learn humility and how to get along with others, lessons that ultimately enable him to win not only release from prison but also the confidence of Pharaoh, who entrusts Egypt's administration and survival to Joseph. It is as a result of his position—and the maturity gained through the suffering he endured to rise from slavery into such a position—that he is then able to save the very brothers who had sold him into Egyptian slavery in the first place, as well as his father, his brother Benjamin, and the rest of his family. In this respect, Joseph's dreams provide a window into his arrogant personality that he would ultimately learn to overcome in order to emerge as a worthy leader and savior of his own family and nation.

Joseph's personality has implications for the nation as well. The Joseph narratives are frequently recognized as a combination of J, E, and P elements,[20] although his role as father of the tribes of Ephraim and Manasseh suggests that he is closely associated with northern Israel as well as the E stratum of the Pentateuch that is identified with the northern kingdom of Israel.[21] Indeed, recent development of source critical analysis of the Pentateuch indicates that E or the Ephraimitic stratum is the foundational stratum of the Pentateuch that was later edited and expanded by the late-monarchic J or Judean stratum and the Persian-period P or Priestly stratum. Given the northern Israelite interests in the narrative, the character of Joseph appears to be based on that of Jeroboam ben Nebat, the first king of the northern kingdom of Israel following its revolt from the house of David ruled by Solomon's son, Rehoboam ben Solomon.[22] Jeroboam first appears as one of Solomon's officers who was in charge of the forced labor imposed on the House of Joseph to carry out Solomon's building projects, such as the royal palace, the Jerusalem Temple, and the fortifications of Jerusalem and many Israelite cities. But when Jeroboam was designated by YHWH, through the prophet Ahijah the Shilonite, to be the next king of northern Israel, Jeroboam began to emerge as a leader rather than as an oppressor of his people. Solomon sought to kill Jeroboam, forcing him to flee to Egypt to save his life. But following the death of Solomon, Rehoboam came north to seek acceptance by the northern tribes. When Rehoboam displayed his own immaturity and evil intent in his answers to the northerners as to how he might rule them, the northern tribes revolted against the House of David and selected Jeroboam, who had just returned from Egyptian exile, as their first king. Although Jeroboam is severely criticized as an idolatrous monarch who led his nation to ruin in the Judean Deuteronomistic Historical narratives in 1 Kgs 11–14, he would have been viewed as the founding hero in northern Israel for releasing the people from the oppressive rule of the House of David. Indeed, Solomon is portrayed as a Pharaoh-like ruler who imposed slavery upon the northern tribes.[23] Starting as a slave master of the House of Joseph under Solomon's rule, Jeroboam emerged as a wise leader

---

20. Campbell and O'Brien, *Sources*, 55–61, 120–31, 175–83, 197–98.

21. Sweeney, *The Pentateuch*, 21–27.

22. For discussion of the relationship between Joseph and Jeroboam, see esp. James L. Kugel, *In Potiphar's House: The Interpretive Life of Biblical Texts* (San Francisco: Harper & Row, 1990).

23. Sweeney, *1 and 2 Kings*, 140–61.

who freed his people from oppressive rule, just as Joseph matured to become the leader of his people who saved them from famine.

Joseph's Interpretation of Dreams (Gen 40–41)

The concern with dream interpretation continues to play an important role in the Joseph narratives. Genesis 40–41 presents Joseph as a skilled interpreter of dreams who uses his skill eventually to win release from prison and to ascend to a position of power in which he is appointed as second only to Pharaoh in authority over Egypt. Although many interpreters regard the Joseph narratives as a quasi-secular composition in which G-d plays relatively little role,[24] the dream narratives in Gen 40–41, like that of Gen 37, employ dreams as a source of divine revelation concerning the future that indicates divine interaction with human beings and guidance concerning their fortunes. Past critical scholarship views Gen 40–41 as J narratives that have been supplemented by E material,[25] but recent advances in Pentateuchal source criticism indicate that the Joseph narratives in Gen 40–41 are fundamentally E or Ephraimite narratives that present an account of the ancestor of the two most important tribes of the northern kingdom of Israel; they have been edited, revised, and supplemented by J or Judean material following the collapse of the northern kingdom of Israel.[26] E is known for its interest in visionary experience and dreams as a means to portray divine-human interaction, whereas J is better known for direct or face-to-face divine-human interaction. The use of dream interpretation to present divine guidance thus indicates the fundamental E character of these narratives.

The dream narratives in Gen 40–41 follow immediately upon Gen 39, which recounts Joseph's imprisonment in Egypt after being falsely charged by his master's wife with attempting to have sexual relations with her. Although the wife in fact proposed sexual relations with Joseph, his refusal to comply with her demands infuriated her and prompted her to accuse him falsely. Joseph is consequently incarcerated in a royal prison where his

24. E.g., Gerhard von Rad, "The Joseph Narrative and Ancient Wisdom," in *The Problem of the Hexateuch and Other Essays*, trans. E. W. Truemen Dicken (London: SCM, 1966), 292–300.

25. Campbell and O'Brien, *Sources*, 120–31, 175–83.

26. Sweeney, *The Pentateuch*, 21–27.

innate wisdom and divine oversight enable him to rise to a level of respect, recognition, and trust, and where he is allowed relative freedom to assume responsibility under the supervision of the prison warden.

Genesis 40–41 introduces two other inmates in the prison, the chief cup-bearer and the chief baker. The narrative does not mention the crimes for which these two men were imprisoned. It only notes that they had angered Pharaoh. But both roles indicate that they would have held some level of re-sponsibility that they must have violated, much as Joseph allegedly had done. A cupbearer is the figure who serves drinks to his master, and who is fre-quently known as one who tastes his master's drinks to be sure that there is no poison. Because of the proximity of a cupbearer to his master, the title came to be used for high royal advisors who had access—and therefore influence—in relation to kings and other powerful figures. A baker may well have played a similar role, insofar as a baker might be responsible for preparing food for a person in power, although the title is not used for royal positions of power.

Each of these men has a disturbing dream while in prison during the same night. Because Joseph is assigned to attend to them, he sees that they are upset and inquires about the cause. The cupbearer relates a dream in which a vine with three branches appeared in front of him. It budded with three shoots that quickly grew into three blossoms that in turn grew and ripened into three bunches of grapes. The chief cupbearer took the three bunches, squeezed them into Pharaoh's cup, and served the wine to Pha-raoh. Although the wine never had a chance to ferment, Joseph interprets this dream as a very positive sign from G-d that in three days' time the chief cupbearer would be pardoned by Pharaoh and returned to service. The chief baker likewise had a dream in which he saw three baskets upon his head filled with the types of food, i.e., breads, cakes, pastries, etc., that a baker would prepare. But birds were eating out of the basket on the chief baker's head. Joseph interprets this dream as a very negative sign: in three days' time, Pharaoh would order that the chief baker be beheaded and that his body be impaled so that birds could eat his flesh.

When Joseph's interpretation of both dreams comes true—the chief cupbearer is released and restored to his former position and the chief baker is beheaded and impaled—Joseph is recognized as a man of wisdom who could correctly interpret dreams from G-d. Although he asks the chief cup-bearer to remember him in hopes of being released from prison, the chief cupbearer quickly forgets about Joseph, who remains incarcerated.

But Joseph's skills are not completely lost. Two years later, the Pharaoh also has disturbing dreams that need interpretation. In the first dream, Pharaoh was standing by the Nile River when he saw seven good-looking and fat cows emerge from the river to graze upon its banks. Shortly thereafter, seven ugly and thin cows emerged from the river and proceeded to eat the first group of seven good-looking and fat cows. Pharaoh then has a second dream in which he sees seven ears of healthy and good grain growing on a single stalk. But then seven ears of thin grain that were scorched by the east wind sprouted on the same stalk and swallowed up the seven fat and good ears of grain. When Pharaoh awakens, agitated and disturbed by his dreams, the chief cupbearer finally remembers Joseph and recommends that Joseph be brought forward to interpret Pharaoh's dreams.

Joseph wisely interprets the two dreams as a divine sign of the future economic state of Egypt. Both dreams point to a period of seven years of plenty in which crops will grow, herds and flocks will flourish, and the nation will have plenty of food. But Pharaoh's dreams also indicate that the seven years of plenty will be followed by seven years of famine in which crops will wither, herds and flocks will diminish, and the people will lack adequate food. Joseph therefore advises that Pharaoh appoint a man of wisdom and discernment to oversee food production and storage over the next fourteen years. He recommends that the man appointed to this position purchase food at bargain prices during the times of plenty and store the food until the time of famine when it is sorely needed. Impressed with Joseph's acumen, Pharaoh appoints Joseph to oversee Egypt's food supply. Joseph lives up to the promise and proves to be a capable administrator who both enables the nation to survive the famine and ensures that it profits in doing so when Egypt becomes a food supplier to surrounding countries during the time of famine. By this means, Joseph rises to power in Egypt, enabling him in the following chapters to save his family and reconcile with his brothers when they come down to Egypt to find food.

The Joseph dream narratives are important for several reasons:

First, they demonstrate that dreams and dream interpretation are an important and accepted means of divine revelation in ancient Israel and Judah. Although past interpreters have noted that the Joseph narratives are largely secular in which G-d appears to play little role, these narratives indicate that G-d is hardly a secondary character in the narrative; rather, G-d is a key character and protagonist in the narrative who gives guidance to Joseph in an effort to ensure that Joseph will overcome threats to his well-being, both from his own inadequacies and from those who would do him harm. G-d does not engage in face-to-face interaction with human beings; rather G-d enters the narrative through the agency of dreams to ensure the ongoing maturation of an originally selfish and childish Joseph so that he can grow into a wise leader who ultimately saves his family's lives, reconciles with his once hostile brothers, and sees to the future of the nation of Israel.

Second, the means of divine revelation through dreams eschews any direct representation of G-d. There are no images of G-d, and G-d is not described in tangible terms. Rather, G-d is an unseen presence who ensures that the images seen in the dreams are conveyed to the dreamer and interpreted by Joseph. Although unseen and undescribed, G-d is nevertheless a key character and protagonist in the narrative. The images employed in the dreams are images that anyone could easily recognize, e.g., grapevines producing clusters of grapes, baskets of bread and pastries eaten by birds, fat and lean cows, and fat and lean ears of grain. But each image is put into motion in the narrative to convey the divine message in each case. Anyone could have seen these images, whether in dreams or in life, but it takes wisdom and discernment to interpret the divine intent conveyed in these images. Joseph emerges as an analytical figure, who employs his innate wisdom and discernment to identify the divine messages conveyed by images that could have been dreamt or seen by anyone.

Third, such a portrayal of G-d as a key character in the Joseph narratives demonstrates that Israel stands in continuity with the larger ancient Near Eastern world in which dreams and dream interpretation play important roles in determining the will and action of the divine in Mesopotamia, Egypt, and Aram. Although YHWH is a distinctive deity, YHWH is understood to employ similar means to those employed by foreign gods to make their wills and presence known. But there is an element of polemic as well. Pharaoh is understood to be a god in Egypt, and yet neither the Pharaoh nor his officers can determine the best course of action for the future to ensure the security and welfare of Egypt and even of themselves. The Joseph narratives make an important point: YHWH is the true G-d of all creation and of humanity, acting not only in the land of Israel, but in Egypt (and Mesopotamia and Aram) as well. YHWH is fully capable of acting on behalf of Israel, but YHWH is also a worldwide G-d.

Moses at the Burning Bush (Exod 3)

The burning bush episode in Exod 3:1–4:17 is a key Pentateuchal narrative; in it, YHWH commissions Moses to confront Pharaoh, with the purpose of releasing the Israelite slaves and demonstrating that YHWH—and not

Pharaoh—is the true creator and G-d of the universe as well as the redeemer of Israel. This episode thereby sets in motion the exodus from Egypt to Mt. Sinai and ultimately to the promised land of Israel.

Exodus 3:1–4:17 is generally viewed as a combined J and E narrative.[27] But with the emerging view that E is the foundational stratum of the Pentateuch, the text would now be recognized as an E or Ephraimite narrative that has been combined, edited, and expanded by J or Judean writers. Within the E tradition, it is the point where YHWH reveals the divine name to Moses for the first time so that Moses, Israel, and the world at large might know that YHWH is the true G-d. It employs the genre of the prophetic call or vocation narrative, a stylized account by which prophets are commissioned to speak to the people on YHWH's behalf (cf. Isaiah 6; Jer 1:4–10).[28] The prophetic call narrative typically includes an introduction of the deity, a commission by the deity for the prophet in question, an objection by the prospective prophet that he or she is somehow not adequate, and a reassurance or sign from YHWH to the prophet that YHWH will support the prophet. All of these elements appear in Exod 3:1–4:17. Although Moses is a Levite, the Levites are not appointed to priestly office until Num 17–18, and so Moses functions primarily as a prophet throughout the exodus narrative.[29]

The key form of the narrative is a vision in which G-d speaks to Moses from a bush that burns but is not consumed. Moses had fled from Egypt after killing the Egyptian taskmaster who was beating an Israelite slave; had found and married Zipporah, the daughter of Jethro, priest of Midian; and was tending his father-in-law's sheep on Mt. Horeb, also known in the Pentateuch as Mt. Sinai, when the vision occurred. Mt. Sinai would later become the site where YHWH revealed divine Torah to the nation Israel at large in Exod 19:1–Num 10:10.

At no point does YHWH appear in tangible form in the narrative. Instead, the vision begins with the notice that an angel of YHWH appeared to Moses in v. 2. Angels are a typical element in E narratives, which are reluctant to portray YHWH or G-d in any physical form. YHWH per se is denoted only by divine speech to Moses, as appropriate for the holy character of YHWH. The image of the burning bush plays an important role in defining YHWH's character in the narrative. At first sight, the notion of

27. Campbell and O'Brien, *Sources*, 132–33, 184–85.

28. George W. Coats, *Exodus 1–18*, FOTL 2A (Grand Rapids: Eerdmans, 1999), 34–42.

29. Jeffrey Stackert, *A Prophet like Moses: Prophecy, Law, and Israelite Religion* (Oxford: Oxford University Press, 2014).

a burning bush that is not consumed seems rather miraculous, but closer study of this image with the flora of the Sinai wilderness indicates that the image of the burning bush is based on the *rubus sanctus*, a common bush found throughout the Sinai region that produces red blossoms in the spring.[30] When viewed from a distance, the blossoming *rubus sanctus* appears as if it is burning even though it is not consumed. Such an image is uniquely typical of the Sinai wilderness.

This is not simply a literary device employed by the author to embellish the narrative; indeed, it is an example of the Pentateuch's concern to portray the exodus-wilderness narratives as a form of creation narrative. The narratives take up the concern with YHWH's role as creator throughout the exodus and wilderness narratives, and they portray YHWH through natural elements of creation and as the author of that creation. The exodus-wilderness narratives therefore function as a form of etiological creation narrative wherein important features of the natural environment of Egypt, Sinai, and Israel/Canaan appear throughout the narrative to indicate YHWH's mastery of creation and human beings. Thus the Israelite slaves display tremendous fertility in giving birth to children, despite Pharaoh's decree that all male Israelite babies be killed. Moses first encounters YHWH amid a burning bush that is native to the Sinai region. The first nine plagues in the Exodus narrative are all elements of nature, e.g., the Nile River turns red like blood every spring as the snows at its headwaters melt and the resulting water carries the red soil of Ethiopia throughout Egypt while the water makes its way to the Mediterranean, overflowing its banks and providing fertile soil for Egypt along its journey. Most of the other plagues, e.g., frogs, flies, gnats, sores, etc., are tied to the annual flooding caused by the Nile, and the other plagues, with the exception of the death of the firstborn, employ other elements of creation native to Egypt and western Asia.[31] Only the tenth plague, the death of the firstborn, is not an element of creation; instead it explains the origins of the ancient Israelite practice of appointing the firstborn sons of Israelite women as the priests of Israel prior to the use of the tribe of Levi for this purpose.[32] The splitting of the Red Sea so that dry land emerges is a classic creation motif that adapts the classic combat myth, in which the creator deity defeats a chaos monster from the sea to ensure the stability

30. Nahum Sarna, *Exodus*, JPS Torah Commentary (Philadelphia: Jewish Publication Society, 1991), 14.

31. Sarna, *Exodus*, 36–51.

32. Sweeney, *The Pentateuch*, 40–41.

of the created world order.[33] Other motifs include YHWH's provision of manna and quails for food in the wilderness; YHWH's provision of water; and the portrayal of Mt. Sinai as YHWH's wilderness sanctuary. Altogether, the Exodus-wilderness narratives point to these elements of creation as part of YHWH's efforts to free Israel from Egyptian slavery and lead the people to the land of Israel where they could be a free people in their own land. Indeed, the Exodus narrative appears to be a response to Egyptian mythological accounts of the conflicts between Seth and Horus for control of creation and Egypt; but in the Exodus account, YHWH, and not Horus, emerges as the winner.

In revealing YHWH to Moses in the world of creation, the narrative portrays Mt. Sinai as a holy temple, in that YHWH commands Moses to remove his shoes since he is standing on holy ground (Exod 3:5). The motif of Sinai as sanctuary will appear once again in Exod 19, which functions as a theophany report in which Moses instructs the people to wash themselves, to abstain from sexual relations, and to not pass beyond the base of Mt. Sinai. All of these features indicate that Sinai is portrayed as a sanctuary insofar as the priests are to immerse themselves in water prior to entering the sanctuary, the people are to purify themselves from sexual relations, and the people are not to enter the holy of holies of the sanctuary. In Judean tradition, the portrayal of Sinai serves as a paradigm for the role of the Jerusalem Temple located on Mt. Zion as the holy center of creation.[34] It is likely that the exodus accounts functioned in a similar fashion in northern Israel as well.

A key element of the narrative is the revelation of the divine name to Moses. When Moses asks YHWH, "who shall I say has sent me," YHWH replies elliptically with the statement, "I am who I am." YHWH's response is an example of the "idem per idem" rhetorical device in which a thing is defined in relation to itself in order to avoid disclosing any characteristics of the thing in question.[35] The reason for such a response is that the divine name of YHWH is holy, and it is not to be desecrated by human use except in the most holy of circumstances, such as when the High Priest enters the holy of holies on Yom Kippur, the Day of Atonement, to atone for the sins of the nation before YHWH. Ancient Egyptian practice included the use of divine names in incantations to curse an enemy or bless someone. Such

---

33. Thomas Dozeman, *Exodus*, Eerdmans Critical Commentary (Grand Rapids: Eerdmans, 2009), 335–41.

34. Jon D. Levenson, *Sinai and Zion: An Entry into the Jewish Bible* (Minneapolis: Winston, 1985).

35. Cf. Sarna, *Exodus*, 17–18.

incantations called for the correct pronunciation of divine names to gain the power of the deity in question to carry out the blessing or the curse. Such usage entailed that the human speaker of the incantation was understood to gain control of the deity's power to carry out the curse or the blessing. Such use of the divine name of YHWH, i.e., using the name of YHWH in vain, is forbidden in the Ten Commandments, which give expression to the most basic principles of Israelite conduct in biblical law.

YHWH's response, "I am who I am," also functions as a means to give expression to the divine character of YHWH. The phrase in Hebrew, *'ehyeh 'asher 'ehyeh*, employs the Hebrew verb, *'ehyeh*, "I am," to interpret the divine name, *yhwh*, as a conjugation of the Hebrew verb, *hayah*, "to be." YHWH's reply to Moses's inquiry thus implies that the divine name itself is a variation of the third person imperfect form, *yihyeh*, "he is," i.e., "he (YHWH) exists," or "he is real." Such a portrayal contrasts YHWH with the Pharaoh, who is considered as a god in Egypt, so that YHWH is identified as the true G-d of creation and human beings. YHWH's victory over Pharaoh and Egypt in Exod 1–15 of course highlights this contention. Following the revelation at the burning bush, the plagues imposed on Egypt by YHWH make sure that both the people of Israel and the people of Egypt know just who YHWH is.

Theophany and Covenant at Sinai (Exod 19–24)

The narrative concerning Moses's ascent to encounter YHWH on Mt. Sinai appears in Exod 24, immediately following the Ten Commandments and the so-called Covenant Code in Exod 20 and 21–23, respectively. Exodus 20 and 21–23 follow the account of YHWH's theophany at Mt. Sinai in Exod 19. These chapters present the first major legal code of Israel in the synchronic narrative sequence of the Pentateuch. Viewed diachronically, these texts have been the subject of much debate. Exodus 20 appears to be an early E or Ephraimitic text from the mid-eighth century BCE.[36] The Covenant Code in Exod 21–23 is oftentimes classified as an independent source due to its character as a legal code.[37] Although some scholars assign it to the exilic or post-exilic periods due to its clear dependence on the Babylonian Law

---

36. Campbell and O'Brien, *Sources*, 188–89.
37. Campbell and O'Brien, *Sources*, 199.

Code of Hammurabi,[38] it appears to date to a much earlier period in the late ninth or early eighth century BCE.[39] This dating is due to Israel's vassal relationship with the Assyrian Empire, indicated first, as mentioned above, by the Black Obelisk of Shalmaneser III (859–824 BCE) that portrays the submission of King Jehu of Israel (842–815 BCE) to Shalmaneser, and also by the Tel Rimlah inscription, which lists Jehu's grandson, King Jehoash of Israel (801–786 BCE), as one of the many tributaries to the Assyrian monarch, Adad Nirari III (811–783 BCE).[40] In addition, laws from the Covenant Code are cited by the mid-eighth century Judean prophet, Amos of Tekoa, who condemned the northern kingdom of Israel for its ill-treatment of Judah in Amos 2:6–16.[41] Hammurabi's Law Code served as a legal template throughout Mesopotamia, and cuneiform fragments of the Code were found in excavations at Hazor.[42] Apparently the Assyrians introduced Israel to the Code, influencing the composition of northern Israel's own law code in Exod 21–23.

Exodus 24 presents an account of the ceremonies employed to ratify the so-called Covenant Code as the basis of the covenant between YHWH and Israel. Such ceremonies would be analogous to those employed in the ratification of covenants or treaties made between Assyria and its various allies and vassals,[43] although the Exodus account clarifies that YHWH—and not an earthly king—is the true monarch of Israel and the creator of the entire world. The narrative begins with YHWH's summons to Moses to appear before YHWH accompanied by his brother Aaron, Aaron's sons Nadab and Abihu, and the seventy elders of Israel. The people of Israel, however, are not invited to approach. The choice of these figures indicates a combination of the religious and political leadership of Israel. Moses is the de facto leader of Israel, chosen by YHWH to guide Israel from Egypt into the wilderness on

---

38. David P. Wright, *Inventing G-d's Law: How the Covenant Code of the Bible Used and Revised the Laws of Hammurabi* (Oxford: Oxford University Press, 2009); cf. John Van Seters, *A Law Book for the Diaspora: Revision in the Study of the Covenant Code* (Oxford: Oxford University Press, 2003).

39. Sweeney, *The Pentateuch*, 44–47.

40. *ANEP*, 351, 355; Page, "A Stela of Adad Nirari III."

41. Marvin A. Sweeney, *The Twelve Prophets*, Berit Olam (Collegeville, MN: Liturgical Press, 2000), 1:214–18.

42. Wayne Horowitz, Takayoshi Oshima, and Filip Vukosavović, "Hazor 18: Fragments of a Cuneiform Law Collection from Hazor," *IEJ* 62.2 (2012): 158–76.

43. Dennis J. McCarthy, *Treaty and Covenant: A Study in Form in the Ancient Oriental Documents and in the Old Testament*, AnBib 21A (Rome: Pontifical Biblical Institute, 1978); McCarthy, *Old Testament Covenant: A Survey of Current Opinions* (Richmond, VA: John Knox, 1972).

its journey to Sinai and later to the promised land of Israel. Aaron, Moses's older brother, is included because Aaron was designated by YHWH in the burning bush episode of Exod 3:1–4:17 to serve as Moses's spokesman and interpreter in communicating YHWH's will to Israel. Aaron and his sons have not yet been chosen to serve as YHWH's priests; that role is first named for them in Exod 28–29. Nevertheless, Exod 24 appears to presuppose a priestly role for Aaron and for his older sons, Nadab and Abihu. The Aaron-ide priest Eli likewise served at the Shiloh sanctuary together with his two sons, Hophni and Phineas; the resemblance suggests that the sons of Aaron were an early Israelite priestly dynasty. The seventy elders of Israel represent the political leadership of Israel prior to the institution of the monarchy. The seventy elders are also the authoritative body that appoints David as King over Israel in 2 Sam 5. Likewise, the House of Omri appears to have utilized a similar body, designated as the seventy sons of Ahab, who were killed along with the House of Omri during Jehu's revolt in 2 Kgs 9–10.

The inclusion of both the religious and the political leadership of Israel in the covenant ratification ceremony makes sense in relation to Assyrian treaty practice. Assyrian treaties were typically concluded with a combina-tion of religious and political leadership.[44] They invoked the gods of both Assyria and the other nation involved in the treaty; to do so would call for the participation of the priesthood. Then, as described above (in relation to Gen 15), the vassal king would walk between the severed pieces of sacrificial animals, declaring that the same should happen to him should he violate the terms of the treaty. Although no such ceremony is evident in Exod 24, the conclusion of a covenant with YHWH—in both capacities, as deity and as suzerain—would call for participation by both the priesthood and by the political body charged with ruling Israel.

Religious practice apparently explains the prohibition of the people from approaching YHWH in the narrative. Ancient Israelite religious prac-tice held that the holy of holies, the innermost room of ancient temples, served as YHWH's throne room. Indeed, Israelite and Judean temples were built according to a common pattern in ancient Syria and Canaan. The pat-tern was a three-room model based upon the structure of royal palace, in-cluding the *ulam* or entry hall for the structure, the *heikhal*, place or main hall of the structure, and the *devir*, or holy of holies, where the deity would normally sit enthroned. Only priests were permitted to enter the temple,

---

44. Moshe Weinfeld, "The Covenant of Grant in the Old Testament and the Ancient Near East," *JAOS* 90 (1970): 184–203.

since it was consecrated space and only the priesthood was consecrated to enter that space. Thus the people would not approach the deity's throne directly; the priesthood, serving as their holy representatives, would approach YHWH on the people's behalf.

The account of the sacrificial offerings begins with the construction of the altar at the foot of the mountain and erection of twelve pillars to represent the tribes of Israel. The building of the altar indicates that the site is to be considered as a holy temple site, and the erection of the pillars indicates the participation of all Israel in a manner analogous to the establishment of the altar at Gilgal following the crossing of the Jordan River in Josh 5. The designation of the young men to assist in the offering is unusual, since they serve as assistants to Moses. It is not clear, however, that they are firstborn sons or Levites, the two groups assigned at different points a role assisting priests, although traditional commentators appear to view the young men as Levites.[45] The offerings include a combination of *'olot*, or whole burnt offerings, and *zivkhei shelamim*, or sacrifices of well-being. The former are standard offerings that are given entirely to G-d, and the latter are also standard offerings that are given in part to support the priesthood. In essence, these offerings are of the types that one would normally expect at a temple service; yet here they are offered as part of the covenant ratification ceremony. The dashing of blood on the people, not a standard part of such offerings in the temple service, appears instead to function as a symbol of the consequences of violating the covenant as in the Assyrian treaties.

The vision of YHWH appears in vv. 9–11 when Moses, Aaron, Nadab, Abihu, and the seventy elders go up to appear before YHWH. There is no bodily description of YHWH other than metaphorical references to YHWH's feet and hands. The reference to YHWH's feet indicates the appearance of divine presence although the feet would have to be understood as a form of metaphor. The pavement of sapphire takes up the imagery of the firmament that divides the heavens above and the waters below in creation. It would appear to emulate the *kapporet* or mercy seat that is built atop the ark of the covenant, which symbolically serves as the throne or footstool of YHWH. If YHWH is understood to be enthroned above the cherubim that sit atop the ark, then the mercy seat would be placed below YHWH's feet. YHWH's royal character is indicated by the fact that YHWH does not raise a hand, again a metaphorical description of divine presence, against the approach of the human characters. Such an action is modeled on that of a monarch who

45. See. e.g., Rashi's commentary on this verse.

might choose to accept or reject visitors appearing before the divine throne. The portrayal of the divine banquet in which Moses and the others eat and drink before YHWH indicates the eating and drinking that would take place at the temple when offerings were presented at the altar. Such offerings signal a banquet for the people before YHWH in later temple practice as well.

Finally, Moses ascends even further up the mountain as he prepares to appear before YHWH in order to receive the tablets of Torah from YHWH. The tablets, inscribed by YHWH, then serve as the basis for the covenant between YHWH and Israel. YHWH's presence on the mountain is portrayed as cloud that covers the mountain, much like the incense smoke that would fill the temple during times of worship. Moses waits seven days, and then enters the cloud to receive the tablets from YHWH. The imagery of divine presence then shifts to consuming fire, much like the flaming wicks of the menorahs that appear together with the incense altars in the heikhal of the temple. Moses ascends to the top of the mountain for forty days as YHWH writes the tablets of the covenant.

Moses's Vision after the Golden Calf (Exod 32–34)

Exodus 32–34 presents the infamous Golden Calf episode in which the people of Israel demand that Aaron construct an idol of a golden calf to worship while Moses remains on Mt. Sinai. The episode is particularly well known for the role that the Levites play in answering Moses's call to purge the people of those who committed apostasy. By this act, the Levites demonstrate their commitment to YHWH, ultimately resulting in their selection by YHWH in Num 17–18 to serve a priestly role assisting Aaron and his sons. For our purposes, the narrative also portrays Moses's vision of YHWH while hidden in a cave on Mt. Sinai as YHWH passes by reciting a litany of divine qualities that demonstrate YHWH's mercy and justice.

The narrative demonstrates a very clear propensity for critique of the northern kingdom of Israel and its use of the golden calves at the sanctuaries at Beth El and Dan.[46] The reason for such a polemic in the narrative is to examine the character of YHWH in the aftermath of the destruction of the northern kingdom of Israel by the Assyrian Empire in 722–721 BCE. As we have seen in our own examination of YHWH's promises to the ancestors in Genesis, YHWH's repeated promises to make Abraham, Isaac, and Jacob

---

46. See Sweeney, *Reading the Hebrew Bible after the Shoah*, 52–57, 67–72.

into a great nation and to grant them the land of Israel are key elements of the covenant enacted between YHWH and the nation of Israel. But the Assyrian conquest of Samaria, the strongly fortified capital of the northern kingdom of Israel, demonstrated to many that YHWH was unable to ensure the divine promises made to the ancestors that stood at the foundation of northern Israel's self-understanding of its identity and place in the world. Indeed, Exod 32–34 portrays YHWH's anger against Israel and willingness to destroy the people and make a new nation out of Moses. But Moses responds by reminding YHWH of the obligations of the covenant, which frees Moses to call for the purging of those who actually engaged in idolatry.

The authors of the narrative in Exod 32–34 were unwilling to charge YHWH with negligence, impotence, dishonesty, absence, or any other of the possibilities that would place the blame for the destruction of northern Israel on YHWH. Instead, they chose to blame the people of Israel, beginning with the northern Israelite kings, for bringing the disaster upon themselves by having failed to observe YHWH's will as expressed in the commandments, the basis for Israel's obligations to YHWH in their covenant relationship. The golden calves erected at the northern sanctuaries at Beth El and Dan were understood to be molten idols of foreign gods that were worshiped in place of YHWH, bringing divine judgment, by means of the Assyrian Empire, upon northern Israel for their rejection of YHWH.

Exodus 32–34 thus appears to have been written by Judean or J stratum authors working in Judah in the aftermath of the Assyrian destruction of Israel.[47] Later redaction by Persian period P authors is also evident, although the basic narrative must be assigned to J during the late monarchic period. The authors appear to have drawn upon several sources in constructing their portrayal of Israel's apostasy at Sinai.[48]

First is the account of the sins of King Jeroboam ben Nebat, the first monarch of the northern kingdom of Israel, in 1 Kgs 12:25–33. Jeroboam is charged with setting up the golden calves at Beth El and Dan to prevent his people from traveling south to Jerusalem to worship YHWH there. But Jeroboam is also charged with cynical motives; the Kings account maintains that Jeroboam commanded his people to worship the golden calves as gods. His language in 1 Kgs 12:28, "This is your god, O Israel, who brought you

47. Campbell and O'Brien, *Sources*, 146–49.

48. Marvin A. Sweeney, "The Wilderness Traditions of the Pentateuch: A Reassessment of Their Function and Intent in Relation to Exodus 32–34," in *SBL 1989 Seminar Papers*, ed. David Lull (Atlanta: Scholars Press, 1989), 291–99.

up from the land of Egypt," is nearly identical to Aaron's charge in Exod 32:4. First Kings 12:25–33 is a key text in the books of the Former Prophets, Joshua–Kings, known to scholars as the Deuteronomistic History (DtrH), which presents a theological evaluation of Israel's and Judah's history in the land of Israel from the time of the conquest under Joshua through the aftermath of the destruction of Jerusalem and exile of Judah to Babylon; the DtrH evaluates this history according to the people's observance of YHWH's instructions in Deuteronomy.

The narrative holds that Israel and Judah failed to observe YHWH's instructions and thereby suffered the punishment of exile from the land, first the northern kingdom of Israel as a result of Assyrian conquest (2 Kgs 17) and later the southern kingdom of Judah as a result of Babylonian conquest (2 Kgs 25). Jeroboam's sins, especially his command to worship the golden calves, were the key reason for the destruction of Israel, as the history maintains that all the northern monarchs followed in the sins of Jeroboam, thereby ensuring Israel's destruction. Judah was destroyed because of the sins of King Manasseh ben Hezekiah (2 Kgs 21). In neither case does the history hold YHWH accountable for the destruction. Jeroboam and Manasseh are the primary culprits in the history. Many scholars believe that an early edition of the DtrH was written during the reign of King Josiah ben Amon of Judah (640–609 BCE; 2 Kgs 22–23), who sought to reunite the nation and dedicate it to YHWH and the observance of YHWH's expectations. But Josiah's death fighting the Egyptian army in 609 BCE put an end to Josiah's ambitions, and the kingdom of Judah was destroyed by the Babylonians twenty-two years later in 587–586 BCE. The critique of Jeroboam in both the DtrH and Exod 32–34 would have been written during Josiah's reign to support his plans.

Both 1 Kgs 12:25–33 (see also 1 Kgs 13) and Exod 32–34 polemicize against Jeroboam as an idolater. Although 1 Kgs 12:25–33 has Jeroboam, followed by Aaron in Exod 32–34, state that the golden calves are to be worshiped as gods by Israel, there is no evidence other than these tendentious claims by the Judean writers of DtrH and Exod 32–34 that the golden calves at Beth El and Dan were ever recognized as gods. Ancient Near Eastern gods were typically mounted on animals or seated on thrones: Hadad, the Aramean storm god, is typically portrayed riding a bull; Hathor, the Canaanite/Egyptian goddess of life and stability, is typically portrayed mounted on a lion. Other such examples abound. Insofar as both Israel and Judah understood that YHWH was not to be portrayed in any tangible form, in northern Israel YHWH would be understood to be mounted atop the golden calves, not identified with them. Judah and the Jerusalem Temple employed different iconography for the same purpose; YHWH sat invisibly enthroned above the cherubim, the winged, composite angelic figures placed atop and around the ark of the covenant in the Jerusalem Temple. Like the golden calves, the ark of the covenant was only a mount or seat for YHWH. But the Judean authors of 1 Kgs 12:25–33 and Exod 32–34 employed the difference in northern and southern iconography as a basis for charging Jeroboam and northern Israel with idolatry, both exonerating YHWH from fault in the destruction of northern Israel and exhorting their own Judean audience to adhere to YHWH and the covenant, in order to protect themselves and their nation from the consequences of idolatry.

A second and third set of texts employed by the authors of Exod 32–34 are the laws of the Covenant Code in Exod 21–23 and the command to avoid marriage with the Canaanite nations in Deut 7:1–6. When Moses comes down from Mt. Sinai to find Israel worshiping the golden calf in Exod 32–34, he breaks the tablets of the covenant dictated by YHWH on Mt. Sinai before he proceeds with the purge of the people. Such an act symbolizes the broken covenant, proceeding to the destruction of northern Israel, that was to be repaired by national restoration enacted by King Josiah in the late seventh century. The scenario of repairing a broken covenant repeats once again, following the Babylonian exile, when according to Neh 8–10 Ezra and Nehemiah gather the people in Jerusalem at the rebuilt Jerusalem Temple to restore the covenant in the late fifth or early fourth century BCE. It is noteworthy that Exod 32–34 posits that YHWH's laws must be rewritten. Consequently, Moses carves two new tablets of stone for a new law code in Exod 34. This law code is essentially a revision of the earlier Covenant Code in Exod 21–23, except that it begins with a command in Exod 34:10–16 to avoid marriage with the Canaanite nations. The reason for such a command at the outset of the new code is that intermarriage with the Canaanites promotes the worship of foreign gods and the abandonment of YHWH. The next command in Exod 34:17 is a prohibition against molten idols, obviously motivated by the calf manufactured from molten gold in the preceding narrative. The later law code of Exod 34 may well have functioned as an early law code together with Deuteronomy in Josiah's reforms.

The third text employed in the composition of Exod 32–34 is 1 Kgs 19, which portrays Elijah's vision of YHWH while in a cave on Mt. Horeb, the DtrH name for Mt. Sinai. Elijah flees to the cave to escape Queen Jezebel, the Phoenician wife of King Ahab ben Omri of Israel, who wants to kill Elijah and the other prophets of YHWH as she promotes Baal worship in the land. While in the cave at Horeb, Elijah sees visions of destructive earth-quake, fire, and wind, but concludes that none of these is to be identified with YHWH. When he hears "a sound of absolute silence" (Hebrew, *qol demamah daqqah*), he recognizes that this represents the true presence of YHWH; the intangible image of the sound of silence signals that YHWH cannot be perceived in any tangible form. Elijah's cave appears to symbolize the holy of holies of Israelite temples where YHWH is believed to appear.

Moses's vision of YHWH is modeled on Elijah's vision, but with different imagery. Like Elijah, Moses is placed in a cave on Mt. Sinai, again a play on the holy of holies of the temple, where he will behold the presence of YHWH. But in its effort to protect the notion that humans cannot perceive the presence of YHWH in tangible form, the text in Exod 34:5–7 merely states that YHWH appeared to Moses in the midst of cloud and stood with him, proclaiming the divine qualities while passing by: "YHWH, YHWH, a compassionate and gracious G-d, slow to anger, great in fidelity and truth, extending fidelity to thousands, pardoning iniquity, rebellion, and sin, but surely not remitting punishment (when it is due), punishing children and grandchildren for the iniquity of their parents to the third and fourth generations." Although later texts would challenge the postulate that later generations would suffer punishment for the sins of the ancestors, the report of the vision of YHWH in Exod 32–34 makes clear that YHWH does not appear in tangible form. Rather, YHWH is experienced in the world by divine acts of mercy and justice that stand as the basis of the covenant between YHWH and Israel. The combination of mercy and judgment represents the tension that ancient Judeans would have experienced in attempting to understand YHWH as a G-d who defended and protected them and a world that thrust suffering upon them in the form of foreign invasion.

YHWH's Enthronement in Tabernacle and Temple (Lev 16)

Ancient Judean thought holds that the divine presence of YHWH resides in the holy of holies of the Jerusalem Temple where the ark of the covenant serves as YHWH's throne. Leviticus 16 makes this understanding clear when it presents YHWH's instruction to Moses in vv. 2–3, "And YHWH said to Moses, 'Say to Aaron, your brother, that he shall not at any time enter the sanctuary behind the curtain that is before the cover atop the ark lest he die, for I appear in the cloud that is above the cover. Only in this manner shall Aaron enter the sanctuary, with a one-year-old bull from the herd for a sin offering and a ram for a whole burnt offering.'" In other words, Aaron, who will eventually become the high priest, may not enter the holy of holies at any time he likes. He enters only at the time that he presents the sin offering together with the whole burnt offering to atone for the nation's sins at Yom Kippur, the Day of Atonement. Leviticus 16 goes on to describe the manner in which Aaron and his successors will present the offerings for Yom Kippur in some detail.

Although we have little information concerning northern Israelite practice, it is likely that Israel held a similar understanding of the divine presence for its various temples, such as Shiloh, Beth El, Dan, and perhaps others. First Samuel 1–3 indicates that the ark of the covenant resided in the Shiloh Temple during Israel's premonarchic period. The golden calves at Beth El and Dan would have served as the mounts for YHWH in the Beth El and Dan sanctuaries. The priest at each of these sanctuaries might likewise appear before YHWH in the holy of holies to make atonement for the nation on Yom Kippur.

The portrayal of the divine presence of YHWH in a cloud associated with the sanctuary in Lev 16 is an important motif in the Pentateuch. We have seen it already in Abram's vision in Gen 15 when he saw a smoking fire pot and a flaming torch as symbols of YHWH passing between the pieces of the severed sacrificial animals. As we observed, such imagery derives from the smoking incense altars and flaming menorahs employed in Judean and likely Israelite temples to portray the divine presence with imagery that is not fully tangible. That is, smoke and fire are clearly present, but they resist any sense of firm imagery or form and thereby make ideal substances for understanding the presence of YHWH. The fire provides light, which aids in symbolizing divine wisdom, and heat, which aids in symbolizing divine power as well as divine presence. Yet the cloud of smoke, whether dark or suffused with the light of fire, obscures human sight, symbolizing the transcendence of the divine beyond the human, even a priest in the closest proximity to YHWH's throne, by frustrating apprehension of a tangible divine form.

We must also note the imagery of the pillar of cloud by day and fire by night to portray the divine presence in Exod 13:20–22, as YHWH leads the people of Israel from Sukkoth to Etham at the edge of the wilderness during the earliest stages of the Exodus from Egypt. The imagery of the pillar of fire and cloud continues to guide and protect Israel on its journey through the wilderness from Egypt to the promised land of Israel. In Exod 14:19, it is called the angel of G-d, and it moves from before Israel to a position between Israel and the Egyptian army in order to protect the nation as it crosses the Red Sea safely to escape. Once again, the pillar of cloud and fire employs the imagery of smoke and flaming lights from the temple, but the use of the pillar imagery suggests the imagery associated with the temple altar at times when the offerings of the people are burned upon it. When the altar is in operation, a pillar of smoke and fire ascends into the sky from the altar, which in turn serves as a signal, visible for miles around, of YHWH's divine presence in the temple.

The pillar of cloud and fire continues to guide Israel through the wilderness to Mt. Sinai in Exod 19. YHWH speaks to Moses from atop the mountain, and YHWH's presence is described as thick cloud, which envelops the mountain together with smoke and lightning flashes, thereby adapting the imagery of the pillar of smoke and fire to the mountain setting. The association of this imagery with the sanctuary is made clear when Moses commands the people not to ascend the mountain to approach the presence of YHWH, much as the people were forbidden to enter the holy of holies of the temple. He also instructs them to wash their clothes, much as the people would need to purify themselves before entering the temple precincts. And he instructs each man not to approach a woman. Sexual relations render both impure, insofar as the emission of semen entails contact with a living substance that dies upon departing the body, thereby defiling a person with the presence of death. As Jon Levenson observes, Mt. Sinai and the Jerusalem Temple are counterparts, insofar as Sinai represents the later temple in the land of Israel, and the temple replicates Mt. Sinai as the locus of divine revelation.[49]

The imagery of the divine presence of YHWH portrayed as smoke or cloud and fire is especially clear in Exod 40, which describes the completion of the wilderness tabernacle and the entry of the divine presence of YHWH into its inner sanctuary. Indeed, the wilderness tabernacle constitutes the template or model for the construction of the temple in later times. Once the people had completed the work of constructing the tabernacle and its various furnishings in Exod 35–39, YHWH instructs Moses in Exod 40 to set up the tabernacle of the Tent of Meeting on the first day of the first month, to place the ark of the covenant in the inner sanctum of the tabernacle, and to place the various furnishings of the tabernacle in their appropriate places. YHWH then instructs Moses to anoint the altar of the sanctuary, and Aaron and his sons to serve as priests of the sanctuary.

Once the work of setting up and sanctifying the tabernacle, its furnish-

---

49. Levenson, *Sinai and Zion*; see also Levenson, "The Temple and the World," *JR* 64 (1984): 275–98.

ings, and Aaron and his sons as priests is complete, the tabernacle is now ready to receive the presence of YHWH. Exodus 40:33b–38 again describes the divine presence with the imagery of cloud, which settles upon and fills the Sanctuary with YHWH's divine presence. From this point on, YHWH's presence is identified with the wilderness tabernacle. Whenever the cloud would lift from the tabernacle, Israel would set out upon the next stage of its journey through the wilderness; and whenever the cloud would settle upon the tabernacle, Israel would stop and remain where it was until the cloud lifted again. From this point on in the Pentateuchal narrative, the tabernacle replaces the pillar of cloud and fire that guides Israel through the wilderness. And from this point on, revelation ceases to come from Mt. Sinai. Instead, revelation proceeds from the wilderness tabernacle, anticipating the revelation of YHWH through the Israelite and Judean temples that were established once the nation took possession of the land of Israel.

Jon Levenson further notes that the establishment of the wilderness tabernacle as the template for YHWH's temple indicates that the Pentateuchal narrative is akin to the creation narratives of the ancient Near East.[50] Once a deity, such as Marduk or Baal, has defeated a chaos monster, such as Tiamat or Yamm, to bring the world of creation into order, the gods build a temple for the creator deity to acknowledge the creator's role in bringing order to the world. The Pentateuchal narrative likewise portrays YHWH's creation of the world and the nation Israel. Once YHWH has completed creation and delivered Israel from Egypt by employing the various elements of creation, such as the natural features symbolized by the burning bush, the plagues, the Red Sea, water from the rock, manna and quail, etc., YHWH has a temple built to acknowledge the divine role in bringing order to creation and delivering the people of Israel from Egyptian slavery.

Michael Fishbane underscores the relationship between the creation narrative of Gen 1:1–2:3 and the creation of the wilderness sanctuary, reiterating the observations of Franz Rosenzweig and Martin Buber, who noted a number of intertextual links between Gen 1:1–2:3 and Exod 39–40.[51] Those links include Gen 1:31, "And G-d saw all that He had made and found it very good," and Exod 39:43, "And when Moses saw that they had performed all the tasks as YHWH commanded, so they had done, and Moses blessed them";

50. Jon D. Levenson, *Sinai and Zion*; see also Levenson, *Creation and the Persistence of Evil: The Jewish Drama of Divine Omnipotence* (New York: Harper & Row, 1988).

51. Michael Fishbane, "Genesis 1:1–2:4a: The Creation," in *Text and Texture: Close Readings of Selected Biblical Texts* (New York: Schocken, 1979), 3–16.

Gen 2:1, "The heavens and the earth and all their hosts were completed," and Exod 39:32, "Thus was completed all the work of the tabernacle of the Tent of Meeting"; Gen 2:2, "On the seventh day, G-d finished the work that He had been doing," and Exod 40:33, "When Moses had finished the work"; and Gen 2:3, "And G-d blessed the seventh day and declared it holy because on it G-d ceased from all the work of creation that He had done"; and Exod 39:43 once again, "And when Moses saw that they had performed all the tasks as YHWH commanded so they had done, and Moses blessed them."

Altogether, the Pentateuch presents a creation narrative modeled on those of the ancient Near East in which YHWH puts creation in order, establishes YHWH's own people, Israel, in the midst of creation, and establishes a sanctuary to honor YHWH as the creator. Throughout the narrative, the depiction of YHWH is accomplished by employing imagery from that sanctuary.

Balaam's Visionary Oracles (Num 22–24)

The Balaam narrative in Num 22–24 presents an example of an ancient Aramean visionary in action. Balaam ben Beor is a known historical figure whose visionary oracles are also preserved in the late ninth- to early eighth-century BCE Deir Alla Inscription.[52] The fragments of the inscription were discovered in the ruins of a temple at a Transjordanian site along the Wadi Jabbok, just east of the Jordan River, often identified as biblical Sukkot. The Deir Alla Inscription presents the oracle of Balaam bar Beor, apparently in celebration of the Aramean victory over Israel in the late ninth century BCE. Balaam's Deir Alla vision recounts the decree of the Transjordanian divine council to plunge the land into chaos without relief until Israel had been defeated and driven out of the land and Aram, Moab, and other nations had then taken control. Insofar as Num 22–24 portrays Balaam as a prophet who is completely under YHWH's control and who may therefore only bless rather than curse Israel, it appears that Num 22–24 was composed in northern Israel as a response to the Deir Alla Inscription following Israel's defeat of Aram during the reign of Joash ben Jehoahaz (801–786 BCE) and the restoration of Israelite control over the Transjordan.[53]

Coats and Knierim identify Num 22–24 as an example of a legend that

52. For discussion of the Deir Alla Inscription, see pp. 36–37 above.

53. Marvin A. Sweeney, "Balaam in Intertextual Perspective," in *Tell It in Gath: Studies in the History and Archaeology of Israel: Essays in Honor of Aren Maeir on the Occasion of His Sixtieth Birthday*, ed. Itzhaq Shai et al., ÄAT 90 (Münster: Zaphon, 2018), 534–47.

highlights the virtue of Balaam ben Beor as a prophet who adheres to the will of YHWH.[54] Nevertheless, we must recognize the influence of the vision report on the Balaam narrative insofar as Balaam presents four oracles that are intended to curse Israel but bless Israel instead, since the prophet may speak only what YHWH permits. The narrative very clearly caricaturizes Balaam, polemicizing against any claim that he might effectively curse Israel. Hired by the Moabite King Balak to curse Israel, Balaam travels from his home in Pethor by the Euphrates River to Moab to fulfill the contract. But during the course of the journey, the renowned seer can see only what YHWH allows him to see. At one point, when an angel sent by YHWH blocks the road, Balaam is not able to see it; but the ass that he is riding does. When the ass balks at the sight of the angel, Balaam beats him. The ass then protests, demanding to know why the seer is beating him. YHWH at last opens Balaam's eyes so that Balaam understands that he is under YHWH's control. Upon arriving in Moab, he attempts to curse Israel but cannot because YHWH does not permit him to do so, and instead he blesses Israel four times. Frustrated, Balak and Balaam return to their respective homes.

Balaam ben Beor appears to function throughout the narrative as an example of a Mesopotamian *baru*-priest.[55] Mesopotamian *baru*-priests were visionary diviners trained to read signs in the world at large in order to discern the will of the gods. Such signs included the entrails of sacrificial animals, the movements of the stars and planets, oil patterns on water, smoke patterns from sacrificial altars, unusual phenomena in the world of creation, etc. The *baru* were a professional class who were well educated in reading and writing cuneiform texts.

Balaam's procedure in Num 23:1–3 is to build seven sacrificial altars and to prepare seven bulls and seven rams for offerings. Although Balak accompanies Balaam, Balaam goes off alone to receive the divine revelation. At the outset of his third and fourth oracles, the introduction to the oracle in Num 24:3b–4 (cf. 24:15b–16) informs us of Balaam's condition as he receives the divine message:

54. Rolf P. Knierim and George W. Coats, *Numbers*, FOTL 4 (Grand Rapids: Eerdmans, 2005), 246–63, esp. 260–61.

55. For discussion of Mesopotamian *baru*-priests, see Frederick H. Cryer, *Divination in Ancient Israel and Its Near Eastern Environment: A Socio-Historical Investigation*, JSOTSup 142 (Sheffield: Sheffield Academic Press, 1994).

Utterance of Balaam son of Beor,
and the utterance of the man whose eye is opened/closed;
Utterance of the one who hears the statements of El
(and who knows the knowledge of Elyon),[56] who sees the vision of
    Shaddai,
falling down as his eyes are uncovered.

These introductions provide us with important insights. First, they indicate that Balaam is having a visionary experience. The text employs an ambiguous phrase, "whose eye is opened/closed," based upon the verb *shetum*, which is understood to mean both "open" and "closed," in an effort to convey that Balaam sees in a manner that other human beings cannot.[57] It indicates his knowledge of "the statements of El," "the knowledge of Elyon," and "the vision of Shaddai," employing divine names originally applied to pre-Israelite Canaanite deities that later come to refer to YHWH. The portrayal of Balaam as "falling" indicates that he is having an ecstatic experience, as was typical for seers in Canaanite and other cultures, as a form of trance possession in which the deity would take control of the seer's body and reveal the vision through the seer's own sight or discernment and through his statements about what he has seen.

The content of Balaam's vision appears to be based on a number of factors, each of which is evident by studying the sequence of his visions. The first in Num 23:6–10 appears to be based on a vision of Israel encamped by the Jordan River prior to their entry into the promised land of Israel. Balaam describes Israel, as seen from the mountain top where he would have been situated, as a people who dwell apart from other nations. He emphasizes the great numbers of the people, employing the imagery of a dust cloud, which draws upon the ancestral blessings of Genesis to assert that Israel will become a great nation.

The second in Num 23:18–24 begins by emphasizing the uniquely divine character of YHWH and the fact that Balaam can say only what YHWH wills him to say. He employs the typical covenant statement that YHWH is with them to emphasize YHWH's promises to protect the nation. He reiterates this point by asserting that their king is in their midst (an apparent reference to YHWH who is conceived as Israel's true king), that G-d delivered them from Egypt, and that Israel must be conceived as a lion that is ready to jump

---

56. Only in Num 24:16aβ.
57. BDB, 1060.

and catch its prey. Most of this oracle is based on the major elements of the Pentateuchal narrative, but the concluding reference to the lion employs an image of the wild lion from nature, which also functions as the symbol of the royal tribe of Judah, to depict Israel's character.

Third is Num 24:3–9 which, following the introduction, begins with a recounting of Israel's tents in keeping with the first oracle. But it quickly moves to the natural imagery of the Jordan River which someone standing atop the Moabite hills would have seen when looking down into the river valley in antiquity. The images are all from creation (palm groves, aloe trees, cedars by the water, etc.) to emphasize the fertility, bounty, and blessing associated with Israel. The oracle then returns to the imagery of the second vision to emphasize how Israel's king will protect the nation from enemies and how G-d delivers them from Egypt.

Finally, the fourth is Num 24:15–24, which depicts a star that will arise from Jacob and a scepter from Israel, clearly a reference to a king who will defeat Israel's enemies and bring victory and peace to the nation as it re-covers Moab and Edom, among other territories, and destroys Amalek, the unremitting enemy of Israel. The concluding elements of the vision refer to Assur and the Kittim. Although the Hebrew term *Kittim* later refers to the Romans in Qumran literature, it appears here as a parallel designation for Assyria. Such a reference indicates Assyria's role in Israel's victory, which makes historical sense. In an effort to free Israel from Aramean attack, King Jehu of Israel (842–815 BCE) submitted to the Assyrian King Shalmaneser III as depicted in Shalmaneser's Black Obelisk.[58] Jehu's grandson, Jehoash ben Jehoahaz (801–786 BCE), is listed as a tributary of the Assyrian monarch Adad Nirai III.[59] Indeed, according to 2 Kgs 13:10–25, it was Jehoash who drove the Arameans out of Israel and restored Israelite rule over the Trans-jordan, thereby enabling his son, Jeroboam ben Jehoash (786–746 BCE), to rule in peace over a kingdom that rivaled Solomon's (2 Kgs 14:23–29).

Balaam's visions as depicted in Num 22–24 differ from those in Israel and Judah that are based on the imagery of the Israelite and Judean temples. But they are based on Mesopotamian cultic practice as well as imagery from the natural creation of the Jordan River, the presumed view of an entire nation encamped by the Jordan, and the imagery of kings (Israelite, Assyr-ian, and divine) that act on Israel's behalf, thereby ensuring its security and prosperity.

---

58. *ANEP*, 351, 355.
59. Page, "A Stela of Adad Nirari III."

Chapter 3

THE FORMER PROPHETS AND PSALMS

Visionary and dream texts throughout the Former Prophets and Psalms convey the experience and presence of YHWH among human beings. As in the Pentateuch, concern with the temple, the Shiloh Temple as well as the Jerusalem Temple, plays a special role. Both sanctuaries housed the ark of the covenant for most—if not all—of the time that they stood. Insofar as the ark represents divine presence in ancient Israelite and Judean thought, the imagery of the ark, the holy of holies in which the ark was housed, and other imagery associated with the temple plays an important role in informing the imagery of the divine in visionary and dream texts. But the imagery extends beyond the temple. Several texts portray angels as military figures who convey divine messages and intent to human beings. In most cases, these figures appear to be based on the images of military figures from the various nations, such as Aram and Assyria, that harassed, attacked, and conquered Israel and Judah during the Iron Age. Other cases are concerned with kingship, particularly the royal House of David. Finally, visionary imagery in the Former Prophets and Psalms is also concerned with creation in order to depict YHWH as the creator and thus the true King of all creation and human beings. Texts treated include Josh 5; Judg 6; 1 Sam 3; 1 Sam 28; 2 Sam 7; 2 Sam 22//Ps 18; Ps 68; 1 Kgs 3; 1 Kgs 9; 1 Kgs 17–2 Kgs 2; and 2 Kgs 2–13.

Joshua and the Commander of the Army of YHWH (Josh 5)

The book of Joshua is the first major element of the Former Prophets in the Jewish Bible. Modern scholars have come to recognize the Former Prophets—Joshua, Judges, Samuel, and Kings—as the Deuteronomistic History (DtrH), in that these books draw language and ideas from Deuteronomy and present a relatively unified and coherent account of the history of the nation of Israel from the time that it entered the Promised Land of Israel under Joshua until the aftermath of the Babylonian Exile when King Jehoiachin ben Jehoiakim, the last legitimate King of Judah, was released from captivity by the Babylonian monarch, Evil Merodach (Amel Marduk), son of Nebuchadnezzar.[1] The final form of the DtrH appears to be a redactional work that demonstrates a relatively consistent theological viewpoint and literary style, while employing a great deal of older material, in an attempt to explain how and why Israel and Judah were exiled from the land promised to them by YHWH. The theological viewpoint and literary form of the DtrH are heavily dependent upon the book of Deuteronomy. Indeed, the DtrH argues that Israel and Judah were exiled as a result of their failure to observe the covenant made between them and YHWH as represented in the book of Deuteronomy. Such an agenda thereby serves as a form of theodicy; it defends the righteousness, power, and presence of YHWH in the face of disaster and instead argues that the human partners to the covenant, Israel and Judah, were responsible for their own demise. Such a theological claim is problematic in the aftermath of the modern experience of the Shoah, but we must remember that the ancients who chose to hold themselves rather than YHWH accountable for their own suffering did so because they were committed to adherence to YHWH and to YHWH's Torah.

Earlier editions of the DtrH are also evident.[2] Many scholars maintain that an earlier edition of the DtrH was written during the late seventh-century reign of King Josiah of Judah (r. 640–609 BCE), who sought to restore the unity of the nations of Israel and Judah under Davidic rule as Assyrian power waned. Indeed, Josiah's program of religious reform and covenant renewal was designed to serve such a purpose by correcting the sins of the kings of the northern kingdom of Israel and by exhorting the people of Israel and Judah to observe YHWH's Torah. But Josiah's restoration efforts ended in 609 BCE when he died in a failed attempt to thwart Pharaoh Necho's advance northward to reinforce Assyria against Josiah's Babylonian allies. In 587 BCE, a short twenty-two years following Josiah's death, Judah was destroyed by the Babylonians just as northern Israel had been destroyed by Assyria in 722–721 BCE. Instead of culminating in the glorious reign of

1. Marvin A. Sweeney, *King Josiah of Judah: The Lost Messiah of Israel* (Oxford: Oxford University Press, 2001); see also Thomas Römer, *The So-Called Deuteronomistic History: A Sociological, Historical, and Literary Introduction* (Edinburgh: T&T Clark, 2007).

2. Marvin A. Sweeney, *1 and 2 Kings: A Commentary*, OTL (Louisville: Westminster John Knox, 2007), 1–32.

Josiah, the DtrH was extended and edited to account for the exile of Judah. Earlier editions of the DtrH and other historical sources are evident in the Hezekian DtrH, the Jehu Dynastic History, the Solomonic History, and other works underlying the present narrative.

Many scholars have followed Richard D. Nelson in noting the interrelationship between Joshua in the book of Joshua and King Josiah of Judah in the Josianic edition of the DtrH.[3] Joshua is portrayed as an ideal figure who leads a united Israel in the conquest and sanctification of the land of Canaan and who reestablishes the covenant between YHWH and Israel on the basis of Deuteronomic Torah. Nelson is correct to argue that the book of Joshua is formulated largely as the introduction to the DtrH, and that the figure of Joshua is model for the ideal kingship of Josiah ben Amon. As part of the agenda to portray Joshua as an ideal leader, the book of Joshua portrays a swift and complete conquest of the land of Canaan in which the conquests of Jericho and Ai mark the conquest of central Canaan, the subjugation of Gibeon and the defeat of its enemies mark the conquest of southern Canaan, and the defeat of Hazor marks the conquest of northern Canaan. But modern scholars have recognized that the conquest of Canaan as depicted in the book of Joshua could never have taken place. Three key cities in the narrative, Jericho, Ai, and Gibeon, were uninhabited tels or ruined city mounds in the 1200s BCE, the time when Israel first appeared in the land of Canaan, as indicated in Pharaoh Merneptah's stele of 1220 BCE.[4] Likewise, Hazor was later defeated by Israel under the leadership of the judge Deborah according to Judg 4–5. Indeed, Judg 1–2 recognizes that Canaanites remained prominently in the land together with Israel, and archeological evidence indicates that warfare in this period did not encompass the entire land but instead appeared along the borders of the hill country of Israel, where the Israelite tribes resided, and the coastal plain, where the Philistines lived. Overall, archeology points to a picture of conflict between the Israelites in the hill country and the Philistines of the coastal plain prior to the rise of the Israelite monarchy ca. 1000 BCE.

Although the account of the conquest of the land of Canaan and the depiction of Joshua ben Nun may not be historically accurate, it should not be dismissed as pure fantasy. The account is deliberately formulated

---

3. Richard D. Nelson, "Josiah in the Book of Joshua," *JBL* 100 (1981): 531–40; cf. Nelson, *Joshua: A Commentary*, OTL (Louisville: Westminster John Knox, 1997), 21–22; Thomas B. Dozeman, *Joshua 1–12*, YAB 6B (New Haven: Yale University Press, 2015), 210–12.

4. *ANET*, 376–78.

to make the theological statement that stands as the foundation of the interpretation of the history of Israel and Judah that DtrH attempts: YHWH demonstrates *hesed* or "fidelity" toward Israel by keeping the covenant. Just as YHWH swore in Deuteronomy, and in the Pentateuch at large, to grant Israel the land of Canaan as part of the covenant, the book of Joshua demonstrates that YHWH keeps YHWH's end of the agreement.[5] This message is accentuated by the miraculous character of the conquest. The waters of the Jordan River part in Josh 3 when the Levites bearing the ark of the covenant enter the water; thereby Israel crosses dry shod into the land just as they crossed the Red Sea in Exod 14–15. Jericho falls miraculously in Josh 6 after Israel marches around the city for six days and blows shofars, or rams' horns, on the seventh to bring about the collapse of the city's walls. Israel is defeated at Ai in Josh 7, not because of any discernable military reason, but because the people had become impure due to Achan's embezzlement of booty consecrated to YHWH after the conquest of Jericho. Once Achan was found and punished, Israel was purified and thus able to take Ai on account of YHWH's intervention in Josh 8. The sun stands still and stones rain down from heaven in Josh 10, enabling Israel to defeat the enemies of their new ally Gibeon and take the southern portion of Canaan. YHWH intervenes miraculously throughout Joshua to ensure Israel's success—and punishes Israel when it fails to reciprocate YHWH's thoroughgoing *hesed* with complete faithfulness to the covenant's demands. Such a portrayal facilitates the agenda of the DtrH: it was never YHWH who failed to observe the covenant; it was Israel who failed to observe the covenant beginning in the book of Judges and continuing through Samuel and Kings until both Israel and Judah were exiled from the land promised to them by YHWH.

It is within the context of this theological portrayal of YHWH's fidelity to the covenant with Israel that we find the significance of the visionary account of YHWH's general in Josh 5:13–15, following the crossing of the Jordan River, the circumcision of the Israelite men, and the celebration of Passover in Josh 3:1–5:12. Each of the preceding acts demonstrated the holy character of the conquest of the land: the parting of the Jordan River demonstrated YHWH's involvement in the conquest; the celebration of Passover provided a religious context for the conquest insofar as Passover celebrates Israel's exodus from Egypt and journey to the promised land of Israel; and

---

5. Sweeney, *King Josiah of Judah*, 125–36.

the circumcision of the Israelite men demonstrated Israel's willingness to abide by the covenant with YHWH.

The brief narrative concerning Joshua's encounter with YHWH's general follows upon this sequence of events. The setting is near Jericho, which will be the scene of the first major encounter with the Canaanites in Josh 6. Joshua sees a man standing before him with his sword drawn and asks him a typical wartime question to identify someone as friend or foe, "Are you with us, or with our enemies?" The man then identifies himself, "No, but I am the commander of the army of YHWH. Now, I have come." Such a statement identifies him as YHWH's emissary and once again demonstrates YHWH's commitment to the covenant with Israel in sending the commander of the divine army to ensure Israel's conquest of the land. When Joshua asks the man, "What does my lord have to say to his servant?" he acknowledges his subordination to YHWH's commander and asks him for orders. When the man responds, "Remove your shoes from your feet, for this place upon which you stand is holy," he identifies the place as holy, much as YHWH identified Mt. Sinai as holy to Moses in the burning bush episode of Exod 3, thereby indicating the holy nature of the undertaking and establishing the parallel between Moses and Joshua. Joshua is thus Moses's successor. Joshua of course complies immediately.

The theological significance of this encounter is clear, but the historical significance of the encounter must also be understood. Many interpreters would be satisfied to allow the military context of the conquest of Jericho and the rest of the land of Canaan to explain the presence of YHWH's military commander. But we must recognize the significance of such an image and assertion in the late seventh-century BCE reign of King Josiah ben Amon. Assyria had been Judah's suzerain from the late ninth century BCE through the reign of Josiah in 640–609 BCE. Indeed, Judah together with its ally Babylon had revolted against Assyria in 705 BCE and suffered the consequences of Sennacherib's invasion of 701 BCE, which devastated the whole of Judah but left King Hezekiah on the throne. When Judah's ally, Babylon, revolted in 652–648 BCE, King Assurbanipal of Assyria dragged King Manasseh ben Hezekiah to Babylon to show him the consequences of Babylon's action and to convince him not to join the revolt. But following the death of Assurbanipal in 631 BCE or later, Babylon revolted a third time in 628–627 BCE under the leadership of Nebopolassar, the father of Nebuchadnezzar, who succeeded in destroying Assur and Nineveh, the religious and political capitals, respectively, of the Assyrian Empire. Josiah's own turn to YHWH took place in the twelfth year of his reign (2 Chr 34:3), indicating his coordination with Nebopolassar's revolt. But when Nebopolassar forced the Assyrian army into a last stand at Haran in 609 BCE, King Josiah of Judah attempted to intervene by blocking Pharaoh Necho of Egypt from moving his army north to Haran to support his Assyrian allies. Josiah was killed at Megiddo, and with him died his reforms and Judah's bid for independence, although he did succeed in stalling the Egyptians long enough so that they arrived at Haran too late to prevent the final defeat of the Assyrian army.

The portrayal of YHWH's military commander appears to be based on Judean experience with the Assyrian army and its officers throughout the two hundred years that Judah was Assyria's vassal. The Assyrians were known to conduct annual *palu* campaigns in which the Assyrian army would march to vassal cities to intimidate them into paying their annual tribute to the Assyrian king.[6] The *palu* campaigns, the Assyrian invasion of Judah in 701 BCE, and the arrest of King Manasseh during the Babylonian revolt of 652–648 BCE would have given Judah plenty of exposure to Assyrian officers whose image informs the portrayal of YHWH's military commander in Josh 5:13–15. This portrayal would then be designed to demonstrate that YHWH, as the true master of creation and human events, was more powerful than the Assyrians; YHWH had an army more powerful than that of any human army and would assure Israel of victory in its conquest of the land of Canaan.

Gideon's Vision and Altar at Ophrah (Judg 6)

The book of Judges follows immediately after the book of Joshua in the literary sequence of the Former Prophets or Deuteronomistic History. But there are major differences between the two works even though they are part of the larger literary framework. Whereas Joshua relates the conquest of all of Canaan by the tribes of Israel, Judges begins with an account of all the Canaanites who remained in the land due to Israel's inability to defeat and dislodge them. Whereas Israel conquered and destroyed Hazor and its King Jabin in Josh 11, Judg 4–5 maintains that Deborah and Barak overpowered Hazor by defeating King Jabin's army led by Sisera. Furthermore, we have also seen that Jericho, Ai, and Gibeon, major cities in the Joshua narrative, were nothing more than ancient ruins ca. 1200 BCE when Israel emerged in the land.

6. Hayim Tadmor, "The Campaigns of Sargon II of Assur: A Chronological-Historical Study," *JCS* 12 (1958): 22–40, 77–100.

Many scholars correctly maintain that Joshua and Judges were composed by different hands, but we must also understand how these conflicting accounts function in relation to each other in the final, synchronic form of the DtrH.[7] They are clearly coordinated by parallel accounts of the death and burial of Joshua in Josh 24:29–32 and Judg 2:6–10a, and as we have seen above, the Joshua narrative is designed to demonstrate YHWH's fidelity to the covenant with Israel. But the continuing presence of the Canaanites in the land, contrary to YHWH's expectations, plays an important role in the Judges narrative. Judges 2 states that an angel of YHWH came up from Gilgal to Bochim in order to relate YHWH's anger at Israel for failing to drive out or destroy the Canaanites. Israel's failure prompts YHWH to charge that Israel has not observed their covenant with YHWH in Judg 2:2. Although YHWH swears not to break the covenant with Israel, YHWH decides to allow the Canaanites to remain in the land so that they will serve as a snare to Israel, thereby leading to Israel's punishment in Judges. The result is a repeating pattern in the book of Judges: (1) Israel begins to serve the gods of the nations that remain in the land, thereby abandoning YHWH; (2) YHWH brings an oppressor against Israel to punish them for their transgressions; (3) Israel cries out to YHWH to deliver them from the oppressor so that they might return to YHWH; and (4) YHWH sends a deliverer who generally defeats the oppressor and gives the land peace until the cycle is repeated. The deliverers are identified as Israel's judges or rulers; the Hebrew term *shophet* ("judge") may refer to a judicial figure, but it more broadly refers to rulers. Indeed, the Akkadian title for the pre-Israelite Canaanite city-state rulers in the Amarna letters is *shappatum*, a cognate word for the Hebrew *shophet*.

This repeated pattern underlies much of the presentation of Israel's early history in the book of Judges, but it also points to a decline in Israel as it becomes increasingly Canaanized and ready to dissolve into chaos by the end of the book. Such a decline points to the need for a king to unite and rule the nation, particularly since the judges of Israel prove increasingly incompetent as the book progresses. The first judge, Othniel from the tribe of Judah, quickly dispatches Israel's Mesopotamian oppressors in Judg 3:7–11. Ehud of Benjamin, the second judge in Judg 3:12–30, can only overcome the Moabite King Eglon by deception due to his left-handedness. Deborah of Ephraim, the third judge, defeats Sisera but is unable to unite the tribes against their enemies. Gideon of Manasseh, the fourth judge, has a

---

7. For critical discussion of Judges, see Sweeney, *King Josiah*, 110–24; and Sweeney, "Davidic Polemics in the Book of Judges," *VT* 47 (1997): 517–29.

dual Israelite-Canaanite identity in Judg 6–8 and builds an idolatrous ephod for Israel to worship. His son, Abimelech, plunges the tribes into civil war in Judg 9 when he attempts to seize power as Israel's king. Jephthah of the Transjordan, perhaps from Manasseh or Gad, sacrifices his own daughter in a manner often ascribed to the Canaanites as he defeats Israel's enemies as well as the tribe of Ephraim when it declares war on him in Judg 11–12. The sixth major judge, Samson of Dan, ignores instructions against marrying foreign women in Judg 13–16. As a result, his Philistine wife, Delilah, is able to overcome him after learning the secret of his great strength. He eventually takes revenge against his Philistine captors, but he can do so only by committing suicide in the process. As a result of Samson's escapades, the tribe of Dan is forced to move away from its tribal allotment along the coastal plain to a location north of Hazor and the Galilee in Judg 17–18 where a man named Micah embezzles money from his mother to build an idolatrous sanctuary in the city of Dan. The final episode in Judg 19–21 relates the despicable rape and murder of the Levite's concubine in the city of Gibeah, which results in a civil war that nearly destroys the tribe of Benjamin. Insofar as Gibeah is the capital city of Israel's first king, Saul ben Kish of the tribe of Benjamin, the narrative is clearly a polemic against Saul as it calls for righteous kingship in Israel. Insofar as the book portrays the initial Judean judge as largely competent and the subsequent judges from northern Israelite tribes as increasingly incompetent, the book of Judges subtly argues for the appointment of a Judean king over all Israel.[8]

Clearly, the continued presence of the Canaanites in the land is an important motif in Judges. The motif is especially important in the Gideon[9] narrative in Judg 6–8, where the judge Gideon ben Joash the Abiezrite of the tribe of Manasseh also has a Canaanite name, Jerubbaal. As Jerubbaal, he built an altar for the worship of Baal. The narrative in Judg 6:32 explains his Canaanite name as meaning "let Baal contend with him," after Gideon tears down his father's altar to Baal; philologically speaking, the name means "may Baal be magnified," a name that clearly honors Baal.

Gideon's mixed Canaanite/Israelite identity plays an important role in the narrative even as he defeats the Midianite enemies of Israel. Prior to the conflict, Judg 6:7–10 relates that YHWH sent a prophet to Israel to charge

8. Sweeney, "Davidic Polemics."

9. For discussion of the Gideon narrative, see esp. Susan Niditch, *Judges: A Commentary*, OTL (Louisville: Westminster John Knox, 2008), 82–116; Jack Sasson, *Judges 1–12*, YAB 6D (New Haven: Yale University Press, 2014), 324–405.

them with disobeying YHWH by worshiping other gods. This charge provides a key expectation of YHWH: because Israel has been punished for worshiping other gods, YHWH therefore expects the people to return to YHWH. Judges 6:11–40 relates the first major requirement that Gideon and Israel must meet before YHWH will deliver them. They must purify themselves and the land by tearing down the Canaanite altar to Baal and replacing it with an altar dedicated to YHWH. Ophrah, the site of the altar, may be located in the Jezreel Valley, north of the Israelite hill country controlled by the tribe of Manasseh.[10]

YHWH's instructions to Gideon come in the form of a vision account, in which YHWH commissions Gideon to serve as YHWH's messenger. It begins with a notice that an angel of YHWH appeared to Gideon to inform him that YHWH is with him. When Gideon questions why his people suffer if YHWH is with him, YHWH addresses him directly and commissions Gideon as YHWH's messenger and Israel's deliverer. The form of the narrative closely resembles prophetic commissioning narratives, suggesting that Gideon is to be a prophet, judge, priest, and warrior, much like Moses or Samuel. Gideon responds to YHWH's commission by offering a goat as an *'olah*, or whole burnt offering (cf. Lev 1), and unleavened bread as a *minhah*, or grain offering (cf. Lev 2), to YHWH. As a result of this offering, YHWH appears to Gideon that night, perhaps in a dream, and instructs Gideon to tear down the older Canaanite altar to Baal, together with its sacred post dedicated to Asherah, and to build a new altar dedicated to YHWH, where Gideon would offer a bull as an *'olah*. After requesting further signs from YHWH, Gideon proceeds to defeat the Midianites and to ward off the Ephraimites who threatened war against Manasseh.

The vision account appears to explain how the tribe of Manasseh dedicated itself to YHWH by the efforts of Gideon, also known as Jerubbaal. Indeed, it may represent an account of how Manasseh became a part of Israel. Overall, it explains the origins of an Israelite or Manassite sanctuary at Ophrah and the ordination of Gideon as its prophetic or priestly founder. Gideon is not a Levite, but he is designated as YHWH's deliverer and, much like a prophet or a priest, has visionary experiences of YHWH and YHWH's angel. No image is ever ascribed to YHWH; YHWH's presence is described only in relation to the angel of YHWH who appears in the narrative, thereby avoiding any tangible description of YHWH. When YHWH appears to Gideon at night, no description of YHWH appears in the narrative. YHWH's appearance to Gideon there-

---

10. Jeffries M. Hamilton, "Ophrah," *ABD* 5:27–28.

fore seems to resemble YHWH's appearance to Samuel in the Shiloh sanctuary (1 Sam 3, below) that identifies Samuel as a prophet and priest.

Unfortunately, the Gideon narrative includes an account of how Gideon demanded that the people of Israel give him the golden earrings that they had won as booty so that he could build an idolatrous ephod for Israel to worship in Ophrah. The act resembles calls for the people to give gold so that a sanctuary might be constructed (Exod 35), but its idolatrous features apparently play a role in signaling the attempt by Gideon's son, Abimelech, to claim kingship over all Israel, thereby plunging the nation in to civil war. Such an episode illustrates the transition from Canaanite to Israelite religiosity.

The Calling of Samuel at Shiloh (1 Sam 3)

The prophet Samuel ben Elkanah is a figure very much like Moses, who combines roles of prophet, priest, judge, and military commander, as overall leader of Israel during the premonarchic period. The narratives about him in 1 Samuel portray him as a transitional figure who serves as the last of Israel's judges and who anoints first Saul ben Kish of Benjamin and later David ben Jesse of Judah as Israel's first monarchs. His father Elkanah is an Ephraimite; but as his mother Hannah's firstborn son, he is donated to the Shiloh sanctuary to be raised under the tutelage of Eli, the high priest of Israel during the period prior to the establishment of the monarchy. The Shiloh sanctuary is where Samuel has a visionary experience that identifies him as YHWH's prophet (and priest) in 1 Sam 3.

The narratives in 1 Sam 1–3 present the background for Samuel's visionary experience at the Shiloh temple. They begin by identifying Samuel's father as Elkanah ben Jeroham ben Elihu ben Tohu ben Zuph, an Ephraimite from Ramathaim of the Zuphites in the hill country of Ephraim. This identification is key because it makes very clear that Samuel's father is not a Levite. First Chronicles 6:1–15 (16–30), esp. vv. 12–13 (27–28), works Samuel's pedigree into the early genealogy of the Levites, although it is noteworthy that the Masoretic Text of 1 Chr 6:12–13 reads, "Eliab, his son; Jeruham, his son; Elkanah, his son; and Samuel, the firstborn, Vashni and Abijah." Such a reading has prompted some discussion insofar as Vashni is sometimes read as "the second" in some textual witnesses and as "Joel" in others (cf. 1 Sam 8:2).[11]

11. See *BHS* notes; Ralph Klein, *1 Chronicles*, Hermeneia (Minneapolis: Fortress, 2006), 172, 182; Gary N. Knoppers, *1 Chronicles 1–9*, AnBib 12 (New York: Doubleday, 2003), 421.

Two issues emerge. First, Chronicles is known for correcting its source materials in Samuel and Kings, particularly to designate persons who fill priestly roles as Levites, even if the text of Samuel or Kings identifies them otherwise. Second, the masoretic punctuation of the text reads "the firstborn" as a designation for Vashni, but the name Vashni itself appears to be a corrupted form of the Hebrew word "and the second," which would suggest an identification of Abijah. Further, because 1 Sam 8:2 identifies Samuel's sons as Joel and Abijah, something may have dropped out of the text of 1 Chr 6:13 (28). Possible readings include, "and the sons of Samuel: the firstborn, Joel, and the second, Abijah," or "and the sons of Samuel, the firstborn: Vashni and Abijah." The second possible reading is especially noteworthy because even in the text of 1 Sam 1, Samuel is the firstborn of his mother Hannah.

The identity of Hannah is key to Samuel's future vocation. First Samuel 1–2 focuses especially on Hannah as one of the two wives of Elkanah, who is initially unable to bear him children. Elkanah's two wives, Peninah and Hannah, have very different experiences. Although Elkanah loves Hannah, she bears him no children, whereas Peninah gives birth to a succession of children. Indeed, the wifely rivalry is very much like that of Leah and Rachel, the two wives of Jacob in Gen 29–31, when Jacob's beloved Rachel is unable to deliver whereas Leah gives birth to four sons, and later two more sons and a daughter.

The narrative in 1 Samuel focuses on Hannah's distress at her inability to bear to set in motion events that demonstrate the incompetence of the High Priest Eli and his sons and that ultimately will introduce a new priestly line.[12] When Hannah goes to the Shiloh sanctuary to pray for the birth of a son, the High Priest Eli mistakes her moving lips for a sign that she is drunk, indicating a flaw in his own character as a priest who did not recognize a person at prayer. After Hannah returns to her home, she becomes pregnant, gives birth to baby Samuel, weans him, and eventually donates the toddler to the Shiloh sanctuary where he will be raised as a priest.

Following the account of Samuel's birth, 1 Sam 2 portrays the lack of integrity of Eli's two sons, Hophni and Phineas, who abuse their own roles as priests by taking undue portions of the offerings presented at the sanctuary for their own consumption and by having relations with the women who are serving at the sanctuary. Such actions on the part of his sons add

---

12. For discussion of 1 Samuel 1–3, see A. Graeme Auld, *1 and 2 Samuel: A Commentary*, OTL (Louisville: Westminster John Knox, 2011), 19–62; Antony F. Campbell, *1 Samuel*, FOTL 7 (Grand Rapids: Eerdmans, 2003), 34–59.

to the portrayal of Eli as an incompetent priest in need of replacement, as indeed 1 Sam 2 concludes with the announcement of an anonymous prophet who condemns the priestly house of Eli and claims that it will be replaced by another.

The portrayal of Samuel as a firstborn son is key to understanding his role in the narrative as a prophet and priest in the service of YHWH, as the leading figure in the transition of Israel's leadership from the judges to the kings, and as the figure who initiates the eventual replacement of the priestly line of Eli and later Abiathar, descended from Aaron's son Ithamar, by the priestly line of Zadok, descended from Aaron's son Eliezer, when Solomon ascends the throne (1 Kgs 2).

Although readers of the Bible normally think of Levi as the priestly tribe of Israel, the Pentateuchal narrative indicates that the firstborn sons of Israel were initially chosen to serve as YHWH's priests, only to be replaced by the Levites at a later time.[13] One of the major features of the narratives in Exod 1–15 is the focus on the death of the firstborn as the tenth plague that YHWH inflicted on Egypt, prompting Pharaoh finally to let Israel go free. Although this plague is noted for its persuasive effect on Pharaoh, its narrative role is not fully understood. Exodus 34:19–20 makes it clear that the firstborn of the herd and flock are to be offered to YHWH at the festival of Passover, but the text also specifies that the firstborn of an ass and the firstborn sons of Israel are to be redeemed and not sacrificed. Exodus 34:19 makes it clear that "all that breaks the womb is mine," i.e., the firstborn to the mother belong to YHWH. Exodus 13:2 likewise makes clear that firstborn animals and sons of Israel are to be consecrated to YHWH. Although our laws stipulate that the firstborn animals must be offered to YHWH as sacrifices, the role of the firstborn sons is not clear. Only much later in the Pentateuchal narrative, in Num 3:5–20; 3:40–51; and 8:5–19, does YHWH tell Moses that the tribe of Levites will replace the firstborn of Israel to perform the sacred service of the sanctuary; i.e., firstborn sons of Israel are consecrated as priests until the Levites are appointed to replace them in that role. The selection of Aaron and the tribe of Levi as YHWH's holy priests in Num 17–18 confirms YHWH's decision.

Such an observation explains Hannah's action in sending her firstborn son, Samuel, to the Shiloh sanctuary to be raised as a priest. Indeed, the

---

13. See Marvin A. Sweeney, "Samuel's Institutional Identity in the Deuteronomistic History," in *Constructs of Prophets in the Former and Latter Prophets and Other Texts*, ed. Lester L. Grabbe and Martti Nissinen (Atlanta: Society of Biblical Literature, 2011), 165–74.

charges of idolatry and religious malpractice made against Jeroboam ben Nebat, the first king of the northern kingdom of Israel, in 1 Kgs 12:25–33 include the charge that he appointed priests from the farthest reaches of the people (of Israel) who were not Levites (1 Kgs 12:31). Figures such as Samuel, Elijah, and Elisha, who are all identified as prophets but not as Levites in the Samuel and Kings narratives, appear to justify this charge because they all engage in priestly activity even though they are not of the tribe of Levi. Perhaps designation of the firstborn sons as priests was a common practice in northern Israel. The above-cited laws and narratives would seem to confirm this view.

Samuel's visionary experience as narrated in 1 Sam 3 confirms his identity not only as a prophet, as stated in the narrative, but as a priest as well. The narrative reports in 1 Sam 3:1 that young Samuel was serving YHWH before Eli in the Shiloh sanctuary, employing a Hebrew term, *mesharet*, which is typically employed for priestly service in the sanctuary. The narrative relates that Samuel sleeps in the sanctuary before the ark of the covenant, a location that also indicates his priestly status, since only priests are allowed access to the holy of holies of Israelite sanctuaries where the ark of the covenant is kept. During the night, Samuel repeatedly hears someone calling him, "Samuel! Samuel!" Young Samuel repeatedly goes to Eli, thinking that Eli has called him, only to be told that he did not. Such an oversight provides further evidence of Eli's initial inability to recognize YHWH, but he finally realizes what is afoot on the third try and tells little Samuel to listen to what YHWH has to say. YHWH condemns the house of Eli to Samuel, and Samuel is thereafter recognized as a prophet insofar as he had a visionary experience in which YHWH spoke to him.

Although the vision is primarily an audial experience in which Samuel hears YHWH's word, this presents little problem. Israelite and Judean visions typically include YHWH's statements as well as visual imagery. The text states in 1 Sam 3:10 that YHWH stood in the sanctuary and called to Samuel, implying some visual presence even if it is not defined. The vision also takes place during the night, suggesting a dream experience. Furthermore, the holy of holies of the temple is the place at which YHWH typically appears (cf. Lev 16:1–2; etc.).

Most importantly, Samuel's vision appears to be an inaugural vision associated with the ordination of young priests. Exodus 29, Leviticus 8, and Numbers 8 all speak of the ordination of young priests, who are incubated for a period of seven days without leaving the sacred space where they will serve. At the end of this time, they are consecrated to serve at the temple altar. The texts state that ordination offerings are presented during the period of incubation, but they provide no clues as to what else might happen during the seven-day period of incubation or where the prospective priests reside. Samuel's example indicates that the prospective young priests were incubated in the temple itself and perhaps even before the ark of the covenant. In such a context, a visionary experience like that of Samuel might well occur.

Saul's Vision of Samuel from Sheol (1 Sam 28)

The present form of 1 Samuel relates the origins of kingship in ancient Israel focusing particularly on the monarchy of King Saul ben Kish, the first king of Israel. The narrative begins with a presentation of the birth and career of Samuel, but one of Samuel's major roles is to designate and anoint the king of Israel on YHWH's behalf, which he does to both Saul and David ben Jesse. Although Saul's portrayal is favorable in some accounts, such as his anointing as king by Samuel while he is looking for his father's lost asses in 1 Sam 9:1–10:16 and his deliverance of the besieged city of Jabesh-gilead in 1 Sam 11, the narrative demonstrates a marked bias against Saul and favor for David.[14]

First Samuel is designed to demonstrate why Saul is an inadequate king who must be replaced, and why David, favored by YHWH, is the one who will ultimately replace him. We have already observed in the discussion of the visions of the judge Gideon (Jerubbaal) above that the narrative concerning the rape of the Levite's concubine in Judg 19–21 is a polemic against Saul. The rape takes place in the city of Gibeah in the area of Benjamin, Saul's capital city and tribal territory. When the city of Gibeah refuses to bring the murderers and rapists to justice, the Levite calls the tribes to action by cutting the concubine's body into pieces and sending a piece to each tribe, a symbolic summons that closely resembles Saul's sending pieces of his slaughtered bovines to call the tribes of Israel together to relieve the city of Jabesh-gilead in 1 Sam 11. Such an action strongly resembles the practice of concluding treaties with a sacrifice and calling on the signatories to walk between the severed pieces of the sacrificial animals, declaring that the same thing should happen to them if they fail to abide by the terms of their treaties. When the tribe of Benjamin is nearly destroyed, brides are found for the

14. For discussion of Samuel, see Marvin A. Sweeney, *Tanak: A Theological and Critical Introduction to the Jewish Bible* (Minneapolis: Fortress, 2012), 207–33.

surviving men of Benjamin by sacking the city of Jabesh-gilead and giving the surviving maidens to the Benjaminites to marry. Jabesh-gilead is not only the city delivered by Saul in 1 Sam 11; it is also the city whose men give Saul a proper burial after the Philistines hang his dead body on the walls of Beth Shean following his death by suicide in the battle against the Philistines at Mt. Gilboa in 1 Sam 31. All of these elements of the narrative of the rape of the Levite's concubine are designed to remind the reader of Saul and thereby to discredit him even before the reader turns to 1 Samuel.

Indeed, 1 Sam discredits Saul. Even when we see positive accounts of Saul's anointing in 1 Sam 9:1–10:16 and relief of Jabesh-gilead in 1 Sam 11, these narratives are framed by episodes that are critical of Saul and of kingship. The people's demand for a king in 1 Sam 8 is presented as a rejection of YHWH, the intervening narrative in 1 Sam 10:17–27 presents Saul as a coward who hides behind the baggage when he is selected as Israel's first king, and Samuel's admonitions to observe the will of YHWH in 1 Sam 12 are followed by two episodes that demonstrate how Saul fails to do so. In 1 Sam 13–14, when he goes to battle against the Philistines, Saul oversteps his bounds as king to offer sacrifices, a duty reserved for Samuel as priest. In 1 Sam 15, Saul disobeys YHWH's instructions to destroy all of the Amalekites and their property. Samuel feels threatened by Saul and is instructed to anoint David as the next king in 1 Sam 16. David proves himself a hero by killing Goliath in 1 Sam 17–18, whereas Saul is afflicted by an evil spirit whose effects on him resemble manic-depressive syndrome. Whereas Saul's son and successor Jonathan and his daughter Michal love David, Saul views David as an enemy and seeks to kill him. Saul's behavior is erratic and irrational. When Jonathan informs Saul of David's absence at a New Moon celebration, Saul hurls a spear at Jonathan, his own son and presumed successor as king. When Saul learns that the priests of Nob gave David shelter and food, one of his officers, an Edomite named Doeg, slaughters the priests of Nob with the exception of Abiathar, who escapes to join David. When David has opportunities to kill Saul in 1 Sam 24 and 26, but declines to do so and swears loyalty to Saul, Saul pursues him nevertheless. Seeking protection from Saul, David becomes a Philistine vassal in 1 Sam 27. But the Philistines leave David behind in 1 Sam 29–31 when they go to battle against Saul and defeat him at Mt. Gilboa. After seeing his sons killed, Saul takes his own life to avoid capture by the Philistines, who then hang his body on the walls of Beth Shean for all to see.

As Saul prepares for his final battle against the Philistines, 1 Sam 28 presents an episode in which Saul is once again discredited by engaging in a type of forbidden visionary experience.[15] Saul, fearful about the impending battle, visits a woman of Endor who is known to engage in divination in order to seek the counsel of the now-dead Samuel; YHWH has refused to answer Saul's inquiries by dreams, Urim, or prophets. Divination and the conjuring of ghosts of the dead were common activities in ancient Canaanite culture, but such actions were forbidden by ancient Israelite laws such as Exod 22:18, "You shall not allow a witch to live." The Hebrew term, *mekhashephah*, commonly translated as "witch," refers to a woman known for divination and conjuring spirits, such as the woman of Endor in our narrative. Indeed, the narrative takes pains to discredit Saul. He disguises himself so that his identity will not be known. The reason for the disguise becomes evident when the woman reminds him that King Saul had issued an order forbidding the conjuring of dead spirits and divination (1 Sam 28:9), apparently a reference to Exod 22:18 from the early covenant code of northern Israel. After Saul's reassurances, she brings up the ghost of the dead Samuel, and she only then realizes that her client is King Saul himself, who has now violated his own order.

There is little description of the ritual, and there is no indication of a temple site at Endor. But insofar as the woman's action is considered an illicit activity, we should hardly expect a consecrated sanctuary, especially since her actions entail contact with the dead, which would render any holy site unclean. The encounter entails a vision of the dead Samuel in which the woman of Endor describes him as a god ascending from the earth. Such a vision would be typical of ancient Near Eastern cults of the dead in which gods and dead spirits are summoned. In ancient Israelite and Canaanite thought, all of the dead descend into Sheol or the netherworld. Sheol is not an attractive place. Isaiah 14 describes the dead kings of the nations lying on their biers rotting as they wait for the descent of the recently killed king of Babylon (originally, Sargon II of Assyria) to join them.[16] The woman of Endor describes the dead Samuel as an old man wrapped in a robe, which confirms his identity to Saul. The encounter does not go well. When Samuel demands to know why Saul has summoned him, Saul tells him that he is in trouble, that YHWH does not answer him, and that he wants to know from Samuel what he should do. Samuel responds that there was no point in

---

15. For discussion of 1 Sam 28, see esp. Auld, *1 and 2 Samuel*, 320–30; Campbell, *1 Samuel*, 276–94.

16. For discussion of Isaiah 14, see Marvin A. Sweeney, *Isaiah 1–39, with an Introduction to Prophetic Literature*, FOTL 16 (Grand Rapids: Eerdmans, 1996), 218–39.

consulting him, as YHWH is doing what Samuel had earlier stated YHWH would do, i.e., taking the kingdom away from Saul because he failed to observe YHWH's instructions in 1 Sam 13–15. Samuel concludes by telling Saul that he and his sons will join him in Sheol, the Netherworld, on the next day, when he is dead and defeated by the Philistines. The narrative concludes with a scene in which the woman of Endor prepares a calf and bread for Saul and his men to eat. Although the narrative employs this motif as a sign of Saul's distress at the news that he has just heard, it may also indicate that an offering would have accompanied Saul's inquiry.

The Prophet Nathan's Capital Idea (2 Sam 7)

David's rise to power as king over all Israel is a key concern of the book of Samuel.[17] Following YHWH's rejection of Saul as king in 1 Sam 13–14 and 15, due to his failure to observe YHWH's commandments, 1 Sam 16–18 introduces David as a young shepherd boy from Beth Lehem in Judah, who is anointed in secret by Samuel. David soothes the increasingly afflicted Saul, and he kills the Philistine giant Goliath, which no one else in the Israelite army seems able to do. David goes on to accomplish heroic feats in battle against the Philistines, to win the hand of Saul's daughter Michal in marriage, and to become the best friend of Jonathan, Saul's oldest son and presumed heir. But with the ongoing collapse of Saul's personality—he appears to suffer from depression, exacerbated by his failure to defend Israel against its enemies and his own fear of David's growing reputation—David flees from Saul to save his own life and ultimately becomes a vassal of the Philistines. As a Philistine vassal, David plays his overlords and protects Judah while satisfying his Philistine masters and building his own constituency in Judah.

Following Saul's defeat and suicide in battle against the Philistines at Mt. Gilboa near the city of Beth Shean in 1 Sam 31, David is well-positioned to take power, first in Judah and then in Israel. Three of Saul's sons, including Jonathan, had died with him at Mt. Gilboa; but another son—known in 2 Samuel as Ishbosheth, Hebrew for "Man of Shame," and in 1 Chronicles as Esh-Baal, Hebrew for "Fire of Baal"—assumes kingship in Israel. Although David is Saul's son-in-law, Saul before his death had married David's wife Michal to another man. David's Philistine overlords would view his moves

---

17. See Campbell, *1 Samuel*; Campbell, *2 Samuel*, FOTL 8 (Grand Rapids: Eerdmans, 2005); Auld, *1 and 2 Samuel*.

to take control of Judah as serving their own interests to control or contain Israel. David proceeds carefully, always making clear that he is loyal to the late Saul. He moves up to Hebron to become king of his native tribe of Judah and wages war against Israel, ostensibly on behalf of his Philistine overlords, although he clearly serves his own interests in taking control of Judah and Israel. After David defeats Ishbosheth's forces at Gibeon in 2 Sam 3, the Israelite army commander Abner comes to David to make an alliance with the rising Judean king but is assassinated by David's own military commander, Joab. When two of Ishbosheth's officers from Gibeon assassinate him, David seizes the moment. He executes the two Gibeonites for raising their hands against YHWH's anointed, and the northern Israelite elders, now kingless, appeal to David to serve as their next king.

Having united Israel and Judah, David must turn to other problems. First, he defeats the Philistines decisively, something that Saul never accomplished, and makes them his vassals. He also turns over most of the surviving men of the House of Saul, with the exception of Jonathan's son, Mephibosheth, to the Gibeonites who execute them due to a grievance that is not fully explained in 2 Sam 21. David then moves to take control of Jerusalem, then inhabited by a Canaanite people known as Jebusites. David's men take the city without bloodshed, and he makes it his capital on the borders between Judah and Israel, securing his power as king of Judah and Israel and suzerain of Philistia, and thereby ensuring the safety of his people. Although the ark of the covenant had resided in Kiriath-jearim following its capture by the Philistines in battle against Israel at Aphek in 1 Sam 4–6, David brings the ark to Jerusalem in 2 Sam 6, likewise ensuring Jerusalem's role as the religious as well as the political capital of all Israel.[18] David also ensures that his own house—and not the House of Saul—will be the future dynasty, refusing to have further sexual relations with his first wife, Michal, so that she will not have a son with a greater right to the throne by virtue of his Saulide bloodline.

Second Samuel 7 presents an account of the visionary experience of the prophet Nathan, who conveys YHWH's promise of an eternal dynasty for David.[19] The narrative begins with David sitting in his palace, since YHWH had granted him safety from all of his enemies; he summons the prophet Nathan and informs him of his plan to build a house or temple for YHWH,

---

18. Campbell, *2 Samuel*, 63–70; Auld, *1 and 2 Samuel*, 405–16.

19. Campbell, *2 Samuel*, 70–79; Auld, *1 and 2 Samuel*, 416–26. See also 1 Sam 25:28 where Abigail announces that YHWH will establish a secure house for David.

to thank YHWH for all that YHWH had done. Nathan's first response is that the king should do as he proposed because YHWH is with him.

But the narrative reports that later during the same night, the word of YHWH came to Nathan with different instructions. The narrative does not elaborate on the nature of the revelation, but v. 17 identifies YHWH's communication with Nathan as a *hizayon*. Although *hizayon* is often translated as "vision," indicating a visual experience, the Aramaic root *hzy*, from which the Hebrew term is derived, refers to both visual and auditory experience, such as that experienced by Samuel in 1 Sam 3 or indicated by the use of the similar term, *hazon*, "vision," in the superscription of the book of Isaiah (Isa 1:1; cf. Isa 2:1; 13:1), which includes both visual and audial prophecy. According to v. 4, Nathan's vision occurs at night, which suggests that it comes as a dream experience while the prophet is sleeping. The installation of the ark of the covenant in Jerusalem in 2 Sam 6 suggests that the presence of the ark played a role in Nathan's visionary experience. Perhaps he was sleeping by the ark when he experienced YHWH's oracle to him, although we cannot confirm it.

Nathan's new oracle contradicts his earlier announcement to David, and it plays on the Hebrew word, *bet*, "house," as a reference both to the temple of YHWH and to the dynasty of King David. Nathan states that YHWH does not need David to build a house, or temple, since YHWH has been wandering about in a tent or tabernacle, apparently referring to the wilderness wandering period that is the setting of most of the Pentateuch as well as to YHWH's exile from Israel following its defeat by the Philistines. But YHWH promises that Israel will dwell secure in its land and that David himself will have a house, or dynasty, that would rule Israel after him eternally. YHWH makes sure to announce that David's descendants will suffer punishment when they do wrong, but YHWH emphasizes in v. 16 that David's house will be established forever. David expresses his gratitude to YHWH for such a promise, presumably while sitting before the ark, in v. 29. When 2 Sam 23:1–7 reiterates this promise, v. 5 refers to it as an "eternal covenant" with the House of David.

The implicit presence of the ark of the covenant is a key element in this narrative. The temple will ultimately become the place where the ark is housed, and the House of David is the monarchy that both builds the Jerusalem Temple during the reign of David's son Solomon and ensures its continuity for the duration of the Davidic house. But both we readers and the narrative know that neither the temple nor the House of David will continue forever. At the conclusion of the Former Prophets or Deuteronomistic

History, some four hundred years after the time of David, the temple is destroyed by the Babylonians in 2 Kgs 25, and David's last ruling descendant, King Jehoiachin ben Jehoiakim, is exiled from Jerusalem in 2 Kgs 24, eventually to be granted the right to eat at the Babylonian king's table in 2 Kgs 25. Although some see Jehoiachin's status in Babylon as a sign that YHWH has guaranteed the promise, the analogy with Jonathan's son Mephibosheth, who also eats at the king's table in 2 Sam 9, indicates that eating at the king's table signals the control of the patron king and the practical end of the dynasty.[20] There was an attempt to restore the House of David in the early Persian period by installing Zerubbabel ben Shealtiel, the grandson of Jehoiachin, as king; but the attempt failed and Zerubbabel disappears from history. Later references to the Davidic promise in 1 Kgs 2:1–4, 8:15–26, 9:1–9, and in Psalms 89, 132, etc., indicate that the promise is qualified: the sons of David shall rule forever, provided they observe YHWH's commandments. By such means the books of Kings and Psalms acknowledge that the House of David did not rule forever and provide a reason why this is so. The House of David would be acknowledged instead in alternative forms. Rabbi Hillel, one of the major Tannaitic rabbis who appears in the Mishnah, was a descendant of the House of David. Jesus, the Messiah of Christianity, was portrayed as a descendant of the House of David. And the Resh Galuta, "Head of the Exile," the civil and political leader of Judaism under Sassanian Persian and Muslim rule in late antiquity and the Middle Ages, was also understood to be descended from the House of David.

Psalms and Divine Imagery (2 Sam 22//Ps 18 and Ps 68)

Second Samuel 7 concludes with an account of David's prayer "before YHWH" in 2 Sam 7:18–29, including praise of YHWH in 2 Sam 7:18–24 and David's petition to YHWH in 2 Sam 7:25–29 to fulfill the divine promise to the House of David.[21] This passage does not present a visionary experience of YHWH, but it does point to the role that psalms can play in narrative literature. In the present instance—by recalling YHWH's praiseworthy history of faithfulness to promises and patronage to Israel, of which the newly revealed promise of a dynasty is another, and because of which he asks YHWH to uphold this promise to David's house—2 Sam 7:21–29 expresses David's

20. Sweeney, *1 and 2 Kings*, 464–65.
21. Campbell, *2 Samuel*, 70–79.

gratitude to YHWH in a manner typically expressed in the context of temple worship. Indeed, the book of Psalms constitutes what many understand to be the psalm- or hymnbook of the temple, and the appearance of psalms within biblical narratives (cf. Exod 15; Judg 5) provides readers the opportunity to see how they might have functioned in ancient Israel and Judah.

Some Psalms do present a visionary experience of YHWH, including the psalm presented in 2 Sam 22, which is nearly identical to Ps 18.[22] Second Samuel 22 appears as part of a supplementary narrative in 2 Sam 21–24 following the David narratives in 1 Sam 16–2 Sam 21. This supplement provides additional perspective on David in several subunits, including the account of David's extradition of the sons of Saul to Gibeon for execution in 2 Sam 21; David's psalm of thanksgiving to YHWH for saving him from his enemies, including Saul, in 2 Sam 22; David's last words in 2 Sam 23:1–7; an account of David's heroes in 2 Sam 23:8–39; and the account in 2 Sam 24 of YHWH's plague against Israel when David takes a census of Israel, in conjunction with his purchase of the threshing floor of Araunah, later the site of Solomon's Temple.

Thus 2 Sam 22 provides further opportunity to view David's piety and gratitude to YHWH—in addition to 2 Sam 7:18–29. The superscription to the psalm in 2 Sam 22:1 presents the psalm as one sung by David after YHWH had delivered him from the hands of his enemies and from Saul. The David narratives make it clear that David's rise to kingship and his exercise of kingship entailed considerable conflict. David's conflict with Saul grows throughout 1 Sam 16–31; Saul views him as a rival and attempts to hunt him down and force him into submission as a vassal to the House of Saul. Following Saul's death, David is engaged in civil war against northern Israel, led by Saul's son, Ishbosheth; in conquest of various nations, to free Israel from foreign control and to establish his own empire; and in suppressing a revolt led by his own son Absalom, dissatisfied with David's handling of the rape of Absalom's sister Tamar and Absalom's murder of the rapist, his own half-brother, Amnon. Although 2 Sam 22 appears in the Psalter as Ps 18 with the same superscription, 2 Sam 22 relates the psalm to the David narratives and there points not only to David's piety and loyalty to YHWH, but also to his musical skills, for which David is credited with writing most of the Psalter.

---

22. For treatment of each text, see esp. Campbell, *2 Samuel*, 188–92; Erhard Gerstenberger, *Psalms, Part I, with an Introduction to Cultic Poetry*, FOTL 14 (Grand Rapids: Eerdmans, 1988), 96–100.

The Psalms provide a means by which the people relate to YHWH through the agency of the temples of Israel and Judah, and they thereby express the people's view of their G-d. Such an occasion is to a certain degree a visionary experience. The book of Chronicles holds that the temple singers were originally viewed as prophets—Heman and Jeduthun are temple singers who are described in 1 Chr 25:1 as figures who prophesied with musical instruments. Indeed, David Petersen's study of Second Temple prophecy points to a shift in conceptualization of the temple singers from prophets to Levites in the book of Chronicles,[23] indicating that music was considered as a form of visionary experience in ancient Israel and Judah.

Second Samuel 22:2–51//Ps 18:2–51 (1–50) combines a song of thanksgiving and a song of praise in which the alleged singer, David, thanks YHWH for protecting him.[24] The psalm describes YHWH in metaphorical imagery that functions as a visual experience of G-d. It begins in vv. 2–25 with an account of the singer's relationship with YHWH, including metaphorical descriptions of YHWH as the singer's rock, fortress, shield, deliverer, etc., prior to a specific portrayal of YHWH's actions on behalf of the singer in vv. 4–25. The metaphorical portrayal continues in this section with the singer's account of deliverance in a time of distress when he called upon YHWH, in v. 4; a metaphorical portrayal of the threat as Death, Belial, and Sheol, in vv. 5–6; and a renewed call for deliverance, in v. 7. YHWH's response appears in vv. 8–21. The presentation begins in v. 8 with theophanic imagery which portrays YHWH's reaction metaphorically as an earthquake. Although we will later see in the discussion of Elijah's vision of YHWH on Mt. Horeb in 1 Kgs 19 that YHWH is not to be identified with earthquake, we must understand that this and the following metaphors portray a deity that cannot be described in finite terms.

Thus, the following verses combine the imagery of human manifestations of anger with the features of the natural world of creation. YHWH's nostrils smoke, YHWH's mouth spouts devouring fire, and YHWH's very person emits blazing coals in a superhuman portrayal of divine anger in v. 9. Such imagery also appears in the visual imagery of the temple during worship, with incense smoke filling the temple and the lights of the *menorot* blazing within the thick incense smoke. Verses 10–13 employ the imagery of YHWH riding the clouds of the heavens in response to the psalmist's plea.

---

23. David L. Petersen, *Late Israelite Prophecy: Studies in Deutero-Prophetic Literature and in Chronicles,* SBLMS 23 (Missoula, MT: Scholars Press, 1977), 55–97.

24. Campbell, *2 Samuel,* 197; cf. Gerstenberger, *Psalms, Part I,* 99–100.

Such imagery is known from ancient Ugarit where Baal is portrayed as the "Rider of the Clouds" and from ancient Assyria where Assur is portrayed riding in a winged sun-disk at the head of the Assyrian armies. Such imagery is typical of fertility deities who are known for bringing about rain and sunlight in order to ensure the growth of crops that will feed their people. YHWH is also a fertility god, and so the imagery naturally applies. Here, YHWH bends the heavens open, descends to earth, and defeats the enemies that threaten the singer. Thick cloud appears below YHWH's feet as YHWH makes the journey from heaven to earth, riding upon a cloud. YHWH mounts a cherub, a composite mythological figure typically portrayed as having a lion's body, bovine legs, eagle's wings, and a human head, which is known as a guardian of divine and human thrones as well as a means of transport for the gods (cf. Ezek 1). The imagery continues with YHWH flying upon the wings of the wind, and then it shifts to imagery of sunlight breaking through the rain clouds to ensure that the sun will nurture the crops that will grow in the aftermath of the rain. The rain clouds therefore begin to dissipate in v. 12 as the sun breaks through in v. 13 to ensure YHWH's deliverance of the psalmist, much as the sun sheds light on the eastward facing temple to ensure the creation of a new day every morning. YHWH's thunder bellows in v. 14, and YHWH's thunder and lightning bolts scatter the psalmist's enemies in v. 15. Verse 16 portrays YHWH's exposure of the sea, a typical enemy in ancient Near Eastern creation myths, and the foundations of the earth as a means to demonstrate YHWH's power as the creator of the earth with the capacity to defeat or deliver whomsoever YHWH might choose. In the present case, vv. 17–20 portray YHWH's rescue of the psalmist from his enemies as one might rescue a sailor adrift in the midst of a raging sea. Verses 21–25 portray the psalmist asserting his own righteousness to explain YHWH's deliverance; and vv. 26–49 express the psalmist's copious praise of YHWH, concluding in vv. 50–51 with the psalmist's efforts to sing in praise of YHWH.

Similar imagery appears in the portrayal of the divine presence of YHWH in Psalm 68.[25] Psalm 68 has received extensive attention since the early study of Ugaritic literature due to its portrayal of YHWH riding the clouds in Ps 68:5, 34 (4, 33), which is very similar to descriptions of Baal as "the rider of the clouds" in Ugaritic mythology.[26] Some interpreters therefore maintain that

25. Erhard S. Gerstenberger, *Psalms, Part 2, and Lamentations*, FOTL 15 (Grand Rapids: Eerdmans, 2001), 34–46.

26. See KTU 1.3 II:39–40, "dew of the heavens, the oil/fatness of earth, the showers of the Rider of the Clouds (*rkb 'rpt*)" (translation mine); for the text see Manfred Dietrich, Oswald Loretz, and Joaquín Sanmartín. *Die keilalphabetischen Texte aus Ugarit, Ras Ibn*

Psalm 68 has very deep pre-Israelite roots in Canaanite mythology;[27] but the imagery of YHWH flying through the clouds while leading an army to defeat Israel's enemies is heavily dependent on Neo-Assyrian depictions of Assur flying through the heavens on a winged sun-disk, while imagery of leading his armies with outstretched bow also has its influence.[28] Gerstenberger's claim of generic inconsistency in Ps 68, discussed below, is also for him a mark of the psalm's redactional growth.[29] Although it is possible that the psalm does indeed have roots in Canaanite culture, its present configuration points to the Neo-Assyrian period of the ninth to seventh centuries BCE when Israel and Judah encountered the Neo-Assyrian Empire and adapted its imagery for Assur to portray YHWH as the more powerful deity who would defeat Israel's enemies and free it from foreign threat. The following discussion presupposes Gerstenberger's structural analysis of Ps 68.[30]

Psalm 68 begins in v. 1 with a superscription[31] directed to the musical director that identifies it as a *mizmor shir*, a type of psalm whose characteristics remain unknown to us, and ascribes it to David. Gerstenberger is correct to note the generic disparity in the body of the psalm in vv. 2–36, but overall, it appears as a highly developed song of praise that calls upon YHWH to defeat the enemies that threaten Israel. The concern with YHWH's defeat of Israel's enemies appears in the prologue for the psalm in vv. 2–4, which portrays G-d rising against enemies to disperse them as smoke is dispersed before the wind and as wax melts before a fire. Such imagery is dependent upon the typical theophanic imagery of the Sinai revelation and the temple insofar as it depicts a combination of smoke and fire, from the clouds and the lightning in the case of Sinai and from the incense smoke and the blazing *menorot* in the case of the temple.

The hymnic introduction to the psalm in vv. 5–7 calls upon the people to sing to G-d and to YHWH's divine name, but it also refers to YHWH as

---

Hani und anderen Orten/The Cuneiform Alphabetic Texts from Ugarit, Ras Ibn Hani and Other Places, 3rd enlarged edition, AOAT 360/1 (Münster: Ugarit Verlag, 2013), 12.

27. E.g., Mitchell Dahood, *Psalms II: 51–100*, AB 17 (Garden City, NY: Doubleday, 1968), 128–52.

28. Thomas W. Mann, *Divine Presence and Guidance in Israelite Traditions: The Typology of Exaltation* (Baltimore: Johns Hopkins University Press, 1977).

29. Gerstenberger, *Psalms, Part 2*, 42–44.

30. Gerstenberger, *Psalms, Part 2*, 35–42.

31. Verse numbers in many English Bibles do not count the superscription, with the result that vv. 2–36 in Hebrew become vv. 1–35; the present discussion refers to the traditional versification of the Tanak in Hebrew.

"the one who rides upon the clouds" (Hebrew, *rokev ba'aravot*), a term that is also employed in reference to Baal in Ugaritic mythology. Insofar as Baal is a storm and fertility deity who brings rain to the earth in order to enable crops to grow, YHWH might be conceived in similar terms. But YHWH is also portrayed as a divine warrior who will use mastery over creation as a means to intervene in the human world and fight on behalf of Israel. Like most ancient Near Eastern deities and monarchs, YHWH fights on Israel's behalf to preserve justice for widows, orphans, the homeless, and the imprisoned against their more powerful enemies.

The hymnic address in vv. 8–11 portrays G-d as a warrior at the head of a divine army, much as Neo-Assyrian mythology and art portray Assur flying through the heavens in a winged sun-disk at the head of his own armies. But because YHWH is also a G-d of creation, the created world trembles before G-d as G-d releases torrents of rain to ensure food for the needy and to ensure the fertility of creation, much like Baal.

The battle hymn in vv. 12–15 retains the military imagery of women bringing news of YHWH's rout of the threatening army and the sharing of spoils. But the imagery of G-d's role as a creator deity appears in ascribing victory to Shaddai, a term meaning either "my mountain" or "my breast" that often refers to G-d's capacity to sustain. In the present case, the battle hymn uses the imagery of a snowstorm, an alternate form of rain, to portray Shaddai's defeat of the enemy kings.

The mountain hymn in vv. 16–19 portrays Mt. Bashan to Israel's north as YHWH's home and refuge, just as Ugaritic mythology associates Baal with Mt. Zaphon, i.e., "Mt. North"; but it also identifies Bashan with Mt. Sinai and depicts it as the place where YHWH's thousands of chariots gather. The congregational response in vv. 20–21 affirms this military imagery by blessing G-d for deliverance from death, again employing a motif from Ugaritic mythology in which Baal defeats Mot, the god of death. The divine oracle in vv. 22–24 likewise portrays YHWH defeating enemies from Bashan in the Trans-Jordan, so that the people of Israel might wade in the blood of their enemies much as the Ugaritic goddess, Anat, a warrior and consort of Baal, wades in the blood of her enemies with their severed hands tied about her waist.

The victory procession of vv. 25–28 looks very much like Mesopotamian Akitu or New Year processions in which the gods of subject nations accompany the Mesopotamian king to the temple so that he might be approved by the ruling deity for another year of service. Here, YHWH is the king, and tribes of Israel, including the royal tribes of Judah and Benjamin as well as the tribes of Zebulun and Naphtali, accompany YHWH to the sanctuary. The hymnic address in vv. 29–32 portrays the nations of the world, such as Egypt and Cush, bringing tribute to YHWH at the Jerusalem Temple, much as subject nations brought tribute to Assur of Assyria or to Marduk of Babylon at the Akitu festivals. The hymnic conclusion in vv. 33–36 portrays the nations singing to YHWH, here portrayed as "the one who rides in the most ancient heavens" (Hebrew, *rokev bishme sheme-qedem*), again employing imagery like that ascribed to Baal in Ugaritic myth.

In sum, Ps 68 employs a combination of creation imagery, like that ascribed to Baal in Canaanite or Ugaritic mythology, and military imagery, like that ascribed to Assur and Marduk in Assyrian and Babylonian mythology, to portray the presence and power of YHWH in the world. The performance of psalms, such as Psalm 68, therefore constitutes a form of visionary experience of YHWH in the temple.

Solomon's Vision and Revision (1 Kgs 3, 9)

King Solomon ben David of Israel is generally lauded as the wisest of Israel's kings. He is known for building up the economy of ancient Israel, thereby making himself and the nation rich. He is known for his wise sayings and Psalms; indeed, the books of Proverbs, Qoheleth, and the Wisdom of Solomon are attributed to him. He is known for his many wives and concubines, a sign of his international standing, insofar as treaties between nations were sealed by a marriage between the royal houses of the nations that entered into the treaties; nevertheless, Solomon is considered to be wise in the ways of love, and so the Song of Songs is also ascribed to him. And finally, Solomon is also known for his visionary experiences of YHWH prior to and following his building of the temple in 1 Kgs 3 and 9, in which YHWH appears to him in order to set the future course of his reign and his dynasty.

But Solomon is also condemned in the account of his reign in 1 Kgs 1–11 for various wrongdoing.[32] Although the core narrative concerning his reign in 1 Kgs 3–10 is quite laudatory, the narratives framing it in 1 Kgs 1–2 and 11 are quite critical and influence the reading of even the laudatory aspects of his reign. First Kings 1–2 reports that David advised Solomon to kill or arrest various figures. David's general Joab was executed; Shimei, a relative

---

32. For discussion of the Solomon narratives in 1 Kings 1–11, see Sweeney, *1 and 2 Kings*, 47–162.

of King Saul, was also executed; the High Priest Abiathar was expelled to Anathoth; and even Solomon's older brother, Adonijah, was put to death because he asked for the hand of David's concubine Abishag in marriage, a move understood as a claim to the throne. First Kings 11 portrays Solomon's many marriages as a source of apostasy. He had married many foreign women, beginning with the daughter of the Egyptian Pharaoh, and 1 Kgs 11 maintains that Solomon allowed them to worship their foreign gods and even built temples and other installations for their worship in Jerusalem. For this reason, maintains 1 Kgs 11, YHWH punished Solomon by dividing his kingdom into the northern kingdom of Israel and the southern kingdom of Judah after his death. First Kgs 12, however, points to Solomon's Pharaonic-like actions in imposing state slavery on the tribes of northern Israel, much like the Egyptian Pharaoh of the book of Exodus, in an effort to complete the building of the temple, the royal palaces, and the many other construction projects completed during his reign.

Solomon therefore emerges as a controversial monarch in Israel's history, insofar as he was both the builder of the temple and the cause of the division of the Davidic-Solomonic Empire in the view of the book of Kings. But fundamentally, he was the founder of the House of David. Although we often think of the first monarch of the line as the founder of a dynasty, it is always the second monarch of the line, the one to claim and secure power in the aftermath of the first monarch's death, who must be recognized as the true founder of the line. And so the visions of Solomon in 1 Kgs 3 and 9 play crucial roles in setting the agendas of Solomon's reign and the House of David as a whole.

First Kings 3:1–3 follows upon the account of Solomon's rise to kingship with some key elements in the portrayal of the new monarch.[33] First Kings 3:1 notes a sign of Solomon's high standing: his marriage to the daughter of Pharaoh, of one of the world's leading monarchs. But this marriage also points to his passion for foreign women, which in 1 Kgs 11 becomes a criticism insofar as foreign wives lead Solomon to apostasy. To underscore the point, 1 Kgs 3:2 remarks on the people's continuing practice of worshiping at the forbidden high places, although the verse also sets the stage for Solomon's building of the Jerusalem Temple by noting that they had nowhere else to go. First Kings 3:3 then follows by noting Solomon's own practice of worshiping at such high places, situating the king in continuity with his people but also setting the stage for his vision of YHWH at Gibeon.

---

33. Sweeney, *1 and 2 Kings*, 78–79.

Gibeon is the site of Solomon's first vision of YHWH in 1 Kgs 3.[34] It is a surprising choice as a place where Solomon would go to worship YHWH, particularly because Josh 9–10 identifies Gibeon as a Canaanite city that tricked Joshua and Israel into an alliance, despite their pledge to eradicate the Canaanites from the land. But Gibeon is also an important city for the house of David. Key to David's own rise to power was his victory at Gibeon over northern Israelite forces led by Abner. In the wake of their defeat, King Ishbosheth and Abner were assassinated; indeed, Ishbosheth was assassinated by two Gibeonite army officers. After David accepted the offer of kingship from the elders of Israel, 2 Sam 21 reports that he handed over Saul's male heirs to Gibeon for execution to satisfy a Gibeonite claim against Saul. Clearly, Gibeon was important to David politically, but Gibeon is also important religiously. According to Josh 9:17 Gibeon led a coalition of cities that included Chephirah, Beeroth, and Kiriath-jearim, all located to the north and west of Jerusalem. The last city of the coalition, Kiriath-jearim, was the site where the ark of the covenant had resided following its capture by the Philistines (1 Sam 4–6; 2 Sam 6). Gibeon's association with Kiriath-jearim suggests its religious significance for the House of David, since David brought the ark up from Kiriath-jearim to Jerusalem in order to make it his new religious as well as political capital.

The identification of Gibeon as the site of Solomon's first vision of YHWH thereby makes sense. Gibeon's shift of alignment from the House of Saul to the House of David demonstrates that Gibeon's support of David was key to the establishment of Davidic rule over Israel. Furthermore, Gibeon's role in relationship to Kiriath-jearim indicates that Gibeon had control over the ark of the covenant, and its release of the ark for movement to Jerusalem also enabled David to consolidate his rule in Jerusalem. Solomon offered sacrifice to YHWH at Gibeon because he had not yet built the temple to YHWH in Jerusalem.

The account of Solomon's vision in 1 Kgs 3:4–15 is clearly a laudatory narrative designed to demonstrate the basis for Solomon's wisdom. The vision takes place during a dream, and it takes place at a site recognized as a temple or high place dedicated to YHWH. YHWH appears to Solomon in the vision, notes Solomon's merits, and states the intention to grant Solomon one wish. Solomon asks for the wisdom and understanding of mind necessary to rule the great people of Israel. When YHWH hears Solomon's request, YHWH is impressed. Solomon could have asked for long life, riches,

---

34. Sweeney, *1 and 2 Kings*, 79–83.

or the lives of his enemies, but upon hearing that Solomon wants the wisdom necessary to rule his people, YHWH grants him the other three possibilities for which Solomon did not ask—long life, riches, and lives of his enemies. However, Solomon must observe YHWH's commandments in order to receive these boons.

Solomon then demonstrates his newly granted wisdom in 1 Kgs 3:16–28 by deciding a case involving two women who both claimed the same living baby as their own. When Solomon proposed to cut the baby in half so that the two women could each have a half of the infant, one accepted this decision, but the other decided to give the other woman her half in order to avoid killing the baby. Solomon therefore recognized the second woman as the true mother of the baby and decided the case in her favor.

There is no attempt to describe YHWH's presence in any tangible form other than the verbal interchange between YHWH and Solomon concerning Solomon's request for wisdom. YHWH is therefore associated with wisdom as an intangible quality that cannot be described in finite terms. Altogether, the episode presents a favorable portrayal of Solomon, although it anticipates the possibility of trouble by stipulating that Solomon will get his wishes only if he observes YHWH's expectations.

The portrayal of Solomon's first vision of YHWH at Gibeon in 1 Kgs 3:1–15 is all the more important when considered in relation to the second vision in 1 Kgs 9:1–9.[35] By the time of the second vision, Solomon has completed the building of the Jerusalem Temple and no longer needs to make use of an apparently Canaanite holy site. But the vision also has implications concerning the character of the House of David. The first vision concluded with YHWH's warning that Solomon must observe YHWH's commandments in order to ensure receipt of the favors that YHWH had granted him, wisdom, long life, riches, and the lives of his enemies. But as the narrative proceeds, it is not clear that Solomon observes YHWH's commands—certainly 1 Kgs 11 charges that he did not, as he married foreign women and built religious installations for their use. Solomon's wisdom comes into question on this point; 1 Kgs 11 portrays Solomon's taste for foreign women as the cause for the dissolution of his kingdom after his death. As for long life, Solomon rules for forty years. Although we are not aware of his age at the time that he ascends the throne, rabbinic tradition maintains that he was twelve, which would mean that he died at the relatively young age of fifty-two. As for riches, Solomon apparently overspent his wealth, and he therefore did

35. Sweeney, *1 and 2 Kings*, 137–40.

not have the funds to pay Hiram of Tyre. He was compelled to cede twenty Israelite cities instead in 1 Kgs 9, thereby giving portions of Israel back to a Canaanite king. And as for the lives of his enemies, 1 Kgs 11 reports the various enemies who broke away from Solomon's rule.

The second vision in 1 Kgs 9:1–9 therefore turns to the theme of YHWH's promise to the House of David. Once again, there is no attempt to portray the presence of YHWH. YHWH is known only through words spoken to Solomon in the context of the vision. The narrative begins with YHWH's reference to Solomon's dedication speech for the temple in 1 Kgs 8, but it then presents the Davidic covenant in conditional terms: YHWH will establish the throne of Solomon's kingdom forever, provided that he and his descendants observe YHWH's commandments. Such a statement resembles David's testament to Solomon in 1 Kgs 2:1–4 and Solomon's speech at the dedication of his temple in 1 Kgs 8:14–26, esp. vv. 25–26. This covenantal condition is a far cry from 2 Sam 7 where YHWH would punish David's descendants when they did wrong, but David's house would last forever. Instead, Solomon does not observe YHWH's commands, nor do most of his descendants—with certain exceptions, such as Asa, Hezekiah, and Josiah.

The House of David will ultimately come to an end at the conclusion of the book of Kings in 2 Kgs 25, where King Jehoiachin ben Jehoiakim is released from prison by the Babylonian king Evil Merodach, son of Nebuchadnezzar, to eat at the king's table. Jehoiachin never returns to Jerusalem, and none of his descendants ever ascends the throne in Jerusalem again. When one compares Jehoiachin's experience of eating at the king's table with that of Mephibosheth, the son of Jonathan and grandson of Saul, we see that such a status marks the end of the effective rule of the Davidic dynasty.

Elijah's Vision at Mt. Horeb (1 Kgs 19) in Context

The account of Elijah's vision of G-d in 1 Kgs 19 appears as part of the Elijah narratives in 1 Kgs 17–2 Kgs 2.[36] They are incorporated into the regnal accounts of King Ahab ben Omri of Israel (1 Kgs 16:29–22:40); King Jehoshaphat ben Asa of Judah (1 Kgs 22:41–51); and King Ahaziah ben Ahab of Israel (1 Kgs 22:51–2 Kgs 2:25). The regnal accounts of these kings are set in the Aramean Wars of the late ninth through the early eighth centuries BCE. King Ahab of Israel was an ally of King Hadadezer (Ben Hadad) of Damascus in 853 BCE when

36. Sweeney, *1 and 2 Kings*, 205–361.

the latter led a coalition of southwestern Asian nations in a bid to stop the Assyrian monarch, Shalmaneser III, from crossing the Euphrates River and expanding his empire into Aram and beyond. Shalmaneser's account of the battle of Karkar identifies Ahab as the leader of a major contingent of forces that included some two thousand chariots and ten thousand soldiers, who joined Hadadezer's twelve hundred chariots, twelve hundred cavalrymen, and twenty thousand soldiers as well as the forces of the other members of Hadadezer's coalition.[37] Although Shalmaneser claims victory in this battle, he was indeed stopped from crossing the Euphrates and made repeated unsuccessful attempts in the years that followed to do so. Although Ahab was an early ally of Hadadezer (Ben Hadad), the relationship was broken for reasons that remain unknown, although it is likely that battling the Assyrians cost Ahab so many of his expensive chariots and well-trained soldiers that he realized he could no longer continue as an ally of Damascus. The biblical narratives portray Ben Hadad's war against Ahab, which include accounts of King Ahab ben Omri's death in battle at Ramoth-gilead in 1 Kgs 22; King Ahaziah ben Ahab's death by accident in 2 Kgs 1; and King Jehoram ben Ahab's overthrow and death as well as the assassination of King Ahaziah ben Jehoram of Judah at the hands of Jehu ben Jehoshaphat ben Nimshi, an Israelite army commander who succeeded Jehoram as King of Israel in 2 Kgs 9–10.

Although some scholars question the historicity of Aram's wars against Israel during this period, the Tel Dan, Deir Alla, and Moabite inscriptions together with the Black Obelisk of Shalmaneser III all provide supporting evidence for the Arameans' advance and its consequences for the northern kingdom of Israel. The Tel Dan Inscription provides an account of an Aramean figure, perhaps Jehu, who claims to have assassinated the kings of Israel and Judah.[38] The Deir Alla Inscription presents the oracle of the Aramean diviner, Balaam bar Beor, who speaks about the defeat of Israel at the hands of the local deities.[39] Balaam's oracles in Num 22–24 appear to represent Israel's response to the Aramean claims.[40] The Moabite Stone

---

37. *ANET*, 278–79.

38. Avraham Biran and Joseph Naveh, "An Aramaic Stele Fragment from Tel Dan," *IEJ* 43 (1993): 81–98; Biran and Naveh, "The Tel Dan Inscription: A New Fragment," *IEJ* 45 (1995): 1–18.

39. For discussion of the Deir Alla Inscription, see esp. Baruch A. Levine, *Numbers 21–36*, AB 4A (New York: Doubleday, 2000), 241–75.

40. Marvin A. Sweeney, "Balaam in Intertextual Perspective," in *Tell It in Gath: Studies in the History and Archaeology of Israel; Essays in Honor of Aren Maeir on the Occasion of His Sixtieth Birthday*, ed. Itzhaq Shai et al., ÄAT 90 (Münster: Zaphon, 2018), 534–47.

presents the claim of victory over Israel, especially the tribe of Gad, by King Mesha of Moab.[41] And the Black Obelisk of Shalmaneser III portrays King Jehu of Israel bowing at the feet of the Assyrian monarch in an apparently successful effort to secure a powerful ally who would pressure Aram to cease its attacks against Israel.[42]

The Elijah narratives in 1 Kgs 17–2 Kgs 2 appear to be a self-contained unit that was combined with the Elisha narratives in 2 Kgs 2–13 and later incorporated into the regnal accounts of the Kings of Israel and Judah mentioned above. Although Elijah is better known, he does not actually succeed in overthrowing the royal House of Omri, and instead ascends to heaven in a fiery chariot in 2 Kgs 2, leaving his disciple, Elisha, to carry on and ultimately succeed in the task of overthrowing the Omride dynasty. In this light, Elijah is only a precursor to the lesser known but more bizarre, powerful, and dangerous Elisha who in fact succeeds in accomplishing the task at hand.

The Elijah narratives present the prophet as a "man of G-d" (Hebrew, *'ish ha'elohim*), who is supported by the world of creation; he drinks the waters of the Wadi Cherith, eats food brought to him by the birds, and goes about wearing a hairy mantle that apparently serves as a source of his divinely granted powers. Although Elijah is always called a prophet or a man of G-d, he seems to function as a priest as well. He builds an altar and offers sacrifice on Mt. Carmel; encounters YHWH in a cave on Mt. Carmel, analogous to the holy of holies in the temple; and anoints Elisha as his successor much as a priest would be anointed.[43] The portrayal of Elijah as a prophet and priest, who is supported by the creation ultimately brought into being by G-d, provides the backdrop for a major theme of the narratives: YHWH, G-d of Israel, is the true G-d of creation, whereas Baal, the Canaanite god of rain and fertility, is not. The occasion that precipitates such a divine encounter is the marriage of King Ahab of Israel to the Sidonian Princess Jezebel bat Ethbaal, in an apparent attempt by Ahab to secure a Phoenician ally to support him in expanding trade into the Mediterranean Sea routes and in defending himself against the Arameans. Insofar as Sidon is a Phoenician—and therefore a Canaanite—seaport, Ahab's marriage to Jezebel violates the Deuteronomic prohibition (Deut 7:1–7) against intermarrying with the

---

41. *ANET*, 320–21.

42. *ANEP*, 351, 355.

43. Marvin A. Sweeney, "Prophets and Priests in the Deuteronomistic History: Elijah and Elisha," in *Israelite Prophecy and the Deuteronomistic History: Portrait, Reality, and the Formation of a History*, ed. Mignon R. Jacobs and Raymond F. Person, AIL 14 (Atlanta: Society of Biblical Literature, 2013), 35–49.

seven Canaanite nations because they will turn Israel away from YHWH and to the worship of foreign gods.

The portrayal of YHWH's conflict with Baal begins in 1 Kgs 17 with Elijah living in the Wadi Cherith and supported by YHWH's creation, but it quickly shifts to Sarafath, a city in Phoenicia, whose god would be Baal, where we see a widow and her young son preparing to die for lack of food due to the drought that plagues the land.[44] The anti-Baal polemic should be clear: not only has the woman lost her husband, but she and her son are about to die because the drought leaves them without sufficient food. As the rain and fertility god of Phoenicia/Canaan, Baal is to blame. YHWH instructs Elijah to go to the widow. When he arrives, he demands food. After she explains her desperate circumstances, Elijah performs a miracle on behalf of YHWH by instructing her to pour out her grain and oil in order to feed him. When she does, she finds that she has an ample supply of grain and oil provided by YHWH and the prophet, Elijah. When her son falls mortally ill, Elijah saves his life, demonstrating once again YHWH's power over against Baal who is tasked with preserving life in Canaanite culture.

The confrontation between YHWH and Baal appears in 1 Kgs 18, which recounts a contest between the two deities.[45] Four hundred and fifty prophets of Baal together with four hundred prophets of Asherah are present to represent the Canaanite side on Mt. Carmel, whereas only Elijah is present to represent Israel. Mt. Carmel, located to the south of Akko and modern Haifa, is a long-standing holy site from well before Israelite times, known for its fertility and capacity to produce grapes for wine. The drought is still on, however, and the terms of the confrontation are for each party to build an altar for their respective gods, call upon them to respond by bringing lightning to light the altar and rain to provide water. The prophets of Baal proceed first by building their altar, then by dancing about it in a halting or limping dance of lamentation and gashing themselves to produce blood. The halting dance would correspond to the 3/2 dirge beat known in the book of Lamentations to represent the halting march employed at funerals when the body is carried to the grave. In this case, Canaanite mythology explains the dry summer season as the time when Baal is dead and residing in the underworld. His consort Anat must descend into the underworld to recover the dead Baal and bring him back to the world of the living where he can inaugurate the rainy season in the fall. The self-gashing and blood are

44. Sweeney, *1 and 2 Kings*, 207–16.
45. Sweeney, *1 and 2 Kings*, 216–30.

meant to represent the reversal of creation in which blood is shed and calls to the gods for action to restore creation to its natural order. Elijah mocks the Phoenician prophets throughout their failed attempts to secure a response from their divine hero.

After the failure of the prophets of Baal, Elijah assumes the role of priest and takes his turn to build an altar to YHWH. He piles wood on the altar, digs a trench around it, and pours water on top of the whole. The purpose of the trench is to mark the holy boundaries of the altar and catch the blood of animal sacrifice to ensure its proper entry into the ground. Although many modern interpreters sneer that Elijah is pouring naphtha on the altar to ignite, in fact he is making a libation offering of water that is characteristic of the temple observance of Sukkot (Booths, Tabernacles), which marks the end of the fruit harvest and the onset of the rainy season in the fall, as well as the wandering of Israel in the desert as they journeyed from Egypt to the land of Israel. When Elijah calls upon YHWH, YHWH responds with lightning, which ignites the altar and signals the onset of rain. Elijah proceeds to slaughter the prophets of Baal and Asherah before heavy rains force him to run before King Ahab's chariot to escape the rushing waters that result from the cloudburst. YHWH wins and does so by bringing what Baal is supposed to bring—rain.

But Elijah's slaughter of the prophets of Baal and Asherah has angered Queen Jezebel, the Phoenician wife of King Ahab, so that she vows to put Elijah to death. In 1 Kgs 19, Elijah flees to Mt. Horeb, also known as Mt. Sinai in the Exodus–Numbers narratives.[46] At first, he is despondent and sits beneath a broom bush where he prays that he might die because he is no better than Israel's ancestors. When he falls asleep, an angel appears—in characteristic northern Israelite fashion—to awaken him, provide him with food, and instruct him to run for forty days until he reaches Mt. Horeb, the Mountain of G-d, where he enters a cave to spend the night. The cave appears to symbolize the holy of holies of ancient Israelite temples in which only a priest might enter.

Elijah's experience of G-d in the cave at Mt. Horeb is analogous to Moses's vision of YHWH at Mt. Sinai in Exod 32–34; indeed, the Elijah narrative appears to be a source for the Moses narrative. YHWH asks Elijah, "Why are you here?" and Elijah responds that he is full of zeal for YHWH. And so Elijah's vision of YHWH proceeds with three major events. First is mighty wind that splits rocks as YHWH passes by, but YHWH is not in the wind.

46. Sweeney, *1 and 2 Kings*, 230–34.

Then a mighty earthquake shakes the mountain, but YHWH is not in the earthquake. Finally, fire engulfs the mountain, but YHWH is not in the fire. Each of these experiences functions as imagery of destruction and power, but the point is that YHWH transcends such finite expressions. It is the fourth experience that makes the point of Elijah's vision. YHWH appears in the *qol demama daqqa*, often translated as "the still, small voice." The phrase actually means "the sound of absolute silence," employing two contradictory expressions for sound (*qol*) and silence (*demama*) and modified by a third (*daqqa*), which conveys the absolute nature of the experience. The use of this phrase is designed to present YHWH as an absolute presence and power in the world of creation that cannot be delimited by any finite or earthly means. YHWH then asks Elijah once again what he is doing here, and Elijah responds again with a statement of his zeal for YHWH. YHWH then gives Elijah three instructions: (1) to anoint Hazael as King of Aram; (2) to anoint Jehu ben Nimshi as King of Israel; and (3) to anoint Elisha ben Shaphat of Abel-meholah as his successor. Anointing is normally reserved for kings and priests. Although Elijah has been identified as a prophet and man of G-d throughout the narrative, he appears to function as a priest.

Although the narrative continues beyond the vision in 1 Kgs 19, Elijah does not fully succeed in carrying out YHWH's instructions. He is able to designate Elisha as his successor, and he condemns King Ahab for the murder of Naboth and the illegal appropriation of Naboth's vineyard for the royal house of Omri (1 Kgs 21). Although Ahab and his son Ahaziah die while Elijah is still alive in the narrative, Elijah ascends to heaven in a fiery chariot in 2 Kgs 2, leaving Elisha as his successor; Elisha is the one who actually succeeds in anointing Hazael and Jehu to overthrow the dynasties of both Aram and Israel.

Elisha's Career and Visions (2 Kgs 2–13)

Elisha's visions differ from Elijah's in that they are more oriented to the notion of YHWH as warrior than they are to imagery of the temple and temple practice. Nevertheless, Elisha is portrayed as both prophet and priest.[47] As noted above, Elijah anointed Elisha as his successor at the conclusion of the account of Elijah's vision of YHWH in 1 Kgs 19. Prophets were not typically anointed, but priests were. In addition, Elisha envisions Elijah's ascent to

---

47. Sweeney, "Prophets and Priests in the Deuteronomistic History."

heaven in a fiery chariot. Although this imagery is military, it evokes the imagery of the ark of the covenant, which was located in the holy of holies of first the Shiloh and later the Jerusalem Temples and served as a throne and chariot for YHWH in visionary texts such as 2 Sam 22//Ps 18; Ps 68; and Ezek 1. The imagery of Elijah's ascent to heaven evokes the role of the temple as the gateway between heaven and earth. When Elijah leaves behind his hairy mantle, Elisha rolls it up and uses it in a manner not unlike the Levitical rod to carry out acts of power and healing on behalf of YHWH. Elisha plays music in keeping with temple practice to accompany his oracles. He also leads a band of prophets who appear to function very much like a priestly community.

The Elisha narratives appear in 2 Kgs 2–13 where they are incorporated into the regnal accounts of Ahaziah ben Ahab of Israel in 2 Kgs 1–2; Jehoram ben Ahab of Israel in 2 Kgs 3:1–8:15; Jehoram ben Jehoshaphat of Judah in 2 Kgs 8:16–24; Ahaziah ben Jehoram of Judah in 2 Kgs 8:25–11:20; Jehoash ben Ahaziah of Judah in 2 Kgs 12:1–21; Jehoahaz ben Jehu of Israel in 2 Kgs 13:1–9; and Jehoash ben Jehoahaz of Israel in 2 Kgs 13:10–25.[48] Like the Elijah narratives, the Elisha narratives appear to be self-contained, and they may predate the Elijah narratives insofar as Elijah serves only as a predecessor to Elisha, and Elisha is the one who actually brings about the overthrow of both Hazael and Jehoram of Israel. Elisha is the truly powerful man of G-d who wields twice the power of Elijah, as noted in the ascent text of 2 Kgs 2.

The vision of Elijah's ascent to heaven employs the imagery of a fiery chariot, which we noted above is linked to the imagery of the ark of the covenant.[49] The ark is generally conceived as a throne for YHWH, as it is topped by two cherubim, winged composite animal figures who typically stand as guards beside royal thrones and the gates of cities in the ancient Near Eastern world. But cherubim have wings, which gives them the capacity to fly and to transport the throne of YHWH wherever it might go. Such imagery appears in 2 Sam 22:11//Ps 18:11, where YHWH mounts a cherub to fly through the heavens; in Hab 3:8–9, where YHWH drives a chariot across the heavens to defeat enemies; and in Ps 68:5, 11, where YHWH rides the clouds to defeat enemies. The imagery is analogous to Assyrian and other Mesopotamian monarchs who frequently fly before their armies in winged sun-disks while drawing their bows to strike down their own

---

48. Sweeney, *1 and 2 Kings*, 263–361.
49. Sweeney, *1 and 2 Kings*, 271–75.

enemies. Such imagery also appears in Ezekiel 1, where Ezekiel, a Zadokite priest exiled from the Jerusalem Temple to Babylonia, experiences a vision of YHWH's throne chariot borne through the heavens by the cherubim to appoint him as a visionary prophet of YHWH. In addition to the imagery of Elijah's flight to heaven in a manner reminiscent of YHWH's own flight through the clouds, Elisha demands a double portion of Elijah's power. He obtains it in the form of Elijah's hairy mantle, which he rolls up and uses like a Levitical rod (cf. Moses during the Exodus plagues) to perform acts of power and healing on YHWH's behalf. Such acts would include purification of the waters of Jericho in 2 Kgs 2.

The second instance of visionary experience in the Elisha narratives appears in 2 Kgs 3, which relates a campaign undertaken by the unnamed King of Israel and his vassal allies, King Jehoshaphat of Judah and the king of Edom, to subdue King Mesha of Moab, who was apparently attempting to break free from Israelite control.[50] When the war party despaired of finding sufficient water while traveling through the southern region of the Dead Sea on their way to attack Moab, King Jehoshaphat called for a prophet who could tell them if YHWH had abandoned them. Elisha was present with the war party and agreed to seek the word of YHWH, but he demanded a musician before he would do so. Insofar as oracular speech typically appears in poetic form that is easily set to music, it should come as no surprise that he should make such a request. But music typically accompanied the prophetic singers of the temple who were later identified by the Chronicler as Levites.[51] For example, 1 Chr 25:1 identifies David's temple singers Asaph, Heman, and Juduthan as leaders of the families who were to "prophesy" with musical instruments. Such musical rendition in the temple enabled the envisioning of the divine, not through sight but through sound. Indeed, the Hebrew-Aramaic root, *ḥzh/ḥzy*, often translated in relation to visionary experience, includes both visual and auditory experience in its range of meaning and is best understood as a reference to perception, whether visual or audial.

The third example of visionary experience in the Elisha narratives appears in the accounts of war between Aram and Israel in 2 Kgs 6:8–7:20.[52] The narrative begins with the king of Aram taking counsel with his officers, who inform him that everything said in confidence to the king is then re-

---

50. Sweeney, *1 and 2 Kings*, 276–84.

51. Petersen, *Late Israelite Prophecy*, 55–97.

52. Sweeney, *1 and 2 Kings*, 302–14.

ported to the king of Israel by Elisha, the prophet and Man of G-d, who seems to know everything spoken in the Aramean king's private councils. The Aramean king therefore determines to capture Elisha and put a stop to his activities. He sends a force to Dothan, where Elisha is residing at the time, to take Elisha prisoner and return him to the king. But when Elisha's servant reports the approach of the Aramean soldiers, Elisha tells him to have no fear. He then calls upon YHWH to open the servant's eyes so that he can see YHWH's fiery chariots on all the hills surrounding Dothan.

As we have seen above, the fiery chariot is the means by which Elijah went up to heaven in 2 Kgs 2. Here it represents YHWH's heavenly army, which will protect Israel from the Aramean assault. The military imagery should come as no surprise. YHWH is typically identified as YHWH *tzeva'ot*, or YHWH of Hosts (often rendered as Sabaoth as in the King James Bible). The Hebrew term *tzava* ("host," plural *tzeva'ot*) refers to an army or other military formation and denotes YHWH's role as a divine warrior who fights on Israel's behalf. Indeed, the term "YHWH of Hosts" is especially related to the ark of the covenant, which resides in the holy of holies of the temple. The term appears in the phrase, "YHWH *tzeva'ot* who sits above the cherubim" (1 Sam 4:4; 2 Sam 6:2; 2 Kgs 19:15//Isa 37:16; Ps 80:1; 99:1), to indicate YHWH's role as the protector of Israel.

As the Aramean forces approach, Elisha again calls upon YHWH to strike the Arameans blind. Elisha then leads the blind Aramean army into the city of Samaria, the capital of northern Israel, where they become prisoners. When the king of Israel proposes to kill them, Elisha responds that they should feed them and make peace with them. As a result, Aramean raids against Israel came to an end according to 2 Kgs 6:23, but they resume once again in the following unit. Second Kings 6:24–7:20 presents an account of the Aramean siege of Samaria, which becomes so severe that people resort to cannibalism due to the lack of food. When several lepers decide to defect to the Arameans because of the lack of food, they find the Aramean camp abandoned. The reason given in 2 Kgs 7:6–7 is that YHWH caused the Aramean army to hear the sound of horses and chariots, an apparent reference to YHWH's heavenly army, which prompted the Arameans to flee. When the Israelites emerged from Samaria to pursue, they found abandoned Aramean equipment and supplies all along the road, indicating that the Arameans had fled the land of Israel altogether due to YHWH's intervention.

Although Elisha is a prophet, at many points his role as a visionary Man of G-d appears to be bound up with priestly identity and temple associations.

Preliminary Conclusions from the Former Prophets

Altogether, the preceding discussion points to a conclusion much like that of the above analysis of texts from the Pentateuch. The Former Prophets and Psalms employ a combination of imagery and motifs from creation, the temples of ancient Israel and Judah, and military imagery from the Assyrian Empire and others in their attempts to depict the presence of YHWH in the world. None ascribes a tangible and unique form to YHWH in keeping with Israelite and Judean expectations that YHWH is not to be portrayed in the imagery of idolatry. Nevertheless, ancient authors employed the use of metaphor and simile to portray the divine presence to their ancient Israelite and Judean audiences to enable them to grasp something of YHWH's character, qualities, and power.

Chapter 4

THE LATTER PROPHETS

The Prophets and Their Books

The Latter Prophets—Isaiah, Jeremiah, Ezekiel, and the Book of the Twelve—are the primary books of the Hebrew Bible identified with visionary and mystical experience concerning the presence of YHWH in the world. Although each of the books currently appears as a literary composition that has been assembled and edited by anonymous editors or redactors, each of the books presents the words and activities of one or more prophetic figures.[1] All of the prophetic books are fundamentally concerned with interpreting their respective contemporary historical situations, in order to understand what happened in the past and is happening in the present as well as to project what might happen in the future. And all are also concerned with understanding the catastrophe of the Babylonian Exile and the prospects for restoration once the exile will be concluded. Most of these prophets are named, but some are anonymous figures, such as the anonymous prophet of the Babylonian Exile in Isa 40–55 known to critical scholarship as Second Isaiah, the anonymous figures of Isa 56–66 known collectively as Third Isaiah, and various other figures whose works appear in the named prophetic works of the Hebrew Bible. Others are figures whose historical identities are uncertain, such as Joel, Obadiah, Malachi, and others, but whose books present visionary and mystical experiences of YHWH like those of prophets who are better known. Discussion of the Latter Prophets demonstrates that they, too, employ imagery drawn from the Jerusalem, Beth El, or other

1. For introductions to the prophetic literature, see Marvin A. Sweeney, *The Prophetic Literature*, IBT (Nashville: Abingdon, 2005); David L. Petersen, *The Prophetic Literature: An Introduction* (Louisville: Westminster John Knox, 2002).

temples with which YHWH is associated; royal ideology, particularly that of the Davidic dynasty; the natural features of the land of Israel and other elements from creation; and other imagery known to them to present their understandings of divine presence and action in the world. Discussion proceeds according to the canonical order of the Tanak.

Isaiah

The book of Isaiah is identified at the outset of the book in its superscription in Isa 1:1 as "The Vision of Isaiah ben Amoz, which he saw concerning Judah and Jerusalem in the days of Uzziah, Jotham, Ahaz, and Hezekiah, Kings of Judah."[2] This identification is reinforced in two subsequent superscriptions in the book: Isa 2:1, "the word which Isaiah ben Amoz saw concerning Judah and Jerusalem," and Isa 13:1, "the pronouncement which Isaiah ben Amoz saw concerning Babylon." Two major issues emerge concerning these superscriptions.

The first is the identification of the book of Isaiah as a visionary book. As we have seen, the Hebrew noun, *hazon*, "vision," and the Hebrew-Aramaic verb, *hzh/hzy*, "to see, envision," are frequently translated in relation to visionary experience, but both terms actually have a much broader range of meaning. Insofar as the terms are used in the superscriptions of Isaiah, readers must recognize that they introduce and characterize not only visually oriented material, such as Isa 6 in which Isaiah envisions the presence of YHWH, but also oracular material throughout the book, such as Isa 1:2–29, and narrative material, such as Isa 7:1–25. Indeed, the Hebrew-Aramaic root, *hzh/hzy*, from which *hazon* and other terms associated with visionary experience are derived, actually refers to both visually oriented material and audially oriented material.

---

2. For commentaries on Isaiah, see esp. Marvin A. Sweeney, *Isaiah 1–39, with an Introduction to Prophetic Literature*, FOTL 16 (Grand Rapids: Eerdmans, 1996); Sweeney, *Isaiah 40–66*, FOTL (Grand Rapids: Eerdmans, 2016); Joseph Blenkinsopp, *Isaiah 1–39*, AB 19 (New York: Doubleday, 2000); Blenkinsopp, *Isaiah 40–55*, AB 19A (New York: Doubleday, 2002); Blenkinsopp, *Isaiah 56–66*, AB 19B (New York: Doubleday, 2003); Hans Wildberger, *Isaiah 1–12*, ContCom (Minneapolis: Fortress, 1991); Wildberger, *Isaiah 13–27*, ContCom (Minneapolis: Fortress, 1997); Wildberger, *Isaiah 28–39*, ContCom (Minneapolis: Fortress, 2002); Shalom Paul, *Isaiah 40–66* (Grand Rapids: Eerdmans, 2012). For studies of the prophetic vision reports, see also Elizabeth R. Hayes and Lena-Sofia Tiemeyer, eds., *I Lifted My Eyes and Saw: Reading Dream and Vision Reports in the Hebrew Bible*, LHBOTS 584 (London: Bloomsbury T&T Clark, 2014).

Second, the superscriptions in Isa 1:1; 2:1; and 13:1 identify the visionary book with the prophet Isaiah ben Amoz, who lived during the latter portion of the eighth century BCE during the reigns of Kings Uzziah (783–742 BCE), Jotham (742–735 BCE), Ahaz (735–715 BCE), and Hezekiah (715–687 BCE). Nevertheless, interpreters since the writing of the Babylonian Talmud have long recognized that Isaiah is not the final author of the book (b. B. Bat. 14b–15a) and that later authors appear in Isa 40–55, Isa 56–66, and elsewhere in the book. Evidence for such a claim appears in the references to King Cyrus of Persia (545–539 BCE) in Isa 44:28 and 45:1, who is identified as YHWH's messiah and temple builder. Because Cyrus lived during the second half of the sixth century BCE, the material in Isa 40–55, which anticipates the downfall of Babylonia and the return of the exiled people of Jerusalem and Judah, appears to date from the last years of the Babylonian Exile in 545–539 BCE when King Cyrus of Persia conquered Babylon and enabled conquered peoples, including Judah, to return to their homelands and restore their respective national lives (under Persian control) as well as to rebuild the temples dedicated to their gods. Isaiah 56–66, which appears to be the work of a number of anonymous authors, anticipates or recognizes the restoration of the Jerusalem Temple and therefore dates to the late sixth and early fifth centuries BCE. Other texts derive from other historical periods, such as Isa 11, which appears to have been written in relation to the reign of King Josiah of Judah. Although the book of Isaiah was written by various prophets working in different historical periods, it has been edited or redacted to form a single book which presents itself as the vision of Isaiah ben Amoz from the late eighth through the mid-fifth centuries. Isaiah ben Amoz is a prophet deeply steeped in the royal tradition of eternal Davidic kingship based in Jerusalem and secured by YHWH's everlasting promise to Jerusalem and the House of David. But the book of Isaiah recognizes that there will be no Davidic monarchy following the return of exiled Jews to rebuild Jerusalem at the end of the exile. It instead declares that Cyrus is YHWH's messiah and temple builder and that the entire nation Israel is the heir of the eternal Davidic promise (Isa 55).

An overview of the book of Isaiah points to its major concerns. The book argues that Jerusalem's experience of invasion, exile, and restoration from the late eighth through the late fifth/early fourth centuries BCE was the result of YHWH's deliberate plans to demonstrate divine sovereignty over Jerusalem/Judah and all creation from Zion.

Diachronic or historically based readings of Isaiah divides the book into three parts, Isa 1–39, 40–55, and 56–66; but a synchronic or literary reading of the book's literary structure points to a two-part division, Isa 1–33 and 34–66.[3] The first portion of the book in Isa 1–33 focuses on YHWH's plans to reveal worldwide sovereignty at Zion, and the second portion in Isa 34–66 focuses on the realization of YHWH's plans for revealing worldwide sovereignty at Zion. The following diagram presents the formal synchronic structure of Isaiah:

The Vision of Isaiah Ben Amoz: Prophetic Exhortation to Jerusalem/Judah to Adhere to YHWH   Isaiah 1–66

I. Concerning YHWH's plans to reveal worldwide
   sovereignty at Zion   1:1–33:24
     A. Prologue to the book of Isaiah: introductory parenesis
         concerning YHWH's intentions to purify Jerusalem   1:1–31
     B. Prophetic instruction concerning YHWH's projected
         plans to reveal worldwide sovereignty at Zion:
         announcement of the Day of YHWH   2:1–33:24
        1. Prophetic announcement concerning the
            preparation of Zion for its role as the center
            for YHWH's worldwide sovereignty   2:1–4:6
        2. Prophetic instruction concerning the significance
            of Assyrian judgment against Jacob/Israel:
            restoration of Davidic rule   5:1–12:6
        3. Prophetic announcement concerning the
            preparation of the nations for YHWH's
            worldwide sovereignty   13:1–27:13
           a. announcements concerning the nations   13:1–23:18
           b. restoration for Zion/Israel at the center
              of the nations   24:1–27:13
        4. Prophetic instruction concerning YHWH's plans
            for Jerusalem: announcement of a royal savior   28:1–33:24
II. Concerning the realization of YHWH's plans for revealing
   worldwide sovereignty at Zion   34:1–66:24
     A. Prophetic instruction concerning the realization of
         YHWH's sovereignty at Zion   34:1–54:17
        1. Prophetic instruction concerning YHWH's
            power to return redeemed exiles to Zion   34:1–35:10

---

3. Sweeney, *Isaiah 1–39*, 31–62; Sweeney, *Isaiah 40–66*, 1–40.

The foundational vision of the book appears in Isa 6:1–13, which presents the prophet's first-person account of YHWH enthroned in the Jerusalem Temple. Isaiah envisions YHWH calling for the services of a prophet who will attempt to render the people of Israel and Judah blind, deaf, and uncomprehending of divine purpose, so that that they will not repent and thereby prevent the punishment to be visited upon the nation, with the result that YHWH will be recognized throughout the world as the true G-d of all creation and the nations of the world, beginning with Israel and Judah. Interpreters have debated the significance of this vision account insofar as some see it as the prophet's call narrative, even though it does not appear at the beginning of the book, whereas others see it as the prophet's later reflection concerning the failure of his prophetic efforts to persuade the people to repent and follow YHWH's guidance.

The vision account opens with Isaiah's first-person statement that he saw YHWH seated upon a high and lofty throne in the year that King Uzziah died.

This statement would place the vision account in 742 BCE at the conclusion of a long period of peace and stability during the reigns of Kings Jeroboam ben Joash of Israel (786–746 BCE) and Uzziah (Azariah) ben Amaziah of Judah (783–742 BCE). Both Israel and Judah would be rocked by a period of political instability in which Israel would suffer a series of royal assassinations as pro-Aramean figures sought to gain control of the Israelite throne, to break Israel's longstanding alliance with Assyria, and to establish a renewed alliance with Aram, from which Israel's ancestors came. The result would be a disaster. When Israel allied with Aram under King Pekah, it attempted to force Judah into its anti-Assyrian coalition. When King Jotham ben Uzziah refused the Israelite overtures, Israel and Aram invaded Judah in 735–732 BCE in an attempt to overthrow the house of David and replace it with a monarchy that would join the Syro-Ephraimitic coalition against Assyria. When King Ahaz ben Jotham appealed to Assyria for assistance following the early death of his father Jotham, King Tiglath-pileser III of Assyria invaded Aram and Israel, destroying Damascus and stripping Israel of most of its outlying lands in the Transjordan, the Galilee, and the coastal plain, leaving Israel with only the hill country of Ephraim and Manasseh. When Israel attempted to revolt in 724–722 BCE, the Assyrians invaded again during the reigns of Shalmaneser V and Sargon II, destroying the capital city of Samaria and exiling major elements of northern Israel's population to other parts of the Assyrian Empire. King Ahaz of Judah may have expected better treatment for his loyalty to Assyria, but the Assyrians demanded even more tribute, prompting Ahaz's son, Hezekiah, to revolt in 705 BCE together with his Babylonian ally, Merodach-baladan. Although the biblical accounts of the Assyrian invasion under Sennacherib claim victory for Hezekiah, Assyrian records make it clear that Sennacherib's forces overran Judah, besieged Jerusalem, and forced Hezekiah's acquiescence to Assyria's terms even as Hezekiah was allowed to retain his throne while Sennacherib invaded Babylonia.

Isaiah's description of YHWH seated on a high and lofty throne presupposes the construction of the Jerusalem Temple as a structure built on the pattern of a royal palace, with an entry porch (Hebrew, *ulam*), a reception hall (Hebrew, *heikhal*), and the holy of holies (Hebrew, *devir*) where the ark of the covenant was placed to serve as YHWH's throne, guarded by the cherubim, composite human-animal angelic figures who typically appeared as the guards of royal thrones and the gates of cities in the ancient Near Eastern world. Indeed, Isaiah's vantage point appears to be from a position by the two columns that stood by the eastern door of the temple structure where the king typically stood during temple services. Such a position allowed him to see into the interior of the temple. He would have stood at this location in his role as a royal counselor.

Isaiah describes the edges of YHWH's robes filling the temple and spilling out of the temple's door as it is opened at the commencement of the temple's liturgical service. The imagery of YHWH's garment apparently derives from the thick incense smoke that would fill the heikhal and the ulam of the temple interior as the ten incense altars in the heikhal were lit; their smoke would simulate the cloud and smoke that typically appear in theophanic texts depicting YHWH's divine presence (e.g., Exod 19). The use of incense smoke provides an ideal metaphor for YHWH's presence; its sweet smell and its amorphous character represent a presence that cannot be defined in tangible form.

Isaiah describes the seraphim flying about YHWH as they sing the liturgy of the temple, "Holy, holy, holy is YHWH *tzeva'ot*! The whole earth is full of his glory!" Such a liturgy would have been sung by the temple priesthood. The depiction of seraphim, a term that refers to angelic figures with six wings, two of which are used to fly, two of which are used to cover their faces before the divine presence, and two of which are used to cover their nakedness, is telling. The Hebrew term *seraph* is derived from the verb root for burning, and the use of the term appears to presuppose the role of the ten temple menorahs, or lampstands, each with seven burning lights, that would burn and flicker in the midst of the smoke emitted from the ten incense altars. The burning and flickering of these seven lamps would suggest the presence of the seraphim flying about YHWH during the course of the vision and thereby contribute to the metaphorical imagery of the divine presence.

The sound of the doorposts rumbling is to be expected from the construction of the temple doors. Two large tree trunks would be used as the basis for the two doors and their planking. The doorposts would be set into the carved bowlike settings of the stone lintels of the temple and lubricated with olive oil to facilitate their movement. The heavy doors would naturally rumble as they were opened at dawn at the outset of the morning Shaharit service—as the sun rose in the east over the Transjordanian lands to fill the interior of the temple with light.

When Isaiah laments his impure state upon seeing this vision of YHWH *tzeva'ot*, one of the seraphim picks up a coal from the altar, perhaps an incense altar, and touches it to Isaiah's lips. Such an act is a typical mouth purification ritual employed by Mesopotamian *baru*-priests and other prophetic figures when they symbolically purify their mouths to prepare to speak on behalf of their respective deities. At this point, Isaiah can hear YHWH asking for someone to send to speak on YHWH's behalf to the people. When Isaiah volunteers for the role, YHWH tells him that his task is to render the people blind, deaf, and uncomprehending, so as to ensure that they will not repent and avert the judgment that YHWH will visit upon them. YHWH makes clear that such judgment will reveal YHWH to be the true G-d of creation and all humanity to the world at large, an agenda that serves as the foundational purpose for the final form of the book of Isaiah. When Isaiah asks how long the judgment will last, YHWH responds that it will last until the land and cities of the land are laid waste without inhabitant, conditions realized as a result of the Assyrian invasions of the land. The vision employs the imagery of a burning tree trunk to make it clear that the destruction will last until only one tenth of the people are left. Then the tree metaphor calls for the burned trunk to take root; the tree will grow once again to produce a restored nation in the aftermath of the punishment and suffering that the people will endure.

Such a scenario of intentional judgment on the people of Israel and Judah, like that imposed on Egypt and Pharaoh in the Exodus narratives, raises moral questions concerning YHWH's actions.[4] The passage presents Isaiah's commission as a prophet of YHWH, but it attempts to interpret YHWH's purposes in bringing judgment against the nation at the hands of the Assyrian Empire. Ultimately, the text presents an example of a theodicy that attempts to explain or justify YHWH's punishment of the nation as an act that will lead ultimately to the restoration of Israel and Judah and the recognition of YHWH throughout the world. It may thereby be recognized as a teleological understanding of divine purpose in which the ultimate goals of YHWH's actions justify the suffering of multiple generations of Israelites and Judeans. Nevertheless, such suffering presents problems when viewed from an ontological moral standpoint, insofar as YHWH's intention to prevent the repentance of the people is an act that is not moral in and of itself. Overall, the intention underlying the text is clearly concerned with explaining the suffering of Israel and Judah as an act of divine righteousness that will ultimately have a positive and justifiable outcome.

Other visionary elements and oracular portrayals throughout the book also employ imagery well-known to an ancient Israelite and Judean audience as metaphors for the portrayal of YHWH and YHWH's actions in the world. The prophetic announcement concerning the preparation of Zion for its

---

4. Marvin A. Sweeney, *Reading the Hebrew Bible after the Shoah: Engaging Holocaust Theology* (Minneapolis: Fortress, 2008), 84–103.

role as the center for YHWH's worldwide sovereignty in Isa 2–4 begins by portraying the nations streaming to Zion to learn YHWH's Torah and inaugurate an era of world peace; this portrayal employs the imagery of pilgrims ascending the Temple Mount in Jerusalem at times of worship in Isa 2:2–4. It concludes in Isa 4:2–6 with a portrayal of a canopy of cloud, fire, and smoke over the city of Jerusalem that is based upon the imagery of smoke and fire rising from the temple altar as the sacred offerings are presented and burned.

The imagery employed in the prophetic instruction concerning the significance of Assyrian judgment against Jacob/Israel in Isa 5–12 likewise employs well-known imagery to depict YHWH's use of the Assyrian Empire to inflict judgment on Israel and Judah, as well as to anticipate subsequent restoration. The vineyard parable in Isa 5:1–7 employs the metaphor of a failed vineyard to illustrate YHWH's frustration with the nation and YHWH's plans to bring judgment against it. The imagery of an enemy army marching against Israel and Judah in Isa 5:25–30 was all too well known during the Assyrian invasions of the land in the late eighth century BCE. The portrayal of the land filling with water as the Assyrian monarch spreads his wings or garments over it is actually a depiction of rape in Isa 8. Likewise, the portrayal of the people walking in darkness until they see the great light of the righteous Davidic monarch in Isa 9:1–6 draws upon the imagery of the morning sunlight entering the opened doors of the temple at sunrise to reveal the ark of the covenant, which functions as the throne of YHWH, in the devir of the Jerusalem Temple. YHWH's outstretched hand against Israel in Isa 9:7–10:4 and the rod used to beat first Israel and then the Assyrian monarch in Isa 10:5–34 draws upon the imagery of Moses's outstretched hand and rod in the Exodus narratives. But the shift to the portrayal of the rod used to beat the Assyrian king draws upon Assyrian mythology, which portrays the Assyrian king as an ideal tree growing from heaven to earth. Just as Israelite farmers beat their olive trees with rods to harvest their fruit, so YHWH beats the Assyrian king with a rod to diminish his branches and power. Once the punishment is complete, the tree imagery shifts to the ideal Davidic monarch in Isa 11, who will emerge as a shoot from the stump of Jesse to become the true ideal monarch; he will defeat Israel's enemies and inaugurate righteous Davidic kingship in the land.

Other well-known images in the first part of the book (Isa 1–33) include the portrayal of animals who know their masters better than Israel knows its G-d in Isa 1, the downfall of the nations who threaten Israel and Judah in Isa 13–23, and the feasting that takes place in the Jerusalem Temple during the sacred holidays in Isa 24–27.

The second part of the book in Isa 34–66 likewise employs well-known imagery to illustrate YHWH's plans to reveal worldwide sovereignty at Zion. Isaiah 35:1–10 picks up the imagery of the highway by which exiled and refugee Jews will return home in Isa 11:15–16 and 27:12–13. That imagery appears once again in Isa 40:1–11 as YHWH prepares to lead the exiled Jews through the wilderness as they return to Jerusalem. Indeed, the imagery of the highway through the wilderness permeates Isa 40–48, which culminates in Isa 48:2–22 with a call to the exiles to depart from Babylon and return to Jerusalem. Their return follows the model of the patriarch Jacob, who exiled himself from the land of Israel, first to find a bride in Aram and later to escape famine in Egypt. Although he returned the first time, it would be left to his descendants to return through the wilderness following the Exodus from Egypt. Throughout Isa 40:12–48:22, the prophet makes a series of contentions to reinforce the view that Jacob/ Israel will return from Babylon to Jerusalem through the wilderness in a second exodus: YHWH is master of creation in Isa 40:12–31; YHWH is master of human events in Isa 41:1–42:13; YHWH is redeemer of Israel in Isa 42:14–44:23; and YHWH will use Cyrus for the restoration of Zion in Isa 44:24–48:22. But as the prophet's argument shifts in Isa 49:1–54:17 to the contention that YHWH is restoring Zion, the imagery likewise shifts: YHWH is restoring the marriage relationship with the bride, Bat Zion, Daughter Zion. This contention builds upon a traditional motif of YHWH's marriage to the bride, Israel or Jerusalem, in Hos 1–3; Jer 2; Zeph 3:14–20; Ezek 16; and now Isa 49–54. Just as Jacob went into exile to find his brides, so YHWH allowed Israel to go into exile so that YHWH could metaphorically find the bride Bat Zion once again.

Finally, Isa 55 exhorts the people to adhere to YHWH as part of its contention that Israel is the recipient of the eternal covenant of David. It thereby introduces the material in Isa 56–66 that envisions the restored nation. A key element appears in Isa 66, which portrays YHWH's announcement that heaven is YHWH's throne and the earth is YHWH's footstool. Such imagery presupposes that of the ark of the covenant in the devir of the Jerusalem Temple, which serves as YHWH's throne. The ark would never be restored to the devir of the Second Temple—no one knows what happened to it—but Isa 66 establishes the relationship between heaven and earth that would characterize the role of the Second Temple as the gateway between heaven and earth. In doing so, it resolves the conundrum concerning Davidic kingship in the book of Isaiah by asserting that ultimately YHWH will be recognized as the true King of Israel.

Jeremiah

The superscription in Jer 1:1–3 identifies the book as "the words of Jeremiah ben Hilkiah from the priests who were in Anathoth in the land of Benjamin, unto whom was the word of YHWH in the days of Josiah ben Amon, King of Judah, in the thirteenth year of his reign, and it was in the days of Jehoiakim ben Josiah, King of Judah, until the completion of the eleventh year of Zedekiah ben Josiah, King of Judah, until the exile of Jerusalem in the fifth month." Insofar as the superscription employs the designation "words of Jeremiah," the book is a chronicle of the prophet's life and career.[5] Although we often think of the Hebrew word, *davar*, as a spoken word, it also refers to "thing" or "matter" and thereby refers to the events of Jeremiah's life as well as his oracular speeches. The book is presented as a chronicle, but it includes a great deal of visionary material, such as the vision reports in Jeremiah 1, 24, and possibly 30–31, as well as a great deal of oracular material that attempts to discern divine intent. Following the initial reference to the words of Jeremiah, the structure of the book is defined by the instances of the prophetic word formula, e.g., "the word of YHWH which came to Jeremiah, saying . . ." The arrangement of the book suggests a chronology from Jeremiah's call to prophesy as a youth and culminates in his exile to Egypt following the destruction of Jerusalem and the failed attempt to revolt against Babylon.

Readers must also recognize that Jeremiah is identified at the outset not as a prophet, but as a priest from Anathoth. He is later identified as a prophet in the book, but his priestly identity is crucial because it entails his experience of the presence of YHWH. Jeremiah's residence in Anathoth indicates that he is a priest of the line of Itamar, Eli, and Abiathar. Abiathar was one of David's high priests who was expelled to Anathoth by King Solomon on the advice of David when he came to the throne. Such a background left Jeremiah with a skeptical view concerning the capacity of the Jerusalem Temple to protect the people, particularly when he considered it in relation to his ancestral sanctuary at Shiloh, which was apparently destroyed early in

---

5. For commentaries on Jeremiah, see esp. Leslie C. Allen, *Jeremiah: A Commentary*, OTL (Louisville: Westminster John Knox, 2008); Georg Fischer, *Jeremia 1–25*, HThKAT (Freiburg am Breisgau: Herder, 2005); Fischer, *Jeremia 26–52*, HThKAT (Freiburg am Breisgau: Herder, 2005); Jack R. Lundbom, *Jeremiah 1–20*, AB 21A (New York: Doubleday, 1999); Lundbom, *Jeremiah 21–36*, AB 21B (New York: Doubleday, 2004); Lundbom, *Jeremiah 37–52*, AB 21C (New York: Doubleday, 2004); Louis Stulman, *Jeremiah*, ACOT (Nashville: Abingdon, 2005).

Israel's history during its conflict with the Philistines. Jeremiah would have been one of the countryside priests of the land of Israel who was invited by King Josiah of Judah to take up residence in the city of Jerusalem in order to serve in the Jerusalem Temple. Although priests from throughout the country were invited, Jeremiah appears to be one of the few who actually accepted the invitation.

As a priest of the line of Ithamar, Jeremiah is firmly grounded in the tradition of Mosaic Torah as the foundational covenant between the people of Israel/Judah and YHWH. He supports the Davidic monarchy, but he insists that the Davidic monarchy must act righteously in accordance with YHWH's Torah. This position puts him at odds with Isaiah, who was grounded in the tradition of the royal house of David. Jeremiah accepts the house of David, but it is clear to him that the Davidic king may suffer judgment if he does not abide by YHWH's Torah.

The book of Jeremiah appears in two very different but related forms in the Hebrew Masoretic Text (MTJeremiah) and the Greek Septuagint text of the book (LXXJeremiah). Of the four Hebrew Jeremiah manuscripts found at Qumran, three support the text and structure of MTJeremiah, but one supports the text, structure, and the apparent Hebrew *Vorlage* of LXXJeremiah. LXXJeremiah is approximately one-eighth shorter than the masoretic form of the book. LXXJeremiah presents a different arrangement for the book, insofar as it places the oracles concerning the nations, Jer 46–51 in MTJeremiah, in the midst of Jer 25, which calls for judgment against the nations that oppress Israel and Judah.

The two forms of the book of Jeremiah present two very different theological outlooks.[6] MTJeremiah is especially focused on the fate and future of the city of Jerusalem, whereas LXXJeremiah begins with concern for the fate of northern Israel as a paradigm for what will happen to Jerusalem and Judah. MTJeremiah envisions the downfall of the nations that oppress Israel/Judah as an act that will take place in the distant future following the restoration of Israel and Judah, but LXXJeremiah sees the downfall of the oppressive nations as a more immediate act that will precede the restoration of Israel and Judah. LXXJeremiah envisions righteous Davidic kingship in LXXJeremiah 23:1–8, but MTJeremiah, like Isaiah, maintains that the Davidic promise will be transferred to the city of Jeru-

---

6. Marvin A. Sweeney, "Differing Perspective in the LXX and MT Versions of Jeremiah 1–10," in *Reading Prophetic Books: Form, Intertextuality, and Reception in Prophetic and Post-Biblical Literature*, FAT 89 (Tübingen: Mohr Siebeck, 2014), 135–53.

salem and its Levitical priesthood. Most interpreters view LXXJeremiah as the older form of the book. The two forms of the book indicate debate concerning the future of Israel, Judah, and Jerusalem during the Second Temple period.

The macrostructure of MTJeremiah appears as follows:

The Words of Jeremiah Ben Hilkiah Concerning
the Restoration of Jerusalem and the Downfall of Babylon   1–52

I. Oracles concerning Israel and Judah	1–6
A. Superscription	1:1–3
B. Commissioning of the prophet	1:4–10
C. Signs concerning YHWH's purpose	1:11–19
D. Oracles calling for Israel and Judah to return to YHWH	2–6
II. Account concerning Jeremiah's temple sermon	7–10
III. Oracles concerning rejection of YHWH's covenant	11–13
IV. Oracles concerning drought and marriage	14–17
A. Drought	14–15
B. Marriage	16–17
V. Oracles concerning shattered pot/judgment against Judah	18–20
VI. Oracles concerning Davidic kingship	21–24
VII. Narratives concerning Jeremiah's warnings to submit to Babylon	25–29
VIII. Oracles concerning restoration of Israel and Judah	30–31
IX. Narrative concerning field at Anathoth	32–33
X. Narrative concerning YHWH's decision to give Jerusalem to Nebuchadnezzar	34:1–7
XI. Narrative concerning reneging on year of release	34:8–22
XII. Narrative concerning fall of Jerusalem	35–39
XIII. Narrative concerning Jeremiah's removal to Egypt	40–43
XIV. Narrative concerning Jeremiah's oracles in Egypt	44
XV. Narrative concerning word to Baruch	45
XVI. Oracle concerning Egypt	46:1–12
XVII. Oracle concerning Babylonian conquest of Egypt	46:13–28
XVIII. Oracle concerning small nations	47–49
XIX. Oracle concerning Babylon	50:1–51:58
XX. Narrative concerning Jeremiah's instructions about Babylon	51:59–64
XXI. Appendix concerning fall of Jerusalem	52

The formal macrostructure structure of LXXJeremiah appears as follows:

The foundational vision accounts of the book, in which YHWH commissions Jeremiah to serve as a prophet, appear in Jer 1:4–19, introduced by the formulas, "and the word of YHWH came unto me, saying . . ." in vv. 4 and 11 (13). Neither vision account attempts to describe YHWH in any detail, but both make heavy use of priestly imagery.

The first in Jer 1:4–10 begins with YHWH's statement to Jeremiah commissioning him as a prophet, "Before I formed you in the belly, I knew you, and before you came out from the womb, I consecrated you as a prophet to the nations." The Hebrew term *hiqdish*, "to consecrate," is a term normally applied to priests. Such language implicitly recognizes Jeremiah's priestly status. It also helps to explain how YHWH "knew" Jeremiah before he was born, since priestly status is tied to being born into the two lines descended from the sons of Aaron: either the line of Ithamar, Eli, and Abiathar, which is the ancestry of Jeremiah, or the line of Eleazar, Phineas, and Zadok, which produces the Zadokite priesthood of the Jerusalem Temple.

Jeremiah's adherence to YHWH's Torah is especially associated with Moses. Consequently, his objections to his prophetic commission establish a parallel with his exemplar. Moses objected to YHWH's commission due to his claim that he was a man of impure lips during the burning bush episode in Exod 3; YHWH therefore appointed Aaron to serve as Moses's spokesman. Jeremiah objects to his commission as a prophet because he is a youth (Hebrew, *na'ar*, which normally refers to an adolescent). It is striking that YHWH responds to Jeremiah's objection as one might speak to a back-talking adolescent by insisting that the young man will go and speak what YHWH tells him to do. The portrayal of YHWH's hand touching Jeremiah's mouth is reminiscent of the seraph touching a coal to Isaiah's mouth in Isa 6. Each action apparently serves as a mouth purification ritual, much like that employed for ancient Mesopotamian *baru*-priests. The commission that Jeremiah will be a prophet to the nations presupposes the role of ancient Israelite and Judean temples—and particularly the Jerusalem Temple in which Jeremiah will serve—as the holy center of creation and the nations that populate it.

The second set of visions in the vision account of Jer 1:11–19 underscores the priestly character of Jeremiah's commission by employing priestly imagery. The first vision in vv. 11–12 employs a standard visionary formula in which the prophet is asked, "What do you see?" The vision is incomprehensible in English because it depends upon a pun in Hebrew, indicating the revelatory power and function of oral speech. Jeremiah responds that he sees "an almond branch" (Hebrew, *maqqal shaqed*). YHWH's response, "You have seen well, for I am watching (Hebrew, *shoqed*) my word to accomplish it," presents a word play on the Hebrew noun, *shaqed*, "almond," with the Hebrew verb, *shoqed*, "to watch." Some interpreters suppose the pun is based on the early blossoming of almond trees, but this phenomenon only partially explains the use of the pun. Almond trees do blossom early, but readers must recall that the temple and its priesthood stand at the holy center of creation and play an important role in ensuring the smooth functioning of that creation, insofar as they promote fertility and the growth of new life, both plant and animal, in creation. The priestly rod thereby symbolizes that role insofar as it appears topped by a blossoming flower. When Aaron and the tribe of Levi are selected as YHWH's priests in Num 17–18, Aaron's rod blossoms to signify YHWH's choice. Archeologists have discovered a ceramic blossoming flower from pre-Israelite Jerusalem that was clearly designed for use as a cap on top of a rod. This artifact is controversial because it is inscribed in paleo-Hebrew with the phrase, "Holy to YHWH," but the inscription has been identified as a forgery insofar as it penetrates the patina that forms over the surfaces of authentic archeological artifacts. Despite the forged inscription, the object itself is authentic, and it points to the form of the typical priestly rod even in pre-Israelite Jerusalem.

The second visionary element in Jer 1:13–19 likewise employs priestly imagery. When YHWH asks Jeremiah a second time, "What do you see?" Jeremiah replies that he sees a boiling pot with its face pouring out from the north. YHWH then explains the vision by stating the intention to summon the peoples from the nations of the north to bring disaster to the inhabitants of the land of Judah and to render judgment against it for having forsaken YHWH and rendering worship to foreign gods. Such a vision clearly has in mind the Babylonian invasions of Judah in the late seventh and early sixth centuries BCE during the career of the prophet. Babylonia must advance against Judah from the north. Although Babylon is situated to the east of Jerusalem, the Arabian Desert prevents the movement of a large army from Babylon to the west to attack Judah. Instead, Babylonian armies must travel north and west through the Tigris-Euphrates River Plain, also known as the Fertile Crescent, in order to find sufficient water and food to support the army. But interpreters frequently overlook the significance of the boiling pot. One of the duties of the temple priesthood is to cook the meat offered in the temple as a festival meal for the priesthood and the people who come to worship. Boiling the meat in a large pot is the preferred way to cook the meat. As a priest of the temple, Jeremiah would have been tasked with boiling the meat in the temple pots, serving it from the pots, and tipping the pot over to clean it as the meat is emptied out. The image of boiling meat poured from the north would lend itself easily to the portrayal of an army invading from the north and making corpses of the people of Judah.

Jeremiah's vision accounts in Jer 1 clearly reflect his role and self-understanding as a priest. His priestly identity remains central to his understanding of divine purpose throughout his lifetime. In the oracles calling for Israel and Judah to return to YHWH in Jer 2–6, Jeremiah calls for adherence to divine Torah as the foundation for the covenant relationship between

YHWH and the people. Such a view is in keeping with his understanding of King Josiah's program of religious reform and national restoration which was based in large measure on the discovery of a Torah scroll, which many identify with an early form of Deuteronomy, during temple renovations early in Josiah's reign (2 Kgs 22–23). Because he is a priest of the line of Itamar, Eli, and Abiathar, Jeremiah is not so adamant concerning the role of the Jerusalem Temple. His ancestor, Abiathar, was expelled from the temple to Anathoth, while Zadok was retained to serve as the ancestor of the Zadokite priestly line in Jerusalem. In his famous temple sermon in Jer 7–10, Jeremiah questions the role of the Jerusalem Temple in securing the safety of the people, a position that his senior colleague Isaiah would have upheld; he argues instead that the people must adhere to divine Torah. Indeed, teaching the people the difference between what is holy and profane and what is clean and unclean is the basic task of the priest (Lev 10:10–11), and Jeremiah holds true to this role. He cites the Ten Commandments in his sermon in Jer 7:9–11 and he then cites the fate of his ancestral sanctuary at Shiloh in Jer 7:12–15 to make his point. The security of the people lies in observance of divine Torah, especially as understood in Deuteronomy, rather than in YHWH's promises of an eternal Davidic dynasty or an eternal temple in Jerusalem.

Jeremiah's priestly identity appears throughout the segments concerning the rejection of YHWH's covenant in Jer 11–13, drought and marriage in Jer 14–17, the shattered pot and judgment against Judah in Jer 18–20, and Davidic kingship in Jer 21–24. Throughout these oracle blocks, readers will encounter the so-called laments or complaints of Jeremiah in Jer 11:18–12:6, 15:10–21, 17:14–18, 18:18–23, and 20:7–18. These passages are written in the form of psalms of lament in which the psalmist presents a lament or complaint to G-d in the context of temple worship. Many modern scholars contend that these texts are secondary to the oracles of the prophet Jeremiah; accordingly, priestly or psalmic speech forms would not enter into prophetic discourse, because the former presuppose the social setting of temple worship rather than prophecy. But Jeremiah is a priest, and his visionary accounts employ priestly imagery to convey their meanings. In this case, the psalmic lament form functions as another means for Jeremiah to make his point. But this time, the visionary experience comes not in a visual understanding of the divine presence and intent. Instead, oral poetic and musical forms serve as the means to express a so-called visionary experience in a manner not unlike that of oracular prophecy. Indeed, one of the roles of the temple priesthood was to sing and to play music for the temple liturgy. The performance of musical forms such as the psalms was a priestly duty (1 Chr

25). As a temple priest, Jeremiah would be expected to perform music and to sing the temple liturgy, including psalmic forms.

Within the laments, Jeremiah talks to YHWH, presents complaints to YHWH, and even questions YHWH in his attempts to discern divine purpose. In Jer 11:18–12:6 he complains of his conflicts with his opponents, apparently the Zadokite priests of the Jerusalem Temple who may have seen him as an intruder and have attempted to exclude him from temple duties as unqualified for holy service. In Jer 15:10–21 he laments the day of his birth because of all the persecution he suffers from his opponents. In Jer 17:14–18, he asks YHWH to heal him and save him from the persecution that he endures and to let his tormentors suffer defeat from YHWH. In Jer 18:18–23, he reminds YHWH of the plots that his enemies have devised against him, reminds YHWH how he has served as YHWH has demanded (see Jer 1), and asks YHWH once again to defeat his opponents. Finally, in Jer 20:7–10, the reader sees the culmination of Jeremiah's complaints in which he characterizes YHWH as a rapist who has seduced Jeremiah, seized him, and overpowered him metaphorically to impregnate him with an unwanted pregnancy. In this case, Jeremiah is unwillingly filled with the word of YHWH, which he cannot hold within himself, just as a new mother cannot hold in the baby that she is about to bear. Once again, Jeremiah laments the day of his birth, wishing instead that he had never been born to endure the suffering to which YHWH's commission as a prophet has subjected him. Jeremiah remains an outsider throughout his combined prophetic and priestly career and suffers throughout, as he challenges the worldviews of his colleagues in the temple who believe that the temple ensures the safety of the nation. But King Josiah's early death at the hands of Pharaoh Necho in 609 BCE and the subjugation of Judah, first to Egypt and later to Babylonia, would have convinced Jeremiah that no such protection for Judah was forthcoming from YHWH unless the people returned to YHWH's Torah.

Jeremiah 21–24 returns to oracular speech to present the prophet's understanding of YHWH's intentions.[7] He critiques King Jehoiakim ben Josiah for building his own magnificent palace rather than serving as a righteous monarch like his father who was concerned with the Torah of YHWH and the welfare of his people. In the end, he condemns Jehoiakim and his son, Jehoiachin, who will suffer the consequences of his father's actions when

---

7. For discussion of Jeremiah's views on Davidic kingship, see esp. Marvin A. Sweeney, "The Reconceptualization of the Davidic Covenant in the Books of Jeremiah," in *Reading Prophetic Books*, 167–81.

he is exiled to Babylonia following the failure of his father's revolt against Babylon. Jeremiah's oracle concerning the future righteous Davidic monarch in Jer 23:1–8 may have had Zedekiah, the brother of Jehoiakim and the successor of both Jehoiakim and Jehoiachin, in mind as an example of a righteous Davidic monarch; but Zedekiah's inadequacy becomes apparent later in the book when he is unable to stop Judah from revolting against Babylon and from ultimately suffering the consequences for doing so (see Jer 34–45). The subsequent diatribe concerning false prophecy in Jer 23:9–40 may well reflect the prophet's disillusionment with Zedekiah when he failed to perform his role as a righteous monarch and sealed the fate of his nation by allowing the ill-advised revolt against Babylon to proceed. Insofar as no Davidic monarch ever claimed the throne in Jerusalem in the aftermath of the destruction of Jerusalem—even until today—it is striking that the two forms of the book differ in their expectations concerning the future of the monarchy. LXXJeremiah includes only the oracle concerning the expectation of a future righteous Davidic monarch in Jer 23:1–8; apparently it expects the resumption of righteous Davidic rule. MTJeremiah, however, includes an oracle in Jer 33:14–26—which is absent in LXXJeremiah—that reassigns the eternal Davidic promise to the city of Jerusalem and to the Levitical priests that serve in the temple. Such a move is not unlike that of Isa 55, which reassigns the eternal Davidic promise to the people and not to a future Davidic king. Whereas LXXJeremiah anticipates a future Davidic king, MTJeremiah and the final form of the book of Isaiah do not.

Jeremiah's vision account in Jer 24, the final component of the oracles concerning Davidic kingship, makes his position clear: Zedekiah is not the righteous monarch anticipated in Jer 23:1–8 and will suffer punishment. The text appears in typical visionary account form with a vision that presupposes Jeremiah's status and activities as a priest. YHWH shows Jeremiah two baskets of fruit before the temple following the exile of King Jehoiachin ben Jehoiakim to Babylonia after the failure of Jehoiakim's revolt in 597 BCE. YHWH asks Jeremiah, "What do you see, Jeremiah?" and Jeremiah correctly answers, "Figs," including good ones and bad ones that cannot be eaten. YHWH then explains the meaning of the vision to Jeremiah. The good figs represent those people who will suffer exile to Babylonia. YHWH intends to build them and plant them and thereby to use them to rebuild the nation in the aftermath of the coming judgment in the form of the Babylonian Exile. The bad figs represent those left in the land, including King Zedekiah whom the Babylonians had apparently installed as a puppet to keep peace in the land. Instead, the result is unmitigated disaster when Zedekiah is unable to control his kingdom, allowing the rebellious elements to revolt against Babylonian rule once again in 588 BCE. This failure of leadership on Zedekiah's part would lead to renewed Babylonian invasion, the destruction of Jerusalem, the destruction of the temple, and the exile of even more surviving Judeans to Babylonia.

Jeremiah envisions the return of exiles from Babylonia and the restoration and reunification of the nation at some point in the future. According to his vision in Jer 25 and the account of his letter to the exiles in Jer 29, he anticipates that restoration will take place in seventy years, a figure that corresponds to Assyrian and Babylonian reckoning of a long time. But it also corresponds roughly to the time between the destruction of Solomon's Temple in 587 BCE and the rebuilding of the Second Temple in 520–515 BCE under Persian rule. In considering the two versions of Jeremiah, each has its own viewpoint as to when that might happen. LXXJeremiah places the oracles concerning the nations that have oppressed Jerusalem and Judah, culminating in Babylon, in the midst of Jer 25—following projections that the nations will drink the cup of the wrath of YHWH. Such a view suggests that Babylon and the nations will suffer judgment prior to the vision of restoration in Jer 30–33 (corresponding to Jer 40–43 in the LXX form of the book). MTJeremiah places the oracles concerning the punishment of the nations in Jer 46–51; such placement follows the vision of restoration in Jer 30–33 and suggests that the masoretic form of the book anticipates the punishment of the nations after the restoration of Israel and Judah to Jerusalem. The masoretic form of the book apparently equates Babylon with the Persian Empire—since the Persians employed Babylon as their administrative capital for the western portions of their empire, including Jerusalem and Judah.

The vision of restoration appears in Jer 30–33. The vision per se appears in Jer 30–31, which calls for the restoration of both Israel and Judah to Jerusalem. The visionary character of these chapters is indicated in Jer 31:26, which indicates that the prophet awakens from sleep and a dream in which he apparently saw the vision. The vision anticipates an eternal covenant at the end in which Jerusalem will be secured forever as YHWH enacts a new covenant. Although some maintain that Jeremiah's new covenant anticipates Christianity (indeed, the term New Testament/Covenant is derived from this term), the new covenant is based on adherence to YHWH's Torah and simply refers to the restoration of Israel, Judah, and Jerusalem as a nation who will observe YHWH's Torah as envisioned by Jeremiah, the prophet and priest. Redaction-critical work indicates that the oracle may originally have been written to envision northern Israel's return to Jerusalem, in keeping with the goals of Josiah's reform, but following Josiah's death, the oracle was expanded to envision the restoration of all Israel and Judah to Jerusalem.[8] Jeremiah points to a sealed and unsealed book, which signals the realization of the vision. Thus, Jer 33 anticipates the recognition that Jerusalem and the Levitical priesthood will become heirs to the Davidic promise as indicated above in keeping with Jeremiah's combined prophetic and priestly identity.

Ezekiel

The book of Ezekiel lacks a formal superscription and generic identification like those of Isaiah and Jeremiah, but instead presents a chronological narrative introduction in Ezek 1:1–3 that provides much information typically found in a formal superscription.[9] The introduction appears initially in v. 1 in first-person narrative form. The speaker, apparently Ezekiel, maintains that the heavens were opened and that he saw "visions of G-d" while in exile by the Chebar Canal during the thirtieth year on the fifth day of the fourth month. Verses 2–3 then follow with third-person narrative from a redactor of unknown identity who maintains that the hand of YHWH was upon the priest Ezekiel ben Buzi by the Chebar Canal in the land of the Chaldeans, i.e., Babylonia, on the fifth day of the month during the fifth year of the exile of King Jehoiachin.

The third-person narrative material in vv. 2–3 is apparently an attempt to explain the enigmatic first-person statement in v. 1. Verses 2–3 therefore identify the speaker as the priest Ezekiel ben Buzi. The fifth year of the exile of King Jehoiachin would be 592 BCE, from the fact that King Jehoiachin ben Jehoiakim of Judah was exiled to Babylonia following the failed attempt by his father, King Jehoiakim ben Josiah, to revolt against King Nebuchadnezzar of Babylon in 598–597 BCE. A large number of prominent Judeans, including various officials, were exiled together with Jehoiachin, and Ezekiel

8. Marvin A. Sweeney, "Jeremiah 30–31 and King Josiah's Program of National Restoration and Religious Reform," in *Form and Intertextuality in Prophetic and Apocalyptic Literature*, FAT 45 (Tübingen: Mohr Siebeck, 2005), 109–22.

9. For commentaries on Ezekiel, see esp. Marvin A. Sweeney, *Reading Ezekiel: A Literary and Theological Commentary*, ROT (Macon, GA: Smyth & Helwys, 2013); Paul Joyce, *Ezekiel: A Commentary* (London: T&T Clark, 2008); Steven Tuell, *Ezekiel*, NIBCOT (Peabody, MA: Hendrickson, 2009); Margaret S. Odell, *Ezekiel*, SHBC (Macon, GA: Smyth & Helwys, 2005); Katheryn Pfisterer Darr, "Ezekiel," in *The New Interpreter's Bible*, ed. Leander E. Keck et al. (Nashville: Abingdon, 2001), 6:1073–1607.

ben Buzi must have been among them due to his status as a Zadokite priest of the Jerusalem Temple. The significance of the thirtieth year in v. 1 is never made clear, but interpreters note that the thirtieth year is the year in which the Kohathite priests would be ordained for service in the Tent of Meeting (Num 4:3; cf. Num 8:23–25, which specifies the years of service of the other families of the Levites beginning with the twenty-fifth year and continuing to the fiftieth year). A priest would then serve for twenty years before retiring at the age of fifty. If Ezekiel was thirty years old in the fifth year of Jehoiachin's exile, he would have been born in 622 BCE, the eighteenth year of the reign of King Josiah of Judah, which is when he commenced his program of religious reform and national restoration (2 Kgs 22:3; 2 Chr 34:8). Having been exiled from Jerusalem to a foreign land at the age of twenty-five prior to his ordination for service in the temple, Ezekiel could no longer be ordained for service as a priest. But the details of Ezekiel's inaugural vision in Ezek 1–3 indicate that he is commissioned as a visionary prophet of YHWH in Babylonian exile at a time when he would otherwise be ordained for priestly service. Readers may note the correlation between Ezekiel's vision of G-d informed by the imagery of the ark of the covenant and the visionary experience of Samuel in 1 Sam 3. Readers may also note the seven-day duration of his commission as a visionary prophet, which corresponds to the time dedicated to the ordination of priests for temple service in Exod 29:1–46, esp. v. 35, and Lev 8:1–36, esp. v. 33 (cf. Num 8:5–26, which takes up the ordination of the Levites).

The chronological statement in Ezek 1:1–3 includes an example of the prophetic word formula in v. 2. Ezekiel 1:1–3 then functions as the first of a series of chronological statements concerning the appearance of the word of YHWH to Ezekiel that define the structure of the book from the fifth year of the reign of Jehoiachin to the twenty-fifth year of Jehoiachin's reign in Ezek 40:1. Such a chronology would then range from Ezekiel's thirtieth year, when he would have been ordained as a priest, until his fiftieth year, when he would have retired from active priestly service. Only one chronological statement in Ezek 29:17 breaks this sequence insofar as it refers to the siege of Tyre in the twenty-seventh year (of Jehoiachin's exile, i.e., 570 BCE), but interpreters note that, although the siege of Tyre began in 585 BCE, it was not concluded until 573 BCE. It appears that the text was modified to the later date to account for the conclusion of Nebuchadnezzar's siege of Tyre. The chronological structure of the book of Ezekiel therefore correlates the years of his service as a visionary prophet of YHWH with the years that he would otherwise have served as a priest in the Jerusalem Temple. It focuses on the significance of the destruction of Jerusalem, which it understands to be a purge of the Jerusalem Temple, and its ultimate restoration. The structure of the book appears as follows:

Ezekiel's Visions concerning the Purge of Jerusalem

The book of Ezekiel, especially Ezekiel's vision of YHWH in Ezek 1–3, has long been recognized as the foundation of the Jewish mystical tradition, in that it gives the most detailed and intentional attempt to describe the presence of YHWH in the entire Bible. Although it is an attempt to describe the presence of YHWH, Ezekiel is trained to serve as a priest, and one of his primary concerns is to avoid portraying YHWH in any tangible form. Consequently, readers note the use of intangible imagery, such as smoke or cloud, light, and water, to describe the divine presence; the prodigious use of simile, using "like," "like the image of," "like the appearance of," etc.; phrases that when properly read convey movement physically impossible for finite beings, such as "they went in the direction of all of their faces"; and the constant interchange of masculine and feminine linguistic forms to describe the figures in the vision account. In this manner, the vision account in Ezek 1–3 employs the finite forms and perspectives of biblical Hebrew in an attempt to describe the intangible presence of YHWH without portraying YHWH in finite forms or language.

The vision report begins in Ezek 1:4 with Ezekiel's description—while standing by the waters of the Chebar Canal—of an apparition of stormy wind coming toward him from the north in the form of a great cloud with flashing and glowing flame all about it that looked to him like something called *hashmal* in the midst of the fire. All the intangible forms are here: water, wind, cloud, and fire. The term *hashmal* is not well understood. In modern Hebrew, it means "electricity," but in ancient Hebrew it appears to refer to a precious yellow sapphire-like stone that has shapes that can be seen within as well as its outer color.

Verses 5–14 convey the basic imagery of the apparition. In its center appear four creatures, which appear to be composite figures or cherubim—indeed, they are identified as such later in Ezek 10—which bear the throne chariot of YHWH through the heavens. Composite figures with bodies of animals, wings of eagles, heads of human beings, etc., typically guard the thrones of kings and the gates of major cities in the iconography of the ancient Near East. In Israelite tradition, cherubim guard the ark of the covenant, which serves as YHWH's throne, with two atop the ark and two built into the holy of holies where the ark resides. Here, they are described as having four faces, which correspond to the four horns or directions of the Jerusalem Temple altar, signifying its place in the holy center of creation, or to the four directions of the world. Each face represents a different quality of G-d: the face of the bull represents the strength or power of YHWH; the face of the lion, symbol of the royal tribe of Judah, symbolizes the sovereignty of G-d in creation; the face of the eagle represents the freedom of YHWH to be anywhere and everywhere in creation; and the face of the human symbolizes the intelligence of G-d to discern good from evil. The gleaming bronze appearance of the creatures apparently represents the bronze used to overlay the ark and its features after Pharaoh Shishak took the gold from the Jerusalem Temple. Other features describe the composite nature of the creatures: each has four wings with which they fly and which spread out to encircle the divine presence, each has a single leg with a calf's foot, each sparkles like burnished bronze, each has human hands under their wings, and each moves in the direction of all of their faces, meaning that they move in all four directions at once. The creatures were dashing back and forth or in and out like lightning.

Ezekiel 1:15–26 turns to the other features of the vision. It begins with the wheels, which are a feature of the ark of the covenant, variously explained as the rings used to carry the ark with poles or the wheels of the cart that carries the ark. One wheel appears by each creature. They gleam like *tarshish*, a term used to describe a precious stone like beryl. Each wheel is described as a wheel within a wheel; though sometimes described as a hub, this explanation does not account for the fact that the wheels—like the creatures—move in all directions at once. The wheel-within-the-wheel imagery is intended to convey the ability of the wheels to travel in all directions at once, which is impossible in a finite world but not so for the divine. The wheels are portrayed as having eyes on their rims and over their features. Such an image presupposes the imagery of the burnished bronze ark of the covenant reflecting the seventy lights of the menorot in the heikhal of the Jerusalem Temple. Spread out above the heads of the four creatures is a firmament like ice, apparently a reference to the *kapporet* or mercy seat of the ark, which symbolizes the division between heaven and earth and serves as the foundation for YHWH's throne. As the creatures bear the throne through the heavens, one pair of wings is used for flight and the other is used to cover their bodies before G-d. The sound of their movement is described as the sound of great waters, as the sound of Shaddai (one of the names of G-d), and as the commotion of a great army. When the throne stops, their wings drop. Atop the apparition is the appearance of a throne with the appearance of a human seated upon it, recalling that in the priestly stratum of the Pentateuch human beings are created in the image of G-d (Gen 1:26–27).

Ezekiel 1:27–3:27 then describes Ezekiel's commission to speak as a visionary prophet of YHWH. He attempts to describe the presence of G-d, but employs metaphorical statements concerning the appearance of a human being from the waist up, engulfed in fire, to ensure the absence of tangible form. Ezekiel falls on his face before YHWH, as one would do in the temple during worship, while YHWH commissions him to speak on YHWH's behalf to Israel. YHWH gives him a Torah scroll to swallow and thereby internalize, much as YHWH did with Jeremiah (cf. Jer 15:16). Ezekiel is returned to his home in Tel Aviv, a Babylonian site identified as Tel Abubi, "Hill of the Flood," by the Chebar Canal, the Babylonian Nar Kabari, that ran through the city of Nippur north of Babylon. Ezekiel 4–7 then follows with a series of symbolic actions, oracles against the mountains of Israel, and oracles of doom to illustrate the coming purge of Jerusalem.

Ezekiel's second major vision in Ezek 8–11 focuses on YHWH's purge of the city of Jerusalem. It takes place in the sixth year, sixth month, and fifth day of Jehoiachin's exile and presents Ezekiel speaking in first-person narrative. The narrative begins with a portrayal of Ezekiel sitting in his house with the elders of Judah seated before him. The text provides no clue concerning the occasion, but it is plausible that the elders came to seek an oracle of YHWH from Ezekiel. They are not disappointed. Ezekiel states that the hand of his Lord, YHWH, fell upon him. He describes the figure from the loins upwards and downwards having an appearance like fire, and he embellishes this imagery with a statement that it was brilliant (Hebrew, *zohar*) like amber (Hebrew, *hashmal*). Such a description recalls the flaming appearance of YHWH in Ezek 1 as well as the brilliant appearance of Mesopotamian gods. The figure lifts Ezekiel by the hair of his head and carries him to Jerusalem where he places the prophet by the north-facing Penimuth Gate of the Jerusalem Temple complex. Insofar as the temple complex formed the northern segment of the city, the figure placed Ezekiel before the northern gate of the city that led into the temple complex. He describes an infuriating image that causes fury (Hebrew, *semel haqqin'a hammaqneh*). The image appears to be a stele erected by Nebuchadnezzar to mark his conquest of Jerusalem in 598 BCE to end Jehoiakim's revolt.

A vision of the divine presence of YHWH like that seen in Ezek 1 appears and commands Ezekiel to dig a hole in the wall by the gate. The reason for such a command is to emulate the means by which the Babylonians would have entered the city. Unlike the east and west walls of the city which come together to form the southern tip of the city wall, the north side of the city is not built on solid rock. Rather, the north wall of the city, which defends the northern side of the temple precincts, is built on land. The Babylonian army typically employed sappers to undermine the walls of a city under siege, and the northern wall of Jerusalem would have been vulnerable to the sappers, who would dig under or through a wall to undermine it and allow Babylonian soldiers to enter the city. Insofar as the temple is located here, the presence of foreign soldiers would desecrate the temple site.

Upon entering the temple compound, Ezekiel sees the abominations that now further defile the temple. In each case, they appear to be activities that would otherwise be normal for the temple, but in the context of Ezekiel's vision in which the temple has already been defiled, they provide further evidence of the temple's desecration. First, he sees the abominable images on the wall of the temple, but these appear to be deformed visionary renditions of the usual Garden of Eden imagery that is carved into the temple's interior walls.

Second, he sees the seventy elders of Israel led by Jaazaniah ben Shaphan with incense burners in hand stating that YHWH does not see them because YHWH has abandoned the now-desecrated temple. Indeed, the exile of Ezekiel and other Zadokite priests would have contributed to the temple's desecration. Burning incense in the temple is hardly forbidden, but offering foreign or unconsecrated incense is strictly forbidden (cf. Lev

10; Num 15–16). The role of Jaazaniah ben Shaphan is noteworthy in that he is the son of Josiah's officer who found the Torah scroll while refurbishing the temple. The Shaphan family were among the major supporters of the priest and prophet Jeremiah, but as a Zadokite priest Ezekiel would have seen Jeremiah and his supporters as figures who lacked the qualifications to serve in YHWH's holy temple.

Third, he sees women weeping for Tammuz. Tammuz is the Babylonian fertility god who dies and goes to Sheol during the dry season before his consort, Ishtar, responds to the mourning of women and brings him up to the world of the living, thereby inaugurating the rainy season in the fall. Mourning rituals are well known in Judaism during the late summer prior to Rosh Hashanah, the New Year, which ushers in Yom Kippur and Sukkot and the onset of the fall rains. It seems likely that some sort of mourning ritual was practiced in Judah at this time and associated with Tammuz in Ezekiel's vision.

Fourth, he sees twenty-five men worshiping the sun, but this is nothing more than a visionary presentation of the temple morning prayer service held at dawn to begin the day.

Altogether, these visionary images indicate that the temple has become defiled and is need of purging. In Ezek 9 YHWH calls for six men, each armed with a weapon, to enter the city accompanied by a seventh man dressed in white linen with a writing case. White linen is the garment of the priests, and this figure appears to be modeled on a temple priest who would record the offerings of the people. He commands the six men to go through the city and mark the men who moan and groan over the city's abominations. He then commands the men to kill the old men, the adolescent boys and girls, the women, and the children, leaving only the marked men alive. Scholars have puzzled over this move, but it appears to be an idealization of the slaughter of the people in the city in which only the men of majority age are spared while everyone else is killed. Insofar as men are the primary temple worshipers, they are responsible for the welfare of everyone else. The portrayal of the killing here demonstrates that they have failed and that their prayers are useless in the face of the desecrated temple and city.

Once the killing is complete, Ezek 10 portrays the divine presence as the throne chariot seen in Ezek 1, except that the beasts are now identified as cherubim. YHWH orders the man in white linen to take a coal from within the wheelwork of the chariot and to use the coal to ignite the city as it is to be purged in fire much like a sacrificial offering. In Ezek 11, YHWH discloses to Ezekiel the plan to take the surviving men outside the city and the land of Israel to form the basis of an exilic community. Although many of these men will be killed as they depart the city and land, YHWH will serve as "a small sanctuary" among them. Some identify this comment as a reference to an early form of synagogue that would serve as a place of study and worship among the exiles, enabling them to cohere as a community and ultimately to form the foundation of identity that would enable them to return to rebuild a purified Jerusalem and temple at the end of the exile.

At the end of Ezek 11, the throne chariot of YHWH departs from the site indicating YHWH's absence from Jerusalem and the site of the temple. Subsequent material throughout Ezek 12–39 provides a detailed chronology of Ezekiel's career and oracles concerning the significance of the destruction of Jerusalem and anticipation of its restoration.

Ezekiel's third and final vision of the restored temple, Israel, and creation at large appears in Ezek 40–48. Although many modern interpreters maintain that this vision is a secondary addition to the text, such a view overlooks the facts that it presents the culminating element of the book of Ezekiel; appears following Ezek 37 and 38–39 which focus on the purification of the land from the bodies of the dead, a necessary precondition for rebuilding the temple; presupposes Ezekiel's dual identity as a Zadokite priest and visionary prophet; and is dated to the twenty-fifth year of the exile of Jehoiachin when Ezekiel would have turned fifty, thereby concluding the twenty-year chronology of the book that correlates to Ezekiel's years of would-be priestly service. Ezekiel's vision of the restored temple corresponds to no known temple in ancient Israel or Judah—certainly not Solomon's Temple nor the Second Temple—and it is much larger than the Temple Mount in Jerusalem could accommodate. Ezekiel's temple is therefore identified as the future temple in rabbinic tradition, first in the rabbinic historical work, Seder Olam Rabbah, and later by Rashi and Radaq in their commentaries on Ezek 40–48. It therefore functions as the Third Temple in Jewish views of the future restoration of the Land of Israel. It also appears to form the basis for the ideal temple in the Temple Scroll of Qumran as well as eschatological visions of the heavenly temple in the New Testament Book of Revelation.

The narrative sequence is actually very simple. The vision is dated to the twenty-fifth year of the exile, which would correspond to Ezekiel's fiftieth year, the year in which a Zadokite priest would normally retire. It takes place at Rosh Hashanah, the Jewish New Year, which precedes the seven-day festival of Sukkot when new priests would likely be ordained and perhaps old ones retired (cf. Exod 29; Lev 8; Num 8). Again, the hand of YHWH was upon Ezekiel and brought him to the site of the restored temple in visions of G-d; he is set upon a very high mountain with a city to the south, the same configuration of the Jerusalem Temple mount and the city of David extending to the south of the temple. Ezekiel's guide is an angelic human-like figure whose body shines like copper. He holds a linen and a measuring rod to give Ezekiel the dimensions of the new temple to report to Israel. Ezekiel 40–42 focuses on the structure of the temple and its courts. Ezekiel 43–46 begins with a notice that the throne chariot of YHWH, earlier seen in Ezek 1–3 and 8–11, returns to the site of the restored temple. These chapters focus on the halakot or laws that are to be observed in the new temple. Notably, the Davidic king, here identified as the Prince in Ezekiel's characteristic fashion (see Ezek 37:15–28, esp. v. 24, which refers to him as king), leads the people in presenting offerings at the new temple. Some of the halakot differ from those of the Pentateuch, which accentuates the revelatory role of Ezekiel's vision. Finally, Ezek 47–48 describes the water that surges forth from the new temple to purify the Dead Sea, thereby renewing creation to make ready for the restoration of all of the tribes of Israel around the new temple.

The grandiose size of the restored temple, the idealization of the restored tribes of Israel, the idealized restoration of creation, and the notice that the city is called "YHWH Shammah," i.e., "YHWH is there," suggests to some that the vision may indicate a heavenly, idealized temple. Alternatively, readers must recognize that the Jerusalem Temple was understood to be the holy center of creation. Creation takes place at the Jerusalem Temple every day with the first appearance of light at the morning Shaharit service. But with the destruction of the Jerusalem Temple, creation ceases to exist and chaos returns to the world. The culminating views of a restored and idealized temple, creation, and Israel suggest that Ezekiel's vision actually entails an entirely new creation in which the restored temple and the restored Israel stand at the center. Such a view then becomes foundational for understanding the role of the temple and creation in the subsequent development of Jewish mysticism and visionary experience.

The Twelve Prophets

The Book of the Twelve Prophets is a composite book that comprises twelve constituent prophetic compositions.[10] It has no comprehensive superscrip-

---

10. For commentaries on the Book of the Twelve Prophets, see esp. Marvin A. Sweeney, *The Twelve Prophets*, 2 vols., Berit Olam (Collegeville, MN: Liturgical Press, 2000);

tion; instead, each constituent book has its own superscription or narrative introduction. In Jewish tradition the Book of the Twelve is read as a single book that includes twelve discrete components. In Christian tradition the Twelve Minor Prophets are read as twelve discrete prophetic books that comprise the Dodekapropheton.

The Book of the Twelve appears in a variety of forms in antiquity. The most prominent witness to the text is the Hebrew Masoretic Text, which presents the order of books as Hosea, Joel, Amos, Obadiah, Jonah, Micah, Nahum, Habakkuk, Zephaniah, Haggai, Zechariah, and Malachi. This order highlights the fate and future of the city of Jerusalem throughout and appears to presuppose the period in the fifth–fourth centuries BCE when the central role of Jerusalem and the Jerusalem Temple figured prominently in the reforms of Ezra and Nehemiah. The so-called Greek Septuagint form of the Twelve Prophets in the fourth-century CE Codex Vaticanus of the Bible presents an alternative sequence—Hosea, Amos, Micah, Joel, Obadiah, Jonah, Nahum, Habakkuk, Zephaniah, Haggai, Zechariah, and Malachi—although readers must recognize most other Septuagint manuscripts followed different orders. Nevertheless, this sequence appears to be a very early sequence that may go back to the early Persian period when the Second Temple was built. It presents Hosea, Amos, and Micah as the first books in the sequence, highlighting the experience of the northern kingdom of Israel as a model for what would happen to Jerusalem. The roots of this sequence may well presuppose the late monarchic period immediately prior to the Babylonian Exile. But the inclusion of Haggai, Zechariah, and Malachi, which envision the building of the Second Temple and posit that a Davidic monarchy will lead YHWH's holy war against the nations, indicates that the early Persian period, when the temple was rebuilt and a new Davidic monarch was envisioned to overthrow the Persian Empire, appears to be the appropriate setting for this order. Other sequences also exist, such as in one of the manuscripts of the Book of the Twelve from Cave 4 at Qumran, 4QXIIa, which indicates a sequence with Jonah following Malachi. Unfortunately, scholars are unable to reconstruct the full sequence of this text, but some maintain that it presupposes an early order in which Jonah was the last book to be added to the sequence.

This discussion will presuppose the Masoretic Hebrew version of the text, which serves as the basis for most biblical translations today, both Jew-

---

James D. Nogalski, *The Book of the Twelve*, 2 vols., SHBC (Macon, GA: Smyth & Helwys, 2011).

ish and Christian. Discussion of the individual books will follow the masoretic order.

The first book in the sequence is the book of Hosea. The superscription
for the book in Hos 1:1 dates the prophet to the reigns of the late-eighth-
century Judean Kings Uzziah, Jotham, Ahaz, and Hezekiah, and to the reign
of the mid-eighth-century Israelite King Jeroboam ben Joash. Hosea is a
northern prophet who would have lived through the destruction of northern
Israel by the Assyrian Empire in 722–721 BCE and apparently spent the rest
of his career in Judah. He is vehemently opposed to Israel's alliance with the
Assyrian Empire, which prompted Israel to trade with its ancient enemy,
Egypt, and kept Israel safe from the Aramean invasions that took the life of
King Ahab ben Omri of Israel. Hosea favors a renewed alliance with Aram,
in large measure because Israel's ancestors came from Aram and because
Assyria's ally, Egypt, was Israel's ancient enemy. Ironically, Israel was destroyed by the Assyrians for breaking its alliance with Assyria and renewing
its alliance with Aram, which suggests that Hosea is at least partly to blame
for Israel's destruction.

Hosea does not present a visionary experience of YHWH. Rather,
he employs a symbolic action in Hos 1–3 based upon his own marriage to
Gomer bat Diblaim, a woman whom the text characterizes as a whore (Hos
1:2), although readers must note that Gomer never speaks for herself in the
text. The purpose of the metaphor is to illustrate Israel's abandonment of
YHWH by making an alliance with Assyria during the reign of the Jehu
dynasty, while abandoning its long-standing alliance with Aram. YHWH
commands Hosea to marry Gomer and to have children with her, each of
whom is named symbolically to illustrate the message of the text. The first
son is named Jezreel to symbolize the place where Jehu assassinated King
Jehoram ben Ahab of Israel, his mother Jezebel, and his ally King Ahaziah
ben Jehoram of Judah, thereby founding the royal House of Jehu (2 Kgs
9–10). Although it is not mentioned in the Bible, King Jehu of Israel is portrayed bowing in submission at the feet of the Assyrian king Shalmaneser III,
inaugurating Israel's alliance with Assyria during the course of the reign of
the House of Jehu. The second child born to Hosea and Gomer, a daughter,
is to be named Lo-ruhamah, No Mercy, to symbolize YHWH's refusal to
show mercy to Israel for the actions of the House of Jehu. The third child,
Lo-'ammi, Not My People, symbolizes YHWH's break with Israel.

Throughout Hos 1–3, it becomes clear that Hosea's failed marriage to
Gomer, whom he charges with having relations with other men, is a model
for the failed relationship between YHWH and Israel, whom the prophet

charges with abandoning YHWH to follow the gods of other nations. The marriage thereby serves as a symbolic action that substitutes for a visionary experience to explain why YHWH would punish Israel despite the covenant by which YHWH swore to protect the nation. The book of Hosea thereby serves as a form of theodicy that does not hold YHWH accountable for Israel's destruction; rather, it charges the nation with abandoning YHWH and thereby justifies the later punishment of Israel.

The second book in the sequence is the book of Joel. The superscription of the book in Joel 1:1 identifies the prophet as Joel ben Pethuel but provides no historical context. The reference to the call to arms against YHWH's enemies in the Valley of Jehoshaphat (Joel 4[3]:9–21, esp. v. 12) suggests a reference to the ninth-century King Jehoshaphat of Judah, but the citation of many Pentateuchal and prophetic books, such as the reversed citation of Isa 2:2–4//Mic 4:1–4 in Joel 4 (3):10, indicates to most scholars that Joel is a late composition from the fourth century BCE. Joel does not present a visionary account of YHWH's divine presence. Rather, it employs the portrayal of a locust horde descending upon Jerusalem as a metaphor for enemies that would assault Jerusalem. Many see Joel as a proto-apocalyptic book, based upon its imagery of the sun turning to darkness and the moon turning to blood (Joel 3:1–5 [2:28–32], esp. v. 4 [31]), but this imagery simply portrays what one would see during the course of a *sharav*, i.e., the dry desert east wind known as khamsin or sirocco, much like the Santa Ana winds of Southern California, that signals the change of seasons in the fall and spring. Such winds carry a great deal of dust that blocks out the sun during the day and makes the moon appear red at night.

The third book in the sequence is Amos. According to the superscription in Amos 1:1, Amos is a sheep breeder from the Judean town of Tekoa, situated to the west of the Dead Sea, during the relatively peaceful reigns of King Jeroboam ben Joash of Israel and Uzziah (Azariah) ben Amaziah of Judah. As noted above, the peace was maintained by means of Israel's alliance with the Assyrian Empire. Judah in turn was subject to Israelite rule as a vassal. During this period, Israel was compelled to pay a heavy tribute to Assyria to maintain the peace, and Judah was compelled to pay tribute to Israel for the same reason. Amos appears to have been delegated by the Judean crown to pay a portion of the Judean tribute to Israel at the royal sanctuary at Beth El in the form of agricultural produce. Amos objected to the payment of such tribute because of the hardship it imposed on Judean farmers, especially in times of locusts, drought, and crop shortages.

Amos 7–9 presents a sequence of five visions of YHWH that apparently constitute Amos's understanding of the foundations for Amos's prophetic role. The vision accounts employ classical visionary language, e.g., "this is what my Lord YHWH showed me," in Amos 7:1, 4. In the first instance, YHWH shows Amos a locust horde that descends upon the land and devours everything in sight, particularly the late-sown crops that follow the king's mowings. The vision takes up a common occurrence, a locust plague, which occurs approximately every seven years in keeping with the gestation periods of locusts. Such a plague typically strips land of its crops. In this case, the timing of the plague following the king's mowings indicates that the portion of the crop to be paid to the Israelite king in tribute had already been harvested, leaving the second harvest to supply the people with food for the year. But with the locust plague, the crops were devastated, leaving the people with little to eat for the coming year. When Amos objects, YHWH relents because Jacob, i.e., Israel and Judah, is so small.

The second vision report, again introduced by the formula, "and this is what my Lord YHWH showed me," portrays fire burning up the fields and consuming the great deep. Such an image is all too typical of a dry Mediterranean climate, such as that found in Israel or in Southern California. At the end of the dry summer season, fires are liable to break out, destroying thousands of acres of crops, forest land, and the like, and leaving devastation everywhere. The outbreak of such fires after a locust plague would have been especially devastating to Israel's farmers. Again, YHWH relents when Amos objects.

In the third vision report, again introduced by the formula, "this is what He (YHWH) showed me," in Amos 7:7, Amos sees YHWH standing by a wall holding a plumb line. Ancient Israelites and Judeans built their homes with stone foundations and mud brick upper courses. In order to ensure the stability of the structures, plumb lines, cords weighted with a tin weight, were used to ensure that the rough stone and mud-brick walls were straight to ensure that they would support the weight of the structure, often a two-story house, and not collapse. In this case, the image of a plumb line provided a metaphorical portrayal of YHWH measuring Israel's righteousness, but it is based on imagery that a Judean sheep breeder and agriculturalist such as Amos would have encountered constantly in his life.

The fourth vision report, again introduced by the formula, "this is what my Lord YHWH showed me," appears in Amos 8:1-3. It portrays a basket of figs, which then becomes the basis for claiming that the end has come for Israel. The vision makes no sense in English because it is based upon a Hebrew pun. The basket of summer fruit, *keluv qayyits* in Hebrew, provides the basis for a pun on the Hebrew word *qets*, "end, that which is cut off," to illustrate YHWH's intention to punish Israel for its failure to care for the needy and poor among the people. The background of an offering at the Beth El altar is crucial here. As a Judean representative, Amos was tasked to present agricultural produce to Israel at the Beth El sanctuary as payment of Judah's tribute. Summer fruit would have been a common offering, especially for a man like Amos, who also tended fig trees in Tekoa. Again, such an offering following the crop shortage caused by the locust plague and the summer fires would have imposed considerable hardship on Judean farmers. But at the same time, Israel needed the tribute. If it failed to pay Assyria, it would face invasion from Assyria.

The final vision report, in which Amos sees YHWH standing by the altar at Beth El, appears in Amos 9:1–15. YHWH calls for the striking of the capitals and the thresholds, the major support structures of a large roofed building such as the northern Israelite sanctuary at Beth El. The oracle then goes on to describe the killing of the people who worship there in a massive slaughter that reaches from the heavens to the depths of the sea. Indeed, the image is based on the imagery of the Israelite sanctuary at Beth El that Amos would like to see demolished. The imagery of slaughter would draw upon the imagery of animal sacrifice at the altar. As animals were killed, their blood drained, their bodies cut apart and burned, Amos would see in such imagery the presence of YHWH calling for the destruction of the sanctuary to which he was compelled to bring offerings despite the agricultural reverses suffered by Judah as a result of the locust plagues and fires mentioned in the earlier visions.

In the end, Amos, a Judean, sees the restoration of Judean rule over both Israel and Judah as in the days of David and Solomon as the solution to the problem. If the fallen booth (Hebrew, *sukkah*) is restored, YHWH will bless Israel and Judah with peace and produce. The imagery of the fallen *sukkah* is especially apt here, as Israelite and Judean farmers typically stayed in temporary *sukkot*, "booths, huts," erected in their fields to ensure that they would harvest as much of the crop as possible before it rotted with the onset of the fall rains that marked the end of the dry summer season.

The fourth and fifth books of the Twelve, respectively, Obadiah and Jonah, do not include material that could be considered visionary.

The sixth book of the Twelve, Micah, presents the work of the late-eighth-century prophet, Micah the Moreshite, a contemporary of Isaiah. According to the superscription in Mic 1:1, Micah spoke during the reigns of the Judean kings Jotham, Ahaz, and Hezekiah. He is from Moresheth Gath, a town on the border between Judah and Philistia, where the Assyrian army concentrated its initial attack when Hezekiah revolted against Assyria in 705–701 BCE. Micah became a war refugee who fled to Jerusalem. He is highly critical of the kings of Israel and Judah for making decisions that had catastrophic impact on their people who suffered under the Assyrian invasions. He does not share Isaiah's adherence to the Zion-Davidic tradition of divine protection for Jerusalem and the Davidic King.

Nevertheless, his book includes the vision of the nations streaming to Jerusalem to learn YHWH's Torah and thereby bring about an end to war; this vision in Mic 4:1–4 also appears in Isa 2:2–4, albeit in a slightly different form. In the case of Micah, the context for this vision differs markedly. Isaiah's version of the vision called upon the House of Jacob to join the nations streaming to Zion in Isa 2:5. The following material in Isa 2:6–22 condemned military alliances with other nations and presented a Day of YHWH oracle that condemned all the arrogant nations that did not recognize YHWH as the ultimate power in the world. Whereas Isaiah maintains that Israel and the nations would suffer punishment on the Day of YHWH, prior to the realization of the ideals in Isa 2:2–4, Micah takes a different approach. Micah 4:4–5 first affirms that everyone should live in peace under his own vine and fig tree and that the various nations worship their own gods. But then Mic 4:6–5:15 lays out an extensive scenario in which a righteous Davidic monarch will arise to punish those nations that oppress Israel and Judah. Insofar as the portrayal of the destruction of enemy weapons and chariots employs language that also appears in Isa 2:6–9, it appears that the two passages were written to engage intertextually in dialogue with each other, although which was written first remains uncertain. In any case, they lay out different scenarios by which the ideals of Mic 4:1–5//Isa 2:2–4 might be achieved. Isaiah calls for punishment of both Israel and the nations to humble them before YHWH, whereas Micah calls for the defeat of the nations that oppress Israel as the necessary precondition for their pilgrimage to Zion.

The seventh book in the sequence of the Twelve is the book of Nahum, which presents the words of Nahum the Elqoshite on the occasion of the fall of Nineveh, the capital of the Assyrian Empire, to the Neo-Babylonian and Median forces led by Nebopolassar of Babylon in 612 BCE. The fall of Nineveh brought the final defeat of Assyria one step closer together with the prospects of an independent Judah ruled by King Josiah ben Amon.

The book is formulated as a disputation speech which argues that YHWH brought about the fall of Nineveh in 612 BCE. Its key visionary element is the partial acrostic hymn of praise in Nah 1:2–8 that celebrates YHWH's power and justice in defeating the enemies of YHWH (and Israel).

No satisfactory explanation has come forward for the partial acrostic form of the hymn, although many note that the first verses focus especially on words that begin with the Hebrew letter *nun* to describe YHWH's anger, power, and zeal in defeating enemies. The letter *nun* is the first letter of Nineveh. The acrostic may continue through vv. 9–10, which culminate in the question, "How (Hebrew, *mah*) do you reckon concerning YHWH, who brings complete destruction; no enemy stands twice . . . ?" If the acrostic continues through the letter *mem*, which precedes *nun*, then it may point to the letter *nun* to accentuate the name, Nineveh, as the target of YHWH's fury. In addition, the acrostic quotes a portion of the formula that describes YHWH's qualities of mercy and justice in Exod 34:6–7. Nahum quotes those portions that focus on YHWH's judgment in celebration of YHWH's justice against the oppressors of Israel in the world. Readers may note that Jonah 4:1–3 quotes the segments concerning YHWH's mercy in its depiction of YHWH's decision to accept Nineveh's repentance. Nahum and Jonah therefore complement each other within the Book of the Twelve in illustrating YHWH's qualities of mercy and justice in relation to Nineveh.

The eighth book of the Twelve Prophets is Habakkuk. The two superscriptions in the book in Hab 1:1 and 3:1 simply refer to Habakkuk the Prophet without specifying context, although the contents of the book make it clear that it is concerned with the Babylonian subjugation of Jerusalem in 605 BCE. The first part of the book in Hab 1–2 is formulated as a dialogue between Habakkuk and YHWH concerning YHWH's role in bringing about Babylon's subjugation of the city and YHWH's intention to bring down Babylon for its oppressive treatment of Jerusalem. Habakkuk 3 presents a theophanic hymn that both anticipates and celebrates YHWH's role in defeating the oppressor; it is designed to underscore YHWH's intention to deliver Jerusalem. The superscription in Hab 3:1 relates the hymn to the Shigionoth, which indicates a complaint form. Indeed, the hymn is formulated as YHWH's answer to Habakkuk's petition to YHWH in Hab 3:2 to act in the face of oppression. Habakkuk 3:3–15 presents a theophany report in which YHWH appears to defeat the oppressor. Habakkuk 3:3–7 portrays YHWH's approach using solar imagery to describe YHWH's rising over the mountains of Teman and Paran to the east; the divine presence shines throughout the skies just as the sun does every morning. Pestilence and plague, which appear as gods in Mesopotamian theophanies, accompany YHWH as YHWH stands to face the foe, causing the earth to shake, nations to tremble, mountains to shatter, and tents to quiver. Habakkuk 3:8–15 then portrays YHWH's combat, using motifs that typically appear in Ugaritic and Mesopotamian combat myths. YHWH defeats Yam, the Sea, by charging in a chariot and shooting a bow, as the winds and rains collaborate to vanquish the foe (cf. Judg 5). YHWH bludgeons the enemy with a club while driving the chariot and horses into the sea to stir the waters into submission. The prophet responds with an expression of his confidence in YHWH in Hab 3:16–19a, and Hab 3:19b concludes the psalm with instructions to the musical director.

The ninth book of the Twelve is Zephaniah. According to its superscription in Zeph 1:1, Zephaniah is a prophet of African and royal descent who speaks during the reign of King Josiah of Judah, sponsor of a major program of religious reform and national restoration. Zephaniah is formulated largely as an exhortation to support the king's reforms. The prophet's oracles concerning the future restoration of Jerusalem culminate in Zeph 3:14–20 with a metaphorical depiction of Jerusalem as Bat Zion, Daughter Zion, or the Bride of YHWH who welcomes her husband home after a long period of judgment and divine absence. The sexual dimensions of this reunion are signaled at the end of v. 17 with the statement, "he (YHWH) will plow in his love," which has been widely misunderstood and mistranslated.

The tenth book of the Twelve is Haggai, which is formulated as the prophet's disputation speech intended to motivate the people to build the Second Temple during the second year of the Persian king Darius, 520 BCE. The final segment of the speech in Hag 2:20–23 presents a vision of YHWH's overthrow of the throne of nations, i.e., Persia, employing language and imagery drawn from the Song of the Sea in Exod 15. It also points to Zerubbabel ben Shealtiel, the grandson of King Jehoiachin of Judah, as YHWH's signet ring, a metaphorical means to suggest the restoration of the House of David.

The eleventh book of the Twelve is Zechariah. According to its narrative introduction in Zech 1:1, Zechariah ben Berechiah ben Iddo spoke during the second year of Darius (520 BCE) to support the building of the Second Temple. Zechariah is both a Zadokite priest and a visionary prophet who returns to Jerusalem with the presumptive high priest, Joshua ben Jehozadak, to assist in reestablishing the Jerusalem Temple.

Zechariah employs a sequence of eight night vision reports in Zech 1–6, each of which is based on imagery associated with the rebuilding and reestablishment of the temple, to make his points.[11] The first appears in Zech 1:7–17, which depicts four horse riders standing among the myrtles that grow

---

11. In addition to the commentaries, see Lena-Sofia Tiemeyer, *Zechariah and His Visions: An Exegetical Study of Zechariah's Vision Report*, LHBOTS 605 (London: Bloomsbury T&T Clark, 2015).

on the Temple Mount. An angelic guide explains to Zechariah that they were sent by YHWH to roam the earth in preparation for the building of the temple. The image of the horsemen is derived from the Babylonian and Persian practice of using horsemen to carry royal decrees throughout the empire. These horsemen would have brought word of authorization to build the temple. The second appears in Zech 2:1–4 (1:18–21) and focuses on smiths building four horns, which the angel explains in relation to divine power. The image is based on workmen building the new temple altar with its four horns that signify the four winds or directions of creation. The third appears in Zech 2:5–17 (1–13), which depicts workmen carrying measuring lines to lay out the lines for the building of new structures. The vision presupposes that Jerusalem has no walls, an accurate depiction of the city at the time. The motif is intended to show that Jerusalem would rival the Persian holy city of Pasargadae, which had no walls but was protected by fire altars along the city's perimeter. The fourth vision in Zech 3 focuses on Satan's accusations against Joshua ben Jehozadak. The vision depicts Joshua's ordination as High Priest of the temple in which he changes from his profane garments into the holy vestments that he wears when serving in the temple. The fifth vision in Zech 4 focuses on the newly constructed temple menorah, which includes seven lamps, each of which has seven olive-oil wicks. The menorah is flanked by the priest, Joshua ben Jehozadak, and the presumptive king, Zerubbabel, both of whom are anointed with oil. The sixth vision in Zech 5:1–4 employs the image of a flying scroll that curses those who are guilty of wrongdoing. The scroll shares the same dimensions as the temple's ulam, or porch, from which the Torah is read to instruct the people in proper behavior (cf. Deut 31:9–13; Neh 8–10). The seventh vision in Zech 5:5–11 focuses on a woman placed in a tub of grain sent to Shinar, the site of Babylon. The woman represents wickedness, apparently for reasons of menstrual impurity, who is sent with the offerings to curse Babylon now that the temple is to be built. The eighth vision in Zech 6 focuses on the inauguration of Joshua ben Jehozadak, the priest, although most scholars maintain that it was supposed to focus on Zerubbabel, who would have been crowned as king. Insofar as Persia likely found a way to eliminate Zerubbabel when the plan to crown him as king was discovered (see Hag 2:20–23), Joshua appears in his place.

Although Zech 9–14 is typically read as a late apocalyptic addition to Zech 1–8 from the Hellenistic period, more recent research establishes that Zech 9–14 was also written in the Persian period and serves as an important component of the book's employment of imagery based in mythology to depict YHWH's apocalyptic war, led by YHWH's Davidic King, against the

Persians and the nations to overthrow the oppressors and prompt them to recognize YHWH at the newly built Jerusalem Temple.

The twelfth and final book of the Twelve is Malachi. Some maintain that Malachi, which means "my messenger/angel," was not an actual prophet, but is based on the imagery of YHWH's angel who would lead Israel through the wilderness in Exod 23:20–33; 33:2). Malachi is formulated as a disputation designed to prompt the people to adhere to YHWH and to observe YHWH's Torah.

Chapter 5

JEWISH APOCALYPTIC LITERATURE

From the Bible to the Heikhalot Literature

The apocalyptic literature of the Bible, the Christian New Testament, and Second Temple Judaism is the bridge between the prophetic literature of the Bible and the heikhalot literature of the early rabbinic period. The term *apocalyptic* is derived from the Greek *apokalypsis*, which means "revelation," in relation to the uncovering of hidden things from the heavenly realm that have an impact on the world of creation. Apocalyptic literature includes the biblical book of Daniel, the New Testament book of Revelation, and a large number of Second Temple Jewish works, such as 1 Enoch, 2 Enoch, 2 Baruch, 3 Baruch, 4 Ezra, the Apocalypse of Abraham, the Apocalypse of Adam, the Apocalypse of Zephaniah, the Songs of the Sabbath Sacrifice, and early Christian works such as the Apocalypse of Peter. Apocalyptic literature generally employs visionary portrayals of the heavenly realm, angelic mediators who guide the visionary through the experience and explain its meaning, portrayals of the heavenly temple and the presence of the divine within that temple, tours of heaven, and lists of revealed things. Some works that lack some of these elements, such as the War Scroll from Qumran and the book of Jubilees, might also be considered.

Apocalyptic literature is heavily influenced by the wisdom literature, such as Prov 8 and Job 28, according to which aspects of the divine may be discerned by observing creation. But apocalyptic literature also grows out of prophetic literature; we frequently see proto-apocalyptic elements in the prophetic books, such as Isa 24–27; 34–35; and 56–66; Ezekiel's visions in Ezek 1; 8–11; and 40–48; Joel; and Zech 9–14. Drawing upon the perspectives of wisdom and prophetic literature, apocalyptic turns its attention to an examination of the heavenly realm in an effort to discern divine intentions and actions in the world of creation.

John Collins has offered a definition of apocalyptic literature that has generally functioned as the standard of the field:

> "a genre of revelatory literature with a narrative framework, in which a revelation is mediated by an otherworldly being to a human recipient, disclosing a transcendent reality which is both temporal, insofar as it envisages eschatological salvation, and spatial insofar as it involves another supernatural world."[1]

This definition arose in the context of a concern with the study of early Christianity, and it reflects those concerns. The concern with "eschatological salvation" is problematic, insofar as it evokes perspectives concerning the end of time and personal salvation in the form of eternal life that are characteristic of early Christianity, although we must note that Collins understands eschatology as cosmic upheaval or fundamental change in the nature of the cosmos. Both terms need to be specified and even replaced. It also fails to address the question of setting, particularly in relation to the Jerusalem Temple. Frances Flannery-Dailey has demonstrated that visionary experience takes place at sanctuaries in both the ancient Near Eastern (including Jewish) and Greco-Roman worlds, and Jon Levenson has demonstrated that the Jerusalem Temple was regarded as the holy center of creation.[2] Indeed, the Jerusalem Temple is the primary locus for the revelation of the divine and the primary gateway to the heavenly realm. Insofar as apocalyptic literature is concerned with visionary experience of the divine, heavenly realm, it is set in relation to the temple, and it envisions the heavenly temple as the locus for discerning divine intent and action. Insofar as apocalyptic literature examines the divine causes of the disruption of the created world order, it is fundamentally concerned with the disruption or destruction of the temple, and it looks forward to the time when the temple will be resanctified or restored so that creation might be resumed or put back into order. Insofar as death and improperly shed blood are key agents in compromising the holiness of

---

1. John J. Collins, "Introduction: The Genre Apocalypse Reconsidered," in *Apocalypse, Prophecy, and Pseudepigraphy: On Jewish Apocalyptic Literature* (Grand Rapids: Eerdmans, 2016), 4–5.

2. Frances Flannery-Dailey, *Dreamers, Scribes, and Priests: Jewish Dreams in the Hellenistic and Roman Eras*, SJSJ 90 (Leiden: Brill, 2004); Jon D. Levenson, "The Temple and the World," *JR* 64 (1984): 275–98.

the temple and creation at large, the absence of death and the presence of eternal life for individuals may be part of the scenario of restoration, but the restoration and resanctification of the temple is the key element in visions of a restored and idealized creation.

We may proceed by examining the proto-apocalyptic and wisdom antecedents of apocalyptic in the Bible; 1 Enoch, the earliest apocalyptic work; Daniel, the Hebrew Bible's only apocalyptic book; Qumran material, including the War Scroll from Qumran and the Songs of the Sabbath Sacrifice; Revelation, the apocalyptic book of the New Testament; and 4 Ezra and 2 Baruch, two examples of apocalyptic literature that are fundamentally concerned with questions of divine justice following the destruction of the temple.

Proto-Apocalyptic and Prophetic Vision

Biblical literature includes two very important antecedents to the development of apocalyptic literature: the proto-apocalyptic literature of the Prophets—including Isa 24–27; 34–35; 56–66; Ezek 1; 8–11; 37; 38–39; 40–48; Joel; and Zech 9–14 among others—and the wisdom literature of the Bible—such as Proverbs, Job, and the Song of Songs. We may begin with the proto-apocalyptic literature before turning to the wisdom literature.

Many interpreters maintain that elements of the book of Isaiah, such as Isa 24–27; 34–35; and 56–66, constitute examples of proto-apocalyptic literature. Although we do not see heavenly mediators, images of the divine, images of the heavenly temple, tours of heaven, or lists of revealed things, the mythological portrayals of creation and their implied role in demonstrating divine intent and action play a key role in the decision to view these texts as proto-apocalyptic. Such mythological portrayals include the imagery of the land languishing in drought, the resurrection of the dead, the twisting serpent Leviathan, and the return of the exiles in Isa 24–27; the defeat of Edom, the command to search and read the book to see what G-d intends, and the portrayal of the highway that will enable the exiles to return to Jerusalem and the land of Israel in Isaiah 34–35; and the portrayal of the ideal restored Jerusalem, the defeat of Edom, the return of the exiles, and the final judgment against the wicked in Isaiah 56–66. Our prior examination of the visions of Isaiah point to the prophet's, whether Isaiah ben Amoz's, Deutero-Isaiah's, or others', mythological portrayal of divine intent. As a consequence, there is a fine line to be drawn between prophecy and apocalyptic in the book of Isaiah, and so it is questionable whether any of these texts may be classified as proto-apocalyptic, especially since the distinction is so frequently presented as based in a conflict between visionary and priestly circles. But it is clear that visionary circles frequently appear among the priesthood, and so it is debatable whether this distinction holds up.

Isaiah 24–27, often called the Apocalypse of Isaiah, appears at the conclusion of the oracles concerning the nations in Isa 13–23 and prior to the oracles concerning Jerusalem in Isa 28–33. Its frequent treatment as a discrete block of oracles within the larger structure of the book of Isaiah has facilitated its identification as a late, proto-apocalyptic insertion into the book.[3] And yet its portrayal of the banquet on Zion in which the nations participate points to its role in concluding the oracles concerning the nations and in paving the way for the following oracles concerning Jerusalem. Although it may well be a later text, it plays an integral role in the larger structure of the book by pointing to YHWH's pacification of the nations at Zion, so that the exiles might return to Jerusalem, and by pointing to the need to prepare Jerusalem/Zion for this role. Isaiah 24–27 was written as part of the sixth-century redaction of the book that built upon the vision of peace among the nations in order to introduce the work of Deutero-Isaiah in Isa 40–55, which looked forward to a time of peace when the exiles could return to rebuild Jerusalem at the outset of the reign of King Cyrus of Persia in the late sixth century BCE.

An examination of the formal structure and contents of Isa 24–27 demonstrates how the passage is designed to fulfill this role. The passage begins in Isa 24:1–23 with a prophetic announcement of YHWH's punishment of the earth. The punishment is portrayed in a mythological imagery of a dry, parched, and devastated earth that would be well at home in Mesopotamian depictions of Tammuz or Canaanite depictions of Baal, dead in the underworld at the end of the dry summer season before Ishtar and Anat respectively bring the dead fertility deities back to life so that they might bring the rains once again to restore the world of creation. The use of such imagery in relation to YHWH is deliberate because it surreptitiously argues that YHWH—and not Tammuz/Ishtar or Baal/Anat—is the true source of rain and life in the world of creation, and that the restoration of creation entails the restoration of Jerusalem, the temple, and the people of Israel and Judah in the holy center of creation. Allusions to earlier prophetic texts reinforce this contention, demonstrating that YHWH had previously stated

---

3. Marvin A. Sweeney, *Isaiah 1–39, with an Introduction to Prophetic Literature*, FOTL 16 (Grand Rapids: Eerdmans, 1996), 311–33.

this scenario would take place, thereby giving credibility to the text's claims concerning YHWH as the true G-d of creation.

Isaiah 25:1–27:13 then follows with a prophetic announcement of blessing for the earth and its results for Zion and Israel. This section includes two major subunits. The first is Isaiah 25:1–12, which depicts YHWH's blessing of the earth. Such a depiction portrays how YHWH will take the ruined city and turn it into a place for banqueting and feasting by the nations of the earth, who will join Israel and Jerusalem in recognizing YHWH as the sovereign of creation. Interpreters frequently miss an important point here: the banqueting and feasting entails temple sacrifice and worship of YHWH. Sacrifice is not simply the slaughter and burning of sacrificial animals; as a sacred meal—or perhaps in modern parlance, a barbecue—it provides the basis for sacred communal celebration. In keeping with Isa 2:2–4 and the ensuing oracles concerning the nations in Isa 13–23, the nations will come to recognize YHWH and join Israel at Zion. Isaiah 26:1–27:13 announces the result, Israel's return to Zion. Isaiah 26:1–21 portrays Judah's petition to YHWH for deliverance, including the portrayal of the dead who will be brought back to life as Zion metaphorically gives birth to a new generation; Isa 27:1 mythologically depicts YHWH's defeat of the chaos monster, Leviathan, in order to portray YHWH defeating and subduing the enemies that have oppressed and exiled Israel; and Isa 27:2–13 calls upon Israel to accept YHWH's offer of reconciliation so that the exiles might return to Jerusalem.

Isaiah 34–35 presents similar issues, and this section is frequently called the Little Apocalypse of Isaiah.[4] Furthermore, many interpreters maintain that Deutero-Isaiah composed chapters 34 and 35, or at least chapter 35. Indeed, both chapters may be assigned to the sixth-century redaction of the book of Isaiah that combined the materials of Isaiah ben Amoz in Isa 1–33 with those of Deutero-Isaiah in Isa 40–55.

Again, Isa 34–35 displays a keen interest in employing mythological imagery to depict YHWH's intent and actions in the world of creation. Isaiah 34–35 is frequently described as a late addition to Isa 1–33, but close analysis of the themes, motifs, and concerns of these chapters demonstrates that they form a parallel with Isa 1; by introducing both YHWH's judgment and restoration, each introduces the material that follows. Just as Isa 1 introduces YHWH's judgment against Israel and the restoration of Zion in the following material in Isa 2–33—including the narrative concerning King Ahaz and the judgment against Jerusalem and Israel in Isa 7:1–9:6—so Isa 34–35 serves the

---

4. Sweeney, *Isaiah 1–39*, 434–54.

same function for Isa 36–39 and 40–55—including the narrative concerning King Hezekiah and the deliverance of Jerusalem and the Babylonian Exile in Isa 36–39.

The formal structure and contents of Isa 34–35 demonstrate its function and role in the book. The whole unit may be characterized as prophetic instruction concerning YHWH's power to return redeemed exiles to Zion. The first subunit of the passage in Isa 34:1–17 includes two addresses to the nations. The first portrays YHWH's destruction of Edom, the nation descended from Jacob's fraternal twin brother, Esau, who represents all the nations that oppress Israel in Isa 34:1–15; and the second address in Isa 34:16–17 confirms YHWH's power by asking readers to search the book of YHWH, i.e., the earlier portions of the book of Isaiah, for confirmation that YHWH said that this would happen. The second subunit in Isa 35:1–10 presents a prophetic oracle of salvation concerning the return of the exiles to Jerusalem; it includes an announcement of the blossoming of nature in the Arabah in Isa 35:1–2 and instruction to the weak concerning YHWH's coming and the appearance of a highway that will return the exiles to Jerusalem in Isa 35:3–10. In keeping with the earlier pronouncement of judgment in Isa 6 and the later announcement in Isa 40–55, the eyes, ears, and hearts (minds) of the people will be opened as YHWH's restoration is revealed.

We may finally turn to Isa 56–66, which portrays the coming restoration of the exiles to Jerusalem as well as the punishment of those deemed to be wicked.[5] In keeping with earlier announcements concerning the inclusion of the nations in the covenant, Isa 56:1–8 calls for the inclusion of foreigners and eunuchs in the covenant, although to be sure it calls upon them to observe the Shabbat as the fundamental observance of Judaism as well as the other requirements of the covenant. In other words, Isa 56:1–8 calls upon them to observe the major requirements of Judaism. Isaiah 60–62 once again employs mythological language to portray the restoration of Jerusalem in which foreigners will take part by facilitating the return of exiled Jews. Although some have seen indications of Second Isaiah's servant in this passage, the figure appears to be a priest; the watchmen on the walls depict a typical function of the priesthood, and the bringing of gifts to Jerusalem entails the presentation of those gifts at the Jerusalem Temple. Isaiah 63:1–6 once more portrays YHWH's defeat of Edom, as YHWH defeats the nations that oppressed Israel. Finally, Isa 65–66 portrays both the punishment of the wicked and the restoration of the righteous as YHWH sits enthroned once

5. Marvin A. Sweeney, *Isaiah 40–66*, FOTL (Grand Rapids: Eerdmans, 2016), 248–385.

again in the Jerusalem Temple, the location of the divine footstool in Isa 66:1, as the nations return the exiles in Isa 66:18–24. Although some maintain that YHWH will take from them priests and Levites, the grammar of the passage indicates that YHWH will take priests and Levites from the exiled Jews who are restored to Zion by the nations.

Mythological language concerning the heavens and YHWH's actions in the world plays important roles in Isa 24–27; 34–35; and 56–66. Such language is a mainstay of prophetic literature; it nevertheless lays the groundwork for the depiction of heaven and the divine in apocalyptic literature.

A second set of potential proto-apocalyptic texts appears in Zech 9–14.[6] Modern critical scholars generally maintain that the book of Zechariah includes two and possibly three major compositions: the accounts of Zechariah's visions in Zech 1–8 and the proto-apocalyptic appendices to the visions in Zech 9–14. Some maintain that Zech 9–14 includes two major compositions, Zech 9–11, often identified as Deutero-Zechariah, and Zech 12–14, sometimes identified as Trito-Zechariah, following the patterns of identification in the book of Isaiah. Zechariah 9–11 mythologically and enigmatically portrays the approach of a royal figure, understood by some to be Alexander the Great, and Zech 12–14 mythologically and enigmatically portrays YHWH's war against the nations that culminates in their recognition of YHWH in the Jerusalem Temple. The distinctions between Zech 1–8 and 9–14 are based on the formal observations that, whereas Zech 1–8 is formulated as vision reports, Zech 9–11 and 12–14 are identified as oracular units insofar as each begins with a superscription that includes the generic designation *massa'*, "pronouncement" or "oracle." The distinctive mythological formulation of the contents of Zech 9–11 and 12–14 reinforces the conclusion that these units appear to be quite distinct both from Zech 1–8 and from each other. An additional factor is the widespread view that Zech 9–14 is a composition of the Hellenistic period, due largely to the reference to the Greeks in Zech 9:13. Many also note the differentiation in intertextual citation and allusion between Zech 1–8, which relates largely to Pentateuchal texts, and Zech 9–14, which relates largely to prophetic texts. Still other scholars maintain that the book of Malachi, which is not a proper name, but simply means "my messenger," may be a third appendix to Zechariah because it, too, is designated as a *massa'* at the outset of the book.

---

6. Marvin A. Sweeney, *The Twelve Prophets*, Berit Olam (Collegeville, MN: Liturgical Press, 2000), 2:559–709, esp. 656–706.

Although the model of Zech 9–11 and 12–14 as later appendices to Zechariah is a potentially attractive diachronic hypothesis for the composition of the book, a synchronic literary analysis of the formal structure of the book demonstrates that all three sections form a coherent whole. The literary structure of the book must be re-envisioned, however, by attention to the chronological introductions evident in Zech 1:1; 1:7; and 7:1. Zechariah 1:1–6 then emerges as the introduction to the book; it calls upon the people to return to Jerusalem and to adhere to YHWH. Zechariah 1:7–6:15 presents the visions of Zechariah concerning the construction of the Jerusalem Temple during the reign of the Persian monarch, Darius I. Zechariah 7–14 presents a narrative account of the transmission of YHWH's words to Zechariah, which are the pronouncements of YHWH that will culminate in the defeat of the nations and their recognition of YHWH at the Jerusalem Temple. Altogether, the final, synchronic form of the book of Zechariah articulates the significance of the construction of the Second Temple as signaling the recognition of YHWH as the G-d of all creation and all the nations.

Several major diachronic considerations support these conclusions. The first is the recognition that Zech 1:1–6 and 7:1–8:23 constitute the literary framework of the book that introduce the vision reports in Zech 1:7–6:15 and the pronouncement in Zech 9–14 respectively. Closer attention to the intertextual relationships within these texts indicate that only the vision accounts in Zech 1:7–6:15 relate intertextually to the Pentateuch whereas Zech 1:1–6 and chs. 7–8 relate intertextually to the Prophets, much like Zech 9–14. Indeed, the configuration of the name of the prophet in Zech 1:1–6 as Zechariah ben Berechiah ben Iddo does not match the mention of his name in Ezra 5:1 and 6:14 as Zechariah bar Iddo. The name has been reconfigured to refer intertextually to Isaiah's witness to the tablet concerning the birth of his son Maher Shalal Hash Baz, "The Spoil Speeds and the Prey Hastens," in Isa 8:1–4, thereby to testify to the outcome of his message. The witness was Zechariah ben Yeberechiah, the latter name meaning "YHWH will bless" once the punishment is over. Zechariah ben Berechiah ben Iddo employs a form of the name Berechiah, "YHWH has blessed," to indicate that with the rebuilding of the temple, the time of blessing has come. We might also note the references in Zech 8 to Isaian oracles concerning Emmanuel in Isa 7:14 and the realization of the famous "swords into plowshares" oracle of Isa 2:2–4, which envisions a time when the nations join Israel at Zion to learn YHWH's Torah. In the view of Zechariah, that time has now come, and the following material in Zech 9–14 will demonstrate how it is to be realized.

Second, Zech 9–14 does not date to the Hellenistic period. Instead, it dates to the Persian period, much like Zech 1–8. The monarch in Zech 9 cannot be Alexander the Great. Zechariah 9 portrays the monarch approaching the land of Israel from Syria, as indicated by his placement in cities such as Damascus and Hamath. Alexander the Great did not approach the land of Israel from Syria; he marched along the Mediterranean coast of Asia Minor and then turned south to follow the Mediterranean coast to the land of Israel. The approach of the monarch from Syria better fits the journey taken by Zerubbabel ben Shealtiel, the grandson of King Jehoiachin ben Jehoiakim of Judah, as he returned from Babylonia to Jerusalem to oversee the building of the Second Temple in 522–520 BCE. The mention of the Greeks fighting Judeans in Zech 9:13 hardly portrays Alexander's approach to Jerusalem. Talmudic sources indicate that Alexander was received in Jerusalem as a friend (cf. Josephus, *Ant.* 11.329; b. Tamid 31b–32b).[7] Judeans and Greeks did not fight at the time of Alexander's approach. But following the conclusion of Darius's efforts to put down revolt throughout the Persian Empire in 517 BCE, he marched north by Judah to begin his campaign against the Greeks. As a vassal of Persia, Judah would have sent a contingent of Judean soldiers to join Darius's campaign, likely led by Zerubbabel.

Third, the anger expressed against the shepherds, i.e., the rulers of Judah, in Zech 10 indicates a lack of confidence in Persian rule that will culminate in the overthrow of the Persian monarchy and the restoration of Davidic rule, as Zechariah's contemporary, Haggai, had anticipated in Hag 2:20–23. The enigmatic three shepherds of Zech 11, whose demise portends the end of YHWH's covenant with the nations, prove to be the three Persian monarchs, Cyrus, Cambyses, and Darius, who had ruled Judah with YHWH's approval, according to the designation of Cyrus as YHWH's messiah and temple builder in Isa 44:28 and 45:1. The book of Zechariah calls for the end of Persian rule over Judah as authorized by the book of Isaiah. Instead, Zechariah calls for the overthrow of Persian rule and the reinstitution of Davidic rule now that the Jerusalem Temple is rebuilt. Perhaps the book of Zechariah anticipated that Zerubbabel would be that Davidic monarch, but with Zerubbabel's absence at the time of the dedication of the newly built Jerusalem Temple in Ezra 6, another Davidic figure would have to fill the role. No one knows what happened to Zerubbabel; perhaps he perished in the course of Darius's campaign against the Greeks. But the building of the temple and Zerubbabel's presence in Jerusalem would have whetted Judean

---

7. "Alexander the Great," *EncJud*, 2:577–79.

appetites for the overthrow of Persian rule and the restoration of the House of David. Zerubbabel might be gone, but a successor could surely be found. In any case, the Persians never again appointed a Davidic descendant as governor (Hebrew, *pekhah*) of Judah. Nevertheless, the portrayal of YHWH's cosmic war against the nations, led by YHWH's Davidic monarch and resulting in the nations' recognition of YHWH in Zech 12–14, gives expression to Judean expectations at that time. Altogether, the book of Zechariah is designed to challenge the book of Isaiah's call for submission to Persian rule as the will of YHWH. As far as the book of Zechariah is concerned, that time is passed, and it is time for Judah to restore the House of David now that YHWH's temple is complete.

Is Zech 9–14 proto-apocalyptic? It presents a view in which the rule of the nations, i.e., the Persian Empire, will be overthrown; the Davidic dynasty will be restored, and the nations will recognize YHWH at the newly built Second Temple in Jerusalem. Surely such a scenario fulfills some expectations concerning the "eschatological" promises of YHWH to Israel and Judah. But Zech 9–14 cannot be recognized as proto-apocalyptic on its own. These chapters are clearly dependent upon the vision reports in Zech 1:7–6:15, which portray the building of the Second Temple and employ heavenly guides who explain to Zechariah the significance of the visions concerning the construction of the temple. Furthermore, the framework material in Zech 1:1–6 and 7:1–8:23 is designed, not only to introduce their respective sections of the book, but to configure them as fulfillments of the book of Isaiah as well. But whereas Isaiah is designed to legitimize Persian rule, Zechariah is designed to call for its end and to anticipate the restoration of Davidic rule as the true outcome of Isaiah's agenda concerning the future recognition of YHWH as the true G-d and sovereign of creation. Zechariah 9–14 alone is not a proto-apocalyptic work. Like the book of the priest Ezekiel, the book of the priest Zechariah is a proto-apocalyptic work.

The book of Joel is frequently cited as an example of a proto-apocalyptic work, especially because of its portrayal of cosmic upheaval as an army of locusts threatens Jerusalem in Joel 1:2–20, the sun turns dark and the moon turns to blood as cosmic order collapses in Joel 3:1–5 (2:28–32), and YHWH calls for holy warriors to beat their plowshares into swords and their pruning hooks into spears as they prepare for battle against the nations in the Valley of Jehoshaphat.[8] Although there are no heavenly guides, tours of heaven,

8. Sweeney, *The Twelve Prophets*, 1:145–87.

lists of revealed things, etc., the imagery of cosmological destruction has convinced many that Joel represents a proto-apocalyptic work in which visionary circles in ancient Judah anticipated the end of cosmic world order.

Critical analysis of Joel needs to consider the role that metaphorical portrayal plays in this book, particularly the imagery of the sun going dark and the moon turning to blood. Indeed, most interpreters are not aware that these images present an example of natural phenomena readily observable both in the land of Israel and in Southern California, the sirocco. The sirocco is a wind condition in which a coastal area located to the east of a major body of sea or ocean and west of a major desert area experiences a wind displacement in which the hot desert air forces prevailing winds to reverse their normal movement, from west to east, to an abnormal movement, from east to west. Such movement often causes high winds that blow hot, dry air and enormous quantities of dirt and sand that blot out the sun during the day and cause the moon to appear red at night. Such conditions appear at times of seasonal change from the wet to the dry season and vice-versa in the land of Israel, where the wind is known as the East Wind of the Bible, the *sharav* in Hebrew, and the *khamsin* in Arabic. In Southern California and elsewhere in the American Southwest, such winds are known as Santa Ana winds. Although the imagery might suggest cosmic upheaval, it merely points to a common natural phenomenon that has been portrayed metaphorically with imagery of the sun turning dark and the moon turning to blood.

Indeed, the lack of historical reference and the use of metaphor in the book of Joel prompts interpretation of the book as a proto-apocalyptic composition. The book is attributed to a prophet named Joel ben Pethuel, but nothing is known of the prophet. Joel is a common name in Hebrew and so there is no symbolic significance to the name. A variety of suggestions for the historical setting of the book and the prophet have been put forward. At the synchronic level, the reference to the coming battle in the Valley of Jehoshaphat points to the ninth century BCE, in that 2 Chr 20:20–26 relates YHWH's defeat of the nations that threatened Jerusalem during the reign of King Jehoshaphat of Judah. At the diachronic level, the numerous citations of literature from the late monarchic, exilic, and Persian periods have prompted interpreters to date the composition of the book to the late fifth or early fourth centuries BCE, which would correspond to the time of Nehemiah and Ezra. Such citations and allusions include Isa 13:6 and Ezek 30:2–3 (Joel 1:15); Mic 4:1–4//Isa 2:2–4 (Joel 4[3]:10); Zeph 1:14–15 (Joel 2:1–2); 2 Chr 20:20–26 (Joel 4[3]:2, 12); Amos 1:2, 9:13 (Joel 4[3]:16, 18); and numerous citations of Obadiah throughout Joel 3–4.

The book of Joel is in the literary form of YHWH's response to Judah's appeals for deliverance from threat. Following the superscription of the book in Joel 1:1, which identifies Joel ben Pethuel as its author, the body of the book in Joel 1:2–4[3]:21 is formulated with this agenda in mind. The first major segment of the book in Joel 1:2–20 presents the prophet's call to community complaint concerning the threat to Jerusalem posed by the locust plague. The basic premise of this section is that a locust plague threatens the agricultural crops of Judah and therefore the livelihood of the people. The imagery draws heavily on the imagery of the locust plague from Exod 10:1–20, and the call for communal lament points to the temple and its priesthood as the setting for the appeal to YHWH to defend the nation against the locust plague as YHWH had done in the days of the exodus. The second major segment of the book appears in Joel 2:1–14, which presents the prophet's call to communal complaint concerning the threat of invasion on the Day of YHWH. The Day of YHWH is frequently employed to portray YHWH's judgment against enemies in the world, including those that threaten Jerusalem. In this case, the metaphorical nature of the so-called locust invasion becomes clear; the invasion so depicted is one of actual warriors, and the people appeal to YHWH at the temple to turn back the invading horde. The solution presented to the people is that they must repent and turn back to YHWH. The third major section of the book appears in Joel 2:15–4[3]:21, which is formulated as the prophet's announcement of YHWH's response to protect the people from threats of invasion. Together with the portrayal of YHWH's intent to protect Jerusalem, the imagery of the East Wind or sirocco, used at the time of the exodus to divide the Red Sea and to deliver Israel from Pharaoh's army (Exod 14–15), appears once again, rendering the sun dark and the moon red as blood, as YHWH prepares to gather forces for the decisive battle at the Valley of Jehoshaphat. Drawing upon the account of Jehoshaphat's defeat of the nations, YHWH calls upon the warriors to beat their plowshares into swords and their pruning hooks into spears as they prepare to confront the enemy in the Valley of Jehoshaphat, which runs east from Jerusalem down to the Dead Sea. YHWH's announcement effectively reverses the message of the famed "swords into plowshares and spears into pruning hooks" oracle of Isa 2:2–4 and Mic 4:1–5, as the imagery of an ideal worldwide peace in which war will no longer be known among the nations now dissolves into a scenario of combat against the nations that threaten Jerusalem. By the end of the passage, Jerusalem will once again dwell in peace as YHWH once again dwells in Jerusalem.

Although the metaphorical language is suggestive of a proto-apocalyptic work, the formal configuration of the book as a divine response to the nation's appeal for assistance in a time of threat indicates that the book of Joel constitutes a form of liturgical composition that was designed to motivate people to turn to YHWH on the Day of YHWH. The setting in the fifth–fourth century BCE indicates the time of Nehemiah and Ezra and their efforts to place the new Jerusalem Temple at the center of Jewish life in the land of Judah, and potentially throughout the entire Jewish diaspora as well. Whether the threat to Jerusalem constitutes a real enemy army is uncertain. There is little evidence of foreign invasion against Jerusalem at this time. Rather, the metaphorical use of the locust plague of the exodus narratives and the temple-based setting of the Day of YHWH tradition points to such characterization of threats to Jerusalem as a liturgical event that was designed to garner popular repentance and return to YHWH as well as greater popular participation in the liturgy of the new Jerusalem Temple on the part of the Jerusalemite and Judean population at large. Considering the form and function of the book of Joel, Joel ben Pethuel may well be a temple singer from the time of Nehemiah and Ezra. Although such singers were often characterized as prophets during earlier periods in Israel's history, they were later recognized as Levitical singers in the temple who were charged with singing and performing the temple liturgy. The Jerusalem Temple was considered as the holy center of creation in ancient Judean thought, and the temple's liturgy and its other holy functions served to maintain the stability of the created world order. In such a case, the disruption of creation in Joel, such as the darkening of the sun and the turning of the moon to blood red, would be seen as a collapse of creation that could be rectified by greater piety and practice on the part of the people as they repented and returned to YHWH. Such an agenda is not only central to the book of Joel; it is also central to the agenda of Nehemiah and Ezra as they sought to make the temple the holy center of Jewish life in Jerusalem and beyond, as well as the holy center of creation at large.

Wisdom Literature and the Discernment of the Divine

Whereas the proto-apocalyptic literature presents a predominantly transcendent understanding of divine presence in the world, insofar as the divine is to be found beyond the confines of the finite and phenomenal world, the wisdom literature presents a predominantly immanent understanding of the

divine, insofar as the divine presence is to be found within the finite and phenomenal world. Both models play important roles in the conceptualization
of visionary and mystical experience in the history of Jewish experience
and thought.

Perhaps the most foundational of the Bible's wisdom books is the book
of Proverbs. Proverbs is ascribed to Solomon, a man credited with wisdom
greater than that of known sages, such as Ethan the Ezrahite and Heman,
Chalcol, and Darda, the sons of Mahol, and attributed with some three
thousand proverbs and one thousand and five psalms (1 Kgs 5:9–14). His
reputation for wisdom was so great that the Queen of Sheba came from one
of the farthest kingdoms known to Israel to test Solomon's wisdom (1 Kgs
10:1–13). According to Ethiopian tradition, she returned to her land with
a son, fathered by Solomon, who founded the ruling dynasty of Ethiopia.

Proverbs holds that the world of creation is infused with divine wisdom,
and that wisdom may be learned by observing firsthand how the world of
creation works.[9] Proverbs is constructed as a book of instruction in which
the father and the mother instruct their children in the ways of the world
based upon their own experience of it. One may study the ants as a source
of wisdom to see how they work hard to organize themselves and accomplish major goals and build a highly structured and complex society (Prov
6:6–11). One may see the results for men who go after married women: the
experience saps their strength, and the jealous husband will undoubtedly
exact his revenge (Prov 6:20–35). One should not withhold discipline from
a child; the rod with which you beat him will not kill him, but it may well
save him from the grave (Prov 23:12–14). Laziness will result in a field filled
with thorns; sleeping late every day will result in poverty (Prov 24:30–34).
The lack of wood causes a fire to go out, and so the lack of a contentious
man stills quarrel (Prov 26:20–22). Whoever digs a pit will fall into it, and
one with a lying tongue will be crushed by it in the end (Prov 26:27–28).
Pay attention to your herds and flocks because wealth does not last forever
(Prov 27:23–27). The wicked flee when no one gives chase, but the righteous
is as confident as a lion (Prov 28:1). A rich man is clever in his own eyes, but
a poor man can see through him (Prov 28:11). The earth shudders at four
things: a slave who becomes king, a scoundrel sated with food, a loathsome
woman who gets married, and a slave girl who supplants her mistress (Prov
30:21–23). And a capable woman is beyond compare (Prov 31:10–31).

9. Richard J. Clifford, *Proverbs: A Commentary*, OTL (Louisville: Westminster John
Knox, 1999).

Altogether, these examples illustrate the foundational principle of the book: the fear of YHWH is the beginning of knowledge (Prov 1:7). But the true foundation of the book is the claim that Wisdom, personified as a woman, was the first of YHWH's creations in the world. Wisdom then advised YHWH and became the fundamental principle of creation (Proverbs 8). Throughout the chapter—and indeed the book—wisdom is presumed to be identified with honesty and integrity and functions as the key to success. It is readily observed in the world and easily understood and emulated.

But what happens when it is not—when honesty and integrity do not always result in reward and those who are wicked often gain the upper hand? The book of Job is designed to address this question, and it clearly has Proverbs' idyllic view of wisdom in mind when it states that the fear of YHWH is the beginning of wisdom in Job 28:28; but throughout Job 28 it portrays wisdom as nearly impossible to find in the world, buried in the earth like precious stones that even the most accomplished of miners can never find.

Indeed, the book of Job illustrates the difficulty of finding wisdom—especially the wisdom envisioned by Proverbs—in the world.[10] Job is described as a righteous man who takes care to ensure that even his ten children are covered when he makes offerings for them every day. When the Satan figure, simply presented as an opponent rather than the demon figure of western imagination, bets that Job would curse YHWH if YHWH caused him to suffer, YHWH accepts the challenge and allows Satan to afflict him, but not to kill him. Ultimately, Job loses all of his property and even the lives of his ten children. When he is visited by his friends, Job contends that there is no righteousness in the world, whereas his friends urge him to confess his sins and repent. When Job's friends fail to persuade him that he has done wrong and therefore deserves the suffering unleashed upon him, YHWH finally appears, demanding to know who has challenged divine righteousness in the world. But when Job responds to YHWH that he rejects YHWH's contentions, YHWH declares to Job that he is right. In the end, YHWH spares the lives of Job's friends for blaspheming against him, restores all of Job's lost property, and grants him ten new children to replace those who had died. Although modern theologians correctly protest that such restoration cannot properly compensate Job for the loss of his original children, the point

10. Leo G. Perdue, *The Sword and the Stylus: An Introduction to Wisdom in the Age of Empire* (Grand Rapids: Eerdmans, 2008), 117-51; Carol A. Newsom, "The Book of Job," in *The New Interpreter's Bible*, ed. Leander E. Keck et al. (Nashville: Abingdon, 1996), 4:319-637; Newsom, *Job: A Contest of Moral Imaginations* (Oxford: Oxford University Press, 2003).

remains: that wisdom is nearly impossible to observe in the world, and it is human beings who must choose to live righteously.

Having made a similar case concerning the difficulty of finding meaning or purpose in life in the world, the book of Qoheleth would concur in calling on human beings to create meaning and purpose in the world themselves.[11] The book is purportedly written by Solomon, especially since the super-scription claims that the author is a son of David (Qoh 1:1), and the speaker claims to have been king of Israel (Qoh 1:12). He claims that everything is futility; there is nothing new under the sun. G-d may grant riches, but another may enjoy them. In the end, Qoheleth claims that despite the folly and purposelessness of life in the world, it is nevertheless wisdom to enjoy life during the brief time that it is granted to us before time and old age take our vigor away and leave us wondering what has just passed us by.

Song of Songs is generally recognized as a wisdom book, in part because it is attributed to Solomon based on his alleged knowledge of women and in part because human sexuality places human beings on a par with G-d insofar as we are able to create new life in the form of human beings.[12] The book portrays a romantic, sexual relationship between a man and a woman, as narrated from the perspective of the woman. The original purposes of the book are obscure. Some interpreters might see it as analogous to Sumerian love poetry, which celebrates the Mesopotamian New Year and New Creation. Others maintain that, like Egyptian love poetry, it was written with entertainment in mind.

Overall, the Song of Songs celebrates human sexuality and sensuality. It comprises four major movements that each conclude with an address by the speaker to the daughters of Jerusalem not to awaken desire until it please. The first movement appears in Song 1:2–2:7 in which the woman anticipates her encounter with the man. She describes herself as black and beautiful, terminology that suggests that she is full of life, insofar as black includes every color of the spectrum, and ready for love. The second movement appears in Song 2:8–3:5 in which she describes the approach of her lover. The third movement appears in Song 3:6–5:8 in which the woman employs a classic *wasf* form, known from Egyptian poetry, in which the man employs metaphorical imagery to portray graphically the beauty of the woman. But the man has vanished, and the woman is left without him. The fourth movement appears in Song 5:9–8:4 in which the woman reclaims her lover. Two more

---

11. Choon Leong Seow, *Ecclesiastes*, AB 18C (Garden City, NY: Doubleday, 1997).

12. J. Cheryl Exum, *The Song of Songs*, OTL (Louisville: Westminster John Knox, 2005).

*wasf*s appear in this section, one in which the woman describes the man and one in which the man describes the woman. At the end of the movement, the relationship is consummated. Finally, Song 8:5–14 concludes the Song with portrayals of the aftermath of love, the passion of which is described as fierce as death, and anticipates the next encounter.

Although interpreters are sometimes at a loss to interpret the sensuality of the Song of Songs, the Song has been read in both Judaism and Christianity as a metaphorical portrayal of the relationship between the human and the divine. In Judaism, the Song is read as a metaphorical lovesong between YHWH and Israel in the context, and thereafter on the pattern, of the exodus from Egypt when they established their relationship in the wilderness. In Christianity, the Song is read as a metaphorical lovesong between Christ and the Church, beginning with the crucifixion and resurrection, which are associated with Passover. In both cases the metaphor conveys the deep bonds and emotions of the relationship. But in both traditions the decision not to define either the divine or the human as the male or female character points to the interchangeability of the roles. Each is reflected in the other. Ultimately, Song of Songs holds that the human being desires to join the divine and the divine desires to join the human, not only that they mirror one another. In other words, the presence of the heavens infuses the earth, and the presence of earth infuses the heavens. Correlation between the two must be recognized.

First Enoch

The book of 1 Enoch is the earliest major apocalyptic book known to scholars. It is somewhat of an enigma in that it is preserved in its fullest form only in the Ethiopic text in the canon of the Ethiopian Orthodox Church, although earlier textual witnesses to the book appear in Aramaic from Qumran and in Greek.[13] It is a composite book that includes five major subunits, which most interpreters view as an attempt to create an Enochic Penta-

---

13. John J. Collins, *The Apocalyptic Imagination* (Grand Rapids: Eerdmans, 1998), 33–67, 142–54; Greg Carey, *Ultimate Things: An Introduction to Jewish and Christian Apocalyptic Literature* (St. Louis: Chalice, 2005), 19–37; E. Isaac, "1 (Ethiopic Apocalypse of) Enoch," in *The Old Testament Pseudepigrapha*, vol. 1: *The Apocalyptic Literature and Testaments*, ed. James H. Charlesworth (Garden City, NY: Doubleday, 1983), 5–89; George W. E. Nickelsburg, *1 Enoch 1*, Hermeneia (Minneapolis: Fortress, 2001); George W. E. Nickelsburg and James C. VanderKam, *1 Enoch 2*, Hermeneia (Minneapolis: Fortress, 2012).

teuch analogous to the organization of the (Mosaic) Pentateuch or Torah. Its components were written at various times from the mid-third century BCE through the aftermath of the Bar Kokhba revolt against Rome in the early second century CE. The five books include the Book of Watchers in 1 En. 1–36, written in the third century BCE; the Similitudes or Parables in 1 En. 37–71, written in the first century BCE through the first century CE, although some proposals extend the date through the third century CE; the Astronomical Book or the Book of the Heavenly Luminaries in 1 En. 72–82, written in the third century BCE; the Book of Dreams in 1 En. 83–90, dating to the period leading up to the Hasmonean Revolt against the Seleucid Empire in 170–163 BCE; and the Epistle of Enoch in 1 En. 91–105, which includes the Apocalypse of Weeks in 1 En. 91:12–17; 93:1–10, dating to the second century BCE.

First Enoch is the first of three works attributed to the primeval figure Enoch ben Jared, the Father of Methuselah, in Gen 5:18–24. Enoch's lifespan in Genesis is three hundred and sixty-five years, a number that associates him with the solar calendar employed in ancient Israel and Judah throughout most of the Iron Age and well into the Second Temple period before the lunar Babylonian calendar supplanted it. At the end of his lifetime, Gen 5:24 reports that Enoch walked with G-d because G-d took him. Later Enochic traditions maintain that Enoch ascended to the heavens, where he was transformed into Metatron, the fiery Angel of the Divine Presence who sits upon the divine throne of YHWH while YHWH resides in the Ogdoad, the eighth level of heaven. YHWH only emerges to sit upon the throne in the seventh level of heaven to hear the praises of Israel at the times of the morning (Shaharit), afternoon (Minhah), and evening (Ma'ariv) worship services in the temple and later in the Synagogue. Such a role suggests that Enoch/Metatron is the heavenly secretary of G-d who keeps the calendar and the times and thereby ensures temporal order throughout all creation.

The Book of Watchers in 1 En. 1–36 relates the disruption of order in the world. It does so by elaborating on the account of the flood in Gen 6–9 by positing that the Watchers, an angelic class that does not sleep and is charged with watching over the world of creation, oversteps its boundaries and descends to earth in order to mate with human women. The mixing of the heavenly Watchers and the human women signals disruption of the stable order of creation, as embodied in their offspring, the Niphilim, a race of bastard giants that then go about the earth spreading chaos. G-d employs the flood as a means to destroy the chaos precipitated by the Watchers. The Book of Watchers also presents tours of heaven and hell. The tours of heaven and hell lay out the parameters of blessing and judgment in the world, and Enoch identifies the names of the angels and demons who oversee these areas. Enoch presents his own meteorological findings by which he had established the solar calendar of three hundred and sixty-four days, thereby bringing temporal order to the world. The Book of Watchers is styled as a blessing for the chosen of G-d for the last days, and it concludes with a celebration of the wonders of creation. Overall, the Book of Watchers advances three major arguments: (1) G-d's world of creation has its own order which may be learned by careful observation, especially of Enoch's revelations; (2) part of that order entails eschatological judgment insofar as G-d has decreed judgment for the angels, the Watchers, and humankind at large, on the analogy of the flood in Genesis; and (3) the chosen should bless YHWH.

The model of cosmic disruption signaled by the mating of the heavenly Watchers with human women and the historical setting in the third century BCE suggest that the Book of Watchers is written in the aftermath of major cataclysmic change in the world. The initiation of such change would have been the invasion of the ancient Near East by the Macedonian king Alexander the Great in 333–323 BCE; Alexander would go on to defeat the Achaemenid Persian Empire and to inaugurate the period of Hellenistic civilization in the ancient Near Eastern world. Following Alexander's untimely death in 323 BCE at the age of thirty-three, his empire disintegrated as his generals went to war against each other to gain control of Alexander's extensive empire. Alexander's general Seleucus gained control of Mesopotamia and married into a powerful Syrian family to establish the Seleucid Empire, and Alexander's general Ptolemy married into a powerful Egyptian family to gain control of Ptolemaic Egypt. The result was the Diadochi Wars that plagued the ancient Near Eastern world from the early third century BCE and continued through the early second century BCE, when the Seleucids defeated the Ptolemies and took control of Judah.

Although Alexander was received in Jerusalem as a hero and ally, some would have seen the foreign incursion into the land of Judah as a sign of foreign desecration. Indeed, the subsequent Hellenization of the priestly class would have furthered such doubts among more traditional priestly Jewish groups, leading some to withdraw from the desecrated temple and to take up residence in the desert, in keeping with Isa 40:1–11, to wait for the time when G-d would wage war against the interlopers and restore the sanctity of the temple and of creation at large. Such a group, led by a priestly figure known as the Teacher of Righteousness, moved out to the desert at Qumran to found a holy community that would study and work in preparation for such a time. First Enoch was important to this group; some eleven copies of the manuscript were found in caves containing other scrolls near the site of Qumran.

The Similitudes in 1 En. 37–71 presents three major parables by Enoch concerning G-d's final judgment against the wicked. Many interpreters maintain that the Similitudes constitute a messianic program for restoring the world of creation to order and sanctity, but such a view is too heavily informed by Christianity's view of a royal messiah. The Similitudes recognize Enoch as the Son of Man/Adam, a term which has messianic significance in the Gospel of Mark, particularly in chapter 13. But the term Ben Adam, Son of Adam/Man, is a term that is applied to the priesthood, particularly to the priest and prophet Ezekiel ben Buzi, by G-d. The term arises from the role of the high priest in the Jerusalem Temple. As Jon Levenson demonstrates, the temple is conceptualized as the entrance to the Garden of Eden, insofar as the cedar walls of the temple are carved and inlaid with images of cherubim, animals, and fruit from the Garden of Eden, and the curtain that separates the holy of holies from the rest of the temple structure is embroidered with the image of the cherub that guards the entrance to the Garden according to Gen 3:24.[14] The high priest, conceptualized as the Son of Adam, attempts to gain entrance to the holy of holies or Garden of Eden every Yom Kippur and thereby restore the relationship between YHWH and humanity that was disrupted by YHWH's expulsion of Adam and Eve from the Garden of Eden. The messianic figure envisioned by the Similitudes must be a priestly figure who will resanctify the temple and thereby enable humanity to have access to YHWH and the Garden of Eden once again. Such an eventuality was anticipated by the Qumran community who expected that their Teacher of Righteousness, apparently a priest expelled from the temple, or his successors would one day facilitate such a restoration.

The Astronomical Book in 1 En. 72–82 presents Enoch's tour of the heavens with a special emphasis on the sun and the moon. The sun and the moon govern time in creation, and therefore the attention paid to them is designed to lay the foundations for determining the times when YHWH might act to restore the Son of Adam and the sanctity of the Jerusalem Temple. It identifies the various angelic figures who are involved in setting the times of the world of creation and who will therefore be instrumental in bringing about the restoration of temple sanctity and therefore of the sanctity and order of creation itself.

14. Levenson, "The Temple and the World."

The Book of Dreams in 1 En. 83–90 presents two distinct visions. The first is a vision of the flood and its role in bringing about punishment for the wicked—and therefore restoration for the righteous. The second is the Animal Apocalypse of 1 En. 85–90, which surveys world history from the beginning of creation, employing animal images that symbolize the major figures of ancient Jewish history from creation through the time of the Seleucid monarch, Antiochus IV (r. 176–163 BCE). The focus on Antiochus IV narrows the date and concern of the Book of Dreams to indicate that the present form of the work is concerned with the overthrow of the Seleucid Empire much like the final vision of the book of Daniel in Dan 10–12. Consequently, the Animal Apocalypse appears to have been written in support of the Hasmonean Revolt against the Seleucid Empire as a means of updating an earlier version of the Book of Dreams.

The Epistle of Enoch in 1 En. 91–105 begins with an exhortation by Enoch to his children to pursue righteousness. It then continues with an epistle directed to all the inhabitants of the earth; it concerns the last days when the wicked will be overthrown and the righteous will be restored to see to the sanctification of the world. Although current forms of the book have rearranged the subunits of this section so that they no longer appear in the correct order, Qumran manuscripts of the book apparently represent the correct order in which they originally appeared. Overall, this section constitutes the culmination of the book that anticipates its ultimate outcome and purpose.

First Enoch 106–7 then concludes with a presentation concerning Noah's birth, signaling the coming of the figure who would lead the efforts at restoration. First Enoch 108 presents a final book of judgment.

Daniel

The book of Daniel is the only fully apocalyptic work in the Bible.[15] Although it is included among the prophetic books in the Christian Old Testament, largely because of Daniel's role in foreseeing the future, the Jewish Tanak includes it in the Ketuvim or Writings that constitute the third major com-

---

15. John J. Collins, *Daniel*, Hermeneia (Minneapolis: Fortress, 1993); Marvin A. Sweeney, "The End of Eschatology in Daniel? Theological and Socio-Political Ramifications of the Changing Contexts of Interpretation," in *Form and Intertextuality in Prophetic and Apocalyptic Literature*, FAT 45 (Tübingen: Mohr Siebeck, 2005), 248–61.

ponent of the Bible. Daniel is pious, prays to G-d, and adheres to tradition as best he can even though he has been exiled from the land of Israel to Babylonia. Although Daniel has visions of G-d and predicts the future, he does not speak on G-d's behalf as the prophets typically do. Rather, he is a sage, who reads the signs of the world in which he lives, such as the dream of Nebuchadnezzar or the course of human history, and the signs of heaven, such as the throne vision of G-d or the positions of the stars, to interpret human events and the will of G-d in relation to those events.

The book of Daniel portrays Daniel as a Jew exiled to Babylonia during the reign of Nebuchadnezzar, but numerous historical discrepancies make it clear that the authors of the book did not know the history of the Babylonian period very well. Daniel 1:1 places the fall of Jerusalem in the third year of King Jehoiakim of Judah; in fact Jerusalem fell during the eleventh year of King Zedekiah. Daniel 5:1–2 portrays Belshazzar as the King of Babylon and the son of Nebuchadnezzar; Belshazzar was a regent, not a king, and his father was Nabonidus, who had no relation to Nebuchadnezzar. Daniel 5:28, 31 portrays the Medes as the ruling world power after Babylon, but the Medes were never the ruling world power; Achaemenid Persia followed the Neo-Babylonian Empire. There is also confusion concerning the Persian kings. Daniel 5:31 claims that Darius is a Mede, but he was a Persian. Daniel 6:1 claims that Darius succeeded Belshazzar, but he succeeded King Cambyses of Persia. Daniel 9:1 claims that Darius was the son of Xerxes; again, Darius succeeded Cambyses. Daniel 6:28 claims that Darius preceded Cyrus, but he preceded Xerxes.

The only time the book exhibits historical accuracy is in the final vision of Dan 10–12, which predicts the events of the Hellenistic period from the time of Alexander the Great's conquest of the ancient Near East in 333–323 BCE, through the Diadochi wars between the Ptolemies and the Seleucids during the late fourth through the third century BCE, and finally, the period of the Hasmonean revolt against the Seleucid dynasty in the early second century BCE. References in Dan 11 clearly relate to the outbreak of the revolt: the portrayal of the contemptible person in Dan 11:21 refers to Antiochus IV (176–163 BCE); the abomination that makes desolate in Dan 11:31 refers to the desecration of the Jerusalem Temple by Antiochus IV; and the reference to a little help in Dan 11:34 refers to the beginning of the Hasmonean revolt in 167–164 BCE. But beginning in Dan 11:40, the future course of events becomes inaccurate. The attack of the king of the south never took place; the submission of Libya and Ethiopia never happened; and the prediction of the death of the king (Antiochus) on his journey back from Egypt never occurred. The accuracy of events leading up to 167–164 BCE and the inaccuracy of events that follow indicate that the book of Daniel was written in relation to the outbreak of the Hasmonean revolt in 167–164 BCE against the Seleucid Syrian Empire led by King Antiochus IV. The book does not say much about Daniel's relationship with Nebuchadnezzar; rather, it employs the setting of the Babylonian exile to address issues relevant to the outbreak of the Hasmonean revolt against Seleucid Syria.

The book of Daniel begins by encouraging its readers to hold true to their Jewish identities, to support the Hasmonean revolt, and to join it. The first part of the book in Dan 1–6 presents six so-called Court Tales to call for Jews to support the Hasmonean revolt.

Daniel 1 portrays the entry of Daniel and his three friends who are being prepared for service into the Babylonian royal court. Each is given a Babylonian name and assigned rations. But the four young men assert their Jewish identities when they request vegetarian food rather than the non-kosher meat that they were to be assigned, and G-d protects them.

Daniel 2 presents the account of Nebuchadnezzar's dream. Without having been told the dream, Daniel correctly related the vision of a Hellenistic colossus made of different minerals that represented a succession of empires. The head of gold was Babylon. The breast and arms of silver were the Medes. The belly and thighs of bronze were the Persians. The legs of iron were the Greeks. The feet of combined clay and iron were the mixed characters of the Ptolemaic and Seleucid dynasties. The final image of the colossus, destroyed by a stone thrown by a non-human hand, indicated that G-d would now bring down the Seleucid and Ptolemaic Empires.

Daniel 3 relates the narrative of the fiery furnace. Daniel's three friends were to be executed in a fiery furnace for refusing to worship Nebuchadnezzar's image, but they were protected by a divine figure. Nebuchadnezzar never demanded such worship, but Antiochus IV did.

Daniel 4 portrays Nebuchadnezzar's madness. Nebuchadnezzar was never associated with madness. But when Antiochus IV declared himself to be a god to be worshiped by the people, he took the title Antiochus Epiphanes, which means Antiochus, Manifest God. Hellenistic writers of the time, however, labeled him Antiochus Epimanes, Antiochus the Mad.

Daniel 5 portrays Belshazzar's feast in which the Babylonian king called for temple vessels to be used for his entertainment. A nonhuman hand then wrote on his wall "Mene, Mene, Tekel, Parsin," Aramaic words that mean "You will be measured, measured; You will be weighed; and You will be scattered/exiled," in reference to the impending downfall of the dynasty.

Daniel 6 portrays Daniel in the lions' den. Daniel was thrown to the lions for refusing orders to desist his prayer as a Jew, but G-d protected him and the lions did not molest him.

Although many scholars maintain that the Court Tales of Dan 1–6 and the Vision Accounts of Dan 7–12 were written separately, the Vision Accounts build upon the Court Tales by illustrating that G-d is about to act to bring down the Seleucid Empire and to ensure the freedom and integrity of the Jewish people.

Daniel 7 begins the vision sequence with a portrayal of a throne vision in which G-d, here portrayed as One Ancient of Days, signals the beginning of action against the Seleucid Empire. The vision employs a sequence of monsters, each of which is slain, that resembles the sequence of Nebuchadnezzar's dream in Dan 2. The first is a lion with eagle's wings that represents Babylon. The second is a bear with three ribs in its mouth that represents the Medes. The third is a four-headed winged leopard that represents Persia. The fourth is an iron-toothed beast that represents Greece. Its ten iron teeth represent a succession of ten Seleucid monarchs, and the final image of a horn with eyes and a mouth speaking great things is Antiochus IV. When the One Ancient of Days, i.e., G-d, slays the beast, the Kingdom of G-d is inaugurated for the Saints of the Most High, thereby signaling the defeat of the Seleucid Empire and the success of the Hasmonean revolt.

Daniel 8–9 portrays a vison apparently based in part on the constellations of the heavens. It portrays a ram charging to the west, which represents the Persian Empire, and a goat charging to the east, which represents the Greek Empire of Alexander the Great. The little horn growing out of the goat, which magnifies itself and defiles the temple, represents the Seleucid Syrian monarch Antiochus IV. But Daniel prays to G-d, and the angel Gabriel comes to him to explain the vision indicating that seventy weeks of years, or four hundred and ninety years, will pass from the time of the Babylonian exile (beginning in 587 BCE) until the ultimate fall of Antiochus IV, whose reign began in 176 BCE. The numbers are drawn from earlier texts. The seventy weeks of years builds upon Jeremiah's statements that the Babylonian exile would last for seventy years in Jer 25 and 29 and upon the calculation of the jubilee year in Lev 25 that calls for the restoration of land to its original owners after a period of seven weeks of years or forty-nine years. The use of such texts in calculating the fall of the Seleucid Empire indicates that the authors of Daniel were searching earlier scriptures for numerical clues indicating the time when G-d would act against the Seleucid Empire.

Likewise, the final vision of the ultimate fall of the Seleucid Empire in Dan 10–12 employs an angelic guide to aid Daniel in interpreting the vision. It includes an account of how Daniel prepares himself for the vision by fasting for three weeks, how the angel appears to him, and how the angel Michael will act on G-d's behalf to realize the Kingdom of G-d. Those Jews who die fighting against the empire will be brought back to life. In the end, a series of numerical projections attempt to predict when the final victory will be achieved.

The Hasmonean revolt took some twenty-seven years before Judah freed itself from Seleucid rule under the leadership of the last surviving Hasmonean brother, Shimon. Although Judah the Maccabee, his father Mattathias, his brother Jonathan, and his other two brothers died during the course of the revolt, Jerusalem was free of Seleucid control in 140 BCE.

The Judean Wilderness Scrolls

The discovery of the Judean wilderness scrolls by the Dead Sea at Qumran, Nahal Hever, Wadi Murabb'at, Masada, and elsewhere revolutionized understanding of the late Second Temple period by pointing to a previously little-known Jewish movement that settled at the site of Qumran, located along the northwestern quadrant of the Dead Sea, beginning in the early to mid-second century BCE until the site was destroyed by the Roman army during the Zealot revolt of 66–74 CE. Archeological excavation of the site following the initial discovery of Hebrew scrolls in 1947 indicated a large community of Jews who hid more than eight hundred scrolls at the outbreak of the war against Rome, including all books of the Bible except for Esther, a number of apocryphal and pseudepigraphical texts, and many works that had previously been unknown. Rachel Elior persuasively argues that the Dead Sea Scrolls include examples of visionary experience and mystical works that anticipate the later heikhalot literature.[16]

The site and the scrolls demonstrate that the community at Qumran belonged to a Jewish sect that believed that the temple in Jerusalem, and therefore the world at large, had become defiled and that G-d would act to restore the sanctity of the Jerusalem Temple and the world at large. The origins of the Qumran sect apparently lie in tensions within the Zadokite

---

16. Rachel Elior, *The Three Temples: On the Emergence of Jewish Mysticism* (Oxford: Littman Library of Jewish Civilization, 2004).

priesthood of the Jerusalem Temple, particularly during the reign of the Seleucid monarch Antiochus IV (r. 176–163 BCE). Antiochus deposed the high priest Onias and replaced him with candidates who were more willing to turn temple resources over to the Seleucid Empire; his policies eventually provoked a revolt against the Seleucid Empire led by the Hasmonean priestly family of Modein. The Hasmoneans ultimately defeated the Seleucid Empire and secured Judean independence by 140 BCE.

There were questions about the fitness of the Hasmonean priests to oversee the temple, particularly as they began to assume more power akin to the power of monarchs. It appears that the Qumran group was founded when a figure identified in the scrolls, especially the Habakkuk Pesher and the Hodayot Scroll, as the Teacher of Righteousness led a group of followers to the Dead Sea to study and sanctify themselves until G-d chose to act. The group was persecuted initially by a priestly figure identified in the scrolls as the Wicked Priest, but it persisted and long outlived its founder until it was destroyed by the Romans in 68 CE. Many interpreters identify the group as the Essenes, whom Josephus and Pliny also mention as having founded a holy community by the Dead Sea, although many questions concerning the identity and practices of the group remain. It is clear from the Temple Scroll, Songs of the Sabbath Sacrifice, and other texts that the Qumran group employed a solar calendar of 364 days like that employed in the Pentateuch. By contrast, the calendar of the Jerusalem priesthood, which Rabbinic Judaism also adopted, was a lunar calendar of 354 days, based on a Babylonian model, which requires an additional month every three years to adjust the calendar to the solar pattern. Calendrical issues appear to be a major issue in the conflict between the Qumran group and the authorities in the Jerusalem Temple.

Although the group was apparently founded by a priestly figure, it appears to have admitted Jews regardless of their priestly status. Women may well have been a part of the community as well, insofar as women's graves are found in the cemetery areas by the Dead Sea, although their relationship to the sacred activities of the community is unclear. Jewish men underwent a probationary period of two years before they were admitted to the group, but only after passing examinations at the end of each of the two years. Once admitted, they joined a general assembly that was seated in a fashion also found in rabbinic yeshivot: with the most learned members in the front, corresponding to their right to speak first on issues under discussion, and the remainder of the membership in rows behind them, according to their levels of knowledge. A vast quantity and rich variety of scrolls that resemble copies of Scripture and interpretive works used by other Jewish groups signify the importance of Scripture and its study at Qumran, as do numerous other works—unknown from elsewhere and apparently unique to the Qumran community—that reuse, imitate, cite, or otherwise interpret Scripture. Torah exegesis appears to include what a number of scholars consider Zadokite or Sadducean forms of exegesis, such as the Temple Scroll or the Damascus Document, insofar as such texts point to the use of written Torah. Others point to a principle of Oral Torah like that developed by the early rabbis, such as the Genesis Apocryphon, insofar as they employed midrashic forms of expanding upon texts. The group held certain views in common with the Zealots as well, insofar as they anticipated an apocalyptic war against infidels, as outlined in the War Scroll, that would ultimately see the defeat of evil and the consecration of the Jerusalem Temple and the world at large. It appears that they died out following the destruction of the community site at Qumran, but traces of their influence appear in medieval reports of manuscript discoveries by the Dead Sea, the discovery of copies of the Damascus Document in the Cairo Geniza, and the emergence of Karaite Judaism, a Jewish group opposed to Rabbinic Judaism and dedicated to the use of the Zadokite written Torah, in the eighth century CE and beyond.

Texts such as the Temple Scroll, the Songs of the Sabbath Sacrifice, and the War Scroll illustrate the apocalyptic and early mystical character of the group.

The Temple Scroll, known especially from 11QTa and several more manuscripts, portrays an eschatological temple and the halakot, or Jewish laws, that are to be observed in relation to that temple; Ezekiel's vision in Ezek 40–48 apparently serves as the model for the Temple Scroll.[17] Ezekiel's temple does not correspond either to Solomon's Temple or to any known structure of the Second Temple, and so it has come to be regarded as a third temple yet to be built. Ezekiel's temple is much larger than any earthly temple that the earthly city of Jerusalem could ever accommodate, and so many interpreters understand it to be a portrayal of the heavenly temple that serves as the model for the building of the Jerusalem Temple. Unfortunately, no surviving copy of the Temple Scroll preserves the initial columns that describe the temple structure itself. The portrayal of the temple courtyards indicates an enormous area that would surpass the area of the Temple Mount in Jerusalem like that of Ezekiel's temple.

17. Florentino García Martínez, *The Dead Sea Scrolls Translated: The Dead Sea Scrolls in English* (Grand Rapids: Eerdmans, 1996), 154–84.

The surviving text of the Temple Scroll focuses primarily on the halakot to be observed, although they are not identical to those of Ezek 40–48. They are derived from Deuteronomy, but the text has been rewritten in first-person form, thereby presenting itself as the transcript of what YHWH said to Moses on Sinai rather than Moses's report of what YHWH said. The combination of all the written texts relating to a particular halakah in order to expound its full meaning accords with the Zadokite principle of deriving halakic interpretations from written Torah. For example, the laws concerning the observance of Shavuot—which in Rabbinic Judaism occurs fifty days after Passover and commemorates the revelation of the Torah and the period of wilderness wandering—appear in a very different form in the Temple Scroll. The Scroll reworks texts devoted to Shavuot in various books of the Torah by combining them all into a single narrative that calls for the observance of three Shavuot festivals, one devoted to grain, one devoted to wine, and one devoted to oil, each of which is observed fifty days following the preceding observance.[18] Likewise, the Temple Scroll presents the "Torah of the King" (Deut 17:14–20) with modifications from other Pentateuchal readings and a lengthy section that explains the laws of kingship by drawing upon numerous scriptural texts concerned with the monarchy.[19] Such examples point to a concern for complete understanding and observance of each halakah in keeping with what is perceived to be the divine will, and to the conviction that the divine will is revealed in the Scriptures.

The Songs of the Sabbath Sacrifice is a liturgical composition that anticipates later heikhalot compositions, such as the Heikhalot Rabbati, the Heikhalot Zutarti, and the Shiur Qomah.[20] One of the best-preserved copies was discovered at Masada; a number of others were found in Qumran caves 4 and 11. Unfortunately, the surviving copies are very fragmentary and even with multiple manuscripts do not provide a complete understanding of the underlying document. The Songs of the Sabbath Sacrifice include thirteen songs, one for each of the Sabbaths for a quarter of the year, thus indicating that the document presupposes a solar calendar of fifty-two weeks and 364 days like that presupposed throughout the Pentateuch. The text portrays a setting before the throne of G-d in the heavenly

18. Marvin A. Sweeney, "Sefirah at Qumran: Aspects of the Counting of the First Fruits Festivals in the Temple Scroll," in *Reading Prophetic Books* (Tübingen: Mohr Siebeck, 2014), 337–45.

19. Marvin A. Sweeney, "Midrashic Perspective in the Torat ham-Melek of the Temple Scroll," in *Reading Prophetic Books*, 346–62.

20. García Martínez, *The Dead Sea Scrolls*, 419–31.

temple where the songs for each Sabbath are sung. It provides a detailed, but fragmentary, description of the heavenly throne of G-d and the various angelic figures that attend upon G-d, apparently as a model for the priests of the Jerusalem Temple. It presents the text of each song, and it highlights the seventh song in the sequence for reasons that are not entirely understood, although it indicates that the seventh Sabbath is especially sacred and marks the midpoint of the thirteen songs presented. In addition to the words of the songs, the text portrays the angelic choir as singing the songs, often indicating details such as a progression of voices, each voice singing in a higher note to achieve the desired effect of the heavenly liturgy. Taken altogether, the fragments of the Songs of the Sabbath Sacrifice present a scenario of worship in the heavenly temple before the heavenly merkavah, the chariot or throne of G-d. Such a function develops the use of psalms in temple worship, as noted above.

Finally, the War Scroll of Qumran presents a scenario of the sect's future expectations.[21] It portrays a forty-year war in which the forces of G-d, including the angels and all righteous Jews in the world, gather to wage war against the evil of the world, including all the demons, all the nations, and all wicked Jews. Insofar as the Qumran group would define itself as the righteous of the world, it appears that they see themselves arrayed against the rest of the world. Two messianic figures emerge to lead the righteous. One is the messiah of David, who will have overall supervision of the combat. The other is the messiah of Aaron, a priestly figure who has overall command and ensures the sanctity of the endeavor. The war proceeds in two stages, apparently based on the chronology of David's own forty-year reign. Six years are devoted to combat to gain control of the Temple Mount, following which a year is spent in sanctifying the temple. Such a pattern appears to be based on David's initial seven years of rule in Hebron, culminating in his capture of Jerusalem, which he established as his capital for all Israel and as the future site of the holy temple. The initial seven years would reunite and sanctify the Jewish people; the remaining thirty-three years would be spent combating the nations of the world in an effort to sanctify all nations and creation at large. Again, the pattern of David's rule comes to mind as he spent the latter thirty-three years of his reign, when he ruled a united Israel, building his empire by conquering foreign nations.

---

21. García Martínez, *The Dead Sea Scrolls*, 95–125; Marvin A. Sweeney, "Davidic Typology in the Forty Year War Between the Sons of Light and the Sons of Darkness," in *Form and Intertextuality in Prophetic and Apocalyptic Literature* (Tübingen: Mohr Siebeck, 2005), 262–68.

Apparently, the War Scroll projects actual earthly conflict. A first edition of the War Scroll appears to presuppose the Hellenistic period and combat against the Seleucid Empire and perhaps the Hasmonean dynasty. The second edition appears to take a Roman model for its detailed description of military equipment, formations, and tactics. If the Qumran group realized its war in the revolt against Rome, the outcome was not what they imagined: the temple was destroyed, Judah was defeated, and the Qumran group ceased to exist as a coherent movement.

The Book of Revelation

The book of Revelation, or the Apocalypse of John, is very clearly a Christian apocalyptic work because it features Jesus Christ as one of the key figures in its visionary accounts concerning the future fall of Babylon or Rome and the inauguration of the New Jerusalem.[22] Its date is disputed. Many note the focus on the significance of the Roman emperor, Nero, who died in 68 CE at the outset of the Roman campaign to put down the Jewish revolt in the land of Israel. Nero was the first major Roman emperor to persecute Christians in Rome, beginning in 64 CE when he slaughtered thousands as a result of his interest in blaming them—and thereby exonerating himself—as the party responsible for the fire that devastated Rome. Revelation 13:18 identifies the number 666 as the mark of the beast. The number 666 is the numerical value of the Hebrew letters that spell the name Nero. Its identification with the beast that must be defeated indicates an interest in the downfall of Nero, as early as 64 CE and continuing through his death in 68 CE, and perhaps beyond, as some believed that he would return from the dead to continue his persecution of Christians. Others maintain that Revelation should be dated prior to the assassination in 96 CE of the Roman emperor Domitian, who was known for his persecution of Christians throughout the empire. Others have pointed to evidence that ties the book to the destruction of the Jerusalem Temple in 70 CE. Many interpreters suggest that Revelation underwent a period of growth from the time of Nero to the time of Domitian to account for the entire period from Nero through Domitian.

22. David E. Aune, *Revelation 1–5*, WBC 52[A] (Nashville: Thomas Nelson, 1997); *Revelation 6–16*, WBC 52B (Nashville: Thomas Nelson, 1998); *Revelation 17–22*, WBC 52C (Nashville: Thomas Nelson, 1998).

The book of Revelation reports to seven churches in Asia the visions of a seer who identifies himself as John. John prefaces the vision reports with an account of his divine commission and with seven messages to the seven churches that are dictated to him by a heavenly figure identified as Jesus. No evidence in the text confirms the identification of this John with any others by the same name who appear in the New Testament or who are the purported authors of other works of the New Testament. John describes himself as a brother who shares in the persecution suffered by the people who constitute the seven churches of western Asia Minor. The identification of the author disregards the usual practice of formulating apocalypses as pseudonymous compositions, but our lack of knowledge concerning the author effectively renders the work as an anonymous composition to modern readers. The author titles the work, "The revelation (apocalypse) of Jesus Christ, which G-d gave him to show his servants what must take place" (Rev 1:1). He claims to have received this revelation through an angel so that he might witness to the word of G-d, the testimony of Jesus Christ, and all that he saw in the vision. The presentation of visionary experience—including a throne vision and tour of heaven, the use of an angelic guide, and the revelation of secret knowledge concerning the divine, creation, and future— all support the identification of this work as an apocalypse. Indeed, recent research places Revelation squarely in the context of the Jewish visionary tradition that leads ultimately to the composition of the Heikhalot Rabbati and subsequent Jewish mystical literature.

The book of Revelation is formulated as an epistle addressed to seven Asian churches that have suffered persecution. It comprises three major subunits: a prologue in Rev 1:1–8 that introduces the work as a whole, a presentation of John's vision and commission in Rev 1:9–3:22, and a disclosure of G-d's eschatological plan for the world in Rev 4:1–22:9. Evident throughout the book is Revelation's dependence on earlier biblical texts, particularly those such as Ezekiel and Isaiah, among others, that present visionary experience of the divine. Its overall goal is to project the downfall of the beast, the Roman Empire that has persecuted early Christians, so that an ideal, eschatological peace might follow.

The prologue to the book in Rev 1:1–8 introduces the whole. It begins with the title of the work in Rev 1:1–2 as noted above. A beatitude that blesses all who read the work as well as those who hear it then follows in Rev 1:3. Revelation 1:4–5 identifies the addressees of the vision report as the seven Asian churches, wishes them grace, and indicates its indebtedness to G-d and to Christ. Two doxologies then follow in Rev 1:7–8. The portrayal of the divine coming in the clouds draws upon portrayals of YHWH's appearance to Ezekiel in Babylonia borne by the four living beings, later identified as cherubim, in Ezek 1. The identification of Christ as the Alpha and Omega, the beginning and the end, signals G-d's totality in the universe.

The account of John's vision and commission in Rev 1:9–3:22 draws heavily on earlier visionary accounts, such as Ezekiel's throne vision in Ezek 1–3 and Daniel's throne vision in Dan 7. Revelation 1:9–20 relates John's reception of the vision in which G-d commands him to write to the seven churches. The image of the seven lampstands draws in part on the imagery of the temple heikhal or main room in which ten lampstands and ten incense altars stand, but the number seven is employed to signal the seven churches. The designation of John as one like a son of man employs terminology that is understood messianically in Mark 13, but in Ezekiel and Daniel the designation Son of Man indicates a priestly figure in the temple who may approach the holy of holies of the temple where G-d is enthroned. The designation Son of Man points to the role of the high priest who represents humankind, i.e., the descendants of Adam, as they approach G-d in the holy of holies, understood as the Garden of Eden. The portrayal of G-d as one with white hair like snow, eyes of flaming fire, feet of bronze, etc., again draws on the imagery of Ezek 1 and Dan 7. The seven stars in G-d's hand are associated with the seven churches. Individual messages to each of the churches then follow in Rev 2–3.

The account of the disclosure of G-d's eschatological plan in Rev 4:1–22:9 comprises seven major sections, all of which build up a scenario of G-d's defeat of the beast, understood to be the persecuting Roman emperor, whether Nero, Domitian, or any subsequent oppressor.

The first section in Rev 4:1–2a signals John's heavenly ascent through a door. Such a portrayal may well build on the imagery of 1 En. 14:14b–15, which portrays a door that provides access to the heavenly realm.

The second section is Rev 4:2b–7:17, which portrays the vision of the heavenly throne room, the breaking of the first six seals, and the sealing of the 144,000. The portrayal of the divine throne room draws upon the imagery of visions of G-d in Exod 24, Isa 6, and Ezek 1. The imagery of G-d enthroned employs precious stones like the *hashmal* of Ezek 1 and the imagery of the blue lapis lazuli pavement from Exod 24. The twenty-four elders seated around G-d are based in the twenty-four courses of priests noted in 1 Chr 24, which provides details concerning the twenty-four priestly courses that guard the sanctity of the temple. The four creatures about the throne are drawn from Ezek 1, and the Kedushah or Trisagion is drawn from Isa 6. The agenda entails the question of who is qualified to open the seals of the book that will disclose the future, an image that is drawn from the open and sealed book of Jer 32. The Lamb, a portrayal of Christ as the Passover sacrificial lamb, proceeds to open the seals as the sun turns dark and the moon turns to blood, an image drawn from Joel 3:4 (2:31). The 144,000 of Israel to be sealed are 12,000 from each of the twelve tribes of Israel, joined by an undefined number of people from the nations who will emerge from the ordeal of persecution to see the final blessing.

The third section in Rev 8:1–11:14 focuses on the opening of the seventh seal and the first six trumpets. The trumpets are portrayed in relation to the plagues of the Exodus narratives to signal divine judgment against the evil of the world. Following the blowing of the trumpets, another angel brings a small scroll that will be eaten by John so that he may prophesy in a manner analogous to the prophet and priest Ezekiel who ate the divine scroll at the conclusion of his vision so that he might speak the divine word (Ezek 3). He is then asked to measure the dimensions of the heavenly temple much as Ezekiel did in Ezek 40–48. The imagery of the two olive trees and two lampstands is drawn from Zech 4 to signify the messianic figures who will witness the blowing of the seventh trumpet that will inaugurate G-d's action to deliver the world.

The fourth section in Rev 11:15–16:21 focuses on the seventh trumpet and the seven bowls. The blowing of the seventh trumpet begins the section to signal the divine theophany that inaugurates G-d's action. This section portrays a cosmic war that breaks out following the birth of a child, apparently Jesus modelled on the birth of Emanuel in Isa 7:14. A seven-headed dragon, apparently Leviathan from Isa 11:15–16 and 27:1, attacks the woman. The child is snatched away to reside with G-d while the woman is expelled to the wilderness. The angel Michael then fights against the dragon who is joined by two beasts, one who is modeled on the fallen Lucifer in Isa 14 and the other who apparently represents the Roman imperial cult in the form of the monster Behemoth. Seven angels are granted seven bowls to pour out the wrath of G-d upon the world to ensure the divine triumph.

The fifth section in Rev 17:1–19:10 portrays divine judgment against Babylon/Rome, which is depicted as a great whore. The portrayal of the woman as Babylon apparently draws on the portrayal of the fall of Babylon in Isa 21 and the presentation of Babylon as a fallen and disgraced woman in Isa 47.

The sixth section in Rev 19:11–21:8 portrays the final defeat of G-d's enemies, including Satan; the resurrection of the dead, apparently derived from Isa 25; Ezek 37; and Dan 12; as well as a portrayal of a New Heaven and Earth derived from Isa 66.

The seventh section in Rev 21:9–22:9 presents the vision of the New Jerusalem, apparently derived from Ezekiel's vision of the new temple in Ezek 40–48.

The epilogue in Rev 22:10–21 closes with a parenesis to motivate and inspire the book's audience, as well as a subscript that resembles the conclusions of epistles.

Fourth Ezra

Fourth Ezra currently appears as part of a Christian apocryphal work known as 2 Esdras, but it appears to be a Jewish apocalyptic work that has been edited and encased in an introductory and concluding literary framework that transforms it into an apologetic Christian work.[23] The basic text of 2 Esdras appears in Latin as part of the Vulgate and in Syriac as part of the Peshitta, and a number of derivative texts appear in Ethiopic, Armenian, Arabic, Coptic, Georgian, and Greek. Scholars maintain that the core of the work in chapters 3–14 was originally written in Hebrew by a Jewish writer following the Roman destruction of the Jerusalem during the Zealot revolt of 66–74 CE. Most understand the reference in 4 Ezra 3:1, which sets the work thirty years after the destruction of the city, to indicate that the work was written in ca. 100 CE The introductory and concluding chapters in 2 Esd 1–2 and 15–16, identified respectively as 2 Ezra and 5 Ezra, recontextualize the work as a Christian theological treatise that polemicizes against Judaism by claiming that the temple was destroyed as a result of Jewish sin. Although Judaism also concluded that Jews had sinned, the polemical aspect appears when the work attempts to use such sin as a justification for G-d's shift to the gentiles and thus to Christianity.

Insofar as G-d is angry with Israel for its failure to abide by the divine will, G-d will now turn to the gentiles as the future foundation for the divine covenant with humankind. It does not appear to presuppose the complete break between Judaism and Christianity that took place following the failure of the Bar Kokhba revolt of 132–135 CE when much of the Jewish population of Judea was destroyed by the Roman army, the land was renamed Palestine by the Roman Empire to erase memory of Jewish existence in the land, and

23. Collins, *The Apocalyptic Imagination*, 156–69; Carey, *Ultimate Things*, 147–56; Bruce M. Metzger, "The Fourth Book of Ezra," in *Old Testament Pseudepigrapha*, 1:517–60; Michael Stone, *4 Ezra*, Hermeneia (Minneapolis: Fortress, 1990).

Jews were forbidden by the Roman emperor Hadrian to practice Judaism. Following the Bar Kokhba revolt, many Christians dissociated themselves from Jews and sought the favor of the Roman Empire.

The core material identified as 4 Ezra in 2 Esd 3–14 is a true apocalypse that employs visionary experience mediated to Ezra by an angelic figure concerning transcendent reality in the world. Ezra is here identified as the son of Salathiel, apparently a rendition of the name Shealtiel, the father of Zerubbabel ben/bar Shealtiel, the grandson of King Jehoiachin of Judah, who was appointed by the Persians as governor of Judah to oversee the construction of the Second Temple. The significance of this identification remains uncertain; it would appear to supply a father for Ezra and connect him with Zerubbabel, even though such an identification would require that Shealtiel and Zerubbabel would be considered as priests.

Fourth Ezra employs seven visionary accounts in 3:1–5:19; 5:21–6:34; 6:35–9:25; 9:26–10:59; 11:1–12:51; 13:1–58; and 14:1–48, which are designed to examine the questions of sin and suffering as well as indications of the impending end of the world as it was known up to that time. The first three visions are distinctive in that they employ Job-like dialogues to address these questions.

The first vision in 4 Ezra 3:1–5:19 portrays Ezra lying in bed, troubled by the questions of human sin and suffering that the destruction of the temple entails. Ezra observes how human beings from the time of Adam on have possessed an evil heart that prompted human beings to engage in wrong behavior. But Ezra's thoughts turn to a comparison between Zion and Babylon as he observes that Babylon has been just as sinful as Zion, if not more so. The angel, Uriel, whose name means "the light of G-d," appears and responds to Ezra's questions. Uriel at first asserts that G-d's ways are inscrutable and that human beings, beginning with Ezra, are in no position to understand G-d's decisions and actions, let alone to challenge them. Such a position is central to the understanding of G-d in the book of Job. When Uriel tells Ezra that he cannot comprehend even the things that he does know, such as the weight of fire or the measure of wind, Ezra exclaims that it would be better for humans not even to exist in a world where such ungodliness and suffering exist. After recounting a parable concerning the limited perspectives of the forest and the sea, Uriel informs Ezra that the present era of suffering is about to come to an end; it is an age of sorrow and suffering, perhaps not unlike the time prior to the flood. Upon awakening, Ezra follows Uriel's instruction in 4 Ezra 5:20 to fast for seven days in preparation for further revelation.

The second vision in 4 Ezra 5:21–6:34 reiterates his concerns about sin and suffering. Ezra demands to know why G-d chose to punish the Jewish people, who had accepted G-d's covenant, by having them overrun by nations that had little to do with G-d's covenant. Uriel first reiterates his earlier point that Ezra cannot understand divine purpose; he then employs the analogy of an aging mother to argue that people born during an age of decline are smaller and less capable than those of earlier generations. Sin consequently increases as the end of the age approaches. But when the humiliation of Zion comes to an end, a new age will be revealed. Ezra then follows Uriel's instructions to fast for another seven days to understand the revelation of what is to come.

The third vision in 4 Ezra 6:35–9:25 begins with Ezra's assertion that creation was made by G-d for Jews to sanctify; why then does Israel not receive its divine inheritance? Uriel responds that the entrance to a better world is narrow; in the case of Judaism, observance of divine Torah is key. Uriel charges that many who were given divine instruction, so that they might live, have disregarded Torah; but a minority of the righteous have indeed observed Torah. When Ezra asks if the righteous might intercede for the wicked, Uriel responds that the righteous cannot always intercede and that all must be responsible for their own actions. When Ezra lists counterexamples, from Abraham through David and beyond, of those who have interceded on behalf of others, Uriel points to resolution in the future age. Then he asks that Ezra go to a field to eat flowers for another seven days to prepare for a new vision.

In the fourth vision in 4 Ezra 9:26–10:59, Ezra goes to the field of Ardat where, as instructed, he eats nothing but flowers for seven days. Ezra's vision begins with the glory of divine Torah, but it turns to a vision of a woman who remained barren for thirty years. She is finally granted a son; but when it comes time for him to marry, he dies, dashing all the hopes in which his mother had believed. The woman is Zion. Uriel explains to Ezra that G-d has revealed to him many secrets concerning the future of Zion, and he asks Ezra to sleep for two more nights and await a dream from G-d.

The fifth vision in 4 Ezra 11:1–12:51 relates the dream of an eagle with twelve sets of wings and three heads that arises to dominate the earth. The eagle is clearly the Roman Empire, and it is identified, by the voice of a lion speaking to it, with the last of the beasts revealed in the book of Daniel. Ultimately, the eagle collapses. When Ezra awakens, he appeals to G-d for an explanation. G-d tells him that the eagle is Rome and the lion is the messiah; Ezra should record these things in a book to teach those who are wise. Ezra is told to wait another seven days for further instruction as he attempts to encourage Israel.

The sixth vision in 4 Ezra 13:1–58 is a dream report in which Ezra sees a man rising from the sea to fly with the clouds of heaven. G-d explains the man as a vision of the figure who will lead to the restoration of Zion. Ezra is instructed to wait three more days for further instruction.

The seventh vision in 4 Ezra 14:1–48 portrays G-d's instructions to Ezra to act as a second Moses, writing books that will instruct the people. G-d tells him to write the twenty-four books of the Jewish Bible that are meant for public instruction, but G-d also tells him to write seventy more hidden works for secret instruction concerning G-d's plans for the future. Such books will facilitate full understanding of divine Torah. They would likely be further apocalyptic and revelatory books, such as the Enochic and heikhalot literature of the rabbinic period, that take up questions very similar to those of 4 Ezra.

Second Baruch

Second Baruch is an apocalyptic book based on the figure of Baruch ben Neriah, the scribe who worked with the prophet and priest Jeremiah in the late seventh and early sixth centuries BCE, during the final years of the Judean monarchy and the early years of the Babylonian Exile.[24] Although Baruch serves primarily a scribal function in the Hebrew Masoretic Text of Jeremiah, Wright demonstrates that Baruch is configured as Jeremiah's visionary successor in the Septuagint version of the book. The book's fifty-two chapters are organized very differently in LXXJeremiah and MTJeremiah. The oracle addressed to Baruch in MTJeremiah 45:1–5 appears instead at LXXJeremiah 51:31–35, thereby placing the prophecy to Baruch, who records Jeremiah's words for the future, at the end of LXXJeremiah.[25] Insofar as Jer 32 speaks of an open and closed book that talks about the future of Jerusalem and Judah, LXXJeremiah provides the basis for developing the figure of Baruch as an apocalyptic seer who will focus on the aftermath of the destruction of Jerusalem.[26]

24. Collins, *The Apocalyptic Imagination*, 170–86; Carey, *Ultimate Things*, 156–68; Albertus F. J. Klijn, "2 (Syriac Apocalypse of) Baruch," in *Old Testament Pseudepigrapha*, 1:615–52.

25. J. Edward Wright, *Baruch ben Neriah: From Biblical Scribe to Apocalyptic Seer* (Columbia: University of South Carolina Press, 2003), 36–39.

26. Andrew G. Shead, *The Open Book and the Sealed Book: Jeremiah 32 in Its Hebrew and Greek Recensions*, JSOTSup 347 (Sheffield: Sheffield Academic Press, 2002).

Second Baruch shares many of the same concerns with 4 Ezra, specifically its concern with questions of divine justice in relation to the suffering of the Jewish people and its contention that Judaism must focus on the observance of divine Torah, a position championed by Jeremiah, to ensure its wellbeing for the future. Some interpreters maintain that 2 Bar. was written as a response to 4 Ezra, not so much to challenge it as to examine its issues more closely. The book appears now in Syriac translation as part of the Peshitta version of the Bible. It was apparently translated from a Greek text, some fragments of which are extant. The Greek version in turn was translated from a Hebrew original which is no longer extant. The book is fully aware of the destruction of the Jerusalem Temple by the Romans in 70 CE, but it does not appear to be aware of the Bar Kokhba revolt. Scholars therefore date it to ca. 100–120 CE.

The literary structure of 2 Bar. is complex, but Collins demonstrates that it comprises seven major segments, based in part on the analogy of the seven visions of 4 Ezra and the interplay of Baruch's instances of fasting for seven days in 2 Bar. 9:1–2; 12:5; 21:1; and 47:1–2, as well as three instances in which Baruch addresses the people in 2 Bar. 31:1–34:1; 44:1–46:7; and 77:1–26. Collins posits that these instances mark the end of the first six structural components of the book and that the letter in 2 Bar. 78:1–87:1 constitutes the final component of the book. The result is seven major subunits in 2 Bar. 1:1–9:2; 10:1–12:5; 13:1–20:6; 21:1–34:1; 35:1–47:2; 48:1–77:26; 78:1–87:1.

Second Baruch 1:1–9:2 begins the book with an account of Baruch's witness of the destruction of Jerusalem. Although the narrative setting of the work is the early sixth century BCE when the Babylonians destroyed Jerusalem, the book addresses the destruction of Jerusalem by the Romans in 70 CE. When Baruch realizes YHWH's intention to destroy Jerusalem, he asks how Israel will continue to observe divine Torah in the face of such a calamity. G-d responds to him that Jerusalem's suffering will last only for a while, but G-d will exist forever; a time of resolution will be realized in the future. Baruch laments and with several companions goes outside the city into the Kidron Valley to witness the destruction. He sees four angels equipped with torches at each corner of Jerusalem and a fifth who is committed to the protection of the holy vessels of the temple. Once the city is destroyed, Baruch weeps and fasts for seven days.

Second Baruch 10:1–12:5 reports that G-d commands Baruch to send Jeremiah to Babylon, in correspondence with the prophet's fate in rabbinic tradition. Baruch remains behind and goes to the gate of the ruined temple, where he raises a lament to G-d concerning the destruction of the city. He then fasts for another seven days.

Second Baruch 13:1–20:6 begins with a divine voice telling Baruch that he has been preserved alive due to his righteousness, but Baruch demands to know, what is the use of such righteousness if one must witness and live through such calamity? G-d responds that the wicked learn righteousness and the righteous learn the merits of struggle until G-d brings about a new future of glory. When Baruch protests that the time until such glory is short and that those who suffered through long lives did so in vain, G-d instructs him to fast for another seven days to prepare for a revelation of G-d.

Second Baruch 21:1–34:1 relates Baruch's vision of G-d in which G-d tells him of the twelve calamities that will precede the coming of the messiah. With the coming of the messiah, the righteous dead will be resurrected, whereas those who were wicked will perish forever. Baruch tells the people to prepare themselves for this future. When Baruch prepares to leave, the people cry out in fear of being abandoned. Baruch therefore promises to go to appear before G-d at the holy of holies of the ruined temple to ask further instruction as to what the people are to do.

Second Baruch 35:1–47:2 relates Baruch's vision at the holy of holies. He falls asleep and in a dream of the night sees a vision of a forest, its trees planted on a plain surrounded by mountains. A vine arose from it, and a spring that submerged the forest in water uprooted it and washed the mountains away until only one cedar was left. When the cedar was brought before the vine, the vine accused the cedar of great wickedness and condemned it. Baruch awakens, prays to G-d, and asks for an explanation. G-d tells Baruch that the vision portends a succession of kingdoms that will exercise power over Zion until only one is left, the cedar, at the time of the messiah, the spring and the vine. In the end, the messiah will judge the last ruler. When Baruch asks for further explanation, G-d tells him to go away and then come back to the place of his ancestors to receive further revelation. After telling his son and the elders to continue to observe divine Torah, Baruch prepares to go to Hebron, where the ancestors are buried.

Second Baruch 48:1–77:26 relates another vision granted to Baruch in which he sees a cloud coming up from the sea. The sea was filled with black waters and many colors with lightning at its top. The black waters overcame the colors in the water twelve times, and twelve streams flowed out from the sea to dominate the entire earth. When Baruch awakens and asks for an explanation of the vision, G-d explains to him that the vision related a succession of twelve catastrophes that were linked to human history from the time of the transgression of Adam, through the entire history of Israel, up to the eleventh time when Jerusalem was destroyed. The twelfth time indicates when Jerusalem will be rebuilt and then destroyed again. At that time, those who escape will be delivered into the hands of G-d's anointed messiah, and the land will show mercy to its inhabitants and protect them. G-d instructs Baruch to go and tell the people to prepare themselves for this time so that they will be among those righteous who will survive and not among those wicked who will perish. As a result, the people ask Baruch to write a letter. Baruch writes two letters, one of which is addressed to Jews in Babylonian exile, exhorting them to observe divine Torah in preparation for what is to come, and the other to the nine and one-half tribes of northern Israel who were carried away by the Assyrians.

Second Baruch 78:1–87:1 presents the text of Baruch's letter to the nine and one-half tribes who were exiled from the land of Israel. The letter warns the lost tribes of the diaspora concerning the coming tribulations and the age of glory to follow. It calls upon them particularly to observe G-d's commandments, to ensure that they will be among those who will survive the tribulation and not among those who will perish.

Like 4 Ezra, 2 Bar. therefore calls upon Jews to observe divine Torah in the aftermath of the destruction of the Jerusalem Temple. Such an agenda constitutes the foundational viewpoint of rabbinic Judaism: to sanctify Jewish life and the world of creation by adhering to divine Torah in preparation for the time when G-d will bring about the restoration, presumably as promised in Ezek 40–48, Isa 40–66, Jer 30–33, and Zech 9–14.

Chapter 6

THE HEIKHALOT LITERATURE

Pious Questions concerning Divine Intent

The heikhalot literature is a rabbinic corpus that was written initially during the talmudic period and early Middle Ages in the aftermath of the failure of three major Jewish revolts against Rome.[1] It is considered to be an esoteric genre of literature insofar as mishnaic and talmudic sources attempt to limit those who would engage in its study. The reason for such concern is not hard to fathom. The heikhalot literature depicts visionary experiences of G-d and heavenly journeys through the seven heikhalot, the "palaces" or levels of heaven, to appear before the throne of G-d and to question G-d concerning divine motives for destroying the temple and exiling the Jewish people from Jerusalem and the land of Israel.

Given the rationalist environment of the Enlightenment and beyond, critical scholarship was loath to spend much effort in the study of literature that posited direct visionary experience of and interaction with G-d in the heavenly sphere. Such works were considered to be subjective forms of devotional and mystical experience that rejected the empirical bases of so-called objective, critical scholarship. Christian scholars largely ignored rabbinic works as they tended to see little purpose to the continued study

---

1. For discussion of the heikhalot literature, see esp. Gershom Scholem, *Major Trends in Jewish Mysticism* (New York: Schocken, 1961), 40–79; Ithamar Gruenwald, *Apocalyptic and Merkavah Mysticism*, AGAJU 14 (Leiden: Bill, 1980); Peter Schäfer, *The Origins of Jewish Mysticism* (Tübingen: Mohr Siebeck, 2009). For text editions, see Shlomo Aharon Wertheimer, *Batei Midrashot*, 2 vols. (Jerusalem: Massad Harav Kook, 1950); Peter Schäfer, *Synopse zur Hekhalot-Literatur* (Tübingen: Mohr Siebeck, 1981). For translation of the heikhalot literature, see James R. Davila, *Hekhalot Literature in Translation: Major Texts of Merkavah Mysticism* (Leiden: Brill, 2013).

of Judaism beyond the origins of Christianity. Judaism was generally portrayed as a dead religion with no future that had descended into pointless
legalism with little sense of direction for the future religious and moral
development of humankind. Christianity, particularly Protestant forms of
Christianity, was viewed as a rational religion that had fulfilled and super-
seded Judaism by developing a rationalistic basis for the future moral development of humankind. Modern Jewish critical scholars were generally
embarrassed by the presence of such work and labeled it as a form of superstition, insofar as it undermined their efforts to demonstrate the rationality
of Jewish thought, belief, and practice as a basis for accepting Judaism as
a rational religion alongside Christianity. Consequently, Jewish scholars
focused on the study of Bible and Jewish philosophy and theology, which
of course ran parallel to Protestant interests in the study of Bible and theology, in their efforts to secure the place of Judaism as a modern, rational,
and moral religious tradition.

But its nonrational character does not hold the underlying reason for
this reluctance to study heikhalot literature. For most of its history since the
emergence of Christianity, Judaism had failed to capture the imagination of
the Western world because it had been defeated by the Roman Empire in
three different revolts against Roman rule: the Zealot revolt in 66–74 CE,
which resulted in the destruction of the Second Temple; the diaspora revolt in Cyprus, Egypt, and the Eastern Mediterranean in 114–117 CE, which
undermined the status of Jews in the Roman Empire; and the Bar Kokhba
revolt in 132–135 CE, which resulted in the destruction of most of the Jewish
population of the land of Israel and resulted in the renaming of the land as
Palestine in an effort to erase the memory of Jews living in the land.[2]

The Zealot revolt resisted Roman efforts to conquer, colonize, and ex-
ploit the land of Judea and the rest of the eastern Mediterranean. Rome had
once been a strategic ally as Judea won independence from the Seleucid
Syrian Empire during the Hasmonean revolt. From its outset in 167 BCE,
the war was hard-fought. Hasmonean forces under Judah the Maccabee re-
captured and resanctified the temple in December of 164 BCE, as the Jewish
festival of Hanukkah commemorates. Although Judah was later killed in battle in 160 BCE, his surviving brothers continued to lead the fight. After Jon-

---

2. For overviews of Jewish history that discuss the Jewish revolts against Rome, see esp.
Robert Seltzer, *Jewish People, Jewish Thought: The Jewish Experience in History* (New York:
Macmillan; London: Collier, 1980); H. H. Ben Sasson, ed., *A History of the Jewish People*
(Cambridge, MA: Harvard University Press, 1976).

athan was killed in 142 BCE, Simon, the last surviving Hasmonean brother, negotiated a truce in 140 BCE that recognized Judean independence and Simon as high priest and leader of the nation. The Hasmonean kingdom was not always stable—Simon was assassinated by his son-in-law, Ptolemy Abubus in 134 BCE—but Simon's son, John Hyrcanus, defeated Ptolemy and took control of the nation to rule during the years 134–104 BCE. His son, Aristobulus, succeeded him and took the title of king as well as high priest. Aristobulus had married Salome Alexandra; when he died in 103 BCE, his brother Alexander Jannai married Salome in a levirite marriage to preserve his brother's name. They had two sons, Hyrcanus II, who would have been Aristobulus's heir, and Aristobulus II, who would have been Jannai's heir. Jannai was not a popular monarch, and traditions preserved both in the Talmud and in the writings of Josephus indicate that Jannai was pelted with citrons while pouring libation offerings at the temple during Sukkot by a crowd that demanded that he step down as high priest. He is also known for crucifying eight hundred of his enemies while feasting and drinking with his concubines. When he died in 76 BCE, his widow Salome Alexandra succeeded him as ruler of Judea. When she died in 67 BCE, Hyrcanus II and Aristobolus II went to war against each other to secure the throne and high priesthood. When both brothers appealed to the Roman general Pompey for support in 63 BCE, Pompey marched his soldiers into Jerusalem, installed Hyrcanus II as high priest, and effectively ended Jewish independence.

Roman rule became harsher and harsher over the years. When the Hasmoneans proved ineffective in ruling Judea, Rome appointed Herod to rule on Rome's behalf in 37 BCE. Herod was the descendant of Idumeans who were forcibly converted to Judaism by John Hyrcanus; he married a Hasmonean princess, Mariamne, but was never accepted by the Jewish population. He attempted to ingratiate himself to Rome by building the seaport at Caesarea and naming it after Caesar, and to Jews by rebuilding the temple compound, the platform of which still stands today. When he died in 4 BCE, Rome continued to experience difficulties in ruling Judea, at last appointing procurators to rule Judea directly, the most notorious of whom, Pontius Pilate, was removed from office for excessive cruelty.

By 66 CE, tensions between Jews and Rome had reached such a point that revolt broke out; its leaders were the Zealots, a Jewish party dedicated to Judean independence. The Roman general Vespasian commanded the Roman army in Syria. He was reinforced by Roman forces under the command of his son, Titus, who moved his troops up from Egypt. Vespasian and Titus launched an invasion of Judea from Syria that first destroyed Jewish resistance under the command of Josephus in the Galilee. They then continued down the Jordan River into Judea, destroying Qumran in 68 CE on the way to lay siege to Jerusalem. Vespasian returned to Rome following the death of Nero and the resulting chaos. Eventually Vespasian emerged as emperor of Rome while Titus broke the siege of Jerusalem, destroyed the city, and demolished the Jerusalem Temple in 70 CE. The war ended in 74 CE with the fall of Masada in which Zealot forces elected to die rather than to fall to the Romans who had used Jewish prisoners to construct a siege ramp up the side of the mountain.

In the aftermath of the failure of the Zealot revolt and destruction of the temple, Rabbinic Judaism, claiming continuity with Pharisaic Judaism, emerged as the dominant form of Judaism. Other factions disappeared or lost influence, such as the Sadducees or Zadokites who formed the temple priesthood; the Essenes at Qumran, who had moved to the wilderness to prepare the way of YHWH; the early Christians, who fled Jerusalem and distanced themselves from the increasingly unpopular Jewish population; and the Zealots, who lost the war. Rabbinic Judaism, led initially by R. Johanan ben Zakkai, focused on the observance of divine Torah as the basis for Jewish identity and practice. Subsequent rabbinic leaders—such as R. Akiva ben Joseph, who set the parameters of midrash and halakah; R. Ishmael, who defined the thirteen means of biblical exegesis; and R. Judah the Prince, who first recorded the Mishnah—laid the foundations for the development of Rabbinic Judaism.

In the meantime, the diaspora revolt of 114–17 CE, which broke out in Cyprus, Egypt, and other eastern Mediterranean locations due to Roman attempts to restrict the rights of Jews, who were increasingly viewed with suspicion, failed.

But the most important revolt was the Bar Kokhba revolt in the land of Judea in 132–135 CE. The Bar Kokhba revolt failed miserably, and the Roman Empire used the revolt as a pretext to commit genocide against the Jewish people by destroying the bulk of the Jewish population of Judea, banning the practice of Judaism, and renaming the land of Israel in an attempt to erase any memory of Jews in the land. Shimon bar Kokhba, so named because of the messianic prophecy in Num 24:17 that a star (Hebrew, *kokhav*; Aramaic, *kokhva'*) would arise in Israel to drive away its enemies, led the revolt. His real name was Shimon ben Kosiba, and his letters indicate that he was an effective military leader who prepared carefully for the revolt by training his men and gathering weapons before choosing the time to strike. The cause of the war was the realization that the Roman Emperor Hadrian would renege on his promise to rebuild the Jerusalem Temple; instead, Hadrian was building a temple to the Roman god Jupiter on the site of the Jewish Temple. The revolt broke out in 132 CE when Bar Kokhba's men drove the Romans out of Jerusalem. Because of Bar Kokhba's preparation, it was a hard-fought war in which an entire Roman legion was destroyed in one encounter. Hadrian eventually took personal command of the army and ultimately killed Bar Kokhba and all his men in a battle at Betar, south of Jerusalem. Intent on destroying Jewish resistance and identity, Hadrian proscribed the teaching and practice of Judaism, executing R. Akiva in a public square, along with other rabbis who continued to teach. He changed the name of Jerusalem to Aelia Capitolina, rebuilt the city, including the temple to Jupiter, and forbade Jews to live in the city. He renamed the land Palestine and then joined it to Syria administratively to eliminate any memory of Jewish presence in the land. Altogether, Hadrian's soldiers killed approximately half a million Jews, effectively ending any major presence of Jews in the land of Israel until modern times.

The Oral Torah and Rabbinic Qualifications for Mystical Study

In the aftermath of the Bar Kokhba revolt, Rabbinic Judaism took measures to preserve and develop the Oral Torah which stood as the basis of the Rabbinic Jewish tradition. The purpose was to define holy Jewish life in the world until such time as Jews could return to the land of Israel to restore Jerusalem, the temple, and the nation of Israel at large. Although Rome relaxed the proscription of Judaism following Hadrian's death in 138 CE, Rome continued to treat Jews with hostility, and the Jewish communities of the Galilee and larger Roman diaspora Jewish community suffered continuous exclusion and persecution, especially when Christianity became the official religion of Rome in late antiquity, in the Middle Ages, and into modern times. Rabbinic Judaism continued to develop in the Galilee, but the Babylonian Jewish community, who lived under Sassanian Persian rule and later under Muslim rule, proved to be the more active branch in developing Rabbinic Judaism in late antiquity and the Middle Ages, despite persistent yet intermittent persecution by Persians and Muslims as well.

The literary development of Rabbinic Judaism began with the initial composition of the Mishnah ("Study [of Torah]") in Hebrew by R. Judah the Prince ca. 200 CE.[3] Following the teachings of R. Akiva, who had been

---

3. For discussion of rabbinic literature, see H. L. Strack and Günter Stemberger, *Intro-*

executed by the Romans at the conclusion of the Bar Kokhba revolt, R. Judah organized the Mishnah into six orders that would provide the basis for the rabbinic understanding of the Oral Torah based on the interpretation of the Written Torah. The orders included Zeraim, "Seeds," laws pertaining to prayer and agriculture; Moed, "Appointed Times," laws related to the observance of Shabbat and Jewish holidays; Nashim, "Women," laws related to marriage, divorce, women, children, and family life; Nezikin, "Damages," civil and criminal laws; Kodashim, "Holy Things," laws related to the temple and temple offerings; and Toharot, "Purities," laws related to food, personal purity, and issues pertaining to death and burial. The Mishnah was later supplemented by Tosefta ("Addition"), also in Hebrew, which included elements of early Oral Torah that had not been included by R. Judah the Prince in the Mishnah. The continuing development of the Oral Torah by the rabbis in the third through sixth centuries, predominantly in the Aramaic widely spoken by Jews in late antiquity, produced the Gemara, "Completion," adding much material to the understanding of the Mishnah. Mishnah and Gemara together form the Talmud, "Teaching," a definitive statement of rabbinic Torah; the Talmud has two forms: the Babylonian Talmud, completed in Mesopotamia, is the more complete and authoritative version of the Talmud, and the Jerusalem Talmud, completed in the Galilee, is shorter than the Babylonian Talmud although it frequently contains different materials. As the tractates indicate, the Talmud was designed to address both the religious and civil aspects of Jewish society in order to provide definition for Jewish life in exile until such time as Jews were able to return to the land of Israel. Additional rabbinic materials include the Targums, authoritative translations of the Torah and the rest of the Bible into Aramaic, and the midrashic literature, which provided authoritative interpretation of the Torah and the rest of the Bible. Rabbinic Judaism continued to develop during the Middle Ages with various works devoted to Jewish halakah (law and practice), liturgy, philosophy and theology, literature, language, and mysticism.

Modern interpreters have often argued that Rabbinic Judaism was hostile to the study of Jewish mysticism. Indeed, modern scholars during the Age of Enlightenment or Reason, from the late eighteenth through the early twentieth centuries, have often labeled Jewish mysticism as nonsense and superstition because of its penchant for positing direct experience of the presence of G-d as opposed to an empirical and objective understanding of

---

duction to the Talmud and Midrash (Minneapolis: Fortress, 1992); Jacob Neusner, Introduction to Rabbinic Literature (Garden City, NY: Doubleday, 1999).

Jewish thought based on reason.[4] Their views were based in large measure on interpretation of the Mishnah's and Talmud's treatment of topics related to Jewish mysticism in tractate Hagigah and on the character of the literature itself, such as the heikhalot literature, which posited visionary journeys through the seven levels or palaces of heaven to appear before the throne of G-d.

Closer study of this material, however, indicates that the early rabbis were not hostile to the study of Jewish mysticism. Rather they were concerned that Jewish mysticism be studied by those most competent and grounded in Jewish study, practice, worship, and life, to ensure that outlandish claims not be made when addressing serious questions concerning the character of G-d, the visionary appearance of G-d, and the reasons why G-d destroyed the temple and sent the Jewish people into exile.

The foundational rabbinic text concerning Jewish mysticism appears in m. Ḥag. 2:1:

> The forbidden degrees may not be expounded before three persons, nor the Story of Creation before two, nor [the chapter of] the Chariot before one alone, unless he is a Sage that understands of his own knowledge. Whosoever gives his mind to four things it were better for him if he had not come into the world—what is above? what is beneath? what was beforetime? and what will be hereafter? And whosoever takes no thought for the honour of the Maker, it were better for him if he had not come into the world.[5]

This mishnah has been taken by many as a warning against the study of Jewish mysticism. But a closer examination of the text and its relation to the associated Gemara indicates that it attempts to define the character of those who would study Jewish mysticism as possessing the highest qualifications among those who study Torah. The Mishnah begins with statements qualifying those who would expound upon three critical texts of the Torah: the "forbidden degrees" or the laws concerning incest and other forms of forbidden sexual relations in Leviticus 18, which would speak to the human capacity to pervert humankind by producing improper offspring; the "Story of Creation" in Gen 1:1–2:3, which takes up G-d's creation of the universe, and which in turn includes understanding of G-d's character that produces

---

4. E.g., Heinrich Graetz, *History of the Jews* (Philadelphia: Jewish Publication Society, 1894), 3:522–62.

5. Herbert Danby, *The Mishnah* (Oxford: Oxford University Press, 1977), 212–13.

the world of creation; and "[the chapter of] the Chariot" in Ezek 1, which presents Ezekiel's vision of the presence of G-d. In the end, the exposition of all of these texts is permitted in Rabbinic Judaism; they are read and studied during the course of the regular cycle of Torah and Haftarah readings through the year as well as on the relevant Jewish holidays. But the Mishnah goes on to state that one who would expound upon these texts must be a sage who understands his own knowledge. The Mishnah does not define what that might mean, but the following statement, that anyone who would take up such questions would be better off if they had never been born, seems rather ominous.

The Gemara for this passage includes a great deal of detailed rabbinic exegesis of the Mishnah's text, including many examples of harm and difficulties that came to those who attempted such study. But a key narrative illustrates the Mishnah's understanding of what a sage who understands of his own knowledge is: the story of the four who entered Pardes. There are several versions of the story in the Tosefta, the Babylonian Talmud, and elsewhere. Although the Tosefta's version is regarded as the oldest, most complete, and original version of the text, the version of the Babylonian Talmud, which illustrates the Gemara's understanding of the matter, reads as follows:

> Our rabbis taught: Four men entered the Garden, namely, Ben Azzai and Ben Zoma, Aḥer, and Rabbi Akiba. Rabbi Akiba said to them: When ye arrive at the stones of pure marble, say not, Water, water. For it is said: He that speaketh falsehood shall not be established before mine eyes. Ben Azzai cast a look and died. Of him, Scripture says, Precious in the sight of the L-rd is the death of His saints. Ben Zoma looked and became demented. Of him, Scripture says, Hast thou found honey? Eat so much as is sufficient for thee, lest thou be filled therewith and vomit it. Aḥer mutilated the shoots. Rabbi Akiba departed unhurt. (b. Hag. 14b)[6]

Interpreters have also argued that this narrative illustrates the dangers of mystical study, and to a certain extent this is true. But the narrative is fundamentally concerned with defining the character of one who would engage in such study: a sage who knows of his own knowledge should be an ideal rabbinic sage like R. Akiva. Entry into the Garden

---

6. For text and translation, see Israel Abrahams, *Hebrew-English Edition of the Babylonian Talmud: Ḥagigah* (London: Soncino, 1990), ad loc.

employs the Rabbinic Hebrew term Pardes, "Garden, Paradise." Although the term is also known in Persian and Greek, Pardes has become a rabbinic acronym for the four dimensions of the study of a Torah text: *peshat*, "simple, plain," a reference to the plain or surface meaning of the text; *remez*, "mystery," a reference to the allegorical meaning of the text; *darashah*, "exposition," a reference to the homiletical dimensions of the text; and *sod*, "secret," a reference to the mystical meaning of the text. Altogether, the reference to entering Pardes indicates the proper study of a Torah text.

The experience of each figure differs, but each experience is related to a characteristic of the figure in question and the scriptural quotation highlights that meaning.[7] Shimon ben Azzai, who "cast a look and died," was one of R. Akiva's disciples; he was so devoted to the study of the Torah that he declined to marry, even when he was offered R. Akiva's daughter. Consequently, he never fulfilled the first commandment of the 613 rabbinic commandments, "Be fruitful and multiply." Having failed to see to the continuation of the Jewish people and of his family, he died upon entering into the Garden, understood simultaneously as the study of Torah and appearing in the seventh heaven before the throne of G-d. "Precious or costly is the death of G-d's saints" indicates the loss of future generations due to this neglect. Like Ben Azzai, Ben Zoma, who "looked and became demented," was never ordained. Although he was known as a great homiletical preacher, he did not complete his halakic studies and thus was never ordained. Hence, his mind was not prepared. The reference to honey indicates his commitment to the sweetness of homiletical study, but he pursued such study overmuch to the neglect of other dimensions. Aher, otherwise known as R. Elisha ben Abuyah, is the classic heretic of rabbinic tradition; he abandoned Judaism and thus became known as Aher, "another person." Rabbi Elisha ben Abuyah was a sage on a par with R. Akiva, but it is said that when he entered the seventh heaven and saw the angel Metatron sitting upon the throne of G-d, he declared, "There are two powers in heaven," mimicking the gnostic teaching of multiple gods in heaven. Other narratives in the Gemara relate how Greek books would fall from his lap when he rose in the yeshivah. But the fundamental reason

---

7. For a detailed analysis of the narrative, see Marvin A. Sweeney, "Pardes Revisited Once Again: A Reassessment of the Rabbinic Legend concerning the Four Who Entered Pardes," in *Form and Intertextuality in Prophetic and Apocalyptic Literature*, FAT 45 (Tübingen: Mohr Siebeck, 2005), 269–82.

for his heresy appears to be his witnessing of punishment for those who adhered to Torah. He saw a man fall and die while attempting to protect the eggs of a mother bird in a nest in keeping with the commands of Deut 22:6–7. But most fundamentally, he witnessed the execution of his teacher, R. Judah Nahtum, by the Romans. When R. Judah Nahtum's tongue was cut out and picked up by a dog, R. Elisha lamented at the treatment of a tongue that had once taught such sweet teachings (y. Hag. 2:1).

Rabbi Akiva was the antithesis of each of the prior three examples. He was an illiterate shepherd when he met Rachel, the daughter of his employer, who promised to marry him if he would learn to read so that he could teach their children. Thus, Akiva ben Joseph was the antithesis to Shimon ben Azzai, who refused to interrupt his studies to marry. Having married Rachel and followed her instructions, R. Akiva became one of the greatest sages of Judaism. Unlike Shimon ben Zoma who limited his study to homiletics, R. Akiva defined midrashic study by focusing on even the most minute features of the Torah texts; for example, he developed the notion of *yetser tov*, inclination for good, and *yetser ra'*, the inclination for evil, in rabbinic ethics based on the two instances of the verb w*ayitser/wayyitser*, "and he created," used for animals in Gen 2:19 and for humans in Gen 2:7. R. Akiva was also known for establishing the six orders of the Mishnah and thereby establishing the foundations for halakic study. R. Akiva also contrasted markedly with R. Elisha ben Abuyah by becoming the quintessential martyr for Judaism during Hadrian's persecution. As he was executed by having his flesh torn from his body by iron combs, he expounded on the Shema in Deut 6, declaring that he finally understood the statement, "and you shall love YHWH your G-d with all your heart, with all your strength, and with all your soul," as he died, in contrast to R. Elisha ben Abuyah, who abandoned Judaism when he could not understand evil in the world.

Consequently, the story of the four who entered Pardes teaches that a sage who understands of his own knowledge should be an ideal sage—like R. Akiva. Each of the heikhalot texts that follows takes up aspects of the teachings of this narrative. Ma'aseh Merkavah explains the prayers and theurgical elements that a prospective mystic must know and employ to see the divine presence. The Heikhalot Rabbati focuses especially on the knowledge of Torah as a qualification to see the divine presence. The Heikhalot Zutarti focuses especially on knowledge of the divine name as a qualification for beholding the presence of G-d. And Sefer Heikhalot, or 3 En., focuses on an understanding of Metatron as a qualification for making the ascent.

Ma'aseh Merkavah

The Ma'aseh Merkavah presents the most basic response to the account of the four who ascended to Pardes, focusing on the hymns and prayers that the prospective mystic must employ to undertake the ascent to the seventh level of heaven.[8] Although many interpreters understand the Ma'aseh Merkavah to be a relatively late text, its focus on hymns and prayers indicates liturgical preparation and basic knowledge of the names of G-d and the angels for the ascent, whereas other merkavah texts presume that the prospective mystic possesses fuller knowledge of elements in addition to the liturgical elements. Heikhalot Rabbati expects full knowledge of Torah; Heikhalot Zutarti expects full knowledge of the divine name; and Sefer Heikhalot, or 3 En., expects knowledge of the names and character of Metatron. Consequently, Ma'aseh Merkavah constitutes a basic gateway text in the heikhalot literature, whereas the other texts are more concerned with the question of what constitutes a sage who understands his own knowledge.

Michael Swartz observes that the Ma'aseh Merkavah is a highly structured text.[9] It comprises primarily poetic, liturgical compositions, but its narrative framework supplies the work with a narrative structure. It presents a dialogue between R. Akiva, who functions as the primary figure involved in the ascent to the seventh level of heaven in the narrative of the four who entered Pardes, and R. Ishmael ben Elisha and R. Nehunyah ben Haqanah, the primary figures featured in the Heikhalot Rabbati, who apparently consult with R. Akiva in preparation for their own journeys.

Section 1 of the Ma'aseh Merkavah (Schäfer, paragraphs 544–59) presents the first portion of the dialogue among the three rabbis concerning various aspects of celestial cosmography and the prayers and hymns necessary to make the ascent to behold the heavens. The dialogue begins in paragraphs 544–51 with R. Ishmael's questions to R. Akiva concerning the prayers employed by a man who wishes to praise RWZZY YHWH, a name based on the movement of the living creatures, or cherubim, in Ezekiel's vision, and R. Akiva's response. R. Akiva emphasizes the need

---

8. For the text of Ma'aseh Merkavah, see esp. Schäfer, *Synopse*, paragraphs 554–96; Gershom Scholem, *Jewish Gnosticism, Merkabah Mysticisim, and Talmudic Tradition* (New York: Jewish Theological Seminary, 1965), 101–17. For translation, see Davila, *Hekhalot*, 245–99. For discussion, see esp. Michael D. Swartz, *Mystical Prayer in Ancient Judaism: An Analysis of Ma'aseh Merkavah* (Tübingen: Mohr Siebeck, 1992); Naomi Janowitz, *The Poetics of Ascent: Theories of Language in a Rabbinic Ascent Text* (Albany: SUNY Press, 1989).

9. Swartz, *Mystical Prayer*, 65–104.

for holiness and purity in the heart of the would-be mystic as he makes his ascent, and he further stresses the need to accomplish the Torah in the world and multiplying learning. R. Akiva states that he saw all the beings of the heavens, including their breadths, heights, and stances. He continues with an account of the twelve thousand myriad bridges that cross the river to the presence of G-d, the twelve thousand rivers of fire, the twelve thousand storehouses of snow, the twenty-four thousand myriad wheels, all of which are arrayed by their halves along the paths that lead the mystic to the throne of G-d in heaven. When R. Ishmael then asks R. Akiva how he would then behold the vision of G-d, R. Akiva responds that he must sing the praises of G-d each day at the break of dawn and purify himself from all iniquity, falsehood, and evil. As a result, G-d would stand by him each day to accomplish righteous acts. He then recounts the hymns which praise the qualities of G-d, culminating in an elaborated version of the 'Aleinu prayer that normally appears near the end of the Jewish prayer service and includes some of the names of G-d. The first word, *'aleinu*, has been modified from a plural ("It is our obligation [to praise]") to a singular, *'alay* ("It is my obligation [to praise]"), to emphasize the individual experience of the would-be mystic ascender.

In paragraphs 552–53 R. Ishmael offers two prayers concerning the praise of G-d. The first meditates upon the divine name spoken with the completely silent voice of G-d described in Elijah's vision on Mt. Horeb in 1 Kgs 19:12, and the second focuses on the divine name as refracted through Moses's vision of G-d after the Golden Calf episode in Exod 34:6. In paragraphs 554–56 R. Akiva enumerates the chariots of fire and the flames that stand guard in each of the seven palaces of heaven, culminating in a rendition of the Kedushah prayer—"Holy, Holy, Holy," from Isa 6:3, combined with Ezekiel's blessing of G-d from his own vision in Ezek 3:12—for each of the seven palaces. R. Ishmael concludes this second part of Ma'aseh Merkavah with his recounting of R. Nehunyah's vision of G-d seated on the throne in the seventh palace in imagery drawn from Isa 6. In paragraph 557 appears R. Akiva's testimony concerning the man who is privileged to stand before the throne of G-d, including a number of specialized names. Then paragraphs 558–59 conclude with R. Akiva recounting to R. Ishmael his experience in ascending through the seven levels of heaven. In the first palace he became pious, in the second he became pure, in the third he became upright, in the fourth he became faultless, in the fifth he brought holiness before G-d, in the sixth he recited the Kedushah, and in the seventh he stood before G-d and recited a prayer to G-d the creator. The first part of Ma'aseh Merkavah concludes with R. Akiva's further description of the measurements of the features of the seventh heaven.

Section 2 of the Ma'aseh Merkavah (Schäfer, paragraphs 560–70) recounts the role of R. Nehunyah ben Haqanah as the teacher of R. Ishmael, particularly his role in teaching R. Ishmael the theurgic prayers, seals, and names he would need to use in his own ascent to the heavens. In paragraphs 560–62 R. Ishmael recounts learning the Sar Torah ("Prince of the Torah") praxis from R. Nehunyah when he was thirteen years old, i.e., the age at which he would have become a Bar Mitzvah. He learned that he must fast for forty days; he must eat his morsel with salt; he must not eat anything foul; he must immerse himself in the mikveh twenty-four times; he must not gaze at dyed things; he must direct his eyes to the ground; he must pray with full vigor; and he must direct his heart to prayer, seal himself with seals, and invoke twelve words of praise for G-d including G-d's holy names. Then paragraphs 563–64 present R. Ishmael's proclamation of the names of G-d, which must be used and not forgotten, and R. Nehunyah's instructions concerning the three names of G-d. But paragraphs 565–68 present an account of R. Ishmael's encounter with the angel of the presence when he forgot elements of the divine name. In the face of the angel's rage, R. Ishmael renewed his efforts at pronouncing the three letters of the name, the three prayers for the holy occasions of the day, and the seals necessary to protect himself from the wrath of the angel of the presence. Further instructions in paragraphs 569–70 from R. Nehunyah to R. Ishmael describe the Sar Torah praxis necessary for a vision of the presence of G-d, including prayer to invoke the angels who stand by the hayot, or living creatures, bearing the throne and the twelve words to behold the vision of G-d.

Section 3 (Schäfer, paragraphs 579–91) presents R. Ishmael's discourse on the angelic names that a prospective mystic would need to know to make the ascent, as well as five key prayers. R. Ishmael gives an account in paragraphs 579–82 of learning from R. Nehunyah ben Haqanah the names of all the angels of wisdom who appear in each of the seven palaces during the latter's vision of the divine presence. R. Ishmael stands as he learns the names with his face illuminated and recites the names himself. The account culminates in the vision of the divine presence itself and the names of the angels who stand to G-d's right and left to sing praise. In paragraphs 583–85 R. Ishmael encounters the angel of the presence, ZBWDY'L, who reproaches him and questions his merit that would enable him to stand before G-d. Recognizing that his merit comes from G-d, R. Ishmael recites the Kedushah prayer, "Holy, holy, holy is YHWH *tzeva'ot*," to acknowledge and praise G-d's holiness. Then paragraphs 586–91 turn to five prayers that R. Nehunyah admonishes R. Ishmael to pray, so as to ensure his safety before the presence of G-d. The text of each prayer follows. The first in paragraph 587 is for Z'WPY'L, Prince of Gehinnom (Hell), to save the people from the judgment of Gehinnom. The second in paragraph 588 is for the holy G-d of heaven and earth and focuses on the divine name and praises YHWH, the holy one in the merkavah, rider of the cherubim. The third in paragraph 589 blesses the holy name of YHWH, who is the incomparable king of all creation. The fourth in paragraph 590 focuses on the holy throne of G-d placed in the uppermost reaches of the heavens. It elaborates once again on the Holy Name of G-d, in this case, TTRWSYH YHWH one hundred and eleven times. The name "TTRWSYH YHWH" combines Greek and Hebrew elements that signify the meaning of the holy name of G-d: TTR from Greek *tetra*, "four," indicates the four-letter name of G-d; WSYH from Greek *ousia*, "being," refers to the explanation of that divine name in Exod 3:14–15 where it is presumed to derive from the Hebrew verb root *hayah*, "being." Hence TTRWSYH YHWH indicates that the four-letter divine name denotes divine existence. The fifth prayer in paragraph 591 presents a modified rendition of the Mi Khamokhah ("Who is like you?"), a prayer from the Jewish liturgy that highlights the incomparability of G-d. Section 3 of Ma'aseh Merkavah concludes with R. Ishmael's quotation of R. Nehunyah that "anyone who prays this prayer with all his vigor is able to have a vision of the splendor of the Shekhinah (the divine presence) and the Shekhinah is beloved to him."[10]

Section 4 (Schäfer, paragraphs 592–96) presents R. Ishmael's questions to R. Akiva concerning the prayers that are necessary for the ascent and R. Akiva's response concerning his own two visions and the prayers he employed during the experience. The return to dialogue with R. Akiva returns to his role as the only one of the four who entered Pardes to succeed in beholding the divine presence; in the Ma'aseh Merkavah R. Akiva now instructs R. Ishmael how he might also do so. In paragraphs 592–94 R. Akiva states that he prayed a prayer for a vision of heaven and then recites the prayer for R. Ishmael. The prayer focuses on the incomparability or oneness of G-d, the foundation of the divine throne in the heavens, and G-d's magnificence and mercy in creating the cherubim, the inhabited world, and all the bands and seraphim who stand before G-d to sing concerning the divine glory, holiness, greatness, and blessedness of the presence of G-d. Then paragraphs 595–96 present a dialogue between R. Ishmael and R. Akiva con-

10. Davila, *Hekhalot*, 292.

cerning a vision of what appears above the seraphim, i.e., above the head of RWZZY YHWH, G-d of Israel. When R. Ishmael asks how to have such a vision, R. Akiva responds by first relating how he ascended to the first palace of heaven and prayed a prayer that enabled him to see all the way to the seventh palace. Once he ascended to the seventh palace, he invoked two angels who enabled him to see what was above the seraphim. The names of the angels were SRYD and HGLYN. When he pronounced their names, they came and took hold of him, advising him not to fear as he looked upon what was above the seraphim. R. Akiva then recites a lengthy prayer that extols YHWH as the incomparable creator and that highlights the silence of the seraphim, drawing upon Elijah's vision in 1 Kgs 19:12. It is noteworthy that the silence of the seraphim's prayer replicates the silence of the priests as they went about the business of preparing the offerings for G-d as they served in the Jerusalem Temple in antiquity. The prayer concludes by extolling the divine name and might of YHWH forever.

Heikhalot Rabbati

The Heikhalot Rabbati portrays the ascent of R. Nehunyah ben Haqanah to heaven to appear before the throne of G-d in the seventh level of heaven. His purpose was to ask G-d why the temple was destroyed, why the rabbinic sages of Judaism were martyred, and why the population of Jerusalem and the land of Judah were exiled. R. Ishmael ben Elisha is the narrator of the Heikhalot Rabbati in which his teacher, R. Nehunyah, presents his account of his ascent to the heavenly throne. Scholem argues that the Heikhalot Rabbati dates to the third to sixth centuries CE, but the fluid character of its text and its continuing use and development by the Hasidei Ashkenaz indicate that its process of composition extends into the seventh–ninth centuries and beyond.[11]

Past scholarship has debated whether the Heikhalot Rabbati is fundamentally concerned with mystical experience or with the interpretation of Torah.[12] Schäfer's analysis of the text, for example, focuses especially on the

---

11. Scholem, *Major Trends*, 40–79.

12. For critical discussion of the Heikhalot Rabbati, see Scholem, *Major Trends*, 40–79; Gruenwald, *Apocalyptic and Merkavah Mysticism*, 150–73; Ra'anan S. Boustan, "The Study of Hekhalot Literature: Between Mystical Experience and Textual Artifact," *CBR* 6.1 (Oct. 2007): 130–60; Schäfer, *The Origins of Jewish Mysticism*, 244–82; Boustan, *From Martyr to*

liturgical elements. Although this is a necessary dimension, he overlooks the emphasis on knowledge of Torah as a qualification for those who would ascend to the seventh heaven to behold the divine presence and to ask G-d why the temple was destroyed and why Jews were exiled from the land of Israel. Indeed, a close reading of the text demonstrates that the Heikhalot Rabbati is fundamentally concerned with both: Torah interpretation is a form of mystical experience insofar as it brings one closer to an understanding of divine presence and purpose in the world of creation.

The Heikhalot Rabbati anticipates an ideal time when Torah—and thus divine presence and purpose—will be fully understood and applied to the sanctification of the world of creation. Indeed, it calls upon its readers to continue their endeavors in mysticism and Torah study to realize that ideal. Three features of the Heikhalot Rabbati demonstrate this perspective. First is the identity and role of the mystical minyan of the Ten Martyrs who gave their lives for the sake of encounter with the divine and the application of Torah in the world. Second is the recall of R. Nehunyah ben Haqanah, illustrating the principle that "those who descend in the chariot" are those who return from the heavenly journey and apply knowledge of Torah to the sanctification of the world—in this case, the laws of Niddah as they are understood by the schools of Hillel and Shammai. And third is G-d's response to the query of R. Nehunyah concerning the destruction of the temple and the martyrdom of the rabbis; G-d admits that the divine decree to destroy the temple and martyr the Rabbis was questionable but nevertheless calls upon Jews to continue their studies of Torah ultimately to understand G-d's presence and purpose in the world.

The first of these three concerns is to identify the qualifications of sages who know of their own knowledge and who thereby would make the ascent through the seven levels of heaven and behold the divine presence. The Heikhalot Rabbati begins with R. Ishmael's question, "What are those songs which he recites who would behold the vision of the merkavah, who would descend in peace and would ascend in peace?" (par. 81).[13] The following material then discusses the qualities of Torah knowledge and faithful obser-

---

Mystic: Rabbinic Martyrology and the Making of Merkavah Mysticism, TSAJ 112 (Tübingen: Mohr Siebeck, 2005).

13. For text editions, see Schäfer, *Synopse*, paragraphs 81–277; Wertheimer, *Batei Midrashot* 1:63–135 (Hebrew). For English translation, see Morton Smith, *Hekhalot Rabbati: The Greater Treatise Concerning the Palaces of Heaven*, ed. D. Karr (2009; www.digital-brilliance .com/kab/karr/HekRab/HekRab.pdf; accessed, January 15, 2019); Davila, *Hekhalot*, 37–157.

vance of Judaism that would qualify them to sing such songs and to behold the divine merkavah.

The identity of R. Ishmael is a key factor in understanding the Heikhalot Rabbati. R. Ishmael ben Elisha was one of the key Tannaitic sages of the first and second centuries CE.[14] He was likely the grandson of the High Priest of the Jerusalem Temple by the same name. He was forced into captivity in Rome but was ransomed by R. Nehunyah ben Haqanah, whom tractate Shabbat identifies as his teacher. R. Ishmael was a contemporary and colleague of R. Akiva ben Joseph. R. Ishmael is known for his Thirteen Midot for the interpretation of the Torah, which emphasized the plain sense of scripture as the basis for interpretation rather than every minor feature of the text as argued by R. Akiva. He is also known as the author of the Mekhilta de R. Ishmael, an early Tannaitic halakic midrash on the legal material in the book of Exodus. He was one of the most prominent rabbinic figures of his day, and he is included in the lists of the Ten Martyrs killed by the Romans in the aftermath of the Bar Kokhba revolt. Some maintain that he died with Bar Kokhba at Betar, although some also maintain that the martyred figure was a namesake of the Sage.

R. Ishmael's question, "What are those songs which he would recite who would behold the vision of the merkavah, who would descend in peace and who would ascend in peace?," indicates the primary agenda of the Heikhalot Rabbati: to define those who would ascend to the seventh heaven to behold the vision of G-d. R. Ishmael's question presupposes the statement in m. Hag. 2:1 that prohibits expounding upon the forbidden sexual relations (Lev 18), the story of creation (Gen 1:1–2:3), and the chapter on the chariot (Ezek 1) unless one is a sage who knows his own knowledge. From this mishnah's subsequent warning, that someone who does not consider the honor of his Maker (G-d) would be better left unborn, it seems clear that one who knows his own knowledge must be a rare sage.

Both the Tosefta (t. Hag. 2:3–4) and the Gemara discussed above (b. Hag. 14b) expound upon the qualifications of such a sage by recounting the story of those who attempted to enter Pardes, in which R. Akiba exemplifies one who knows his own knowledge.[15] Analysis of the Babylonian Talmud's version of the story demonstrates that part of its purpose is to contrast the characteristics of R. Akiva with those of three others who were not prop-

---

14. Shmuel Safrai, "Ishmael ben Elisha," *EncJud* 9:83–86.

15. See my study, "Pardes Revisited Once Again: A Reassessment of the Rabbinic Legend Concerning the Four Who Entered Pardes," in *Form and Intertextuality*, 269–82.

erly prepared for the experience of the vision of G-d in the seventh level of heaven. But the Tosefta's version of the narrative places greater emphasis on biblical interpretation than the version of the Babylonian Gemara. The Gemara's version only associates biblical verses with Shimon ben Azzai and Shimon ben Zoma to explain the reasons they failed in their attempt to enter Pardes. Ben Azzai's early death prior to marriage and his commitment to Torah are associated with Ps 116:15, "Precious/expensive in YHWH's eyes is the death of his saints." Ben Zoma is associated with Prov 25:16, "Have you found honey? Eat (only) what is sufficient for you, lest you be filled with it and vomit it," a criticism of his commitment to aggadic preaching at the expense of his expertise in halakah. But the Tosefta's version also adduces Qoh 5:5, "Do not allow your mouth to cause your flesh to sin," for R. Elisha ben Abuya's apostasy and Song 1:4, "Draw me after you, let us run; the king has brought me to his chambers," to express R. Akiva's intimate relationship with G-d and Judaism. Each of these citations expresses the respective experience of the figure with which it is associated in his attempt to enter Pardes.

R. Akiva, because of his expertise in the study of Torah and his commitment to Judaism, therefore exemplifies the sages who were qualified to behold the vision of the merkavah. He joins R. Ishmael as a member of the havurah of the Ten Martyrs; these sages form a mystical minyan who hear the exposition of R. Nehunyah ben Haqanah concerning his journey through the seven levels of heaven to behold the merkavah and the presence of G-d. The eight other sages who comprise this minyan are the traditional martyrs of Judaism who were murdered by the Romans in the aftermath of the Bar Kokhba revolt: R. Judah ben Baba, R. Jeshbab the Scribe, R. Hananyah ben Teradyon, R. Hozpit the Interpreter, R. Elazar ben Shammua, R. Hanina ben Hakinai, R. Shimon ben Gamliel, and R. Eliezer ben Dama. Although versions of the rabbinic lists of the Ten Martyrs vary in their identification of the victims, they signify the major sages of the time who gave their lives as martyrs for the sake of G-d and divine Torah. They are the ones qualified to sing the songs that would allow them to behold the divine merkavah. They are seated together before the crowd of eight thousand students in the fashion typical of yeshivot, where the sages are seated first and those of lesser accomplishment and status sit behind them.

The Heikhalot Rabbati also makes it clear that the Ten Sages are the ten victims of their generation who are executed to atone for the ten sons of Jacob who sold their brother, Joseph, into slavery in Egypt. As the faithful sages of their generation who knew their own knowledge, they were qualified to learn why they must be sacrificed.

The second feature of the Heikhalot Rabbati pertains to the recall of R. Nehunyah ben Haqanah from heaven and the expertise in Torah interpretation that is necessary to make his recall possible. R. Nehunyah ben Haqanah describes the mystic ascent to appear before the throne of G-d as a journey in which one must pass through the seven gates into the seven palaces or levels of heaven. Each gate is guarded by eight angels, and the prospective mystic must know the name of each angel and correctly recite the incantation that addresses each angel, thereby allowing him to pass through the gate without harm. Insofar as there are eight angels for each of the seven gates, the mystic must learn one hundred and twelve angelic names and incantations to ascend safely to the seventh level of heaven and to descend safely once the encounter has concluded. Such a procedure is analogous to the ascent of Adapa to heaven in the Babylonian tradition following his action to stop the south wind from blowing and threatening his boat.[16] This action enabled Adapa to appear before the throne of Anu to receive the bread and water of life. It is also analogous to the Greek magical papyrus in which the prospective mystic must correctly open the seals and recite the incantations that will allow him to pass through the seven levels of heaven in the gnostic tradition.[17]

But a problem arises when R. Nehunyah arrives at the sixth level of heaven. The angels of the sixth heaven are especially fierce, threatening to destroy any prospective mystic who is not absolutely pure enough to appear before the throne of G-d. When R. Ishmael states (par. 224) that the gate keepers of the sixth level would destroy those who "do and do not" descend to the merkavah because they act without permission, the havurah of the Ten Martyrs and the crowd of colleagues that listen to R. Ishmael's narration of R. Nehunyah's journey want an explanation of what is meant by those who "do and do not" descend to the merkavah. A halakic means must be devised to recall R. Nehunyah from his journey to the sixth level of heaven so that he can answer the question without coming to harm at the hands of the angels who guard the sixth gate. R. Nehunyah must be rendered minimally impure so that he will be dismissed from the heavenly setting but not killed by the guardian angels.

R. Ishmael devises a procedure to recall R. Nehunyah that requires detailed knowledge of the laws of Niddah, menstruation, to render R. Nehu-

---

16. *ANET,* 101–3.

17. Hans Dieter Betz, *The Greek Magical Papyri in Translation, Including the Demotic Spells* (Chicago: University of Chicago Press, 1986).

nyah minimally impure so that he might be recalled from the sixth palace without harm.[18] R. Ishmael takes a soft white woolen cloth, known as a parhava, which is used to check the purity of a woman following the conclusion of her menstrual cycle. He gives it to R. Akiba, who in turn gives it to a servant with instructions to lay the parhava by a woman who immersed herself in the mikveh at the conclusion of her cycle, but did not become pure, and then immersed herself again, so that she did become pure. The woman will then come before the havurah of the Ten Martyrs to declare the circumstances of her purity. One member of the havurah will declare her to be impure and forbid her to her husband, whereas the other members of the havurah will declare her pure and permitted to her husband. She is instructed to touch the parhava very lightly as one might remove a hair from one's eye. The parhava is then taken to R. Ishmael, who takes a branch of myrtle soaked in spikenard oil laid up in balsam to pick it up and place it upon the knees of R. Nehunyah. R. Nehunyah is then dismissed from the sixth level of heaven without harm, so that he might answer the question and then return to the sixth level of heaven to continue his journey.

What does this action mean? It serves to distinguish between the stricter halakah of R. Shammai as understood in heaven and the more lenient understanding of halakah as understood and applied by R. Hillel on earth. The woman in question has a regular menstrual cycle and immerses herself in the mikvah without checking; according to the strict halakah of R. Shammai the uncertainty of her status would leave her impure. Although a second immersion would ensure her purity in the eyes of the school of R. Hillel, R. Shammai still would not be persuaded. By lightly touching the parhava she renders it minimally impure in the school of R. Shammai, but it is pure in the school of R. Hillel. The parhava is then picked up with the myrtle branch soaked in spikenard oil laid up in balsam, a formula used in Jewish magical texts to protect one against impurity. Laying it upon the knees of R. Nehunyah renders him as minimally impure as possible in the eyes of the school of R. Shammai, as understood in the halakah of heaven, whereas R. Nehunyah remains halakically pure as understood in the school of R. Hillel on earth. Hence R. Nehunyah is able to return to earth to explain the difference between those who "do and do not" descend on the merkavah. Those who do descend on the merkavah are the havurah of the Ten Martyrs who witness

---

18. For discussion of R. Ishmael's actions, see esp. Lawrence H. Schiffman, "The Recall of Rabbi Nehuniah ben ha-Qanah from Ecstasy in the Hekhalot Rabbati," *AJSRev* 1 (1976): 269–81.

R. Nehunyah's ascent and will make the journey themselves; those who do not descend are the crowd of colleagues who listen and record the narration, but who will not yet make the journey themselves. R. Nehunyah then safely returns to the sixth level of heaven to continue his journey to appear before the throne of G-d.

R. Ishmael's use of the parhava tests whether a prospective mystic fully understands divine Torah on the laws of Niddah. The choice of subject takes up a halakic concern far removed from the experience of the typical male yeshivah student, one that demands a level of halakic sophistication to distinguish between the strict halakic understanding of the school of R. Shammai, which regards a woman with a known regular menstrual cycle as impure even after two immersions, and the more lenient halakic understanding of the school of R. Hillel, which would see a woman known to have a regular cycle as pure after two immersions even without checking. The basic premise underlying this example is that the prospective mystic must understand even the most arcane differences in halakic understanding of such a topic as menstrual purity. That is, in the words of m. Hag. 2:1, the prospective mystic must be a sage who understands his own knowledge.

The third point pertains to G-d's response to R. Nehunyah. As R. Nehunyah prepares to pass through the gate of the sixth palace, he meets a special challenge in the form of the angels Katzpiel and Dumiel. Katzpiel represents the wrath of G-d and therefore symbolizes submission to the divine will by means of the observance of Torah. Dumiel represents the silence of G-d. Dumiel is also named Avir Gahidariham, representing the four basic elements of creation in ancient Greek thought: *aer*, or air, expressed with the Hebrew term, *avir*; *ge* or earth; *hudor*, or water; and *pur*, fire, expressed through the Hebrew term for heat, *ham*. With a name comprising the basic elements of the created world, Dumiel symbolizes submission to G-d through discernment of the natural world. The combination of Katzpiel, representing submission to G-d through Torah, and Dumiel, representing submission to G-d through understanding the world of creation, constitutes the two basic elements of rabbinic thought: the Torah is studied to understand the will of G-d, but Torah can also be learned by understanding the world of creation. The wisdom tradition of the Bible maintains that G-d created the world first by creating wisdom, personified as a woman in Proverbs 8, and then by consulting her as the rest of creation proceeded. Rabbinic thought similarly holds that it is possible to learn Torah by studying creation. Such study is known as gaining an understanding of *derek eretz*. Although an understanding of *derek eretz* constitutes a path to understanding the divine will, rabbinic thought maintains that the Torah was revealed at Sinai to save time by offering a more expeditious way to learn the divine will. The combination of Katzpiel and Dumiel therefore represents a full comprehension of the divine will as a basis for earning the right to appear before the throne of G-d.

When R. Nehunyah produces the divine seal that admits him through the seventh gate into the seventh palace, Katzpiel sheathes his sword, mounts R. Nehunyah on a wagon of radiance borne by the storm wind, and ushers him into the seventh palace to appear before the throne of G-d. Dumiel constitutes an entirely different challenge. He poses two questions: the first is whether or not R. Nehunyah repeatedly studies the Torah, Prophets, and Writings, i.e., the Bible, and the second is whether or not R. Nehunyah repeatedly studies the Mishnah, halakah, and aggadah, and observes the entirety of the Torah tradition. If the answer is yes, Dumiel approves the admission, calls upon Gabriel to record the virtues of R. Nehunyah on parchment, and carries the document before the wagon of radiance that bears R. Nehunyah. Satisfied that R. Nehunyah has studied and observes the entire Torah tradition, Katzpiel, Dumiel, and Gabriel form a procession that escorts R. Nehunyah through the seventh gate and into the presence of G-d.

An objection emerges, however, when R. Shimon ben Gamliel is angered because R. Nehunyah did not reveal the names of the angels who guard the entrance to the seventh heaven. Not knowing the names could lead to death (par. 238). R. Nehunyah responds that the name can be revealed, but the names of the guards of the seventh palace all have names that are derived from the names of G-d. He therefore agrees to reveal the names on the condition that the haverim stand and bow at the mention of each name. Following this liturgical acknowledgment of the names of the angels guarding the seventh palace, the angel Anaphiel, Branch of G-d, opens the gates of the seventh palace and allows the procession bearing R. Nehunyah to pass.

Upon entry into the seventh palace, R. Nehunyah will see the 512 eyes of the four hayot, or living creatures, of the divine throne-chariot, the eyes of the cherubim of the divine throne-chariot, and the eyes of the ophanim, or wheels, of the divine throne-chariot gazing upon him, each of which is like torches of fire and conflagrations of coals of juniper. These eyes clearly constitute a threat to R. Nehunyah, but Anaphiel supports R. Nehunyah, bids him to fear not, enter and see the king of heaven, and not be destroyed. At that point, a horn sounds from above, and the cherubim and ophanim avert their gaze so that R. Nehunyah might enter. When he does so, the "Throne of Glory" hymn, which extols G-d's royal glory in creation, is sung by the angels.

The Sar Torah, "Prince of the Torah," section then follows. Here, R. Ne-hunyah appears before the throne of G-d and asks the question he came to ask concerning the great tasks that G-d had enjoined Israel to fulfill, the building of a great house or temple for G-d and the study of the Torah. The question becomes, what tasks should Israel fulfill, insofar as he presupposes that the two tasks are a great burden on Israel? G-d's response is telling. G-d tells R. Nehunyah that Israel had a long rest between captivities, and that G-d longed to hear the words of Torah emanating from the mouths of Israel. G-d states, "You have not done well, and I have not done well," a shocking statement that charges both Israel and G-d with having done wrong and thereby bringing punishment upon Israel. G-d explains that Israel did not observe G-d's expectations and that, in divine anger because of what they had done, G-d sealed a decree of judgment against Israel that might endure for all time. But G-d concludes by stating that Israel has rebuked G-d and that they did well in doing so. G-d states, "Already, I accept your rebuke," and adds that the words of Israel are sweet in G-d's ears and that the words of Torah shall not depart from Israel's mouth. G-d claims to know what Israel wants: knowledge of Torah and Talmud, a multitude of halakic teachings, and the increase of such knowledge among a great number of students, academies, and kallahs, or rabbinic conferences. G-d's response therefore asserts that the role of Israel is to continue to learn Torah until such time as it understands the whole and thereby understands the full will of G-d. The Heikhalot Rabbati thus casts such understanding of Torah, and thereby the will of G-d, as an eschatological goal of Rabbinic Judaism.

Scholars have debated whether the Heikhalot Rabbati depicts mystical ecstatic experience or the study of divine Torah. This discussion demonstrates that it depicts both. Although the Heikhalot Rabbati is concerned with liturgy, it focuses first and foremost on the study of Torah. The minyan that hears R. Nehunyah's account of his journey to the seventh level of heaven comprises the Ten Martyrs who gave their lives for the study of Torah during the Roman persecution of Jews following the failed Bar Kokhba revolt. The recall of R. Nehunyah from the sixth level of heaven requires detailed knowledge of the laws of Niddah, at a level and on a topic far from the experience of the typical male yeshivah bahur, so that a procedure that would render R. Nehunyah impure according to the heavenly halakah of R. Shammai but pure according to the earthly halakah of R. Hillel might be devised to recall him from the sixth palace without harm. G-d's response to R. Nehunyah's query about the task of Jews is that they must continue to be preoccupied with the study of Torah until they understand fully divine

Torah and the will of G-d. Such an endeavor is consistent with rabbinic understanding of the eschatological task of Jews, the completion of the study of Torah to bring about the complete sanctification of creation. But such study of Torah must be seen as an ecstatic mystical journey as well, as one learns the *peshat*, plain meaning of the text, the *remez*, the allegorical meaning of the text, the *darashah*, the homiletical meaning of the text, and *sod*, the secret or mystical meaning of the text in order to enter into Pardes, the Garden, and thereby appear before the throne and presence of G-d.

Heikhalot Zutarti

Heikhalot Zutarti, or Lesser Palaces, is generally considered to be the oldest of the heikhalot texts, although Schäfer maintains that it is dependent on the Heikhalot Rabbati.[19] The reasons for viewing Heikhalot Zutarti as the earliest text are its relatively short length in relation to the heikhalot corpus, the relative lack of stability in its text as indicated by the variations in the Schäfer edition of the heikhalot literature, and the relatively simple premise of the Heikhalot Zutarti in relation to other heikhalot literature. Scholem argues that it would have been composed during the third–sixth centuries CE, the latter talmudic period, although the fluidity of its text and its use by the Hasidei Ashkenaz movement during the massacres perpetrated against Ashkenazi Jewish communities at the time of the Crusades suggest that the text was under development for a long period of time.[20]

Although heikhalot mysticism was known in Judea and the Galilee during Roman rule, the motif of the seven palaces through which the rabbinic mystic would travel as he ascended and descended to and from heaven to see the vision of the holy presence of G-d ultimately derives from a Mesopotamian context.[21] The notion of seven levels of heaven and of the underworld was known in Mesopotamia already in the third millennium BCE. It appears in the Sumerian mythological portrayal of the descent of

19. For text editions of Heikhalot Zutarti, see Schäfer, *Synopse*, paragraphs 335–426; Rachel Elior, *Heikhalot Zutarti* (Jerusalem: Magnes, 1982). For translation, see Davila, *Hekhalot*, 187–243. For studies, see esp. Gruenwald, *Apocalyptic*, 86–92, 142–49; Schäfer, *The Origins*, 282–306.

20. Scholem, *Major Trends*, 40–79.

21. See, e.g., Alasdair Livingstone, *Mystical and Mythological Works of Assyrian and Babylonian Scholars* (Oxford: Clarendon, 1986); Vita Daphna Arbel, *Beholders of Divine Secrets: Mysticism and Myth in the Hekhalot and Merkavah Literature* (Albany: SUNY Press, 2003).

Inanna to the underworld in which she traveled through the seven levels of the underworld to rescue her consort, the fertility god Dumuzi, in order to restore the rains and therefore fertility to the land of Mesopotamia at the conclusion of the hot, dry summer season.[22] The Sumerian myth ultimately evolved into the descent of Ishtar to the netherworld to rescue her consort, the fertility god Tammuz. Like Inanna, Ishtar also traveled through the seven levels of the netherworld in order to rescue Tammuz from the dead, and thereby restored fertility in the world. The motif also appears in the myth of Adapa's ascent to heaven.[23] Adapa was an early human who gained the notice of the gods and was invited to heaven to be granted immortality by eating the bread of life and drinking the water of life. He traveled through the seven levels of heaven and acknowledged the gods who guarded each level to gain passage. But he had been warned that the invitation was a trap, and so he declined the bread and water of life, thereby consigning human beings to mortality. Both the Inanna/Ishtar and the Adapa myths present models for understanding the journey through the seven heavenly palaces and the need to acknowledge the divine beings who grant passage through each level in the heikhalot literature.

Some would also point to the Greek Magical Papyri, which posit that the soul travels through seven levels of heaven and breaks the seals to read the appropriate incantations for the deities who guard each level on their way to join Pistis Sophia, the gnostic deity, in the highest levels of heaven. The texts are from Greco-Roman Egypt, reflect a gnostic background, and date from the second century BCE through the fifth century CE. Although the Greek Magical Papyri predate the heikhalot literature, they likewise suggest dependence upon Mesopotamian conceptualizations of the structure of heaven and the cosmos at large.[24]

The Heikhalot Zutarti appears to presuppose the rabbinic story of the four who attempted to enter Pardes. In developing this story, the Heikhalot Zutarti appears to be designed to specify the experience of the prospective mystics, explaining what it means to be qualified to engage in the study of Jewish mysticism and what it means to appear before the presence of G-d to expound upon the true meaning of Torah. In the case of the Heikhalot Zutarti, the experience entails revelation of the divine Name and the importance of understanding the divine name for a true understanding of divine Torah.

---

22. *ANET*, 52–57, 106–9.
23. *ANET*, 101–3.
24. Betz, *The Greek Magical Papyri*.

Several underlying premises require examination here. First is the Jewish prohibition against pronouncing the divine name. The prohibition appears in both versions of the Ten Commandments, which warn against profaning the Holy Name of YHWH by pronouncing it. In Jewish practice, the divine name is uttered only once a year on Yom Kippur when the high priest enters the holy of holies of the temple to invoke the holy name of G-d in an effort to atone for the sins of the nation. The notion also comes into play in the first revelation of YHWH to Moses in Exod 3, in which YHWH informs Moses that he should tell Pharaoh that "I am who I am" has sent him to demand the freedom of the Israelite slaves. As discussed above, this response employs the *idem per idem* rhetorical device to avoid revealing the name to Moses and to suggest that the divine Name YHWH is associated with the imperfect/future conjugation of the verb *hyh*, indicating that YHWH's name means, "He exists." It addresses the background of Egyptian magical practice expressed in the Egyptian execration texts that hold that proper pronunciation of the name of an Egyptian deity gives the speaker the power of that deity to curse or bless human parties in the earthly world. Such a practice would compromise the sanctity and power of YHWH in Israelite practice, and thus the pronunciation of YHWH's name was forbidden as such pronunciation entailed tremendous power to create, bless, destroy, and curse.

The Heikhalot Zutarti begins in paragraph 335 with the following statement concerning how one who is presumably qualified to do so would behold a vision of the presence of G-d:

> If you want to be singled out in the world so that the secrets of the world and the hidden things of wisdom will be revealed to you, study this Mishnah and be careful about it until the day of your passing. Do not attempt to understand what will be after you, and do not examine the words of your lips. What is in your heart, you should try to understand, and remain silent about it so that you will be worthy of the beauty of the merkavah. Be careful with the honor of your creator, and do not descend to him. And if you have descended to him, do not enjoy anything from it. Your end would be to be expelled from the world of the glory of G-d. Hide the matter so that you will not be expelled from the world.[25]

Such an introductory instruction sets the agenda for the rest of the work. Beholding the divine presence is to be a secret experience in which the

25. Schäfer, *The Origins*, 283–84.

would-be mystic studies "this Mishnah," i.e., the Heikhalot Zutarti itself, to learn how to conduct himself for the rest of his life as he engages in the study of Jewish mysticism. Such an instruction builds upon the teachings of m. Hag. 2:1, which calls upon one to avoid expounding upon texts concerned with incest, creation, and Ezekiel's vision, unless he is a sage who understands of his own knowledge. Part of that knowledge is the recognition that such exposition should be presented to those who are themselves worthy and educated enough to understand it. Although it does not constitute a prohibition of the study and exposition of Jewish mysticism, this instruction does define the boundaries of such study with an eye to protecting the honor of G-d as stated in the Mishnah. It also addresses the issue of asking what is to come after, as instructed in the Mishnah passage. It is noteworthy that the Hebrew word warning to keep such confidence "until the day of your passing" (lit., "your separation," *perishteka*), can also be used to refer to "your interpretation or study," indicating that the vision of the divine presence is fundamentally concerned with the study of Torah in order to achieve an understanding of the vision of G-d.

The reference to understanding what is in your heart rather than what is on your lips recognizes that the mystic might not be able to describe what he sees and understands, much as in Ezekiel's vision of G-d in Ezek 1 where simile, metaphor, and paradoxical imagery attempting to describe the presence of G-d convey the inadequacy of human language to do so, e.g., "and they went in the directions of all of their faces," a reference to the movement of the four creatures who bore the throne of G-d and went in the direction of all four of their faces at once, movement that would be impossible in the finite human world. The reference to the beauty of the merkavah alludes to the statement in Isa 33:17, "When you behold the king in his beauty." The references to expulsion from the presence of G-d indicate the punishment that awaits one who is not properly prepared for the vision of the presence of G-d, nine hundred million bars of iron that would be thrown at the miscreant, killing him and expelling him from the divine presence.

Heikhalot Zutarti differs from the later Heikhalot Rabbati by focusing on R. Akiva as the figure who will ascend through the seven levels of heaven to behold the divine presence. This focus on R. Akiva points to the central role that the story of the four who entered Pardes plays in this work; Heikhalot Zutarti in part presents an exposition concerning the meaning of this narrative. But it does much more than that by also focusing on what R. Akiva learns from his vision of G-d, i.e., the meaning of the divine name. Heikhalot Zutarti paragraph 337 takes up this issue as follows:

> This is the name that was revealed to R. Akiva when he looked at the work of the merkavah. And R. Akiva went down and taught it to his students. He said to them, My sons, be careful with this name. It is a great name, it is a holy name, it is a pure name. For everyone who uses it, in terror, in fear, in purity, in holiness, in humility, will succeed in all his endeavors, and his days will be long. Blessed are you, O YHWH, who sanctified us with his commandments concerning the sanctification of the name.[26]

Several issues emerge here. First is the focus on R. Akiva as the exemplar of the worthy mystic who would look upon the divine presence. Moses, Isaiah, Ezekiel, and others would have preceded R. Akiva, but they are not named. Here readers may note that Rabbinic Judaism maintains that there is a progression in the revelation of and understanding of the Torah. Although both the Written and the Oral Torah were revealed to Moses on Mt. Sinai, the extent to which Moses was able to look upon the divine presence and his understanding of what was revealed are questions in rabbinic literature. For example, the Babylonian Talmud relates in b. Men. 29b that when Moses ascended to heaven, he found G-d making little crowns for all of the letters of the Torah. When Moses asked G-d what they were for, G-d responded that there will come a time when Akiva ben Joseph will come and deduce halakic rulings from every little curve and crown of the letters of the Torah; even these penstrokes will become the basis of the halakah. When Moses asked to see Akiva, G-d took him to R. Akiva's yeshiva where he sat in the back with all of the beginning students. Moses was dismayed and dumbfounded as he listened to R. Akiva speak because he could understand nothing of what R. Akiva said. But Moses was pleasantly surprised when an advanced student asked R. Akiva how a particular halakah was derived. When R. Akiva responded that we learned this particular ruling from our teacher Moses, Moses then understood that he introduced the basis for the tradition, but later interpreters would build upon what Moses had done in bringing about the full understanding of the Written and Oral Torah to all generations.

The reference to R. Akiva's descent is also a key feature of the narrative. In contrast to Moses who ascended Mt. Sinai to receive the revelation of the Torah from G-d, R. Akiva ascends in peace and descends in peace in

---

26. Schäfer, *The Origins*, 285.

various versions of the account of the four who entered Pardes, as well as in the present text. This is no accident. When Moses descended from Mt. Sinai in Exod 32–34, he met disaster in the form of the people worshiping the golden calf. Later in the wilderness, in Num 20, G-d declared that Moses would never enter the promised land of Israel because of his transgression in the episode concerning water from the rock. Moses had faults as a leader, and he was punished for them by being denied entry to the land of Israel; there he would have been able to actualize the Torah that had been revealed to him at Sinai. Despite his faults, he nevertheless served as a role model for R. Akiva. R. Akiva for his own part was an ideal figure when compared to Shimon ben Azzai, Shimon ben Zoma, and R. Elisha ben Abuyah, and the story of these four who entered Pardes lauds him for being able to ascend in peace and descend in peace. Indeed, R. Akiva had faults—he was wrong in declaring Bar Kokhba to be the messiah—but he nevertheless lived long enough to actualize the teachings of Torah in the land of Israel and died as a martyr for Judaism in doing so. Like Moses, R. Akiva serves as a role model for future generations of Jews. As Schäfer argues, R. Akiva's knowledge of the holy name of YHWH is what enables him to fulfill this role in the Heikhalot Zutarti.[27]

A version of the account of the four who entered Pardes then follows in the Heikhalot Zutarti. As Schäfer points out, this version of narrative is not designed simply to portray R. Akiva's vision of the divine presence or even his knowledge of Torah.[28] Rather, the Heikhalot Zutarti version is designed to demonstrate that R. Akiva learned the meaning of the divine name during his journey to Pardes, and this is what enabled him to ascend in peace and descend in peace so that he might walk on dry ground, apparently a reference to the dry ground that emerged from the Red Sea in Exod 14–15, in his understanding of divine revelation. By learning the meaning of the divine name in his journey to and from Pardes, R. Akiva became the sage par excellence in Judaism; he understood that the water imagery of the exodus narrative did not simply refer to the plain meaning of the text. Such imagery was the gateway to a deeper understanding of the Torah narrative that would enable R. Akiva to walk on dry ground, as it were, i.e., to actualize the teachings of the Torah in the lives of the people of Israel in this world. By this reasoning, a heavenly vision of the divine is useless if it does not have an impact on the world of the living. Schäfer notes the narrative's extensive

27. Schäfer, *The Origins*, 286.
28. Schäfer, *The Origins*, 286–88.

dependence on Ezekiel's vision of Gd in Ezek 1–3, but also noteworthy is that Ezekiel's vision came at the beginning of his book. Following his vision of G-d in Ezek 1–3, Ezekiel spent the next twenty-five years actualizing the divine will among the people in exile. Heikhalot Zutarti recognizes this lesson when it states about R. Akiva:

> But R. Akiva said, He is, so to speak, like us, but He is greater than everything, and this is His glory that is concealed from us. Moses says to them, to these ones and those ones, Do not investigate your words, but rather He should be blessed at His place. Therefore it is said, Blessed be the Glory of YHWH from His place (in Ezek 3:12).[29]

Like Ezekiel, R. Akiva recognizes the need to bless YHWH. Ezekiel includes halakic statements that are not found in the Torah, and rabbinic tradition maintains that R. Hananyah ben Hezekiah burned three hundred barrels of oil while trying to reconcile Ezekiel's statements with those of the Torah. He ultimately recognized that Ezekiel was a halakic teacher on a par with Moses (b. Shab. 13b). Consequently, the chain of tradition in Heikhalot Zutarti is Moses, Ezekiel, and then R. Akiva. Moses is a model for Ezekiel, Ezekiel is a model for R. Akiva, and R. Akiva is a model for his disciples who would expound upon the Torah; but each perceives and understands G-d from his own unique position. R. Akiba concludes concerning the holy name of G-d:

> He used to say, Whoever spreads his name, loses his name, and who does not study, deserves death. Who makes use of the crown, vanishes. Who does not know Qintamisa' shall be put to death, and who knows Qintamisa' will be desired in the world to come.[30]

From R. Akiva's standpoint, a combination of worship and study is necessary to understand the divine. But he identifies knowledge of the name Qintamisa', though we do not know what this means, as essential knowledge of the divine name for anyone who would understand the divine presence and the will of G-d. When R. Akiva appears before the throne of G-d in the seventh heaven, he ascends on a wagon of fire and beholds the whole universe:

29. Schäfer, *The Origins*, 290.
30. Schäfer, *The Origins*, 292.

R. Akiva said, I looked and saw the whole universe, and I have perceived it as it is. I ascended in a wagon of fire and contemplated the palaces of hail, and I found . . . sitting on . . .[31]

One might be tempted to conclude that R. Akiba ascends to heaven in a chariot of fire like Elijah in 2 Kgs 2, but the term is *'agala'*, Aramaic for wagon or cart, which is how the ark of the covenant is conveyed to Jerusalem when David brings it up from Kiriath-jearim in 1 Chr 16. The palaces of hail are drawn from the Enoch tradition when Enoch is brought to heaven to behold the heavenly temple with its storerooms of hail and fire. R. Akiba sees a figure with many names sitting in a place which also has many names, all of which are incomprehensible to us, although each name is likely a reference to a quality of G-d or a quality of the holy of holies or the ark of the covenant where G-d metaphorically resides. The multiple names point to Heikhalot Zutarti's interest in the holy power of names to convey the holy power of G-d.

The power of the use of holy names comes to expression in Heikhalot Zutarti paragraph 367, where R. Akiba describes the spells and seals that make his journey to heaven possible:

This is the spell and the seal by which one binds the earth and by which one binds the heavens. The earth flees before it, and the universe trembles before it. It opens the mouth of the sea and closes the books of the firmament. It opens heavens and floods the universe; it uproots the earth and mixes up the universe.[32]

In other words, knowledge of the names embedded in the spells and seals gives one the power of the divine name to control the earth, the seas, the heavens, and other elements of creation, much as knowledge of divine names in the Egyptian execration texts gives one sufficient knowledge of the god in question to curse or to bless others in the world. In the case of the Heikhalot Zutarti, knowledge of divine names makes both the creation and the destruction of the universe possible.

Schäfer observes that the Heikhalot Zutarti turns to consider Metatron, the angel of the presence who sits upon the throne of G-d in the seventh heaven at times when G-d is not present.[33] Metatron developed

31. Schäfer, *The Origins*, 293.
32. Schäfer, *The Origins*, 293.
33. Schäfer, *The Origins*, 294–98.

out of the figure of Enoch, who lived for three hundred and sixty-five years. Genesis 5:24 states of him, "And Enoch walked with G-d, and then he was no more for G-d took him." Later Enochic and heikhalot literature indicates that Enoch was transformed into an angel as he ascended to heaven, where he was renamed Metatron and took on the role of the angel of the presence. The meaning of the name Metatron is disputed. The most cogent meaning is "the guardian," derived from the Aramaic term *mattara'*, "keeper of the watch," or the verb *memattar*, "to watch, guard."[34] Many maintain that the name is derived from Greek, *meta* and *thronos*, with or by the throne, but the two words do not appear separately with this meaning in any context, and the suggestion must therefore be rejected.[35] The Heikhalot Zutarti identifies Metatron as "the Great Prince of the testimony," who informs R. Akiva concerning the measurements of the body of G-d. Because the divine measurements are derived from the Shiur Qomah, Schäfer argues that this section may well be a later redactional addition to the Heikhalot Zutarti. The text continues with material concerned with the divine name and its application in the world. Metatron utters the name of G-d but blocks the ears of the angels with the fire of deafness so they cannot hear either G-d or him. Thus, Metatron emerges as the angel closest to G-d, whose names and form are nearly identical with those of the divine presence.

Heikhalot Zutarti concludes with instructions concerning the proper preparation for ascent to appear before the divine throne and further discussion concerning the understanding of the Holy Name of G-d. A very telling statement about preparation for the ascent in paragraph 424 reveals the Heikhalot Zutarti's concern with the divine name:

> R. Akiva said, Everyone who wishes to learn this Mishnah and to explain the Name shall fast for forty days. He shall rest his head between his knees, until the fast has taken complete hold of him. He shall whisper to the earth but not to heaven so that the earth will hear it, but not heaven. If he is a youth, he should say it before he has an ejaculation. If he is a married man, he should be prepared for three days, as it is said, Be prepared for the third day (do not go near a woman).[36]

34. Marcus Jastrow, *Dictionary of the Targumim, the Talmud Babli and Yerushalmi, and the Midrashic Literature* (1943; repr., Peabody, MA: Hendrickson, 2006), 767.
35. Scholem, *Major Trends*, 69; Scholem, *Jewish Gnosticism*, 91, 43.
36. Schäfer, *The Origins*, 302.

The instructions for preparation are based in part on a number of biblical sources, such as Elijah's preparation for his own encounter with G-d (1 Kgs 18:42, 19:8); Daniel's preparation for his vision of angelic interpretation of prophecy (Dan 10:2–3); and Moses's instructions to Israel prior to the theophany at Mt. Sinai (Exod 19:15). Such preparations appear to anticipate the mystical study of Torah in an effort to understand the meaning of the divine name. As such, Heikhalot Zutarti appears to anticipate the Sefer Yetzirah and Abraham Abulafia's later practice in studying Torah.

Sefer Heikhalot, or Third Enoch

Sefer Heikhalot, also known as 3 Enoch, focuses especially on the heavenly ascent of R. Ishmael and his vision of Metatron, the angel who sits on the throne of G-d except when G-d is present to hear the praises and worship of Israel.[37] The Sefer Heikhalot does not include a detailed account of R. Ishmael's ascent; instead it focuses on Metatron's speeches to R. Ishmael, in which he explains his origins as Enoch ben Jared, the father of Methuseleh, who lived for three hundred and sixty-five years and then walked with G-d. Metatron further explains his seventy names, his close association with G-d, and the features of heaven to R. Ishmael.

Because of its dependence on 1 En., the Heikhalot Rabbati, the Heikhalot Zutarti, and the Shiur Qomah, many interpreters consider 3 En. to be a relatively late heikhalot composition that may date as late as the tenth century CE. The use of the heikhalot motif of the seven levels of heaven suggests a Babylonian origin, although some elements originating in the Galilee during a long period of composition are also apparent.

Third Enoch appears to be conceptualized as a response to and reflection upon the story of the four who entered Pardes. Whereas 1 En. focuses on the character of the heavenly temple and its associated fixtures, the Heikhalot Rabbati focuses on the interpretation of Torah, the Heikhalot Zutarti focuses on the meaning of the Holy Name of G-d, and the Shiur Qomah focuses on describing the dimensions of the divine presence of G-d,

37. For text editions of Sefer Heikhalot or 3 En., see Schäfer, *Synopse*, 855–946; Hugo Odeberg, *3 Enoch or the Hebrew Book of Enoch* (New York: Ktav, 1973). For translations, see Odeberg; Philip S. Alexander, "3 (The Hebrew Apocalypse of) Enoch," in *The Old Testament Pseudepigrapha*, vol. 1: *Apocalyptic Literature and Testaments*, ed. James H. Charlesworth (Garden City, NY: Doubleday, 1983), 223–315. For studies, see those of Odeberg and Alexander already named and Schäfer, *The Origins*, 315–27.

3 En. focuses on the visualization of Metatron. According to the account of the four who attempted to enter Pardes, R. Elisha ben Abuyah "cut the shoots" and became *aher*, "another person," i.e., he abandoned Judaism. The traditions concerning R. Elisha ben Abuyah in the Jerusalem Talmud (y. Hag. 2:1) attribute his apostasy to events he witnessed and questions they raised of divine justice for people who are righteous and scrupulous in adhering to the divine will as expressed in halakah: the death of man attempting to protect the eggs in the nest of a bird, as Deut 22:6–7 commands, and the Roman execution of his teacher R. Judah Nahtum as a dog carried off his severed tongue. Another tradition (b. Hag. 15b) states that when he would rise in the yeshivah, forbidden Greek books would fall from his lap. But for the present purposes, the most pertinent explanation is that R. Elisha ben Abuyah saw Metatron sitting on the throne of G-d when he entered the seventh heaven. G-d would only enter the seventh heaven from the Ogdoad, the eighth level of heaven, at times of Jewish worship—during the Shaharit (morning), Minhah (afternoon), and Ma'ariv (evening) services. Otherwise, Metatron would be seated in the seventh heaven in place of G-d. When R. Elisha ben Abuyah saw Metatron sitting on the throne of G-d, he declared, "There are two powers in heaven," indicating that there are two G-ds in heaven, in complete contradiction to the fundamental Jewish belief that there is only one true G-d (y. Hag. 2:1). Such a view is characteristic of gnosticism, which holds that Pistis Sophia is the supreme goddess of creation who dwells in the Ogdoad or eighth heaven of the universe, whereas Sabaoth, who dwells in the seventh heaven, rules the lower worlds. Because of this statement, R. Elisha ben Abuyah was declared to be Aher, another person, and was excommunicated from Judaism. Insofar as 3 En. attempts to describe the character and presence of Metatron, it appears to be an attempt to describe what R. Elisha ben Abuyah saw when he beheld Metatron in the seventh level of heaven and mistook him for G-d's very own self.

Third Enoch begins in its first two mishnayot (paragraphs) with an account of R. Ishmael's ascent to the seventh level of heaven. The focus on R. Ishmael ben Elisha, as in Heikhalot Zutarti, as opposed to R. Akiva, as in Heikhalot Rabbati, is key; it points to the later composition of this text and its presuppositions of the earlier texts noted above. R. Akiba was the one who succeeded in ascending and descending according to the account of the four who entered Pardes, and so he was featured in the Heikhalot Rabbati, the earliest of the heikhalot narratives; R. Akiva's role emphasized the full understanding of Torah necessary to become a sage who understands of his own knowledge and who would then be qualified to enter the seventh heaven to behold the divine presence. But R. Ishmael was a peer of R. Akiva, who also developed a system of exegesis in his thirteen Middot, measures or guidelines for deriving halakah from the biblical text; these include practical guidelines for understanding the plain meaning of the text as well as theological premises that ensure proper understanding. His system was applied in halakic midrash, such as the Mekhilta de R. Ishmael, which focused on the interpretation of the legal texts in Exod 12–35. R. Ishmael's method was considered to be more logical than that of R. Akiva, and R. Ishmael was known to seek a balance between competing viewpoints; as a result, more found his halakic decisions convincing. His ability to reconcile opposing viewpoints apparently played a role in his selection as the merkavah mystic of the Heikhalot Zutarti and 3 En., as a figure with greater credibility than R. Akiba, who despite his reputation and erudition was deemed to have been mistaken in declaring Shimon bar Kokhba to be the messiah.

R. Ishmael's ascent to heaven in 3 En. appears rather truncated when compared to the Heikhalot Rabbati, which spends considerable time on the dynamics and problems of the ascent, so as to ascertain the qualities necessary for one who would make the ascent and behold the divine presence. Because Heikhalot Rabbati has already portrayed this process, it is not necessary for 3 En. to do so. R. Ishmael's priestly status plays a role in his admission to the seventh heaven and enables him after some delay to sing the praises of G-d that would be necessary for beholding the divine presence at a time of worship. When R. Ishmael's presence is challenged because he is human, Metatron, who himself was the human Enoch before being transformed into an angel, is the one who vouches for R. Ishmael before the heavenly host of angels.

As just noted, one of the problems encountered by R. Ishmael in his ascent into the seventh level of heaven is the objections of the angels to a human being among them. The reason for such objections is that in previous Enochic literature, following the book of Genesis, the interrelationship between human women and the sons of G-d in Gen 6:1–4 was a major cause of the breakdown of holy cosmic order that brought about the flood. The issue was treated in 1 Enoch as the cause of the dissolution of cosmic order. But when Metatron identified R. Ishmael as a Levite and son of Aaron who presented the sacred offerings to G-d, the angels relented and allowed him to remain in heaven. This encounter prompted R. Ishmael in 3 En. 3 to ask about Metatron's identity, especially since he holds authority over the other angels. Metatron's response aids in understanding why R. Elisha ben Abuyah believed that Metatron was G-d. Metatron states that he has seventy names, which correspond to the seventy nations of the world, and each one of them is based on the name of the King of Kings, i.e., G-d. In essence, Metatron's seventy names are like the seventy names of G-d, but he goes on to explain that G-d refers to him as "the youth," because he is a relative latecomer to heaven when compared to the angels. The notion of a god having a multiplicity of names actually has Mesopotamian roots; Marduk is addressed by fifty names in the Babylonian Creation Epic, the Enuma Elish, following his defeat of Tiamat and his ordering of the world of creation.[38] Insofar as Marduk becomes chief of the gods by virtue of his victory over Tiamat, he also becomes chief of the nations, which entitles him to the Etemenanki temple or ziggurat in Babylon and his fifty names that signify his rule over all creation and nations.

When R. Ishmael observes that Metatron is greater than all the other angels, Metatron goes on to explain his human origins. He tells R. Ishmael that he was Enoch ben Jared, the father of Methuseleh, known in Gen 5:21–24. Metatron further tells R. Ishmael that when human beings persisted in their sins and rejected G-d, G-d took Enoch from among human beings so that he might serve as a witness against them for their sins and thereby justify their punishment by flood. Metatron raises questions of divine justice. Did these people commit enough sin to justify such punishment? What about their wives and children who would suffer punishment with them? Metatron explains that G-d appointed him to witness against the sins of future generations as well, brought him up to the heights of heaven, and placed him above the angels so that he might fulfill this role. When three angels, Azzah, Uzzah, and Aza'el, protested that humans had no right to ascend to heaven to be placed in such a position, Metatron reports that G-d objected to being interrupted by the angels and that G-d would do what G-d willed. At that point, the angels prostrated themselves before Enoch/Metatron and accepted the divine decision. Because he is a latecomer among the angels, G-d therefore refers to him as the youth.

Metatron goes on to explain that the holy Shekhinah, the divine presence of G-d, resided in the Garden of Eden under the tree of life and radiated light three hundred and sixty-five thousand times more brilliant than the sun. All was well until the time of Enosh, son of Seth, who is deemed to be the first major idolater, according to a rereading of the text of Genesis that says at that time humans began (*huhal*) to call upon the name of G-d.

38. *ANET*, 60–72, esp. 69–72.

The reading takes *huhal*, "began," as a reference to *hullin*, "profane things," asserting that humans profaned the calling of the name of G-d in the time of Enosh. The angels therefore protested the Shekhinah's residence on earth among idolatrous human beings and took action to prompt the Shekhinah to ascend from earth into heaven to escape the profanation of earth. G-d consequently decided to bring Enoch to heaven in a fiery chariot together with the Shekhinah. When the angels again protested the presence of a human in heaven, G-d responded that Enoch was the best of them. Enoch would serve as G-d's sole reward for engaging in the process of creation that led to such a despicable lot.

Third Enoch 7–16 then explain how Enoch was transformed into an angel. G-d first grants him three hundred thousand measures each of understanding, prudence, life, grace and favor, love, Torah, humility, sustenance, mercy, and reverence. G-d laid the divine hand on him and blessed Enoch with 1,365,000 blessings so that Enoch was enlarged to a size that matched the world in length and breadth. Enoch grew seventy-two wings so that each covered an entire world, and 365,000 eyes so that he would see all. G-d then made for Enoch a throne covered with splendor and brilliance, like the throne of glory on which G-d sits, and placed it at the door of the seventh palace of heaven. Enoch would sit there as G-d's servant to speak on G-d's behalf and in G-d's name and would have charge over all the stores of the palaces of the Arabot. G-d then revealed to Enoch all the wisdom of what has happened and will happen, granted him a robe and a crown, and called him the lesser YHWH, stating, "My name is in him," i.e., G-d's name is in Enoch. The crown was inscribed with all the letters of the alphabet by which all creation was created; this detail anticipates the Sefer Yetzirah, or Book of Creation, which examines the roles played by the letters of the Hebrew alphabet in the creation and workings of the world. Enoch received all the homage of the angels, and he became a being of fire to signify his transformation from human to angel; thus Metatron became like G-d and the angels, having intangible form comprised of light and flame.

In 3 En. 16, Metatron explains what happened when R. Elisha ben Abuyah entered the seventh heaven to find Metatron enthroned with an appearance like G-d and speaking on behalf of G-d. R. Elisha exclaimed, "There are two powers in heaven," confusing Metatron for G-d and reiterating the gnostic belief in two powers in heaven, Pistis Sophia and Sabaoth. At that point, the angel Anaphiel YHWH struck Metatron with sixty lashes of fire, forcing him to stand upon his feet.

In 3 En. 17–40, Metatron gives an account of the hierarchies of angels that dwell in the heavens, including their organization and their activities in the heavenly realm. He begins with the seven main angels, Michael, Gabriel, Shatqi'el, Shahaqi'el, Baradiel, Baraqi'el, and Idri'el, each of whom governs one of the seven levels of heaven from the seventh to the first. Under them is Galgalli'el, who is in charge of the orb of the sun. The rest of the angelic organization and functions then follow in detail, many of which are identified with features of the visionary experience of G-d, such as Isaiah's vision of the seraphim in Isa 6 or Ezekiel's vison of the ophanim, wheels, eyes, beasts, etc., in Ezek 1. The description culminates in a discussion of the proper means of singing the Kedushah, the heavenly prayer, "Holy, Holy, Holy is YHWH *tzeva'ot*, the whole earth is full of his glory," which features in Isaiah's vision in Isa 6, the Jewish worship service, and later the Christian worship service. If the angels do not sing the Kedushah properly, fire emanates from YHWH and destroys them all. Then with one word, YHWH creates them all once again for the next singing of the Kedushah.

Third Enoch 41–48 then focus on the various stores of heaven, including the cosmic letters by which creation was brought into being, the power of divine names, the souls of the righteous, the souls of the wicked and the intermediate, the souls of the patriarchs, the heavenly curtain, the spirits of the stars, the spirits of the punished angels, and the right hand of G-d.

Altogether, Sefer Heikhalot or 3 En. presents an overview of the role of Metatron in response to the account of the four who entered Pardes, especially to explain what R. Elisha ben Abuyah saw that made him cut the shoots or abandon Judaism when he declared, upon seeing Metatron enthroned in the seventh level of heaven, that there are two powers in heaven. Third Enoch also builds upon the heavenly tours of Enoch and other apocalyptic works in explaining the organizations and functions of the angels, as well as the stores of the various elements of creation and the souls of those who have inhabited or will inhabit it; this all serves to explain the function of Metatron, who was once the biblical figure Enoch but who has now been transformed into a heavenly angel that helps to guide qualified humans in their attempts to appear before the divine presence.

Conclusion

In sum, the heikhalot literature presupposes the transcendent character of G-d and the need for full expertise in Torah interpretation and commitment to Judaism on the part of those who would approach G-d. The use of the seven-palace heikhalot motif facilitates the notion of the holy transcendence of G-d, but the fact that the would-be mystic actually approaches G-d through liturgical prayer, theurgic practice, and Torah study indicates that G-d also has an immanent character, insofar as G-d is to be found in the holy practice and study of Judaism within the world of creation.

Chapter 7

FROM HEIKHALOT TO EARLY
KABBALISTIC LITERATURE

The Diaspora Context of Pre-kabbalistic Jewish Mysticism

The aftermath of the failed Bar Kokhba revolt in 132–135 CE saw a marked change in the status and self-conceptualization of Judaism. Having seen the Roman destruction of the temple in 70 CE during the Zealot Revolt against Rome in 66–74 CE and the Roman genocide committed against the Jewish population of Judea in the Bar Kokhba war, Jews were compelled to rethink their status as a nation living in its own land. They therefore began to adopt the identity of an exiled people living as an ethnic and religious minority in foreign lands. Although there was an important Jewish population in the Galilee that produced the Jerusalem Talmud, Roman persecution against Jews continued, ensuring that Galilean Judaism would remain a relatively minor population within the larger Jewish world. Roman persecution also curtailed Jewish life throughout the Roman Empire, including the major Jewish population in Egypt as well as the Jewish populations of Rome, Greece, Western Asia, and Europe. Jews in Europe would continue to suffer persecution and exclusion in Roman society, particularly after the early-fourth-century reign of the emperor Constantine, when Christianity emerged as the official religion of the Roman Empire and sought to suppress Jews, gnostics, pagans, and others in an effort to ensure its domination throughout the Roman Empire.

Although Western scholars tend to focus on the European Middle Ages, the major centers of Judaism shifted to Babylonia and the Persian Empire. Babylonia and Persia generally had little to do with emerging European societies during the second through fifteenth centuries CE and instead enjoyed periods of prosperity and progress interspersed with wars that upheld or overthrew a succession of empires, as had been the case from the Achaemenid Persian (550–330 BCE) to the Seleucid (312–63 BCE) Empires, now followed by the Parthian Persian (247 BCE–224 CE), Sassanian Persian (224–607 CE), and finally the Islamic Empire beginning in 637 CE.

Under the rule of both the Sassanian Persian and Islamic Empires, Jews were granted the right to local autonomy as an ethnic and religious community able to govern its own internal affairs. It did so under the supervision of rabbis and of three major leaders of Jewish community: two Gaons (Excellencies), or heads of the two major rabbinic yeshivot in Babylonia (in Sura and Pumbeditha), as well as the Resh Galuta (Head of the Exile), a civil leader of the Jewish community who was believed to be descended from the House of David. This Jewish community system in exile is generally known as the kehillah (community), a system of Jewish local autonomy submitting to the authority of the larger state. The talmudic statement by R. Samuel (ca. 200–260 CE), *"dina' demalkuta' dina',"* in Aramaic, "The law of the state is the law," is generally taken as a rabbinic recognition of state authority at the outset of Sassanian rule following 224 CE (b. Ned. 28b; b. Git. 10b; b. B. Qam. 113a; b. B. Bat. 54b–55a). State recognition of the kehillah continued through the period of Islamic rule and on into other Asian, African, and European Jewish cultures—in Europe until it was abolished by Napoleon Bonaparte, emperor of France, in 1805 as an attempt to assimilate the Jews into French, and the larger European, society. Indeed, the origins of the kehillah system may be traced back to the Achaemenid Persian Empire, which granted local autonomy to Jews in the land of Judah under the supervision of Ezra and Nehemiah and their successors.[1] The kehillah model suffered disruptions during the Seleucid and Roman Empires, at times when both attempted unsuccessfully to impose their own religious observance on Jews; but apparently it continued into the Parthian Persian Empire.

The late Parthian and the Sassanian periods of Persian rule saw the gradual establishment of Rabbinic Judaism as the primary expression of Jewish religious, cultural, and national life, along with the composition of the Mishnah, the Jerusalem and Babylonian Talmuds, and the early midrashic literature as the foundations for Rabbinic Jewish life. Although some of this literature was composed by the rabbis of the Galilean Jewish community, Babylonian Judaism, which emerged as the leading and most influential movement in Rabbinic Judaism, produced the Babylonian Talmud and other works. As noted in the discussion of the composition of this literature in the

---

1. Joel Weinberg, *The Citizen-Temple Community*, JSOTSup 151 (Sheffield: Sheffield Academic Press, 2009).

last chapter, the talmudic rabbis attempted to define the parameters for a stable, just, and holy Jewish life in exile, all the while anticipating an eventual restoration to the land of Israel when G-d saw fit to restore the Jerusalem Temple and to reestablish the royal House of David in Jerusalem.

But no such restoration ever came during the Middle Ages, and Jews had to adapt themselves to lives as often-despised minorities under foreign rule, especially when Christianity and Islam became the dominant religions of the empires that ruled over them. Throughout the early Middle Ages, more Jews—by some estimates, approximately 90 percent of the worldwide Jewish population—lived under Islamic rule in Western Asia, North Africa, and in some parts of Europe.[2] At the outset of Islamic rule, Jews were attacked by Muslim armies, particularly in the Arabian Peninsula.

Although Islam traces its origins to Adam, it was founded by Muhammad, an illiterate Arabian caravaneer, who claimed to have experienced visions from Allah (G-d) mediated by the angel Jibril (Gabriel). Through his visions, G-d revealed the Qur'an, which would serve as the foundational Muslim scripture and the capstone of divine revelation from G-d to humanity in Muslim thought. As the prophet of Islam, an Arabic term that refers to submission to G-d, Muhammad began to speak publicly and to attract followers to the new movement in his home city of Mecca. But experiencing resistance in Mecca, Muhammad accepted an invitation to come to the city of Yatrib in 622 CE where he set up the first Muslim state as a basis for establishing order, justice, and holiness in the world. Yatrib therefore became known as al-Medinah an-Nabiwiyah, "the City of the Prophet," or simply Medina, "the City." The year 622 CE therefore marks the Hijrah or pilgrimage of Muhammad to Medina and the founding of the Muslim ummah, the "people" constituted by Islam.

Insofar as Muhammad saw Islam as the fulfillment of Judaism and Christianity, he anticipated that Jews and Christians would flock to the new movement, and he therefore directed that worship of G-d be directed toward Jerusalem. Jews did not convert to Islam, by and large. During Muhammad's military campaign against Mecca, Jews in Medina refused Muhammad's call to side with him against the Meccans in battle because the day on which the battle took place was Shabbat. After Muhammad defeated the Meccans,

---

2. John Efron et al., *The Jews: A History*, 2nd ed. (Boston: Pearson, 2014), 150. For discussion of Judaism during the Middle Ages, see Efron et al., *The Jews*, 149–208; Robert Seltzer, *Jewish People, Jewish Thought: The Jewish Experience in History* (New York: Macmillan, 1980), 323–453; H. H. Ben Sasson, ed., *A History of the Jewish People* (Cambridge: Harvard University Press, 1976), 385–723.

he turned against several major Jewish tribal groups in Medina.[3] The first were the Banu Qaynuqa, a Jewish tribe of craftsmen and artisans, who were expelled from Medina when the Khazraji chieftain, Abd Allah b. Ubayy, demanded that Muhammad show mercy to the Jews. The second were the Banu al-Nadir, who surrendered and were initially expelled from Medina to Khaybar, but Muhammad attacked Khaybar two years later, killing the men who did not convert to Islam and appropriating their wealth and their women. The third were the Banu Qurayza, who were executed publicly in Medina, thereby securing Muhammad's reputation as a leader with whom to be reckoned. Following these encounters, Muhammad directed Muslim worship toward Mecca.

In general, Islam did not tolerate the existence of pagans in areas of Muslim rule, but Jews and Christians were understood to be "Peoples of the Book" to whom divine revelation had already been granted, albeit without the complete revelation of G-d's will to Muhammad as recorded in the Qur'an. Consequently, toward the end of his life Muhammad issued instructions that Jews and Christians were to be allowed to live in areas of Muslim rule in the expectation that they would eventually convert to Islam. They were to be subjected to a poll tax, known as the jizya, which would enable them to live under Muslim rule. Their status was finalized after Muhammad's lifetime, attributed traditionally to the Pact of Umar, the Second Caliph of Islam, although other authorities consider this to be a later development. Jews and Christians would be recognized as People of the Book and granted the right to live under Islamic rule as dhimmi.[4] The Arabic word *dhimmi* signifies protected status, like that of women, that would permit Jews and Christians to live as second-class citizens under Islamic rule. In addition to the payment of the jizya, dhimmi would be expected to live under a series of restrictions that would demonstrate their protected status. Dhimmi would be forbidden to build new synagogues or churches or to repair older ones; they would be forbidden to hang religious symbols on their houses of worship; Muslims would be allowed to enter Jewish and Christian houses of worship at any time; synagogues and churches would acknowledge the Muslim times for prayer by ringing a small bell; dhimmi would be forbidden to raise their voices in worship; dhimmi houses of worship and homes would be built so as

---

3. See esp. Norman A. Stillman, *The Jews of Arab Lands: A History and Source Book* (Philadelphia: Jewish Publication Society, 1979), 3–22.

4. For discussion of dhimmi status, see Bat Ye'or, *The Dhimmi: Jews and Christians under Islam* (London and Toronto: Associated University Presses, 1985).

not to tower over Muslim houses of worship and homes; such houses would compel dhimmi to bow upon entering or exiting to remind them of their low status; dhimmi would not ride horses or use saddles; dhimmi would not bear arms; dhimmi would wear distinctive clothing, i.e., Jews would wear yellow turbans and belts and Christians would wear blue turbans and belts; dhimmi would not impede those who would convert to Islam; dhimmi would not sell alcohol to Muslims; dhimmi would not beat a Muslim; dhimmi would give up their seats to a Muslim; dhimmi would not engrave seals with Arabic; dhimmi would not buy a Muslim prisoner or slave; dhimmi would not wear insignia of honor; and many others as well.

In general, Jews did not suffer the pogroms that their counterparts in Europe suffered, but there were exceptions, such as the attack against the Jewish community of Granada in 1066 in which some four thousand Jews were killed. For the most part, Jews lived as minor merchants, shopkeepers, craftsmen, and workers in similar trades, while enduring the second-class status imposed upon them as dhimmi. Throughout the history of Jews under Islamic rule, several messianic movements emerged, but overall no clear movement for the restoration of Jews to the land of Israel emerged until modern times. The majority of Jews' experience of absence from Jerusalem and the land of Israel at large contributed to the continuing development of Jewish mystical thought, which began to shift from models of divine transcendence, such as the journey to the heavenly presence of G-d in the heikhalot literature, to models of divine immanence, in which divine presence may be found and experienced in the world of creation, as found in the kabbalistic literature. In addition, the roles of Jews under Muslim rule in trade and crafts facilitated contact with foreigners and foreign ideas, especially from South and East Asia, which markedly influenced the development of later kabbalistic literature.

Jews living under Roman rule generally faced greater socio-economic barriers and exclusion than those who lived under Persian and later Islamic rule. Although Jews were to be found throughout the Roman Empire, particularly in Egypt and North Africa, Asia Minor and Western Asia, Greece, and the Roman homeland itself, the Jewish revolts against Rome, including the Zealot Revolt of 66–74 CE, the Diaspora Revolt of 114–117 CE, and the Bar Kokhba revolt of 132–135 CE, did much to turn the Roman government and Roman public opinion against Jews because of the losses suffered in putting down the revolts and because of the perceived refusal of Jews by and large to integrate fully into Roman society, particularly with regard to worship of Roman gods and adherence to distinctive Jewish practice, such as kashrut, Shabbat observance, and the general avoidance of intermarriage.

In the aftermath of the revolts, many Jews who survived the wars were taken as prisoners to serve as slaves elsewhere in the Roman world. Many were placed on the frontiers of the Roman Empire, such as the Rhine River Valley on the borders between the Roman Empire and the generally un-Romanized tribal areas known as Germania. Trade along the Rhine River was emerging as an important economic development during late antiquity and the early Middle Ages, but the dangers of a frontier life left the Jewish population of the Rhine River Valley oftentimes under threat and relatively isolated from the rest of the Roman world. Overall, northern Europe was a very primitive and undeveloped area during the periods of late antiquity and the early Middle Ages.

Although Jewish life under Roman rule was never easy in the centuries following the defeated revolts, conditions became much worse when Christianity became the dominant religion of the Roman Empire in the aftermath of the reign of Emperor Constantine (r. 306–337 CE). Constantine established a second capital in Constantinople (modern Istanbul), which straddled the European and Asian continents and served as the capital of the eastern Roman or Byzantine Empire. Although Constantine was a pagan for most of his life, he attributed the military victories that brought him to the throne to Christ and converted to Christianity on his deathbed. His mother and his successors did much to solidify Christianity's grasp on the empire, which resulted in persecution of Jews and adherents of other traditions, such as gnosticism, Samaritanism, and others, as outcasts in Roman late antiquity due to their refusal to accept Christ—and therefore the authority of the Christian Roman Empire. In the case of Jews, charges that Jews had called for the crucifixion of Jesus and claimed that "his blood be upon us and our children" (Matt 27:25) would justify persecution of those who allegedly murdered and denied Jesus—and therefore the Roman state. Indeed by 400 CE Christianity and the Roman state were fully identified.

Roman persecution of Jews appeared especially in the legal realm as the Roman Empire would enact laws that would discriminate against Jews, Samaritans, and others as early as the reign of Constantine.[5] The laws of Constantine enacted in 315 CE would punish Jews and other non-Christians for attacks against those who had converted to Christianity. Anyone who

5. Jacob R. Marcus, *The Jew in the Medieval World: A Source Book: 315–1791* (New York: Atheneum, 1981), 3–7.

attempted to stone those who had converted to Christianity would be punished by fire, i.e., burning at the stake. The laws that Emperor Constantius
enacted in 339 CE dissolved marriages between Jewish men and Christian
women and required that such women be returned to the weaving facto-
ries where they would be required to work and support themselves rather
than share the "shameful" lives of their Jewish husbands. Any Jew who attempted to circumvent this law would be put to death. Likewise, the laws
of Constantius forbade Jews to own Christian slaves; these slaves were to be
appropriated for the imperial treasury when discovered. Jewish owners who
circumcised their slaves would be fined and would also suffer capital punishment. A law of Theodosius II, enacted in 439 CE, forbade Jews from holding
public office, such as the administration of a city, or of jails; it further forbade
the building of synagogues that might approach the size and magnificence of
local churches. Such synagogues were subject to confiscation by the church
should they be deemed to have violated this law. Furthermore, any Jews who
converted a slave or a freeman to Judaism would be punished with death.

As Germanic and other European kingdoms replaced the Western Roman Empire, they maintained allegiance to its church and perpetuated its
policies toward Jews, with the result that Jews in much of Europe experienced increasing economic isolation. For much of the early Middle Ages,
the European economy was largely based on a feudal structure of land own-
ership by elites, usually recognized as royals, who presided over an agricultural economy worked by serfs who were bound to the lands on which they
worked. Jews were barred from owning land in many European countries
and could therefore not take part in this economy. But as the economy developed, Jews engaged in crafts and skilled trades, such as metalworking,
woodworking, leatherworking, baking, and small manufacturing. Such
trades developed with the growth of urban areas that supplied the needs of
feudal agriculture; but as these trades grew in importance, so did efforts to
exclude Jews. As trade guilds grew to dominate the various trades, Jews were
excluded from guild membership, and thus from practicing many trades
except within the much smaller Jewish community. Many Jews adapted by
moving into commerce, aided by common languages such as Hebrew, Aramaic, Yiddish, and Ladino that made Jews well-suited for communication
with other Jews outside of their local areas to facilitate the trade of goods,
the development of a financial system for such trade, and the conveyance
of ideas between other regions and their home territories. Jews therefore
played an important role in developing banking and a cash economy in medieval Europe that enabled feudal landlords to sell their produce and goods

abroad. It also enabled Jews who rose to prominence in such trade and financial activities to support their co-religionists who were so frequently denied the bases for economic self-support, as well as the feudal landlords who frequently found themselves in financial straits and looked to Jews for loans and beneficial trade connections.

Jews were often subject to physical assault, especially pogroms against Jewish communities, and especially during the Crusades. When Pope Urban II declared the First Crusade of 1095–1099, Crusader armies gathered in northern Europe to begin their march, eastward to Turkey and then southward to Palestine, to liberate Jerusalem from Muslim rule. Jewish communities around the Rhine River Valley in western Germany and eastern France, in towns such as Speyer, Worms, Mainz, Cologne, and elsewhere, were attacked by Crusader armies who demanded money to finance their campaigns, converts to support the church, and lives to satisfy their lust for infidel blood. Although there were instances when church officials intervened in often futile attempts to save Jewish lives, thousands were killed up and down the Rhine Valley. Pogroms against Jews also broke out during the period of the second great plague in 1346–1348 because Christians accused Jews of alliance with the Devil to undermine Christian civilization; actually, ships returning from trade with regions outside of Europe had picked up rats that transmitted diseases against which Europeans had developed no immunity. In efforts to explain why G-d did not come to their deliverance in these pogroms, many Jews turned to the study of the heikhalot literature, and Jewish mysticism flourished. Consequently, the Hasidei Ashkenaz (the Pious of Germany) movement developed under the leadership of the Kalonymus family, beginning with R. Judah Hehasid, author of Sefer Hasidim, in the twelfth to thirteenth centuries. Consequently, the Hasidei Ashkenaz (the Pious of Germany) movement developed in the twelfth to thirteenth centuries. The Hasidei Ashkenaz were known for the view that martyrdom represents a form of piety, insofar as the martyr devotes his or her life to G-d in such cases of persecution and death.

Ironically, the Crusades opened Western (and Central) Europe to foreign trade as the Crusader armies traveled back and forth to the Holy Land through Mediterranean ports and overland routes. Indeed, as European trade developed in the latter Middle Ages, a Christian middle class of traders began to develop and assert its own power. Jews who had formerly taken part in international trade were frequently pushed out of business as Christian traders took control. The result was the increasing expulsion of Jews in Western Europe: from England in 1290, from France in 1394, from Spain in 1492, and from Portugal in 1497. In countries that were not politically united, such as Italy and Germany, ghettos were established to isolate the Jewish populations of major cities. Indeed, the term ghetto, derived from the Italian word *getto*, "foundry," recalls the establishment of the first major Jewish ghetto in Venice in 1516. Because the foundry district was known for its heat, smoke, and filth, the city fathers of Venice decided that the vicinity of the foundry district would be a suitable place to isolate its Jewish community.

Like Jews of the Muslim world, European Jews longed for a time when the restoration of Jewish life to Jerusalem and the land of Israel would take place; but as the Middle Ages progressed, such an outcome seemed increasingly unlikely. Also like Jews of the Muslim world, European Jews were heavily engaged in trade. Against a background of persecution in both the Christian and the Muslim worlds and of engagement in trade between both, Jews were in a position to begin thinking seriously about the presence and integrity of G-d in the world of creation. Under such circumstances, older beliefs in the notion of a transcendent G-d in heaven, as depicted in the heikhalot literature, began to give way to works that would consider the immanent presence of G-d in the world of creation, a subject of inquiry that would be expressed in the emergence of later kabbalistic movements and literature.

Shiur Qomah

The Shiur Qomah, "The Measure of the Body (of G-d)," is generally included among the merkavah or heikhalot texts because of its depiction of the body of G-d, presumably as a visionary experience.[6] But what is never clear is whether the vision is of the heavenly presence of G-d, as in the heikhalot literature, or is a manifestation of divine presence on earth. The absence of specification on this matter suggests that the Shiur Qomah is a text that is instrumental in the shift in Jewish mysticism and visionary experience in

---

6. For text, translation, and commentary on Shiur Qomah, see Martin Cohen, *The Shi'ur Qomah: Texts and Recensions*, TSAJ 9 (Tübingen: Mohr Siebeck, 1985); Cohen, *The Shi'ur Qomah: Liturgy and Theurgy in Pre-Kabbalitic Jewish Mysticism* (Lanham: University Press of America, 1983). See also Marvin A. Sweeney, "Dimensions of the Shekhinah: The Meaning of the Shiur Qomah in Jewish Mysticism, Liturgy, and Rabbinic Thought," *Hebrew Studies* 54 (2013): 107–20; Joseph Dan, *The Ancient Jewish Mysticism* (Tel Aviv: MOD, 1993), 63–77.

the Middle Ages from a heikhalot model that posits visionary experience of the transcendent presence of G-d in the heavens to a kabbalistic model that posits the immanent presence of G-d in the earthly realm.

The Shiur Qomah is easily one of the most problematic, controversial, and misunderstood writings in all of Jewish tradition.[7] It is known primarily for its discussion of the measurements of the body of G-d. The Shiur Qomah grows out of the merkavah mystical tradition of the late talmudic period.[8] It elaborates upon the experience of the priest and prophet Ezekiel, upon whose foundational vision of G-d in Ezek 1–3 the Jewish mystical tradition stands. Yet Ezekiel is careful throughout the vision to use the language of simile, thereby avoiding any statement that would violate biblical prohibitions against portraying G-d in human or any other tangible form.[9] Nevertheless, the Shiur Qomah portrays G-d in human terms, and its interest in the measurements of the body of G-d therefore raises serious theological questions about the work, insofar as attempts to portray G-d in any physical form are associated in Judaism with idolatry and apostasy.[10]

Although the Shiur Qomah's focus on the measurements of the body of G-d has generally embarrassed past interpreters, it raises several issues that demand attention: (1) the midrashic elaboration of earlier biblical texts concerned with the portrayal of G-d; (2) the incomprehensibility of the measurements given; (3) the mythological portrayal of G-d as the creator and primary power of the universe; and (4) the role of Shiur Qomah in public prayer. The Shiur Qomah is fundamentally a liturgical text intended for public recitation. The various depictions of the measurements of G-d's body are interspersed among liturgical texts that, when read together, construct a heavenly liturgy based upon the standard Jewish prayer service. The incomprehensibility of the divine measurements observed by Jellinek

7. For a brief overview, see Gershom Scholem, "Shi'ur Komah," *EncJud* 14:1417–19.

8. But see now Howard M. Jackson, "The Origins and Development of *Shi'ur Qomah* Revelation in Jewish Mysticism," *JSJ* 31 (2000): 373–415, who traces the origins of the work to the early Tannaitic period and the destruction of the Jerusalem Temple in 70 CE.

9. For discussion of Ezekiel, see my studies, "Ezekiel's Debate with Isaiah," in *Congress Volume: Ljubljana 2007*, ed. André Lemaire, VTSup 133 (Leiden: Brill, 2010), 555–74; *The Prophetic Literature*, IBT (Nashville: Abingdon, 2005), 127–64; "Ezekiel: Zadokite Priest and Visionary Prophet of the Exile," in *Form and Intertextuality in Prophetic and Apocalyptic Literature*, FAT 45 (Tübingen: Mohr Siebeck, 2005), 125–43; *Reading Ezekiel*, Reading the Old Testament (Macon, GA: Smyth & Helwys, 2013).

10. But see Benjamin D. Sommer, *The Bodies of G-d and the World of Ancient Israel* (Cambridge: Cambridge University Press, 2009), who demonstrates the interest in portrayals of the body of G-d in ancient Israel.

is deliberate.[11] Such a technique is intended to impress the audience of the Shiur Qomah with the majesty of the divine presence. By placing the divine measurements in the midst of a heavenly liturgy, the Shiur Qomah prompts those engaged in Jewish worship to attempt to imagine themselves before the incomprehensible grandeur and glory of G-d.

Although physical representation of G-d is forbidden in Judaism, the Bible is filled with statements that suggest a physical character for G-d. Genesis 1:26 states, "Let us make humankind in our image." Numbers 12:8 states, "with him [Moses] I [G-d] speak face to face, and he beholds the form of YHWH." Isaiah 33:17 states, "Your eyes will see the king in his beauty." Ezekiel 1:26 portrays "a throne in appearance like sapphire and seated above the likeness of the throne was something that seemed like a human form." Psalm 147:5 states, "Great is YHWH and abundant in power, His understanding is above measure." And Song 7:8 states, "This is your body like a palm tree and your breasts are like its clusters." All of these texts have been understood as portrayals of G-d, and interpreters have struggled throughout the history of Jewish interpretation to ensure that they are not read as expressions of idolatry. Indeed, Hos 12:10 provides a key criterion for reading such passages as metaphors, "I spoke to the prophets; it was I who multiplied visions, and through the prophets I speak in similes/silence."[12]

The ark of the covenant served as a tangible symbol for the presence of G-d in the holy of holies of the First Temple. Thus, biblical references to YHWH enthroned above the cherubim attempt to portray the divine presence in relation to the cherubim atop the ark in the holy of holies of the Jerusalem Temple (e.g., Isa 6; Ezek 1). But the absence of the ark in the Second Temple prompted mythological speculation concerning the portrayal of the divine presence, both during the Second Temple period itself and in the period following its destruction. For example, Dan 7 portrays G-d as one "ancient of days" with a garment like white snow and hair like lamb's wool. The imagery of G-d's throne portrays fire streaming forth before G-d and myriads of attendants.

Ezekiel's vision in Ezek 1:26–27, as noted above, is a key text in apprehending the presence of G-d: "And above the firmament which was above their head, like the appearance of a stone of sapphire, was the likeness of a

11. Adolf Jellinek, *Bet ha-Midrasch*, 2nd ed. (Jerusalem: Bamberger & Wahrmann, 1938), 6:xlii–xliii.

12. For discussion of Hos 12:10, see Marvin A. Sweeney, *The Twelve Prophets*, Berit Olam (Collegeville, MN: Liturgical, 2000), 1:125.

throne, and above the likeness of the throne was a likeness like the appearance of a human being from above. And I saw like a sight of *hashmal*, like the appearance of fire encasing it round about, a vision of his loins and above and a vision of his loins and below. I saw what was like a vision of fire, and it was shining all about."

As a Zadokite priest, Ezekiel is fully aware of the prohibition against the tangible portrayal of G-d—here in human form—and interpreters have observed the book's extensive use of the language of simile to avoid a direct statement that G-d takes any tangible form. Readers may further note the use of the imagery of fire here, and of wind and water earlier, to portray G-d because these elements are tangible; but they function admirably as metaphors insofar as they are tangible elements that have no inherit delimitation to their forms.

The Song of Songs must also factor in to attempts to envision the presence of G-d. Modern interpreters consider the Song of Songs an example of ancient love poetry in which a woman anticipates union with her lover, generally in very explicit sexual terms. Rabbinic tradition regards Song of Songs as an allegory concerning the intimate relationship between G-d and Israel. Indeed, m. Yad. 3:5 recalls an ancient debate as to whether Song of Songs should be considered as sacred Scripture; R. Akiva ultimately rules it so, declaring the Song of Songs to be the holy of holies of sacred Scripture that was revealed to Moses at Mt. Sinai so that the book is now read as part of the liturgy for Pesah.

An important text in the discussion of the Shiur Qomah, Song 5:10–16 is an example of the *wasf* poetic form, a device in ancient Egyptian love poetry that employs explicit descriptions of the body of the male or female beloved.[13] In this case, the beloved is male:

> My beloved is clear skinned and ruddy, distinguished among ten
> thousand.
> His head is finest gold, His locks are curled and black as a raven.
> His eyes are like doves by watercourses, bathed in milk, sitting by a brim-
> ming pool.
> His cheeks are like beds of spices, enhanced by perfumes.
> His lips are like lilies; dripping flowing myrrh.
> His hands are rods of gold, filled with beryl;

13. See Roland Murphy, *Song of Songs*, Hermeneia (Minneapolis: Fortress, 1990), 46–47, 66, 169.

His belly a tablet of ivory, decorated with sapphires.
His legs are like marble pillars set in sockets of fine gold.
His appearance is like Lebanon, choice as the cedars.
His mouth is sweet and all of him is delightful.
This is my beloved, and this is my darling, O daughters of Jerusalem.

The imagery is clearly erotic and, when applied to an understanding of the presence of G-d, portrays G-d metaphorically in very human terms. Of course, we do not know that the male lover must represent G-d and the female lover Israel. And so the portrayal of the female lover in Song of Songs 7:1–9, which might also describe G-d:

How beautiful are your feet in sandals, O daughter of nobles!
Your rounded thighs are like jewels, the work of a master's hand.
Your navel is like a round goblet—mixed wine shall not be lacking!
Your belly like a heap of wheat entwined with lilies.
Your two breasts are like two fawns, twins of a gazelle.
Your neck is like a tower of ivory; your eyes, pools in Heshbon by the gate
      of Bath-Rabbim.
Your nose is like the Lebanon tower that looks toward Damascus.
Your head upon you is like crimson wool, the locks of your head are like
      purple—
A king is held captive in the tresses.
How beautiful you are, how lovely! Love with all its rapture!
This, your body is like a palm; your breasts are like clusters.
I say, I will climb the palm; I will take hold of its branches;
May your breasts be like clusters of grapes; may your breath be like the
      fragrance of apples,
And your mouth like fine wine.
Let it flow to my beloved as new wine, gliding over the lips of sleepers.

Interpreters note v. 7, "This, your body is like the palm; your breasts are like clusters," particularly because the Hebrew word qomatek, "your body," is employed to describe the body of the female lover. It is the same term employed in the title of the Shiur Qomah. The proposal to climb the palm and take hold of its branches may be read as an act of adherence to G-d. So then, the portrayal of the woman in the Song of Songs can also be read as a metaphorical portrayal of G-d.

Scholem also cites Ps 147:5 as a very clear allusion in Shiur Qomah:[14] *gadol adoneinu verav koach*, "Great/Big is our L-rd, and mighty of strength." This verse also describes G-d in tangible terms, this time in terms of size and strength. But the significance of this verse is tied to its gematria. Interpreters have observed that the Hebrew phrase, *verav koach*, "and mighty of strength," has a numerical equivalence of 236, i.e., the total value of *vav* = 6, *resh* = 200, *beth* =2, *kaph* = 20, and *heth* = 8. Cohen argues that this number is significant for the Shiur Qomah because it provides the basis for the assertions that the height of G-d in Shiur Qomah section B is 2,300,000,000 parasangs and that the crown of G-d's head is 600,000 parasangs.[15] Reflection on a verse from the Psalms that portrays G-d in sexual terms, like the Song of Songs, forms the basis for calculating at least some of the basic measurements for G-d's body employed in the Shiur Qomah.

Hints of the liturgical character of the Shiur Qomah are also evident. Already some view the Shiur Qomah as a text that calls for reflection on the presence of G-d and is designed for public recitation. An overview of the text demonstrates that it includes all the basic elements of a Jewish prayer service.

Shiur Qomah section A begins with the superscription for the work, *sefer haqomah 'inyenei merkavah*, "The Book of the Body, Topics Concerning the Chariot." [16] Immediately following, the Shiur Qomah opens with a very familiar prayer that initially corresponds to the opening paragraph of the Amidah: "Blessed are you, O L-rd, our G-d, G-d of Abraham, G-d of Isaac, G-d of Jacob, the great, mighty, and awesome G-d, G-d Most High . . ." But then the text diverges from the standard form of the Amidah, "Creator of heavens and earth, You are king, king of kings, etc.," in place of the expected "the one who keeps fidelity and who creates everything, etc." Indeed, as the Shiur Qomah's version of the opening paragraph of the Amidah continues, it focuses on the throne of G-d and the fiery presence of G-d upon it: "And your seat on the throne of glory and the celestial creatures ascend to the throne of glory. You are fire, and your throne is fire, and your celestial creatures and servants are fire, etc." Readers will recognize that the version of the opening paragraph

---

14. Gershom Scholem, *On the Mystical Shape of the G-dhead* (New York: Schocken, 1997), 23–24.

15. Cohen, *The Shi'ur Qomah: Texts and Recensions*; Cohen, *The Shi'ur Qomah: Liturgy and Theurgy in Pre-Kabbalitic Jewish Mysticism*.

16. Cohen, *The Shi'ur Qomah: Liturgy and Theurgy*, 187–89; Cohen, *Shi'ur Qomah: Texts*, 125–26.

of the Amidah presented in the Shiur Qomah is influenced by biblical texts that present the presence of G-d as a flaming presence: Ezekiel's portrayal of a flaming presence of G-d in Ezek 1:26–27; Isaiah's portrayal of the seraphim as flaming angels around G-d in Isa 6; and Daniel's portrayal of a stream of fire breaking out from below the throne on which G-d sits in Dan 7. Such a flaming presence of G-d suggests a heavenly vision of G-d, and the liturgy that accompanies and conveys this vision of G-d's flaming presence suggests that it is a heavenly liturgy, analogous to the earthly liturgy that Jews pray as part of the standard worship service on earth.

Section B treats the dimensions of the body of G-d.[17] R. Akiva, the speaker in this section, reports what Metatron, the angel of the presence of G-d, has told him:

> "From the place of the seat of his glory and up is a distance of 1,180,000,000 parasangs. From his glorious seat and down is a distance of 1,180,000,00 parasangs. His height is 2,300,000,000 parasangs. From the right arm across until the left arm is 770,000,000 parasangs, and from the right eyeball until the left is a distance of 300,000,000 parasangs. The skull of his head is 300,000,003 and a third parasangs, and the crown of his head is 600,000 parasangs, corresponding to the 600,000 Israelite minions. Thus is He called the great, mighty, and awesome G-d."

This statement is followed by a series of unpronounceable names, concluded by the familiar statement from the Shema, "Blessed be He and blessed be the name of the glory of His kingdom forever." Here readers see an interest in relating the dimensions of the divine body to a key statement from the Amidah, understood as a reference to G-d's size and other qualities, as well as to a statement from the recitation of the Shema, a proclamation of G-d's eternal royal glory. But the numbers for the dimensions of G-d's body also confront readers. These numbers are derived in part from the numerical equivalents of the statement in Ps 147:5 understood as a reference to G-d's stature; as already noted, the 2,300,000,000 parasangs of G-d's height derive from 236, the numerical equivalent of *verav koach*, "[Great is G-d] and mighty of strength." The number 230 is accounted for in the height of G-d; the remaining number 6 is then related to the 600,000 who witnessed G-d's revelation at Mt. Sinai in Exod 19 (see Num 2:32).

17. Cohen, *The Shi'ur Qomah: Liturgy and Theurgy*, 189–92; Cohen, *Shi'ur Qomah: Texts*, 127–28.

The opening statement in section C reads, "And all who know this secret are certain to acquire the world to come."[18] Following references to G-d's protection of the righteous, the text appears to presuppose the Kaddish that marks the conclusion of the Amidah in the standard Jewish prayer service. It deviates from the standard form: "and therefore we are obligated to praise, beautify, glorify, and to exalt, to bless, and to magnify the great king, the mighty king, the strong king, etc." The passage goes on to heap praise upon G-d for all of G-d's actions on behalf of creation and Israel, much as the standard form of the Kaddish does in the standard Jewish prayer service. G-d's qualities are here magnified beyond those of the standard Kaddish, reflecting of the role that this Kaddish plays in a heavenly liturgy. Readers may note that in an alternative paragraph identified by Cohen for this portion of the Shiur Qomah, section Cx, a new and embellished version of the Mi Khamokhah also appears: "Who is like our L-rd? Who is like our G-d? Who is like our King? Who is like our Savior? There is none like our G-d. There is none like our L-rd. There is none like our King. There is none like our Savior." Again the embellishments of this version of the Mi Khamokhah point to a heavenly liturgy.

Section D initially presents a statement by R. Ishmael;[19] it is remarkably akin to the Kedushah of the Jewish prayer service: "I saw the king of king of kings, the Holy One, blessed be He, as He was sitting on an exalted throne and His soldiers were standing before Him to the right and to the left." This statement introduces another section concerned with the bodily measurements of G-d. R. Ishmael recounts that Metatron spoke to him and that he then asked Metatron the measurements of the body of G-d. He recounts Metatron's lengthy statements concerning the measurements and holy names of each of the body parts of G-d: the feet, the soles of the feet, the calves, the thighs, the loins, the heart, the neck, the head, the mouth, the beard, the face, the cheeks, the forehead, the eyes, the arms, the shoulders, the palms of the hands, the fingers, etc. Section D once again concludes with the familiar statement from the Amidah, "Therefore is He called the great, mighty, and awesome G-d." Again, the measurements of the body of G-d are related to a liturgical context.

Following a large number of sections concerned with descriptions of the holy and awesome presence of G-d, section M then presents another familiar statement from Jewish liturgy akin to the 'Aleinu prayer that comes

18. Cohen, *The Shi'ur Qomah: Liturgy and Theurgy*, 193–96; Cohen, *Shi'ur Qomah: Texts*, 129–34.

19. Cohen, *The Shi'ur Qomah: Liturgy and Theurgy*, 197–214; Cohen, *Shi'ur Qomah: Texts*, 134–47.

near the conclusion of the Jewish prayer service.[20] Section M reads, "We are obligated to praise you, to beautify you, and to bless you, and to magnify you, and to crown you, and to declare your unity, O L-rd of all creation, G-d of all souls, G-d of all life, the Life of Lives, the First and the Last, etc." Again, the modified form of a standard liturgical prayer points to a worship service in the heavenly realm, beyond normal human experience. The concluding section of the Shiur Qomah, section N,[21] calls upon its audience to fall on their faces before G-d who resides in heaven; it continues with a detailed portrayal of the heavenly temple and all of its retinue at a time of worship. Cohen's alternative section Nx states that the worshipers are to go out into the world to do acts of Torah following their encounter with the divine.

This survey of the Shiur Qomah points to a very significant feature of this text: the portrayals of G-d's presence and the measurements of G-d's body are interspersed among sections that present a modified version of the Jewish worship service, including the Amidah, the Kaddish, the Mi Khamokhah, the Kedushah, and the Aleinu, followed by instruction to go out into the world and practice the teachings of Torah. The modified wording of the prayers suggests a heavenly liturgy in which the worshipers pray the major sections of the Jewish worship service before G-d, whose bodily form and measurements are provided among the major segments of the liturgy. Although many interpreters assume that G-d must be portrayed in masculine terms, whereas the Jewish people is portrayed in feminine terms, Jewish mysticism is also capable of envisioning feminine images of G-d, e.g., as a nursing mother who sustains Israel.[22]

Several conclusions may be drawn from these observations. First, the Shiur Qomah is based in reflection on scriptural texts that portray G-d in tangible terms or that suggest such a portrayal. Texts such as Ezek 1, Song, Ps 147, and others indicate that, like many ancient Near Eastern cultures, ancient Jews employed imagery of tangible bodily forms to portray the presence of G-d. Such portrayal is considered metaphorical, as indicated in Hos 12:10 and elsewhere. Even the names given to the body parts of G-d are ap-

---

20. Cohen, *The Shi'ur Qomah: Liturgy and Theurgy*, 245–48; Cohen, *Shi'ur Qomah: Texts*, 165–68.

21. Cohen, *The Shi'ur Qomah: Liturgy and Theurgy*, 248–65; Cohen, *Shi'ur Qomah: Texts*, 169–82.

22. See Peter Schäfer, *Mirror of His Beauty: Feminine Images of G-d from the Bible to the Early Kabbalah* (Princeton: Princeton University Press, 2002); Ellen Davina Haskell, *Suckling at My Mother's Breasts: The Image of a Nursing G-d in Jewish Mysticism* (Albany: SUNY Press, 2012).

parently intended to express divine qualities, although what they are is not always clear. Given that the tangible portrayal of G-d is intended to provide a foundation for reflection on the divine character, the Shiur Qomah employs such portrayal in its own reflection on the divine.

Second, among the prominent numerical features of such a portrayal, gematria appears to play a role in the Shiur Qomah's reflection on the body of G-d. This discussion has noted how Ps 147:5 yields the number 236 when read through the lens of gematria, and that this number is instrumental in calculating major dimensions of the divine body. Other numerical measurements may be similarly derived, although interpreters do not yet know them all. But there is another dimension to the numerology apart from the numerical equivalents themselves, and this is the gargantuan dimensions employed in the Shiur Qomah. The Shiur Qomah maintains that G-d's height is 2,300,000,000 parasangs. Although that is a calculable number, it is a figure beyond normal human comprehension. Such a feature is an indispensable aspect of the Shiur Qomah's depiction of G-d, i.e., G-d has a massive divine presence, but the divine presence is beyond human capacity to comprehend in any meaningful way. The point of such numbers is to demonstrate the overwhelming dimensions of the divine presence.

Third, the Shiur Qomah's liturgical character is evident in its composition, as it is structured around the major elements of the Jewish prayer service. It includes versions of the Amidah, the Shema, Kaddish, the Mi Khamokhah, the Kedushah, and the Aleinu, and the depictions of the divine body are interspersed among these liturgical elements. Such a strategy is quite deliberate insofar as the Shiur Qomah places its readers in the context of worship of the divine presence of G-d. But in doing so, it reformulates the Jewish prayer service as one that must be identified as a heavenly prayer service. In the context of the merkavah or heikhalot literature, such a strategy is hardly surprising; this literature constantly employs liturgical features in its portrayals of the divine and human attempts to relate to G-d. But the liturgical model of the Shiur Qomah is foundational; liturgy sets the structure of the text, and the depiction of the body of G-d is intended to be read within the context of that structure—and not vice versa. Recognizing this fundamental feature of the Shiur Qomah, one finds that the Shiur Qomah addresses its readers with the bodily dimensions of G-d as a means of asking them to imagine the overwhelming presence of G-d before them as they pray. The Shiur Qomah emerges in this reading as a text that asks readers to remember before whom they pray and to contemplate before whom they live throughout their lives in the world of creation where G-d has placed them.

Sefer Yetzirah

Whereas the Shiur Qomah focuses on the worshiper in the world of creation who envisions the heavenly presence of the divine during prayer, the Sefer Yetzirah, "Book of Formation," focuses on language as the means by which the divine presence of G-d manifests in creation.[23] It is an example of Ma'aseh Bereshit, a "Work of Creation," as opposed to previously studied texts which are understood to be Ma'aseh Merkavah, a "Work of the Chariot." Whereas the heikhalot texts look to Ezek 1 to focus on visionary experience as the basis for their understanding of visions of G-d, Sefer Yetzirah looks to Gen 1:1–2:3 for understanding of creation.

Sefer Yetzirah was already known in talmudic times. The Babylonian Talmud cites Sefer Yetzirah in b. San. 65b, where it is related that R. Hanina bar Homa and R. Oshaia, both students of R. Judah haNasi', studied Sefer Yetzirah in an effort to create a one-third grown calf so that they could slaughter it and eat it. This talmudic reference suggests that Sefer Yetzirah dates to the fourth century CE, but its date is disputed.[24] The Gemara follows this incident with Raba's distinction between the creative powers of humans and those of G-d; absolute purity enables a human to become like G-d and thereby to perform acts of creation. The text then reports Raba's creation of a golem, which he then sends to R. Zera, who dismisses it. Commenting on this passage, Rashi maintains that creation proceeds by means of the mystic combination of the Hebrew letters of the divine Name, insofar as knowledge of the use of the divine Name gives one the creative power of G-d. Likewise, in b. Ber. 55a R. Judah, in the name of Rab, relates that Bezalel, the architect of the tabernacle, knew how to combine letters by which heaven and earth were created. The text goes on to compare Bezalel's own qualities with those by which heaven and earth were created, likening Bezalel's qualities in Exod 35:31 to those of G-d in Prov 3:19, 20 and Dan 2:21.

Sefer Yetzirah focuses on the creative power of human speech; the capacity to name and define elements in the world of creation serves also as a means to create them. To a certain degree, such a conceptualization of the world is rooted in Platonic philosophy, which posits an ideal conceptualization for all phenomena in the world, such as the ideal concept of a table;

---

23. For text, translation, and commentary on Sefer Yetzirah, see A. Peter Hayman, *Sefer Yeṣira*, TSAJ 104 (Tübingen: Mohr Siebeck, 2004); Knut Stenrung, *The Book of Formation: Sepher Yetzirah* (New York: Ktav, 1970).

24. See, e.g., Dan, *Ancient Jewish Mysticism*, 198–211.

all the various individual instances of tables that one might encounter in the world together imply an ideal table. The idea also finds expression in the Memphite Theology of Creation, written in Egypt ca. 700 BCE, in which the cosmos comes into being when the creator god Ptah speaks.[25]

Sefer Yetzirah, apparently written during the talmudic period of the third–sixth centuries CE, focuses on the Hebrew alphabet as the basis for its understanding that all creation comes into being through speech. It presumes that Hebrew is the language in which YHWH created the world in Gen 1:1–2:3 by speech; after all, Gen 1:1–2:3 is written in Hebrew. Insofar as Hebrew is constructed from the sounds signified by the twenty-two letters of the Hebrew alphabet, those twenty-two letters then convey the epistemological foundations for the world of creation. One who is pure by observance of the Torah and who understands the epistemological character of the Hebrew alphabet and divine speech is then capable of engaging in creation.

The first mishnah (paragraph) of the first chapter of the Sefer Yetzirah (i.e., 1:1) begins by stating the thirty-two wonderful paths of wisdom are the foundational epistemological foundations for creation. This statement presupposes the thirty-two times that the term *'elohim*, "G-d," appears in the text of Gen 1:1–2:3. It is also based on the two other sets of elements. One is the twenty-two letters of the Hebrew alphabet that form the basis for all words in the Hebrew language. The other is the Ten Sefirot, countings or enumerations, which combine with the twenty-two letters of the Hebrew alphabet to form the ten statements that G-d utters in Gen 1:1–2:3. Although Gen 1:1–2:3 posits that G-d creates the world in six days of work and inaugurates the seventh day of rest, the holy Shabbat, G-d actually speaks ten times during the course of creation. Each of G-d's ten utterances follow the Hebrew phrase *wayomer 'elohim*, "and G-d said" (Gen 1:3, 6, 9, 11, 14, 20, 24, 26, 28, and 29), indicating that G-d spoke and thereby created the world in ten statements in Hebrew. The term *sephirah*, singular for the plural *sephirot*, refers to counting, as in the counting of the Omer or sheaf of the elevation offering for seven full weeks or fifty days between Passover and Shavuot (see Lev 23:15–16). Such a reckoning indicates the time for the ripening of the grain from Passover until its first harvest at the time of Shavuot.

Having identified the combination of the Ten Sefirot and the twenty-two letters of the Hebrew alphabet with the thirty-two instances of *'elohim* in Gen 1:1–2:3, Sefer Yetzirah 1:1 then states three basic principles of word for-

---

25. Miriam Lichtheim, *Ancient Egyptian Literature*, vol. 1: *The Old and Middle Kingdoms* (Berkeley: University of California Press, 1975), 54–55.

mation in Hebrew, employing three iterations of the Hebrew word root *spr*: *besapher*, "by number/counting"; *vesepher*, "and letter"; and *vesippur*, "and word/utterance." In other words, every Hebrew letter functions as a number as well as a signifier of a sound, and these functions together form the basis for every Hebrew word. The interplay of numerical and lexical meaning is the basis for later uses of gematria in Jewish mysticism, associating Hebrew words with their numerical values, their lexical meanings, or both.

Sefer Yetzirah 1:2 then proceeds to make a fundamental distinction between the Ten Sefirot and the twenty-two letters of the Hebrew alphabet. The Ten Sefirot are identified as the ten *sephirot belimah*, meaning "intangible enumerations." The Hebrew term *belimah* appears in Job 26:7 where it refers to G-d, "who suspended the earth over *belimah*," and is understood to refer to "nothingness." This meaning derives from analyzing the word as the combination of the linguistic elements *beli*, "without," and *mah*, "what"; taken together, "without what" would indicate nothingness. In Job 26:7 the term is also parallel with *tohu*, a word that together with *vavohu*, indicates "chaos" or "nothingness," in Gen 1:2. The term *belimah* in Sefer Yetzirah 1:2 is then understood as a reference to the intangible or undefinable character of the Ten Sefirot in Sefer Yetzirah.

Sefer Yetzirah 1:2 then continues by dividing the Hebrew alphabet into three categories, each of which is based upon its linguistic characteristics: the three mothers, *aleph, mem*, and *shin*, which will be treated in Sefer Yetzirah 3; the seven doubles, *bet, gimel, dalet, kaph, pe, tav*, and *resh*, which will be treated in Sefer Yetzirah 4; and the twelve simple letters, *he, vav, zayin, khet, tet, yod, lamed, nun, samek, ayin, tsade*, and *qoph*, which will be treated in Sefer Yetzirah 5. Sefer Yetzirah 2 will deal with the alphabet in general, and the rest of Sefer Yetzirah 1 will deal with the Ten Sefirot.

Sefer Yetzirah 1:3 focuses on the Ten Sefirot as a basis for determining the basic distinctions between the material world and the spiritual world. The paragraph begins with a statement that the Ten Sefirot signify the ten fingers and ten toes in the human body. The Hebrew word *etzba'ot* refers to both fingers and toes; there is no individual word for either. It continues by dividing the ten digits into five and five to demonstrate the principle of duality in the material and spiritual worlds. By material and spiritual, Sefer Yetzirah understands the distinctions between the tangible and the intangible characteristics of the world, the concrete and the abstract principles of the world, and the good and evil characteristics of the world. It then continues by positing that two symbols of the covenant between G-d and Abraham are set in the middle of the ten digits (fingers and toes) of the human body. The references to these two symbols of the covenant are signified by a Hebrew pun based on the two words. The first is "the word (*millah*) of the tongue"; *millah* is the Rabbinic Hebrew word for "word," apparently derived from the Aramaic term that replaces the biblical Hebrew word *davar*, "word." The expression refers to the oaths or promises spoken by G-d and Abraham in making their covenant. The second is "the covenant of circumcision (*milah*)," a reference to the circumcised penis which symbolizes the covenant between G-d and Abraham. The Hebrew words *millah*, "word," and *milah*, "circumcision," are two different words that are spelled differently but sound the same. These two dimensions of the covenant between G-d and Abraham as expressed in Gen 17 then symbolize two aspects of the covenant, the abstract word and the material circumcision. They are associated with the abstraction of the divine statements which enact creation by G-d in Gen 1:1–2:3 and the material means of sexual intercourse by which human beings engage in the creation of new life.

Sefer Yetzirah 1:4 calls for the reader to set the Creator ("G-d") in his place. In this respect, one may note that the circumcised penis marks the dividing point between the upper dimensions of the (male) human body where the ten digits or fingers are found and the lower dimensions of the (male) human body where the ten digits or toes are found, so that the human body is divided into two parts, the upper part where abstract thought is found and the lower part where material sexuality is found.

Sefer Yetzirah 1:5–8 then turns to the basic definitions of the borders of reality by articulating a principle of duality in each case. These include: (1) the borders of temporal reality, which comprise first and last; (2) the borders of moral reality, which comprise good and evil; and (3) the borders of physical reality, which comprise height and depth, east and west, and north and south. The metaphorical descriptions of a circle without beginning and end and the interrelationship between fire and coal is meant to convey that these opposite dimensions have no firmly defined boundary between them; rather, each pair is understood as two opposite ideals that are defined in relation to each other. One can never understand first without last, good without evil, height without depth, east without west, north without south, and vice versa. Each is relative to its opposite. These sections thereby illustrate a basic principle of thought in Sefer Yetzirah that will ultimately become foundational in kabbalistic thought: dialectical thinking in which each phenomenon is understood relative to its opposite.

Sefer Yetzirah 1:9–14 then turns to the enumeration of the Ten Sefirot and their role in creation. The text begins with "the spirit/wind of G-d" (Hebrew, *ruah 'elohim*), which appears at the outset of creation hovering over the waters of the deep in Gen 1:1–2. The spirit/wind of G-d then brings forth four sefirot which correspond to the four basic elements of creation known from Greek thought: earth (Greek, *gē*), which is without form; darkness, which represents fire (Greek, *pyros*) without light; air/wind (Greek, *aēr*) which sweeps over the face of the deep without shape or form; and water (Greek, *hydor*) which again lacks shape and form. Each is discussed further in turn. The first sefirah, the spirit/wind of G-d, is defined in relation to sound or voice, spirit or air, and speech, each of which points to phenomena that appear within creation but are nevertheless intangible. The spirit/wind of G-d then denotes the creative principle of G-d that brings forth the following sefirot. The second sefirah, air, then emerges as the realm in which the twenty-two letters of the alphabet are combined to form speech. The third sefirah, water, represents the moisture of the breath of G-d, or the realm of *tohu vavohu* ("formless and void," Gen 1:2), as a basic potential element of the reality of earth. The fourth sefirah, fire, represents the warmth of the breath of G-d, which constitutes the realm of the divine, including the heavenly, fiery beings such as angels, seraphim, ophanim, and hayot; fire represents the reality of heaven. Sefirot five through ten then emerge in relation to every possible combination of the three different letters in the divine name YHWH: height (YHW), depth (YWH), east (HYW), west (HWY), south (WYH), and north (WHY). Sefer Yetzirah 1:14 then summarizes by defining the spirit of the living G-d as the basic source of reality; air or the letters which produce the basic element of air; water or matter which produces the basic element of earth; and fire or angels which produce heaven. The basic dimensions of height, depth, east, west, south, and north in the world then follow.

Sefer Yetzirah 2:1 then turns to an examination of the letters of the alphabet for understanding the character of creation. The chapter begins by naming the three mother letters, the basic sounds uttered by a human infant human: *'aleph*, which stands for "air" (Hebrew, *'avir*); *mem*, which stands for the "water" (Hebrew, *mayim*) that also produces earth; and *shin*, which stands for the "fire" (Hebrew, *'esh*) that also produces heaven. The three mother letters are then employed to represent the basic structure of creation in which heaven above and earth below are separated by air in the middle. This structure then illustrates Sefer Yetzirah's principle of equilibrium in which two opposites are separated by an intangible element. This structure is correlated with linguistic considerations in which two basic sounds uttered by humans, the sibilant *shin* and the labial *mem*, are separated and balanced by *'aleph*, the aspirated glottal stop.

Sefer Yetzirah 2:2–6 then turns to the implications of the principle of equilibrium in which two opposites are held in balance. When this principle is applied to the Hebrew alphabet, which forms the basis for all speech, each of the twenty-two letters is then paired with each of the other letters of the alphabet to produce 231 combinations of letters in which each pair is held together in balance. The pairs also include every possible sequence for the two letters. The 231 pairs are then identified as 231 gates for understanding the role of speech in creation. They are arranged as a wheel with twenty-one spokes, a number derived from the numerical equivalents of the three letters that comprise the holy name, YHWH: Y = 10, H = 5, and W = 6, totaling 21. The wheel is arranged with eleven circles, derived from the letters H = 5 and W = 6. Each circle includes two letters of the alphabet with all of its possible combinations with the other letters. The result is a wheel with eleven spokes or circles, each of which contains two letters and all of their possible combinations. To be properly employed, the wheel must be properly aligned. Sefer Yetzirah 2:4 presents the proper principle of alignment: there is no goodness above pleasure/delight (Hebrew, *'oneg*), and there is no evil below pain/affliction (Hebrew, *nega'*). Each of the two Hebrew words is the equivalent of its opposite spelled backwards. Attempts to explain this system are many, but often fail. The basic principle appears to be solved when the inner circle, in which the balancing letter *'aleph* appears, is turned ten spaces in keeping with the ten sefirot, and the wheels align to produce *'oneg* and *nega'* aligned with each other. The inner circle with *'aleph* then functions as a wheel within a wheel, the enigmatic image in Ezekiel's vision of G-d in Ezek 1. Thus, the inner *'aleph* wheel is the balancing principle, the turning of ten spaces is the Ten Sefirot, and the twenty-two letters then constitute all possible combinations, resulting in the thirty-two paths of wisdom that are held together in balance. Although the function of the wheel is not fully understood, it appears to be a means for associating words in the Torah to produce pre-kabbalistic interpretations of the text based on the principle of the balance of the covenant of word and circumcision, indicating in turn that the heavenly is balanced with the earthly and good is balanced with evil.

Sefer Yetzirah 3 then returns to the significance of the three mother letters, *'aleph*/air, *mem*/water, and *shin*/fire. These three letters point to the three basic categories of reality, the universe, the time and year, and the human body and the moral sphere. The three letters define the basic structure of the universe in which fire/*shin* denotes heaven above, water/*mem* denotes earth below, and air/*'aleph* stands between the two to balance them in the world of creation. They also denote the basic times of the year, such that

fire/*shin* denotes the heat of summer, water/*mem* denotes the cold of winter, and air/*'aleph* denotes the balance between these two opposites in the
year. Finally, the three mother letters also denote the basic structure of the
human body: fire/*shin* denotes the upper body where thought takes place;
water/*mem* denotes the lower parts of the body where fluids, food, and waste
reside; and air/*'aleph* denotes the middle of the body where the air of the
lungs strikes the balance between the upper and lower parts.

Sefer Yetzirah 4 turns to the significance of the seven doubled letters,
bet, gimel, dalet, kaph, pe, tav, and *resh*. The doubled character of these letters indicates the principle of opposites in Sefer Yetzirah. The seven letters
denote the seven blessings, life, peace, wisdom, wealth, beauty, fruitfulness,
and dominion, and their opposites, death, misfortune, folly, poverty, ugli-
ness, devastation, and slavery. They point to the seven dimensions, height,
depth, east, west, south, north, and the holy temple in the center. They point
to the seven known moving stars or planets of antiquity, Saturn, Jupiter,
Mars, the Sun, Venus, Mercury, and the Moon. They denote the seven days
of the week, the six days of work and Shabbat. And they denote the seven
gates or openings in the human body, two eyes, two ears, two nostrils, and
one mouth.

Sefer Yetzirah 5 then focuses on the twelve simple letters, *he, vav, zayin,
khet, tet, yod, lamed, nun, samek, 'ayin, tsade*, and *qoph*. These letters are tied
to the twelve dimensions of the material world, which combine to produce
a three-dimensional cube. They form the twelve months of the year, Nisan,
Iyyar, Sivan, Tammuz, Av, Elul, Tishri, Marheshvan, Kislev, Tevet, Shevat,
and Adar. They indicate the twelve signs of the zodiac, Aries, Taurus, Gem-
ini, Cancer, Leo, Virgo, Libra, Scorpio, Sagittarius, Capricorn, Aquarius,
and Pisces. And they indicate the twelve organs and members of the human
being, two hands, two feet, two kidneys, the liver, the spleen, the gallblad-
der, the stomach, the colon, and the bowels.

Sefer Yetzirah then concludes with a summary of chapters 4, 5, and 6
above as well as the assertions that Sefer Yetzirah originates with Abraham,
taking Gen 12:5 as a reference to "the souls he made" at Haran.

Altogether, Sefer Yetzirah attempts to trace the role by which the presence of G-d manifests in the world by means of the power of speech. Insofar
as G-d creates the world by speech in Gen 1:1–2:3, divine presence infuses
the world of creation and is best experienced and comprehended by understanding the capacity of speech, both in human beings and in G-d, as an
abstract quality that nevertheless exercises an ongoing role in creation and
thus remains a presence in the finite or material world of creation.

Sefer Habahir

Sefer Habahir, the Book of Brilliance, is generally recognized as the first major kabbalistic work.[26] Kabbalah, meaning "tradition" or "that which is received," is the major medieval movement of Jewish mysticism that emerges in the mid-twelfth century CE in southern France and northeastern Spain. Kabbalah is characterized by its focus on the Ten Sefirot, the enumerations of the ten qualities or characteristics of G-d that emanate from the transcendent G-d, who exists beyond the finite world of earthly existence, in order to manifest the divine presence (Hebrew, *shekhinah*) in that same finite world of earthly reality. In kabbalistic thought, the Shekhinah manifests throughout the world of creation, including within each individual human being.

Sefer Habahir appears to have originated in the region of Provence in southern France in approximately the middle of the twelfth century CE. The title of the *sefer*, Bahir, derives from Job 37:21, "And now, they have not seen the light (the sun); it is brilliant (*bahir*) in the clouds, and a wind passes by and purifies them," quoted in the initial paragraph of the work to initiate discussion of the nature of creation. The Bahir is written in a Mishnaic Hebrew style to present a succession of textual components that discuss the major premises of the book. The speakers include R. Nehunyah ben Haqanah, the primary narrator of the Heikhalot Rabbati, and R. Akiva and R. Ishmael, the two great sages of rabbinic interpretative tradition, although it is clear to modern interpreters that the Bahir does not present their authentic words; rather, they serve as mouthpieces for the Bahir's authors. Other speakers include fictitious characters, such as R. Amora or Amorai, a name derived from the Amoraim, the Talmud's post-mishnaic teachers, and R. Rehmai, or Rehumai, a name which alludes to a fourth-century talmudic figure. Others include figures known from the aggadic midrashim. Most scholars follow Scholem in maintaining that the Bahir is a highly disorganized and convoluted text that makes discernment of its literary structure impossible. Such a view is based on the premise that the text has been heavily and carelessly edited over the course of centuries, resulting in a confused and disorganized text, although we will see below that there is some basis for determining structure in the Bahir.

In articulating its understanding of the Ten Sefirot, the Bahir is heavily influenced by gnosticism, insofar as it posits a duality between the infinite

---

26. Gershom Scholem, *The Origins of the Kabbalah* (Philadelphia: Jewish Publication Society, 1987); cf. J. H. Laenen, *Jewish Mysticism: An Introduction*, trans. David E. Orton (Louisville: Westminster John Knox, 2001), 84–115.

world of heaven and the finite world of earth. Indeed, the gnostic movement known as Catharism, which the Roman Catholic Church sought to suppress, was active in northern Italy and southern France during the twelfth through the fourteenth centuries CE. It apparently originated in the eastern Byzantine Empire and spread westward by means of the trade routes which extended through the Mediterranean coast, southern Europe, and on through the Rhine River region to the Netherlands and beyond during the Middle Ages. In gnostic thought, the infinite world is identified with the Greek *plērōma*, "fullness," the realm of the divine, spirit, absolute perfection, and harmony. The lower worlds of finite existence emerged from the *plērōma* during the process of creation, which progressed by degrees of material form in the finite world. Gnostic thought employs the image of the cosmic tree, which grows from heaven to earth and thereby conveys the infinite qualities and powers of the divine into the finite material world. Such an image arises from ancient Mesopotamian thought, which identifies Mesopotamian kings as examples of the ideal human being, descending from the divine through the seven levels of the earthly realm to govern human empires on behalf of the gods. Gnostic concepts in the Bahir are then correlated with biblical texts.

Beginning with the Bahir, kabbalistic thought employs the gnostic concept of the *plērōma*, the fullness, to posit the heavenly realm of G-d whose infinite qualities are manifested in the finite earthly realm. The gnostic *plērōma* is then identified with the Hebrew term *melo'*, "fullness," in the liturgical formula chanted by the seraphim in Isaiah's vocation vision in Isa 6:3: "Holy, holy, holy is YHWH *tzeva'ot*; the whole earth is full (*melo'*) with his glory." The fullness is then identified with Mahshavah, "thought," as the basis for the kabbalistic system in the Bahir. Like kabbalistic thought in general, the Bahir presupposes the mishnaic tradition that the world was created by means of the ten sayings of G-d, as expressed in m. Avot 5:1, which in turn presupposes the ten statements in Gen 1:1–2:3 by which G-d brought about the world of creation. This notion of creation by ten divine utterances then served as the basis for the conceptualization of creation articulated in Sefer Yetzirah, discussed above. Whereas Sefer Yetzirah focused on the Ten Sefirot as the basis for the creative power of language and its expression through the Hebrew alphabet, Sefer Habahir reconceptualizes the Ten Sefirot by identifying them with the infinite qualities or emanations of the divine.

Despite legitimate reservations concerning his work, Kaplan's analysis provides at least a general indication of the progression of thought in the Bahir.[27] Scholem rejected Kaplan's work as worthless due to its popular character. Although a full systematic analysis of the formal structure of the Bahir remains to be done, it is nevertheless possible to see in Kaplan's work a basis for understanding the Bahir's sequence of major concerns. Kaplan maintains that the Bahir focuses on creation in paragraphs 1–16, the alphabet in paragraphs 17–44, the seven voices of Sinai and the Sefirot in paragraphs 45–122, the Ten Sefirot in paragraphs 123–193, and the mysteries of the soul in paragraphs 194–200.[28]

The first major division of the Bahir in paragraphs 1–16 takes up the character of creation as the basis for the further definition of the interrelationship between the divine and the earthly realm and its understanding of the divine Sefirot. As noted, it begins in paragraph 1 with R. Nehunyah ben Haqanna's quotation of Job 37:21, "And now, they have not seen light (the sun); it is brilliant (*bahir*) in the clouds, and the wind passes by and purifies them." The purpose of this quote is to introduce the concept of brilliant light as the first act of creation in Gen 1. R. Nehunyah follows immediately with a quote of Ps 18:11, "He appointed darkness as his hiding place," a reference to the darkness that preceded light in creation. R. Nehunyah then follows with Ps 139:12, "Darkness is not dark for you, and night shines like day; darkness is like light," to resolve the apparent contradiction between the first two quotations. Altogether, these three quotes introduce the concept of dualist thought or dialectical thinking that is characteristic of both gnosticism and kabbalistic thought. Two opposing ideas are inherently linked together so that each is defined in relation to the other; they function together in creation to produce a synthesis of the two. Darkness is not light, and light is not darkness; and yet both work together in the finite world to produce the varying shades of light and dark manifested in the world of creation. Absolute darkness and absolute light exist only in the heavenly realm. Much the same might be said of other sets of polar opposites: heat and cold, life and death, truth and falsehood, good and evil, motion and stillness.

Then paragraph 2 quotes R. Berakhiah, who analyzes Gen 1:2, "the earth was formless (*tohu*) and void (*vavohu*; alone, without 'and,' *bohu*)." This is

27. Aryeh Kaplan, *The Book Bahir: Illumination* (York Beach, ME: Samuel Weiser, 1979). The range given for the sections on the alphabet is a misprint; the first section is not 27 (*sic*) but 17, as correctly indicated below.

28. For the primary edition of the Hebrew text of the Bahir, see Reuven Moshe Margaliot, *Sefer ha-Bahir* (Jerusalem: Massad Harav Kook, 1978). For an English translation, see Kaplan, *Bahir*. For commentary, see Gershom Scholem, *Das Buch Bahir*, 4th ed. (Darmstadt: Wissenschaftliche Buchgesellschaft, 1989).

a statement concerning the past in which the formlessness of *tohu* is con-trasted with the potential for form in *bohu*, here read as *bo hu*, "it is in it," i.e., there is substance in *bohu* but not in *tohu*. Thereby he reads into Gen 1:2 the distinction and interrelationship between infinite formlessness and finite form.

A discussion in paragraphs 3–16 begins with the question why the Torah begins with the Hebrew letter *bet*, i.e., *bereshit bara' elohim et hashamayim ve'et ha'aretz*, "When G-d began to create the heavens and the earth" (Gen 1:1). The initial answer is that the *bet* is meant to indicate "blessing" (*bera-khah*), and blessing in turn is examined for its various dimensions. This dis-cussion introduces Moses's blessing of Naftali in Deut 33:23, "Naftali is sated with favor and full (*male'*) of the blessing of YHWH; the sea (west) and the south is (his) possession." This verse becomes the basis for defining the goal of the Torah as the bringing of the blessing of divine presence into the finite world by means of the terms *yam*, "sea," and *darom*, "south." By examining the uses of *bereshit*, "in (the) beginning," from Gen 1:1, the Bahir associates *reshit*, "beginning," with *hokhmah*, "wisdom," in Ps 111:10, "The beginning of wisdom is the fear of YHWH," and in 1 Kgs 5:12, "And YHWH gave wisdom to Solomon," both of which are examples of blessing. This leads to Prov 8:30 in which wisdom, personified as a woman, states that she was with G-d at the outset of creation, frolicking before YHWH and bringing both wisdom and praise into the world. Discussion concludes by returning to the original question as to why the Torah begins with *beth*. In paragraph 14 *bet*, because it also signifies "house" (*bayit*), points to the blessing of establishing the holy temple, or house of G-d, first built by Solomon, in the finite world where the infinite character of YHWH may be encountered and praised. Thus the *bet* through the course of the discussion in paragraphs 1–16 points to the establishment of the divine presence in the world by means of the temple to bring about blessing and wisdom in the world of creation.

Bahir paragraphs 17–44 then turn to an examination of the first eight letters of the Hebrew alphabet, *aleph, bet, gimel, dalet, he, vav, zayin, khet*, in an effort to correlate them with the Ten Sefirot. The sequence stops prior to *tet*, which does not appear in the Ten Commandments and stands at the center of the Hebrew word, *beten*, belly, which divides the pure upper part of the human body from the impure lower part. Such an understanding de-rives from Sefer Yetzirah, which conceived of the Ten Sefirot, countings or emanations of G-d, with the ten utterances of G-d in Gen 1:1–2:3, all of which are formed by the letters of the Hebrew alphabet, to bring about the creation of the finite world.

Discussion begins with the letter, *aleph*, the first letter of the Hebrew alphabet. *Aleph* has no pronunciation and therefore functions as a silent letter that holds a vowel. R. Amorai states that *aleph* appears at the beginning, even before the Torah. His statement presupposes that the Torah does not begin with *beth*, the second letter of the Hebrew alphabet, which appears at the head of the first word of the Torah, *bereshit*, "in the beginning." R. Amorai's statement therefore entails several conclusions. First, *aleph* presides over creation. Second, *aleph* is silent and therefore indicates the unnamed and unformed reality that existed prior to the process by which the finite world emerged. Third, *aleph* is identified with the first sefirah, Keter Elyon, or Crown of the Most High, which alludes to G-d as the source or author of creation.

R. Amorai follows with observations concerning *bet*. It is first, i.e., it is the first letter of the Torah, which initiates the process of the creation of the finite world. Second, *bet* has a tail, which points back to something. Consequently, *bet* must presuppose that something precedes both its order in the alphabet and that something precedes creation. This of course will be *aleph*, the Keter Elyon, which represents the first emanation of G-d in the world of creation. *Bet* therefore represents *Hokhmah*, Wisdom, the second sefirah or emanation of G-d in the finite world. In this case, *Hokhmah* indicates the quality of conceptualization and planning that must inform the creation of a well-ordered finite world. It presupposes Prov 8:30, where *hokhmah*, personified as a woman, is the first of G-d's creations, whom G-d consults while she dances before him as he creates the rest of the world.

Gimel then appears as the third letter in the Hebrew alphabet which "bestows" (*gomelet*) kindness into the finite world of creation. *Gimel* has three parts. The first is a head on top which draws from what precedes; in this case, *gimel* draws from *bet*, here associated with *Hokhmah*. The second part of *gimel* is a pipe, which conveys what it draws from the head to the tail, the third part of the letter. Insofar as *gimel* draws from *Hokhmah*, the second sefirah, and conveys to kindness (*hesed*), the fourth sefirah, *gimel* is identified with *Binah*, or Understanding, the third of the sefirot by which the infinite G-d is manifested within the finite world. *Binah* plays a very practical role in the way it channels *Hokhmah* to the rest of the sefirot. *Binah* therefore indicates practical knowledge, which is necessary to convey the theoretical knowledge of *Hokhmah* into the world in a manner that gives it form and makes it manifest in the finite world. Whereas *Hokhmah* may be identified with the theoretical knowledge necessary to conceptualize and plan the building of a house, *Binah* indicates the knowledge of craftsmen who take that knowledge and turn it into a practical reality; they build the house.

The Bahir next takes up the letter *dalet*, the fourth letter of the Hebrew alphabet. *Dalet* is associated with the tenth and final sefirah in the sequence, known as *Malkhut*, the Kingdom (of G-d), or as *Shekhinah*, the Presence of G-d in the finite world. There arises therefore a question as to whether *dalet* should come next or if *he* should come next. The conclusion is that *he* should come next because the form of *dalet* actually includes the form of the letter *he*. Insofar as *he* appears twice as the second and third letters of the divine name, YHWH, *dalet* signifies that *he* should come next; *dalet* points forward to the culminating presence of G-d in the world as the tenth sefirah, *Malkhut/Shekhinah*. *He* then represents the divine name, YHWH, in which *yod*, the tenth letter, indicates the Ten Sefirot by which YHWH becomes manifest in the world. Likewise, *vav*, the sixth letter, indicates the other six sefirot—*Hesed*, kindness/fidelity; *Gevurah*, power; *Tiferet*, beauty; *Netzah*, endurance/dynamism; *Hod*, majesty/stability; and *Yesod*, foundation—that appear between *Binah* and *Malkhut/Shekhinah* to manifest G-d in the finite world. These six sefirot are identified with the six dimensions of the universe, up, down, east, west, north, south, which together define the dimensions of a house, i.e., the Jerusalem Temple, by which YHWH is manifested in the finite world.

Finally, the vowels—*qamets, patakh, tsere, segol, shewa, holem, hireq, shureq, qibbuts*, and no vowel—are also identified with the Ten Sefirot by which the infinite G-d is manifested in the finite world.

Sefer Habahir paragraphs 45–122 focus on the interpretation of the seven voices of G-d that the people of Israel saw at Mt. Sinai according to Exod 19:16: "And all the people were seeing the voices (*haqolot*, the thunders) and the lightning and the voice (*qol*, sound) of the shofar and the mountain smoking; and the people saw, and they moved away, and they stood from afar." Exodus 19:16 portrays the people's reaction to witnessing the divine theophany at Mt. Sinai, including the imagery of thunder and lightning and the sound of the shofar as the divine presence of YHWH manifested on Mt. Sinai. This verse is part of the Torah portion, Exod 19:1–20:23, for the first day of Shavuot, which celebrates the revelation of the Torah at Sinai. The haftarah portion is Ezek 1:1–28; 3:12, which relates Ezekiel's vision of the merkavah, the foundation of Jewish mysticism and kabbalistic thought.

The "voices" at Sinai are correlated with Ps 29:4–9, verses that relate the role of YHWH's voice in the creation of the universe. The Bahir thereby cites seven statements from Ps 29: "the voice of YHWH is upon the waters" (v. 3); "the voice of YHWH is in power" (v. 4a); "the voice of YHWH is in majesty" (v. 4b); "the voice of YHWH breaks cedars" (v. 5a); "the voice of

YHWH kindles flames of fire" (v. 7); "the voice of YHWH overpowers the wilderness" (v. 8); and "the voice of YHWH prompts hinds to labor" (v. 9). The Bahir concludes that this sequence demonstrates that the Torah was also revealed with the seven voices of YHWH. Because Exod 19:16 appears as part of the narrative in which the Ten Commandments are revealed, the Bahir takes the opportunity to examine how the seven voices of G-d are related to the Ten Commandments, expressing the same pattern evident in creation when G-d speaks ten times to carry out creation in seven days.

A wide-ranging intertextual discussion ensues, with special emphasis on Isa 55 (pars. 51–56) and Hab 3 (pars. 68–81). Isaiah 55 begins with an invitation in Isa 55:1 to come eat and drink: "Hoy, all who are thirsty, come for water; and whoever has no money, come, break (bread), and eat; come, break without money." This invitation conveys YHWH's invitation to the people of Israel to return to G-d. In the end, YHWH promises that the eternal covenant of David (2 Sam 7) will be manifested in the people of Israel at large. In other words, the divine presence will be manifested in Israel forever. Habakkuk 3 is the prophet's account of his theophanic vision of YHWH, who rides through the heavens to defeat Israel's (Judah's) enemies and restore the nation to safety as promised in the covenant. Habakkuk 3 is the haftarah portion read on the second day of Shavuot, and so it also celebrates the revelation of Torah at Sinai and the covenant between Israel and YHWH. This section also takes up the mystical names of YHWH and provides special focus on the importance of the number thirty-two, the numerical equivalent of the Hebrew word *lev*, "heart," which is understood in the Bible as the seat of the mind and intellect. The number thirty-two also corresponds to the thirty-two wonderful paths of wisdom that open the Sefer Yetzirah and to the combination of the Ten Sefirot or utterances of YHWH at creation and the twenty-two letters of the Hebrew alphabet which comprise YHWH's statements.

Sefer Habahir paragraphs 123–93 focus on the Ten Sefirot. The discussion begins with Lev 9:22, "And Aaron raised his hands to the people, and he blessed them, and he came down from making the sin offering and the whole burnt offering and the well-being offering." This verse describes the actions of the high priest when officiating over the offerings in the tabernacle, but its significance for the Bahir lies in the imagery of Aaron's raised hands that are placed together, his ten fingers acting as a symbolic canopy for the people as he recites the priestly blessing. Aaron's ten fingers signify the Ten Sefirot of the divine presence manifested in the world, much like the ten utterances of YHWH at creation and the Ten Commandments at Sinai. A lengthy intertextual discussion then names and characterizes each of the Ten Sefirot. Beginning in paragraph 179, the Ten Sefirot are correlated with ten spheres or emanations from the divine that create the channels of connection to the finite world of earth and that thereby ensure the infinite divine presence in the finite world of creation.

Sefer Habahir paragraphs 194–200 conclude the work with an intertextual reflection on the human soul that was breathed into the first human being by G-d at creation. Insofar as Gen 1:26–27 claims that G-d created the first human (*adam*, singular) "male and female," the Bahir examines both the male and female aspects of the human soul. The Bahir identifies the snake in the Garden of Eden with the evil angel Samael. It maintains that Samael seduced Eve in the Garden, introducing evil into the world and thereby disrupting the infinite divine presence of G-d in the finite world of creation.

The preceding discussion of Sefer Habahir describes features that qualify it as the first known major kabbalistic work. The Bahir is formulated as a synthesis of Jewish texts, including the Bible and earlier works of Jewish mysticism, such as the heikhalot literature and the Sefer Yetzirah, and gnostic concepts, such as the notion of an infinite and transcendent deity residing in the *plērōma* and associated with pure thought and wisdom, who influenced the formation of the finite earthly world. Nevertheless, the lines of gnostic influence that instigated the formation of kabbalistic thought and literature are not entirely clear. Provence and Languedoc in southern France and Gerona in northeastern Spain are the regions where the kabbalah first developed. These regions are well-positioned for gnostic influence due to the volume of Mediterranean trade with North Africa and the Middle East that would have played an important role in bringing gnostic thinkers, texts, and ideas to the Jewish communities in the area. The regions are also known for the wide influence of the Cathars, a gnostic group that competed with the Roman Catholic Church for influence and adherents.

Despite the potential for gnostic influence in the region of southern France and northeastern Spain, interpreters raise questions concerning the sources of gnostic teachings that fed into the development of early kabbalah. For one, gnostic influence is apparent well beyond southern France and northeastern Spain as indicated by the Hasidei Ashkenaz or German Pietism movement that appeared in northern Italy, Switzerland, and the Rhine River region in the tenth–twelfth centuries CE, itself apparently influenced by gnostic movements originating in the Middle East rather than in southern Europe. Indeed, Scholem demonstrates that the influence of the antisemitism that permeated the Catharist movement, particularly its assertion that the finite world is governed by the demonic Jewish deity who is entirely evil, appears to have no influence on kabbalistic thought. Rather, the influence of rational philosophy, beginning with the work of the Egyptian Jewish scholar R. Saadia Gaon of Baghdad (892–942 CE) and continuing through the work of R. Moses ben Maimon, or Maimonides (1135–1204 CE), of Spain and Egypt, appears to be the basis for the development of kabbalistic thought. Dan points out that only in the twelfth century CE, when earlier philosophical works written in Judeo-Arabic were translated into Hebrew, did they begin to have an impact on the Jewish community of southern Europe. Indeed, kabbalah appears to originate in opposition to the work of the rationalist philosophers who posited a deity like that of Aristotle, an unmoved Mover who set creation into motion but had nothing to do with it afterwards. Such philosophy was initially opposed by R. Judah Halevi (1175–1241 CE) of Spain and Egypt, who wrote the Sefer Hakuzari to demonstrate that the Jewish experience of, and relation with, G-d in history stood as the basis of Jewish thought—rather than any sterile notions of an unmoved First Mover. Sefer Habahir, with its development of the Ten Sefirot as the Ten Emanations of G-d into the finite earthly world, appears intended to demonstrate the means by which the infinite G-d is manifested in the finite world precisely so that G-d may interact with human beings in the finite world of human events and develop a relationship with them in order to complete the ongoing work of creation and to perfect the world as understood in Jewish thought and tradition. In Scholem's view, such an agenda was quintessentially Jewish and shows no evidence of western gnosticism.[29] Rather, such a movement appears to have developed in the Middle East, in Mesopotamia and Egypt, prior to making its appearance in southern and northern Europe. At the same time, he holds that kabbalistic thought may have functioned as an answer to the anti-Semitic views of the Cathars in terms that they—and Jews—would readily understand.

Other Key Movements and Figures: The Hasidei Ashkenaz, Isaac the Blind and His Students, and Abraham Abulafia

One of the major pre-kabbalistic movements of the Middle Ages was the Hasidei Ashkenaz, the German Pietists, who formed under the leadership of the Kalonymus family of northern Italy, the Albun family of France, and

29. Scholem, *Origins*, 232–38.

others, who moved into Germany during the tenth century CE.[30] They were especially influenced by Jewish suffering during the First Crusade of 1096 CE in which thousands of Jews living along the Rhine River and elsewhere were murdered by rampaging Crusader armies who decided that they would first attack infidels in Europe itself before going on to Palestine to capture Jerusalem from its Muslim rulers. The early Hasidei Ashkenaz were known for their commitment to Judaism to the point of martyrdom, an experience all too common for Jews during the Crusades, and their study of the heikhalot literature, such as the Heikhalot Rabbati, the Shiur Qomah, and the Sefer Yetzirah, in an effort to understand the hidden presence of G-d in the world.

One of the major leaders of the Hasidei Ashkenaz was R. Yehuda Hehasid, R. Judah the Pious (1150–1217 CE) of Regensburg (Ratisbonne in southeastern Germany). R. Judah was the author of the Sefer Hasidim, the Book of the Pious, which laid out the major teachings of the movement. Hasidei Ashkenaz teachings held that the world was created for one purpose: to distinguish the righteous from the wicked based upon observance of the divine commandments. G-d originally intended to create a world of evil, which is a major contention of gnosticism, but relented because G-d recognized that not one righteous person could ever emerge in such a world. Consequently, G-d included elements of good that might prompt the righteous to action and thereby justify the finite world of creation. Insofar as pleasure is the result of sin, suffering becomes a measure of righteousness, so that martyrdom becomes the ultimate measure of human righteousness before G-d.

In order to facilitate their view of righteous response to G-d, the Hasidei Ashkenaz developed a concept of the Kavod, the Glory of G-d, to explain the infinite G-d's relationship to the finite world. Saadia Gaon had already argued that the Kavod of G-d was a revelatory angel of G-d that pointed forward to the Shekhinah or divine presence in the world. R. Abraham Ibn Ezra (1089–1164 CE) developed this idea in his commentary on Exod 33 to claim that the Kavod of G-d is not an angel, but a divine aspect of G-d that facilitated G-d's transcendent presence with the immanent presence of G-d in the world. R. Judah the Pious developed the concept even further in a

30. For discussion of the Hasidei Ashkenaz, see Joseph Dan, *The Early Kabbalah*, Classics of Western Spirituality (New York: Paulist, 1986), 14–23; Gershom Scholem, *Major Trends in Jewish Mysticism* (New York: Schocken, 1961), 80–118; Ivan G. Marcus, "The Devotional Ideals of Ashkenazi Pietism," in *Jewish Spirituality*, ed. Arthur Green (New York: Crossroad, 1986), 356–66; Marcus, *Piety and Society: The Jewish Pietists of Medieval Germany* (Leiden: Brill, 1981).

supercommentary on Ibn Ezra's work to demonstrate a hierarchy of such divine manifestations and the role of divine providence in Hasidei Ashkenaz thought. R. Judah's system thereby anticipates the concept of the Ten Sefirot or Ten Emanations of G-d in kabbalistic thought.

There were of course early kabbalistic thinkers in southern France as well. One of the most influential was R. Isaac the Blind of Provence (ca. 1160–1235 CE), who some scholars believe may have been the author of Sefer Habahir although conclusive evidence is not forthcoming. R. Isaac the Blind came from a circle of talmudic and kabbalistic scholars who flourished in southern France during the twelfth and early thirteenth centuries CE. The first of these was R. Abraham ben Isaac of Narbonne (1116–1179 CE), a talmudic scholar who served as President of the Rabbinic Court. He was careful not to spread kabbalist ideas among those who were not properly prepared for kabbalist thought, although he is known for producing a key list of kabbalistic terms that could only be understood by those properly initiated.[31] A second was R. Abraham ben David of Posquières (known as the Rabad, 1125–1198 CE), the son-in-law of R. Abraham ben Isaac and a famed talmudic scholar and philosopher in his own right. Although he never wrote a known kabbalistic work, some passages in his writings include mystical dimensions which he keeps deliberately vague. He does claim that some of his halakic work is based on direct revelation. The third figure was R. Jacob ben Saul of Lunel (late twelfth century CE), also known as Jacob the Nazirite. He was a colleague of the Rabad who was known for his ascetic practice and devotion to the study of Torah. R. Jacob ben Saul received some mystical traditions and concepts of angelology while in Jerusalem, and developed mystical prayer based on what he had learned.

With such precedents, R. Isaac the Blind was heavily influenced by a combination of talmudic and halakic thought as well as an interest in mysticism that remained less publicly expressed.[32] Blind from birth, he developed a contemplative form of pre-kabbalistic thought that first comes to expression in his commentary on Sefer Yetzirah. Although the Bahir retains Mahshavah (thought) as the factor that stood at the beginning of the process of creation, R. Isaac the Blind makes allusions to something that stands above Mahshavah as the ultimate cause of creation. He does not label this "something" Ein Sof, the term that describes the Infinite character of G-d

---

31. For the following, see Laenen, *Jewish Mysticism*, 95–96.

32. See esp. Dan, *Early Kabbalah*, 31–34; for full discussion, see Scholem, *Origins*, 248–309.

in Zoharic kabbalah, and he continues to view Mahshavah as the first of the Sefirot. Yet R. Isaac the Blind develops the symbols of the Ten Sefirot employed throughout later kabbalistic work. In addition to Mahshavah, Hokhmah, and Binah, he bases his terminology of the seven lower sefirot on David's prayer to G-d in 1 Chr 29:11: Hagedullah (Greatness; later Hesed, Fidelity or Mercy); Hagevurah (Power to Punish); Tiferet (Beauty); Netzah (Endurance); Hod (Majesty); Hamamlekhah (Kingship; later Shekhinah, Divine Presence); and Hamitnasse' (All That Is Lifted Up; later Yesod, Foundation). In R. Isaac's thought, the emanation of the Ten Sefirot precedes physical creation itself, insofar as divine thought must first emerge before it achieves its realization in the creation of the finite world. His portrayal of creation entails that G-d began with the primordial Torah, derived from the quarry of repentance and from the source of wisdom. G-d then hewed out each sefirah and named it prior to actualizing it in creation, indicating the close interrelationship between naming and actuality, derived in part from Sefer Yetzirah.[33] Despite R. Isaac's blindness, he makes extensive use of the imagery of light and color to describe the process of creation, which clearly influences subsequent kabbalistic thought. Likewise, his notions of *devequt* or cleaving to G-d become key to later kabbalistic thinking.

Kabbalistic influence also began to spread to Spain, particularly in the work of two major students of R. Isaac the Blind, R. Ezra ben Solomon (late twelfth century CE) and especially his younger colleague R. Azriel ben Menahem (1160–1238 CE) of Gerona, active in Catalonia (northeastern Spain).[34] Whereas R. Isaac the Blind attempted to keep kabbalistic thought and writings hidden and available only to those who were properly prepared for kabbalistic study (cf. m. Hag. 2:1), R. Ezra ben Solomon and R. Azriel ben Menahem attempted to disseminate the teachings of kabbalah to a larger Jewish reading public through their many writings. R. Isaac the Blind wrote a letter to Gerona, admonishing the kabbalists there for their attempts to publicize kabbalistic thought. Apparently, the Geronese kabbalists listened to their teacher; their writings ceased after R. Isaac's letter. Although R. Isaac was invited to visit Gerona, he declined the invitation and sent his nephew, R. Asher ben David, in his place.[35]

33. See Dan's translation in the *Early Kabbalah*, 71–79, esp. 73. See also pp. 80–86, in which R. Isaac describes the process of emanation.

34. For full discussion of R. Azriel's work and the Geronese school, see Scholem, *Origins*, 365–475; cf. Dan, *Early Kabbalah*, 34–36, 87–150; Laenen, *Jewish Mysticism*, 99–104.

35. Dan, *Early Kabbalah*, 34–35.

R. Azriel was particularly prolific, apparently prior to R. Isaac's admonition. His work presents the beginnings of the classical kabbalistic understanding of the Ten Sefirot insofar as he is the first writer to name the Ein Sof, the Infinite character of G-d, as the foundation of the Sefirotic system of divine emanation.[36] He also employs the term *Keter*, "Crown," generally understood as the manifestation of the divine will, as the name of the first Sefirah to emanate from the Ein Sof during the process of creation. R. Azriel's work addressed the needs of both the scholars of kabbalah and those who were just beginning their study as part of his efforts to popularize the kabbalah and spread its influence throughout the Jewish community of his time. One of his works was a discussion of the mystical aspects of prayer. Such an effort would have challenged the influence of neo-Aristotelian thought among Jews, particularly the work of Maimonides, by attempting to demonstrate that G-d was not a First Mover who remained transcendent and unaffected by the experience of human beings and the world of creation. Instead, the emanation of the Ten Sefirot demonstrated that G-d was not only immanent or present in the world but was profoundly affected by human prayer and experience. In other words, G-d maintained active involvement in the world of creation and was transformed by the experience. Humans were likewise transformed by prayer. The Tefillah, "Prayer," or Shemoneh Esreh, "the Eighteen Blessings," constitutes the major prayer of the Jewish worship service. R. Azriel points out that the human body has eighteen vertebrae, which convey the *kavvanah*, "intention," of the worshiper from the brain throughout the rest of the body to ensure that the entire being of the person is involved with G-d in prayer.

R. Azriel's influence continued through his most important student, R. Moshe ben Nahman (Nahmanides or Ramban, 1194–1270 CE). The Ramban followed his teacher's example following the admonition of R. Isaac the Blind, by keeping his kabbalistic teachings more or less secret. Nevertheless, he makes allusions to kabbalistic thought, most notably the notion of the transmigration of the soul, throughout his commentary on the Torah, Job, halakic works, and other writings.[37]

The work of R. Abraham Abulafia (1240–ca. 1291), founder of the school of Prophetic kabbalah, also plays an important role in kabbalistic practice,

---

36. See R. Azriel's discussion of the Ten Sefirot, beginning with the Ein Sof, in Dan, *Early Kabbalah*, 89–96.

37. For full discussion of the thought of Nahmanides, see David Novak, *The Theology of Nahmanides Systematically Presented* (Atlanta: Scholars Press, 1993).

especially in its influence in later Lurianic kabbalah and Hasidism.[38] Abulafia was born in Zaragosa, Spain, and was later raised in Tudela, Navarre. He embarked on travel throughout his life, first going to the land of Israel to seek out the River Sambatyon and the Ten Lost Tribes of Israel, but he got no further than Akko (Acre) due to rampant lawlessness in the land under Muslim rule. He settled, studied, and taught in many localities, such as Barcelona, Capua, Messina, Patros, and eventually the Maltese island of Comino in 1291, after which evidence of his life disappears. He was a prolific writer, who developed kabbalistic commentary and practice in works such as Sefer Hayei Ha'olam Haba' (Book of the Life of the World to Come); Sefer 'Or Hasekhel (Book of the Light of the Intellect); Sefer Hakheshek (Book of Desire); and Imrei Shefer (Words of Beauty), all written between 1280 and 1291. Abulafia concentrated on meditation techniques that were designed to clear the mind and thereby enable it to engage in intense focus or *hitbodedut* on the Name of G-d. Techniques included free-style writing, gematria, pronunciation of the Name of G-d, and shifting of the letters of the Divine Name, as well as of other terminology from the Torah, to enable the mystic better to understand statements in the Torah and other texts. Abulafia's techniques were often controversial, especially because he engaged in pronunciation and writing of the Divine Name. He was denounced for such activity in Patros and eventually was excluded from the early Spanish kabbalists due to the controversial nature of his work.

38. See esp. Moshe Idel, *The Mystical Experience in Abraham Abulafia* (Albany: SUNY Press, 1988); Idel, "*Hitbodedut* as Concentration in Ecstatic Kabbalah," in *Jewish Spirituality: From the Bible Through the Middle Ages*, ed. Arthur Green (New York: Crossroad, 1986), 405–38; Scholem, *Major Trends*, 119–55.

Chapter 8

THE ZOHAR

Overview of the Zohar's Components, Context, and Concepts

The Zohar is the quintessential work of Jewish mysticism in general and of kabbalistic literature in particular.[1] The Hebrew term *zohar* means "splendor" or "radiance." It appears in Ezek 8:2 to describe the appearance of the human-like figure who lifted the prophet by the hair to transport him to Jerusalem where he would witness its destruction. It also appears in Dan 12:3 to refer to the radiance, like the firmament of the sky, of those who are knowledgeable concerning G-d's plans for the nation of Judah. As a title, the word *zohar* functions much like the word *bahir*, "brilliance," to indicate the infinite nature of knowledge concerning the presence of G-d in the finite world of creation.

The Zohar offers a mystical commentary on the Torah, elucidating the secret, hidden meaning of the Torah text associated with the letter *samek* of the word *pardes*, understood as an acronym of the four levels of interpretation; *samek* signifies the *sod* or secret meaning of the Torah text. The Zohar is not a literarily unified work. Rather, several discrete compositions, apparently all by the same author over the course of a lifetime, together

---

1. For introductions to the Zohar, see Gershom Scholem, *Major Trends in Jewish Mysticism* (New York: Schocken, 1961), 156–243; Daniel Chanan Matt, *Zohar: The Book of Enlightenment*, Classics in Western Spirituality (New York: Paulist, 1983), 1–39; Isaiah Tishby, *The Wisdom of the Zohar: An Anthology of Texts*, 3 vols. (Oxford: Littman Library of Jewish Civilization, 1983), 1:1–225; Boaz Huss, *The Zohar: Reception and Impact* (Oxford: Littman Library of Jewish Civilization, 2016). For a Hebrew-Aramaic text edition, see Reuven Moshe Margaliot, ed., *Sefer ha-Zohar*, 6th ed., 3 vols. (Jerusalem: Massad Harav, 5744/1984). For English translations of texts from the Zohar, see Tishby, *Wisdom*; Daniel Chanan Matt et al., *The Zohar: Pritzker Edition*, 11 vols. (Stanford: Stanford University Press, 2004–2017).

form the whole of the work. Tishby provides a convenient overview in the introduction to his anthology of texts from the Zohar. He maintains that the core of the Zohar is the Zohar on the Torah.[2] This is a collection of commentaries, written in Aramaic, on the various *parashiyot* (plural of *parashah*), or sections of the Torah that are read on each Shabbat.

The Zohar does not cover all the *parashiyot* of the Torah. It focuses especially on Genesis, Exodus, and Leviticus; many sections of Numbers and Deuteronomy are entirely absent. Furthermore, the commentary on each *parashah* is selective. Rather than provide a complete or systematic commentary on the entire *parashah*, the Zohar on the Torah comments selectively on individual verses from within the *parashah* that are particularly relevant for addressing the *sod*, or secret meaning of the passage, in keeping with the kabbalistic concerns and character of the Zohar. The commentary forms a midrashic treatment of the passage, yielding either shorter comments or sometimes extensive treatises on the verses at hand. As is typical of homiletic midrash, each section of commentary opens with a *petihah*, an opening or introduction, which typically quotes a passage or verse from the Psalms that raises the issue to be treated in the commentary on the *parashah*. Oftentimes, the commentary can appear as a dialogue among rabbinic figures, often R. Shimon bar Yohai, as well as other known rabbinic sages and many sages who were invented for the Zohar; together they constitute the circle of scholars gathered around R. Shimon bar Yohai to examine and comment upon the issues raised in the *parashah*.

Tishby also identifies the Zohar on the Song of Songs, which presents a midrashic, kabbalistic commentary on the Song similar in form and content to that on the Torah.

Scholem identified the Midrash Hane'elam (The Hidden Midrash) on the Torah as an older work that apparently preceded the Zohar on the Torah discussed above. The Midrash Hane'elam is written in a combination of Hebrew and Aramaic, and focuses on the interpretation of *parashiyot* from Genesis, the first *parashah* from the book of Exodus, and elements from other *parashiyot*. It does not work systematically through the entire text of the Torah, and it was apparently employed as a framework for the presentation of the Zohar on the Torah. It presents far more rabbis than the Zohar on the Torah, although it presumes little connection or discussion among them in comparison to the Zohar on the Torah. Tishby notes that the Midrash Hane'elam addresses a much narrower range of topics than the Zohar

2. Tishby, *Wisdom*, 1:1–13.

on the Torah, focusing on creation, the soul, the afterlife, and the messianic age, whereas the Zohar on the Torah takes up issues of the mysteries of the divine as well as "the other side" (Sitra Ahra), which refers to the question of evil. Unlike the Zohar on the Torah, which probes the language of the Torah text to derive its kabbalistic midrashic comments, the Midrash Hane'elam focuses more on allegory as the basis for its interpretation of the text.

Tishby also points to a Midrash Hane'elam on Song of Songs, Ruth, and Lamentations. Those on Song of Songs and Lamentations are largely incomplete and fragmentary, whereas the one on Ruth is largely complete and forms a commentary much like the Midrash Hane'elam on the Torah. The Sitrei Torah, "Secrets of the Torah," appear to be individual comments on selected passages from Genesis; likewise, the kabbalistic Matnitin (Aramaic for *mishnayot*) and Tosefta represent discrete passages that appear within the commentaries on selected passages.

The Sava de-Mishpatim (The Old Man of Parashat Mishpatim) presents the discourse of an old man who works as an ass driver. Although he at first appears to be a complete ignoramus, he proves to be a sage named R. Yava Sava who is well versed in the kabbalistic interpretation of the soul. Most of his discourses appear with the Zohar's commentary to Parashat Mishpatim, on the halakic section in Exod 21–24, particularly the laws pertaining to slaves in Exod 21:1–11.

The Yanuka (The Child) presents a series of homilies spoken by a child identified as the son of R. Hamnuna Sava. The child proves to be a sage who is far wiser than the other rabbinic colleagues present for his discourses. The Yanuka appears especially in Parashat Balak (Num 22:2–25:9) although it has little to do with Balaam or the narratives that constitute the parashah.

The Rav Metivta (The Head of the Academy) presents an account of discourses learned by R. Shimon bar Yohai and his circle while they are in the Garden of Eden. The teachings come from the Head of the Heavenly Yeshivah, and they appear in Parashat Shelah-Lekha, Num 13–15, which takes up the divine decree that the wilderness generation will perish in the wilderness so that only a new generation who did not know slavery will enter the promised land of Israel.

The Sifra de-Zeni'uta, "The Book of Concealment," focuses on Parashat Bereshit (Gen 1:1–6:8), although it appears in Parashat Terumah (Exod 25:1–27:19), where it focuses on the mysteries of the G-dhead as an important summation of the Zohar's teachings on the character of G-d. The Idra Rabba (The Great Assembly) is a section that develops the ideas of the G-dhead found in the Sifra de-Zeni'uta, based on discussion by R. Shimon bar Yohai and his circles. It appears in Parashat Naso (Num 4:21–7:89). The Idra Zutra (The Small Assembly) presents the last discourses on the Idra Rabba by R. Shimon bar Yohai to his gathered disciples prior to his death. It appears in Parashat Ha'azinu (Deut 32) as a conclusion to the Zohar.

Other discrete sections in the Zohar include the Heikhalot (Palaces) which describes the heavenly palaces scattered among various *parashiyot*; the Raza de-Razin (Secret of Secrets) which treats physiognomy and chiromancy in Parashat Yitro (Exod 18–20); the Sitrei Otiyot (Secrets of the Letters) which focuses on the character of the G-dhead as revealed in the letters of the divine Name; the Ma'amar Kav Hamiddah (The Standard of Measure) which focuses on the unity of G-d based on the Shema in Deut 6:4; and an untitled commentary on Ezekiel's chariot.

The Raya Mehemna (Faithful Shepherd) is a discourse on the Ten Commandments; originally a unified composition, it is now found scattered among various passages. The Tikkunei Hazohar (Corrections of the Zohar) is a discrete work with seventy main sections as well as additional appendices; each of the seventy sections begins with the word *bereshit*, "in the beginning," and comments on verses from Parashat Bereshit (Gen 1:1–6:8). Together, the Raya Mehemna and the Tikkunei Hazohar constitute the Zohar Hadash (New Zohar), which can circulate as a separate book, independent of the other contents of the Zohar.

The primary narrator of the Zohar is R. Shimon bar Yohai (Rashbi), the second-century Tannaitic rabbi who was a student of R. Akiva during the years following the destruction of the Second Temple in 70 CE and the Bar Kokhba war in 132–135 CE. According to rabbinic legend, R. Shimon and his son, R. Eleazar Ben Shimon, hid in a cave for thirteen years to escape Roman persecution of Jews. During those thirteen years, R. Shimon and his son subsisted on the fruit of a carob tree which grew near the mouth of the cave while R. Shimon taught his son the secret meaning of the Torah and recorded his teachings in the form of a Torah commentary that came to be known as the Zohar. According to tradition, therefore, R. Shimon bar Yohai is the author of the Zohar which dates to the second century CE.

Modern critical scholars of Rabbinic Judaism have been very skeptical of this assertion concerning the Zohar's authorship for a number of reasons.[3] First, the character of the Aramaic language used to write the Zohar does not correspond to that used in second-century CE Judah. Rather, the dialect is characteristic of those used for rabbinic literature during the Middle

---

3. Scholem, *Major Trends*, 156–204; Tishby, *Wisdom*, 1:55–87.

Ages up to about the thirteenth century CE, and it includes many words of Spanish origin. Second, the Zohar cites or makes reference to a number of rabbinic works, such as the commentaries of Rashi, Radaq, Ibn Ezra, Ramban (Nahmanides), and Rambam (Maimonides), as well as mystical works, such as the Heikhalot Rabbati, the Sefer Yetzirah, and the Bahir, that were known only in the Middle Ages and not in the second century CE. Third, the imagery of the countryside described in the Zohar as R. Shimon walks about the land discussing Torah looks nothing like the land of Israel in the second century CE, but instead it resembles Spain during the Middle Ages. Fourth, scholars have been unable to find any reference to the Zohar prior to ca. 1280 or 1290 CE. Finally, R. Moses ben Shemtov de León, a kabbalistic rabbi from Avila, was known as the scribe who sold copies of the Zohar. R. Isaac of Akko determined that he would visit de León to ascertain the provenance of the Zohar because of his own suspicions about its authorship. He recounts traveling to Spain ca. 1290 to meet with de León; but when he arrived, de León had already passed away. R. Isaac spoke with de León's widow, attempting to locate the original manuscript of the work from which de León had copied. But de León's widow told him that her husband never copied the Zohar from an earlier manuscript. Rather, he wrote the Zohar entirely on his own and attributed it to R. Shimon bar Yohai in the belief that it would be more profitable if people believed that R. Shimon, and not R. Moses ben Shemtov de León, was the true author of the work. On these bases, modern scholars such as Gershom Scholem maintain that R. Moses ben Shemtov de León was in fact the true author of the Zohar.

Indeed, R. Moses ben Shemtov de León should have given himself more credit for writing the Zohar.[4] As the quintessential text of kabbalistic Judaism, the Zohar develops earlier conceptualizations of the ascent to heaven in the heikhalot literature and the conceptualization of the Ten Sefirot of G-d in Sefer Yetzirah and Sefer Habahir. The Zohar addresses the fundamental question: how is the infinite character of G-d manifested as the divine presence of G-d in the finite world? The Zohar identifies the infinite character of G-d as the Ein Sof, Hebrew for "infinity." It then conceptualizes the Ten Sefirot of G-d, earlier understood as G-d's divine utterances at creation, as ten emanations of the various qualities of G-d that together sustain the divine presence of G-d in the finite world of creation; the divine presence of G-d in the finite world is identified as the Shekhinah, a Rabbinic Hebrew term that refers to G-d's dwelling or presence. The Ten Sefirot are organized into

---

4. Tishby, *Wisdom*, 1:269–307; Marvin A. Sweeney, "Ten Sephirot," *DDD*, 487–93.

three intangible triads—mental, moral, and material—each one of which is constituted as a pair of ideal dialectical opposites that is balanced by a third. Each of the sefirot appears as part of the divine personality as well as elements of the human personality and of creation at large. Altogether, they provide a model for understanding the immanence of G-d in the world of humanity and creation.

The three mental sefirot include a first sefirah that emanates two specified aspects. The first is Keter Elyon, which means "Crown of the Most High (G-d)" in Hebrew. The Keter Elyon represents the mental quality of the will to create or act in the world. The Keter Elyon is often closely identified with the Ein Sof, but it may be distinguished as an initial specification of the character of the Ein Sof. It is often explained by the metaphor of building a house, bearing in mind that the House of G-d is embodied in the Jerusalem Temple, which is understood in Jewish thought as a manifestation of divine presence and as the holy center of creation. In this case, Keter Elyon would represent the divine will to create the world, culminating in the creation of the temple at its center. For humans, Keter Elyon would represent the will to create or act in the world. The second sefirah is Hokhmah, "Wisdom." Hokhmah refers to the theoretical knowledge or capacity for conceptualizing and planning. In the case of G-d, it refers to the wisdom necessary for conceptualizing and planning the world of creation. For humans, it represents the capacity to conceptualize and plan any action or project that human beings might undertake, beginning with the fulfillment of G-d's commands to build the temple and to engage in study and worship at the behest of G-d. In the metaphor of building a house, Hokhmah might best be understood in relation to the blueprints. But planning also requires practical knowledge to bring the plan to fruition. The need for actualizing a plan leads us to the third mental sefirah, Binah, which means "Understanding" in Hebrew. Binah refers to the practical knowledge necessary for realizing an abstract conceptualization or plan. In the case of G-d, Binah entails the capacity for building or constructing all aspects of the world of creation. In relation to the human world, Binah entails the practical knowledge of cutting wood, laying brick, nailing pieces together in their proper place, painting, sealing, etc.: all the elements of the house, each in its proper place.

The three moral sefirot include two dialectically opposite sefirot that are balanced by a third. Thus, the fourth sefirah is Hesed, which is Hebrew for "Fidelity," although it is also understood to refer to "Mercy." It is identified with the right hand and arm of the human body and indicates the capacity to give or to reward. One might think of Hesed in relation to a child who is given everything in life because the parents love the child. But when the child is given everything, the child becomes spoiled; never having learned to fend for itself, the child always expects to be given everything that it needs or wants. Such a child sees itself and itself alone as important; everyone and everything else is unimportant and disregarded. The dialectical counterpart to Hesed is the fifth sefirah, Gevurah, "Power," although this sefirah is also known as Din, "Judgment." Gevurah/Din is associated with the left hand and arm of the human body and refers to the capacity to take or punish. One might think of Gevurah or Din in relation to a child who is given nothing by parents who do not love the child, who force it to fend for itself, entirely neglected. Again, such a child is problematic, not because it is spoiled, but because it has no sense of self-worth; everyone and everything is considered more important than the child. Neither the spoiled child of Hesed nor the neglected child of Gevurah or Din represents a well-balanced human personality; each is an ideal or extreme that cannot sustain itself in life. Consequently, the Moral Sefirot require a balancing principle, a concept known from medieval Aristotelian philosophy and the works of Maimonides as the golden mean or balance of human moral action. In the case of the Zohar, the moral balance is expressed by the sixth sefirah, Tiferet, "Beauty." Tiferet balances the capacity to give or reward inherent in Hesed and the capacity to take or punish inherent in Gevurah or Din. Tiferet is generally identified with the torso of the human body. When one thinks of the paradigmatic children noted in relation to Hesed and Gevurah/Din discussed above, the balancing effects of Tiferet yield a child or human personality who experiences a balanced mix of giving and reward together with taking or discipline. The result is a child with an appropriately balanced personality, knowing both reward and punishment, who can therefore function effectively in the world.

The three material sefirot likewise include two dialectically opposed principles balanced by a third. The seventh sefirah is Netzah, Hebrew for "Endurance." The material sefirot might be likened to the Chinese dialectical pair of Yin and Yang, which refer to the masculine and feminine principles of material reality in the world of creation. Alternatively, one might think of the interplay of Shiva, the Destroyer, or principle of change in the world, and Vishnu, the Preserver, or the principle of stability, in the Hindu pantheon. Thus, Netzah refers to the dynamic principle of material reality, i.e., those aspects of the material world that are in motion and thereby generate heat or change in the world. Netzah is generally identified with the right leg and foot of the human body. One might think of Netzah in relation to examples of absolute motion in the material world, such as a nuclear explosion or cancer in the body, in which motion and change become so extreme that they destroy the world or the body in which they occur. Obviously, such an idealization of motion or change cannot sustain the world or the body in which it might exist, and so there must be a dialectical opposite. Therefore, sefirah number eight is Hod, Hebrew for "Majesty." Hod refers to the feminine principle of material reality that represents no change or stability. Hod is generally identified with the left leg and foot of the human body. When one applies the ideal of stability to the material world, Hod then represents the complete lack of motion; this generally entails death and decline in the world of creation. One might think of a world or a human body that dies for lack of motion or change. The material world cannot sustain itself by either absolute dynamism or absolute change, and therefore requires a balancing principle that holds the two dialectical opposites together. Sefirah number nine is therefore identified as Yesod, "Foundation," which holds Netzah and Hod together to create a perfect balance, both in the material world and within the human body. The interplay of dynamism and stability in the human body might be recognized by the changing character of the human face over the course of a lifetime, from infant to child to adolescent to young adult to mature adult and finally to elderly adult. But even though the human face changes over the course of a lifetime, its stability remains, as the changing face is recognized as the same face during the course of a lifetime.

As the sefirot correspond to the human form, Yesod is generally identified with the male penis, and so it points to a sexual dimension of the sefirot. When all of the first nine sefirot function in perfect balance, their infinite character is channeled through yesod, the male penis, into sefirah number ten, Shekhinah, the Hebrew word for the divine dwelling or presence of G-d in the finite world of creation. The tenth sefirah is sometimes also known as Malkhut, "Kingship" or "Sovereignty," to indicate divine sovereignty and presence in the finite world of creation. As both terms, Shekhinah and Malkhut, are feminine nouns in Hebrew, they are often metaphorically identified with the human vagina. When the infinite essence of the divine is channeled through the Yesod to the Shekhinah, continuing the metaphor of sexual intercourse, the Ten Sefirot produce a perfectly balanced expression of the ten infinite qualities of G-d, establishing divine presence in the finite world. Such an ideal balance entails ideal order in the world of creation. By contrast, it is only when this balance is disrupted that the finite world also suffers disruption or chaos. Given the metaphor of sexual intercourse, the channeling of the sefirot through Yesod into Shekhinah points to the human capacity for creating new life in the finite world.

The Zohar follows the general narrative structure of the Torah with treatment of many topics scattered among the commentaries on the various *parashiyot* of the Torah. However, a coherent overview of the Zohar's concerns requires that the following discussion proceed thematically. Topics treated include Interpretation of the Torah, G-d, the Sefirot, the Shekhinah, the Sitra Ahra, Creation, Human Beings, and the Role of Temple and Torah.

The Torah

Kabbalistic interpretation of the Torah arose during the Middle Ages as a response to the influence of Jewish rational philosophy. Fundamentally, medieval Jewish philosophy was based on the interpretation of the Torah with the use of human reason to elucidate the hidden meaning behind the literal reading (*peshat*) of the Torah text. Such an understanding was ultimately based on the rabbinic concept of the Oral Torah, which probed the written text of the Torah to determine the true meaning of that text. By such means, for example, the Mishnah defined the thirty-nine categories of work that were forbidden on Shabbat, deriving them from the various types of work that would be necessary to build the tabernacle in the wilderness. Such interpretive effort was necessary because the text of the Torah never explicitly defined what constituted "work" when it issued prohibitions against performing work on Shabbat. Likewise, the Babylonian Talmud probed the meaning of *lex talionis*, i.e., the legal notion that wrongdoing should be punished on the principle of a life for a life, an eye for an eye, a hand for a hand, etc., because the Amoraim recognized that such a principle when applied literally could never result in true justice. Punishing a one-eyed man who destroyed the eye of another person would actually produce a worse fate by rendering him blind. And the reciprocal injury of those who harmed others would only produce a class of injured perpetrators who not only would be unable to replace what they had taken from their victims but would themselves become dependent on others. Consequently, the Talmud interpreted the principle in opposition to its literal statement: the text did not literally demand an eye for an eye, but instead it indicated a principle of monetary compensation. The perpetrator would supply the needs of the injured and would not in turn become dependent upon others due to a court-imposed injury.

The medieval Jewish philosophers, beginning with R. Saadia ben Joseph al-Fayumi, better known as R. Saadia Gaon (892–942 CE), responded to challenges on several sides at once: from Islam, which adapted Greco-Roman philosophy to support the claims of Islam; from Christianity, which likewise adapted Greco-Roman philosophy to support the claims of the church; and from Karaite Judaism, which originated in Mesopotamia and Persia in the mid-eighth century CE, a Jewish movement analogous to Shiite Islam that rejected the Oral Torah of Rabbinic Judaism and based its understanding of Judaism on the written text of the Torah. Jewish philosophers such as Saadia were well-versed in rabbinic tradition but based their argumentation on the use of human reason and observations of the finite world of creation, a view found in the wisdom literature of the Bible. Indeed, the philosophers accepted the principle of the Oral Torah, that the meaning of the written text of the Torah continued to unfold in the tradition of its study and elucidation, a purpose served by their use of reason. Thus Saadia could argue in his Sefer Emunot Vede'ot, "Book of Opinions and Beliefs," that G-d must be One because the ordered design of the world of creation must presuppose a single Creator—multiple creators would produce chaos—and that the Torah's notions of reward and punishment require reward and punishment in the afterlife in order to ensure just reward and punishment for the righteous and the wicked. Likewise, R. Moses ben Maimon, better known as Maimonides (1135–1204 CE), attempted rational explanations for animal sacrifice and anthropomorphic depictions such as the hand of G-d. Anthropomorphism was metaphorical, necessary to convey to human beings the concept of divine action in the world; animal sacrifice was a means to socialize human beings into the concept of prayer. Ultimately, Maimonides argued that the prophets possessed the necessary intellect to encounter aspects of the true nature of G-d due to the abstract qualities of the human intellect and the infinite nature of G-d.

But medieval Jewish mystics were not satisfied with the contention of the philosophers that the hidden meaning of the Torah could be elucidated by human reason, particularly when they considered the holy Presence of G-d in the finite world of creation. Earlier works of Jewish mysticism, such as the heikhalot literature, had pointed to the heavenly or infinite dimensions of divine presence and purpose that manifested in the finite world in ways that human reason could not fully understand. An example from the Heikhalot Rabbati is G-d's response to R. Nehunyah ben Haqanah: G-d's punishment in the destruction of the temple and the defeat of the Bar Kokhba revolt may have been mistaken, and additional study of Torah would be necessary to understand why G-d had done so.

Consequently, kabbalistic literature, particularly the Zohar, probed the written text of the Torah to elucidate its hidden or secret meaning, particularly its understanding of the true nature of the infinite or heavenly nature of G-d and G-d's relationship to the finite world of creation. An important text on this issue appears in Zohar 3:152a, which begins with a discourse by R. Shimon with his circle of followers.[5] He begins by castigating those who hold that the Torah intended only to relate stories and the words of common people, i.e., the simple or plain meaning of the text, because a human could have done a better job in composing such a work, as many human works of the time would attest. Instead, R. Shimon asserts that the words of the Torah convey supernal mysteries that require a different form of interpretation. He notes parallels between the heavenly world and the earthly world and contends that, when the heavenly angels descend to this world (basing his interpretation on Ps 104:4), they would don earthly garments in order to enable the finite world to withstand their presence. R. Shimon reasons that if the heavenly angels need earthly garments, so much more so does the Torah of G-d on which everything depends. The plain meaning of the narratives of the Torah is the garments of the Torah that enable the Torah to exist in the finite world, but one cannot expect to understand the true meaning of divine Torah from only those garments. Just as garments cover a human body, and a human body contains a human soul, so one must look underneath the garments to see the body of the Torah, and within the body of the Torah to see its soul, and within the soul to see the "soul of the soul." Such a notion is consistent with the rabbinic concept of the Oral Torah in addition to the written form of the text; and the image of the soul's garments nuances the four dimensions of Torah interpretation expressed in the mnemonic use of the Pardes, the Paradise or Garden that is the setting of the Torah scholar's mystical ascent in the heikhalot literature, to recall the four levels of interpretation, i.e., the *peshat* or plain meaning of the text; *remez* or allegorical meaning; *darashah* or homiletical meaning; and *sod*, the hidden, secret meaning of the text. The hidden secret of the Torah, the Sod, is now clothed in the garments of the other three dimensions of the Torah.

A second narrative in Zohar 1:134b–135a focuses on the role of Torah in sustaining the world.[6] Such a concept is especially important to the book of Proverbs, which posits that fear or reverence of G-d is the beginning of all wisdom (Prov 1:7) and that G-d created Wisdom first, then consulted her in creating the rest of the world (Prov 8). Solomon's wisdom in Proverbs

---

5. Tishby, *Wisdom*, 3:1126–27.
6. Tishby, *Wisdom*, 3:1123–24.

is the recognition that divine Torah sustains the world and may be learned by studying the world of creation to discern its underlying basis. R. Hiyya begins the Zohar's discourse by stating that G-d created the world by first looking into Torah, equated with Wisdom in Prov 8:30, for its guidance in creation. R. Hiyya turns to the problem of punishment of humans for wrong-doing; but G-d responds to him, stating that repentance was already in place before the world was created to provide humans recourse to divine mercy. The world exists for the sake of human beings, that they might observe the laws of the Torah and thereby sustain the world. All elements of the world are put into order, just as the various elements of the body of a human are joined together, to ensure the life of the human being, who is in turn responsible for ensuring the order of the world in all of its parts. Although both Solomon and David attempted to understand the world of creation, they were unable to complete the task, so future generations of humans must carry on the work to sustain and sanctify the world of creation based on the teachings of divine Torah.

A third section in the Zohar on the Song of Songs (Zohar Hadash 70d) outlines the obligations of humans to learn the true knowledge of the Torah so that they might fulfill their obligation to sustain and sanctify the world.[7] One who knows what is expected is exempt from punishments. Such a person must know how to understand the mystery of G-d: what is G-d's infinite character and how is it manifested in the finite world. Such a person must therefore know one's own body because the presence of G-d is manifested within it as well as in all creation. One must know how the body was created, where it came from, and where it will go when the person comes to judgment before G-d. Such a person must understand the secrets of the soul: what is the life force within, from where did the soul come, and why was it placed in this particular body, which is only a temporary home that will ultimately pass away. Such a person must also understand the world: upon what it is based, and the supernal mysteries of the heavenly world above. All of this is necessary so that one may understand G-d and G-d's expectations of us. Without knowledge, one will still be expelled from this world, and so it is the obligation of the human being to study divine Torah. In this case, such knowledge entails the secret knowledge of the Torah which the Zohar and the rest of the kabbalistic tradition are designed to teach.

7. Tishby, *Wisdom*, 3:1131–33.

G-d

Rabbinic Judaism shies away from any attempt to describe or define the form of the Holy G-d because any such attempt to portray G-d in terms available through human conceptualization and language is potentially limiting and idolatrous.[8] And yet the presence and action of the infinite and intangible G-d are the foundations of Jewish life and understanding of the world in which we live. So how is that human beings can perceive the presence of G-d in the world of creation? The medieval philosophers attempted to address this issue by positing that the human intellect, which is itself an intangible aspect of the human being, constitutes the means by which humans might begin to perceive, understand, and interrelate with the holy presence of G-d in the finite world. Such a position meant that human perception and reason were key to encountering the divine. In the view of the philosophers, the human intellect was able to draw conclusions about and come to an understanding of G-d by means of the knowledge derived from observing and studying the world in which we live, the finite world of creation. Even the prophets were human beings, but according to Maimonides the prophets had developed the most advanced intellects among humankind that were capable of understanding at least the essence of the eternal divine that not only created but also stood both behind and within our finite world. On the basis of their encounter with the divine—by means of the human intellect—the prophets were able to understand, interpret, and communicate the divine will to us human beings.

But the kabbalists were hardly satisfied with a view of G-d based upon human perception, reasoning, analogy, and deduction as the means to understand the transcendent presence of G-d in the heavenly realm. The kabbalists were fundamentally interested in the means by which the transcendent, infinite, and heavenly presence of G-d manifested immanently in the finite world, as well as in the means by which finite human beings and creation at large embodied the heavenly divine, perceived it within themselves and the world at large, and consequently acted upon its qualities and expectations. For the kabbalists, the interrelationship between the infinite, supernal G-d and the finite, tangible world of creation was a two-way street, a dialogue, and an experience of encounter, and they set out to uncover the nuances by which the divine personality took on its various layers and aspects so that its different qualities might find expression in the world and motivate humans

8. Tishby, *Wisdom*, 1:229–305.

to establish relationship with the divine. Consequently, the interrelationship between the Ein Sof, the infinite and supernal transcendent presence of G-d in the heavens, and the Shekhinah, the tangible, immanent presence of G-d in the finite world, is key to kabbalistic thinking in the Zohar.

Zohar 2:239a presents a discourse on the nature of the Ein Sof and Ayin, "Nothingness."[9] The discourse is based on a reading of the whole burnt offering in Lev 1, and it begins with R. Eleazar's question to R. Shimon bar Yohai concerning the heights to which the attachment of the will of the priests, the Levites, and the people of Israel at large might extend while the whole burnt offering is burned on the temple altar before the holy of holies as a gift to G-d. R. Shimon answers that their attachment extends all the way to the Ein Sof, which is actually beyond any concept of beginning or end in the finite world. The Ein Sof is kept secret from human experience in relation to the will of wills, i.e., G-d. But the Ayin or supernal nothing does entail beginning and end. Consequently, the Ein Sof, being closest to G-d, reveals nothing of the divine presence.

A discourse from the Tikkunei Hazohar (Zohar 1:22b) begins with R. Shimon bar Yohai's quote of Deut 32:39, "See now, I, even I, am He, and there is no god with Me."[10] Such a quote points to G-d as the cause of all causes, suggestive of Aristotelian philosophy; but R. Shimon points out that this is the first cause before all the prior things. Consequently, G-d's statement in Gen 1:26, "Let us make a human in our image," indicates not one but two, insofar as some aspect of G-d stands beyond G-d's capacity to create and is therefore necessary to authorize the creation that the other will carry out. As R. Shimon's companions consider the matter, they recognize that something caused the first sefirah, the Keter Elyon, to create the first human being. R. Shimon then points out to them that the cause above the Keter Elyon must be the cause of all causes, which in the larger context of the Zohar can be nothing other than the Ein Sof, the infinite nature of G-d, which stands beyond the Ten Sefirot that manifest divine presence in the world of creation.

A paragraph from the Raya Mehemna in Zohar 3:225a begins with statements that G-d understands all, but there is none that understands G-d.[11] Such a conception of G-d is inherent in the practice of never addressing G-d by the Divine Name (the letters *yod*, *he*, *vav*, and *he*) nor by any other name

---

9. Tishby, *Wisdom*, 1:257.
10. Tishby, *Wisdom*, 1:258–59.
11. Tishby, *Wisdom*, 1:259.

that might be applied to G-d and thereby make it possible for G-d to be known. G-d is deep so that no light can reach G-d without going dark first; but G-d encompasses all of the world and fills the entire world, though none fill G-d. Throughout this paragraph, this aspect of G-d is clearly identified with the Ein Sof.

A selection from the second preface of the Tikkunei Hazohar (17a–b) focuses on the conduct of the world through the sefirot.[12] Elijah, the prophet who does not die but ascends to the heavens in a fiery chariot (2 Kgs 2), begins the discourse with statements directed to G-d as Master of the Worlds. Elijah states that G-d is one, but not in number, the highest of the high, the secret of all secrets, and in a slam against the philosophers, that G-d is beyond the reach of all human thought. Elijah identifies G-d as the creator of the Ten Sefirot that conceal G-d as the Ein Sof from all humankind, but that nevertheless enable the manifestation of the divine presence in the world of phenomena. Elijah states the sequence of the three moral sefirot— Hesed, identified with the right arm; Gevurah, identified with the left arm; Tiferet, identified with the torso—and the three material sefirot—Netzah and Hod, identified with the two legs, and Yesod, identified as the completion of the (male) body—and last of all, Malkhut, the tenth Sefirah, is here identified with the inner mouth that speaks the Oral Torah. Elijah then turns to the mental sefirot: Hokhmah, identified with the brain and inner thought, and Binah, identified with the heart that understands. He finally identifies the first sefirah, Keter Elyon, as the crown of Malkhut that declares the end from the beginning (Isa 46:10) and as the headpiece of the tefillin or phylacteries that are worn on the head at times of prayer. Elijah lauds the workings of the Ten Sefirot that enable the Ein Sof, the cause of all causes, to be manifested in the world.

The Zohar Hadash on Parashat Yitro (Venice edition, 55b–d) focuses on the acts of the Ein Sof by stating at the outset that the Ein Sof brings everything from potentiality to actuality.[13] The Ein Sof varies its deeds, but there is no variety in the Ein Sof. The Ein Sof puts the Ten Sefirot into order, but there is no order in the Ein Sof. The Ein Sof created everything with Binah, but there is none that created the Ein Sof. The Ein Sof designed everything with Tiferet, but there is none that designed the Ein Sof. The Ein Sof formed everything with Malkhut, but none formed the Ein Sof. The Ein Sof is within the Ten Sefirot in unity, but anyone who separates the constit-

---

12. Tishby, *Wisdom*, 1:259–62.
13. Tishby, *Wisdom*, 1:266–68.

uent elements of the Ten Sefirot makes a separation within the Ein Sof. The
Ein Sof unites the letters of the divine Name, binds all of the chariots of the
heavenly angels, and supports the upper and the lower worlds. The Ein Sof
is everywhere in creation, but there is no limit to the Ein Sof above, below,
or beside the world of creation. The Ein Sof is only recognizable through
the Ten Sefirot as witnessed in creation. The Ein Sof is wise, but not with
known wisdom; understanding, but not with known understanding; loving,
but not with known love; powerful, but not with known power. It is beauty
in every place, but not with known place; majesty and glory in every place,
but not with known place. It is sovereign, but not with known sovereignty;
one, but not in number. It sustains the upper and lower worlds as well as all
the worlds, even though no one sustains the Ein Sof. The Ein Sof grasps all
thought, but no thought knows the Ein Sof, and there would be no need
to think of the Ein Sof apart from humankind. Ultimately, humankind is
created with all created beings in order that human beings might recognize
G-d through the Ten Sefirot. Such an assertion corresponds with the rabbinic belief that the task of human beings is to serve as partners with G-d to
sanctify and complete the world of creation.

The Sefirot

The Sefirot, their characteristics, and the process of their emanation from
the Ein Sof receive extensive discussion throughout the Zohar.[14] The process
of emanation of the Sefirot appears in Zohar 1:15a–b, in comments on the
expression *bereshit*, often mistranslated as "in the beginning," in Gen 1:1.[15]
At the very outset of creation, the Ein Sof, here called "the King," made
engravings in the supernal purity. Such a statement indicates that the Ein
Sof introduced a concealed existence on the powers that would carry out
creation in the world; this concealed existence in turn would have existed in
the Ayin or nothingness from which creation emerged. A spark of darkness,
i.e., a concealed light, emerged in the sealed-within-the-sealed, concealed
in mist within matter, implanted in a ring with no color. The imagery here
indicates the intangible and undefinable character of the first act of creation.
Colors to provide light emerged as a basis for the later acts of creation. All of
these primary acts of creation are embedded within the expression *bereshit*,

14. Tishby, *Wisdom*, 1:269–307.
15. Tishby, *Wisdom*, 1:309–13.

"in the beginning," as the first word of the creation narrative—and indeed, of the Torah itself.

Light is an important metaphor for expressing the emanation of the Ten Sefirot, and Zohar 1:16b–17a begins its discourse on the chain of the sefirot by analyzing Gen 1:3, "And G-d said, Let there be light; and there was light."[16] The Zohar's focus on the text of creation in Gen 1:1–2:3 is important, because its argumentation indicates that it is building on the discussion of the Sefirot in Sefer Yetzirah. But instead of limiting itself to Sefer Yetzirah's conceptualization of the Sefirot as the ten utterances of G-d at creation, correlating them with the letters of the Hebrew alphabet, the Zohar appears to be interested in building upon the work of Sefer Yetzirah by defining the function and characteristics of each sefirah as well. The Zohar therefore notes that the first word of the command in Gen 1:3, *yehi 'or*, "Let there be light," is spelled with the Hebrew consonants, *yod, he, yod.* The first two consonants *yod* and *he* are also the first two consonants of the divine Name of G-d, YHWH; they refer back to G-d, the Ein Sof, as the origin of the sefirot that begin to emerge by means of the Keter Elyon (Most High Crown), which represents the divine will. But as noted in the discussion of the sefirot above, Keter Elyon is only the first of the three mental sefirot. Consequently, the passage argues that the second *yod* in *yehi* ("Let there be") must refer to Hokhmah (Wisdom), the second of the mental sefirot. Insofar as the first *yod* and *he* refer back to G-d, the second *yod* must refer to some aspect of G-d. The form of the Hebrew letter *yod* is often described as a point. By referring to the second *yod* as a primal point, the Zohar asserts that Hokhmah must represent the primal point through which light is conveyed into the world by means of Hesed (Fidelity, Love, Mercy), the first of the three moral sefirot. The light of Hesed in turn brought about the darkness of Gevurah (Power), the second of the moral sefirot; and then Tiferet (Beauty) had to emerge as the third of the moral sefirot to maintain the balance between Hesed and Gevurah. The creation of the letters of the Hebrew alphabet coincided with the creation of Hesed as light and Gevurah as darkness; the letters are the means to engrave the Torah, to introduce YHWH's Torah into the world, and thus to bring light to that world. Insofar as Hesed and Gevurah are held in balance by Tiferet, Tiferet functions as the center of the sefirotic system, and so it brings about the creation of Yesod (Foundation), the third sefirah of the material sefirot. The statement in Gen 1:4, "And G-d saw that the light was good," is associated with the central role of Tiferet. Tiferet, the central

16. Tishby, *Wisdom*, 1:313–18.

pillar, was then able to bring about Netzah (Endurance, Dynamism) and Hod (Majesty, Stability) as the right and left pillars of the material world, which Yesod in turn holds in balance. As the ninth sefirah, Yesod then can channel into the tenth sefirah, Malkhut (the sovereignty of G-d) or Shekhinah (the presence of G-d), in the finite world of creation.

One aspect of the emanation of the sefirot that manifest the Ein Sof, the infinite character of G-d, as the Shekhinah or presence of G-d is the dimension of color. Color in and of itself is an ideal, intangible element in the world of experience. Zohar 2:23a–b addresses this issue in a discourse by R. Shimon with his son R. Eleazar and R. Abba. The discourse begins with R. Eleazar's question to his father about Exod 6:3, "And I appeared to Abraham, Isaac, and Jacob, but by My Name YHWH I did not make myself known to them."[17] R. Eleazar wants to know why the passage reads, "And I appeared," as opposed to "And I spoke." R. Shimon's response focuses on the verse as an indication of the dimensions of color in the revelation of G-d. He associates the supernal colors with the revelation of the name El Shaddai, instead of YHWH, and indicates that there are four of them, citing Dan 12:3, "And the perceivers shall shine as the brightness (*zohar*) of the firmament; and they that turn the many to righteousness, as the stars for ever and ever." By pointing to the brightness (*zohar*) that stands above the firmament, R. Shimon signals the heavenly nature of the colors that are revealed to the ancestors, Abraham, Isaac, and Jacob, in the finite world below. The colors may be seen in heaven, but they do not shine below. One is revealed as the light that shines, and the other three are sealed. The three sealed colors are associated with the eye, including the white sclera, the black pupil, and the color of the iris. The light that shines is associated with the Name, YHWH, and revealed by means of the mirror or speculum that shines (b. Yeb. 49b). R. Shimon explains that one may perceive this supernal light by closing one's eyes and witnessing the points of light that then appear in the colors visible to the closed eye. Such light then provides a hint of the eternal presence of G-d or Ein Sof that will be manifested as Shekhinah or Malkhut in the finite world of creation.

Thought, voice, and speech are also intangible elements of the world of creation which, even though unseen, are nevertheless indispensable to motivating action in the finite world of creation. Zohar 1:246b focuses on the interrelationships of these qualities.[18] The passage begins by quoting Gen

17. Tishby, *Wisdom*, 1:322–24.
18. Tishby, *Wisdom*, 1:325–26.

49:21, "Naphtali is a hind sent forth; he gives beautiful words," and Song 4:3, "Your speaking is comely." These verses illustrate the principle that speech and the words it conveys derive from voice, and voice derives from thought in order to give expression to thought. Thought, i.e., Hokhmah (Wisdom), is the beginning of everything; it extends into Binah (Understanding), by which thought is expressed through voice and speech and thereby is conveyed into the world. Such a conception builds upon the teachings of the Sefer Yetzirah, which identifies the Ten Sefirot as the ten speeches of G-d that produced the world of creation in Gen 1:1–2:3. The Zohar here attempts to explain the teachings of Sefer Yetzirah by identifying the abstract principles of the divine that are then manifested in the world by means of the speech that ultimately derives from the thought of the Ein Sof.

One of the essential concepts of the Zohar is the dialectical interrelationship between two ideal opposites, e.g., how good is defined in relation to evil, and evil in relation to good, and the essential combination of the two ideals in any finite manifestation in creation. An example might appear in the experience of a flood, which is destructive and therefore evil on the one hand, but also good because the provision of water sustains creation. Zohar 3:65a–b takes up this issue with a discourse on the names of G-d, Elohim and YHWH.[19] The name YHWH generally conveys divine mercy in Jewish tradition; Elohim, judgment. But both aspects of G-d are often conveyed together. The principle is illustrated in R. Shimon's quotation to his son R. Eleazar from Deut 4:39, "Know this day, and lay it to your heart that YHWH is Elohim." R. Shimon explains the principle by referring to instances in which the written name YHWH is read aloud as Elohim. For example, when the words *Adonai YHWH* ("My L-rd YHWH") are written together (e.g., Ezek 2:4), the phrase is read aloud as *Adonai Elohim* ("My L-rd G-d"). The word *Adonai* ("My L-rd") is generally read in place of the ineffable Name YHWH, but wherever Adonai is written as a title along with the Name, YHWH must be read aloud as Elohim instead, to avoid confusion from repeating Adonai, Adonai ("My L-rd, my L-rd"). In R. Shimon's discourse, this practice illustrates the interrelationship between the two names, Elohim and YHWH, and likewise the interrelationship between the two concepts, Judgment and Mercy, that the two names represent. This principle then explains the interrelationships between the ideal sefirotic opposites that are held together by a balancing principle: Keter Elyon (the Crown of the Most High, signifiying the divine will) holds in balance Hokhmah (Wis-

19. Tishby, *Wisdom*, 1:344–47.

dom) and Binah (Understanding); Tiferet (Beauty) holds in balance Hesed (Fidelity, Mercy) and Gevurah (Power, Judgment); and Netzah (Endurance, Dynamism) and Hod (Majesty, Stability) are held together by Yesod (Foundation) to produce the ideal balance of qualities that then manifest Malkhut (Kingship) or Shekhinah (the presence of G-d) in the finite world.

The metaphor of sexuality and love is also a key concept in the Zohar, insofar as sexuality and love give human beings the capacity to serve as creators on analogy with G-d's capacity for creation. Love and sexualities are intangible aspects of human existence by which to understand both the human and divine wills and their capacities to create. Indeed, the Song of Songs, with its celebration of sexual love between human beings, is generally read in Judaism as a portrayal of the relationship between G-d and Israel, due in large measure to prophetic texts that speak about the divine marriage between G-d and Israel (e.g., Isa 54; Jer 2; Ezek 16, 20; Hos 1–3; Zeph 3:14–20). Zohar 2:146a–b examines the role that love and sexuality play in the interrelationship between G-d and Israel by focusing on the kiss as metaphor for that relationship.[20] The passage begins with a quotation of Song 1:2, "Let him kiss me with the kisses of his mouth," an expression of the woman's desire for her male lover in the Song of Songs. The passage follows immediately by asking what Solomon, the traditional author of the Song of Songs, meant by introducing such words of love between the upper and the lower worlds, i.e., between G-d and Israel. The passage notes that kisses are given by the mouth, through which the spirit is also conveyed, and the two spirits of the lovers are thereby intertwined by the act of kissing. This image becomes the metaphorical basis for understanding the emanations of G-d as intangible aspects of the Ein Sof conveyed to the finite world of creation and the role of Israel within that creation. Consequently, the metaphor of the kiss conveys the presence of the divine emanation of the Ten Sefirot within each human being and the world of creation at large. Zohar 3:61b–62a extends the metaphor of the kiss into one of sexual intercourse, quoting Gen 2:10, "And a river goes out from Eden to water the garden," to describe how the divine sefirot are introduced into the finite world of creation.[21] The passage draws upon the male imagery of the ninth sefirah, Yesod, as a penis uniting with the tenth sefirah, Shekhinah, imaged as female, in the culminating act that manifests the divine presence in the finite world of creation.

20. Tishby, *Wisdom*, 1:364–65.
21. Tishby, *Wisdom*, 1:365–66.

The Shekhinah

The Hebrew term *Shekhinah*, literally "Dwelling," conveys the divine presence of G-d in the world of creation.[22] It is also used for the tenth sefirah in kabbalistic literature. The Hebrew term *Malkhut*, "Sovereignty," is also employed for the tenth sefirah, insofar as when the divine presence appears in creation, it establishes divine sovereignty in that world, sanctifying and perfecting creation. Both nouns are grammatically feminine, so they can convey the feminine aspects of G-d at the culmination of the process of emanation as well as the feminine aspect of Israel in relationship with G-d. Insofar as the ninth sefirah, Yesod (Foundation), is generally identified with the male penis, the unification of Yesod and Shekhinah/Malkhut is generally identified metaphorically as a sexual union of the sefirot, or more specifically a sexual union between G-d and Israel that points to Israel as the means by which divine holiness is manifested in the world. Clearly, the sexual imagery of Song of Songs stands behind such a conceptualization of the relationship among the sefirot and between G-d and Israel. Such imagery enables the kabbalists to conceive of Israel as a bride or partner of G-d in creation whose task it is to complete and thereby sanctify the finite world of creation according to the will of G-d, the Ein Sof, as expressed in the revelation of divine Torah.

The Zohar employs conventional gender associations between women and flowers as it takes the imagery of flowers in the Song of Songs to elaborate the role of Israel as the bride of YHWH, based not only on the language of the Song of Songs itself, but also on the conceptualization of Israel as the bride of G-d in the prophetic literature, e.g., Isa 54; Jer 2; Ezek 16, 20; Hos 1–3; Zeph 3:14–20. Such a conceptualization is evident in Zohar 1:1a, which begins with R. Hezekiah quoting Song 2:2, "as a lily (*shoshanah*) among thorns."[23] The Hebrew word *shoshanah* (whence the English name Susan) clearly refers to a flower, sometimes understood as a lily and sometimes as a rose. Here, R. Hezekiah identifies the lily with the congregation of Israel and focuses on the colors of the lily as metaphors for the principles of Judgment and Mercy that are associated with Israel. Just as the colors of the lily are both red and white, so judgment (red, for blood) and mercy (white, for purity) convey these concepts in relation to Israel. But the metaphor is not limited only to color. The lily has thirteen petals, which are then correlated

22. Tishby, *Wisdom*, 1:371–87.
23. Tishby, *Wisdom*, 1:391.

into the thirteen attributes of mercy that G-d extends to Israel, to protect the bride. The number thirteen is derived from Gen 1:1–2 in which thirteen words appear between the first and second instances of the word *Elohim*. Those thirteen words, which portray the process of creation, are then explained as an expression of G-d's mercy for Israel in the world of creation. Five leaves surround the petals of the lily, referring to the five gates of salvation G-d makes available to Israel. The number five is derived from the five words that appear between the second and third mentions of Elohim in Gen 1:2–3. The passage then cites Ps 116:13, "I will lift up the cup of salvation," to indicate the five fingers of the hand that lifts the cup of salvation, which in turn correlate with the five leaves that enclose the lily and thereby offer it salvation.

A second passage, in Zohar 1:221a, also focuses on the flower imagery of the Song of Songs to portray allegorically the Shekhinah or divine presence of G-d in the finite world of creation.[24] The passage begins with R. Shimon's quotation of Song 2:1, "I am a rose (*havatzelet*) of Sharon, a lily (*shoshanah*) of the valleys," to portray the community of Israel as the bride of G-d. The metaphor conveys how beloved the assembly of Israel is to G-d. As G-d blesses Israel, so Israel sings its praises for G-d, as indicated by the term *Sharon*. Sharon normally refers to the flat coastal plain to the south of Akko and modern Haifa, west of the hill country of Ephraim and Manasseh in the land of Israel. But the passage takes the term *Sharon* as derived from the root of *shir*, meaning "to sing." The passage therefore understands the designation "rose of *Sharon*" to be a reference to Israel's capacity to sing the praises of G-d in the Jerusalem Temple, where the Psalms constitute a major portion of the Jewish worship designed to praise G-d. The passage likewise takes the imagery of the rose of Sharon as one of well-watered fertility, recalling the waters of the river in Eden that were understood as a sexual metaphor for the emanation of the sefirot and the manifestation of the Shekhinah in the world; here the union is between G-d and Israel, as noted above. The changing colors of the Yellow Rose and the Red or White Lily then convey the changing dimensions of G-d's relationship with Israel for both Mercy and Judgment.

The role of the Shekhinah is sometimes portrayed in the Zohar in gendered expectations of the role of the wife to provide food for her husband. This is the case in Zohar 3:97a, from the Raya Mehemna, which discusses the presentation of the sheaf offering at the temple.[25] The passage begins

24. Tishby, *Wisdom*, 1:391–92.
25. Tishby, *Wisdom*, 1:396–97.

with a reference to Lev 23:11, "And he shall wave the sheaf." The offering indicates the purity of the relationship between husband and wife insofar as the offering and the priests who present it must be purified to appear before G-d in the holy temple. Therefore the metaphorical portrayal of the purity of the wife's offering to G-d points to her, i.e., Israel, as an ideal bride of G-d, in contrast with women who pursue men other than their husbands.

But the reality of the divine relationship between G-d and Israel includes the destruction of the Jerusalem Temple and the exile of the people of Israel, first by the Babylonians in 587–586 BCE and later by the Romans in 70 CE. Zohar 1:202b–203a portrays the problem of exile in a discourse that draws heavily on Isa 22.[26] It portrays the people going to the rooftops of Jerusalem to celebrate the deliverance of the city from the Assyrians, likely following the withdrawal of Assyrian forces from Jerusalem in 701 BCE, when King Hezekiah was left on the throne while the Assyrian King Sennacherib pursued Hezekiah's enemy, Prince Merodach Baladan of Babylonia. R. Hezekiah begins the discourse by quoting Isa 22:1, the oracle concerning the Valley of Vision: "What ails you now that you have gone up entirely to the roofs?" Although the historical meaning of the oracle is linked to the deliverance of Jerusalem in 701 BCE, the Zohar's understanding of Isa 22 indicates the Babylonian destruction of the city. The presumption of destruction introduces the portrayal of the Shekhinah of G-d going about the country to mourn the losses among the people, here illustrated by the reference to Jer 31:15, "Thus says the L-rd, A voice is heard in Ramah, lamentation and bitter weeping, Rachel weeping for her children." The portrayal of destruction entails the cessation of the temple offerings in which Israel, the bride of YHWH, would bring food to her husband, prompting the passage to look forward to the time when Israel would be restored to the land, and the offerings—as well as the relationship that they presuppose—would be restored.

The Zohar examines the implications of the disruption of the relationship between G-d and Israel in Zohar 3:69a, which examines the problem of the Dismissal of the Queen.[27] The passage begins with R. Shimon's contention that Israel has become the lowest of the nations due to G-d's dismissal of Israel in favor of all the nations of the world. He asserts that the King, G-d, has dismissed the consort, understood as a reference to Adam's first wife, Lilith, and brought in a maidservant to take her place. He then quotes Prov 30:21–23, "For three things the earth quakes . . . for a servant when he reigns

26. Tishby, *Wisdom*, 1:406–7.
27. Tishby, *Wisdom*, 1:408–9.

... and for a servant girl that is heir to her mistress." R. Shimon then mourns for the implications of the disruption of the relationship between G-d and Israel for our understanding of G-d. He states that a king without a consort is not called a king, i.e., G-d's dismissal of Israel raises questions concerning the power, righteousness, and fidelity of G-d who promised Israel an eternal covenant. He attempts to resolve the problem of G-d's abandonment of Israel by positing a restoration of the relationship, quoting Zech 9:9, "Rejoice greatly, O Daughter of Zion; shout, O Daughter of Jerusalem; look, your King comes to you; righteous and victorious is he," apparently indicating a future restoration of the relationship, as envisioned in the Prophets. Such a view posits a teleological resolution to the problem: G-d will eventually return and restore the relationship, negating the effects of the exile. But of course, the ontological problem still remains: G-d has violated the eternal covenant by not protecting Israel as promised. Just as G-d delivered Israel from Egyptian bondage, so G-d will act on Israel's behalf again. But such assertions raise questions about G-d: to what extent is G-d evil, unreliable, and powerless to deliver Israel?

The Zohar portrays G-d's mourning for Israel in Zohar 1:210a–b, where R. Hiyya begins by quoting Isa 66:10, "Rejoice with Jerusalem and be glad with her; all you that love her; rejoice with joy for her."[28] The passage describes G-d's departure at the time of Jerusalem's destruction and Israel's exile, and it also portrays G-d's return after the punishment had taken place, only to find the destruction that resulted. R. Hiyya then returns to Isa 22, quoting v. 12, "In that day, the L-rd, the G-d of Hosts, proclaimed weeping, and lamentation, and baldness, and girding with sackcloth." Such a claim indicates divine mourning for the loss of Israel as the bride of YHWH. It also appears to develop the major conclusion of the Heikhalot Rabbati, that G-d recognized that the divine decision to destroy Jerusalem and send Israel into exile was not quite right. Such a conclusion once again raises questions about G-d: was G-d wrong to impose judgment upon Israel?

The Sitra Ahra and the Problem of Evil

The problem of evil is one of the key issues of the Zohar.[29] Earlier gnostic works that played important roles in the conceptualization and develop-

---

28. Tishby, *Wisdom*, 1:409.
29. Tishby, *Wisdom*, 2:447–74.

ment of kabbalistic thought posited multiple deities that were frequently in conflict with each other for control over the world of creation. Such conflict between deities vying for power in turn led to the introduction of evil into the world. But kabbalistic thought, because it is Jewish, presupposes that there is only one G-d in the world. Consequently, kabbalistic thought holds that there can be no conflict between multiple deities, although it allows for conflict involving angels. Early kabbalistic thinkers, such as Isaac the Blind, posited that evil arose from the imbalance of the moral sefirot, i.e., Gevurah would grow to overpower its balance over Hesed, and thus he explained the existence of evil in the world. This position appears in the Zohar, perhaps in earlier layers of its composition. But later models posited in the Zohar indicated that evil arose through earlier attempts at divine emanation that failed to produce a sustainable finite world. Such models are heavily influenced by the Neoplatonic conceptualizations that influenced gnostic thought. In the Neoplatonic model, creation proceeds by the emanation of light, but that light becomes increasingly opaque as it makes its way through its levels of emanation until it ultimately becomes material, thus finite in form and character, creating a finite world. In the kabbalistic thought of the Zohar, earlier failed attempts at emanation left residue, particularly in the form of angels which had no independent existence in the world, but nevertheless caused chaos and conflict.

Insofar as kabbalistic thought presumed Jewish monotheism, evil had to be derived from G-d. As a creation of G-d, Jewish thought holds that evil, such as the *yetzer hara* or inclination to evil in human beings, serves divine purpose in directing the world. Insofar as human beings possess free will, the inclination for evil allows for the introduction of punishment, to assist humans in learning to follow and to cultivate the *yetzer hatov*, or inclination for good, in order that humans might fulfill their role of bringing about the completion and sanctification of the world. Such a teleological ethical model, of course, raises moral questions in that humans are forced to suffer punishment for wrong decisions that lead to punishment; but the conflict between teleological and ontological moral models remains unresolved, both in Jewish thought and in general ethical theory at large.

The dimensions of evil in the kabbalistic system of the Zohar became known as the Sitra Ahra, Aramaic for "the Other Side" of G-d and of creation. The Sitra Ahra is ultimately derived from the sefirot of the one G-d, but it is expressed in the form of angels that adopted a course of evil action and thereby introduced evil and chaos into the world of creation. The angel Samael is the head of the Sitra Ahra who oversees the punishment of the wicked, and who thereby introduces evil into the world in the form of punishment. Indeed, the role of Samael and his angels is to instill the fear of punishment for wrongdoing into humankind; they serve the purposes of G-d helping to protect creation from becoming compromised by evil actions. The Sitra Ahra has the authority to punish individuals, but it does not have the authority to punish the world at large.

But this model for the emergence of evil in the world runs into problems because it ultimately asserts that evil arises out of the emanation of the sefirot themselves, which are supposed to function as a force that introduces order into the world. De León apparently had some problems with this issue; the Zohar posits that there must have been some early faulty emanation from the sefirah Hokhmah that left some residue or imperfection in the world. The Zohar refers to these faulty emanations as worlds that were destroyed or kings that died. They were concealed in divine thought where they functioned as corruptions of the sefirotic system, insofar as they produced chaos from within the emanations of G-d. As these faulty worlds or kings were destroyed, they left fragments or residue within the world at large which then explains the problem of evil in the finite world. The Zohar therefore has two explanations for evil in the world. One is that it emerges from Gevurah or Judgment, and the other is that it is residue from an earlier emanation from Hokhmah.

The Zohar discusses in 3:70a the flawed emanations from Hokhmah, the sefirot of uncleanness.[30] It asserts that G-d produced ten holy crowns in the world above, identified with G-d as a flame is identified with the coal from which it burns. But it also asserts that G-d produced ten unholy crowns in the world below that are attached to the filth that comes from under the fingernail of a holy crown. Because the lower ten are flawed, they are called Wisdoms. Of the ten created, Egypt picked up nine of them, from which the Egyptians learned sorcery.

Examples of the judgmental character of the flawed residue from earlier emanations in the world appear in the Zohar's discussion of Ezekiel's vision of the throne-chariot of YHWH in Ezek 1. Zohar 2:203a–b examines the stormy wind that conveys YHWH's throne-chariot at the outset of the vision in Ezek 1:4.[31] R. Isaac first associates this with Nebuchadnezzar's destructive power unleashed against Jerusalem, and later associates it also with the wind from Elijah's vision in 1 Kgs 19:11, a wind that destroyed mountains, as well

30. Tishby, *Wisdom*, 2:482.
31. Tishby, *Wisdom*, 2:490–92.

as with the evil that will come from the north in Jer 1:14. Zohar Hadash on Yitro 38a–b returns to the imagery of the stormy cloud in Ezek 1:4 to argue that the cloud was intended to reveal secrets to those prepared to receive them.[32] But Ezekiel's statement that he saw this vision (*wa'ere*, "and I saw") is a shortened form of the verb *wa'ereh* in Ezek 1:28. The difference between them concerns the letter *he*. The absence of *he* in v. 4 indicates the lower worlds, whereas the presence of *he* in v. 28 indicates that Ezekiel was there concerned with higher worlds. The passage understands the stormy wind of Ezek 1:4, the destructive wind of 1 Kgs 19:11, and enemy from the north in Jer 1:14 as examples of husks that conceal the light within and thereby constitute flawed matter that brings about judgment and chaos in the world of creation. Raya Mehemna, in Zohar 3:227a–b, examines Elijah's images of destructive wind, fire, and earthquake in 1 Kgs 19; in each case G-d was not in them.[33] It concludes that these, too, represent the shells of a nut, husks of flawed matter, that conceal or exclude divine presence in the world and bring about chaos instead.

The forces of impurity in the Sitra Ahra exist only in the form of dross and waste, and therefore have no independent existence or life. But they nevertheless thrive and grow through the influence of human wrongdoing and thereby threaten to overturn the order of the Shekhinah or presence of G-d in the world when they grow large enough. Regarding the fertility of the world of creation infused by the Sefirot, Zohar 2:103a quotes Gen 2:10, "And a river goes out of Eden to water the garden."[34] But the "other god," a reference to the Sitra Ahra, is emasculated and lacks all desire, so it is unable to bear fruit. Any person associated with the Other Side becomes evil, insofar as that person's actions feed the Sitra Ahra, making it more powerful and therefore threatening to destroy the world of creation.

The Sitra Ahra is ruled by Samael, an angel of destruction that attempts to undermine the created order of the sefirot. He is joined by Lilith, a female demon who was the first wife of Adam in an earlier world of creation. Together, they intend to create demons to undermine world order. Some are created from persons who were to be created immediately prior to Shabbat, but the onset of Shabbat disrupted the process of creation and left these persons incomplete to become demons bent on the destruction of the world. Others were created when Adam and Cain had intercourse

32. Tishby, *Wisdom*, 2:492–93.
33. Tishby, *Wisdom*, 2:493–94.
34. Tishby, *Wisdom*, 2:517.

with female demons or when the snake in the Garden had intercourse with Eve to produce Cain.

The Zohar discusses the creation of blemished creatures in Zohar 1:47b–48a.[35] The passage begins with a citation of 2 Sam 7:14, "And I will chasten him with the rod of men and the blows of the children of men," from YHWH's oath to punish David's descendants when they do wrong, but to uphold the house of David for all eternity. The passage asks what the blows of the children of men are and concludes that they must be demons who will bring the world to ruin. The passage explains the presence of such demons in the world by stating that, while they were being created, Shabbat was sanctified, and they were left incomplete as spirit with no body. Because their creation was incomplete, the holy presence of G-d does not dwell in them; they cannot dwell in the upper world. Following the completion of Shabbat, they went out into the world in all directions; they attempt to corrupt that world with the support of human beings who commit wrongdoing.

A second female demon is Na'amah, who is considered to be the mother of all demons. R. Hiyya states in Zohar 1:55a that Na'amah was the sister of Tubal-Cain in Gen 4:22.[36] Her role is to assist Lilith in seeking the death of children, whereas Lilith attempts to kill the infants. The means to defend oneself and one's children from the threats posed by Lilith and Na'amah is to sanctify oneself in purity, so that neither of these demons can approach.

Altogether, Samael, Lilith, and Na'amah are demons or flawed angels, who take on the roles played by opposing gods in non-Jewish models of creation and conflict in the universe. But insofar as they are angels or demons who lack independent power, they do not threaten the notion of YHWH as the One G-d of Jewish kabbalistic thought expressed in the Zohar.

Creation

Creation—or more properly, cosmogony—is a central concern of the Zohar. It explains the creation of the universe as a process that takes place within the divine character of Ein Sof and that results in the establishment of a finite world of creation that stands outside of or apart from G-d.[37] Tishby correctly maintains that creation is actually a theogonic process of divine

35. Tishby, *Wisdom*, 2:535–37.
36. Tishby, *Wisdom*, 2:541–42.
37. Tishby, *Wisdom*, 2:549–60.

revelation and embodiment in the Zohar, although it is not entirely clear to what extent the embodiment of the finite world is actually separate from the divine revelation that originates from within the Ein Sof. This interrelation between the infinite revelation within the Ein Sof and the finite world of creation that allegedly exists outside of or apart from the Ein Sof remains a central problem for the Zohar; its resolution is left to later Lurianic kabbalah. The Zohar largely conceives of creation as *creatio ex nihilo* or creation out of nothing insofar as it begins in the infinite Ein Sof but manifests itself in the finite world of creation. Such a conception points to the problematic nature of creation in the Zohar as de León developed his own understanding of the process. The notion of *creatio ex nihilo* is not supported by the Hebrew text of Gen 1:1; Rashi's analysis shows that the initial Hebrew phrase, *bereshit bara' elohim et hashamayim ve'et ha'aretz, veha'aretz hayetah tohu vavohu*, could not read, "In the beginning, G-d created the heavens and the earth, and the earth was formless and void," i.e., indicating that earth was initially created as formless and void. Instead, the grammar and syntax of the Hebrew must read, "When G-d began to create the heavens and the earth, the earth was formless and void," etc. That is, the earth existed in chaotic form prior to creation. But insofar as the Zohar posits that creation takes place within the Ein Sof, the notion of *creatio ex nihilo* becomes an absolute necessity.

When related to the emanation of the sefirot from within the Ein Sof, the first three mental sefirot, Keter Elyon (Will), Hokhmah (Wisdom), and Binah (Understanding, Practical Knowledge), are identified with the Ein Sof as examples of intangible aspects of the being of G-d. The other seven sefirot—Hesed (Fidelity, Mercy), Gevurah (Power, Judgment), Tiferet (Beauty), Netzah (Endurance, Dynamism), Hod (Majesty, Stability), Yesod (Foundation), and Malkuth/Shekhinah (Divine Sovereignty/Presence)—are identified with the six days of creation and the seventh holy day, the Shabbat, when divine sovereignty and presence manifest in the finite world. Again, the interrelationships between the infinite or intangible aspects of each sefirah and its respective finite or tangible aspects remains a problem: how can both aspects exist together at once? The Zohar posits that the intangible aspects dwell in the upper or heavenly world and that the tangible aspects dwell in the lower or earthly world, but their exact interrelationship remains without full explanation. The problem is compounded by the fact that in most of the Zohar, creation takes place through a process of emanation from the Ein Sof in which the letters of the Hebrew alphabet are assembled, illuminated, and engraved, forming the conceptual bases on which finite creation takes place. But in the earlier Midrash Hane'elam, creation takes place as a series of acts by the Creator (G-d) who carries out creation outside of the divine Self in the realms of the chariot and the angels.

The later parts of the Zohar, the Raya Mehemna and the Tikkunei Hazohar, make an attempt to resolve the relationships between the infinite and finite realms. They posit four worlds in which the acts of creation take place: Atzilut (Emanation), Beriyah (Creation), Yetzirah (Formation), and Asiyah (Making). The terminology is derived from Isa 43:7, "I have created him for my glory, I have formed him; indeed, I have made him." Atzilut, or Emanation, is identified with the world of the sefirot; Beriyah, or Creation, is associated with the realm of the divine chariot, the throne of glory, the seven palaces, and other aspects of the power of the chariot. Yetzirah, or Formation, is associated with the realm of the angels, beginning with Metatron; and Asiyah, or Making, with the finite world of creation. Each aspect moves from the infinite to the finite insofar as each represents a progressive grade of embodiment or tangibility. The system represents an expression of greater nuance in the interrelationship between the intangible and tangible aspects of the world, but it nevertheless still does not explain the full interrelationship between the elements.

Zohar 2:234a–b describes the process of creation beginning with forty-two letters, corresponding to the forty-two letters employed to write the Hebrew text of *bereshit bara' elohim et hashamayim ve'et ha'aretz, veha'aretz hayetah tohu vavohu*, from the first *bet* of *bereshit* to the *bet* of *bohu* (with "and," pronounced *vavoh*).[38] When they were joined, the letters ascended to create the world above and then descended to create the world below. They are the foundation and mystery of all the worlds, indicating that they give expression to the abstract conceptualization and language that identify and therefore create the various worlds of creation.

The earlier Midrash Hane'elam posits a different process for the creation of the upper and the lower worlds. Midrash Hane'elam, in Zohar 2:20a, begins with R. Shimon's statement that human beings do not understand the true nature of the world with both its upper and lower realms.[39] He maintains that all of the worlds were created by G-d with one thought, and supports this notion by citing Ps 104:24, "With wisdom you have made them all." This quote identifies Wisdom or Hokhmah as the basis of creation by means of thought. The passage then posits that G-d's right hand created the world above, and G-d's left hand created the world below, citing Isa 48:13,

38. Tishby, *Wisdom*, 2:361–62.
39. Tishby, *Wisdom*, 2:569.

"My hand has laid the foundations of the earth, and my right hand has spread out the heavens. I call to them. They stand up together." All were created at the same time to enable the upper and lower worlds to correlate with each other. Such an understanding was apparently an early attempt by de León to posit a kabbalistic model for understanding the creation of the world; it later developed into the model presented above which looked to the letters of Gen 1:1–2 as the basis for the creation of the world.

Jerusalem and the temple serve as the holy center of creation in Jewish thought, and the Zohar reinforces this notion by identifying Jerusalem as the site of the foundation stone that supports the world of creation. Zohar 2:222a–b begins with a quotation of Ps 48:3 (2), "Beautiful in elevation, the joy of the whole earth, Mount Zion, the uttermost parts of the earth, the city of a great king," as a signal of Jerusalem's central role. R. Judah states when G-d created the world, G-d threw down a precious stone from beneath the throne of glory to serve as a foundation stone in the deep for creation of the world.[40] Three circles then expanded out from this point, symbolic of emanation. The first was clear and pure and situated above the entire earth. The second was situated around the first, but not quite as clear, although it was as clear as dust could be. The third was darkness and the coarsest form of dust. All of this was surrounded by the waters of the deep, which encompass the whole world. The first is the temple with all of its halls and palaces and Jerusalem enclosed within. The second is the holy land of Israel. And the third is all the other lands and the nations that live in them. The sea surrounds it all.

The realm of the chariot is the place just below the eighth level of heaven where G-d descends to hear the praises of Israel three times per day; it is where the mystics of the heikhalot literature ascend to the seventh level of heaven in order to appear before G-d.[41] It is the site of the throne of G-d, represented by the ark of the covenant in the holy of holies of the Jerusalem Temple, and it is borne by four angels (cf. Ezek 1), Michael, Gabriel, Uriel, and Raphael. Zohar 1:41a–45b presents a detailed description of the seven heikhalot or palaces that constitute the realm of the divine chariot. The first heikhal is associated with Exod 24:10, "Under his feet there was a kind of sapphire pavement, and like essence of heaven in purity." It includes precious light on all sides and a pavement of spirits, from which the wheels (Ophanim) are created. The second heikhal is associated with the same verse, which continues, "and like the essence of heaven in purity."

40. Tishby, *Wisdom*, 2:570–71.
41. Tishby, *Wisdom*, 2:587–95.

The spirit located here is called Zohar, "radiance," and its light is white to avoid mixing with other colors. It creates the various spirits, such as the six seraphim that surround the divine presence (cf. Isa 6). The third heikhal is called Nogah, "brightness." Its pure light creates the twenty-two letters of the Torah. The fourth heikhal includes a spirit called Zekhut, "merit," which moves all things and inscribes the three different letters of the divine name. The fifth heikhal flashes lightning in all the brilliant colors that illumine the world below, with a figure like that of a human being. The sixth heikhal includes the scarlet thread, understood to be the kiss on the lips that differentiates life and death. Moses was gathered here upon his death. The seventh heikhal has no image; it is entirely concealed, representing the holy of holies and establishing divine sovereignty and presence in the world.

The realm of the angels, who interact on behalf of the divine with the finite world, is represented in Zohar 3:217a as a realm in which the angels are all farming fire and grass that is cut down every day and yet grows back.[42] One of the roles of the angels is to sing the heavenly liturgy each day as a model for the singing of the temple liturgy by the priests and Levites. In Zohar Hadash, Parashat Yitro 39d–40a portrays Metatron, formerly known on earth as Enoch, as the chief of the angels who holds the twelve celestial keys that unlock the secrets of the Master of the Universe.[43]

The natural world then provides the arena in which the chariot and the angels interact with human beings.

Human Beings

Human beings occupy a position of primary importance in the Zohar because they play a primary role in establishing the relationship between the upper and lower worlds.[44] In rabbinic thought generally, human beings are responsible for assisting G-d in completing and sanctifying creation by means of their observance of divine Torah; and in the Zohar human beings are a primary venue for channeling the Ten Sefirot that enable the Ein Sof to manifest in the finite world of creation as the Shekhinah. By channeling the sefirot in a holy and balanced manner, human beings hold back the influence of the Sitra Ahra in the world of creation and thereby enable the world's

---

42. Tishby, *Wisdom*, 2:623–36.
43. Tishby, *Wisdom*, 2:643–45.
44. Tishby, *Wisdom*, 677–722.

completion and sanctification. Although human beings have suffered dam-age due to the sins of Adam and Eve in the Garden of Eden, it is incumbent upon them to avoid further sins by observing divine Torah in order to carry out their task.

Unlike classical rabbinic thought which views the human soul in relation to the throne of glory, which is not itself a part of the divine (b. Shab. 152b; b. Hag. 12b), the Zohar traces the soul of human beings all the way back to G-d by means of the Ein Sof. According to the Zohar, human beings have three souls, the *nephesh*, the *ruah*, and the *neshamah*. The *nephesh* is the lowest dimension of the soul, and it receives sustenance from the *ruah*. The *ruah* is the next lowest dimension of the soul, and it receives substance from the *neshamah*. And the *neshamah* is the highest dimension of the soul, which re-ceives light and sustenance from the upper world. The *nephesh* is associated with the human body of the finite world of creation; it both nourishes the body and it depends upon it for sustenance. The *neshamah*, breathed into Adam by G-d at creation in Gen 2:7, is closely connected to the divine and the upper world; and therefore it serves as the basis for human study and understanding of divine Torah. When humans understand divine Torah, they are obligated to activate their bodies into observing the divine will, implementing its teachings in the world of creation and thereby manifesting the divine Shekhinah or presence in the finite world. Although *ruah* stands between *nephesh* and *neshamah*, the Zohar has little to say about it, appar-ently because de León did not develop his understanding of *ruah* sufficiently. In sefirotic terms, the earthly *nephesh* represents Malkhut or Shekhinah, the mediating *ruah* represents Tiferet, and the divinely associated *neshamah* represents Binah. The tripartite view of the soul also has its relationship to Greek philosophy insofar as both Plato and Aristotle posited a tripartite soul. For Plato, the soul included intellect, power or anger, and desire, whereas Aristotle posited an intellectual faculty, an animal faculty, and a vegetative faculty. But the Greek philosophers did not relate their concepts of the soul to G-d like the Zohar. Rather, their concepts of the soul appear to be the models for those of Jewish philosophy, especially Maimonides.

In contrast to the later sections of the Zohar, the earlier Midrash Hane'elam holds that the soul originates not in the sefirot, but in the throne of glory as in classical rabbinic thought. Apparently, de León developed his kabbalistic understanding of the soul following the composition of this early Zoharic midrash.

Midrash Hane'elam to Bereshit, in Zohar Hadash 10b–c, begins with G-d's statement in Gen 1:24, "Let the earth bring forth a living soul after its kind."[45] This quotation provides the basis for R. Bo's observation that G-d looked and saw that Israel would one day stand to receive the holy Torah. G-d therefore hewed out all the souls of Israel from the throne of glory and made a storehouse in the upper world where all of these souls would wait in the "body of souls" until such time as they would descend to earth. This place is called the Aravot, an area of the heavens above the celestial throne of glory in the seventh heaven. Midrash Hane'elam to Bereshit further states (Zohar Hadash 10c–11a) that when the *neshamah* is blown in to the nostrils of Adam, it becomes the *nephesh hayyah* or living soul.[46] But R. Johanan states that G-d blew a *nishmat hayyah* into the nostrils of Adam (the highest human soul); if one does not study Torah, it becomes a *nephesh hayyah* (the lowest soul). Thus, Jews who study Torah possess a *nishmat hayyah* whereas those who do not possess only a *nephesh hayyah*.

Midrash Hane'elam to Ruth, in Zohar Hadash 82c–d, begins with R. Bun's quotation of Isa 26:9, "with my soul (*nephesh*), I desired You in the night, and with my spirit (*ruah*) within me I have sought You early."[47] He concludes from this that G-d gave humans two fine crowns, the *nephesh* to sustain the body by means of the commandments, and the *ruah* to stimulate the body by means of the Torah and to guide it in this world. If they are worthy enough, then a greater eminence, a *neshamah*, will be bestowed on humans to stimulate supernal wisdom for service in the upper world. By the *neshamah* and the supernal wisdom associated with it, humans are prompted to *teshuvah*, or repentance, and good deeds.

Before it descends into the finite world of creation, a soul spends thirty days in the Garden of Eden in order to see the spirits of the righteous standing row upon row.[48] This motivates the soul to take an oath to study Torah and thereby assist in the manifestation of the Shekhinah. Jewish thought maintains that human beings possess free will in that they are able to choose between *yetzer hatov*, the inclination for good, and *yetzer hara*, the inclination for evil. But the soul must be properly motivated and prepared to make its choices in life by means of the study of divine Torah and the supernal wisdom that it inculcates in the souls of human beings. Zohar 1:179a–b begins with R. Hiyya's quote of Ps 34:20 (19), "Many are the evils of the righteous, but the L-rd rescues him from them all." He goes on to state that G-d

---

45. Tishby, *Wisdom*, 2:723–24.
46. Tishby, *Wisdom*, 2:724–29.
47. Tishby, *Wisdom*, 2:729–31.
48. Tishby, *Wisdom*, 2:749–76.

provides a human with a soul in order to preserve him because, as Gen 4:7 states, "Sin crouches at the door"—the evil *yetzer* is always waiting to trap them.[49] Animals are always ready to protect themselves by running away from danger, but humans are far less able to do so because they are always tempted to pursue evil action. Whereas the evil *yetzer* is ready to join humans on the day that they are born, so that they learn to trust the evil *yetzer* and not the good *yetzer*, the righteous person through study and wisdom learns to trust the *yetzer tov* and reject the *yetzer ra* instead, thereby enabling the manifestation of the divine presence or Shekhinah into the finite world.

Sleep and dreams are important dimensions for understanding the human soul in the Zohar.[50] When a person sleeps at night, the experience is likened to death insofar as the Talmud repeatedly states that sleep is a sixtieth part of death (e.g., b. Ber. 57b). Death is associated with the Sitra Ahra, because it represents evil in the world, and also with the Shekhinah, because it is associated with Judgment (i.e., Gevurah) and appears as the Tree of Death when it is dissociated from the other sefirot. The human soul separates from the body during sleep and ascends to the Shekhinah to assess the human's actions during the day. The virtues of the soul enter the Shekhinah like semen, and she gives birth to the righteous soul once again each morning. Dreams represent the experiences of the soul during sleep. The dreams of the righteous are understood to relate the soul to the realm of the angels, and those of the wicked relate them to the realm of the demons.

Zohar 1:83a begins with R. Shimon's quote of Isa 26:9, "With my soul, I have desired You at night, and with my spirit within me I have sought You earnestly," while on a journey.[51] He explains that the soul of human leaves at night to ascend to the heavens, but he asks whether all souls ascend. He answers by stating that not everyone sees the face of G-d. If a soul is pure, it goes to the higher realms; but if it is not, it joins dimensions of impurity and does not ascend all the way. Zohar 2:121b maintains that the soul is judged during sleep as it tastes death. When it ascends, it gives an account of a person's deeds during the day. If the account indicates righteousness, the soul ascends all the way to the upper realm, but if not, its sins are recorded against it and the soul is sent back. Raya Mehemna, in Zohar 3:222a–b, teaches that a wicked person will dream of the forces of evil that come and place the evil soul in difficult situations because of its sins, whereas the righteous person

---

49. Tishby, *Wisdom*, 2:795–98.
50. Tishby, *Wisdom*, 2:809–14.
51. Tishby, *Wisdom*, 2:818–19.

will dream of the living creatures of Ezekiel's vision (Ezek 1) before the divine throne and prophetic visions of the divine.[52]

Death is when the soul leaves the body and final judgment is realized.[53] The Zohar quotes Song 8:6, "For love is as strong as death," to express the emotions and the importance of G-d's judgment concerning the soul, which is decided between Rosh Hashanah and Yom Kippur. At this point, a dying person may see visions of relatives and friends who have already passed away and wait in the beyond. If the person is righteous, they rejoice at his entry into the world beyond; but if the person is wicked, they grieve. The dying person might also see Adam and have a brief conversation with him. Adam asks why the person is leaving the world of the living and explains that he transgressed once and was punished, whereas the dying person has transgressed many times. The death of the righteous is described as a kiss when the dying person stands before the angels for final judgment. The shackles of the body are then released so that the soul may ascend and contemplate the sefirot among the angels. Midrash Hane'elam, in Zohar 1:99b, portrays R. Johanan's description of death as the twinkling of an eye. He quotes Qoh 6:6, "Though he live a thousand years twice over . . . ," to indicate that everything from the past appears only as a single day.[54]

The Roles of the Temple and Torah in the Thought of the Zohar

The temple is the holy center of creation in Jewish thought, and therefore it serves as the locus where human beings appear before the divine presence in the world.[55] It is the place of worship, offerings, and prayer as well as a place of study; divine Torah continues to be revealed there. In rabbinic thought, a heavenly temple was established corresponding to the earthly temple to facilitate establishing the relationship between the divine and the earthly realms. When the temple was destroyed, first by the Babylonians in 587 BCE and again by the Romans in 70 CE, the heavenly temple continued to function as the holy center of creation; the heavenly temple would prompt human beings to continue in their roles as partners with G-d to complete and sanctify the world of creation. Though the First Temple was

---

52. Tishby, *Wisdom*, 2:820–21.
53. Tishby, *Wisdom*, 2:831–35.
54. Tishby, *Wisdom*, 2:837.
55. Tishby, *Wisdom*, 3:867–908.

destroyed by the Babylonians, it served as a model for the reconstruction of the Second Temple. Although the First Temple had housed the ark of the covenant as a visible symbol of the presence of YHWH in the world, the ark of the covenant had disappeared and the holy of holies remained empty in the Second Temple, symbolizing the invisible and intangible presence of G-d in the world. When the Second Temple was destroyed by the Romans, the offering of animal sacrifice ceased altogether; and worship, prayer, and the study and implementation of Torah, both in the home and in the synagogue, replaced the temple ritual in Jewish practice until such time as the Third Temple might be established to complete and sanctify the world once again.

The Zohar builds upon the understanding of the temple in classical rabbinic thought by positing an even higher edifice above the heavenly temple. The tabernacle is the model for the construction of the temple; thus the tabernacle qua temple is established in both the upper and lower realms so that the earthly temple depends upon the heavenly one. But the Zohar posits a third temple above that serves as the source for the heavenly temple insofar as G-d dwells in the eighth level of heaven or Ogdoad, and only descends to the seventh level of heaven to hear the praises of Israel at times of worship. That eighth level of heaven is symbolized by the construction of the binyan or building behind the holy of holies in Ezekiel's vision of a temple yet to be built in Ezek 40–48, regarded as a Third Temple.

Zohar 2:220b–21a presents R. Shimon's discourse on the construction of the tabernacle beginning with a quotation of Gen 1:1, "In the beginning, G-d created the heavens and the earth," to illustrate the principle that creation entailed the creation of the world above and the world below.[56] He continues by stating that G-d created the world by first looking into the Torah and then by carrying out the process of creation. He states that the world is created by three principles: Hokhmah (Wisdom), Binah (Understanding), and Da'at (Knowledge), which is equated with Tiferet (Beauty). R. Shimon quotes Prov 3:19–20 to justify this point, "By wisdom He created the Heavens . . . , by understanding He created the earth, . . . and by His knowledge the depths were broken up." When G-d instructed Moses to build the tabernacle, Moses was confused because he did not know how to do it. So R. Shimon cites Exod 25:40, "See that you make them according to their pattern that is shown you on the mount." Moses studied the patterns that G-d showed him and thereby learned how to construct the tabernacle. Moses then had to account

56. Tishby, *Wisdom*, 3:909–11.

to G-d for the entire construction of the tabernacle to ensure that nothing had been left out.

The Zohar continues in Zohar 2:241a with an account of the three tabernacles, by quoting R. Jose's citation of Num 9:15, "And on the day that the tabernacle was erected the cloud covered the tabernacle, even the tent of the testimony; and in the evening there was on the tabernacle as it were the appearance of fire until morning," to ask R. Shimon why there are three instances of *tabernacle* in the verse and not a house or temple.[57] The question presupposes that the first tabernacle or dwelling is Binah, which houses Hokhmah; the second tabernacle is Malkhut, which houses the lower six sefirot from Hesed through Yesod; and the third tabernacle is the house or temple which serves as the dwelling place for Malkhut or the Shekhinah. R. Shimon then employs the model of the tabernacle, the temple at Shiloh, and the Jerusalem Temple to demonstrate the interlocking interrelationship between the three tabernacles or dwelling places of G-d, so that the divine presence could remain close to Israel.

Although the temple was the site where Israel worshiped G-d by means of animal offerings, the destruction of the temple meant that animal sacrifice was suspended, and the rituals and prayers that accompanied the sacrifices would constitute the bases of the home and synagogue worship services. Such prayer is labeled by the Talmud as worship of the heart (b. Ta'an. 2a).[58] The Zohar's understanding of worship of the heart entails foci on prayer and *kavvanah*, "intention," as bases for the human relationship with G-d. Such an understanding of prayer entails that prayer does not only constitute the visible aspects of Jewish prayer, but instead contends that true prayer comes from the innermost dimension of the human being, the manifestation of the mental, moral, and material sefirot in the human. Thus all aspects of the human being, i.e., one's thought, moral impulses, and action in the world, must be involved in prayer. In this case, *kavvanah* (intention) indicates the innermost motivation for prayer; it stems from the relationship of the human being to the Ein Sof, beginning with the Keter Elyon (Will), Hokhmah (Wisdom), and Binah (Understanding), signifying the intentional sincerity of prayer. Such intentional sincerity in prayer holds off the Sitra Ahra and makes possible the introduction of the Shekhinah into the world—and into the inner being of the human engaged in prayer. When properly motivated in the heart, prayer then manifests itself in the moral worldview of the human in question

57. Tishby, *Wisdom*, 3:911–13.
58. Tishby, *Wisdom*, 3:941–1016.

and in the actions that the human being undertakes in the world, resulting in the manifestation of the holiness of the divine presence, the Shekhinah.

The Raya Mehemna, in Zohar 2:59b–60a, maintains that the synagogue below should be built on the pattern of the celestial temple above to facilitate the ongoing relationship between the infinite G-d and the finite world of creation.[59] The synagogue then becomes the place where prayer enables the unification of Israel with G-d. Zohar 2:133b–134b focuses on the recitation of the Shema, "Hear (*shema*), O Israel, the L-rd our G-d, the L-rd is One" (Deut 6:4), as a central element of Jewish prayer; asserting the unity of G-d in turn unifies the congregation of Israel and each individual within that congregation, unifying the body with the single intention to engage the divine.[60] Likewise, Zohar 2:138b focuses on the Eighteen Benedictions of the Amidah, the central prayer of the Jewish worship service, as a means to cleave to G-d.[61] Raya Mehemna, in Zohar 3:93a, focuses on the Kedushah, the prayer in the Amidah that sanctifies the divine name.[62] The Tikkunei Hazohar, Tikkun 21, 44b–45b, contends that proper prayer enables the Shekhinah to ascend and descend like a bird feeding her young, establishing the relationship between the divine and human and thereby unifying the upper and lower realms of the world of creation.[63]

Finally, study of the Torah is a central aspect of the Jewish worship service along with prayer. [64] When the temple was destroyed and animal sacrifice suspended, Rabbinic Judaism set the reading and study of the Torah as the central act of the Jewish worship service in their place. Zohar 2:206a–b emphasizes that when the Torah is taken from the ark for reading during the worship service, the gates of heaven are opened.[65] The passage provides instructions for reading the Torah, including the proper mode of blessing the Torah and the preparation of the reader of the Torah for his task in the synagogue, to ensure the holy integrity of the act. He must prepare beforehand and read the words of the Torah exactly as Moses intended them when he wrote them down at the dictation of G-d on Mt. Sinai.

As for the interpretation of Torah, we have already discussed the need to understand the hidden or secret understanding of the Torah, in keeping

---

59. Tishby, *Wisdom*, 3:1017–18.
60. Tishby, *Wisdom*, 3:1023–29.
61. Tishby, *Wisdom*, 3:1029–30.
62. Tishby, *Wisdom*, 3:1030–33.
63. Tishby, *Wisdom*, 3:1053–56.
64. Tishby, *Wisdom*, 3:1077–1131.
65. Tishby, *Wisdom*, 3:1037–39.

with the dimensions of Sod in the Pardes or Garden of Torah interpretation.[66] Here, we may reiterate the role of Torah as sustaining the world. Zohar 1:134b–35a emphasizes this point, opening with R. Hiyya's quotation of Ps 106:2, "Who can express the mighty acts of the L-rd or declare His praise?"[67] He follows with comments about how G-d looked into the Torah to create the world and prepared repentance so that human beings could seek restoration at times when they commit sins that impede their sanctity and relationship with G-d. Such repentance is necessary because human beings were created with the special task of serving as partners with G-d to complete and sanctify the world, and the study and implementation of divine Torah is the means to carry out that task. In R. Hiyya's view, one who studies Torah sustains the world. Such study involves the entire being of the human, so that all the mind, body, and limbs are engaged to manifest divine knowledge and the holy presence of G-d, through the Shekhinah, in the world. In R. Hiyya's view, such a person is the answer to his initial question, "Who can express the mighty acts of the L-rd, or declare His praise?"

66. See "The Torah," pp. 293–300 above.
67. Tishby, *Wisdom*, 3:1123–24.

Chapter 9

Lurianic Kabbalah

Lurianic kabbalah proved to be one of the most innovative, far-reaching, and influential movements in Jewish thought and practice during the transition from the Middle Ages to Modernity.[1] Based upon the interpretation of kabbalistic thought developed by R. Isaac Luria (also known as the Ari, i.e., Ha'ahkenazi Rab Yitzhaq, 1534–1572), Lurianic kabbalah provided a compelling conceptualization and interpretation of the Zohar's understanding of the presence of G-d in the world that changed kabbalah from a largely esoteric and marginal movement in Judaism to a popular movement prompting Jews to adopt kabbalistic spiritual practice and study in anticipation of the messianic age when the messiah would appear, the temple would be reestablished, and the world of creation would be completed, with Jews reestablishing Jewish life in Jerusalem and in the land of Israel as the holy center of all creation. Lurianic kabbalah grew out of attempts by Luria and his circle of teachers and disciples, based in the Galilean town of Sefad, to interpret the Zohar and to understand the expulsion of Jews from Spain in 1492. It laid the groundwork for the emergence of Shabbetai Zevi (1626–1676) as a false but widely influential messianic figure who galvanized the Jewish people to renew their efforts to serve as partners with G-d to complete and sanctify creation. In the aftermath of the Shabbetean debacle, Lurianic kabbalah also laid the groundwork for the emergence of Hasidic Judaism as the major spiritual movement of Judaism in modern times.

1. For overviews of Lurianic kabbalah, see Gershom Scholem, *Major Trends in Jewish Mysticism* (New York: Schocken, 1961), 244–86; J. H. Laenen, *Jewish Mysticism: An Introduction*, trans. David E. Orton (Louisville: Westminster John Knox, 2001), 143–88.

Reconquista, Expulsion, and the Shattered Sparks of Spain

An understanding of Lurianic kabbalah must begin with an understanding of the Spanish expulsion of Jews from Spain in 1492.[2] Jews had lived in the Iberian Peninsula since the immediate aftermath of the Babylonian destruction of Jerusalem in 587 BCE, if not before. There is little information on Jewish life in Iberia from this time, but insofar as many scholars identify the Iberian Peninsula as ancient Tarshish, it seems likely that ancient Jews were heavily involved in trade, most likely due to their association with the Phoenicians, who first developed seagoing trade relations with most of the nations settled along the Mediterranean coast, including the Iberian Peninsula. Indeed, the term "Ships of Tarshish" may well indicate Iberia as it would have been one of the farthest destinations from Phoenicia. Jews are much better documented in Iberia during the period of the Roman Empire, since the Romans were heavily involved in Iberia, and Jews would have been especially engaged in trade during that time.

But Spain proved to be a border territory between Christianity and Islam during the Middle Ages, and the fortunes of Jews rose and fell depending on the nature of the ruling powers, whether Christian or Muslim. Following the collapse of the Roman Empire in the West, the Visigoths took control of the Iberian Peninsula. Although the Visigoths were originally pagan and opposed to the Roman Catholic Church, by 587 the Visigoth ruler Recared converted to Roman Catholicism, and he and his successors actively persecuted Jews and other non-Christian peoples in efforts to convert them to Christianity. The later Visigoth ruler Sisebut (612–620) ordered the forced conversion of babies born to Catholic and non-Catholic parents, and he also issued an edict of expulsion against the Jewish community, wishing to consolidate his rule over an entirely Christian population. A succession of Councils at Toledo called for the expulsion of Jews; the forced baptism of Jews; seizing children born to those who continued Jewish practice following conversion to Christianity; punishments for circumcision, Shabbat observance, and other Jewish practice; and other measures that were generally hostile to Jews and Judaism.

Because of the hostile stance of the Catholic Visigoth rulers of Iberia, Jews generally supported the Moorish invasion of Iberia in 711 by Tariq Ibn

2. For histories of the Jews in Spain, see Elyahu Ashtor, *The Jews of Moslem Spain*, 2 vols. (Philadelphia: Jewish Publication Society, 1973–79); Yitzhak Baer, *A History of the Jews of Christian Spain*, 2 vols. (Philadelphia: Jewish Publication Society, 1961); Haim Beinart, *The Expulsion of the Jews from Spain* (Oxford: Littman Library of Jewish Civilization, 2005).

Ziyad who brought Muslim rule to Spain. The Moorish invasion of Iberia opened what many consider to be a golden age in the history of relations between Muslims and Jews. To be sure, Muslims were the rulers of Iberia, and Jews continued in their status of Dhimmi. Nevertheless, the Moorish rulers of Iberia generally treated Jews as close allies in military, economic, political, and cultural matters. With the reign of the Ummayid ruler Abd al-Rahman I (731–788), Jews participated in the defense of the city of Toledo and many other Iberian cities. Jews from other parts of the world migrated to Iberia and formed there the foundations of Sephardic Jewish culture. Rabbinic academies were established; Jews learned to speak Arabic and participated fully in Arabic cultural life, even as they developed Jewish studies under the influence of the rabbinic academies of Islamic Babylonia. During the reign of Abd al-Rahman III (882–955), the Caliphate of Cordoba was established, and the caliph promoted intellectual life; Jews participated fully in the literary, economic, military, political, and professional life of the caliphate. During this time, a Sephardi Jewish literary culture, writing in Arabic, emerged in all fields of inquiry—literature, poetry, philosophy, science and medicine, etc.—that had much exchange and much in common with Muslim counterparts. Such intercultural cooperation would constitute what many call the golden age of Jewish life in Spain.

With the collapse of the Ummayid dynasty in the eleventh century CE, the Cordoba Caliphate also declined and disintegrated, giving way to a number of Taifa or independent principalities that controlled cities and territories in Iberia. Jews continued to thrive, but the transition marked the beginnings of Jewish decline in Iberia as well. The 1066 pogrom against the Jewish community of Granada marked a turning point as some four thousand Granadan Jews were murdered by Muslim mobs.

As the Muslim position in Iberia declined, the Christian Reconquista of Iberia gained ground. When Toledo fell to the Christians in 1085, the Muslim leaders of Seville appealed to the al-Moravides of North Africa to come to Iberia to lend support. The al-Moravides pursued a far more conservative understanding of Islam, and many Jews were forced to convert to Islam under al-Moravide rule. Nevertheless, their position softened as they absorbed more and more of the liberal Andalusian culture of Iberia, but the al-Moravides were eventually forced to withdraw as conflict and civil war continued to plague their native North Africa.

With the withdrawal of the al-Moravides, Christian forces resumed their advance into Iberia, prompting Iberian Muslims to appeal once again to North Africa for assistance. The al-Mohades responded to the Iberian request and by 1172 had conquered much of the Islamic territories of Iberia. But the al-Mohades were far more conservative than the al-Moravides as they issued decrees of expulsion for non-Muslims in both Iberia and Morocco. Jews were forced to convert or flee to Muslim lands, such as Egypt, that were more tolerant. Indeed, the family of Maimonides was forced to flee, first to Morocco and then to Egypt, even though the Rambam's father was a respected jurist in Spain. Because of the family's sojourn in Morocco, there are questions as to whether Maimonides converted to Islam. He later ruled that converts to Islam should leave the oppressing country at their first opportunity and revert to Judaism once they reached more tolerant lands. Maimonides himself eventually made his way to Egypt where he served as physician to the Kurdish Muslim ruler, Salah-edh-Din (Saladin), as well as chief rabbi of the Egyptian Jewish community.

As the Christian Reconquista gained ground, the Catholic rulers of Castile and León continued to persecute Jews without mercy, much like the al-Mohades. But as the Christian conquest of Iberia progressed, Christian rulers began to recognize the utility of having Jewish support, and frequently gave Jews greater privileges even as persecution of Jews also continued. Alfonso VI, the conqueror of Toledo in 1085, gave many privileges to Jews, including service in his armies. But the opposition of Pope Gregory VII, who warned against giving Jews authority over Christians, prompted many to resist Alfonso's policies. As Alfonso's health declined, anti-Jewish riots broke out in Toledo, resulting in the massacres of thousands of Jews and the conversion of thousands more. Later Christian monarchs sometimes gave privileges to Jews, but for the most part, the Christian rulers of Spain pursued a decidedly anti-Jewish policy. Although a Crusade called in Spain to support Christian warfare against the Muslims relied heavily on Jewish support, following the holy war of 1212 in Toledo, Christian forces attacked the Jewish community of Toledo until Alfonso VIII checked his renegade supporters with his own knights. Although Alfonso VIII continued to give privileges to the Jews in recognition of their support, the rising tide of anti-Jewish sentiment in Christian Spain would ultimately prevail.

During the reigns of Ferdinand III (1199–1252), who united Castile and León, and James I (1208–1276), ruler of Aragon, Jews were compelled to wear a yellow badge as they did in France to identify them as Jews to the majority Christian population. The purpose of the badge was allegedly to protect them from violence, but more often than not, it actually encouraged attacks. With the papal bull of Pope Innocent IV in 1250, Jews were forbidden to build synagogues, eat and drink with Christians, live under the same roof as Christians, employ Christian servants, use the same bath as Christians, or proselytize among Christians. Spanish Christian kings began to think of Jews as their property, and they acted accordingly to control and restrict the lives of Jews in their realms.

The growing anti-Jewish sentiment in Christian Spain led to more massacres in 1366 when a number of Jewish communities were attacked and their inhabitants killed. Although the interest in unifying Iberia under a single religion, either Christianity or Islam, served as a general background for the persecution of Jews during this period, other factors also played a role. The Christian kingdoms in Iberia during this period were generally disunited principalities: Aragon, Castile, Portugal, León, Navarre, and others, each with its own monarch. These principalities were often competing with each other as well as fighting against Muslims, conditions that reinforced their interests in promoting unity amongst their populations. Furthermore, Jews had attained high ranks in governmental roles in many of these kingdoms; this provoked jealousy on the part of the working-class population. The fact that Jews were often used as tax collectors often exacerbated hard feelings toward Jews, especially when coupled with New Testament imagery of Jews as tax collectors, Christ-killers, hypocrites and vipers, etc. The Crusades, beginning in 1096, and the outbreak of the Great Plague in 1346 also had deleterious effects on Iberian Jews, as these events often resulted in charges against Jews: infidelity and Christ-killing in the case of the Crusades and plots in league with the Devil to poison the water of Europe in order to kill Christians in the case of the Plague, as well as outbreaks of rioting and pogroms that incited the murder of thousands and the forced conversions of thousands more. Many Jews forcibly converted to Christianity would continue to practice Judaism in secret, resulting in charges and executions on the part of the Inquisition of the Roman Catholic Church.

Massacres occurred once again in 1391 as Ferrand Martinez, the confessor of Queen Leonora and Deacon of Seville, began to incite violence against the Jewish communities of Spain in an effort to convert them to Christianity. Many thousands of Jews died in mob riots when Martinez and his supporters broke into synagogues during times of worship with crosses in hand and mob support to demand immediate conversion to Christianity. Thousands more were forcibly converted. The violence spread from Seville to cities throughout the Iberian Peninsula, and many Jews began to leave for more hospitable lands in North Africa and elsewhere to escape the growing anti-Semitism. In the aftermath of these riots, Jews were required once again to wear the yellow badge and they were forbidden to use Christian names so that they could be publicly identified as Jews and suffer discrimination and persecution.

In the aftermath of the 1391 anti-Jewish riots, Martinez called on the Inquisition of the Roman Catholic Church, which was charged with identifying apostates from Christianity, to step up its efforts to investigate Jews who were forcibly converted to Christianity but continued to practice Judaism in private. Such persons were known in Spanish as *conversos* or converts, but more popularly they were called *marranos* or pigs to indicate Christian outrage at infidelity to the Church. Thousands were investigated and put on trial, often ending in a conviction with the punishment of death.

In 1469, King Ferdinand of Aragon and Queen Isabella of Castile married and by 1479 their united kingdoms formed the basis for a united Spanish kingdom. They continued to pursue the war of reconquest against Muslims in the south and they stepped up their persecution of Jews, both from a desire to rid their lands of non-Christian presence and out of fear that Jews would join the Muslims in fighting against Christian armies. In Toledo and other cities under Christian control, Jews were forced to live in separate barrios or ghettos to ensure that they would not mix with Christians. In 1481, the first Auto de Fe, Act of Faith, took place when six converso men and six converso women were burned at the stake for apostasy against the Church. The purpose behind the burning was so that the conversos could demonstrate true repentance and purge themselves of their alleged sins. In 1483, Thomas Torquemada, Queen Isabella's Dominican confessor, was appointed to lead the Inquisition in Spain after converso Jews were caught celebrating Passover. Torquemada himself was rumored to be the descendant of converso Jews, but this rumor has never been confirmed. With Torquemada's appointment, the Inquisition proceeded in earnest. Thousands of Acts of Faith followed as converso Jews were purged by the Roman Catholic Church in Spain.

But Torquemada found that the Inquisition was failing as case after case was found of converso Jews who continued to practice Judaism following their conversions to Christianity. Torquemada believed that such heresy was prompted by the continuing presence of Jews who had not converted to Christianity, who would attempt to sway the conversos to return to Jewish practice. As a result, Torquemada began to demand the complete expulsion of Jews from Spain, eliminating in turn the problem of heresy. But one of the realities of the situation of King Ferdinand and Queen Isabella was that they needed Jewish support as they continued to prosecute their war against the Muslims in the southern portions of the Iberian Peninsula.

Jews were frequently tax collectors and wealthier Jews were frequently the sources of funds for the Spanish monarchs. Consequently, Ferdinand and Isabella refused Torquemada's demands that they expel the Jewish population of Spain; they needed the Jews too much to expel them even as they continued to persecute them. But even while Ferdinand and Isabella refused Torquemada's demands, further charges of heresy came forward. In 1490, for example, accusations were made against a group of conversos who allegedly used a consecrated host to bring about the downfall of Christianity. In addition, they were charged with crucifying a young Christian boy. The charges were demonstrably false and typical of the anti-Jewish charges so frequently made during the Middle Ages and the transition to early Modernity; but in the heavily charged anti-Semitic climate of the time, such charges were taken seriously and greatly influenced public opinion concerning Jews.

On January 2, 1492, Granada fell to the forces of Ferdinand and Isabella and effectively ended the war. The Iberian Peninsula was now entirely under Christian rule, and Ferdinand and Isabella no longer needed the Jews. They consequently issued an edict of expulsion against the Jews of Spain on March 30, 1492, ordering the removal of all Jews from Spain by July 30, 1492. The edict was protested by Abraham Senior and Isaac Abrabanel, two Jews who heavily financed Christian efforts to defeat Muslim control of Iberia. Abrabanel offered a substantial sum of money to persuade Ferdinand and Isabella to give up their persecution of Jews. But while Abrabranel was conferring with the royals, Torquemada burst into the room carrying a huge cross, which he threw to the floor at the feet of the king and queen of the country, shouting that Judas Iscariot sold out Christ for thirty pieces of silver. Will you now sell him for 300,000 ducats of silver? Here he is, take him and sell him. Ferdinand and Isabella refused Abrabanel's offer and the order of expulsion went forward.

Although the expulsion order was scheduled for July 30, 1492, it actually took effect on August 2, 1492, which coincidently was the ninth day of Av, the traditional date of mourning in the Jewish calendar for the destruction of both the First and the Second Temples as well as other disasters that had taken place in Jewish history. The Sephardi or Spanish Jewish community was compelled to leave Spain for destinations throughout the Mediterranean basin: Turkey, the Middle East, North Africa, as well as the Netherlands, England, and even the new world of the Americas. Many conversos were crew members on Christopher Columbus's ships for his voyage of discovery of the New World. Indeed, Hebrew inscriptions in his ship's log have led to speculation that Columbus himself may have been a converso or a descendant of conversos, although no definitive answer to this question has been forthcoming.

The Jewish world was shocked by the Spanish expulsion of its Jewish community. The Sephardi or Spanish Jewish community had been considered the leading Jewish community in the medieval Jewish world for centuries. It was known for its high culture, intellectual life, and its political influence during its so-called golden age and beyond, during which Jews frequently attained high office, political power, and economic success. The collapse of the Spanish Jewish community would be analogous to the collapse of the American Jewish community if such a development were to occur in modern times. Sephardi Jews spread throughout the Jewish world and took root once again wherever they could, bringing a very distinctive Jewish rite of worship and two languages, the Ladino dialect, a medieval form of Spanish spoken by Jews, analogous to the Yiddish or Germanic dialects spoken by Jews of Ashkenazi origin, and Judeo-Arabic, which had become the language of Jewish intellectual and cultural life in Spain. Many Jews also fled to the Americas in an effort to escape the reach of the Spanish Inquisition and the later Portuguese expulsion of 1497. Crypto-Jews in the Portuguese colony of Recife, Brazil, for example, rejoiced and openly resumed their Jewish lives when the Dutch conquered the colony. But when the Portuguese reconquered Recife from the Dutch, the Portuguese Jews were compelled to leave Recife in 1654 for the Dutch colony of New Amsterdam in North America. Although the Dutch permitted Jews to live in New Amsterdam, the Dutch governor, Peter Stuyvesant, placed restrictions on the Jews, such as refusing to allow them to bear arms in the defense of the colony. When the British captured the colony in 1664, they renamed it New York and lifted the restrictions on the Jews.

Essentially, Jews regarded the Spanish expulsion as another instance of Jewish exile, analogous to the Babylonian Exile following the destruction of the First Temple in 587 BCE and the exile of Jews from Judea following the failures of both the Zealot revolt in 66–74 CE, which saw the destruction of the Second Temple, and the Roman genocide against the Jewish population of Judea following the failure of the Bar Kokhba revolt in 132–135 CE, which saw, in addition to the destruction of Jewish life in the land of Judea, the Roman attempt to remove any memory of Jewish life in the land by renaming it Palestine.

Regathering the Sparks in Safed with Cordovero and Karo

The town of Safed (pronounced Tzephat) in the upper Galilean hill country was the site where Lurianic kabbalah originated.[3] Safed is not mentioned in biblical sources, and it is only mentioned briefly in the Jerusalem Talmud as a site from which fire signals were sent to announce the new moons and festivals in the Second Temple period. Safed comes to prominence in the twelfth century CE as the site of a Crusader fortress, and in the sixteenth century as the site of the Jewish community in which Lurianic kabbalah originated. It is also known as the site near where R. Shimon bar Yohai, the alleged author of the Zohar, and other renowned rabbinic figures are buried.

Although there was a Jewish community in Safed from the time of the Crusader period on, the Jewish population of Safed began to grow during the early sixteenth century under Ottoman Turkish rule. Following his defeat of the Mamluk sultanate in Egypt in 1516–17, the Ottoman Sultan Selim incorporated the former Mamluk territories into his empire. Safed became the capital of the administrative district within the larger province of Damascus. Safed was already an important hub in the growing textile trade of the time, and Selim ordered Egyptian Jews who were engaged in the textile industry to relocate to Safed in order to produce textiles and to ship them to domestic and foreign markets. Insofar as Safed was the site of R. Shimon bar Yohai's burial, it attracted the interest of many kabbalistic thinkers who made their living in the textile trade, and Safed began to develop as a center for the study of kabbalistic thought. In the aftermath of the Spanish expulsion in 1492, many Jews in Safed were refugees from Spain; and the question of why G-d had exiled the most prominent, cultured, and highly educated Jewish community in the world was paramount.

Safed therefore became the site of numerous Jewish study circles; as scholars came to Safed, they began to attract circles of disciples who wanted to study with them. Among them were R. Joseph Karo (Caro), R. Moses Cordovero, R. Isaac Luria, and R. Hayim Vital.

R. Joseph ben Ephraim Karo (1488–1575) is best known as the author of the Shulkhan Arukh, a semi-popular compendium of halakha that contin-

---

3. See esp. Solomon Schechter, "Safed in the Sixteenth Century: A City of Legists and Mystics" in *Studies in Judaism*, Second Series (Philadelphia: Jewish Publication Society of America, 1908), 202–85.

ues to serve as an authoritative text in traditional Jewish circles.[4] Karo was likely born in Toledo, Castile, in 1488, although some authorities maintain that he was born in Portugal. His family was forced to leave Spain following the 1492 Edict of Expulsion by King Ferdinand and Queen Isabella. They initially moved to Portugal, but Portugal expelled its Jews in 1497, and the family moved on to Turkey, where Karo lived for about forty years. Karo became an expert in Jewish law, first studying with his own father and later with other teachers, including R. Solomon Molcho, a descendant of conversos who returned to Judaism and declared himself to be the messiah. Molcho was convicted of heresy by the Inquisition and burned at the stake in 1532, prompting Karo to declare his own longing for martyrdom, although Karo lived to be eighty-seven and died of natural causes. Other teachers and colleagues included R. JosephTaitazak, a prominent Sephardi talmudic scholar and kabbalist from Salonica, and R. Solomon Alkabetz, a kabbalistic authority known especially for his composition of Lekhah Dodi (Come, My Beloved), a metaphorical hymn sung at the outset of Shabbat evening services to welcome the Shabbat Bride into the congregation.

Karo began work in 1522 on one of his most important works, the Beit Yosef, House of Joseph, a comprehensive analysis of Jewish halakah meant to clarify the entirety of halakah for the Jewish community. The work was motivated in part by the decline of halakic studies among Sephardi Jews in the aftermath of the Spanish expulsion and the emergence of halakic treatises among the Ashkenazi community that now threatened to emerge as the leading scholarly community in Judaism. It would take Karo some twenty years to complete this work. In 1536, Karo left Turkey with the intention to settle in Safed, but he first moved to Egypt where he may have begun to study with R. Jacob Berab, a noted talmudic scholar known especially for his efforts to reintroduce traditional rabbinic ordination in Judaism. The problem was that many rabbis at the time had been conversos, or were the descendants of conversos, and the means for them to repent from their sins had to be established so that they could then receive semikhah or traditional rabbinic ordination. Karo was ordained as rabbi by Berab in 1538, but he apparently did not consider his ordination to be sufficiently authoritative. Karo apparently studied with Berab in Safed as well.

Karo became a member and eventually the head of the Beit Din or Rabbinic law court in Safed, which ruled on all aspects of Jewish life in the city.

---

4. For discussion of Joseph Karo, see esp. R. J. Zwi Werblowsky, *Joseph Karo: Lawyer and Mystic* (Philadelphia: Jewish Publication Society of America, 1980).

His role as head of Safed's Beit Din prompted him to write hundreds of rabbinic responsa to inquiries concerning proper Jewish observance; in the context of those writings he continued work on the Beit Yosef and later on the Shulkhan Arukh and his other halakic studies. Karo also served as the head of a major yeshivah or rabbinic academy in Safed with some two hundred students. His aim in writing the Beit Yosef, which he completed in 1542, although it was not published until 1555, was to provide an authoritative discussion of all issues in Jewish halakah, including the citation of all sources and discussion of competing positions as well as those recognized as authoritative. He intended to replace the halakic work of Maimonides, who offered his own interpretations of halakah without citing sources or opposing viewpoints. In doing so, he hoped to restore Sephardi scholarship to its leading role in Judaism over against the challenges that were written by Ashkenazi scholars. The Shulkhan Arukh, or Set Table, published 1564–65, was intended as a pocket summary of halakah for students, but its clarity prompted the work to be read throughout the Jewish world, and the Shulkhan Arukh is currently recognized as an authoritative halakic work throughout traditional Judaism.

Although his halakic work is most widely known, Karo was also heavily engaged in the study of kabbalah, which he saw as foundational for his halakic work. Throughout his life, Karo claimed that he was visited by a *maggid*, an angelic member of the heavenly rabbinic academy, who would come to him in dreams and other visionary experiences to teach him concerning both halakah and kabbalah. The *maggid* claimed to be a personification of the Mishnah and the Shekhinah. Karo was known to channel this *maggid* vocally when a faint voice would speak through him in rendering halakic decisions and in teaching various aspects of halakic and kabbalistic thought. Karo wrote down his various experiences of the *maggid* throughout his lifetime in a mystical diary which was eventually published under the title *Maggid Mesharim* (Preacher of Righteousness) in 1646.

Karo was one of the most prominent halakic authorities of his day, but Isaac Luria, who came to Safed while Karo was still alive and who studied briefly with Karo's student Moses Cordovero, refused to admit him to his own kabbalistic circle, apparently due to doubts concerning the interrelationship between his understandings of halakah and kabbalah. Karo consequently led his own kabbalistic circle in Safed throughout his life in the city. Karo's work in kabbalah is not particularly original, but it is an important source for understanding the state of kabbalistic thought in Safed during the sixteenth century, particularly because Luria wrote down so little of his own thoughts.

One of Karo's disciples was Moses Cordovero, who went on to become a major kabbalistic thinker in his own right.[5] R. Moses ben Jacob Cordovero (1522–1570) was the leading kabbalistic thinker in Safed prior to Isaac Luria. His birthplace is unknown, but it is presumed to be in Spain, likely in or near Cordova as suggested by his family name, Cordovero. He was a student of R. Joseph Karo and R. Solomon Alkabetz as well as a teacher of R. Isaac Luria. His background in both Jewish philosophy and kabbalah enabled him to write a succession of works that attempted to engage the interrelationships between both fields of inquiry. Significant works include the *Pardes Rimmonim* (Garden of Pomegranates, 1548), which served as a systematic introduction to kabbalistic thought and especially to the problems raised in the Zohar's understanding of G-d; *Elimah Rabbati* (Great Work of Elim, 1567–68; cf. Exod 15:27, where Elim is an oasis of twelve streams and seven palm trees), which attempts to explain the relationship between the Ein Sof and the subsequent emanations of the sefirot; *Or Yaqar* (Precious Light), a commentary on the Zohar that focuses especially on understanding the Ein Sof; and *Tomar Devorah* (The Palm Tree of Deborah, 1588), which examines the ethical aspects of the Ten Sefirot, especially how one might manifest the divine qualities in daily life. A major agenda in his work is to reconcile the differences amongst the various elements of the Zohar, particularly the basic Zohar text, the Tikkunei Hazohar, and the Raya Mehemna, which have been recognized as distinctive compositions by modern scholars. The result was a highly systematic assessment of the Zohar's teachings on the nature of G-d that served in part as the basis for Luria's ideas.

Cordovero draws heavily on philosophy in his attempts to explain the interrelationships between the Ein Sof and the sefirot that manifest the divine presence in the finite world of creation. Cordovero likens the Ein Sof to the First Mover in Aristotelian thought as understood by Maimonides. In Aristotelian thought, the First Mover is likened to G-d as the entity who sets the world of creation into motion, although the First Mover plays no other role in creation and therefore has no personal relationship with creation once it is put into motion. Maimonides modified this understanding of Aristotle's First Mover when he identified it with G-d as understood in Judaism and posited a very active relationship between G-d and creation in which G-d would intervene directly in human affairs and take a very close interest in the activities of human beings, particularly of Israel. Maimonides

5. For an overview discussion of Cordovero's work, see Joseph B. Schechtman, "Cordovero, Moses ben Jacob," *EncJud* 5:967–70.

was preoccupied with explaining anthropomorphisms in Jewish thought as necessities by which G-d made it possible for human beings to understand the divine and the requirements that G-d imposed upon humans. Nevertheless, Maimonides had posited that the human intellect or spirit would develop its intangible character, so that humans might interrelate to G-d in a world in which the finite elements of creation lay at the center of the universe, but emanated out to the infinite or transcendent G-d who would be found beyond the finite world.

Like Maimonides, Cordovero is also fundamentally concerned with the relationship between G-d and human beings, but unlike Maimonides whose foundations for understanding the relationship between G-d and humans lay in Aristotelian philosophy, Cordovero's foundations lie in kabbalah and especially in the Zohar and its understanding of the relationship between the Ein Sof and the Ten Sefirot. In Cordovero's thought, it is the sefirot that make possible the manifestation of the Ein Sof as the Shekhinah in the finite world of creation, but his understanding of the sefirot moves far beyond the understanding of the Zohar. His fundamental question about the sefirot is whether they represent divine substance or whether they are only *kelim*, vessels, made of increasingly finite or tangible earthly substances as they convey the intangible Ein Sof into the finite world. Such a conception draws upon Aristotelian and Platonic philosophy, which posit a fundamental distinction between the intangible substance of the divine and the tangible substance of the earthly. Cordovero's position draws upon an early principle seen in the Sefer Yetzirah and in the various elements of the Zohar, i.e., the interrelationship between the intangible and tangible is like the relationship between flame and the coal on which it feeds; they are different substances but inextricably linked together. In the Zohar, the sefirot are both the substance of the Ein Sof and the *kelim* (vessels) by which that substance is conveyed at the same time. In other words, G-d's substance is immanent in the Kelim. Cordovero therefore considers the sefirot as the Kelim that bear divine substance, and in doing so, the sefirot enable the intangible character of G-d to be present and active in the world of creation. Hence it is the divine substance of the Ein Sof that permeates and gives life to the successively tangible sefirot. Cordovero nevertheless makes a distinction between the purely intangible substance of G-d and the transmission of divine substance into the world. The transcendent intangible G-d has undergone no process of transformation, but once divine substance permeates the sefirot, it is immutably changed into divine substance that increasingly becomes inherently tangible in relation to its degree of emanation. Insofar as the process begins with the expression of the divine will in the form of the first sefirah, Keter Elyon, the divine will is transmitted to the finite world through the process of emanation.

Cordovero argues that the process of emanation conveys the divine will, but the divine will transforms in its essential character as it undergoes the multiple processes of emanation. In Cordovero's understanding, G-d's will is an emanation from G-d, but it is manifested in a series of emanations, each one of which is transformed by its interrelationship with the tangible form of the sefirot by which it is emanated. Some describe this process as asymptotic, that is, the divine will approaches the tangible through the process of the emanation of a succession of wills, but it never touches the tangible and therefore never becomes fully tangible itself.

For Cordovero, the process of emanation is inherently dialectic in that divine substance must be concealed within the sefirot, which in turn reveal the divine substance as the sefirot are emanated into the finite world. Concealment enables revelation, and revelation therefore prompts concealment. The process of revelation manifests itself through a constant process by which the inner aspects of the sefirot change; as the sefirot are manifested in the world in their various forms, the transition from intangible to the various aspects of tangible changes the inherent aspects of the sefirot by giving them tangible form. In philosophical terms, Plato's ideal table takes multiple forms, and each expression of a tangible form changes the understanding of the ideal table by giving it a sense of finite manifestation. Such transformation constitutes a reflective process within the emanation of the sefirot that both distinguishes the sefirot and enables their emanation, each from the other, in their succession of emanation. The sequential emanation of manifestations of the divine Will (Keter) requires that each manifestation inherently embodies Hokhmah (Wisdom), in order to conceptualize each manifestation of Will. And each manifestation of Hokhmah successively embodies Binah (Understanding), in order to render each conceptualization workable in the finite world; and so on through all of the sefirot. In this manner, Keter, together with Hokhmah, Binah, and the other sefirot, embody all of the possible manifestations of divine will, or in a more tangible form, all of the possible forms of Plato's table, that are both manifested in actuality or remain as yet unmanifested in reality and yet are potential. By this means, the process of emanation transmits all the potential realities of the tangible world, both those that have been manifested and those that remain possible.

Cordovero's notion of the possible manifestations of divine will actually constitutes a reversal of the Zohar's concept of prior creations that had failed. He refers to them as the Kings of Edom who ruled prior to the Kings of Israel (cf. Gen 36). In the Zohar, these earlier creations were destroyed by acts of divine judgment because they were somehow deemed unsuitable for the purposes of the divine will. In Cordovero's view, these earlier creations failed because they did not manifest enough judgment to enable them to develop in accordance with the divine will; the reason was that they were not under sufficient control or guidance. In Cordovero's view, Judgment (Din) is a necessary aspect of creation insofar as Judgment is one of the Ten Sefirot, i.e., Gevurah (Power), which often goes by the name Din (Judgment). Judgment is necessary to counterbalance Hesed (Fidelity, Mercy, or Compassion), insofar as Judgment gives discipline to control the potential excesses of Compassion, just as the magnanimity of Hesed is necessary to counteract the destructive influences of Din. In keeping with the sefirotic system, Hesed and Gevurah/Din must exist dialectically in interrelationship with each other balanced by Tiferet, Beauty.

Cordovero's understanding of the dialectic nature of the process of emanation likewise entails that influence move upward and downward through the sefirot, as well as within each. Thus, the process of emanation produces *or yashar*, Direct Light, which moves the process of emanation downward from the Ein Sof to the Shekhinah. But it also produces *or hozer*, Returning or Reflected Light, that moves back up from Shekhinah to Ein Sof during the process of emanation. In other words, the dialectical process of emanation moves in two directions at once; the emanation influences the final manifestation of Shekhinah just as it influences the original manifestation of the Ein Sof. Such motion, both downwards and upwards, is continuous in Cordovero's understanding. It constitutes a continuous movement to and from divine Nothingness, or Ayin, and the First Being of the world of creation. Fundamentally, each influences the other so that G-d brings into being the finite world of creation, and the finite world of creation influences and changes G-d.

Cordovero's understanding of the relationship between the Ein Sof and the sefirot also has moral dimensions, and the moral dimensions of the process of emanation are the central concern of his work Tomar Devorah (The Palm Tree of Deborah).[6] The ten chapters of the Tomar Devorah discuss the means by which a man might learn the qualities of each of the sefirot and apply those qualities to living his life. Cordovero does not discuss how

6. See Rabbi Moses Cordovero, *The Palm Tree of Deborah*, translated from the Hebrew with an introduction and notes by Louis Jacobs (New York: Sepher Hermon, 1974).

a woman might learn such qualities because in his world only men were required to study, but modern readers might consider his work in relation to women as well.

The first chapter takes up learning from the Keter Elyon or Divine Will. In rabbinic interpretation (see b. Rosh Hash. 17b), the words of Exod 34:6–7 that G-d proclaims to Moses, instead of allowing Moses to see G-d's face, present thirteen divine attributes of mercy which constitute the highest such attributes. Cordovero identifies and enumerates each of the qualities presented in Exod 34:6–7 and advises how they might be applied in life as an expression of the divine will. Chapter 2 continues discussion of the Keter Elyon, treating human humility; concentration on worthy thoughts; kindness to all; perfection of hearing, sight, and speech; and the eradication of pride, all in imitation of G-d. Chapter 3 focuses on the imitation of Hokhmah (Wisdom) by loving all things and extending care to all creatures. Chapter 4 focuses on Binah (Understanding), which entails sincere repentance. Chapter 5 takes up Hesed (Fidelity, Mercy, Compassion) by employing methods discussed in the chapter, e.g., feeding and circumcising a child, visiting and healing the sick, giving charity to the poor, welcoming guests, tending to the dead, bringing a bride under the huppah (wedding canopy), and making peace between people, to ensure the smooth functioning of the sefirot. Chapter 6 takes up Gevurah (Power), i.e., managing the *yetzer ra'* or inclination to evil in humans so that it serves G-d. Chapter 7 focuses on Tiferet (Beauty), which entails the obligation to study and thereby to serve G-d. Chapter 8 takes up Netzah (Endurance or Dynamism), Hod (Majesty), and Yesod (Foundation) to support Torah students and the purity of life. Chapter 9 focuses on Malkhut (Sovereignty), also known as Shekhinah (Presence of G-d), to make the sacrifices necessary for Torah and to engage in marriage for holiness in the world. Chapter 10 concludes with discussion of general conduct in relation to the sefirot so as to bring about the presence of G-d in the world.

Cordovero's understanding of the interrelationship between the Ein Sof and the sefirot is fundamental to Isaac Luria's understanding of kabbalistic thought.

Lurianic Kabbalah, from Tzimtzum to Adam Kadmon

Both Cordovero and Luria continued to work on the question of the interrelationship of the infinite G-d to the finite world throughout their lives, i.e., how is the infinite G-d manifested and known in the finite world of earth and human beings? Cordovero was the first to posit that the infinite G-d is manifest in all finite reality, but that finite reality does not encompass the totality of G-d.[7] Expressed metaphorically or mythologically, the infinite G-d may be expressed as divine light in the world, whereas the finite world may be expressed as the ten vessels or jars that contain the divine light in the finite world. Interpreted, such an image means that G-d's infinite presence appears throughout the finite world, although it cannot be seen; it is hidden in the finite world of earthly phenomena. Nevertheless, the infinite presence of G-d can be recognized through the infinite qualities and sensitivities of the human intellect or soul, as well as through those intangible forces that can be perceived and experienced throughout all creation.

Following Cordovero's death in 1570, R. Isaac ben Solomon Luria (1538–1572) became the principal kabbalistic teacher of Safed.[8] Luria is known in kabbalistic circles as Ha'ari, "The Lion," the letters for *ha'ari* deriving from the moniker *ha'elohi rabbi yitzhaq*, "The Divine/G-dly Rabbi Isaac." His contemporaries in Safed, however, referred to him as R. Isaac Ashkenazi, apparently because his father, R. Solomon Luria, was originally from Germany (Ashkenaz) or Poland and immigrated to Jerusalem where he married into the Sephardi Frances family. Unfortunately, Solomon Luria died while Isaac was still a child, and his mother took the boy to Egypt to live in the home of her brother, Mordecai Frances, who was a wealthy tax farmer. Young Isaac studied with R. David ben Solomon ibn Abi Zimra and later with R. Bezalel Ashkenazi, with whom he collaborated in writing halakic works. Luria proved to be a prodigy in the study of Jewish halakah, but he also was engaged in business, specifically the importing and sale of spices and grain, in order to support his family. He continued in this line of work throughout his lifetime until his death in Safed in 1572.

Luria began kabbalistic studies while still in Egypt, retiring to an island called Jazirat al-Rawda in the Nile River near Cairo. The island was owned by his uncle, who also became his father-in-law. Luria's time on Jazirat al-Rawda enabled him to deepen and formulate his own understanding of kabbalah, especially the Zohar, earlier kabbalistic works, and the works of Moses Cordovero. He later studied with Cordovero himself, both in Egypt and in Safed. Cordovero was very influential in Luria's understanding of kabbalah.

---

7. Scholem, *Major Trends*, 252–53.

8. In addition to the overviews cited above, see also Gershom Scholem, "Kabbalah," *EncJud* 10:489–653, esp. 540–51.

Although the exact dates of his sojourn are uncertain, he remained on the island for some seven years. During this time, Luria wrote his only known extant kabbalistic work, a commentary on Sifra de-Zeni'uta, The Book of Concealment, which Luria's disciple Hayim Vital published as part of his Sha'ar Ma'amrei Rashbi. Around 1569 or 1570, Luria moved to Safed, where he continued to study with Cordovero until the latter's death in 1570. Luria had already begun to gather his own followers, and following Cordovero's death in 1570, Hayim Vital became one of his closest disciples—or at least Vital portrays himself as Luria's closest disciple—and eventually wrote the primary accounts of Luria's teachings.

In true kabbalistic fashion, Luria wrote down practically none of his teachings, as teaching face-to-face was considered the only valid way to convey such ideas in keeping with the traditions of the early rabbis who developed and taught the oral Torah of the Mishnah. Luria's circle of disciples includes over thirty named individuals, including Vital, who always makes a special effort to portray himself as Luria's chief disciple. Some who applied to join Luria's circle, including celebrated scholars such as R. Moses Alshek and R. Joseph Karo, were rejected as Luria did not consider them to be adequate. Indeed, Vital maintains that Luria refused to write his ideas down because Luria claimed that the outpouring of his ideas defied systematization and completeness, so Vital took on the task of writing down Luria's teachings, both before and after Luria's death. In point of fact, we cannot always be sure whether Vital's accounts of Luria's teachings accurately portray Luria's ideas or only Vital's understanding of Luria's ideas. Luria's teachings took place before his disciples in the Ashkenazi Synagogue in Safed and on long walks with some of his closest disciples through the environs and forests around the city of Safed. A major portion of his teachings focused on the spiritual dimensions of kabbalah; indeed, he was able to identify the many kabbalistic teachers buried in the vicinity of Safed, many of whom had been previously unknown. Such an alleged ability was evidence of his *kavvanah*, here referring to his mystical meditation in prayer, which enabled him to commune with the souls of the tzaddikim, "righteous ones," who had passed on before him and were now buried in the vicinity of Safed.

As understood primarily from the writings of Luria's disciple Hayim Vital, Lurianic kabbalah includes three basic principles, expressed metaphorically or mythologically, that are designed to explain the interrelationship between the infinite presence of G-d and the finite reality of the world. These principles include Tzimtzum, the contraction of the presence of G-d to create the finite world; Shevirat Hakelim, the shattering of the vessels of the finite world and the infinite presence of G-d; and Tikkun Olam, the repair or mending of the finite world and the infinite presence of G-d in that world.

Tzimtzum refers to the contraction of G-d's infinite presence to create the finite world. The concept does not originate with Luria; it is in fact first mentioned in the Sefer Ha'iyyun, identified by Scholem only as "a preface to a commentary on the 32 paths of wisdom found in the Florence Ms." Sefer Ha'iyyun refers to G-d's first act prior to emanation as one of contraction, "like a man who gathers in and contracts his breath . . . so (G-d) contracted His breath into a handbreadth (Isa 40:12) . . . and the world was left in darkness, and in that darkness (G-d) cut boulders and hewed rocks."[9] The statement refers to the creation of Keter, the first of the sefirot, at the outset of the process of emanation of the Ten Sefirot. Although Luria does not originate the concept, he develops its fullest understanding by positing that it is not an act of revelation and emanation, but instead it is an act of concealment and limitation of the Ein Sof.

Luria's understanding of Tzimtzum holds that G-d's infinite presence encompasses all reality, leaves no room for anything else in the yet-unformed universe, and therefore includes all ten of the sefirot. The original midrashic use of the verb *metzamtzem*, "contract," entailed the withdrawal of the divine presence from the holy of holies of the Jerusalem Temple. But Luria's understanding of the term entails G-d's withdrawal and concealment from creation itself at a given point in primordial space. In this space, remnants of the light of Ein Sof remained to mix with elements of Din (Judgment), which were concentrated in one location or point at the moment of divine withdrawal and concealment, so that Tzimtzum becomes an act of judgment. When G-d's love is manifested, G-d desires to create the finite world. When G-d creates the world out of love, the creation of this new entity compromises the finite character of G-d by manifesting Din (Judgment), or Gevurah (Power), as a counterbalance to Hesed (Fidelity, Love, Mercy, Compassion). Because something else then exists together with G-d, G-d's presence is no longer fully infinite, and by means of Din, Punishment, G-d's infinite presence contracts or withdraws in order to conceal the divine presence, allowing the finite world to exist. The finite world then becomes a series of *kelim* or vessels that contain the divine essence of G-d, but the creation stores it in delimited finite containers that then constitute the finite world of creation. In the case of the human being, the first major container for the collection of divine essence is Adam Kadmon, the Primal Adam or Primal Human.

9. Scholem, "Kabbalah," *EncJud* 10:588–89.

But the contraction of G-d's infinite presence has consequences. Because G-d is no longer infinite, the various sefirot or qualities of G-d no longer operate in harmonic balance with each other. Such contraction therefore allows Gevurah or Din (divine Power or Judgment) to be manifest without the balancing effects of Hesed (Lovingkindness). Through the creation of the finite world, brought about by G-d's Hesed, that divine Power or Judgment is released into the world, unchecked by divine Hesed. Such a conception of the divine builds upon Cordovero's understanding of the influence of both the Ein Sof on the Ten Sefirot and the Ten Sefirot on the Ein Sof, indicating that the eternal divine presence of G-d is influenced by what takes place in the finite world where the Ten Sefirot conveying divine presence are manifested. In other words, the Ein Sof of G-d is vulnerable in relation to the world of phenomena as G-d may be changed by the finite world. G-d therefore is dependent upon the finite world and especially in need of human beings to act as partners with G-d in completing and sanctifying the world of creation.

The second major principle of Lurianic kabbalah is Shevirat Hakelim, the Shattering of the Vessels. Shevirat Hakelim posits that the ten finite vessels that received the infinite presence of the divine light poured into them at creation were unable to withstand the infinite presence of the divine. The result is that seven of the vessels shattered, scattering sparks of divine light throughout the world where they are encased in the broken fragments of the seven shattered vessels.

The metaphorical or mythological dimensions of this image must be understood. When Tzimtzum takes place, the Ein Sof is compelled to withdraw or become concealed at a given point in the *tehiru* or primordial space that exists at the outset of creation. When this point in space is vacated, the primordial intangible lights that are released by the process of emanation or contraction shine into the *tehiru*, where they are gathered together within the tangible forms or vessels created by the *reshimu* or tangible residue from earlier attempts at creation. As this light is emanated, gathered, and formed, the point of creation expands in two ways, the circle and the line. The circle constitutes the substance of creation which will first become the substance of Adam Kadmon; the line constitutes the direction or goal of creation which will ultimately become the form of the Adam Kadmon. Within Adam Kadmon, the *reshimu* therefore forms ten vessels that are to contain the emanated divine light in order to give it its tangible form. The ten vessels are therefore the Ten Sefirot, the qualities of G-d that emanate from the intangible character of the Ein Sof to be manifested in the tangible world of creation.

Of the ten vessels or sefirot within Adam Kadmon, only the mental qualities can withstand the divine presence, i.e., the human mind has its own intangible qualities of spirit and intellect. It can therefore comprehend the divine presence in the world because in fact these qualities stand closest to G-d. The other vessels, emanations, or sefirot of G-d, the three moral qualities, the three material qualities, and the tenth manifestation of divine presence or holiness in the world were unable to withstand the presence of the divine in creation. This inability is due in part to the fundamental distinction between the intangible sefirot or qualities of G-d and the moral and material qualities of the tangible world of creation in which they are encased. How can the pure, ideal moral and material dimensions of the Ein Sof come to expression in the tangible world? That is, to what extent is it possible to realize ideal goodness or evil as well as ideal dynamism and stability? The ideal and intangible moral and material dimensions of G-d must be compromised by their encounter with the limited nature of the tangible universe, i.e., the intangible divine presence or holiness is hidden in the tangible world. This means that the moral and material dimensions of G-d are not yet manifested in the moral and material realms of human life in the world. The divine presence is therefore disconnected from the moral and material dimensions of human life in the world of creation.

As a result of the fundamental incompatibility of the divine and intangible aspects of the moral and material dimensions with the finite and tangible world, the seven vessels that contain the moral and material dimensions within the Adam Kadmon shatter before the power of the supernal divine light, thereby scattering the divine lights of morality, materiality, and divine presence throughout the world of finite creation. Adam Kadmon is therefore shattered, and the divine light that constitutes his presence in the world is scattered about and in need of collection and reassembly in order to ensure the integrity of the divine Ein Sof, Adam Kadmon, and the tangible world of creation.

This concept of the shattering of the vessels, Shevirat Hakelim, points to the fundamental character of the finite world of creation: it is flawed, shattered, and in need of gathering, reintegration, and completion. Tikkun Olam, the mending of the world, points to the role of human beings in the world as partners with G-d to bring about the restoration of the flawed and shattered world. The task of human beings is metaphorically or mythologically described as gathering all of the fragments of the infinite divine presence that were shattered and scattered throughout the world when the seven vessels broke. With the breaking of the vessels, the Ten Sefirot reorganized themselves into several aspects, *partzufim*, or faces of the divine presence in the world. The first face is the Arikh Anpin, the Long Face of G-d, i.e., the Patient or Long-Suffering Face, or the Attika, the Ancient Face of G-d. The Arikh Anpin represents the sefirah Keter Elyon (Crown of the Most High), i.e., the will of G-d to create. As the expression of the divine will to create, the Arikh Anpin constitutes the foundation of the Lurianic system and it will therefore be the first element to act in creating the world and the last element to be restored as the process of Tikkun, Mending, takes place.

The second *partzuf*, or face, in the Lurianic system is actually two: the Abba (the Father) and the Imma (the Mother), treated as separate aspects of the same face. The Abba is identified with the sefirah of Hokhmah (Wisdom) and the Imma is identified with Binah (Understanding). Together, they carry out the reindividuation and redifferentiation of all the following sefirot within the Adam Kadmon. They are the foundation of the dialectical character of the Lurianic understanding of the sefirotic system insofar as the mental and material groupings of sefirot each entail two ideal opposites balanced by a third, much as creation takes place by the sexual and spiritual union of the Father and the Mother in human creation. Hokhmah and Binah by their interaction determine the character of the following sefirot just as human parents determine the character of their children, both by their physical characteristics as expressed in their DNA as well as by their spiritual and intellectual elements as expressed in their personalities and worldviews.

The union of Abba and Imma forms a third *partzuf*, the Zeir Anpin, the Short-faced or Impatient One. The Zeir Anpin represents a combination of six lower sefirot from the moral and material triads. It includes the three moral sefirot, Hesed (Fidelity, Compassion, Love), its opposite, Gevurah (Power) or Din (Judgment), and what balances them, Tiferet (Beauty), as a means to determine the moral foundations of the world of creation. The material sefirot have a similar structure of two opposites balanced by a third. Thus, the material aspects of the Zeir Anpin include the sefirah Netzah (Endurance), which expresses the material property of dynamism in the tangible world of material creation, and its opposite sefirah Hod (Majesty), which expresses the material property of stasis in the tangible world of material creation. Balancing the opposing pair is Yesod (Foundation), which ensures that the material world includes both dynamism and stability. Yesod is also understood to represent the phallus of the Adam Kadmon, which unites with the final face of the Lurianic *partzufim*, the tenth sefirah, Malkhut (Sovereignty), or Shekhinah (the Presence of G-d in the world). As in the other sefirotic systems, because both Malkhut and Shekhinah are feminine nouns, they complete the sexual metaphor when combined with Yesod and thereby ensure the proper channeling of all Ten Sefirot, expressing intangible divine qualities into the tangible and finite world of creation.

The Lurianic understanding of the emanation of G-d into the finite world of creation constitutes a marked change in the conceptualization of the sefirot as expressed in the Zohar and earlier kabbalistic works. Whereas the Zohar was concerned principally with explaining how the infinite character of G-d could be manifested in the finite world of creation, Lurianic kabbalah moves well beyond a fundamental concern for the relationship between the infinite and the finite to one which employs the metaphors of withdrawal and concealment to define how it is that the presence of G-d has been exiled from the world—and how it is that human beings can take action to restore the divine presence to the world and thereby sanctify it. The exile of G-d from the world of creation becomes an epistemological metaphor for the exile of the Jewish people, exile from the land of Israel, from Spain, and from elsewhere in the world, that then provides the foundation for determining the purpose of exile. By acts of holiness as defined in Jewish practice, the Jewish people are tasked with going into exile into the world to gather the various sparks of the divine presence that are hidden in the broken shards of the seven shattered vessels of the moral and material realms; regathered, they then realize the holy presence of G-d in the world. In the Lurianic system, human beings act as true partners with G-d in the world of creation insofar as G-d is dependent upon human beings. Because G-d's presence has been shattered and scattered through the inability of an as yet unsanctified world to bear the divine presence, human beings must act in a holy manner to secure the holiness of creation, gathering and reassembling the scattered sparks of G-d, and thereby sanctify the finite world of creation for the infinite divine presence of G-d to dwell within it.

Intention, Transmigration, and Redemption in Lurianic Kabbalah

It is the task of human beings to ensure the smooth and proper functioning of this system of sefirot and divine *partzufim* in the world of creation.[10] By

10. For discussion of Lurianic practice, see Lawrence Fine, *Safed Spirituality*, Classics of Western Spirituality (New York: Paulist, 1984); Fine, *Physician of the Soul: Isaac Luria and His Kabbalistic Fellowship* (Stanford: Stanford University Press, 2003); David R. Blumenthal, *Understanding Jewish Mysticism: The Merkabah, and the Zoharic Tradition* (New York: Ktav, 1978), 159–80.

acting in a holy and moral manner within the material world of creation, human beings collect and reassemble the fragments of the divine presence in the world and thereby restore the holy presence of the infinite G-d piece by piece throughout the finite world of creation. Such action includes the performance of mitzvot, acts of Jewish observance; avodah and tefillah, i.e., worship and prayer; *yihudim* or "unions" with special dead; and Idra Rabba, the Great Assembly in which metempsychosis and messianic redemption complete the system of Lurianic kabbalah.

Insofar as the Lurianic system is a Jewish system, it calls for Jews to live life in a holy manner based on the performance of mitzvot, commandments or good deeds, consistent with the practice of halakah or Jewish law. Mitzvot include all the moral and ritual or liturgical commandments of Judaism that are designed to ensure the holiness of Jewish life in the finite world. Their performance must begin with the mental qualities that express the divine qualities within the human being: the will to create or act, the wisdom to create or act, and the understanding necessary for creation and human action. When human beings act in full accordance with divine instruction or Torah, the world then becomes a perfectly holy place and the divine presence is wholly manifested in the moral and material worlds. In this respect, Lurianic kabbalah points to the traditional Jewish understanding of the role of human beings as partners with G-d who act in accordance with the divine will to ensure the completion and sanctification of creation at large.

The Lurianic understanding of the performance of mitzvoth begins with the efforts of individuals to purify their souls of sinfulness and impurity. Such efforts are consistent with the understanding of traditional Orthodox Judaism, but Lurianic kabbalah moves beyond traditional Judaism by stipulating that personal sanctification entails a combination of theurgical and experiential efforts at promoting holiness within the self and the world in which we live. They entail the release of the divine sparks of the divine presence in the world from the *qelippot* or husks of material substance in which they are encased and trapped, which thereby constitute the shattering of the divine elements of the last seven sefirot. Such efforts would not simply repair the shattered cosmos as postulated in Lurianic mythology; it would actually constitute a new cosmos that would manifest divine sanctity at its most basic ontological levels. In contrast to Jewish philosophy, which looked to thought or intellect as the foundation for sanctity and purity in the world, Lurianic kabbalah looked to human action in the world as the basis for the sanctification of human life and thought, i.e., holy action would lead to holy thought just as holy thought would lead to holy action. Mitzvot influence the sefirot, just as the sefirot influence mitzvot; and ultimately the mitzvot influence G-d or the Ein Sof, just as G-d or the Ein Sof influences mitzvot.

In Lurianic kabbalah, human beings are obligated to observe and perform all of the commandments in Judaism except for those that they are constitutionally unable to perform. By such observance of the mitzvot, one purifies one's soul. This concept is known in traditional Judaism from the teaching that there are 613 commandments incumbent upon human beings, or specifically, Jewish men in traditional Judaism, including 365 negative commandments or prohibitions and 248 positive commands. These numbers correspond to the 613 elements of the human body according to traditional Judaism. Consequently, the performance of mitzvot, or the failure to perform them, respectively, supports the 613 elements of the human body or injures the 613 elements of the body. The mitzvot are to be performed with joy, because it is a privilege and a pleasure to live in the world of creation and to perform the will of G-d; it is not a burden to be alive in the world of creation. Such performance constitutes serving the will of G-d, and such service is considered to constitute joy. Such joy is expressed with sexual metaphor. The observance of negative mitzvoth or prohibitions motivates the love between the Abba (Hokhmah, Wisdom) and the Imma (Binah, Understanding), and the performance of positive commandments motivates the coupling of the Abba and the Imma that together prompt the emanation of the following seven sefirot to complete the creation, i.e., to bring about Tikkun (Repair) of the world. Indeed, the sexual metaphor points to the Lurianic understanding of marriage: the coupling of a man and a woman produces children whose inner intellectual and spiritual aspects must be created or fashioned just as much as their physical aspects, beginning with the teachings of their parents and continuing through life with the efforts of other teachers and mentors.

But the performance of mitzvot is not limited to marriage or sexual union. Acts of tzedakah, righteousness or charity, are required to train the inner soul to give of itself to benefit those in need. The study of Torah as a mystical rite by which one learns the sanctity of the tradition and the will of G-d is paramount to Lurianic kabbalah. The *kavvanah*, intention, of Pentateuchal recitation or reading out loud is crucial to Lurianic thought, particularly understanding the basic structure of Adam Kadmon in relation to the four letters of the divine Name, *yod*, *he*, *vav*, and *he*. Thus, the basic structure of the face of Adam Kadmon includes four dimensions, the eyes, ears, nose, and mouth, by which one senses by seeing, hearing, smelling, and tasting. Each of these elements corresponds to the various combinations of letters that constitute the divine name. These combinations are used to identify the number of verses in the Torah portion that are to be read for each day of the week and the correspondence between each segment of the Torah portion and the sefirah that is emphasized for the day. In addition to the contemplative reading of the Torah, Lurianic kabbalah also calls for the contemplative study of Jewish halakah as a basis for redeeming the sparks of the divine presence from their *qelippot* and thereby bringing about Tikkun Olam, Repair of the World.

Traditional Judaism calls for all persons to engage in worship and prayer. Such worship and prayer are not to be engaged in casually; rather, they are to be performed with *kavvanah*, intention, to concentrate the mind on the task of acknowledging, sanctifying, honoring, and activating G-d as well as the self. In kabbalistic thought, proper worship and prayer entail *kavvanah*, intention, to activate awareness of and engagement with the sefirot or elements of divine presence that are within each and every human being. One does not pray by rote, but with proper attention to and engagement with the text with which one prays. In Lurianic kabbalah, one should approach the mindfulness of worship and prayer with proper joy at the prospect of encountering and sanctifying G-d in thanks for the life that G-d has given us on earth as well as the opportunity to sanctify and complete that life in relation to creation at large. But together with joy, one should also observe proper humility, fear, and reverence of G-d. Thus, in Lurianic practice, the major prayers of the Jewish worship service, such as the Amidah or Shemoneh Esreh (Eighteen Benedictions), are whispered during the week, but pronounced aloud and with joy on Shabbat and the festivals. Luria himself would pray from memory, with his eyes closed to concentrate on the words of the service leader and his left hand over his right hand on his heart to symbolize the combination of the left side of the sefirotic elements with those of the right, thereby to ensure the proper intimate interaction of the Zeir Anpin or the six sefirot of the moral and material spheres with the Shekhinah or presence of G-d in the finite world.

Proper kabbalistic and Lurianic *kavvanah*, intention, during prayer entails intensive engagement in prayer as though it were an act of intimate union that brings one near to death. When praying the Amidah or Shemoneh Esreh, the main prayer of the Jewish worship service, one stands and prays with reverence and joy to sustain the unity of the world above with the world below. But following the Amidah when one prays Tahanun (Petition), one prostrates oneself, face to the ground, to symbolize the humility and reverence that one must feel when appearing before the presence of G-d. Such an act of falling upon one's face symbolizes the death of the body following the intensive joy of the Amidah and handing one's soul over from the Tree of Life to the Tree of Death as a pledge of complete devotion to the Shekhinah or Presence of G-d in the world. Such an act is understood as an enactment of *teshuvah* or repentance, in which after confessing one's sins before G-d, one prepares oneself to accept the consequences of one's sins by preparing to hand one's life over to G-d in punishment for wrongdoing. Only divine mercy enables a person to survive such an act and thereby to bring about the purification of the soul during an act of prayer and worship. In Lurianic thought, the worshiper therefore engages in *devequt*, cleaving to the Shekhinah by throwing oneself down to the deepest depths of the created world to retrieve the sparks of divine presence in one's soul, thereby enabling them to rise from their encasement in the *qelippot* or husks of material form to be reunited in a process of Tikkun, the repair or restoration of the holy presence of G-d in the world. Such an act represents a form of symbolic martyrdom that may symbolize actual martyrdom such as that experienced by Rhineland Jews during the pogroms prompted by the Crusades and the Plague, or by the later instances of the Chmielnitzki Massacres in Poland and the Ukraine in 1646–1648, or even the Shoah during World War II. Martyrdom in Jewish thought represents an act of absolute holiness or *qiddush hashem*, Sanctification of the Divine Name of G-d when one willingly gives one's life for G-d and G-d's Holy Name.

More joyous *kavvanot* are also known in Lurianic practice, such as the singing of the psalm Lekhah Dodi (Come, My Beloved) at the beginning of the Shabbat Evening service to welcome Shabbat, metaphorically understood as the bride of G-d, into the congregation as the holiness of the divine presence and divine union is manifested in the congregation.

Luria was known for his innovation in the performance of traditional Jewish practices such as observing mitzvot and engaging in Jewish prayer and worship. But he was also known for creating new traditions and practices that had little or no basis in Jewish tradition. One of his primary innovations was the performance of rituals for communion with the dead, known in Hebrew as *yihudim*, "unions." As part of the larger Lurianic effort to purify the soul in preparation for Tikkun Olam, Repair of the World, such rituals enabled one to consult with the souls of departed *tzaddikim* or righteous ones who might advise concerning proper action, prayer, study, and repentance.

Such communions might take place at the burial site of the departed tzaddik or in the home of one who sought such communion. When the ritual was performed at the grave of the tzaddik, the disciple would first lie face down on top of the grave and stretch himself out, as Elijah did when he revived the soul of the dead son of the woman from Zarephath (1 Kgs 17:17–24) or as Elisha did when he revived the dead soul of the son of the Shunemmite woman (2 Kgs 4:8–37). Such an action presumes that the soul of the dead tzaddik hovers over the body and gravesite of the departed. By lying face down on top of the grave or upon the soul, the disciple then aligns himself physically with the body of the dead and concentrates his own efforts on binding his soul with that of the departed tzaddik. Such an action is considered a form of *devequt*, "binding" one's soul to that of another, or even to G-d. The disciple finally seeks to assimilate their souls together so that he might raise them to the upper realms whereby they would then join with the root of the original soul of Adam. When performed at home, the disciple forgoes the first step and concentrates on the two meditative steps described above to achieve *devequt* with the soul of the departed tzaddik. It should be noted that the practice engages only the *nephesh*, "life force," of the dead tzaddik, the lowest of the three parts of the human soul. By engaging the *nephesh*, *devequt* makes possible the rising of the two other aspects of the departed soul, i.e., the *ruah* or "spirit," of the departed tzaddik and his *neshamah* or "intellect." Such practice remains unknown in the Zohar, but Cordovero speaks in his Zohar commentary of the secret of the soul bound up with the soul when one pours out his soul on the grave of a departed tzaddik, thereby cleaving soul to soul.

Much like the practice of imitating death during the recitation of the prayer service described above, the disciple again engages death to bring about new life in the world of creation as part of the process of Tikkun Olam. Contact with the dead is an act of extreme defilement in Judaism, such that the *kohanim* or priests of the temple were forbidden to have contact with the dead except in the case of the burial of a blood family member, a parent, a brother, a virgin sister, or a child (Lev 21:1–4). In antiquity when the Jerusalem Temple was still standing, burial sites for the dead normally lay outside of inhabited space to avoid the contact between the living and the dead that was practiced in some aspects of Canaanite and Greco-Roman societies. But in post-temple times, pilgrimages to the grave sites of dead holy figures became a common feature of both Christian and Jewish practice. Although the practice of visiting the graves of sages is discussed in the Talmud (see, e.g., b. Sot. 34b; b. Ta'an. 23b; and b. B. Metz. 85b), the rabbinic understanding of *hishtathut*, "bowing down," likely meant little more than simple prostration before the grave of the departed. But by modeling Hashtathut on the actions of Elijah and Elisha, each of whom is described throughout their narratives as a "man of G-d," the Lurianic practice not only intensified the concept of what it meant to bow, or more literally, to stretch oneself out upon the grave of the departed tzaddik, but it also provided the means by which the disciple might in some respect bring the soul of the dead tzaddik back to life.

Part of the practice of binding the souls of the disciple and the departed tzaddik together involves meditation upon the divine name, YHWH, which is always viewed as holy and capable of utmost power. But there are other names of G-d as well, such as 'EHYEH, "I am" (see Exod 3). In order to facilitate the combination of the souls, the disciple might meditate based on a combination of the names in which the consonants of one are interspersed and pronounced with the other, e.g., Y'HHVYHH, as well as the numerical equivalents of the various divine names to invoke the Hokhmah/Abba and Binah/Imma to stimulate the process of emanation whereby the lower sefirot are activated and empowered to raise the souls of the dead tzaddikim. By such means, the sanctity and power of the divine name are invoked to help ensure the success of the process of *devequt* as a foundation for the larger concern with the Tikkun Olam or restoration of the world. Such practice might also involve spirit possession whereby the spirit of the dead tzaddik speaks as a Maggid through the disciple, as noted in the discussion of Cordovero's practice above.

One of the most distinctive concepts of Lurianic thought is the transmigration of souls, whereby the soul of a past tzaddik is embodied in the soul of a later tzaddik. For example, Luria believed that he embodied the soul of R. Shimon bar Yohai and others of his disciples embodied the souls of the Rashbi's (R. Shimon bar Yohai's) disciples. The manifestation of such transmigration takes place in a segment of the Zohar, 3:127b–145a, which discusses the Idra Rabbah or Great Assembly, in which a minyan or quorum of ten sages discusses important aspects of the Zohar's teachings, such as the Sifra de-Zeni'uta or Book of Concealment, known from 2:176b–79a. Here, R. Shimon bar Yohai gathers a minyan of his disciples, including his son R. Eleazar, R. Abba, R. Judah, R. Yose bar Jacob, R. Isaac, R. Hizqiyah bar Rav, R. Hiyya, R. Yose, and R. Yesa, to engage in the discussion. The discussion among this mystic minyan is so intense a spiritual experience that three of the colleagues die as a result, R. Yose bar Jacob, R. Hizqiyah, and R. Yesa. Although such a death might be understood to be a form of punishment for engaging in the most esoteric teachings of the divine (cf. m. Hag. 2:1), R. Shimon explains that the soul of each of the sages bonded with that of G-d at the moment of death, so that their deaths might be considered the most sublime death, the kiss of G-d. The kiss of G-d is the type of death that rabbinic tradition ascribes to Moses, Aaron, Miriam, Abraham, Isaac, and Jacob, indicating that each experienced a communion or cleaving with G-d that took them to the highest realms of divine experience.

Transmigration of souls does not appear in biblical or in classical rabbinic tradition. Rather it appears to have originated in Iraqi Jewish circles during the eighth to tenth centuries CE under the influence of Mutazilite Muslims or Ismailian gnostics. The concept was accepted by Anan ben David, the traditional founder of Karaite Judaism, which was heavily influenced by Shiite Islam and rejected rabbinic tradition. R. Saadia Gaon, who defended rabbinic tradition against Karaite, Muslim, and Christian polemics, and wrote the first major philosophy of Judaism, attacked the concept of transmigration of the soul as madness and confusion. The concept took root in early kabbalist circles in Provence and Spain, apparently based on the teachings of travelers from Baghdad and its environs who made their way to southern Europe.

Luria adopted the concept and gathered his own disciples, each of whom he considered as embodying the soul of one of the original Idra Rabbah participants, to reenact the ritual and thereby continue the efforts of R. Shimon bar Yohai and his disciples; apparently he based the practice on the teachings of Cordovero and others who had fled Spain in the late fifteenth century and found their way to Egypt and Safed. The primal Adam's (Adam Kadmon) soul apparently contained all the souls that would ever exist in humankind, but because of his sin, his 613 limbs dropped off from him and these souls were scattered throughout creation, hidden in the *qelippot* or husks that would conceal them. There were five classes of souls: (1) those that were new and differentiated from Adam and would ascend to heaven prior to his sin; (2) those new souls that were present with Adam when he sinned and can perfect themselves; (3) the souls of Cain and Abel and their descendants who are also capable of perfecting themselves; (4) those old souls that fell into the *qelippot* at the time of Adam's sin and must go through a series of transmigrations to perfect themselves; and (5) those old souls that enter the bodies of converts to Judaism and thereby perfect themselves by practice and repeated transmigrations (e.g., R. Akiba was descended from converts). All of the last four soul types would enter the realm of *qelippot* and would therefore be responsible for purifying themselves as part of the larger effort to repair the world of creation.

In this manner, R. Isaac Luria became what Lawrence Fine describes as a Physician of the Soul, a messianic-like figure much like Moses and R. Shimon bar Yohai before him, who would enable disciples to engage in self-purification of the soul through the use of worship, study, observance, and *devequt* or cleaving to G-d and the souls of departed tzaddikim. Such a role plays a key part in the larger effort to gather and reassemble the scattered sparks of the divine sefirot and thereby bring about Tikkun Olam, the restoration of the world by means of the restoration of the presence of G-d within the finite world of creation. Indeed, as we will see later in relation to Shabbetai Zevi, the Baal Shem Tov, and the Lubavitcher Rebbe, this role as Physician of the Soul continues as a key element in the development of Jewish mysticism into the present day.

Between Tragedy and Tikkun:
Shabbetean Messianism and Apostate Mystics

Lurianic kabbalah had tremendous influence in Judaism in the century following the death of R. Isaac Luria. At the most fundamental level, it changed the character of kabbalah itself from a contemplative and esoteric movement, based on the study of the Zohar and other kabbalistic literature by a small number of adherents who were well-schooled in both kabbalistic and classical rabbinical writings, to a widely popular movement that had major impact on all parts of the Jewish world. Much of the credit for such change must be given to Hayim Vital and other disciples of Luria who wrote, traveled, and talked extensively about Lurianic kabbalah to an ever-growing audience of Jews who were hungry for spiritual teaching that would help to make sense of the suffering of the Jewish people, both throughout history in general and in relation to the expulsion from Spain and elsewhere in particular. The expulsion of the Jews from Spain shook the entirety of Judaism much as the modern experience of the Shoah or Holocaust has shaken the Jewish world in modern times. Especially important were the Lurianic *kavvanot*, acts of worship, study, and practice that became widely influential throughout the Jewish population that was eager for redemption. Indeed, Lurianic kabbalah offered an explanation: G-d had gone into exile at the very outset of creation due to the Tzimtzum, the contraction or withdrawal of divine presence to make room for creation, resulting in the Shevirat Hakelim, the shattering of the vessels that could not sustain the divine, thereby scattering divine sparks throughout the finite world. It would be the task of human beings, by acts of study, worship, and action, to act as partners with G-d, to gather and restore the sparks of divine presence and bring about Tikkun

Olam, Repair of the World, which in turn would bring to an end the exile of G-d from the world and the exile of Judaism from Jerusalem and the land of Israel, thereby ushering in the Messianic Age in which G-d, Judaism, and creation would be sanctified and restored.

But Lurianic kabbalah and its notions of Tikkun Olam would ultimately have a major impact on the whole of Judaism as well. Not only would Lurianic kabbalah lead to the emergence of modern Hasidism as a kabbalistically based Jewish movement to engage the masses of Judaism, particularly the working-class Ashkenazi Jews of Eastern Europe, in kabbalistic study, worship, and practice. It would also influence the foundations of non-kabbalistic movements, such as the development of the modern Orthodox and Reform movements in Judaism, and the development of modern Zionism as a Jewish political movement meant to restore Jewish life in the land of Israel. Hasidism, modern Orthodoxy, modern Reform Judaism, and modern Zionism all share in the Lurianic ideal of bringing about Tikkun Olam or the repair of a very damaged world.[11]

A key element in the spread and influence of Lurianic kabbalah in the centuries after Luria's death was the career of the false messiah, Shabbetai Zevi (1626–1676), and the emergence of the Shabbetean movements that emerged following the failure of his messianic claims, his conversion to Islam, and his death.[12] The Shabbetean movements attempted deliberately to emulate Shabbetai Zevi's career and teachings in an effort to bring about the Tikkun Olam anticipated by Lurianic kabbalah. In addition to the Doenmeh and Frankist movements, modern Hasidism—with all of its offshoots—would be an example of a Shabbetean movement, but one that clearly surpassed earlier Shabbetean movements to become one of the most widespread Jewish mystical, kabbalistic, and spiritual movements in the modern world.

The background for the emergence of Shabbetai Zevi and the derived Shabbetean movements is the contexts of the Cossack-Polish War of 1648–1657, the Russo-Polish War of 1654–1657, and the Chemielnicki or Chmielnitzki massacres of Jews in 1648–1667.[13] By 1648, the Polish-Lithuanian

11. Marvin A. Sweeney, "The Democratization of Messianism in Modern Jewish Thought," in *Biblical Interpretation: History, Context, and Reality*, ed. Christine Helmer and Christof Landmesser, SBLSym 26 (Atlanta: Society of Biblical Literature, 2005), 87–101.

12. For discussion of Shabbetai Zevi, see Scholem, *Major Trends*, 287–324; Scholem, *Sabbatai Sevi: The Mystical Messiah* (Princeton: Princeton University Press, 1973).

13. For background, see Paul Robert Magocsi, *A History of Ukraine* (Seattle: University of Washington Press, 1996).

Commonwealth had come to dominate not only its home territories of Poland and the Baltic states, but much of the Ukraine as well. Such domination played an important role in containing and hindering the interests of the Ukrainian Cossacks, as well as the Russian empire, and in raising resentment against Polish rule. In addition, Sweden was a major power at the time and had its own interests in expanding its influence in the Baltic region and beyond. Insofar as Poland was a patchwork of cultural and ethnic groups, the various nations and groups named above began to recognize that Poland was vulnerable to internal revolt and outside attack. Religion also entered into the divisions; the Poles were Roman Catholic, the Cossacks and Russians were Eastern Orthodox, the Swedes were Lutheran, and the Jews were Jewish.

Bogdan Chmielnitzki was a Cossack who was educated in Jesuit schools. His early life was spent in helping his father join forces with the Polish nobility to battle against the growing Ottoman Turkish Empire, which sought to expand its influence into the Ukraine and elsewhere in Eastern Europe. After having served time as an Ottoman hostage in Constantinople, Chmielnitzki returned to his hometown of Subotiv in the Ukraine with his wife and children. Chmielnitzki had been an important asset to the Cossacks; he had participated in campaigns led by the Grand Crown Heman Stanislaw Koniecpolski, led delegations to King Wladyslaw IV Vasa in Poland, and had thereby attained great respect in both Cossack and Polish circles. But when Koniecpolski's heir Aleksander Koniecpolski attempted to seize Chimielnitzki's lands, Chmielnitzki appealed to King Wladyslaw of Poland for support only to find his appeals ignored, apparently because Wladyslaw saw the younger Koniecpolski as an important ally in his attempts to strengthen and expand Polish influence in the Ukraine. Chmielnitzki turned to Cossack supporters who readily responded to charges of Polish attempts to undermine Cossack power in the Ukraine. Chmielnitzki's revolt broke out in 1648. Although Chmielnitzki would have failed if he relied only on his Cossack supporters, he persuaded the Tartars to join his revolt, which gave him a combination of Cossack infantry and Tartar cavalry that together could face the Polish cavalry, then viewed as the finest and most capable cavalry in all of Europe.

The result was a melee. As the Cossacks and their Tartar allies fought the Poles, both the Russians and the Swedes intervened to serve their own interests together with guerilla groups of various ethnicities. Although the Polish nobility and cavalry did not attack the Jews—Jews were used widely by the Polish-Lithuanian Commonwealth for tax collection, commerce, and other economic tasks that were considered onerous to the Poles—the Cossacks, Tartars, Russians, Swedes, and Polish partisans all treated Jews as enemies allied with the Polish nobility and attacked indiscriminately. Thousands of Jews were slaughtered, pushed off their own lands, and forced into exile to flee the violence. The revolt ended at some point between 1654 and 1657 (the date of Chmielnitzki's death) with the Poles pushed out of the Ukraine and the Russians gaining a toehold in the region. Most authorities maintain that approximately 100,000 Jews were massacred during the uprising and most Jewish communities were destroyed or severely damaged. As a result, Judaism at large viewed the Chmielnitzki massacres as another serious disaster that followed on the heels of the Spanish expulsion, and many began to press for the realization of a messianic redemption along the lines proposed by Lurianic kabbalah.

It was against the background of the Chmielnitzki massacres that Shabbetai Zevi entered the scene. Zevi was born in Smyrna (Izmir) on the ninth of Av, 1626. The ninth of Av was the traditional date on which the messiah was to be born in the view of many Jewish traditionalists at the time. His father, Mordecai, and his brothers, Elijah and Joseph, were relatively well-to-do poultry merchants, whose trading activities expanded and whose fortunes rose with the rise of Smyrna as a major center of trade in the early seventeenth century. Young Shabbetai pursued a traditional Jewish yeshivah education, and he was recognized as an *ilui*, a genius, very early in life. He was deemed to be the family *hakham*, learned sage, who would someday become a great rabbi. He studied under major teachers, R. Isaac de Alba and R. Joseph Escapa, and was ordained at age eighteen. He reportedly left yeshivah at age fifteen, however, because he had already mastered the Talmud and most of the rest of the Jewish tradition and was capable of studying on his own. Indeed, he isolated himself as an ascetic who would study the Zohar and other kabbalistic works from age fifteen through age twenty-two (1642–1648).

Unfortunately, during this period of his life, Zevi began to show symptoms of cyclothymia or manic-depressive syndrome, which could explain his charismatic and ecstatic personality combined with bouts of deep depression and potentially suicidal behavior.[14] At the time, his moods were described as being illuminated like Moses, falling, and hiding the face, which lent themselves easily to Lurianic notions of the hidden presence of G-d that would be revealed as sparks hidden among the *qelippot* in Lurianic parlance.

14. For discussion of Shabbetai Zevi's illness, see Scholem, *Sabbatai Sevi*, 125–38.

He engaged in *ma'asim zarim,* strange acts that were considered forbidden in Jewish tradition but were also considered by some to be hints of his messianic identity. Examples of such acts included pronouncing the Holy Name of G-d; strange rituals, such as observing Passover, Shavuot, and Sukkot all at once; and engaging in two marriages between 1646 and 1650, both of which remained unconsummated because he refused to approach either of his wives.

The year 1648 proved to be decisive for the young Shabbetai Zevi when he was twenty-one or twenty-two years old. It was at this time that word of the Chmielnitzki massacres began to reach the Jewish community of Smyrna. It was also the year that, in the view of many, the Zohar predicted that the messiah would come. Young Shabbetai Zevi, maintaining that great tribulation would introduce the advent of the messiah in the world, announced that he was the messiah after publicly uttering the Holy Name of G-d. No one took his claims seriously, and by ca. 1651–1654, the rabbis of Smyrna, including his teacher R. Joseph Escapa, banished him from the city. Zevi then traveled to Greece and Thrace. He ultimately settled in Salonika, where he was again expelled for another one of his strange acts; this time he celebrated a wedding ceremony between himself and the Torah, perhaps on the model of Shimon ben Azzai, a disciple of R. Akiba, who himself married the Torah and never took a wife.

During the years 1662–1665, Zevi settled in Jerusalem and Cairo. He married a woman named Sarah, who is described as a woman of doubtful reputation, in an effort to establish an analogy between himself and the prophet Hosea, who married a woman named Gomer. Gomer is described as a woman of harlotry, although Gomer never has a chance to speak for herself in the book of Hosea to challenge or confirm this accusation.

By 1664–1665, Zevi was troubled by his bizarre behavior, and began to seek help. He began by asking G-d to take away his abnormal states, but when his prayers proved ineffectual, he turned to other sources for help. He heard about a "man of G-d," the same designation given to the prophets Elijah and Elisha in the Bible, in the city of Gaza. Nathan of Gaza was a twenty-year-old kabbalistic faith healer who had a reputation for telling others the secrets concerning the roots of their souls so that they might find the means to achieve Tikkun within their own souls. It is unclear whether Nathan was an opportunist or if he was taken by surprise, but after meeting with Shabbetai Zevi, he became convinced that Zevi was indeed the messiah and did everything in his power to prompt Zevi to continue in his efforts to reveal himself as the messiah to the world. On May 31, 1655, Nathan the

Prophet and Shabbetai Zevi together in Gaza proclaimed that Shabbetai Zevi was indeed the messiah who had come to bring about Tikkun Olam in the world at large. It is testimony to the desperate state of Judaism in the aftermath of the Spanish Expulsion and the Chmielnitzki massacres that they were able to convince the entire Jewish population of Gaza concerning Zevi's messianic claims.

In June 1655 Shabbetai Zevi and Nathan of Gaza traveled to Jerusalem and circled the city seven times to declare Zevi to be the messiah. The local rabbinic authorities were appalled by this claim and opposed Zevi and Nathan of Gaza. But despite the rabbinic opposition, the general population of Jerusalem was willing to accept Zevi's claims and welcomed him as the messiah within their midst. By September 1655 Nathan of Gaza had a new revelation and addressed letters to the leadership of the Jewish population of Jerusalem and beyond. He made a number of claims concerning the significance of Shabbetai Zevi's appearance:

1. Lurianic meditations or *kavvanot* are no longer valid;
2. The inner structure of the universe had changed insofar as no more holy sparks of divine presence remained under the domination of the *qelippot* or material husks;
3. Shabbetai Zevi will take the crown of the Turkish sultan without war, and he will make the sultan his servant;
4. After four to five years, Shabbetai Zevi will go to the River Sambatyon to recover the Ten Lost Tribes of Israel; there he will marry Rebekah, a thirteen-year-old daughter of the resuscitated Moses;
5. The sultan will rebel against the efforts of Shabbetai Zevi, which is to be expected as part of the period of birth pangs of redemption;
6. The expected redemption will constitute the Tikkun Olam anticipated in Lurianic kabbalah.

In the aftermath of Nathan's announcements, Shabbetai Zevi attracted a mass following, in Jerusalem and beyond, of people who believed him to be the messiah who would usher in the Messianic Age of Tikkun Olam. Many began displaying aspects of prophetic behavior in anticipation of the final redemption of the world.

Shabbetai Zevi and Nathan of Gaza then returned to Smyrna. On December 11–12, 1655, Shabbetai Zevi broke off his Shabbat prayers and made his way to the Portuguese Synagogue in the city; the Portuguese Jews were his opponents. He took up an ax to smash the locked doors of the synagogue so that he could enter, read the Torah, announce himself to be the messiah, and proclaim that 15 Sivan, 5426 (June 18, 1666), would be the day of redemption.

Shabbetai Zevi then traveled to Constantinople by boat. But the sultan, recognizing that Shabbetai Zevi constituted a threat to his royal authority by making such claims, ordered his arrest on December 30, 1665. Shabbetai Zevi was intercepted in the Sea of Marmara on February 6, 1666. He was arrested and brought ashore in chains on February 8, 1666. But contrary to usual policy concerning rebels, Shabbetai Zevi was not executed immediately, and this only lent authority to his messianic claims. Shabbetai Zevi was imprisoned but refused an attempt to bribe the prison officials to ease the conditions of his incarceration. His refusal of such efforts again lent even more authority to his messianic claims. In prison, he maintained normalcy, presenting himself as a dignified scholar who bore his suffering. Nevertheless, later efforts to bribe the guards were successful, and Shabbetai Zevi was allowed to receive visitors as though he maintained a royal court.

The Turks saw Shabbetai Zevi's growing reputation in prison as a threat to Turkish authority. The climax came in September 1666, when a Polish kabbalist by the name of Nehemiah Hakohen visited Shabbetai Zevi in prison. There are conflicting accounts of the encounter. One account holds that Nehemiah failed to see how Shabbetai Zevi corresponded to earlier predictions of the messiah in Jewish tradition. Another account holds that Nehemiah Hakohen disagreed with Shabbetai Zevi over the nature and role of the Messiah ben Joseph who would precede the Messiah ben David. In the end, Nehemiah Hakohen claimed to be the predecessor Messiah ben Joseph, but Shabbetai Zevi denied that Nehemiah Hakohen filled this role in Judaism.

In the aftermath of this encounter, Nehemiah Hakohen informed the guards that Shabbetai Zevi was ready to convert to Islam. Zevi was taken to Adrianople on September 16, 1666. He was tried by a divan, or judge, in the presence of the Ottoman sultan and given the choice either to suffer immediate execution or convert to Islam. Shabbetai Zevi chose to convert to Islam, and he adopted the Muslim name Aziz Mehmed Effendi.

Nathan of Gaza stepped in following Shabbetai Zevi's conversion to Islam to explain what Zevi had done. Nathan held that Shabbetai Zevi was actually fulfilling his role as messiah because only the true messiah could restore some of the last sparks of the divine presence of G-d that were covered with the evil of the *qelippot* and that thereby prevented the full repair of the world of creation. The messiah must descend to the deepest depths of sin and shame to accomplish his messianic task.

Shabbetai Zevi continued for some ten years following his conversion to Islam leading a double life as an outward Muslim who taught as the head of a small group of converted Jews who had followed his example by themselves converting to Islam as well. During this last period of his life, Shabbetai Zevi still saw himself as the messiah and taught kabbalah to his followers in an effort to prepare them for the final restoration. He died on September 17, 1776, at the age of fifty.

Nathan of Gaza explained Shabbetai Zevi's death as a case of occultation and argued that Shabbetai Zevi had not actually died. Rather, Zevi had ascended to the realm of the heavenly lights and been absorbed into the G-dhead. Nathan's explanations of Shabbetai Zevi's death set the stage for other messianic and mystical expectations among the Jews of Eastern Europe that called for redemption through sin on the Shabbetean model.[15] As a result, two major Shabbetean movements arose. One was the Doenmeh sect, which comprised volunteers who converted to Islam like Shabbetai Zevi and continued to observe Judaism in secret in an effort to imitate the example of Shabbetai Zevi in bringing about the redemption of the world.[16] The other was the Frankist movement led by Jacob Frank (1726–1791) of Poland. Frank claimed to be a reincarnation of Shabbetai Zevi. He declared that the nullification of the Torah was in fact its true fulfillment. Eventually, he converted to Catholicism, attempting to establish a hidden Jewish presence that would bring about the final restoration of the world.

15. On the concept of redemption through sin in Shabbetean kabbalah, see Gershom Scholem, "Redemption Through Sin," in *The Messianic Idea in Judaism and Other Essays on Jewish Spirituality* (New York: Schocken, 1971), 78–141.

16. See Scholem, "The Crypto-Jewish Sect of the Dönmeh (Sabbatians) in Turkey," in *The Messianic Idea*, 142–66.

Chapter 10

HASIDISM

The Besht

Hasidism represents the modern manifestation of Jewish mysticism.[1] The term *Hasidism* has appeared before in relation to the Hasidei Ashkenaz movement in the German Rhineland and elsewhere in Central Europe during the twelfth–thirteenth centuries CE. The Hebrew term *hasid* simply means "one who is pious," and it is applied throughout the history of the Hebrew language to individuals and movements that manifest religious piety in its various forms. Modern Hasidism has nothing to do with the earlier movement. Instead, it constitutes an entirely new and different Jewish mystical and pietistic movement beginning from the early eighteenth century under the leadership of R. Israel ben Eliezer, otherwise known as the Baal Shem Tov, and continuing in various Hasidic movements through the present time.

Although R. Israel ben Eliezer (ca. 1700–1760) is universally recognized as the founder of the Hasidic movement, modern Hasidism actually grows out of earlier forms of Lurianic kabbalah and the Shabbatean movements that followed from the failed messianic claims of Shabbetai Zevi.[2] This is not to say that Hasidism replicates the earlier Lurianic and Shabbatean

---

1. For surveys of Hasidism, see Gershom Scholem, *Major Trends in Jewish Mysticism* (New York: Schocken, 1961), 325–50; J. H. Laenen, *Jewish Mysticism: An Introduction*, trans. David E. Orton (Louisville: Westminster John Knox, 2001), 215–50; Moshe Idel, *Hasidism: Between Ecstasy and Magic* (Albany: SUNY Press, 1995); Gershon David Hundert, ed., *Essential Papers on Hasidism: Origins to Present* (New York: New York University Press, 1991); Rivka Schatz Uffenheimer, *Hasidism as Mysticism: Quietistic Elements in Eighteenth Century Hasidic Thought* (Princeton: Princeton University Press, 1993); David Biale et al., *Hasidism: A New History* (Princeton: Princeton University Press, 2017).

2. See esp. Biale et al., *Hasidism*, 43–75.

movements. Rather, Hasidism develops out of the earlier movements, although it constructs its own distinctive worldview that frequently draws on Lurianic and Shabbatean thought, but in some respects also rejects or moves well beyond earlier beliefs and practice. Hasidism does not represent a Jewish intellectual movement following the example of its Lurianic and Shabbetean forebears. Rather, it developed among the largely uneducated Eastern European Jewish working class of Podolia, the Ukraine, Belorussia, and Lithuania. Laenen, drawing on the work of Meijers, points to the major economic downturn that followed the Chmielnitzki rebellion against the Polish-Lithuanian Commonwealth in 1648–1657 and the other conflicts, such as the Russo-Polish War (1654–1667) and the Second Northern War (1655–1660), that grew out of, coincided with, and followed the rebellion. These wars killed some 100,000 Jews and left the Jewish community—as well as much of the region at large—economically depressed for a century or more. The result was that most of the Jewish communities of this region were unable to see to the education of their children. Although there were still wealthy Jews and Jewish communities, such as Vilna (Vilnius), which became a major intellectual Jewish community, the majority of the Jewish working class were left largely illiterate and ignorant of most of the Jewish literary tradition. As a result, Hasidism emerged initially as a largely anti-intellectual movement that relied more on individual spirituality and magical practice led by charismatic faith healers who constituted the initial leadership of the movement.

Hasidism arose in the aftermath of the Shabbetai Zevi debacle as the Jewish people and the world at large began to recognize that Shabbetai Zevi was a false messiah. In the aftermath of his conversion to Islam and death ten years later, many kabbalistic faith healers began to appear among the Jewish communities of Eastern Europe to promote forms of spiritual action, healing, and demon expulsion at a time when traditional Jewish education was declining among the population and magical practice was gaining in appeal. Magic, amulets, and faith healing had always been a part of the kabbalistic tradition, but in the absence of a strong intellectual tradition magic became the primary form of kabbalistic practice among the working-class Jewish population. Such faith healers were called *baalei shem*, "masters of the Name (of G-d)," insofar as their knowledge and practices were based on alleged knowledge and application of the Holy Power of the Name of G-d, YHWH. Such *baalei shem* generally presupposed a Lurianic worldview, insofar as Lurianic kabbalah had taken such deep root among the Jewish people of Eastern Europe and beyond, due to its emphasis on Lurianic prayer and practice that so frequently called for *kavvanot* or meditations on the divine Name as a basis for activating the sefirot within the human soul and thereby raising the sparks of divine presence from among the *qelippot* or husks that constituted the finite, material world. By such means, the *baalei shem* maintained that they could purify a human soul from evil and enable individuals to overcome illness and impurity in the process of sanctifying their lives and the world in which they lived.

Israel ben Eliezer gained his reputation as a *baal shem*, and because he rose to prominence as the epitome of the Baalei Shem and was credited with the founding of Hasidic Judaism, he is known as the Baal Shem Tov, i.e., The Master of the Good Name (of G-d), an epithet generally abbreviated as "the Besht." Most knowledge about the Baal Shem Tov is derived from legendary sources, such as the Shivhei Habesht, "Praises of the Baal Shem Tov," which was first published in 1814 as an adulatory and legendary account of his life for the edification of the Hasidim and the promulgation of Hasidic Judaism amongst the people.[3] Other collections of Hasidic legends about the Besht and his teachings include Tzvaat Haribash, "The Testament of Rabbi Israel Baal Shem," which presents the Besht's teachings concerning the need for the expression of joy in worship and study. Although the Baal Shem Tov taught in Yiddish, Shneur Zalman of Liady observes that it is written in Hebrew, which indicates its later origins among disciples. The Keter Shem Tov, "Crown of the Good Name," published in 1794, apparently by later disciples, is a collection of teachings by the Baal Shem Tov. Because of the legendary character of these works, it is difficult to tell how much goes back to the Besht himself and how much represents the understandings of his later disciples. Such legendary accounts are typical of major religious leaders as exemplified by Moses in the Torah and rabbinic literature, Jesus in the Gospels, Siddhartha Gautama in Buddhist literature, and many others.

Israel ben Eliezer was born in the town of Okopy, Podolia, not far from Kamieniec Podolski, near the Polish-Turkish border between Podolia and Moldavia.[4] The legends about his birth indicate that he was born during a period of peace, which would have begun with the peace agreement signed between Poland and the Ottoman Turkish Empire at Karlowice in 1699.

---

3. Dan Ben-Amos and Jerome R. Mintz, trans. and eds., *In Praise of the Baal Shem Tov [Shivhei ha-Besht]: The Earliest Collection of Legends about the Founder of Hasidism* (New York: Schocken, 1984).

4. Avraham Rubenstein, "Israel ben Eliezer," *EncJud* 9:1049–58; Simon Dubnow, "The Beginnings: The Baal Shem Tov (Besht) and the Center in Podolia," in *Essential Papers*, ed. Hundert, 25–57.

Consequently, most authorities place his birth at approximately 1700, although the exact date remains unknown. Israel's father, Eliezer, had been taken prisoner by armed men, presumably Tartars involved in the conflict. According to the legends, Eliezer was taken to a place where there were no Jews and forced to serve as a servant in the house of the Viceroy. Because of the favorable impression he made, Eliezer was eventually appointed as counselor to the king, but he was allowed to return home when it was learned that he was Jewish and already married. The prophet Elijah appeared to him and revealed that his wife, Sarah, would bear him a son—even though they were both close to one hundred years old—who would bring enlightenment to all Israel. Consequently, they named him Israel.

Young Israel was orphaned early in life. His father told him on his deathbed to remember, "G-d is with you; do not fear anything." After the death of his father, young Israel was entrusted to the Jewish community in Okopy who sent him to study at the local *heder* and *Talmud Torah*, terms for traditional Jewish religious schools. Israel was able to support himself by serving as a supervisor for younger boys, making sure that they found their way to school each day, leading them in the chanting of simple prayers, and other duties necessary to keep the school in order. Although young Israel was capable enough in his studies, he was not very interested in them, and he frequently skipped classes to spend his time in the forests of the Carpathian Mountains, where he communed with nature, studied kabbalistic texts, and began to recognize the presence of G-d in the finite world of nature all about him. Dubnow points out that the Kitvei Ha'ari, or Writings of the Ari (Ashkenazi Rabbi Isaac Luria), a work that dealt with the practical aspects of Lurianic kabbalah, was widely known at the time and may therefore have been a work that the young Israel ben Eliezer might have studied on his own.

Scholars such as Dubnow and Scholem have noted that among the works that young Israel ben Eliezer would have read was a collection of manuscripts delivered to him by the son of a Rabbi Adam Baal Shem. Rabbi Adam instructed his son to deliver the manuscripts to Israel ben Eliezer after his death because the son was not worthy of them, but the future Baal Shem Tov was. When the son delivered the manuscripts after his father's death, he stated that they came from his father's patrimony and that he had been instructed to deliver them to the young Israel ben Eliezer. After delivering the manuscripts and watching how young Israel ben Eliezer studied them, the son asked to remain so that he might learn the material found in the manuscripts under the tutelage of the young Israel ben Eliezer. The manuscripts apparently included extensive teachings that would make young Israel ben

Eliezer a Baal Shem, and he agreed to allow the son to remain and study with him, provided that he keep the matter secret. Such an instruction was consistent with the insistence in the legends that young Israel deliberately presented himself as an ignoramus so as not to reveal his true character until the time for his revelation had come. As for the manuscript material attributed to R. Adam Baal Shem in the legends, modern scholarship has postulated an identification for the man and his work. Insofar as the name Adam would not have been used by Jews at the time, Scholem argues that Rabbi Adam must be identified with R. Heshel Zoref of Vilna, a Shabbatean Baal Shem who died in 1700 and wrote an approximately 1,400-page manuscript entitled "Sefer Hatzoref," which takes up the mysteries of the prayer Shema Yisrael. Scholem maintains that the Baal Shem Tov had a copy of this work which he treasured and studied all his life. Later scholars have demonstrated that Scholem is wrong in this claim.[5] Scholem never analyzed the contents of this manuscript to demonstrate its relationship to Hasidic thought. Furthermore, the Baal Shem Tov opposed the Shabbateans, and frequently allied with the classical rabbinic authorities in Vilna to do so. Shortly before his death, the Frankist movement converted to Christianity. Upon news that the Frankists had converted, the Besht commented that as long as a branch remains connected to a tree, it is possible to save, but once the branch is cut off from the tree, there is no longer any hope of saving it.

Young Israel ben Eliezer was eventually engaged to be married to a woman named Chana bat Ephraim. Young Israel had aided her father, Ephraim of Brody, in some legal matters by acting as the *dayyan* or judge in the case. He had so impressed the older man that he offered his daughter to him in marriage. Israel agreed to the marriage, provided that it remained confidential for a period of time. Unfortunately, Ephraim died before informing his daughter of her betrothal, but she agreed to marry Israel ben Eliezer upon finding a document of betrothal among her late father's papers. Her brother, R. Abraham Gershon Kutower, regarded Israel ben Eliezer as an uneducated ignoramus, apparently because he was not a talmudic scholar. But as we have seen above, Israel ben Eliezer was in fact educated, albeit in kabbalistic and Shabbatean texts, especially those that dealt with practical issues. Nevertheless, R. Gershon was so scandalized by the marriage that he bought Israel and Chana a horse and wagon and told them to leave Brody to find a home elsewhere.

5. Moshe Idel, *Kabbalah: New Perspectives* (New Haven: Yale University Press, 1988), 266–67.

They settled in a valley in the Carpathian Mountains between Kutow and Kosow where young Israel isolated himself in the forests, perhaps on the model of young Isaac Luria in Egypt, to commune with nature, meditate, and study kabbalistic texts. Twice a week Chana brought the cart to Israel, who would load the cart with clay that he had dug from the side of a hill for sale in town. Otherwise, young Israel continued his earlier communion with nature to learn the meaning of the phrase from the Kedushah, "The whole earth is filled with His (G-d's) glory." Later, Chana ran a small tavern, again provided by her brother, while young Israel continued his isolation. It was common for Jews to run taverns in this period as they were commissioned by the Polish and Russian governments during this period to collect taxes on the sale of alcohol. Such a policy redirected public resentment at alcohol taxes from the government to the Jews. Later, R. Gershon became an admirer of the Baal Shem Tov after hearing his exposition of rabbinic texts, realizing that he was not an ignoramus at all.[6]

Although Israel ben Eliezer deliberately hid his future status as the Baal Shem Tov, the legends emphasize that he was at times recognized, apparently building anticipation for his coming revelation. Various stories were told about how local rabbis summoned young Israel ben Eliezer for simple lessons in Talmud and other Jewish texts. In an effort to conceal his true identity, he would put on his simpleton's mask to appear before the rabbi, but he would remove the mask from time to time to reveal who he truly was. In another case, the legend of the Mad Woman of Brody, a woman who was believed to be demented and spent much of her time mumbling to herself regained her senses when she encountered the young Israel ben Eliezer, and declared to him, "I know who you are, and I am not afraid of you! I know that you possess certain powers, and I also know that you may not use them until the age of thirty-six!" Young Israel responded to her simply, "Be quiet, or I will evict the evil spirit from you!"

According to legend, Israel ben Eliezer did indeed begin his career as the Baal Shem Tov at age thirty-six. Insofar as thirty-six is twice eighteen, and eighteen is the numerical value of the Hebrew word *hay*, "life," the age of thirty-six is an especially auspicious time for success. One Shabbat, a student of R. Gershon was traveling and stayed at the tavern run by Chana and

---

6. For a study of R. Gershon Kutover, particularly his later life in the land of Israel, see Abraham Joshua Heschel, "Rabbi Gershon Kutover: His Life and Immigration to the Land of Israel," in *The Circle of the Baal Shem Tov: Studies in Hasidism*, ed. S. H. Dresner (Chicago: University of Chicago Press, 1985), 44–112.

Israel ben Eliezer. As usual, Israel presented himself as an ignoramus, but in the middle of the night, the student awakened in fear to see a huge flame burning on the fireplace hearth. But when he ran to extinguish it to prevent the tavern from burning down, he was surprised to find that the flame was actually Israel ben Eliezer flooded in light. Israel told him simply, "One does not look where one should not," and sent him back to bed. After Shabbat concluded, the student returned home and announced that there was a new source of light in the world. As a result, the men of the community ran to the forest to build a new throne for the Baal Shem Tov with branches and leaves as the Besht announced, "I shall open a new way."

Many of the legends emphasize the various miracles undertaken by the Baal Shem Tov to save the lives and livelihoods of others, much like the legends of Elijah and Elisha in the book of Kings. One such legend concerned a rich man who traded in goods with the city of Leipzig, but he had no children. Upon the advice of a friend, he went to visit the Baal Shem Tov, who told him to cease his trade with Leipzig, sell all of his merchandise, rent an *arrendeh* (lease) from the governor in Leipzig, and inform him when his wife gave birth to a son. He did as instructed, and his wife gave birth the following year; but he neglected to inform the Besht, thinking that it was just a coincidence. When the boy grew up, he became wild and incorrigible, and the man finally visited the Baal Shem Tov again. The Baal Shem Tov told him to sell the *arrendeh*, go to Leipzig, and spend a year traveling, after which the son would be a changed man who would study Torah. The rich man did as instructed, but after four months he bought more merchandise and ran out of money to travel. He placed his merchandise in a wagon while in a town and stopped to observe the Shabbat. Following Shabbat, a man offered to buy his merchandise on half credit. The value of the merchandise was established as 160,000 red coins. The man paid him half and gave him a note for the rest. The rich man bought more merchandise but could not buy more than 80,000 coins' worth because his note was only signed "Jonah," and no one knew who he was. Despairing that he would never see the rest of his money, the rich man prepared to return home, but as he approached the city gate, the man who had bought his merchandise and given him the note signed "Jonah" met him there and, after some discussion, paid the remaining money and told the rich man to give his regards to the Baal Shem Tov. Upon returning home, he found that his son had changed and had begun to study Torah diligently. The rich man went to see the Besht and give him Jonah's greetings, to which the Besht responded, "That was Jonah ben Amittai, the prophet of the Bible."

Such a portrayal is consistent with that of a Shabbetean faith healer, which one might expect from a figure who was apparently influenced by a Shabbetean master like Heshel Zoref. But Scholem makes special efforts to demonstrate that Hasidism differs markedly from the Shabbatean masters and movements that emerged following the failure of Shabbetai Zevi. Shabbetai Zevi was a self-styled messiah, and his efforts were directed to redeeming the Jewish people in particular and the world at large from the evil of the Sitra Ahra, whose husks had hidden the sparks of the divine presence that had been scattered throughout the world, according to Lurianic tradition. Shabbetai Zevi's role was to identify and raise the last of those sparks so that the world at large might be redeemed. Nathan of Gaza argued that Zevi's conversion to Islam was a deliberate act to find the last sparks by descending to the deepest levels of sin, so as to ensure their gathering, rising, and reintegration, resulting in the repair of the divine presence in the world.

The subsequent Shabbatean movements, the Doehnmeh in Islam and the Frankists in Roman Catholicism, converted to other religions in an effort to emulate Shabbetai Zevi and thereby to bring about the final redemption. But Sholem points out that the Baal Shem Tov and the early Hasidic movement never saw themselves as messianic in character insofar as there was no focus on the redemption of the Jewish people or the world at large; rather, the Baal Shem Tov and his followers focused on the redemption of individuals. Indeed, Shabbetai Zevi had been discredited, and that called for a revision in strategy. In this respect, Scholem misses an important point: the final redemption may focus on the Jewish people, humankind, and creation at large, but one must remember that the Jewish people and the world at large comprise all the individuals that forge and constitute the corporate identity of the larger groups. The Baal Shem Tov's strategy appears to be to redeem each of the individual souls that constitute the people of Israel and thereby to bring about the redemption of the Jewish people and the world at large. But the process would focus on each individual Jew, one by one, and likewise each individual gentile. By this means, the Baal Shem Tov and the Hasidic movement in general would be able to concentrate on recovering all the individual sparks of the divine presence, one by one, and in doing so to bring about the redemption of the entire Jewish people and the world of creation at large.

At least in this respect, the early Hasidic movement was indeed messianic, even as it concentrated only on individuals. Hasidism inaugurates a messianic process in which the Baal Shem Tov and his successors point the way as individuals who bring about the redemption of other individuals by enabling them to discover the divine spark or element within. Such a strategy takes seriously the Lurianic—and to a certain degree, the Shabbatean—element of hiddenness or concealment of the divine or the holy in the finite world of creation. The purpose of hiddenness was not to engage in sin to bring about the final redemption, as Nathan of Gaza explained Shabbetai Zevi's conversion, or as the Shabbatean sects counseled in imitation of Shabbetai Zevi; rather, the purpose of hiddenness was to call upon people to make the special effort to activate their intangible souls and thereby to find the sanctity or sparks of the divine that were concealed within their own tangible and finite beings. Thus, the Baal Shem Tov and early Hasidism focused on *kavvanah*, proper intention or meditation, to motivate the soul to act, engaging and realizing the holiness within, and on *devequt*, cleaving to the divine as the means to engage the inner holiness and to bring it to realization within one's own life and actions. Unlike the Zohar and earlier Lurianic kabbalah, early Hasidism did not develop a theoretic or intellectual approach to the engagement of holiness that required an adherent to gain great knowledge of the tradition through study. The Baal Shem Tov was known for study, but he was not a rabbinic Talmud scholar like those of Vilna. Instead, he called for study with proper intention, such as meditating on the letters of the text rather than focusing on the contents of the Talmud's teaching.[7] Recognizing the relatively uneducated character of the Jewish people at the time, the early Hasidic tradition focused on the uneducated working class; the movement recognized that this neglected class was the very basis in which the final sparks of the holy in the world would be found. One did not have to be a sage in early Hasidism; rather, one could be the simplest working person, much as Israel ben Eliezer made himself seem during his earlier years, and yet nevertheless discover the depth of holiness within the self as well as within others and the world in which one lived.

Indeed, the messianic character of the early Hasidic movement is accentuated by the role that the prophet Elijah plays in communicating with the Baal Shem Tov. In Jewish tradition, Elijah is the precursor to the messiah who visits Jewish homes during the Passover Seder to answer the halakic question of whether four or five cups of wine are to be drunk during the seder for each of the passages in the Torah that call upon Jews to teach

---

7. See Joseph Weiss, "Torah Study in Early Hasidism," in *Studies in Eastern European Jewish Mysticism*, ed. D. Goldstein, Littman Library of Jewish Civilization (Oxford: Oxford University Press, 1985), 56–68.

their children the Passover story so that the Jewish people might be able to return to the land of Israel. According to one legend, the Baal Shem Tov responded to the demands of his disciples to show them the prophet Elijah. He told them, "Open your eyes wide," so that they might see. Three figures then appeared before them in succession. The first was a beggar who entered a house of study from which he emerged with a book that he had stolen. The second was another beggar who entered a banquet hall and emerged with a silver spoon that he had stolen. The third was a soldier sitting on his horse asking for someone to light his pipe. The disciples asked the Baal Shem Tov, "Where is Elijah?" The Baal Shem Tov responded, "It was he; the secret is in the eyes," i.e., all depends upon one's perspective in the world. Each of the figures that the disciples had seen was a most unlikely model for Elijah, the precursor to the messiah. The first two were thieves, hardly the kind of righteous figure that one might expect the holy prophet Elijah to be. The third was a threat, i.e., a soldier, who was generally the type of figure that would persecute and kill Jews on behalf of the local gentile authorities of the time, hardly a likely model for the prophet Elijah who would precede the redemption of the Jews and the world. But in the eyes of the Baal Shem Tov, each was a likely Elijah if each would recognize the presence of the divine within. The point of the legend is that anyone could be Elijah, no matter how lowly, dishonest, and even threatening one might be. Even persons of the lowest and most suspect status had the capacity to find holiness within the self and act thereon on behalf of the divine to redeem the world in which we live.

Such a view presaged the advent of the messiah in Hasidic thought as each individual had the capacity to bring about the messiah much as Elijah was reputed to do. Indeed, the prophet Elijah in the Bible was the lowest of the low. According to 1 Kgs 17, Elijah lived in the Wadi Cherith, where the crows supported him by bringing his food. And yet Elijah was the figure who provided food for the woman of Zarephath and brought her son back to life, before having his vision of G-d on Mt. Horeb in 1 Kgs 19 and ascending to heaven in a fiery chariot in 2 Kgs 2 as his disciple Elisha emerged with even greater power to take his place.

As the Baal Shem Tov's life began to draw to a close, the question of the leadership of Hasidic Judaism became paramount. Although the Baal Shem Tov had a son, Hersheleh Zevi, the legends indicate that his son was considered incapable of assuming leadership. On the day of the Baal Shem Tov's death, his followers asked him, "Why do you not instruct your son (in what needs to be done following the Besht's death)?" The Besht responded

"What can I do? He is asleep." So his followers awakened Hersheleh and brought him to his father. The Besht told his son that he knew that he had given the boy a holy soul, for when he joined with his wife, the heavens shook. But the Besht continued that he could have brought the soul of Adam, but he refrained from doing so because he already had all that was necessary. So Hersheleh asked his father, "Tell me something!" When the Besht started to speak, Hersheleh said that he did not know what his father was saying, so the Besht told Hersheleh that there was nothing he could do. So he taught his son a name and told him that when he uttered the name, the Besht would come to study with him after his death. Hersheleh asked, "What if I forget the name?" Although the Besht instructed his son in the means to remember the name, the narrator states that Hersheleh did not remember what the Besht said.

The Baal Shem Tov died on the first day of Shavuot, May 22, 1760. Shavuot is a special occasion because it celebrates the revelation of Torah at Sinai as narrated in Parashat Jethro, Exod 18–20, and the Haftarah portion is Ezek 1, which relates Ezekiel's vision of G-d in the divine throne-chariot. The narrative states that R. Pinhas, a disciple of the Besht, had come to visit, but he had neglected to go to the mikveh prior to the holiday. During the course of his prayers, he perceived that the Besht would die because of his opposition to the Shabbateans who wanted to burn the Talmud on Yom Kippur. Although R. Pinhas strengthened his prayers, the Besht told him that the deed was done, and nothing would then prevent his death. On Shavuot night, the Besht taught Torah as was customary, but by morning the Angel of Death was on his way. The soul of a dead man came to the Besht to ask for a blessing, but the Besht rebuked him and sent him away. When the Angel of Death appeared before him, he granted the angel two hours, but asked that he not torture him. When the Besht's followers asked to whom he spoke, the Besht responded that it was the Angel of Death, "Do you not see him?" At this point, it was clear that the Besht was losing his power because he could not expel the Angel of Death. The Besht gave his followers a sign that when he would die, two clocks would stop. When he washed his hands, one clock stopped, and his followers blocked his view so he would not know. So the Besht told them that he was not concerned—when he leaves through one door, he would enter through another. He expounded on the texts concerning the ascent from the lower heavens to the upper heavens, began his prayers, and then became quiet until his followers realized that he had passed away. At that point, the second clock stopped.

Hasidim and Mitnagdim

By the time of the Baal Shem Tov's death, he had gathered a following that had spread well beyond Polonne into the Ukraine and other areas of Eastern Europe.[8] There have been attempts to estimate the numbers, but none have proved to be reliable. Among his followers were Nahman of Horodenka, Menahem Mendel of Premishlan, Pinhas of Korzec, Menahem Mendel of Bar, and Nahman of Korsov. According to Hasidic legend, the Baal Shem Tov appeared to his followers in a vision shortly after his death to inform them that he had chosen R. Dov Ber, the Maggid of Mezritsh, located in the region of Volonne. In actuality, it appears that there was some difficulty in establishing a successor. The Baal Shem's son, Hersheleh Zevi, proved to be an inadequate leader and stepped down after about a year. There were a number of other contenders for leadership, most notably Jacob Joseph of Polonne and Dov Ber. Although Jacob Joseph was the more senior and perhaps better educated, and Dov Ber suffered major health issues that kept him bedridden for much of his later life, Dov Ber emerged as the Baal Shem's successor.[9] He had a very charismatic personality and a systematic and organizational mind, and he proved to be far more adept at building the movement and attracting followers. Even so, not all of the Baal Shem's disciples accepted Dov Ber's leadership, and the seeds were sown for a movement that would lack central authority in later generations. Whereas the Baal Shem Tov had lived in Mezhbizh in Podolia, Dov Ber lived initially in Mezritsh in Volhynia and later in Hanipol (Annopol).

The term *Maggid* refers to Dov Ber's role as a kabbalistic preacher, who through his charismatic personality gathered many more followers to the movement, began to systematize the teachings of the Baal Shem Tov and laid the organizational foundations for the movement. The dates of the Maggid's birth are uncertain, ranging from 1700 to 1710. He was given a classical Jewish education and was known for his expertise in Talmud and kabbalah. He initially made his living as a teacher and lived as an ascetic to devote himself to the study and teaching of Torah. But his abstinence from sufficient food caused his health to decline, and he turned to the Baal Shem Tov for healing.

---

8. For historical background, see esp. Biale et al., *Hasidism*, 76–99, who stress that the early movement was constituted by a circle of largely independent followers who led small groups in various villages through the region.

9. Esther Zweig Liebes, "Dov Baer (The Maggid) of Mezhirech," *EncJud* 6:180–84; Simon Dubnow, "The Maggid of Miedzyrzecz: His Associates and the Center in Volhynia (1760–1772)," in *Essential Papers*, ed. Hundert, 58–85; Biale et al., *Hasidism*, 76–99.

The Baal Shem taught the Maggid that his regimen of study and fasting was not in accord with G-d's will; instead, G-d called for attention to the soul with joy and religious enthusiasm as the basis to establish communion with G-d and thereby to raise the divine sparks in the world to bring about Tikkun Olam. Nevertheless, the Baal Shem taught him that he needed to eat as well, although Dov Ber still continued to practice some self-denial which ensured that he would endure poor health for most of his life. Indeed, it was on the basis of the Baal Shem's focus on the soul that Dov Ber became his disciple. With his classical rabbinic training, Dov Ber was not initially convinced by the Baal Shem Tov's teachings until the Besht summoned him in the middle of the night to ask him to interpret a passage from Hayim Vital's Etz Hayim, which summarized Lurianic kabbalah. The Maggid read the passage and gave a standard rabbinic interpretation of the text, but the Besht told him that he was wrong. The Maggid looked again and held to his position. It was only when the Besht explained to him that although his interpretation was technically correct, it lacked any sense of soul or enthusiasm for the ideas expressed therein. Seeing the angels that had entered the room as the Baal Shem Tov explained the issue, the Maggid then decided to remain and study with the Besht to learn from his great wisdom. Because the Maggid suffered from poor health and could not travel about to Eastern European Jewish communities, he remained homebound throughout most of his life as the leader of the Hasidic movement and sent emissaries out to teach on behalf of himself and the movement. His residence in Volhynia in central Poland, rather than in Polonne where the Baal Shem lived, proved to be an important strategic decision. Whereas Polonne was located in the south near the Turkish border, Volhynia was more centrally located in central Poland between Lithuania, Germany, and the Ukraine, and the location better enabled the Maggid to send emissaries to these regions to ensure the growth of the Hasidic movement.

Unfortunately, Dov Ber wrote very little, and his teachings are known through the works of legend and of his followers. His teachings apparently focused especially on the notion of *devequt*, cleaving to G-d or establishing a special holy relationship with G-d. Dov Ber's focus on *devequt* and his charismatic personality prompted the Hasidic movement to begin developing the image of the tzaddik, the righteous person or teacher, like the Baal Shem Tov or the Maggid of Mezritsh, who due to his righteous and saintly persona would represent the divine presence to others and serve as the instigator for others to imitate and learn from him how to activate and redeem the sparks of the divine within. The Hasidic tzaddik developed into a major figure in the Hasidic movement insofar as the holiness and purity of his soul better enabled him to raise the sparks of the divine presence to restore the holiness and integrity of creation. The tzaddik therefore emerged as a figure who had a special relationship with G-d and thereby was able to intercede with G-d on behalf of others. Because of Dov Ber's role in developing the image of the tzaddik, there are numerous examples in Hasidic legend of how a disciple would hide under the Maggid's bed at night to see how he made love to his wife, how he laced up his boots in the morning, and other such actions, all in an effort to emulate the great tzaddik. The theory behind such an act is that even the smallest or most insignificant acts of the tzaddik convey holiness that can be learned, emulated, and transmitted for the ultimate redemption or repair of the world.

Such an understanding presupposes that the world is filled with the divine sparks of the holy presence of G-d and that even the most insignificant of those sparks must be recovered, redeemed, and reassembled to restore the holiness of the tangible world of creation. Indeed, the Maggid appears to have rethought the Lurianic doctrine of Tzimtzum. Tzimtzum was no longer understood to be a moment of contraction in which the divine presence had somehow withdrawn from the world leaving only fragments or scattered sparks of the divine presence that littered the finite world and had to be recovered from the husks that concealed them. Rather, the Maggid understood Tzimtzum to be an act of emanation or explosion in which the sparks or fragments emerged from the Ayin or Nothingness to permeate the world of finite creation. Thus, the divine sparks were indeed scattered and hidden throughout the finite world of creation, and they still needed to be recovered and gathered together to ensure the sanctity and integrity of the world of creation. But whereas individual effort was the norm during the time of the Baal Shem Tov, the tzaddik or Hasidic master increasingly took on this role on behalf of his own followers. Any man could become a tzaddik, and having become such, would act on behalf of others and especially exemplify holiness that would serve as a model for others who would follow suit, much like the figure of the Bodhisattva in Buddhism.

Among the Maggid's disciples were many of the founders of the various Hasidic sects that emerged in Eastern Europe following the Maggid's lifetime, i.e., Elimelekh Weissblum of Lizhensk , Shneur Zalman of Liady, Nahum of Chernobyl, Levi Yitzhak of Barditshev, Menahem Mendel of Vitebsk, Jacob Isaac Horowitz (the Seer of Lublin), Israel ben Shabetai Hopstein (the Maggid of Kozhenits), and Shlomo of Karlin. Dov Ber employed his skills as a Maggid and focused on teaching his followers the developing Hasidic thought of the Baal Shem Tov, which he expounded in relation to his own expertise in rabbinical and kabbalistic literature. He would then send his followers out into Eastern Europe to act as maggidim themselves and then to return periodically for further study and communion with their fellow Hasidic masters. On this basis, Dov Ber established the initial, decentralized organization of Hasidic Judaism insofar as his disciples established synagogues and bases for the teaching and spread of Hasidic Judaism, and thereby ensured the growth and future of the movement throughout Eastern Europe. R. Dov Ber apparently lived for some twelve years after the death of the Baal Shem Tov and died in 1772, but his impact on the movement was significant as Hasidic Judaism began to grow and challenge the authority and standing of the more classically oriented rabbinic figures from Vilna and elsewhere who relied on their vast knowledge of rabbinic tradition to assert their leadership of Eastern European Ashkenazi Judaism.

The Hasidic movement, with its emphasis on the souls of the simplest of working-class Jews who lacked such education, therefore presented a major challenge to the rabbinic elite of the time. As the Hasidic movement grew, opposition began to grow in classical rabbinic circles. By the time of the Maggid's death in 1772, R. Elijah ben Solomon Zalman (1720–1797), otherwise known as the Vilna Gaon or Hagra' (Hagaon Rabbeinu Elijah, the Gaon our Rabbi Elijah), was recognized as the leading rabbinic authority of his time. The Vilna Gaon represented the epitome of the Jewish intellectual tradition as an authority in rabbinic literature, halakah, Jewish philosophy, and kabbalah. During the mid-eighteenth century, Vilna, modern-day Vilnius in Lithuania, was a Jewish-majority city known as the capital of Eastern European Judaism. Because of his view that Jews required extensive knowledge of the classical Jewish tradition, he regarded the Hasidim as heretical because of their lack of attention to Jewish knowledge and their prayer like madmen. He therefore issued an edict of excommunication for the entire Hasidic movement as unfit to be considered as Jews. Indeed, the tension caused by the Vilna Gaon's excommunication of the Hasidic movement is frequently cited as a contributing factor to the Maggid's death.

But the Hasidim for their part were not fazed. By 1781, R. Jacob Joseph, one of the Baal Shem Tov's original disciples, published *Toledot Jacob Joseph*, The History of Jacob Joseph, which was the first major publication of Hasidic thought and practice. The *Toledot* was a polemical work in which R. Jacob Joseph, an accomplished and educated preacher like the Maggid, argued that admonishment of the leadership of his generation was just as important as blessing, i.e., the admonishment of the prophet Ahijah the Shilonite against

King Solomon was more important than the blessings of Balaam ben Beor for Israel. Such a position apparently grew out in part from his anger and frustration at being passed over by Dov Ber as the leader of the Hasidic movement. Indeed, R. Jacob Joseph argued that Ahijah was the teacher of the prophet Elijah and as noted above, Elijah was the teacher of the Baal Shem Tov in visionary form. On this basis, the Hasidim would proceed with their critique of the Vilna rabbinical authorities and to a certain degree of the Hasidic leadership. The Hasidim therefore excommunicated the Vilna Gaon and the Mitnagdim (Opponents) and their followers in turn for their alleged lack of attention to the Jewish soul. The Mitnagdim in turn issued further orders of excommunication against the Hasidim and even approached the Czarist Russian government to denounce the movement, resulting in the imprisonment of some Hasidic leaders.

Although Jacob Joseph ben Zevi Hakohen of Polonne was embittered at being passed over as the successor of the Baal Shem Tov, his *Toledot* and other writings established him as a major intellect who profoundly shaped the ideology of the movement. He had a rabbinic education and had served as rabbi in various locations in Podolia before finally settling in Polonne where he spent the rest of his life. In addition to his critique of the rabbinic leadership of his day, he taught that the presence of G-d is manifested everywhere in the world and in every human thought. It is therefore necessary for human beings to recognize the divine element within the self and work assiduously to improve and uplift it so as to bring about Tikkun within the self and from there in the greater world of finite creation. By manifesting within the soul joy in the material and form of the finite world, humans overcome the inclination to evil to become a force for holiness and good in the world and thereby to achieve or better to recognize *devequt* or cleaving with G-d. Prayer undertaken with a purified and joyful soul enables one to commune with G-d and change an evil decree to a favorable one on behalf of others and society at large. In the case of an ignoramus who understands nothing of Judaism or of G-d, it is the task of the tzaddik to pray on his behalf to ensure his cleaving to G-d as well as the lifting of his own sparks.

Habad Hasidism

Although there was tremendous tension between the Hasidim and the Mitnagdim, it is clear that the Hasidic movement turned increasingly to Torah study in the aftermath of the Baal Shem Tov's life. Indeed, many of the legends suggest that the Baal Shem Tov himself was a competent rabbinic scholar insofar as he knew rabbinic scholarship but critiqued it for its lack of soul as indicated in the legend concerning Dov Ber's initiation as a disciple of the Besht, noted above. It is also clear that a number of his first disciples, Dov Ber, Jacob Joseph of Polonne, Shneur Zalman of Liady, and others, were indeed competent rabbinic scholars who were able to respond to the charges leveled against the movement by the Mitnagdim, but it is unclear if the later turn to rabbinic study influenced the presentation of the Baal Shem Tov in the legends about him. It is well known that the Baal Shem Tov allied with the rabbinic authorities to oppose the Shabbatean movements, particularly the Frankist sect which converted *en masse* to Christianity near the end of the Baal Shem Tov's life, so it is plausible that the Baal Shem Tov had at least some sympathy for rabbinic studies even if he did not subscribe to the rabbinic viewpoint in its entirety.[10]

One of the best-known and most influential Torah scholars in the Baal Shem Tov's inner circle was Shneur Zalman of Liady (1745–1813), the founder of the Schneersohn family line and the founder of Habad Hasidism, later known as Lubavitcher Hasidism.[11] Shneur Zalman was born in Liozna, Belorussia. He devoted himself to Torah study early in life, but finally concluded that he needed to learn something about prayer as well, and so went to Dov Ber of Mezritsh to learn from him. He quickly became part of the Maggid's inner circle, and in 1770, Dov Ber commissioned him to write a new version of Joseph Karo's Shuhan Arukh, the authoritative guide to halakah that informed traditional Jewish life. Unfortunately, only about a third of his work was published, and the rest has been lost. In addition to his mastery of talmudic and kabbalistic thought, Shneur Zalman was also known for his mastery of non-religious subjects, such as mathematics and astronomy, which set a pattern for future Rebbes of the Habad or Lubavitcher line. Following the initial edict of excommunication issued by Elijah ben Solomon Zalman against Hasidism, Shneur Zalman and Menahem Mendel of Vitebsk went to visit the Vilna Gaon in order to attempt to resolve the issues between the rabbinic authorities and the Hasidim. The reasoning behind the proposed visit would have been that Shneur Zalman and Menahem Mendel were accomplished talmudic scholars who could discuss such issues with the Vilna

10. See Weiss, "Torah Study in Early Hasidism," 56–68.

11. Avrum Stroll, "Shneur Zalman of (Liozna-) Lyady," *EncJud* 14:1432–40; Biale et al., *Hasidism*, 125–36.

Gaon, but he refused to receive them, apparently to demonstrate his disdain for the movement that in his view could not be considered Jewish.

Menahem Mendel was apparently the leader of the Belorussian Hasidim, and when he went to the land of Israel with many followers, he appointed Shneur Zalman as his deputy in Reisen, Belorussia. Shneur Zalman attracted many followers in Reisen, and later Menahem Mendel recognized his accomplishments by designating him as the full leader of the Hasidic community in Reisen. During the period of his leadership in Reisen, Shneur Zalman composed his collected teachings, which he titled *Likkutei Amarim*, Collections of Sayings (1797), but it is better known in later editions as the *Tanya*, Teaching.[12] The Tanya is the foundational document of Habad Hasidism which presents a very systematic analysis of Habad doctrine and identifies it as a very distinctive understanding of Hasidic thought. As Shneur Zalman gained increasing influence in Hasidic Judaism, he was denounced by rabbinic authorities as a threat to the Russian state, for which he was arrested in 1798 and again in 1801. In the first instance he was acquitted by trial, and in the second he was pardoned by Czar Alexander I. In addition, Hasidic rivals, such as Abraham Katz of Kalisk and Baruch of Mezhbizh, began to emerge as well. During the Franco-Russian War, Shneur Zalman sided with the Russians, and died in Pienna in 1813 while fleeing with the defeated Russian armies. He was buried in Hadich.

The Tanya, supplemented by related Habad writings, presents the theological foundations of the Habad movement.[13] The term *Habad* is an acronym that stands for the modified form of the three basic mental sefirot as understood in Habad, i.e., *H* for Hokhmah, wisdom; *B* for Binah, understanding; and *D* for Da'at, knowledge. In the Habad system, Keter Elyon is considered so close to the Ein Sof that they are practically indistinguishable, whereas Da'at or Knowledge of the Jewish tradition as well as other branches of knowledge in the world completes the three-part mental and intellectual foundations for the emanation of the divine presence in the finite world of creation.

Shneur Zalman's thought developed in relation to his engagement with Dov Ber's understanding of Hasidic Judaism and rabbinic knowledge. His

12. Shneur Zalman of Liadi, *Liqqutei Amarim: Tanya* (bilingual edition) (Brooklyn: Kehot, 5770/2009).

13. For the following, see esp. Rachel Elior, "ḤaBaD: The Contemplative Ascent to G-d," in *Jewish Spirituality: From the Sixteenth-Century Revival through the Present Age*, ed. Arthur Green (New York: Crossroad, 1989), 157–205; Elior, *The Paradoxical Ascent to G-d: The Kabbalistic Theosophy of Habad Hasidism* (Albany: SUNY Press, 1993).

Tanya is fundamentally concerned with laying out a systematic understanding of the mystical foundations for understanding the presence of G-d in the world of creation at large and in the soul of human beings in particular, and the means by which human beings then relate to G-d. It is concerned first and foremost with the Beinoni, the average human being, and not the tzaddik, an exceptional human being who already possesses the means to gain full understanding of G-d and the world and is capable of inspiring others to do so. Rather, it is the Beinoni who must learn to understand the true nature of the world in which we live, the true nature of G-d who is the only substantive reality in the universe, and the means by which one understands and performs the divine will. It is also concerned with clarifying the relationship between Lurianic kabbalah and Hasidic worship, prayer, and comprehensive attention to living a holy Jewish life in relation to Jewish tradition (Avodat Hashem, Service or Worship of G-d). Thus Habad is interested in establishing the relationship between its theological understanding of the relationship between G-d and humankind and the practical application of that understanding to living a wholly and holy Jewish life.

In order to accomplish these goals, Habad gives special emphasis to the concept of Yihud, Unification, which includes two aspects: the *yihud ha'elyon*, the Upper Unification, and the *yihud hatahton*, the Lower Unification. The Upper Unification entails the spiritual worship of G-d and the negation of the finite aspects of the world and its inclusion within the divine reality of G-d, and the Lower Unification entails drawing the divine into the lower world through understanding of Torah, the practice of mitzvot or righteous acts in the Jewish tradition, and the proper Jewish worship of G-d. In essence, Habad is fundamentally concerned with the dialectical relationship between divine transcendence and divine immanence. Habad is especially interested in developing the holy soul and consciousness of the Beinoni, the average person, as opposed to the tzaddik, insofar as tzaddikim are rare and Beinonim are ubiquitous in keeping with the Lurianic/kabbalistic understanding of the scattering of divine sparks throughout the world of creation.

The Tanya includes five basic portions or books: Sefer shel Beinonim, the Book of the Average People; Sha'ar Hayihud Veha'emunah, the Gate of Unity and Belief; Iggeret Hateshuvah, the Letter of Repentance; Iggeret Hakodesh, the Letter of Holiness; and Kunteres Aharon, Last Theses. Elior maintains that Habad has four basic concerns as articulated in the Tanya and related Habad literature: Torat Ha'elohut, the teaching concerning the divine or a mystical theology of G-d; Torat Hanefesh, the teaching concerning the soul or the psychological understanding of divine service; Avodat Hashem, or divine service, which entails both worship and the manner in which one lives one's life; and Avodah Sheme'ever Leta'am Veda'at, a confrontation with the religious problematics that follow from the contradictions in mystical axioms, their Hasidic interpretation, the demands of halakah, and personal experience. In contrast to earlier Hasidic thought and practice, Habad and the Tanya call for strict observance of rabbinic expectations as defined in the classical talmudic tradition and beyond, together with the spirituality and concern for the soul exhibited in the thought, teachings, and practices of the Baal Shem Tov and the other early Hasidic masters.

Habad theology is rooted in the notion that G-d is the only reality of the universe, and all other reality is illusory. In this respect, Habad has great affinity with Buddhism, although Buddhism regards divinity as illusory as well. The world therefore has no independent existence, and all finite reality is dependent upon G-d. This notion is expressed in the formula, "There is nothing apart from Him" (Deut 4:35). Apart from G-d, all reality or existence (*qiyyum*) is lacking in substance (*yishut*) which means that any perception of reality, insofar as it lacks substance itself, is illusory. Existence is therefore only an image that emanates from the divine. Any tangible sense of divine existence is absent to human perception and therefore constitutes insubstantial illusion, whereas the divine is the only substantial reality even as it remains undetected by human perception. Habad theology therefore postulates that the tangible world of finite reality conceals (and reveals) the substantial and yet intangible divine presence. It is the task of the human being to uncover and therefore engage that divine presence.

Therefore, "G-d is One" is Habad's understanding, and all reality is a manifestation or emanation of the divine unity. Habad therefore teaches seven basic facets of the relationship between G-d and the world:

1. Pantheism: G-d is the exclusive substance, and the world is nothing more than a projection or emanation of the divine which in turn depends upon the divine for its own illusory or insubstantial existence;
2. Acosmism: From the standpoint of G-d, the world lacks any true or substantive existence; creation does not constitute change within G-d, contrary to the Lurianic understanding of Tzimtzum articulated above;
3. Creation: G-d is the creator, originator, and sustainer of the world at all times, even as the world undergoes a process of constant change instigated continuously by G-d;

4. Immanence: G-d is present everywhere in the world at all times and in all places; there is no distinction between the substantive nature of G-d in either the upper or the lower realms;

5. Panentheism: Everything that exists is within G-d; all that might be understood to exist outside of G-d in fact does not exist at all;

6. The Finite World is a Manifestation of G-d: The world is a necessary and essential manifestation of G-d; G-d incorporates the world into the divine Self;

7. Dialectical Reciprocity: G-d has no independent existence apart from the world insofar as the world is nothing but a manifestation of G-d and stands as an expression of G-d's infinite perfection and G-d's continuing desire for self-perfection.

These seven postulates give expression to the Habad concept of *hashva'ah* or *coincidentia oppositorum*, i.e., the notion that divine substance or reality is one and the same in the infinite and finite or the upper and the lower worlds, and that the two worlds are in constant interaction with each other within the divine presence. The Lurianic *qelippot* or husks in which the sparks of the infinite divine presence reside are in fact manifestations of that infinite divine presence that cannot be separated from them. G-d entails everything and its opposite, nothingness and existence, transcendence and immanence, infinity and finitude at once. Tzimtzum was not a process of inner contraction or limitation; rather, it is a process in which the divine presence fills the finite world of creation. These aspects of G-d must be recognized in human perception.

Habad maintains that the dialectical nature of G-d also finds expression in the human soul. The Ein Sof pours itself into the human soul by the process of emanation. Insofar as the divine entails infinite substance and finite expression, so, too, the human soul entails both of these dimensions. The human soul therefore comprises both the divine soul and the animal soul. The divine soul is a portion of G-d above, which originates in the sefirot emanated from G-d by means of the Ein Sof working through the Keter Elyon and the rest of the sefirot. The animal soul is rooted in the bright husk that combines good and evil within itself and manifests itself in the world of differentiated phenomena which does not recognize its relationship with the divine. The divine and the animal soul are interdependent, insofar as the divine soul is the source of all vitality and the necessary condition for the existence of the animal soul, whereas the animal soul is the husk, shell, or garment that enables the divine soul to manifest itself in the finite world.

The interrelationship between the divine and animal souls is not static. The divine soul strives to transform the animal soul in order to incorporate it into the G-dhead or Ein Sof, and the animal soul wishes to transform the divine soul into an expression of finite physical reality. The purpose of the descent of the divine soul into the realm of finite reality is to reveal the divine glory in the lower realms. Thus the physical realm cannot exist without the spiritual or divine realm that sustains it, and the divine realm cannot come to expression without the physical realm in which it is embodied. The animal soul is the central focus and impetus of religious life, insofar as it seeks the manifestation of the divine in the midst of a world of perception and differentiation, and the divine soul represents mystical consciousness of the divine nature of the cosmos and its unity.

Habad's understanding of divine worship is rooted in its dialectical understanding of the character of G-d and the soul of the human. Whereas creation entails a finite existence that seemingly exists separately from the divine, worship is intended to overcome that sense of separation in order to lead finite and illusory reality back to the infinite reality of G-d. Thus the purpose of worship is to negate the illusory reality of the tangible world to recognize the divine as the true substance and reality of the world, and thereby to restore the divine unity of creation. Worship as understood in Habad entails both spiritualistic and non-spiritualistic aspects that work together to facilitate the recognition of the illusory nature of the finite world of creation and the reality of the divine world that is concealed within the finite realm.

Two commandments therefore relate to the worship of G-d. The first is to draw down the divine into the finite, and the second is to draw down the divine will into the finite world by means of the understanding of Torah and the performance of its Mitzvoth in order to ensure abnegation of self-will before the presence of the divine, i.e., to promote the understanding and performance of the divine will over against the understanding and performance of the self-will. These dimensions of worship then define Habad's understanding of the Lurianic concepts of the Shevirat Hakelim (the Breaking of the Vessels) and Tikkun Olam (the Repair of the World). Shevirat Hakelim constitutes the outpouring of divine presence and substance to constitute the illusion of finite creation, and Tikkun Olam constitutes repair and reintegration of that seemingly broken world by recognizing its true unity and sanctity by means of Torah, mitzvot, and avodah (worship). For human beings, divine worship constitutes the recognition of the two aspects of both the divine and the finite world, including the human soul, and the reintegration of them by self-abnegation of the human will in favor of the divine will.

Self-abnegation is a key concept in Habad thought because it provides a means by which one moves from the state of Shevirat Hakelim, in which the divine essence is poured to form the tangible world of finite creation, to the state of Tikkun Olam, in which the finite world is reintegrated with the divine presence. Habad thought employs the Hebrew term *avodah bebittul*, "worship through negation," to express the concept. The concept expresses the notion that the human being is nullified in relation to the divine, and the human's relationship to reality is negated in relation to the divine element that sustains finite reality. The notion of bittul or negation constitutes a stage in the acquisition of the highest human perfection that enables communion between the human and G-d. It thereby enables the transition from finite to infinite and profane to holy in Habad thought.

The concept of bittul in Habad worship constitutes spiritual practice that makes this transition possible. It presumes that the divine spirit within the human being is able to negate physical reality by pointing the human soul to the element of the divine that is encased in the tangible and illusory world. The service of bittul begins with the practice of *hitbonenut*, self-understanding or contemplation, concerning the interrelationship between the infinite and the finite or being and nothingness. Such contemplation aims to facilitate understanding of the simultaneous distance of the divine from finite reality and the nearness of the divine within finite reality, so as ultimately to recognize the G-dhead as the exclusive and ultimate source of reality beyond and within the finite world. Contemplation on G-d reveals both G-d's existence and non-existence or hiddenness in the tangible world. To attain knowledge of such divine unity in the world, one must employ rational contemplation to understand Tzimtzum, emanation, and the sefirot as a means to excite the soul to break out of its finite worldview and thereby achieve unity with the divine element that stands both beyond and within the finite world. Such rational contemplation enables pneumatic-spiritual and transrational experience, or intellectual ecstasy, in which to comprehend the divine presence in the finite world.

There are three such levels of negation in Habad thought. The first is negation in relation to the transrational substance. From the divine point of view, the finite lacks substance in relation to its own existence and serves only as a means to conceal the divine from created beings. From the human point of view, there is no sense of feeling or self-consciousness at all since the human ascends from finite reality—much like the heikhalot mystics of old who encountered the divine through the study and contemplation of texts—to encounter the divine beyond and within.

The second level of negation is the negation of understanding and knowledge, which recognizes the unification of the divine with the world. That is to say, G-d expands in the process of creation to fill the entire created world, and the entire created world therefore does not exist except as the divine. Finitude may still see itself as a separate existence from the divine, but full progression of the negation ultimately reveals that finitude is only an expression of the divine. Upon the attainment of understanding and knowledge, finitude understands the divine as its source and its true substance.

The third level of negation is the negation of feeling and ecstasy, here understood as emotion, which enables the human to move beyond sensory experience to recognize the sensation of distinctive manifestation of essence as a unity in which their differentiations are recognized as non-existent or insubstantial. As the relationship between divinity and existence grows closer and closer, one recognizes that love and ecstasy ultimately dissipate as one approaches understanding of divine presence behind emotional feeling and ecstatic expression.

As a result of these three forms of negation, human beings come to realize that G-d is the ultimate and only reality in the world; the world itself is only an illusory projection or manifestation of G-d, completely lacking in substance. Such recognition entails the complete denial of human will and the complete affirmation of divine will within the self and the world at large. These forms of negation lead to transrational faith in which one recognizes the limits of knowledge and understanding in order to move beyond them and thereby grasp the interrelationship between divine transcendence and divine immanence. Such a position is similar to that of Taoism in which Tao permeates and informs all tangible reality as an expression of Tao. Alternatively, one might draw an analogy to Buddhism, which defines substantial reality to the finite world, but does not attribute substantial reality to the world beyond, other than to understand it as nothingness.

Within the system of Habad thought, understanding of Torah and the performance of mitzvot then serve as vehicles by which the Beinoni, the average human being, might understand the negation of the self-will and recognition of the divine will as the only substantial reality of creation.

Following the death of Shneur Zalman in 1813, he was succeeded by his oldest son, Dov Ber (1773–1827), who settled in the town of Lubavitch, or Lyubavitchy, in Belorussia, which gave the movement its name as Lubavitcher Hasidisim.[14] Dov Ber was a prolific writer who often ex-

---

14. Avrum Stroll, "Shneur Zalman," *EncJud* 14:1434–36.

plained and expanded his father's ideas in his own work. He called upon the Lubavitchers to engage in productive employment and established a Lubavitcher settlement in Hebron in 1820 to establish Jewish presence in the Land of Israel. Like his father, he was imprisoned for a time because of the accusations of an informer. Menahem Mendel (1789–1866), the grandson of Shneur Zalman by his daughter and son-in-law and uncle, Dov Ber (Dov Ber married his nephew's daughter), succeeded his father-in-law and uncle as leader of the Habad movement. Again, he was a prolific writer who was especially well known for his halakic work. He was acknowledged by the Russian government as a major Jewish leader, although he opposed government efforts to assimilate Jews into Russian society. His sons were unable to agree on a leader, and so they established several rival branches of the Habad movement: in Kopys under Judah Leib (1811–1866), in Liady under Hayim Shneur Zalman (1814–1880), and in Nezhin under Israel Noah (1815–1883). Menahem Mendel's youngest son, Samuel (1834–1882), succeeded his father in Lubavitch, and Samuel's son, Shalom Dov Ber (1860–1920), founded the first Hasidic yeshivah (rabbinical school), which enhanced Habad's educational efforts and its viability as an ongoing Jewish movement.

Joseph Isaac (1880–1950), the son of Shalom Dov Ber, was a dynamic leader during the Russian Civil War, the Communist Revolution, and World War II. He was a great organizer who was recognized as the leading figure in Russian Jewry. Joseph Isaac led a major Jewish revival in Russia, fought the secularization efforts of the new Communist regime, and was imprisoned for his efforts. He later went to Riga in Latvia, then Poland, and ultimately to Brooklyn in the United States to organize and expand the Habad movement throughout the world with synagogues, schools, and publications. His son, Menahem Mendel Schneerson (1902–1994), known as the Rebbe, studied mathematics and sciences at the Sorbonne in addition to Jewish studies and Habad thought prior to assuming leadership of the movement in 1950. He expanded the movement greatly and promoted the use of Habad emissaries to go out into the Jewish community to bring young Jews back to traditional Judaism. Ultimately, Menahem Mendel was responsible for making Habad the best known and most influential Hasidic movement, with Habad Houses established throughout the world. Many in the movement regarded him as the messiah. Insofar as there was no successor to Menahem Mendel Schneerson, many continue to regard him as the leader of the movement and the future messiah as Habad leadership continues with a ruling council of Habad sages known as the Agudas Chasidei Chabad, the Organization of the Habad Hasidim. Overall, the purpose of the organization is to reinvigorate Judaism to bring about the revelation of the messiah and Tikkun Olam in the world. Habad's membership constitutes some 40,000–200,000, although these figures are disputed, making it one of the largest of the Hasidic movements in the contemporary world.

Bratzlaver, Satmar, and Other Hasidic Movements

There are a number of Hasidic movements besides Habad active in the world today.

One influential movement is the Bratzlaver Hasidim, founded by R. Nahman of Bratzlav (1772–1811).[15] The Bratzlavers hold to Torah study and, like the Habad movement, anticipate the coming of the messiah. R. Nahman ben Simha of Bratzlav (also known as Breslau in German or Wroclaw in Polish) was the great grandson of the Baal Shem Tov; his mother, Feige, was the daughter of Udel, who was the Baal Shem Tov's daughter. He was also the grandson of one of the Baal Shem Tov's major disciples, Nahman of Horodenka (Gorodenka) after whom he was named. Indeed, his grandfather's line was descended from R. Judah Loew, the Maharal, of Prague (d. 1609), who claimed descent from the royal house of David. Little is known of his father, Simha, who is simply described in Hasidic sources as retiring. R. Nahman was born in Mezhbizh, the Baal Shem Tov's later hometown. After he was married, he later settled in Medvedevka in the province of Kiev and began to assume the role of a Hasidic tzaddik with a growing number of followers. He went to the land of Israel in 1798, and traveled in Haifa, Jaffa, Tiberias, and Safed. In part, he was following the example of his grandfather, Nahman of Horodenka, who settled in Israel together with Menaham Mendel of Premishlan, apparently to establish the first Hasidic settlement there. The elder Nahman died and was buried in Tiberias in 1772. His grandson was intent on visiting his grandfather's grave in order to commune with him, much as he had done at the grave of the Baal Shem Tov. But Nahman of Bratzlav was forced to leave the land of Israel prematurely due to Napoleon's invasion.

R. Nahman settled in Zlatopol, again in the province of Kiev, and found himself in conflict with his great-uncle, Aryeh Leib "the Zeyde" ("Grand-

---

15. Esther Zweig Liebes, "Naḥman (ben Simḥah) of Bratzlav," *EncJud* 12:782–87; Biale et al., *Hasidism*, 111–17; Arthur Green, *Tormented Master: The Life and Spiritual Quest of Rabbi Nahman of Bratzlav* (Woodstock, VT: Jewish Lights Publishing, 2013); Martin Buber, *Tales of Rabbi Nachman* (New York: Avon, 1956).

father") of (nearby) Shpole, the brother of his grandfather, who charged that R. Nahman adhered to Shabbatean and Frankist beliefs. He further raised questions about R. Nahman's moral character. Nahman was also later denounced by his maternal uncle, Baruch of Mezhbizh. Even when he moved to Bratzlav in 1802, controversy about him followed and dogged him all his life. One of the major problems was that R. Nahman apparently considered himself to be the messiah, which would appear to draw on Shabbatean and Frankist beliefs. Such a claim would have provoked the opposition and torment that R. Nahman experienced throughout his life. He undertook various journeys during his time at Bratzlav. There is much speculation concerning his mystical goals—perhaps they were intended to demonstrate his messianic status—but it also appears that he sought healing from his tuberculosis. Shortly before his death, he moved to Uman, where he died and was buried in 1811.

The charges of Shabbatean and Frankist sympathies are rooted in R. Nahman's belief that his soul had a messianic status and that the messiah, including the Messiah ben David and the Messiah ben Joseph, would be one of his descendants. He held that his role as the ideal tzaddik entailed his messianic status and that the various controversies that he provoked pointed to his role in relation to the Suffering Servant of Isa 52:13–53:12. But he also maintained that the role of the messiah was to aid the sinful souls of others and that it was his task as the messianic tzaddik to engage such souls and assist them in recognizing their own divine characters so that they might participate in the process of Tikkun Olam, repair of the world. Although faith in G-d is not a requirement for Jewish identity—one is a Jew by birth or conversion, not by a statement of belief—R. Nahman placed great stress on one's Jewish faith in G-d as a basis for Tikkun, and he held that it is essential that one also believe in G-d's tzaddik, i.e., himself, as part of the expression of such faith. Whereas most Hasidic tzaddikim received Hasidic pilgrims every Shabbat, R. Nahman received them in his Hasidic court only on Rosh Hashanah, the Shabbat of Hanukkah, and Shavuot. He required pilgrims to visit him and pray with him on those days. R. Nahman demanded loyalty from his followers. Bratzlav Hasidim were required to confess before him as an initiation rite in order to enter into the Bratzlav Hasidic community, and especially on Erev Rosh Hashanah as an ongoing practice, both to purify their souls and to demonstrate loyalty to the master. The practice of gathering at Rosh Hashanah was continued after R. Nahman's death by his disciple, Nathan, who played a major role in leading and organizing the sect through the first half of the nineteenth century. But no successor has ever been appointed to R. Nahman by the Bratzlaver Hasidim, apparently because R. Nahman was considered a hidden messiah. The Bratzlaver Hasidim ultimately settled in Jerusalem and other parts of the land of Israel. R. Nahman's teachings appear in two volumes, *Likkutei Moharan*, Gleanings of Reb Nahman (1806, 1811) and a collection of legends, *Sippurei Ma'assiyot*, Stories of Deeds (1815).

Reb Nahman's teachings are always based on kabbalistic tradition attributed to Shimon bar Yohai (Rashbi), Isaac Luria (the Ari), and Israel ben Eliezer (the Besht), but they display considerable innovation. He maintains that in its efforts to reveal mercy, the Ein Sof created the universe with the presence of the divine inherent in all creation, ruled by the Ein Sof. Divine presence appears in everything, even the *qelippot* that encase the sparks of divine presence and manifest evil in the world. Even though human beings are encased in evil, it is always possible to find G-d in the world, engage in *teshuvah* or repentance, and thereby repair what has been broken. R. Nahman's understanding of Tzimtzum raised a great deal of doubt about his beliefs in kabbalistic thought and therefore played a role in promoting opposition to his ideas. Tzimtzum entails withdrawal of the divine, as postulated in Lurianic kabbalah, but it also resulted in the manifestation of divine presence throughout the world in hidden form. This model constitutes a paradox, which allows for the assertion that the Creator of the universe does not exist. Doubts about the answer to the question of whether the Creator exists then provide the impetus to seek and recognize the Creator in this world and thereby to carry out the process of Tikkun Olam by recognizing the divine within the self and the world at large.

R. Nahman also postulates questions concerning the Shevirat Hakelim, the Breaking of the Vessels, in Lurianic kabbalah. The Breaking of the Vessels referred to the shattering of the material form in which the sparks of the divine presence were encased; thereby it indicates the continuing existence of finite form and evil in the world even after the act of creation. The *qelippot* therefore constitute a sphere of existence separate from that of the divine, and this sphere becomes the source of evil. Insofar as R. Nahman holds to classical rabbinic education, such a sphere of *qelippot* points to the origins of doubt and consequent evil thought, such as modern secular studies and heretical questions. Such doubts and questions constitute a vacuum known as the realm of silence, which calls upon the faith of the believer in G-d to answer and thereby to negate them. Faith conquers all doubts and gives expression to the free will of the believer as understood in classical Rabbinic Judaism. Rational thought, however, is the antithesis of faith; it raises doubts that cannot be answered except in relation to itself. R. Nahman holds to the worship of G-d as a pure act of faith in naïveté, lacking in crafty thought; faith thereby gives expression to the true love of G-d as expressed in rabbinic tradition and manifested through the performance of mitzvot, as specified in Torah. R. Nahman opposes study of philosophy because the rational view and argumentation of philosophy contradict faith. Lack of faith explains the perpetuation of Jewish exile from the land of Israel.

R. Nahman claims that there is only one true tzaddik in the world. He viewed himself as this one true tzaddik, who is destined to become or to father the messiah. The tzaddik is a figure like Moses who gives redemptive force to the prayers of the people. Reflection on questions of doubt gives humans the faith that they need to overcome doubt. And the tunes of the songs that he sings also play a role in bringing about the spiritual growth of the people. The tzaddik continues to live even after his death. One must believe in the tzaddik despite any doubts that one might have so that the tzaddik can rise above the level of the Ayin or Nothingness of the world of creation, not only to teach human beings about their relationship with G-d, but also to teach G-d about how to deal with human beings. In this regard, the tzaddik emerges as the true mediator between G-d and human beings. Consequently, humans must travel to the tzaddik when he is alive and after he is dead to seek his wisdom and guidance as they confess before him.

Human beings must show absolute faith in G-d (and in G-d's messiah), which is especially expressed in prayer and the study of Psalms, but only when one identifies with their content and thereby embodies the outlook presented in the Psalms. The human soul must approach G-d without despair or doubt, but with joy, dancing, song, self-critique, communication with the tzaddik, and direct relationship with the Creator. Such a relationship with the Creator promotes dialogue with G-d in isolation from the rest of the world. Nahman was heavily preoccupied with the purification of his own soul and the overcoming of doubt concerning G-d. He would pour out his doubts alone before G-d in a process he called (in Hebrew) *hitbodedut*, making oneself alone (before G-d). Through the use of *niggunim*, tunes or songs to express joy, the human being thereby engages G-d and evokes response from G-d. Such responses appear in the form of self-revelations to the human being and thereby enable the manifestation of holiness, both within the person who approaches G-d with such faith and within the world of creation in which the human lives and in which G-d is manifested.

Unfortunately, R. Nahman died young in 1811 of tuberculosis, but he forbade his followers to appoint a successor. Bratzlaver Hasidism continues, under the guidance of a number of influential rabbis, to call upon its followers to establish personal communion with G-d on the model of R. Nahman. Many Bratzlaver Hasidim were murdered during the Shoah (Holocaust), and so the movement has relocated today to the US, the UK, and Israel, especially Jerusalem.

Another influential movement is the Satmar Hasidism.[16] Satmar (or Szatmar) Hasidism is a relatively recent movement, having been founded in 1905 in the city of Satu Mare, Hungary (now in Romania), by R. Joel Teitelbaum (1887–1979). Like Bratzlaver Hasidism, Satmar places special emphasis on the role of the tzaddik in relationship to G-d, and it anticipates a future messiah, although human beings seem to have little role in bringing about the messiah's arrival.

Teitelbaum's Hasidic roots go back to his ancestor, R. Moshe Teitelbaum, known as the Yismach Moshe (1759–1841), the Rebbe of Uzhely in Hungary. The elder Teitelbaum signed his name *Tamar*, meaning "palm tree," in Hebrew also the meaning of the Yiddish name Teitelbaum. He was a disciple of R. Jacob Isaac Horowitz, the Seer of Lublin (1745–1815), a disciple of Dov Ber, the Maggid of Mezritsh, who had sent R. Jacob to Poland to expand Hasidism in its early years. R. Moshe Teitelbaum was a key figure in the foundations of Hungarian Judaism in Sighet and Satmar. His great-grandson was Hananiah Yom Tov Lipa Teitelbaum, the Grand Rabbi of Sighet (1836–1904). R. Hananiah was known for his Hasidic background, his resistance against modernity, and his opposition to modern Zionism.

When R. Hananiah died in 1904, he was succeeded as rabbi in Sighet by his older son, R. Haim Tzvi Teitelbaum, although many concerned believed his younger son, Joel, to be the more capable leader, particularly because he was already known for his strong intellect at an early age. In 1905, R. Joel Teitelbaum moved to Satu Mare, where his followers opened a study hall for him, and he began to attract a following and referred to himself as the Rebbe of Satmar. In 1911, he accepted an invitation to serve as rabbi in Ilsova in the Austro-Hungarian Empire where he opened a yeshivah to promote Hasidic teachings. At the outbreak of the First World War, he returned to Satu Mare to find that his old study hall had developed into a full-fledged yeshivah. Teitelbaum continued to follow his father's understanding of Judaism, rejecting modern influence in Judaism and Jewish life and strictly opposing modern Zionism. The basis for his opposition to Zionism was the traditional belief that only G-d could restore Israel in the time when the messiah would

16. Biale et al., *Hasidism*, 393–96, 631–32, 685–92.

come. Early Zionism was a largely secular Jewish movement; its supporters were mainly Jews who were influenced by the Haskalah or Enlightenment that promoted rational thought and empirical observation as its foundations for understanding truth in the world. Although early Zionism had some traditionally religious supporters, particularly the religious Mizrahi movement, major religious support would only come later under the influence of Rav Kook and the apparent miracle of Israel's victory in the Six-Day War of 1967. One might question traditionalist opposition, particularly due to the role played by the emanation of the Ein Sof into the human soul by means of the sefirot, which would suggest that G-d does indeed act through human beings, but Teitelbaum did not recognize such an understanding of divine emanation or the sefirot.

Teitelbaum served in several rabbinical posts until he was finally named rabbi of Satmar, following a long and conflicted process, in 1934. With the outbreak of World War II, Teitelbaum was forced to flee from Hungary and ultimately made his way to Williamsburg, Brooklyn, in the United States. By 1948, Teitelbaum and his followers had established a synagogue. He became a leader of the Jewish anti-Zionist movement in the United States. Later, in 1974, the Satmar Hasidim purchased a tract of land in Monroe, New York, where they established Kiryas Yoel (Kiryat Yoel, the Town of Joel), a Satmar community where the Satmar could pursue their distinctive understanding of Jewish life apart from modern influences. Teitelbaum suffered a stroke in 1968, and later died in 1974. His nephew, R. Moshe Teitelbaum, succeeded him as leader of the Satmar Hasidim.

As noted above, Teitelbaum opposed modern Zionism due to the view that only G-d could restore Israel by means of the Jewish messiah. The Satmar approve and encourage members who settle in Israel in self-sustaining communities that do not accept assistance from the modern state, but they forbid Satmar Hasidim from making aliyah, immigrating to Israel and becoming citizens of the state. Teitelbaum's opposition is further based on three "oaths": (1) the people of Israel should not return to the land by force; (2) Israel should not rebel against the other nations; and (3) the nations should not oppress Israel too harshly. He saw modern Israel as an act of impatience that was designed to bypass the divine will with human action. Therefore, the establishment of modern Israel constituted a great threat of divine punishment to the people. Even if a religious government were formed prior to the appearance of the messiah, it would be contrary to the will of G-d all the same and would still place the Jewish people in danger of attack by the nations who would attempt to destroy it. Indeed, the Satmar sent a delegation to Iran following Iran's threats against modern Israel to demonstrate good Iranian-Jewish relations.

Teitelbaum's views called for extraordinary conservatism in Jewish life. In contrast to other rabbis who argued that the *mehitsah* that separates Jewish women from Jewish men in the synagogue need only be shoulder high, Teitelbaum argued that the *mehitsah* should completely block the women from view, to prevent impure thoughts. He required married Hasidic men to wear a large fur hat; although such hats were not commonly worn in Hungary, Teitelbaum called for such hats as a means to distinguish Satmar men from the men of the modern secular world, which he saw as a source of corruption. Boys and girls should not meet more than two or three times before getting engaged. Women must wear opaque stockings to ensure their modesty. He insisted that women shave their heads each month prior to immersion in the mikveh at the conclusion of menstruation, although they should wear a turban rather than a wig. Televisions were prohibited because they broadcast promiscuous content, but a Satmar Yiddish press was established to counter the destructive influence of outside ideas.

Today, with some 75,000 followers, Satmar Hasidism may be the largest Hasidic movement.

Jerusalem and Brooklyn, Almost Holy Lands of Twentieth-Century Hasidism

Although Satmar Hasidism, like most early Hasidic movements, does not anticipate a return to the Land of Israel until the time of the messiah, modern Zionism has begun to have an impact on other Hasidic movements, particularly the Habad movement, which have established communities in Israel. Although Israel's victory over overwhelming Arab forces in the Six-Day War of 1967 had much to do with convincing many traditionalists, including Habad Hasidim, that G-d was bringing about the restoration of the Jewish people to the land of Israel, R. Abraham Isaac Kook (1865–1935), the chief rabbi of Mandatory Palestine and a noted halakic and kabbalistic scholar, laid much of the groundwork for this shift in attitude.

Rav Kook was born in Griva, now in Latvia, and proved to be an *ilui* or genius in the study of Talmud.[17] His father, R. Shlomo Zalman Hakohen

17. Aviezer Ravitzky, *Messianism, Zionism, and Jewish Religious Radicalism*, trans. Michael Swirsky and Jonathan Chapman (Chicago: University of Chicago Press, 1996), 86–124;

Kook, was a student at the Volozhin Yeshivah, the most respected yeshivah among the Lithuanian rabbinic schools, and his maternal grandfather was a follower of the Kopust Hasidic movement, founded by R. Yehudah Leib Schneersohn, the son of R. Menahem Mendel Schneersohn. Consequently, Kook's ancestors included significant representation among both the Mitnagdim and the Habad Hasidim. Kook himself studied at the Volozhin Yeshivah, beginning at age eighteen, for about a year and a half and demonstrated his mastery of Rabbinic Jewish tradition. He served as rabbi in Latvia and elsewhere; and he was a prolific writer on halakic, kabbalistic, and Zionist issues, among other topics, and gained a great reputation as a rabbinic sage. In 1904, he moved to Jaffa to become chief rabbi of the city and the Zionist agricultural settlements in the area. During the First World War, he moved temporarily to London and Switzerland due to wartime conditions, and in 1921 he moved to Jerusalem to become the first Chief Ashkenazi Rabbi of Mandate Palestine. In 1924 he established the Yeshivat Merkaz Harav Kook, the Yeshivah of the Rabbi Kook Center, which functions as the major yeshivah of religious Zionism. Throughout his career, he held that modern Zionism did indeed represent the divine will, despite its secular origins, and in his writings he attempted to demonstrate the religious significance of modern Zionism. He died in 1935.

Kook's first foray into discussion concerning modern Zionism took place in 1898, one year after the first World Zionism Congress in Basel, when he published a Hebrew pamphlet entitled "On Zionism." He attempted to defend Zionism, then a largely secular Jewish movement, from the critiques leveled against it by traditionalist rabbis who charged that it would divide Judaism much as they alleged that the modern Reform movement had done. But Kook also rejected in strong terms the secular character of the movement. He called for the creation of the Great Sanhedrin and the renewal of the historic chain of the ordination of rabbis in the land of Israel in order to give the revived Jewish nation a Jewish religious identity. His work was messianic in orientation, but it was distinctive at the time because it did not call for the miraculous appearance of a messiah as traditionalists had typically expected; instead he called for the recognition of messianic redemption through the course of historical process. Thus, the messiah is not the impetus to the advent of the Messianic Age, but instead constitutes its ultimate out-

---

Ben-Zion Bokser, *Abraham Isaac Kook* (Mahwah, NJ: Paulist, 1978); Sholomo Avineri, *The Makings of Modern Zionism: The Intellectual Origins of the Jewish State* (New York: Basic Books, 1981), 187–97; Biale et al., *Hasidism*, 644–51.

come. He sees the messiah as representing the time when the people of Israel would return to the land of Israel, and he further argued that a restored Israel would function as a source not only of political renewal for the Jewish people but of spiritual renewal as well. He maintained that nationalism alone, without spiritual or moral depth, has the capacity to debase and dehumanize the nation. Such nationalism devoid of moral and spiritual foundation would only lead to crude patriotism and degeneration of the nation, much as the example of the French Revolution had shown; but nationalism infused with the spirit of G-d as understood in the Prophets would enable the nation to achieve its goals of creating an ideal nation with the necessary spiritual and moral value and thereby prevent it from descending into totalitarianism. In other words, Kook maintains that there can be no national revival without G-d and Judaism at its foundations.

Shortly after making aliyah to the Land of Israel in 1904, Kook presented a eulogy of Theodor Herzl, the chief organizer of the World Zionist Congress, who had recently died. His eulogy angered many traditionalist rabbis at the time because of his avoidance of traditional messianic imagery and concepts and his adherence to the historical process noted in his earlier pamphlet. Kook was well aware of Herzl's and the Zionist movement's secular orientation, and he dismissed the traditionalist view that Herzl would have returned to Jewish religion had he lived longer. Instead, he envisions Herzl within a historical messianic process and associates him with the Messiah ben Joseph of classical rabbinic tradition. The Messiah ben Joseph is a preliminary figure in rabbinic thought who will battle Israel's enemies and ultimately fall in battle against them, much like Shimon bar Kokhba and his followers in the Bar Kokhba revolt against Rome in 132–135 CE. But the Messiah ben Joseph would lead ultimately to the Messiah ben David, a utopian figure who would bring about the full restoration and idealization of Israel at the center of a utopian world. Ravitzky maintains that this characterization of Herzl's association with the Messiah ben Joseph points to the dialectical character of Kook's thinking on modern Zionism as a historical process that would suffer reverses in its initial stages as a secular movement but that would ultimately find its way to the restoration of Israel as a religious nation of Judaism set at the center of a restored world in which G-d would be recognized.

Indeed, Kook's understanding of the "footsteps of the messiah" as an expression for the historical process of the restoration of Israel would inform later writings, such as *Orot Hakodesh 1* (Lights of Holiness, vol. 1), where he would begin to speak of "the lights of tohu (chaos)," in relation to the reverses that Zionism would experience as it worked its way through historical experience. Such language very clearly draws upon the Lurianic concept of the sparks of divine presence that are scattered throughout the world and hidden in the *qelippot* or husks of finite existence. Such a process entails the redemption not only of the Jewish people but of the world at large, as each stage in the historical process, or steps of the messiah, raises creation to higher and higher states of holiness as the sparks of the divine are gathered and assembled to restore or recognize the presence of the divine in the world at large. Kook's use of Lurianic concepts and imagery effectively provides a reconceptualization of the secular, Enlightenment (Haskalah) understanding of the progress of history—such as that promoted by Ahad Ha'am, who himself had come from a Hasidic background before turning to modern secular Zionism—casting it instead in the messianic terms of Lurianic kabbalah. Kook thereby conceives of modern Zionism as a religious process sanctioned and impelled by G-d. Modern secular Zionism constitutes an expression of the Shevirat Hakelim of Lurianic thought, itself a reaction to the historical events of the expulsion from Spain; but Ravitzky sees Kook's understanding of the Breaking of the Vessels as an expression or stage of the contemporary historical process in which modern secular Zionism would be a failed stage in the process that would ultimately lead to the Tikkun Olam or restoration of the world. For Kook, Tikkun Olam is not repair of a damaged world, but a positive stage in the recognition of the hidden divine character or holiness of the world in which we live. In this respect, Kook is much closer to the Habad understanding of the process as articulated by Shneur Zalman of Liady in the Tanya and his other writings. The challenges of secularism, particularly in modern Zionism, are the birth pangs of religious revival in Judaism that will culminate in the restoration of the Jewish people as a religious people in their own land.

In essence, Kook embraces secular Zionism by seeing it as part of a larger process of religious restoration. But he also views the secular Zionists of his time as pawns in the hands of G-d who do not fully understand their purpose in the divine scheme of world history and the creation of the world. Their efforts are instigated and informed by the divine even if they do not realize it. Kook's understanding thereby provides a new understanding of the notion of divine concealment in Lurianic kabbalah and in Shabbatean thought and practice because it understands the divine to require elements of sin or unholiness as part of a larger process that will see the ultimate revelation of the holiness of the divine in the world. Although modern secular Zionism was largely rejected by the traditionalist Jewish establishment of the day, Kook identifies it as an element in G-d's plans for the sanctification of all creation. Just as Lurianic kabbalah recognized the sparks of the divine within the *qelippot* or husks of materiality; just as Shabbetai Zevi would descend into the depths of sin to recover the last sparks of holiness in the world; and just as the Habadnik had to find and activate the sparks of holiness within oneself: even so, in Kook's view, modern secular Zionism, though viewed by traditionalists as a sinful rejection of traditional Jewish belief and practice, must be recognized as a movement in accordance with the divine will. To be sure, Kook did not see a future for secular Jewish expression, whether Zionist or otherwise, but he nevertheless laid out an understanding whereby modern Zionism could be accepted as an expression of the will of G-d.

Kook's work and ideas have had tremendous impact in convincing much of the traditionalist Jewish world to support modern Zionism. Although the early modern Zionist movement was primarily a secular enterprise, a product of the Haskalah or Jewish Enlightenment of the late nineteenth and twentieth century, Kook's work helped to convince traditionalists to see modern Zionism and modern Israel as an expression of the footsteps of the messiah, insofar as they believed that modern Israel would ultimately become a halakically governed Jewish state, rather than its current form as the social-democratic state of the Jewish people. Indeed, traditional Jews pray every day for the restoration of Israel when they lay tefillin, although they envision a halakically based kingdom rather than a secular democracy. Although many traditionalists see the current Jewish state as a transitional stage in the development of a halakically based Jewish state, Israel's victory against the overwhelming Arab forces amassed against it in the Six Day War of 1967 did much to convince traditionalists of divine support of the modern state of Israel and its role as an element in the divine plan of messianic redemption of the world, with a halakically based Jewish state at its center.

Among traditionalist Jewish movements that support modern Israel, Habad merits special attention.[18] Although we have treated the foundational Habad movement and thought above, the modern experience of Habad Hasidism, particularly the life and work of its last Rebbe, R. Menahem Mendel Schneerson, demands consideration.[19] Schneersohn (1902–1994), best known as the Lubavitcher Rebbe or simply the Rebbe, was a dynamic and influential leader—indeed, he is considered in many circles as the most dynamic and influential Jewish leader of the twentieth century—who trans-

18. Biale et al., *Hasidism*, 694–700.
19. Ravitzky, *Messianism*, 187–206.

formed Habad from a marginal Jewish sect into a movement that, under Schneerson's leadership, has expanded greatly in the latter half of the twentieth century, established Habad Houses worldwide, and laid out an agenda for the return of the Jewish people to traditional Jewish practice and thought, as well as a role for the nations in recognizing G-d and sanctifying their own lives through the laws of Noah according to traditional Jewish thought.

Schneerson was born in Nikalaev in what was then the Russian empire in 1902; Nikolaev is now Mykolaiv, Ukraine. His father was R. Lev Yitzhak Schneerson, and his mother was Chana (Yanovski) Schneerson. From an early age, young Menahem Mendel was recognized as an *ilui* or genius and talmudic prodigy. He married Chaya Mushka Schneersohn, the daughter of the sixth Habad rabbi, Joseph Isaac Schneersohn. Although Menahem Mendel and Chaya Mushka had a long and happy marriage, they did not have children. In addition to his Jewish studies, Menahem Mendel studied mechanics, electrical engineering, and mathematics in France at the Sorbonne and elsewhere. When Germany invaded France in the Second World War, the Schneersons were forced to flee to the United States. During the war, Schneerson volunteered his services to the US Navy and drew the electrical wiring schemes for the battleship USS *Missouri* which was under construction in the Brooklyn Navy Yard. Due to his talents, Menahem Mendel worked in his father-in-law's office, and he ultimately became the chairman of the Agudas Chasidei Chabad, the Association of the Habad Hasidim, the umbrella agency that oversees the Habad movement. When Joseph Isaac died in 1950, Menahem Mendel was persuaded to assume leadership of the Habad movement, although it took a year to convince him to do so.

Contemporary Habad Hasidism continues to hold to Shneur Zalman's view that the presence of G-d permeates all reality and that all finite reality is illusory and only conceals the divine presence. Although Habad supports modern Israel, it holds that ultimately modern Israel must become a halakic Jewish state that will then facilitate the revelation of the messiah in the world, and the messiah will then complete the process of Tikkun Olam. Habad presence in modern Israel is intended to aid in bringing about the revelation of the messiah.

But Menahem Mendel Schneerson was far more entrepreneurial than his predecessors had been in envisioning the sanctification of the entire world as the outcome of the process of Tikkun Olam. He viewed past Habad efforts as largely defensive, and he called on his adherents instead to go on the offensive in their efforts to bring Jews back to traditional Judaism—and gentiles also to their roles in the worldview of Habad. Schneerson called on

his followers to send out mitzvah mobiles, small trucks loaded with *kippot,
tallitot, tefillin,* and other Jewish ritual objects, in search of Jewish men on
the street to invite them to lay tefillin and thereby begin the process of renewing traditional Jewish practice. Indeed, the request to lay tefillin and
pray in the traditional Jewish manner is the hallmark of encounters between
Habadniks and non-observant Jewish men. Likewise, Schneerson called for
the establishment of Habad Houses throughout the world, including in Asia,
Africa, and Australia, as well as in Europe and the Americas, so as to spread
Habad influence throughout the world. A Habad House is generally staffed
by a Habad rabbi, his wife or rebbetzin, and their family. The purpose is to
provide a place for Jews to come to join traditional Jewish worship, engage
in traditional Jewish study, eat kosher meals, and meet other Jews—to form
a community in the host cities and countries. Habad makes major efforts
to ensure that rabbis, rebbetzins, and children all have the opportunity to
gather and meet their counterparts wherever they might be located in the
world; e.g., Habadniks in East Asia regularly gather about once a month for
such purposes to ensure that they will continue to function effectively to
create holy Jewish communities in places where Jews are few. In keeping
with the Tanya and Lurianic kabbalah, Jews are to go out into the world to
reveal the holiness of G-d throughout.

But Schneerson did not limit his efforts to Jews alone. He called for the
lighting of Hanukkah Menorahs in public as a means to raise the consciousness of both Jews and gentiles, and he reasoned that the Christian season
of Christmas would be an ideal time for such efforts since many Christians
(and Jews) view Hanukkah as a sort of Jewish Christmas—even though the
analogy does not apply. Likewise, Schneerson called on Jews to make every
encounter with a gentile a teaching moment in which the gentile would
learn more about Judaism and traditional Judaism's expectations that gentiles should practice the laws of Noah, i.e., laws that attempt to build in-
terreligious relationships with Judaism by calling upon them to recognize
G-d, avoid blaspheming G-d, establish courts of justice, prevent murder,
avoid theft, avoid illicit sexual relationships, avoid eating meat with the life
(blood) still in it, and other commands that would help to achieve holiness
and divine expectations in the finite world. The purpose of the laws of Noah
is to ensure the sanctity of gentiles according to what is expected of them as
understood from the Torah and before G-d.

Menahem Schneerson employed his education in electrical engineering
and mathematics to support his efforts by promoting Habad broadcasts of
Jewish teachings. When traditionalist rabbis criticized him for employing

modern innovation in a world that had been created by the divine, Schneerson responded that G-d had created the radio waves as part of creation and that they, too, should be employed in efforts to sanctify creation. Indeed, it is Schneerson's position that modern science will lead to the recognition of cosmic monism as an expression of divine reality, and so modern science must be engaged in his religious worldview.

When Schneerson's wife, Chana, died in 1988, he moved into his study at Habad Headquarters in New York. In 1992, he suffered a major stroke that left him speechless and mostly incapacitated, although he continued to work. He passed away in 1994. Many Habadniks view him as the messiah, but, so far, he has not returned as such. Because he had no children, there was no one to follow him in his position. The Agudas Chasidei Chasidim continues to govern Habad Hasidism since his death. Today, Habad is recognized as the fastest-growing and most influential movement in Judaism.

Conclusion

Jewish visionary experience and mysticism have been among the most innovative and influential movements in the entire history of Judaism, Jewish thought, and Jewish practice. Even in the pre-Israelite Canaanite period, visionaries in Canaan, Egypt, Mesopotamia, and elsewhere developed visionary and dream experiences as a means to portray divine presence and action in the world of creation and human events, thereby to influence the outlooks and actions of human beings. Such experience also proved to be highly influential in the Torah, Former Prophets, and the Psalms in portraying YHWH's presence and actions in the world. Indeed, the Latter Prophets in the Bible not only called attention to the presence and will of G-d, but also attempted to persuade their contemporaries and the later readers of their writings, so that their audiences would understand and adhere to the divine will. The apocalyptic literature of the Bible and works of the Persian, Hellenistic, and Roman periods were instrumental in conceptualizing divine intentions in relation to the building of the Second Temple, threats leveled against the temple and the Jewish people at large, and the destruction of the temple in 70 CE and the failure of the Bar Kokhba revolt in 132–135 CE.

Even with the destruction of the Second Temple, rabbinic forms of Jewish mysticism and visionary experience influenced the identification of divine presence and purpose in the world; they also significantly helped to reconceptualize Judaism in relation to life in exile from the land of Israel and the many challenges faced by Jews living in foreign and frequently hostile lands. The visionary authors of the heikhalot or merkavah literature posited that it was possible to apprehend the presence of G-d in the seventh heaven above the world of creation, as well as divine purpose in bringing about the destruction of the temple and the dispersion of the Jewish people among the nations. The works of the Ma'aseh Bereshit and the early kabbalah began the process of examining the intangible aspects of G-d in relation to the Ten Sefirot, understood first as the ten utterances of G-d during the creation of the universe and later as the abstract qualities of G-d found within all human beings and all creation. The teachings of the Zohar, the pinnacle of medieval kabbalistic thought, refined the concept of the Ten Sefirot into a new understanding of the epistemology of the world of creation and human events. Lurianic kabbalah began the process of making kabbalistic thought a pervasive movement in Jewish thought and life, rather than the preserve of a small number of esoteric specialists who had developed the various earlier forms of heikhalot and kabbalistic thought and literature. And finally, the Hasidic movement averred that all Jews had access to G-d and Jewish tradition through its understanding of the divine presence that permeated all of creation.

The democratization of Jewish mysticism has exerted a defining influence in most aspects of Jewish thought and life.[1] The pervasive influence of Jewish mysticism began with the emergence of Lurianic kabbalah, which through its mythological understanding of the character and presence of G-d at the outset of creation and its theological influence on Jewish liturgy and practice ensured the widespread understanding and application of kabbalistic thought and practice. Through its pervasive influence, Lurianic kabbalah was instrumental in founding the Hasidic movement, initially under the leadership of R. Israel ben Eliezer, known as the Baal Shem Tov, as well as later figures, such as R. Dov Ber and R. Shneur Zalman, which has played such an important role in redefining Jewish life and worship in the modern world. Indeed, Habad Hasidism is the fastest growing movement in all of Judaism today. But with its doctrines of Tzimtzum, the withdrawal of G-d at creation, and Tikkun Olam, the repair of the world, Lurianic kabbalah was also influential in the foundations of the modern Jewish movements of Reform and Orthodox Judaism, insofar as both are rooted in the work of Moses Mendelssohn, who sought to define Judaism as a true religion which was concerned with the sanctification and idealization of the world at large as well as the Jewish people within that world.

Lurianic kabbalah also played an important role in the origins of modern Zionism, the modern Jewish political movement concerned with the reestablishment of Jewish state and homeland for the Jewish people in the land of

---

1. Cf. my study, "The Democratization of Messianism in Modern Jewish Thought," in *Biblical Interpretation: History, Context, and Reality*, ed. Christine Helmer and Christof Landmesser, SBLSym 26 (Atlanta: Society of Biblical Literature, 2005), 87–101.

Israel. Asher Ginzburg, better known as Ahad Ha'am, was a former Hasidic rabbi who adopted the principles of the Haskalah or Jewish Enlightenment to become one of the major leaders of the early Zionist movement in Russia. He was instrumental in defining the interrelationship between Jews living in the modern homeland in the land of Israel and those living in the diaspora in order to bring about the betterment of the world at large as well as of the Jewish people, in keeping with the teachings of Lurianic kabbalah.

Jewish mysticism has also had a pervasive influence in the larger literary world, as exemplified by the works of Franz Kafka, a late-nineteenth- and early-twentieth-century Jewish writer whose works demonstrate his understanding of a wholly other world beyond what can be sensed but not touched,[2] or Chaim Potok, a twentieth-century Jewish writer whose works helped a larger public to understand the world, thought, and life of Hasidic Jews.[3]

In all cases, Jewish visionary and mystical experience prompted the rethinking of Jewish concepts and life. The eighth-century BCE prophet, Isaiah ben Amoz, laid the foundations for understanding divine punishment against Jerusalem and Judah as demonstrations of divine sovereignty worldwide, as well as for recognizing the divine capacity to restore the exiled Jewish people to Jerusalem and the land of Israel. The exilic priest and prophet, Ezekiel ben Buzi, likewise provided the basis for thinking of YHWH as a worldwide G-d, whose divine presence could be experienced in the farthest reaches of the earth as well as in Jerusalem and the land of Israel. The visions of Daniel demonstrated that G-d could intervene in the world's affairs to ensure the sanctity of the Jerusalem Temple and to defeat foreign powers that sought to compromise that sanctity. The authors of 1 Enoch considered how human beings might approach G-d in the heavens and thereby understand divine actions on earth. The Heikhalot Rabbati demonstrated that not only was an approach to the heavenly throne of G-d possible through the study of Torah, but that G-d might admit mistakes in bringing excessive punishment against the Jewish people, calling upon them to continue their study of Torah in order better to understand the will and purposes of the divine. The Shiur Qomah prompted Jews to understand the overwhelming majesty of the divine presence before whom Jews would pray. The Sefer Yetzirah

---

2. Moshe Idel, *Kabbalah: New Perspectives* (New Haven: Yale University Press, 1988), 271; see Franz Kafka, *The Complete Stories* (New York: Schocken, 1971). My thanks go to my former PhD student Dr. Soo J. Kim, herself an expert in literary interpretation, for her suggestions concerning Franz Kafka.

3. Chaim Potok, *The Chosen* (New York: Simon & Schuster, 1967); Potok, *The Promise* (New York: Alfred A. Knopf, 1969).

explored the various dimensions of the Hebrew language and alphabet to uncover hidden teaching in the Ten Sefirot or the ten utterances of G-d in the process of creation. Early kabbalistic works, such as Sefer Habahir, and later kabbalistic works, such as Sefer Hazohar, developed the Ten Sefirot as expressions of the intangible aspects of the presence of G-d that were manifested in all human beings as well as in creation at large. Lurianic kabbalah emphasized how divine love enabled G-d to produce creation and thereby to limit the divine self on behalf of the world of creation and human beings. Not only did Lurianic kabbalah provide the means by which Jews might act as partners with G-d in restoring the integrity and sanctity of creation; it also made sure that Jews throughout the world had access to Lurianic teachings. Hasidism reinvigorated Jewish worship, study, and practice, but it did so in a way that even Jews with little in the way of Jewish knowledge could come to understand and put into practice. Indeed, the emerging understanding of the vulnerability of G-d and the divine need for relationship with human beings has played a major role in demonstrating divine presence and involvement in the world, even in the face of the Shoah or Holocaust.[4]

As Judaism moves through its fifty-eighth century in the Jewish calendar and the beginning of the twenty-first century in the secular calendar, Jewish mysticism is well poised to continue its influence in Jewish thought and worship and Judaism's capacity to meet the challenges of Jewish life in the modern world.

4. See Abraham Joshua Heschel, *G-d in Search of Man: A Philosophy of Judaism* (New York: Farrar, Straus, and Cudahy, 1955); Marvin A. Sweeney, *Reading the Hebrew Bible after the Shoah: Engaging Holocaust Theology* (Minneapolis: Fortress, 2008).

Bibliography

Abrahams, Israel. *Hebrew-English Edition of the Babylonian Talmud: Ḥagigah*. London: Soncino, 1990.

Aharoni, Miriam. "Arad." *NEAEHL* 1:75–87.

Alexander, Philip S. "3 (The Hebrew Apocalypse of) Enoch." Pages 223–315 in *The Old Testament Pseudepigrapha*. Vol. 1 of *Apocalyptic Literature and Testaments*. Edited by James H. Charlesworth. Garden City, NY: Doubleday, 1983.

Allen, Leslie C. *Jeremiah: A Commentary*. OTL. Louisville: Westminster John Knox, 2008.

Arbel, Vita Daphna. *Beholders of Divine Secrets: Mysticism and Myth in the Hekhalot and Merkavah Literature*. Albany: SUNY Press, 2003.

Ashtor, Elyahu. *The Jews of Moslem Spain*. 2 vols. Philadelphia: Jewish Publication Society, 1973–79.

Auld, A. Graeme. *1 and 2 Samuel: A Commentary*. OTL. Louisville: Westminster John Knox, 2011.

Aune, David E. *Revelation 1–5*. WBC 52A. Nashville: Thomas Nelson, 1997.

———. *Revelation 6–16*. WBC 52B. Nashville: Thomas Nelson, 1998.

———. *Revelation 17–22*. WBC 52C. Nashville: Thomas Nelson, 1998.

Avineri, Sholomo. *The Makings of Modern Zionism: The Intellectual Origins of the Jewish State*. New York: Basic Books, 1981.

Baer, Yitzhak. *A History of the Jews of Christian Spain*. 2 vols. Philadelphia: Jewish Publication Society, 1961.

Bat Ye'or. *The Dhimmi: Jews and Christians under Islam*. London: Associated University Presses, 1985.

Beinart, Haim. *The Expulsion of the Jews from Spain*. Oxford: Littman Library, 2005.

Ben-Amos, Dan, and Jerome R. Mintz, trans. and eds. *In Praise of the Baal Shem Tov [Shivhei ha-Besht]: The Earliest Collection of Legends about the Founder of Hasidism*. New York: Schocken, 1984.

Ben Sasson, H. H., ed. *A History of the Jewish People*. Cambridge: Harvard University Press, 1976.

Betz, Hans Dieter. *The Greek Magical Papyri in Translation, Including the Demotic Spells*. Chicago: University of Chicago Press, 1986.

Biale, David, et al. *Hasidism: A New History*. Princeton: Princeton University Press, 2017.

Biran, Avraham, and Joseph Naveh. "An Aramaic Stele Fragment from Tel Dan." *IEJ* 43 (1993): 81–98.

———. "The Tel Dan Inscription: A New Fragment." *IEJ* 45 (1995): 1–18.

Blenkinsopp, Joseph. *Isaiah 1–39.* AB 19. New York: Doubleday, 2000.

———. *Isaiah 40–55.* AB 19A. New York: Doubleday, 2002.

———. *Isaiah 56–66.* AB 19B. New York: Doubleday, 2003.

Blumenthal, David R. *Understanding Jewish Mysticism: The Merkabah Tradition and the Zoharic Tradition.* New York: Ktav, 1978.

Bokser, Ben-Zion. *Abraham Isaac Kook.* Mahwah, NJ: Paulist, 1978.

Bottéro, Jean. *Religion in Ancient Mesopotamia.* Chicago: University of Chicago Press, 2004.

Boustan, Ra'anan S. *From Martyr to Mystic: Rabbinic Martyrology and the Making of Merkavah Mysticism.* TSAJ 112. Tübingen: Mohr Siebeck, 2005.

———. "The Study of Hekhalot Literature: Between Mystical Experience and Textual Artifact." *CBR* 6.1 (Oct. 2007): 130–60.

Buber, Martin. *Tales of Rabbi Nachman.* New York: Avon, 1956.

Campbell, Antony F. *1 Samuel.* FOTL 7. Grand Rapids: Eerdmans, 2003.

———. *2 Samuel.* FOTL 8. Grand Rapids: Eerdmans, 2005.

Campbell, Antony F., and Mark A. O'Brien. *Sources of the Pentateuch: Texts, Introductions, Annotations.* Minneapolis: Fortress, 1993.

Carey, Greg. *Ultimate Things: An Introduction to Jewish and Christian Apocalyptic Literature.* St. Louis: Chalice, 2005.

Clifford, Richard J. *Proverbs: A Commentary.* OTL. Louisville: Westminster John Knox, 1999.

Coats, George W. *Exodus 1–18.* FOTL 2A. Grand Rapids: Eerdmans, 1999.

———. *Genesis, with an Introduction to Narrative Literature.* FOTL 1. Grand Rapids: Eerdmans, 1983.

Cohen, Martin. *The Shi'ur Qomah: Liturgy and Theurgy in Pre-Kabbalitic Jewish Mysticism.* Lanham: University Press of America, 1983.

———. *The Shi'ur Qomah: Texts and Recensions.* TSAJ 9. Tübingen: Mohr Siebeck, 1985.

Collins, John J. *The Apocalyptic Imagination: An Introduction to Jewish Apocalyptic Literature.* 2nd ed. Grand Rapids: Eerdmans, 1998.

———. *Daniel.* Hermeneia. Minneapolis: Fortress, 1993.

———. "Introduction: The Genre Apocalypse Reconsidered." Pages 1–20 in *Apocalypse, Prophecy, and Pseudepigraphy: On Jewish Apocalyptic Literature.* Grand Rapids: Eerdmans, 2016.

Cordovero, Rabbi Moses. *The Palm Tree of Deborah, Translated from the Hebrew with an Introduction and Notes by Louis Jacobs.* New York: Sepher Hermon, 1974.

Cryer, Frederick H. *Divination in Ancient Israel and Its Near Eastern Environment.* JSOTSup 142. Sheffield: Sheffield Academic Press, 1994.

Cunningham, Graham. "Sumerian Religion." Pages 31–53 in *The Cambridge History of Religions in the Ancient World,* vol. 1: *From the Bronze Age to the Hellenistic Age.* Edited by Michele Renee Salzman and Marvin A. Sweeney. Cambridge: Cambridge University Press, 2013.

Dahood, Mitchell. *Psalms II: 51–100.* AB 17. Garden City, NY: Doubleday, 1968.

Dalley, Stephanie. *Myths from Mesopotamia: Creation, the Flood, Gilgamesh and Others.* Oxford: Oxford University Press, 1991.

Dan, Joseph. *The Ancient Jewish Mysticism*. Tel Aviv: MOD, 1993.

———. *The Early Kabbalah*. Classics of Western Spirituality. New York: Paulist, 1986.

Danby, Herbert. *The Mishnah*. Oxford: Oxford University Press, 1977.

Darr, Katheryn Pfisterer. "Ezekiel." Pages 1073–1607 in vol. 6 of *The New Interpreter's Bible*. Edited by Leander E. Keck et al. Nashville: Abingdon, 2001.

Davila, James R. *Hekhalot Literature in Translation: Major Texts of Merkavah Mysticism*. Leiden: Brill, 2013.

Dietrich, Manfred, Oswald Loretz, and Joaquín Sanmartín. *Die keilalphabetischen Texte aus Ugarit, Ras Ibn Hani und anderen Orten/The Cuneiform Alphabetic Texts from Ugarit, Ras Ibn Hani and Other Places*. 3rd enlarged edition. AOAT 360/1. Münster: Ugarit Verlag, 2013.

Dijkstra, Meindert. "Is Balaam Also among the Prophets?" *JBL* 114 (1995): 43–64.

Doxey, Denise M. "Egyptian Religion." Pages 177–204 in *The Cambridge History of Religions in the Ancient World*, vol. 1: *From the Bronze Age to the Hellenistic Age*. Edited by Michele Renee Salzman and Marvin A. Sweeney. Cambridge: Cambridge University Press, 2013.

Dozeman, Thomas B. *Exodus*. Eerdmans Critical Commentary. Grand Rapids: Eerdmans, 2009.

———. *Joshua 1–12*. YAB 6B. New Haven: Yale University Press, 2015.

Dubnow, Simon. "The Beginnings: The Baal Shem Tov (Besht) and the Center in Podolia." Pages 25–57 in *Essential Papers on Hasidism: Origins to Present*. Edited by Gershon David Hundert. New York: New York University Press, 1991.

———. "The Maggid of Miedzyrzecz: His Associates and the Center in Volhynia (1760–1772)." Pages 58–85 in *Essential Papers on Hasidism: Origins to Present*. Edited by Gershon David Hundert. New York: New York University Press, 1991.

Efron, John, et al. *The Jews: A History*. 2nd ed. Boston: Pearson, 2014.

Elior, Rachel. "ḤaBaD: The Contemplative Ascent to G-d." Pages 157–205 in *Jewish Spirituality: From the Sixteenth-Century Revival through the Present Age*. Edited by Arthur Green. New York: Crossroad, 1989.

———. *Heikhalot Zutarti*. Jerusalem: Magnes, 1982.

———. *The Paradoxical Ascent to G-d: The Kabbalistic Theosophy of Habad Hasidism*. Albany: SUNY Press, 1993.

———. *The Three Temples: On the Emergence of Jewish Mysticism*. Oxford: Littman Library of Jewish Civilization, 2004.

Exum, J. Cheryl. *The Song of Songs*. OTL. Louisville: Westminster John Knox, 2005.

Fine, Lawrence. *Physician of the Soul, Healer of the Cosmos: Isaac Luria and His Kabbalistic Fellowship*. Stanford, CA: Stanford University Press, 2003.

———. *Safed Spirituality*. Classics of Western Spirituality. New York: Paulist, 1984.

Fischer, Georg. *Jeremia 1–25*. HThKAT. Freiburg am Breisgau: Herder, 2005.

———. *Jeremia 26–52*. HThKAT. Freiburg am Breisgau: Herder, 2005.

Fishbane, Michael. "Genesis 1:1–2:4a: The Creation." Pages 3–16 in *Text and Texture: Close Readings of Selected Biblical Texts*. New York: Schocken, 1979.

Flannery-Dailey, Frances. *Dreamers, Scribes, and Priests: Jewish Dreams in the Hellenistic and Roman Eras*. SJSJ 90. Leiden: Brill, 2004.

García Martínez, Florentino. *The Dead Sea Scrolls Translated: The Dead Sea Scrolls in English*. Leiden: Brill; Grand Rapids: Eerdmans, 1996.

Gerstenberger, Erhard S. *Psalms, Part 1, with an Introduction to Cultic Poetry*. FOTL 14. Grand Rapids: Eerdmans, 1988.

———. *Psalms, Part 2, and Lamentations*. FOTL 15. Grand Rapids: Eerdmans, 2001.

Graetz, Heinrich. *History of the Jews*. 6 vols. Philadelphia: Jewish Publication Society, 1891–1898.

Green, Arthur. *Tormented Master: The Life and Spiritual Quest of Rabbi Nahman of Bratzlav*. Woodstock, VT: Jewish Lights Publishing, 2013.

Gruenwald, Ithamar. *Apocalyptic and Merkavah Mysticism*. AGJU 14. Leiden: Bill, 1980.

Hamilton, Jeffries M. "Ophrah." *ABD* 5:27–28.

Hamori, Esther J. "When Gods Were Men." *The Embodied God in Biblical and Ancient Near Eastern Literature*. BZAW 384. Berlin: Walter de Gruyter, 2008.

Haskell, Ellen Davina. *Suckling at my Mother's Breasts: The Image of a Nursing G-d in Jewish Mysticism*. Albany: SUNY Press, 2012.

Hayes, Elizabeth R., and Lena-Sofia Tiemeyer, eds. *I Lifted My Eyes and Saw: Reading Dream and Vision Reports in the Hebrew Bible*. LHBOTS 584; London: Bloomsbury T&T Clark, 2014.

Hayman, A. Peter. *Sefer Yeṣira*. TSAJ 104. Tübingen: Mohr Siebeck, 2004.

Heschel, Abraham Joshua. *G-d in Search of Man: A Philosophy of Judaism*. New York: Farrar, Straus, and Cudahy, 1955.

———. "Rabbi Gershon Kutover: His Life and Immigration to the Land of Israel." Pages 44–112 in *The Circle of the Baal Shem Tov: Studies in Hasidism*. Edited by S. H. Dresner. Chicago: University of Chicago Press, 1985.

Hundert, Gershon David, ed., *Essential Papers on Hasidism: Origins to Present*. New York: New York University Press, 1991.

Hurowitz, Victor Avigdor. "Babylon in Bethel—New Light on Jacob's Dream." Pages 436–48 in *Orientalism, Assyriology, and the Bible*. Edited by Steven W. Holloway. Sheffield: Sheffield Phoenix Press, 2007.

Huss, Boaz. *The Zohar: Reception and Impact*. Oxford: The Littman Library of Jewish Civilization, 2016.

Idel, Moshe. *Hasidism: Between Ecstasy and Magic*. Albany: SUNY Press, 1995.

———. "Hitbodedut as Concentration in Ecstatic Kabbalah." Pages 405–38 in *Jewish Spirituality: From the Bible Through the Middle Ages*. Edited by Arthur Green. New York: Crossroad, 1986.

———. *Kabbalah: New Perspectives*. New Haven: Yale University Press, 1988.

———. *The Mystical Experience in Abraham Abulafia*. Albany: SUNY Press, 1987.

Isaac, E. "1 (Ethiopic Apocalypse of) Enoch." Pages 5–89 in *The Old Testament Pseudepigrapha*, vol. 1: *The Apocalyptic Literature and Testaments*. Edited by James H. Charlesworth. Garden City, NY: Doubleday, 1983.

Jackson, Howard M. "The Origins and Development of Sh'ur Qomah Revelation in Jewish Mysticism." *JSJ* 31 (2000): 373–415.

Jacobsen, Thorkild. *The Sumerian King List*. Chicago: The University of Chicago Press, 1939.

———. *The Treasures of Darkness: A History of Mesopotamian Religion*. New Haven: Yale University Press, 1976.

James, William. *The Varieties of Religious Experience*. New York: The New American Library, 1958.

Janowitz, Naomi. *The Poetics of Ascent: Theories of Language in a Rabbinic Ascent Text*. Albany: SUNY Press, 1989.

Jastrow, Marcus. *Dictionary of the Targumim, the Talmud Babli and Yerushalmi, and the Midrashic Literature*. 1943. Repr., Peabody, MA: Hendrickson, 2006.

Jellinek, Adolf. *Bet ha-Midrasch*. 2nd ed. Jerusalem: Bamberger & Wahrmann, 1938.

Jones, Rufus M. *Studies in Mystical Religion*. London: Macmillan, 1909.

Joyce, Paul. *Ezekiel: A Commentary*. New York: T&T Clark, 2008.

Kafka, Franz. *The Complete Stories*. New York: Schocken, 1971.

Kaplan, Aryeh. *The Book Bahir: Illumination*. York Beach, ME: Samuel Weiser, 1979.

Katz, Steven T. "The Conservative Character of Mysticism." Pages 3–60 in *Mysticism and Religious Traditions*. Oxford: Oxford University Press, 1983.

Klein, Ralph. *1 Chronicles*. Hermeneia. Minneapolis: Fortress, 2006.

Klijn, Albertus F. J. "2 (Syriac Apocalypse of) Baruch." Pages 615–52 in *The Old Testament Pseudepigrapha*, vol. 1: *The Apocalyptic Literature and Testaments*. Edited by James H. Charlesworth. Garden City, NY: Doubleday, 1983.

Knierim, Rolf P., and George W. Coats. *Numbers*. FOTL 4. Grand Rapids: Eerdmans, 2005.

Knoppers, Gary N. *1 Chronicles 1–9*. AB 12. New York: Doubleday, 2003.

Kugel, James L. *In Potiphar's House: The Interpretive Life of Biblical Texts*. San Francisco: Harper & Row, 1990.

Kuhrt, Amélie. *The Ancient Near East, c. 3000–330 BC*. London: Routledge, 1998.

Laenen, J. H. *Jewish Mysticism: An Introduction*. Translated by David E. Orton. Louisville: Westminster John Knox, 2001.

Lambert, Wilfred G., and Alan Ralph Millard. *Atra-Ḫasīs: The Babylonian Story of the Flood*. Oxford: Clarendon, 1969.

Levenson, Jon D. *Creation and the Persistence of Evil: The Jewish Drama of Divine Omnipotence*. New York: Harper & Row, 1988.

———. *Sinai and Zion: An Entry into the Jewish Bible*. Minneapolis: Winston, 1985.

———. "The Temple and the World." *JR* 64 (1984): 275–98.

Levine, Baruch A. *Numbers 21–36*. AB 4A. New York: Doubleday, 2000.

Lichtheim, Miriam. *Ancient Egyptian Literature*, vol. 1: *The Old and Middle Kingdoms*. Berkeley: University of California Press, 1975.

———. *Ancient Egyptian Literature*, vol. 2: *The New Kingdom*. Berkeley: University of California Press, 1976.

———. *Ancient Egyptian Literature*, vol. 3: *The Late Period*. Berkeley: University of California Press, 1980.

Livingstone, Alasdair. *Mystical and Mythological Works of Assyrian and Babylonian Scholars*. Oxford: Clarendon, 1986.

Lundbom, Jack R. *Jeremiah 1–20*. AB 21A. New York: Doubleday, 1999.

———. *Jeremiah 21–36*. AB 21B. New York: Doubleday, 2004.

———. *Jeremiah 37–52*. AB 21C. New York: Doubleday, 2004.

McCarthy, Dennis J. *Old Testament Covenant: A Survey of Current Opinions*. Richmond: John Knox, 1972.

———. *Treaty and Covenant: A Study in Form in the Ancient Oriental Documents and in the Old Testament*. AnBib 21A. Rome: Pontifical Biblical Institute, 1978.

Magocsi, Paul Robert. *A History of Ukraine*. Seattle: University of Washington Press, 1996.

Mann, Thomas W. *Divine Presence and Guidance in Israelite Traditions: The Typology of Exaltation*. Baltimore: Johns Hopkins University Press, 1977.

Marcus, Ivan G. "The Devotional Ideals of Ashkenazi Pietism." Pages 356–66 in *Jewish Spirituality*. Edited by Arthur Green. New York: Crossroad, 1986.

———. *Piety and Society: The Jewish Pietists of Medieval Germany*. Leiden: Brill, 1981.

Marcus, Jacob R. *The Jew in the Medieval World: A Source Book: 315–1791*. New York: Atheneum, 1981.

Margaliot, Reuven Moshe, ed. *Sefer ha-Bahir*. Jerusalem: Massad Harav Kook, 1978.

———. *Sefer ha-Zohar*. 6th ed. 3 vols. Jerusalem: Massad Harav Kook, 5744/1984.

Matt, Daniel Chanan. *Zohar: The Book of Enlightenment*. Classics in Western Spirituality. New York: Paulist, 1983.

Matt, Daniel Chanan, et al. *The Zohar: Pritzker Edition*. 11 vols. Stanford: Stanford University Press, 2004–2017.

Metzger, Bruce M. "The Fourth Book of Ezra." Pages 517–60 in *The Old Testament Pseudepigrapha*, vol. 1: *The Apocalyptic Literature and Testaments*. Edited by James H. Charlesworth. Garden City, NY: Doubleday, 1983.

Morenz, Siegfried. *Egyptian Religion*. Ithaca: Cornell University Press, 1973.

Murphy, Roland. *Song of Songs*. Hermeneia. Minneapolis: Fortress, 1990.

Nelson, Richard D. *Joshua: A Commentary*. OTL. Louisville: Westminster John Knox, 1997.

———. "Josiah in the Book of Joshua." *JBL* 100 (1981): 531–40.

Neusner, Jacob. *Introduction to Rabbinic Literature*. Garden City, NY: Doubleday, 1999.

Newsom, Carol A. "The Book of Job." Pages 319–637 in vol. 4 of *The New Interpreter's Bible*. Edited by Leander E. Keck et al. Nashville: Abingdon, 1996.

———. *Job: A Contest of Moral Imaginations*. Oxford: Oxford University Press, 2003.

Nickelsburg, George W. E. *1 Enoch 1*. Hermeneia. Minneapolis: Fortress, 2001.

Nickelsburg, George W. E., and James C. VanderKam. *1 Enoch 2*. Hermeneia. Minneapolis: Fortress, 2012.

Niditch, Susan. *Judges: A Commentary*. OTL. Louisville: Westminster John Knox, 2008.

Nogalski, James D. *The Book of the Twelve*. 2 vols. SHBC. Macon, GA: Smyth & Helwys, 2011.

Novak, David. *The Theology of Nahmanides Systematically Presented*. Atlanta: Scholars Press, 1993.

Odeberg, Hugo. *3 Enoch or the Hebrew Book of Enoch*. New York: Ktav, 1973.

Odell, Margaret S. *Ezekiel*. SHBC. Macon, GA: Smyth & Helwys, 2005.

Oppenheim, A. Leo. *Ancient Mesopotamia: Portrait of a Dead Civilization*. Chicago: University of Chicago Press, 1964.

———. *The Interpretation of Dreams in the Ancient Near East*. Philadelphia: American Philosophical Society, 1956.

Page, Stephanie. "A Stela of Adad Nirari III and Nergal-ereš from Tell al Rimlah." *Iraq* 30 (1968): 139–53.

Paul, Shalom. *Isaiah 40–66*. Grand Rapids: Eerdmans, 2012.

Perdue, Leo G. *The Sword and the Stylus: An Introduction to Wisdom in the Age of Empire*. Grand Rapids: Eerdmans, 2008.

Petersen, David L. *Late Israelite Prophecy: Studies in Deutero-Prophetic Literature and in Chronicles*. SBLMS 23. Missoula, MT: Scholars Press, 1977.

———. *The Prophetic Literature: An Introduction*. Louisville: Westminster John Knox, 2002.

Potok, Chaim. *The Chosen*. New York: Simon and Schuster, 1967.

———. *The Promise*. New York: Alfred A. Knopf, 1969.

Pritchard, James B., ed. *The Ancient Near East in Pictures*. Princeton: Princeton University Press, 1969.

———. *Ancient Near Eastern Texts Relating to the Old Testament*. 3rd ed. Princeton: Princeton University Press, 1969.

Rad, Gerhard von. "The Joseph Narrative and Ancient Wisdom." Pages 292–300 in *The Problem of the Hexateuch and Other Essays*. Translated by E. W. Truemen Dicken. London: SCM, 1966.

Ravitzky, Aviezer. *Messianism, Zionism, and Jewish Religious Radicalism*. Translated by Michael Swirsky and Jonathan Chapman. Chicago: University of Chicago Press, 1996.

Redford, Donald B. *Akhenaten: The Heretic King*. Princeton: Princeton University Press, 1984.

———. *Egypt, Canaan, and Israel in Ancient Times*. Princeton: Princeton University Press, 1992.

Römer, Thomas. *The So-Called Deuteronomistic History: A Sociological, Historical, and Literary Introduction*. Edinburgh: T&T Clark, 2007.

Rubenstein, Avraham. "Israel ben Eliezer." *EncJud* 9:1049–58.

Safrai, Shmuel. "Ishmael ben Elisha." *EncJud* 9:83–86.

Sarna, Nahum. *Exodus*. JPS Torah Commentary. Philadelphia: Jewish Publication Society, 1991.

———. *Genesis*. JPS Torah Commentary. Philadelphia: Jewish Publication Society, 1989.

Sasson, Jack. *Judges 1–12*. YAB 6D. New Haven: Yale University Press, 2014.

Schäfer, Peter. *Mirror of His Beauty: Feminine Images of G-d from the Bible to the Early Kabbalah*. Princeton: Princeton University Press, 2002.

———. *The Origins of Jewish Mysticism*. Tübingen: Mohr Siebeck, 2009.

———. *Synopse zur Hekhalot-Literatur*. Tübingen: Mohr Siebeck, 1981.

Schatz Uffenheimer, Rivka. *Hasidism as Mysticism: Quietistic Elements in Eighteenth Century Hasidic Thought*. Princeton: Princeton University Press, 1993.

Schechter, Solomon. "Safed in the Sixteenth Century: A City of Legists and Mystics." Pages 202–85 in *Studies in Judaism*, Second Series. Philadelphia: Jewish Publication Society of America, 1908.

Schechtman, Joseph B. "Cordovero, Moses ben Jacob." *EncJud* 5:967–70.

Schiffman, Lawrence H. "The Recall of Rabbi Nehuniah ben ha-Qanah from Ecstasy in the Hekhalot Rabbati." *AJSRev* 1 (1976): 269–81.

Schneider, Tammi J. "Assyrian and Babylonian Religions." Pages 54–83 in *The Cambridge History of Religions in the Ancient World*, vol. 1: *From the Bronze Age to the Hellenistic Age*. Edited by Michele Renee Salzman and Marvin A. Sweeney. Cambridge: Cambridge University Press, 2013.

Scholem, Gershom. "The Crypto-Jewish Sect of the Dönmeh (Sabbatians) in Turkey." Pages 142–66 in *The Messianic Idea in Judaism and Other Essays on Jewish Spirituality*. New York: Schocken, 1971.

———. *Das Buch Bahir*. 4th ed. Darmstadt: Wissenschaftliche Buchgesellschaft, 1989.

———. *Jewish Gnosticism, Merkabah Mysticism, and Talmudic Tradition*. New York: Jewish Theological Seminary, 1965.

———. "Kabbalah." *EncJud* 10:489–653.

———. *Major Trends in Jewish Mysticism*. New York: Schocken, 1961.

———. *On the Mystical Shape of the G-dhead: Basic Concepts in the Kabbalah.* Mysticism and Kabbalah. New York: Schocken, 1997.

———. *The Origins of the Kabbalah.* Philadelphia: Jewish Publication Society; Princeton: Princeton University Press, 1987.

———. "Redemption Through Sin." Pages 78–141 in *The Messianic Idea in Judaism and Other Essays on Jewish Spirituality.* New York: Schocken, 1971.

———. *Sabbatai Sevi: The Mystical Messiah.* Princeton: Princeton University Press, 1973.

———. "Shi'ur Komah." *EncJud* 14:1417–19.

Sefati, Yitschak. *Love Songs in Sumerian Literature: Critical Edition of the Dumuzi-Inanna Songs.* Ramat Gan, Israel: Bar Ilan University Press, 1998.

Seltzer, Robert. *Jewish People, Jewish Thought: The Jewish Experience in History.* New York: Macmillan, 1980.

Seow, Choon Leong. *Ecclesiastes.* AB 18C. Garden City, NY: Doubleday, 1997.

Shead, Andrew G. *The Open Book and the Sealed Book: Jeremiah 32 in Its Hebrew and Greek Recensions.* JSOTSup 347. Sheffield: Sheffield Academic Press, 2002.

Smith, Mark S. *The Ugaritic Baal Cycle.* Vol. 1. Leiden: Brill, 1994.

———. *Where the Gods Are: Spatial Dimensions of Anthropomorphism in the Biblical World.* New Haven: Yale University Press, 2016.

Smith, Morton. *Hekhalot Rabbati: The Greater Treatise Concerning the Palaces of Heaven.* Edited by D. Karr. 2009. www.digital-brilliance.com/kab/karr/HekRab/HekRab.pdf; accessed, January 15, 2019.

Sommer, Benjamin D. *The Bodies of G-d and the World of Ancient Israel.* Cambridge: Cambridge University Press, 2009.

Speiser, Ephraim A. *Genesis.* AB 1. Garden City, NY: Doubleday, 1965.

Stackert, Jeffrey. *A Prophet like Moses: Prophecy, Law, and Israelite Religion.* Oxford: Oxford University Press, 2014.

Stenrung, Knut. *The Book of Formation: Sepher Yetzirah.* New York: Ktav, 1970.

Stillman, Norman A. *The Jews of Arab Lands: A History and Source Book.* Philadelphia: Jewish Publication Society, 1979.

Stone, Michael. *4 Ezra.* Hermeneia. Minneapolis: Fortress, 1990.

Strack, H. L., and Gunter Stemberger. *Introduction to the Talmud and Midrash.* Minneapolis: Fortress, 1992.

Stroll, Avrum. "Shneur Zalman of (Liozna-) Lyady." *EncJud* 14:1432–40.

Stulman, Louis. *Jeremiah.* ACOT. Nashville: Abingdon, 2005.

Swartz, Michael D. *Mystical Prayer in Ancient Judaism: An Analysis of Ma'aseh Merkavah.* Tübingen: Mohr Siebeck, 1992.

Sweeney, Marvin A. *1 and 2 Kings: A Commentary.* OTL. Louisville: Westminster John Knox, 2007.

———. "Balaam in Intertextual Perspective." Pages 534–47 in *Tell It in Gath: Studies in the History and Archaeology of Israel; Essays in Honor of Aren Maeir on the Occasion of His Sixtieth Birthday.* Edited by Itzhaq Shai et al. ÄAT 90. Münster: Zaphon, 2018.

———. "Davidic Polemics in the Book of Judges." *VT* 47 (1997): 517–29.

———. "Davidic Typology in the Forty Year War Between the Sons of Light and the Sons of Darkness." Pages 262–68 in *Form and Intertextuality in Prophetic and Apocalyptic Literature.* FAT 45. Tübingen: Mohr Siebeck, 2005.

———. "The Democratization of Messianism in Modern Jewish Thought." Pages 87–101 in *Biblical Interpretation: History, Context, and Reality*. Edited by Christine Helmer and Christof Landmesser. SBLSym 26. Atlanta: Society of Biblical Literature, 2005.

———. "Differing Perspective in the LXX and MT Versions of Jeremiah 1–10." Pages 135–53 in *Reading Prophetic Books: Form, Intertextuality, and Reception in Prophetic and Post-Biblical Literature*. FAT 89. Tübingen: Mohr Siebeck, 2014.

———. "Dimensions of the Shekhinah: The Meaning of the Shiur Qomah in Jewish Mysticism, Liturgy, and Rabbinic Thought." *Hebrew Studies* 54 (2013): 107–20.

———. "The End of Eschatology in Daniel? Theological and Socio-Political Ramifications of the Changing Contexts of Interpretation." Pages 248–61 in *Form and Intertextuality in Prophetic and Apocalyptic Literature*. FAT 45. Tübingen: Mohr Siebeck, 2005.

———. "Ezekiel: Zadokite Priest and Visionary Prophet of the Exile." Pages 125–43 in *Form and Intertextuality in Prophetic and Apocalyptic Literature*. FAT 45. Tübingen: Mohr Siebeck 2005.

———. "Ezekiel's Debate with Isaiah." Pages 555–74 in *Congress Volume: Ljubljana 2007*. Edited by André Lemaire. VTSup 133. Leiden: Brill, 2010.

———. "Form Criticism." Pages 58–89 in *To Each Its Own Meaning: An Introduction to Biblical Criticisms and Their Application*. Edited by Steven L. McKenzie and Stephen R. Haynes. Louisville: Westminster John Knox, 1999.

———. *Isaiah 1–39, with an Introduction to Prophetic Literature*. FOTL 16. Grand Rapids: Eerdmans, 1996.

———. *Isaiah 40–66*. FOTL. Grand Rapids: Eerdmans, 2016.

———. "The Jacob Narratives: An Ephraimitic Text?" *CBQ* 78 (2016): 236–55.

———. "Jeremiah 30–31 and King Josiah's Program of National Restoration and Religious Reform." Pages 109–22 in *Form and Intertextuality in Prophetic and Apocalyptic Literature*. FAT 45. Tübingen: Mohr Siebeck, 2005.

———. *King Josiah of Judah: The Lost Messiah of Israel*. Oxford: Oxford University Press, 2001.

———. "Midrashic Perspective in the Torat ham-Melek of the Temple Scroll." Pages 346–62 in *Reading Prophetic Books: Form, Intertextuality, and Reception in Prophetic and Post-Biblical Literature*. FAT 89. Tübingen: Mohr Siebeck, 2014.

———. "Pardes Revisited Once Again: A Reassessment of the Rabbinic Legend concerning the Four Who Entered Pardes." Pages 269–82 in *Form and Intertextuality in Prophetic and Apocalyptic Literature*. FAT 45. Tübingen: Mohr Siebeck, 2005.

———. *The Pentateuch: Foundations of Identity in Israel and Judah*. CBS. Nashville: Abingdon, 2017.

———. *The Prophetic Literature*. IBT; Nashville: Abingdon, 2005.

———. "Prophets and Priests in the Deuteronomistic History: Elijah and Elisha." Pages 35–49 in *Israelite Prophecy and the Deuteronomistic History: Portrait, Reality, and the Formation of a History*. Edited by Mignon R. Jacobs and Raymond F. Person. AIL 14. Atlanta: Society of Biblical Literature, 2013.

———. *Reading Ezekiel: A Literary and Theological Commentary*. ROT. Macon, GA: Smyth & Helwys, 2013.

———. *Reading the Hebrew Bible after the Shoah: Engaging Holocaust Theology*. Minneapolis: Fortress, 2008.

———. "The Reconceptualization of the Davidic Covenant in the Books of Jeremiah." Pages

167–81 in *Reading Prophetic Books: Form, Intertextuality, and Reception in Prophetic and Post-Biblical Literature*. FAT 89. Tübingen: Mohr Siebeck, 2014.

———. "Samuel's Institutional Identity in the Deuteronomistic History." Pages 165–74 in *Constructs of Prophets in the Former and Latter Prophets and Other Texts*. Edited by Lester L. Grabbe and Martti Nissinen. Atlanta: Society of Biblical Literature, 2011.

———. "Sefirah at Qumran: Aspects of the Counting of the First Fruits Festivals in the Temple Scroll." Pages 337–45 in *Reading Prophetic Books: Form, Intertextuality, and Reception in Prophetic and Post-Biblical Literature*. FAT 89. Tübingen: Mohr Siebeck, 2014.

———. *Tanak: A Theological and Critical Introduction to the Jewish Bible*. Minneapolis: Fortress, 2012.

———. "Ten Sephirot." *DDD* 487–93.

———. *The Twelve Prophets*. Berit Olam. Collegeville, MN: Liturgical Press, 2000.

———. "The Wilderness Traditions of the Pentateuch: A Reassessment of Their Function and Intent in Relation to Exodus 32–34." Pages 291–99 in *SBL 1989 Seminar Papers*. Edited by David Lull. Atlanta: Scholars Press, 1989.

Tadmor, Hayim. "The Campaigns of Sargon II of Assur: A Chronological-Historical Study." *JCS* 12 (1958): 22–40, 77–100.

Tiemeyer, Lena-Sofia. *Zechariah and His Visions: An Exegetical Study of Zechariah's Vision Report*. LHBOTS 605. London: Bloomsbury T&T Clark, 2015.

Tishby, Isaiah. *The Wisdom of the Zohar: An Anthology of Texts. Littman Library of Jewish Civilization*. 3 vols. Oxford: Littman Library of Jewish Civilization, 1983.

Tuell, Steven. *Ezekiel*. NIBCOT. Peabody, MA: Hendrickson, 2009.

Van Seters, John. *A Law Book for the Diaspora: Revision in the Study of the Covenant Code*. Oxford: Oxford University Press, 2003.

Weinberg, Joel. *The Citizen-Temple Community*. JSOTSup 151. Sheffield: Sheffield Academic Press, 2009.

Weinfeld, Moshe. "The Covenant of Grant in the Old Testament and the Ancient Near East." *JAOS* 90 (1970): 184–203.

Weiss, Joseph. "Torah Study in Early Hasidism." Pages 56–68 in *Studies in Eastern European Jewish Mysticism*. Edited by D. Goldstein. Littman Library of Jewish Civilization. Oxford: Oxford University Press, 1985.

Werblowsky, R. J. Zwi. *Joseph Karo: Lawyer and Mystic*. Philadelphia: Jewish Publication Society, 1980.

Wertheimer, Shlomo Aharon. *Batei Midrashot*. 2 vols. Jerusalem: Massad Harav Kook, 1950.

Wildberger, Hans. *Isaiah 1–12*. ContCom. Minneapolis: Fortress, 1991.

———. *Isaiah 13–27*. ContCom. Minneapolis: Fortress, 1997.

———. *Isaiah 28–39*. ContCom. Minneapolis: Fortress, 2002.

Wolfson, Elliot R. *Through a Speculum That Shines: Vision and Imagination in Medieval Jewish Mysticism*. Princeton: Princeton University Press, 1994.

Wright, David P. *Inventing G-d's Law: How the Covenant Code of the Bible Used and Revised the Laws of Hammurabi*. Oxford: Oxford University Press, 2009.

———. *Ritual in Narrative: The Dynamics of Feasting, Mourning, and Retaliation Rites in the Ugaritic Tale of Aqhat*. Winona Lake, IN: Eisenbrauns, 2001.

———. "Syro-Canaanite Religions." Pages 129–50 in *The Cambridge History of Religions in the Ancient World*, vol. 1: *From the Bronze Age to the Hellenistic Age*. Edited by Michele Renee Salzman and Marvin A. Sweeney. Cambridge: Cambridge University Press, 2013.

Wright, J. Edward. *Baruch ben Neriah: From Biblical Scribe to Apocalyptic Seer.* Columbia: University of South Carolina Press, 2003.

Wyatt, N. *Religious Texts from Ugarit: The Words of Ilimilku and His Colleagues.* BibSem 56. Sheffield: Sheffield Academic Press, 1998.

Zalman, Shneur, of Liadi. *Liqqutei Amarim: Tanya.* Bilingual edition. Brooklyn: Kehot, 5770/2009.

Zweig Liebes, Esther. "Dov Baer (The Maggid) of Mezhirech." *EncJud* 6:180–84.

———. "Naḥman (ben Simḥah) of Bratzlav." *EncJud* 12:782–87.

Index of Authors

Index of Subjects

Index of Scripture and Other Ancient Texts